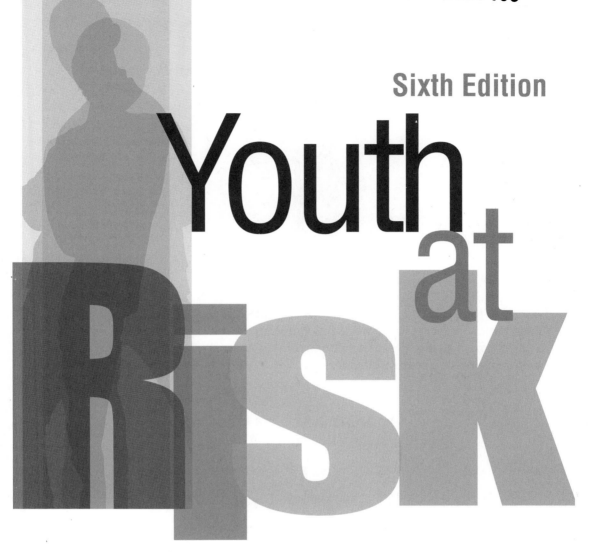

Sixth Edition

Youth at Risk

A PREVENTION RESOURCE FOR COUNSELORS, TEACHERS, AND PARENTS

edited by David Capuzzi and Douglas R. Gross

AMERICAN COUNSELING
ASSOCIATION

6101 Stevenson Avenue | Alexandria, VA 22304 | www.counseling.org

Sixth Edition

Youth at Risk

A PREVENTION RESOURCE FOR COUNSELORS, TEACHERS, AND PARENTS

10   9   8   7   6   5   4   3   2

American Counseling Association

6101 Stevenson Avenue | Alexandria, VA 22304

Associate Publisher | Carolyn C. Baker

Production Manager | Bonny E. Gaston

Editorial Assistant | Catherine A. Brumley

Copy Editor | Kimberly W. Kinne

Cover and text design by Bonny E. Gaston.

Library of Congress Cataloging-in-Publication Data

Youth at risk : a prevention resource for counselors, teachers, and parents/edited by David Capuzzi, Douglas R. Gross.—Sixth edition.
  pages cm
Includes bibliographical references and index.
ISBN 978-1-55620-330-5 (alk. paper)
  1. Youth with social disabilities—United States.   2. Youth—Counseling of—United States.   3. Deviant behavior.   4. Adolescent psychopathology—United States.   5. Adolescent psychotherapy—United States.   6. Dropout behavior, Prediction of.   I. Capuzzi, David.   II. Gross, Douglas R.
  HV1431.Y68 2014
  362.74—dc23   2013017481

Table of Contents

Preface   v

Acknowledgments   vii

Meet the Editors   ix

Meet the Authors   xi

Part 1   Introducing the Problem

Chapter 1 | Defining Youth at Risk   3
Douglas R. Gross and David Capuzzi

Chapter 2 | Prevention: An Overview   23
David Capuzzi and Douglas R. Gross

Chapter 3 | Resilience: Individual, Family, School,
and Community Perspectives   43
Rolla E. Lewis

Part 2   Examining the Problem

Chapter 4 | The Impact of Dysfunctional Family Dynamics
on Children and Adolescents   69
Cass Dykeman

Chapter 5 | "Who Cares What I Think?":
Problems of Low Self-Esteem   93
Sandra S. Meggert

Chapter 6 | Identifying and Preventing Mood Disorders
in Children and Adolescents   125
Marilyn J. Powell and Colleen R. Logan

Chapter 7 | Stress and Trauma: Coping in Today's Society   139
Savitri V. Dixon-Saxon and J. Kelly Coker

Part 3 Working With Youth at Risk: Prevention and Intervention

Chapter 8 | "Who Am I?": Unique Issues for Multiracial Youth   169
Laura R. Haddock and Jeannie Falkner

Chapter 9 | The Secret and All-Consuming Obsessions:
Eating Disorders   197
Meredith J. Drew, Ann M. Ordway, and Mark D. Stauffer

Chapter 10 | "I Don't Want to Live": The Adolescent at Risk
for Suicidal Behavior   229
David Capuzzi and Douglas R. Gross

Chapter 11 | A Future in Jeopardy: Sexuality Issues in Adolescence   265
Melinda Haley, Jessica C. Gelgand, and Alberto Ivan Rodriguez

Chapter 12 | "I Am Somebody": Gang Membership   291
Lisa Langfuss Aasheim

Chapter 13 | "It Takes a Village": Advocating for Sexual Minority Youth   319
John F. Marszalek III and Colleen R. Logan

Chapter 14 | Death in the Classroom: Violence in Schools   337
Abbé Finn

Chapter 15 | "Escaping Reality": Adolescent Substance Abuse   367
Matthew V. Glowiak

Chapter 16 | Nowhere to Turn: The Young Face of Homelessness   395
Melissa A. Stormont and Rebecca B. McCathren

Chapter 17 | "This Isn't the Place for Me": School Dropout   421
Lea R. Flowers and Dawn M. Robinson-McDonald

Chapter 18 | A Nation at Risk: Bullying Among Children and Adolescents   441
Jennifer E. Beebe

Index   465

Preface

Youth at Risk: A Prevention Resource for Counselors, Teachers, and Parents is a revision of the 2008 fifth edition. In this sixth edition, major emphasis has again been placed on prevention efforts with at-risk populations as well as on practical guidelines for successful intervention with behaviors most often identified as placing youth at risk. Selected chapters include case studies that explore prevention efforts from individual, family, school, and community perspectives. Every effort has been made to address the complexities of working with vulnerable youth in a way that provides professionals, as well as parents, with an information base and guidelines for working within the parameters of the prevention–intervention paradigm. This text differs from similar texts because of the attention placed on counseling and systems applications with youth at risk.

The text is developmental in orientation. Part 1 presents information dealing with population identification, definition, and behaviors and causal factors descriptive of youth who are at risk. Information is also included that serves as a foundation for understanding the prevention–intervention paradigm. Part 1 also addresses prevention from the point of view of identification and promotion of resiliency in our youth.

Part 2 of the text deals with parameters that often serve as causal factors for the development of at-risk behaviors. Included in this section are chapters dealing with the effects of a dysfunctional family, low self-esteem, depression, bipolar disorders, mood disorders, and stress and trauma. Each chapter in this section not only identifies various aspects of the causal factors, but also presents information on prevention strategies for dealing with these factors and on adaptations for diversity.

Part 3 of the text deals with issues and behaviors most often identified as placing youth at risk. Chapters 8 through 18 focus on such issues as racial and ethnic identity, eating disorders, suicide, sexuality issues in adolescence, gang membership, counseling sexual minority youth, violence on the school campus, substance abuse, homelessness, school dropout, and bullying. Each chapter in Part 3 provides definitive information related to the specific issues and/or behavior; includes a case study to illustrate the information presented; and provides approaches to prevention and intervention from individual, family, school, and community perspectives. For each case example in this book that is not fictitious, client confidentiality was maintained by disguising aspects of the case material so that the client and third parties (e.g., family members) are not identifiable. Adaptations for diversity are also addressed because prevention and intervention efforts usually need to be modified to meet the needs of minority and disenfranchised youth served by the schools, communities, and mental health practitioners.

New to This Edition

- Chapter 8, "'Who Am I?': Unique Issues for Multiracial Youth," has been heavily revised.
- Chapter 9, "The Secret and All-Consuming Obsessions: Eating Disorders," written by three writers who are new to this edition, provides a fresh perspective on the topic.
- Chapter 13, "'It Takes a Village': Advocating for Sexual Minority Youth," is also written by new authors who approach the topic differently than in the fifth edition.
- Chapter 15, "'Escaping Reality': Adolescent Substance Abuse," addresses adolescent substance abuse in a way that readers will find helpful and presents the new perspective of a different author.
- Finally, Chapter 18, "A Nation at Risk: Bullying Among Children and Adolescents," is totally new to this edition and is quite pertinent to a textbook such as ours.
- In addition to the above, each chapter in this sixth edition includes sidebars designed by the authors to create greater reader self-awareness and to enhance the presentation and understanding of the concepts, skills, roles, and applications of the chapter material.
- For those who will adopt our text for use in a community college or university classroom, we provide in this sixth edition a test manual for instructors. This edition also contains PowerPoint slides that can be used by any instructor who wishes to make use of them.

Every effort has been made by the editors and contributors to provide the reader with current and relevant information in each of the 18 areas of focus. We hope that this new edition of *Youth at Risk: A Prevention Resource for Counselors, Teachers, and Parents* will prove to be an invaluable resource for individuals committed to assisting young people in the often difficult transition between adolescence and adulthood.

Acknowledgments

We would like to thank the 24 authors who contributed their expertise, knowledge, and experience in the development of this text. We would also like to thank our families, who provided the freedom and encouragement to make this endeavor possible. Our thanks are also directed to Carolyn Baker and other members of the American Counseling Association staff for their encouragement and assistance with copy editing and ultimately the production of the book.

Meet the Editors

David Capuzzi, PhD, NCC, LPC, is a counselor educator and member of the core faculty in mental health counseling at Walden University and professor emeritus at Portland State University. Previously, he served as an affiliate professor in the Department of Counselor Education, Counseling Psychology, and Rehabilitation Services at Pennsylvania State University and scholar in residence in counselor education at Johns Hopkins University. He is past president of the American Counseling Association (ACA; formerly the American Association for Counseling and Development) and past chair of both the ACA Foundation and the ACA Insurance Trust.

From 1980 to 1984, Dr. Capuzzi was editor of *The School Counselor*. He has authored a number of textbook chapters and monographs on the topic of preventing adolescent suicide and is coeditor and author with Dr. Larry Golden of *Helping Families Help Children: Family Interventions With School Related Problems* (1986) and *Preventing Adolescent Suicide* (1988). He coauthored and edited with Douglas R. Gross *Youth at Risk: A Prevention Resource for Counselors, Teachers, and Parents* (1989, 1996, 2000, 2004, 2008, and 2014), *Introduction to the Counseling Profession* (1991, 1997, 2001, 2005, 2009, and 2013), *Introduction to Group Work* (1992, 1998, 2002, 2006, and 2010), and *Counseling and Psychotherapy: Theories and Interventions* (1995, 1999, 2003, 2007, and 2011). Other texts are *Approaches to Group Work: A Handbook for Practitioners* (2003), *Suicide Across the Life Span* (2006), and *Sexuality Issues in Counseling*, the last coauthored and edited with Larry Burlew. He has authored or coauthored articles in a number of ACA-related journals.

A frequent speaker and keynoter at professional conferences and institutes, Dr. Capuzzi has also consulted with a variety of school districts and community agencies interested in initiating prevention and intervention strategies for adolescents at risk for suicide. He has facilitated the development of suicide prevention, crisis management, and postvention programs in communities throughout the United States; provides training on the topics of youth at risk and grief and loss; and serves as an invited adjunct faculty member at other universities as time permits.

An ACA fellow, he is the first recipient of ACA's Kitty Cole Human Rights Award and is also a recipient of the Leona Tyler Award in Oregon. In 2010, he received ACA's Gilbert and Kathleen Wrenn Award for a Humanitarian and Caring Person. In 2011, he was named a distinguished alumni of the College of Education at Florida State University.

Douglas R. Gross, PhD, NCC, is a professor emeritus at Arizona State University, Tempe, where he served as a faculty member in counselor education for 29 years. His professional work history includes public school teaching, counseling, and administration. He is currently retired and living in Michigan. He has been president of the Arizona Counselors Association, president of the Western Association for Counselor Education and Supervision, chairperson of the Western Regional Branch Assembly of the ACA, president of the Association for Humanistic Education and Development, and treasurer and parliamentarian of the ACA.

Dr. Gross has contributed chapters to seven textbooks: *Counseling and Psychotherapy: Theories and Interventions* (1995, 1999, 2003, 2007, 2011), *Youth at Risk: A Resource Guide for Counselors, Teachers, and Parents* (1989, 1996, 2000, 2004, 2008, and 2014), *Foundations of Mental Health Counseling* (1986, 1996), *Counseling Theory, Process, and Practice* (1977), *The Counselor's Handbook* (1974), *Introduction to the Counseling Profession* (1991, 1997, 2001, 2005, 2008, and 2013), and *Introduction to Group Work* (1992, 1998, 2002, 2006, 2010). His research has appeared in the *Journal of Counseling Psychology, Journal of Counseling & Development, Association for Counselor Education and Supervision Journal, Journal of Educational Research, Counseling and Human Development, Arizona Counselor's Journal, Texas Counseling Journal,* and *AMHCA Journal.*

During the past 15 years, Dr. Gross has provided national training in bereavement, grief, and loss.

Meet the Authors

Lisa Langfuss Aasheim, PhD, is an associate professor in the counselor education program at Portland State University. She coordinates the school counseling master's program and is the director of the community counseling clinic. Dr. Aasheim specializes in clinical supervision and counselor development and is the author of the book *Practical Clinical Supervision for Counselors: An Experiential Guide,* which focuses on the practical application of clinical supervision theories and techniques.

Dr. Aasheim takes great delight in working with counselors to become their most ideal counselor selves. She believes that counselors do their greatest work when they are prepared with a wide breadth of knowledge and information, then combine that knowledge with reflective and collaborative practices. Dr. Aasheim encourages counselors of all experience levels to find creativity, passion, and meaning in their work and play. Her many areas of professional passion and interest include clinical supervision, motivational interviewing, risk factors related to child development and achievement, addictions counseling experiences, and organizational factors that impact the counseling process.

Jennifer E. Beebe, PhD, is an assistant professor at Canisius College in Buffalo, New York. She received her doctorate in counselor education and supervision from the University of Northern Colorado. In addition to being a counselor educator, she is a national certified counselor as well as a certified K–12 professional school counselor in New York and Hawaii. Dr. Beebe has served as a delegate for the American School Counselor Association and is on the editorial board of the *New York State Counseling Journal.*

Dr. Beebe has been researching bullying and cyberbullying for the past 7 years and has published several articles on the topic. She has presented numerous times at the state, local, and national levels on the topics of bullying and cyberbullying. She has also collaborated with community agencies to provide workshops for parents and guardians on strategies to increase awareness about bullying and cyberbullying. Dr. Beebe has partnered with local schools and communities to increase awareness, education, and intervention efforts on these same topics. She is currently the lead researcher on a community-based intervention program targeting the reduction of bullying among elementary and middle school students in Illinois.

J. Kelly Coker, PhD, is the program director for the PhD in counselor education, and the MS in school counseling at Walden University. She is a licensed professional counselor in North Carolina. Dr. Coker has worked as a drug prevention and intervention school counselor in North Carolina and as a counselor in an art therapy department for a residential adolescent treatment facility in Nevada. She has also worked as a counselor in private practice in North Carolina, focusing primarily on working with children and adolescents. Dr. Coker has been a counselor educator in programs accredited by the Council for Accreditation of Counseling & Related Educational Programs (CACREP) since 1998. She also serves on the editorial board for the *Journal of Counseling & Development* and the *Journal of International Counselor Education*, and she serves as a CACREP site team reviewer. Dr. Coker has several publications in professional journals and has presented her research at local, state, and national conferences.

Savitri V. Dixon-Saxon, PhD, is the associate dean of the School of Counseling at Walden University. Previously, she served as the program director for the master's of science in mental health counseling. She has over 20 years experience in higher education and has been a counselor educator for the last 10 years.

Meredith J. Drew, MS, LPC, NCC ACS, holds a master's of science in education from Fordham University with a concentration in counseling. She is currently working toward her PhD in counselor education and supervision at Walden University. She is a licensed professional counselor in New Jersey, a national certified counselor, and an approved clinical supervisor. Meredith is an assistant professor of psychology at Centenary College and teaches in the undergraduate and graduate counseling programs. She is the internship coordinator for the graduate program. She has extensive experience as a school counselor and previously worked with the homeless, substance abusers, and adolescents. Her areas of interest include online education, the role of personal counseling with newly graduated students from graduate programs, supervision of counselors, and wellness counseling for the counselor and the client.

Cass Dykeman, PhD, is an associate professor of counselor education at Oregon State University. He earned his PhD in counselor education from the University of Virginia. He holds a national counselor certification (NCC) as well as national specialty certifications in school counseling (NCSC) and addiction counseling (MAC). Before becoming a counselor educator, Dr. Dykeman served as a school counselor in Seattle, Washington. He served as the principal investigator for two federal grants and is the author of numerous books, book chapters, and scholarly articles in the area of counseling.

Jeannie Falkner, PhD, LCSW, has dual academic degrees in counselor education and social work. Prior to accepting a core faculty appointment in the mental health program for Walden University, she held the rank of tenured associate professor of social work at Delta State University in Cleveland, Mississippi. During this appointment, Dr. Falkner served on the National Association of Social Work (NASW) board's task force in Culpepper, Virginia, to develop practice analysis of clinical mental health social work supervision. The completion of this work is *An Analysis of Supervision for Social Work Licensure: Guidelines on Supervision for Regulators and Educators* (2009).

Dr. Falkner is a member of the ACA, the Association for Counselor Education and Supervision, and the NASW. She has served on the boards of the Mississippi chapter of the NASW and the Mississippi Association of Marriage and Family Therapy. Dr. Falkner has numerous publications, with research interests in cultural diversity and counselor wellness, including financial wellness. She is a frequently invited guest speaker and provides postgraduate training in redecision therapy.

Abbé Finn, PhD, is a licensed professional counselor, program leader for counseling programs, and associate professor at Florida Gulf Coast University. She earned a BA and MEd from Tulane University, an MS from Loyola University in New Orleans, and a PhD from the University of New Orleans. Dr. Finn has a variety of clinical experiences in crisis management and the prediction of violence. She was an employee assistance professional with the U.S. Postal Service for 6 years. Many of her clients there had substance abuse problems. While working with postal employees, she was a team leader on the National Crisis Response Team. Dr. Finn spent a week in New York City counseling survivors following the destruction of the World Trade Center, and she worked with the Red Cross as a counselor working with survivors of Hurricane Katrina and with survivors of the earthquake in Haiti. While working for the U.S. Postal Service in New Orleans, she initiated the management training in violence prevention. Dr. Finn has written and lectured on numerous occasions regarding the importance of school crisis response plans—including the identification of students most at risk for harming others—and identification and management of employees at risk for harming others.

Lea R. Flowers, PhD, LPC, NCC, holds a doctorate in the area of counselor education from the University of New Orleans. She is a licensed professional mental health counselor (LPC) in the state of Georgia and is certified as an NCC by the National Board of Certified Counselors. Dr. Flowers is a former assistant professor at Georgia State University, specializing in the area of counselor training and trauma with an emphasis on posttraumatic growth.

Currently, Dr. Flowers is the owner and director of Chrysalis Counseling and Consulting. She is also a dedicated advocate for students and families who live with disabilities and serves as the co-chair of the Georgia Statewide Human Rights Council for Developmental Disabilities.

Jessica C. Gelgand, MEd, received her master's degree in counseling from the University of Texas at El Paso. She also received a BS in biology from the University of Texas at San Antonio. Currently, she is working on research within her field and gaining a greater knowledge about the counseling process. As a result of a master's degree in counseling, Jessica wants to work with adolescents, children, adults, and the military. Along with fine-tuning her skills so that she can serve her clients more successfully, she is also pursuing a license for marriage and family therapy (LMFT) to have a better understanding in this area. In the future, Jessica hopes to become an LPC and aspires to continue her education.

Matthew V. Glowiak, MS, NCC, LPC, is a third-year doctoral student in Walden University's Doctor of Philosophy: Counselor Education & Supervision Program. Matt has made contributions along a broad spectrum of counseling-related activities. He has served as teaching assistant under Dr. David Capuzzi, acts as an alumni ambassador, was coeditor and committee chair of the Omega Zeta chapter of Chi Sigma Iota newsletter, and was nominated the Omega Zeta outstanding doctoral student of the year. As a writer, he has coauthored two chapters for books published in 2011 and is preparing another chapter for a 2014 publication.

Upon completion of his doctorate, Matt's professional goals include, but are not limited to, becoming a tenured professor of counselor education and supervision (CES); developing multiple clinics geared toward children and adolescents; writing for professional publications; conducting research; performing professional and community advocacy; and being an active member in various state, regional, and national professional associations. His ultimate goal is to continue to make a positive impact on the counseling field and to promote positive social change.

Laura R. Haddock, PhD, LPC-S, is core faculty for the counselor education and supervision PhD program at Walden University. Dr. Haddock has been a counselor educator since 2005, supported by more than 20 years as a mental health clinician. She is an LPC, an NCC, and approved clinical supervisor. Dr. Haddock maintains a private practice and has served on the Mississippi Licensed Professional Counselors' Board of Examiners as well as the executive board for the Mississippi Counseling Association and the Mississippi Licensed Professional Counselor Association. She has presented research on the state, national, and international levels and has published scholarly writings for professional counseling journals and textbooks. Research interests include counselor wellness and secondary trauma, spirituality, crisis response, and cultural awareness.

Melinda Haley, PhD, received her doctorate in counseling psychology from New Mexico State University in Las Cruces, New Mexico, and is currently a core faculty member in the PhD program in counselor education and supervision at Walden University. Dr. Haley has written numerous book chapters and multimedia presentations on diverse topics related to counseling and psychology. She has extensive applied experience working with adults, adolescents, children, inmates, domestic violence offenders, and culturally diverse populations in the areas of assessment, diagnosis, treatment planning, crisis management, and intervention. Dr. Haley's research interests include multicultural issues in teaching and counseling, personality development over the life span, personality disorders, the psychology of criminal and serial offenders, trauma and posttraumatic stress disorder, bias and racism, and social justice issues.

Rolla E. Lewis, EdD, NCC, is a professor in educational psychology and the school counseling coordinator at California State University, East Bay. Before becoming a counselor educator, he worked for 16 years in the public schools as a teacher and counselor. His current scholarly interests involve helping school counselors collaborate with school administrations in using a participatory inquiring and action research process focused on enhancing students' resilience, learning power, wellness, connectedness to the living environment and community where they live. He is the recipient of the Oregon Counseling Association's Leona Tyler Award for outstanding contributions to professional counseling.

Colleen R. Logan, PhD, LPC, LMFT, NCC, serves as the program coordinator for the master's in marriage, couple, and family counseling; career counseling; and addictions counseling programs at Walden University. Previously, she held academic and administrative positions at Argosy University and the University of Houston–Victoria, serving in the roles of vice president of academic affairs and associate dean, School of Psychology and Behavioral Sciences, respectively. Dr. Logan provided counseling services in a private practice from 1997 to 2009, specializing in HIV services, adolescent intervention, and enrichment counseling.

In addition to acting in such academic and administrative positions, Dr. Logan also served as the president of the ACA (2008–2009) and president of the Texas Association for Lesbian, Gay, Bisexual, and Transgender Issues in Counseling, a division of the Texas Counseling Association (2009–2010). She has been recognized for her contributions to the field of counseling and affirmative therapy with lesbian, gay, bisexual, and transgender individuals and their significant others. Dr. Logan has been instrumental in working with school counselors and administrators to institute and implement zero tolerance policies toward bullying, with an emphasis on creating an affirmative environment for all students.

John F. Marszalek III, PhD, received his BA from Canisius College in Buffalo, New York. He received an MS in counselor education and PhD in counselor education at Mississippi State University. Dr. Marszalek is an NCC and LPC in Mississippi. He has been a counselor educator for over 10 years, currently serving as a core faculty member and program coordinator for the master's in counseling program at Walden University. Previously, Dr. Marszalek served on the faculty of Barry University in Miami and Xavier University in New Orleans. He has been a counselor for over 15 years, maintaining private practices in Fort Lauderdale, New Orleans, and Columbia, Mississippi. He also previously worked in psychiatric and community counseling settings and taught elementary education. His research interests include gay, lesbian, and bisexual identity development theory and factors promoting and inhibiting long-term gay relationships.

Rebecca B. McCathren, PhD, is an associate professor in special education at the University of Missouri. She was a practitioner for 20 years working with young children in diverse, integrated settings including residential treatment and respite care programs, teaching young children with disabilities and those with multiple risk factors in inner-city settings, working with parents and their preschool-age children, and teaching in a public school setting where a third of the children spoke a language other than English. Her academic credentials include an elementary teaching certificate, an early childhood certification, a master's degree in early childhood special education, and a doctorate in early childhood special education from Vanderbilt University.

Dr. McCathren has been the recipient of four personnel preparation grants supporting students at the master's level. She is the author of Missouri's Part C training modules and has collaborated on the development of three online modules focusing on children with autism and their families. Her interests include promoting early communication and language development for children with disabilities, including those with autism; supporting children with disabilities in integrated settings; supporting families of children with disabilities or those who are at risk; and preventing language and behavioral challenges in young children.

Sandra S. Meggert, PhD, is on the teaching faculty at Antioch University, Seattle, Washington. She also is a consultant/diagnostician for Payne & Associates in Olympia, Washington, where she does assessment and diagnosis of adults with learning disabilities. From time to time, she also does Creative Humor at Work seminars. She has written a book by that name and is currently collaborating with a colleague to write another book about humor. In her spare time, she still enjoys baseball and is considering renting a villa in Europe when she retires and inviting all of her friends to visit.

Ann M. Ordway, JD, MA, EdS, is a licensed family law attorney in New Jersey with master's and EdS degrees in counseling. She is presently completing her PhD in counselor education and supervision at Walden University, with a specialization in forensic mental health. Ann is an instructor in the Psychology and Counseling Department on the Florham Campus of Fairleigh Dickinson University in New Jersey, where she teaches on the graduate level. She has worked extensively through the New Jersey court system as a parenting coordinator, a mediator, and a child advocate for children caught in the middle of high-conflict family court litigation and for other youth at risk. Ann has worked extensively with children and adolescents affected by high-conflict divorce, domestic violence, child abuse and the child welfare system, and parental alienation.

Marilyn J. Powell, PhD, serves as the associate dean for the School of Psychology at Walden University. Previously, she held academic and administrative positions at Argosy University, serving in the roles of program chair, vice president of academic affairs, and campus president. Dr. Powell has provided counseling services, in a limited private practice, from 2006 to the present, specializing in couples therapy and clinical supervision.

In addition to acting in such academic and administrative positions, Dr. Powell also provided therapy, assessment, and crisis management services in state prisons and county jails. She worked extensively with co-occurring substance abuse and mental health services, primarily with homeless and other significantly marginalized populations. In addition, Dr. Powell worked in non-profit administration creating programs for underserved populations at the nexus of substance abuse, family welfare, child protective services, corrections, and mental health systems. She helped create and establish enduring programs effectively serving those often seen as beyond assistance.

Dawn M. Robinson-McDonald, PhD, is an assistant professor in the counselor education program at Columbus State University. She is an LPC, is an NCC, and is certified as a professional school counselor in Georgia and Texas. Dr. Robinson-McDonald recently completed her doctorate in counselor education and practice at Georgia State University. She has over 12 years of experience in working with children and adolescents in Title I schools. She obtained a bachelor of social work and master's of education at the University of Texas at Austin and completed her educational specialist degree in school counseling at Georgia State University. She has previously served as the assistant to the editor for the *Journal of Personnel Evaluation in Education.* Her current research interests include gender and racial micro-aggressions, leadership in school counseling, gang prevention and intervention, and systemic interventions with youth.

Alberto Ivan Rodriguez, BS, developed an interest in psychotherapy early in his life because of his strong interest in philosophy. Studying philosophy convinced him that the understanding of one's mind is the road toward happiness. This belief has now transcended and evolved into his current interest in psychology. After taking an introductory course in psychology as an undergraduate, Ivan was able to link the influences philosophy has had on psychological theory. This ability to link the two fields allowed for an easy transition from one field of study to the other.

After receiving his BS in psychology, Ivan decided to continue his studies by entering a graduate program in the field of counseling. He has since developed a sense of duty to contribute as much as he can to further his knowledge of psychotherapy in order to provide the best possible therapeutic services to those in need. His research interests include counseling intervention and suicide prevention.

Mark D. Stauffer, PhD, NCC, serves as a core faculty member in the mental health counseling program at Walden University. He specializes in couples, marriage, and family counseling and worked in the Portland metro area in Oregon at crisis centers and other non profit organizations working with individuals, couples, and families. He has been a counselor and advocate for homeless and at-risk youth in drop-in centers, shelters, a residential program, and a family counseling center. He has coedited three textbooks: *Introduction to Group Work* (2006–2010); *Career Counseling: Foundations, Perspectives, and Applications* (2006, 2012); and *Foundations of Addictions Counseling* (2008, 2012).

Melissa A. Stormont, PhD, is a professor of special education at the University of Missouri. Dr. Stormont has published extensive research related to the educational and social needs of young children who are vulnerable for failure in school, who have attention-deficit/hyperactivity disorder, or who are homeless. Dr. Stormont spent 3 years as a preschool teacher and has spent years conducting field research in Head Start and early childhood special education settings. She has focused the majority of her research efforts on contributing factors in early behavior problems in young children.

Dr. Stormont has published more than 60 articles and book chapters related to the needs of children at risk for failure. She has also written three books on young learners who are at risk for failure. Dr. Stormont is on the editorial boards of *Psychology in the Schools, Behavior Disorders, Intervention in School and Clinic, School Psychology Quarterly,* and the *Journal of Applied School Psychology.* Currently, Dr. Stormont is a co-principal investigator on a $2.9 million efficacy trial to evaluate a teacher training program funded by the Institute of Education Sciences.

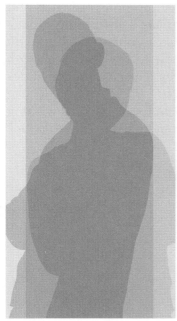

PART 1

Introducing the Problem

Any person who either works with or lives with youth becomes increasingly aware of the potential that exists for the development of at-risk behaviors. This awareness is enhanced by media coverage, educational reform, mental health programming, governmental mandates, and law enforcement reporting. This ongoing bombardment of the vulnerability of youth provides a call to action for all persons involved with this population. Prior to taking such action, however, one must understand not only the demographics of this population but also current definitions, at-risk behaviors, generic causal factors, and prevention and intervention approaches to dealing with youth at risk. Part 1 of this text provides the reader with this foundational information. Chapter 1, "Defining Youth at Risk," introduces the topic of *at-riskness* by providing the reader with foundational information related to definitions, at-risk behaviors, and causal factors that enhance the development of at-risk behaviors. The chapter concludes with an introduction to the concept of resilience and the prevention and crisis management paradigm.

Building on this foundation, Chapter 2, "Prevention: An Overview," lays the groundwork for understanding the various strategies incorporated in the term *prevention*. Information presented in this chapter includes goals and purposes of prevention; primary, secondary, and tertiary concepts related to prevention; and program examples to illustrate prevention's place in the broad spectrum of helping. Some discussion of schools' efforts to develop tragedy response plans is included. The chapter concludes with an explanation of how to plan prevention strategies.

Chapter 3, "Resilience: Individual, Family, School, and Community Perspectives," adds dimension to the prevention paradigm by offering counselors, teachers, and parents an alternative view that sees youth "at promise" rather than "at risk." This chapter provides key research, effective practices, professional possibilities, and definitions. It sets forth ideas for practices that promote resilience, and it establishes a framework for seeing youth as having innate self-righting capacities for changing their life trajectories. Also included are discourses dealing with risks, racism, and poverty and an outlook that asks people to slow down enough to listen deeply to the stories embedded in everyday lives. The chapter concludes with adaptations for diversity.

These first three chapters provide a necessary foundation for all persons wishing to reduce the vulnerability of youth for the future development of at-risk behaviors.

Chapter 1

Defining Youth at Risk

Douglas R. Gross and David Capuzzi

As John Patron sat down at the large table in the conference room, he hoped that something positive could come from this meeting—perhaps something finally could be done to help some of the students in his classroom. He knew that he had been instrumental in forcing Ms. Callis, his principal, to call this meeting. He hoped that all of his colleagues attending shared his view on the urgency for taking some positive action.

This was John's third year of teaching, and each day he was confronted with problems in his classroom. The problems were not those of math, his subject area, but problems that he observed and that were reported to him by many of his students. The problems covered a wide range of areas, including pregnancy, gangs, drugs and alcohol, violence, eating disorders, and dropping out of school. Certainly he was not the first to notice these problems or the only teacher in whom students confided. If these problems were so obvious to him, why hadn't something been done to deal with them? Most of his students were now juniors in high school, and he was sure that the problems did not have their origins in attaining junior status.

He did the best he could, but he was not trained to handle these issues. In seeking direction, he talked with the school counselor, the school psychologist, and Ms. Callis. Although all of the people contacted wanted to help, they were also overwhelmed by the demands on their time. John's questions for the most part went unanswered. If he was correct that these problems did not begin during the junior year in high school, why hadn't something been done earlier? Hadn't former school personnel recognized the difficulties these students were having? Hadn't parents asked for help with their children? Why hadn't something been done to prevent these problems from developing? John hoped that answers would be forthcoming at the meeting.

After the meeting John sat in his classroom and reflected on what had happened. He was very pleased that he was not alone in his concern about the students and that his colleagues had raised many of the same questions that plagued him. He was also pleased that many of his colleagues saw a need for adding trained personnel to work with teachers, students, and parents in developing strategies to intervene in the disrupted lives of many of the students before it was too late. John felt that several helpful outcomes resulted from the meeting. The first of these was that of exploring the development of prevention strategies aimed at early identification of problem behaviors and establishing programs directed at impeding their development. This outcome generated much discussion centering around such questions as, "What constitutes prevention?" "How does prevention differ from crisis management?" "What have other schools tried and what has worked?" "Do we need to go beyond the school to build a prevention program?" and "What part will the community and parents play in the prevention program?"

The second outcome dealt with the identification of other at-risk issues, such as low self-esteem; issues in the family; suicide; increased sexual activity and the danger of sexually transmitted diseases, including AIDS; and the impact of homelessness on a small percentage of the students. This outcome led to a discussion of the questions, "Are there community resources we can use to aid us in better dealing with these identified problems?" and "What do we need to do to effectively utilize these resources?"

A third outcome dealt with the concept of resilience and the related questions, "What makes some young people resilient to high-risk environments while others succumb to these same environments?" and "What are the characteristics of both the individual and his or her environment that make him or her resistant to these high risks?" John had not thought much about resilience and was excited over finding answers to these questions. He sensed that the questions came more easily than would the answers.

The major directives that came from the meeting were (a) the establishment of a committee to investigate what is currently being done by other schools to develop an approach to prevention, (b) the development of a list of community mental health services that could be utilized by the school to supplement the work currently being done by the school staff, and (c) the collection of data relating to the concept of resilience and how these data would affect the development of a prevention program. John had volunteered to serve as chairperson of the committee investigating current programs and to assist in gaining more information about the issue of resilience. He looked forward to the next meeting that was scheduled in 2 weeks.

■ ■ ■

This hypothetical situation has been repeated over and over in school districts across the United States as teachers, counselors, administrators, community leaders, and parents attempt to better understand what needs to be done to provide effective programs to help with the growing numbers of young people who are labeled *at risk* because of their involvement in certain destructive behaviors and to help prevent the development of these destructive behavioral patterns. The question these concerned professionals are striving to answer is, "Do we continue to deal with the problem behaviors of young people from a crisis management perspective, or do we take a preventive approach to attempt to stop these problem behaviors from developing?"

The answer to both parts of this complex question is yes. With the growing numbers of young people entering the educational systems identified as at risk, it is not possible to say no to continuing the crisis management strategies. Because of these increasing numbers, however, most educational systems are not equipped to address this problem from a purely crisis management perspective. Therefore, steps must be taken to attempt to stop its development. Such steps are usually described in terms of prevention modalities aimed at providing programs that will identify young people with the highest potential for developing at-risk behaviors, prevent these destructive behaviors from developing, and work to identify individual and environmental characteristics that enhance the resilience of the individual and his or her environment. Thus, we must continue to intervene at the points of crisis and at the same time set into place prevention programs that will eventually reduce the need for crisis intervention.

This chapter first provides a foundational perspective on at-risk youth by presenting definitions, identifying the population, and describing the population's behavioral and causal characteristics. The chapter then introduces the concept of resilience and concludes with a discussion of a prevention and crisis management paradigm.

A Foundational Perspective

Many problems are encountered in attempting to understand the concepts and issues that surround the term *at-risk youth*. Such problems center on defining cause and effect, calculating and determining the population, and developing and implementing both prevention and crisis management programs that have an impact on the various destructive behaviors that place youth at risk. According to Conrath (1988), "Principals and teachers have known at risk youth for a long time. They have recently been discovered by policy makers and budget sculptors" (p. 36). Simple answers and agreed-on definitions do not currently exist. The best we have at this time are experimental programs; a host of opinions, definitions, and population descriptors; and a high motivation to find workable solutions. The concepts that surround the students at risk and the most effective ways to deal with this at-riskness are complex, filled with frustration for those who attempt to understand them, filled with despair for those who attempt to affect them, and often filled with tragedy for the individuals so labeled.

Sidebar 1.1 ■ Taking a Stand on Crisis Management Versus Prevention

As with the hypothetical situation presented at the beginning of this chapter, we are often called on to take a position regarding how best to handle difficult situations. Where do you stand with crisis management versus a preventive approach? Place yourself at the meeting and identify questions and concerns you would raise. What advice would you give John Patron as he seeks workable solutions to what he sees as insurmountable problems? Are the outcomes and directives from the meeting sufficient to address the identified problems? If not, what outcomes and directives would you add?

■ ■ ■

Overwhelming statistics place the concepts and issues surrounding at-risk youth high on the priority lists of educators, mental health workers, counselors, social workers, psychologists, parents, community leaders, and governmental programs (Capuzzi & Gross, 2008; Finn, 2008; Hamilton, Martin, & Ventura, 2012; National Center for Education Statistics, 2012). According to the Children's Defense Fund (2011), each day in America:

- 5 children are killed by abuse and/or neglect.
- 5 children or teens commit suicide.
- 8 children or teens are killed by firearms.
- 32 children or teens die from accidents.
- 186 children are arrested for violent accidents.
- 368 children are arrested for drug offenses.
- 2,058 children are confirmed as abused or neglected.
- 3,312 high school students drop out of school.
- 4,133 children are arrested.
- 18,493 school students are suspended.

It is important to keep in mind that each day steps are being taken to reduce these staggering numbers. Educational, psychological, sociological, governmental, and community-based entities are developing and applying prevention and crisis management strategies directed toward a society at risk. The major purpose of this book is to provide these entities with information and direction in meeting their difficult tasks.

The Definition

Tracing the exact origins of the term *at risk* as it applies to education and youth is difficult. The term seems to have come into use after the 1983 article "A Nation at Risk," which was published by the National Commission on Excellence in Education (Placier, 1993). During the past 30 years, the term has appeared frequently in educational literature, federal reports, and legislative mandates from the individual states. In 1988, *Education Week* reported that three out of four states either had adopted or were preparing a definition of their populations determined to be at risk (Minga, 1988); it is assumed that all states have by now established legislative parameters for their at-risk populations. A review of the known definitions reveals not only a lack of clarity and consensus but also that the term is explained most often from an educational perspective and indicates individuals at risk of dropping out of the educational system. The characteristics of at-risk youth presented in these definitions include the well-known risk factors of chronically being tardy, earning poor grades, having low math and reading scores, and failing one or more grades (Beekhoven & Dekkers, 2005; Dynarski & Gleason, 2002; Flowers & Hermann, 2008).

A more interesting listing of characteristics was adopted by the Montana State Board of Education in April 1988. This definition (reported by Minga, 1988) is as follows:

> At-risk youths are children who are not likely to finish high school or who are apt to graduate considerably below potential. At-risk factors include chemical dependence, teenage pregnancy, poverty, disaffection with school and society, high-mobility families, emotional and physical abuse, physical and emotional disabilities and learning disabilities that do not qualify students for special education but nevertheless impede their progress. (p. 14)

This definition speaks directly to the confusion that surrounds the issue of being at risk and somewhat indirectly addresses concerns regarding cause versus effect. From this definition, it could be concluded that behaviors such as tardiness, truancy, and low grades are the effects of identified causal factors, for example, chemical dependency, teenage pregnancy, and poverty (Bazargan & West, 2006; Brook, Brook, & Phal, 2006; Haber & Toro, 2004).

If programs dealing with at-risk youth first attempt to deal with factors such as tardiness, truancy, and low grades, they may be placing the proverbial cart before the horse. If the desired effects are to reduce tardiness and truancy and to improve grades, with the ultimate aim of reducing the dropout rate, perhaps more attention needs to be directed toward such identified causal issues as those listed by the Montana State Board of Education.

Underlying much of the confusion surrounding at-risk youth is the amount of emphasis placed on either cause or effect (behavior) or both. Whichever position is selected often determines both definition and strategies to operate within that definition. For example, if we approach this area from an effect (behavior) point of view, then what we need to do is identify the behaviors that place the individual at risk and develop strategies to change these behaviors. Or if we approach this area from a causal perspective, then we must try to determine what caused the development of the effect (behavior) and attempt to develop strategies that eliminate the causal factors, thereby stopping the development of the effect (behavior). If we approach from both cause and effect perspectives, then we must develop strategies to identify and eliminate the causal factors and at the same time put into motion programs that will change the behavior.

This last approach—from both cause and effect perspectives—forms the basis for our definition of at risk. In this book, the term *at risk* encompasses a set of causal/effect (behavioral) dynamics that have the potential to place the individual in danger of a negative future event. This definition not only considers the effect (behavior) that may lead to a negative future event but also attempts to trace the causal factors that led to the development of the effect (behavior). For example, with school-age persons, one of these negative future events may be that of dropping out of school. The causal/behavioral approach identifies not only the behaviors that led to this event but also the myriad causal factors that aided in the development of this behavior. This definition speaks directly to the need for programs to change existing negative behaviors and for prevention programs to tackle the precipitating events that serve as causal factors in the development of the negative behavior. When viewed from the causal/effect (behavioral) perspective, the concept of being at risk broadens, and dropping out is only one of many possible outcomes. Other risks include, but are not limited to, graduating without an education, without goals and objectives, without direction for what comes next, without an understanding of potentials and possibilities, without appreciation for self, or without a knowledge of one's place in the larger society.

When viewed from this causal/effect (behavioral) perspective, the concept of being at risk takes on new dimensions and places the emphasis on individual and systemic dynamics that may or may not lead to a wide range of destructive outcomes. Such a viewpoint emphasizes the vulnerability of all youth to be at risk and provides a strong rationale for the development of prevention programs directed toward stemming the negative impact of certain individual and systemic

Sidebar 1.2 ■ The Case of Ann

Ann is a junior in high school. She is above average in intelligence and until 2 months ago she was active in school functions and maintained a high grade point average. Teachers report that during the past 2 months, Ann has missed several days of school, has stopped participating in school activities, and has had declining grades. Using the causal/effect definitions found in the preceding paragraphs, what steps would you take to better understand and perhaps change her current behavioral patterns?

■ ■ ■

dynamics. This viewpoint directs attention to a set of causal issues and resultant behaviors that often have proved to be significantly related to the development of many personal and educational dilemmas faced by today's youth. Any one of these dilemmas could result in personal and educational impairment. In combination, the results could be both personally and educationally fatal. This book uses the causal/effect (behavioral) definition of being at risk and presents both information and strategies to deal with at-riskness from a preventive perspective.

The Population

One of the basic issues confronting those wishing to work in the area of at-risk youth focuses on identifying the population. Who are these youth identified as being at risk? Is it possible to identify young people who, by behavior or circumstance, are more at risk than others? On the basis of behaviors, environments, and developmental patterns, are not all young people at risk? Specific answers to these questions are not readily available. The research literature in this area is replete with more opinion and supposition than fact. Interest in this population is recent. Population identification may be possible only after the fact, as exemplified by the studies that deal with placing the label of at-risk youth on those who drop out of school, abuse alcohol and/or drugs, become involved in gangs, and attempt and/or complete suicide. In such studies, the population is identified by the specific behaviors manifested. Such an approach to identification, although interesting, limits the identification process of at-riskness to those who currently manifest the specified behaviors.

Another factor that may hinder gaining a comprehensive perspective on the population of at-risk youth is the fact that the terms *at-risk youth* and *adolescence* are used somewhat interchangeably. It seems that to be at risk is to be between the ages of 13 and 18. Such parameters are understandable when we realize that most of the behaviors that are used to describe at-risk youth are those that coincide with the turbulent and exploratory developmental period of adolescence. Factors such as sexual experimentation, first-time drug and alcohol use, ego and self-concept development, bullying, and peer inclusion or exclusion are descriptive of both adolescence and of the population labeled *at-risk youth*. Such age-specific parameters, however, are limiting and often rule out a large segment of youth, namely, those younger than 13, who also need to be a focus in any discussion of at-risk youth.

According to Stevens and Griffin (2001), it is alarming to realize the age at which youth begin to engage in risk behaviors. Large numbers of children ages 9 through 12 experiment with chemical substances. Stevens and Griffin reported, on the basis of a 1996 report, that 32.4% of those who reported having had at least one drink in their lifetime were under 13 years of age, 7.6% had tried marijuana, and 9% had become sexually active. It is easy to see that such early behavior choices put young people at risk for poor outcomes in later life.

If we limit our identification process of at-risk youth to adolescence, we may also limit issues of cause and effect. From this perspective, both causal and behavioral dynamics are correlated with entrance into and exit from the developmental stage termed *adolescence*. On the basis of the definition of at-risk youth stated earlier and knowledge of human development, we take a somewhat different viewpoint in identifying this population and view adolescence as simply the emerging period for behaviors that have been developing over a much longer period of time.

In keeping with this definition and viewpoint, the population identified as at risk includes all youth regardless of age. All young people have the potential for developing at-risk behaviors. The key words in this statement are *potential for*. All young people may move in and out of at-riskness depending on personal, social, educational, and family dynamics. No one can be excluded.

By expanding the at-risk population to include all youth, the doors are open to begin work with this population at a much earlier age, to identify causal factors in the individual's environment that may either encourage or impede the later development of at-risk behaviors, and to develop prevention programs for all youth regardless of age or circumstance. If all youth have the potential to develop at-risk behaviors, preventive steps can be taken to see that the young person does not reach his or her at-risk potential. If this population also includes those who have achieved their at-risk potential, then crisis management steps can be taken to reduce the level of at-riskness and return them to a level more descriptive of "potential for."

Behaviors and Causal Factors

If we assume that all youth have the potential for at-riskness, how then are we able to identify both behaviors and causal factors that make these behaviors a reality? Is it possible to spell out a direct cause–effect relationship, or is this relationship much more indirect and circular in nature? The answers to these questions are at best speculative and perhaps best understood by looking at the developmental period that describes this population and then by identifying the behaviors and causal factors related to this population from school, mental health, and home perspectives.

The developmental period from childhood through adolescence is characterized by rapid physical change, the quest for independence, exploration and implementation of new behaviors, the strengthening of peer relationships, sexual awakening and experimentation, and the pursuit of clarity relating to self and one's place in the larger society. Pressures exerted by family, school, peers, and society to conform or not conform to established standards contribute to the highly charged environment in which this developmental process takes place and the degree of

Sidebar 1.3 ■ Defining the Population

On the basis of the information presented in the last section, how would you define the term *population* as it applies to at-risk youth? In addressing this question, take into consideration all of the various organizations within your community that deal with youth. If you were given the opportunity to speak to these groups, what advice would you give them regarding your definition of the population labeled *at-risk youth*?

■ ■ ■

vulnerability that exists within it for the individual. Ingersoll and Orr (1988), in an article about adolescents at risk, discussed G. Stanley Hall's 1904 view of adolescence as a phase of "storm and stress" and painted a graphic picture of this developmental process in which adolescence is simply the emerging period for behaviors that have been developing over a much longer period of time:

> Still, for those who deal with adolescents in a therapeutic context, there remains a subgroup that does experience storm and stress, whose transition to adulthood is marked by turmoil and trial. Further, only a recluse could be unaware of the statistics that show an upsurge in adolescent suicide, pregnancy, and venereal disease, as well as continued patterns of drug and alcohol use and abuse, school dropouts, and delinquency. For some young people, adolescence is an extended period of struggle; for others the transition is marked by alternating periods of struggle and quiescence. During periods of stress and turmoil, the latter group's ability to draw on effective adaptive coping behaviors is taxed. The resulting maladaptive behavior risks compromising physical, psychological, and social health. These young people are at risk. (p. l)

Terms such as *turmoil, trial, struggle, compromise,* and *stress* lend credence to the difficulty that surrounds this developmental period of youth. Research dealing with this developmental period includes, but is not limited to, such factors as eating disorders (Von Ransom & Robinson 2006; K. S. Wright & Blanks, 2008), homelessness (National Coalition for the Homeless, 2009; Stormont, 2007; Stormont & McCathren, 2008), sexual behaviors (Bohon, Garber, & Horowitz, 2007; Haley & Vasquez, 2008), abuse (Coldwell, Pike, & Dunn, 2006; Dykeman, 2008), affective disorders (Hamrin & Scahill, 2005; McWhirter, McWhirter, McWhirter, & McWhirter, 2007; Meggert, 2008), substance use and abuse (Burrow-Sanchez, 2006; Gagliardi-Blea, Weber, Rofkahr, & Robinson-Kurpius, 2008; Inaba & Cohen, 2000), pregnancy (Blake & Bentov, 2001; Haley & Sherwood-Hawes, 2004), suicide and suicidal ideation (Capuzzi & Gross, 2008; Maples et al., 2005; National Institute of Mental Health, 2007), and violence (Derzon, 2006; Finn, 2008; Finn & Remley, 2002; Ross, 2003). Each of these factors is descriptive of either behaviors or causal factors that can be identified from the perspective of the school, the mental health community, or the home. The behaviors and causal factors are separated for purposes of discussion only. Many items could appear in each perspective's listing.

From a School Perspective

At-risk behaviors. From an educational perspective, there seems to be a good deal of consistency regarding the behaviors of youth who fall within the parameters of the at-risk population. According to Brooks, Schiraldi, and Ziedenberg (2000); Davis (2013); Flowers and Hermann (2008); Jimerson, Anderson, and Whipple (2002); Reschly and Christenson (2006); and White and Kelly (2010), the following behaviors are red flags for those at risk:

- tardiness,
- absenteeism,
- poor grades,
- truancy,
- low math and reading scores,
- failing one or more grades,
- rebellious attitudes toward school authority,

- verbal and language deficiency,
- inability to tolerate structured activities,
- dropping out of school, and
- aggressive behaviors or violence.

Causal factors. Behaviors such as those just listed, viewed either individually or in combination, aid in the identification process. However, this type of identification focuses on existing behaviors that need crisis management strategies to attempt to change them. A different approach, and one we support, identifies the causal factors that lead to these behaviors and suggests prevention programs that may keep these behaviors from developing.

Ekstrom, Goertz, Pollack, and Rock (1986) attempted to address these causal issues in their analysis of data from the U.S. Department of Education's High School and Beyond national sample of 30,000 high school sophomores and seniors. The researchers looked at sophomores in 1980 and 1982 and concentrated on the differences between graduates and nongraduates. Their findings indicated that behavioral problems and low grades were major determinants of dropping out. Other determinants included family circumstances with few educational supports and parents who were uninvolved in the ongoing process of their child's education. Furthermore, students who dropped out tended to have close friends whose attitudes and behaviors also indicated alienation from school.

In a study of a comprehensive high school in upper Manhattan, Fine (1986) concluded that the structural characteristics that may lead to dropping out include a school that has a disproportionate share of low-achieving students and insufficient resources to provide for this population; overcrowded classrooms; teachers who are predominantly White, which can lead to poor communication with minority students and a lack of understanding; and teaching styles based more on control than conversation, authority than autonomy, and competition than collaboration.

Barber and McClellan (1987) and Paulu (1987) addressed the dropout problem from the students' perspective and reported that the reasons students gave for leaving school included personal reasons, such as family problems, pregnancy, and academic problems. Other reasons that spoke directly to problems inherent in the educational structure included the absence of the following: individual help; challenging classes; smaller classes; consistent discipline; and understanding, support, and help from teachers. Other explanations included the presence of boredom and communication problems with teachers, counselors, and administrators.

According to Garnier, Stein, and Jacobs (1997) and Rumberger (1993), socioeconomic status plays a large role in adolescent dropout from school, with the highest dropout rate stemming from those in the lowest 20th percentile of income. Dropping out was also seen as a gradual disengagement from school activities that begins in childhood.

Flowers and Hermann (2008) and Kushman, Sieber, and Heariold-Kinney (2000), reporting on studies of early warning signs, identified a variety of school and personal factors that aid in predicting dropping out. These factors are described by the following four categories: (a) poor academic performance (low grades, low test scores, behind in grade), (b) behavior problems (disruptive classroom behavior, acting out, truancy, suspension), (c) affective characteristics (poor self-concepts, alienation), and (d) personal circumstances (teen pregnancy, teen parenting, having to work, caring for family members).

From a Mental Health Perspective

At-risk behaviors. Today, more and more young people are seen by mental health agencies either in terms of clients who present for treatment or through the mental health agency's consulting relationships with schools. Regardless of the nature of the involvement, the following behaviors are most often presented:

- drug and alcohol use and abuse,
- eating disorders,
- gang membership,
- pregnancy,
- suicide or suicidal ideation,
- depression,
- sexual acting out,
- aggression,
- withdrawal and isolation,
- low self-esteem,
- school-related problems, and
- family problems.

Causal factors. On the basis of the behaviors identified, it is easy to realize that no single causal factor provides the answer as to why such behaviors develop. The answer probably is better understood in terms of combinations of causal factors leading to somewhat predictable behaviors. Often listed as causal factors for many of the behaviors just identified are dysfunctional family dynamics; peer group pressure for inclusion/exclusion; lack of positive adult models; an uninspired educational system; learning difficulties that go untreated; increased violence within the community and the school; homelessness and economic hardship; single-parent households; living in a highly stressed society; and physical, sexual, or psychological abuse (Adams, 2006; Bagdi & Pfister, 2006; Beaumont, 2002; Gaffney, 2006)

From the Perspective of the Home

At-risk behaviors. Parenting in today's society presents many challenges, not the least of which is attempting to understand children and the various factors that affect them. Parents do not have the objective, somewhat clinical, viewpoint of at-risk behaviors as do either school personnel or members of the mental health profession. Because of the parents' close relationship with their children, the following is descriptive of what parents might list if asked to identify behaviors that place their children at risk:

- failing to obey rules or directives,
- avoiding taking part in family activities,
- spending a great deal of time alone in their room,
- being secretive about friends and activities,
- not communicating with parents or siblings,
- displaying values and attitudes different from family,
- resisting going to school or discussing school activities,
- arguing about everything, and
- staying away from home as much as possible.

Causal factors. As the family and its dynamics are generally viewed as one of the major contributors (causal factors) to at-risk behaviors, what does the family identify as causal factors and where do they look for explanations? Families must look inside the family structure as well as to entities outside the family to arrive at causal factors. These factors include the educational system; the peer group; the media; the economic conditions that necessitate both parents working; the lack of time for family interaction; the absence of extended family; the availability of drugs and alcohol; the lack of funds or governmental support for child care; and the violence so common in the community, the school, and the society at large (Capuzzi & Gross, 2008; Dykeman, 2008; Houseknecht & Hango, 2006; Jones & Prinz, 2005).

Origins of Causal Factors

The three perspectives illustrate not only the differing behaviors identified but also the differing opinions as to the origins of the causal factors that aid in the development of these behaviors. Is one perspective more accurate than the other two? Does one provide a better answer than the other two? Are all three perspectives accurate? The answer to all three of these questions could be yes, depending on the setting, the perspective of the person in the setting, and the individual under evaluation. No one single factor can explain the development of at-riskness; only in combination are we able to understand the impact these factors have on the developmental process. For example, the young person growing up in a dysfunctional family often internalizes aspects of this dysfunction. Such internalization may stem from physical, sexual, or psychological abuse and may result in low self-esteem, poor school performance, drug and alcohol use, or gang membership. The causal factors stem from both the degree of dysfunctionality within the family and how the young person reacts to that dysfunctionality. We know that not all young people who live in a dysfunctional family environment achieve at-risk status. We do know, however, that the potential for at-riskness in this type of environment is high.

This same situation exists when we move from the family environment to the school environment. The child who enters school for the first time may find this environment both frightening and difficult. So much depends on what is done to recognize these reactions in the child and to develop programs to aid the child in making the transition from home to school. First impressions can have a far-reaching impact on this child's movement through the educational system—an impact that has the potential for such future behaviors as poor grades, lack of interest in learning, disruptive behaviors, and eventually dropping out of the educational system.

Aligned closely with the school environment is the developing pressured environment of the peer group. Part of the developmental process from childhood through adolescence is the growing importance of the peer group and the need to conform or to belong. The peer group affects youth in areas such as self-identification, self-esteem and self-worth, interactive styles, attitudes, values, and beliefs. As youth develop, the peer group is like a magnet that continually pulls them away from family and often encourages behaviors that are decidedly different from those espoused by the family. Young people attempting to find their place in the world are faced with making choices, choices that for the most part place them at odds with one of two pulling forces: the family or the peer group. The ensuing stress demands the use of coping strategies and decision-making skills, both of which are often not part of the young person's behavioral repertoire. Unless something is done to relieve this pressure, the young person may develop a wide range of emotional reactions or behavioral dynamics in an attempt to relieve the stress, including depression, aggressiveness, use of alcohol and drugs, development of eating disorders, and suicide or suicidal ideation. Any one of these classifies the young person as being at risk.

Society provides a further environment that has the potential for causing at-riskness in young people. One influencing element within today's society is conflicting standards for youth. On the one hand, through legislative actions, persons under the age of 18 have few rights. Decisions regarding many aspects of their lives are made by parents or other adults. The message is clear: You are too young to make these important decisions. On the other hand, the media, which permeates so much of society, provides and promotes all types of models that encourage youth to be more adult in terms of behaviors, clothes, physical appearance, and relationships. The pull that the media holds for youth is like that of the peer group. The only difference is that the pull may be even stronger and again may encourage youth to move away from the demands of the family, culture, racial and/or ethnic orientations, and religious teachings.

A second influencing element on youth in today's society is best summed up in the term *violence.* It is difficult to read a newspaper or view a news program without being confronted with stories detailing robbery, rape, assault, murder, drive-by shootings, gang-related retaliations, and terrorism. From an educational perspective, between 1999 and 2013 schools in Pearl, Mississippi; West Paducah, Kentucky; Jonesboro, Arkansas; Edinboro, Pennsylvania; Springfield, Oregon; Conyers, Georgia; Moses Lake, Washington; Green River, Wyoming; Littleton, Colorado; and Newtown, Connecticut, made national headlines as armed individuals killed or wounded both peers and school personnel. All of these violent incidents involved young people and took place in environments generally thought of as safe: elementary and high school playgrounds and campuses.

The terrorist attack of September 11, 2001, added yet another layer of violence, and again this took place in an environment generally viewed as safe: America. Faced with vivid examples of such violent responses together with the death of family, friends, peers, and teachers, young people experience a great deal of uncertainty about their future. Such uncertainty creates stress, frustration, and often an attitude of hopelessness and helplessness. Any one of these enhances the at-riskness potential of youth; in combination, they almost ensure it. Because of the growing significance of violence in schools, we again devote an entire chapter (Chapter 14) to a discussion of the issues surrounding violence in schools together with prevention information from an individual, family, school, and community perspective.

Within these four environments—the family, the school, the peer group, and society—are found most of the causal factors that lead to at-riskness in youth. However, the individual's internal environment (what the individual brings to and takes from these environments) also must be considered in terms of its place in this causal paradigm. What part does the individual play in response to these various environments? Are youth simply victims without recourse, or do they play an active role in determining their own at-riskness? Answers to these questions may be found in the growing body of research surrounding the concept of resilience.

Sidebar 1.4 ■ The Impact of Diversity

It is important to keep in mind that within and across each of these environments concepts surrounding diversity play major roles in determining the impact each has on the individual. It would be naïve to believe that factors such as race, culture, ethnicity, gender, and gender identity would not factor into each environment. The degree of impact is impossible to determine with any accuracy. On the basis of your life experiences, what impact has diversity played in your own development? Within the four environments identified, where would you see diversity having the greatest influence?

■ ■ ■

Resilience

The term *resilience*, when applied to at-risk youth, describes certain skills, abilities, personal qualities, or attributes that enable certain youth who are exposed to significant stress and adversity to cope with and even thrive in spite of the stress and adversity. These youth, unlike many of their peer counterparts, do not succumb to the stresses and adversities present in their environment and in fact may develop strength and positive coping strategies from the exposure (Bernard, 2004; Friesen & Brennan, 2005; Goldstein & Brooks, 2006; Werner, 2006).

The research on resilience (Cosden, 2001; Deater-Deckard, Ivy, & Smith, 2006; Felner, 2006; Kaplan, 2006; Lewis, 2008; Marshall, 2004; Unger, 2004, 2005) identifies various sets of characteristics that, when present in youth, provide a screening device that allows them to adjust to and cope with the negative conditions within their environments. Such listings often include, but are not limited to, the following:

- approaching life's problems in an active way;
- constructively perceiving pain, frustration, and negative experiences;
- gaining positive attention from others;
- having a view of life as both positive and meaningful;
- possessing positive self-esteem;
- comprehending, appreciating, and producing humor;
- being willing to risk and accept responsibility;
- being proactive;
- being adaptable; and
- being competent in the school, social, and cognitive dimensions.

There are no data to indicate what percentage of youth fit this profile. On the basis of the staggering figures presented earlier, it seems that the percentage is perhaps small. The research on resilience, however, does provide direction for those working with at-risk youth (Bernard, 2004; Lewis, 2008; Marshall, 2004; Vaillant, 2002; Werner & Smith, 2001; M. O. Wright & Masten, 2006). Given our view of the growing importance of resilience in prevention programming, we have devoted an entire chapter (Chapter 3) to a discussion of resilience and its application to prevention programs for at-risk youth.

Prevention and Crisis Management Paradigm

The descriptions of at-risk youth in terms of causal factors, behaviors, and factors of resilience provide a logical entry into a discussion of the prevention and crisis

Sidebar 1.5 ■ The Significance of Resiliency

Resilience, as a concept in human development, presents a picture of youth "at promise" rather than "at risk" (Lewis, 2008). It addresses the potential that exists not only within the individual but also within the environments in which the individual must operate to produce positive rather than negative results. Among researchers and other professionals, there is still much debate and controversy regarding resiliency as to its nature and nurture; however, the concept does speak to the development of healthy systems within which the individual can grow and prosper.

■ ■ ■

management paradigm as this relates to developing programs that will assist in preventing the development of the problem behaviors, treating the problem behaviors that have developed, or enhancing resilience factors.

Prevention

Two basic criteria underlie the development of effective prevention programs for at-risk youth: The causal factors that lead to at-riskness can be enumerated, and the population of young people who are affected by these factors can be identified. Causal factors are enumerated for a variety of identified problems in this chapter and the chapters that follow, and there seems to be a good deal of similarity across these factors. The population of young people affected by these factors is also identified in this chapter: All young people have the potential for at-riskness. With these two basic criteria established, prevention programs can be developed to keep the identified population from achieving its at-risk potential.

Prevention programs can be and have been developed for a wide range of potential at-risk behaviors. The theory behind prevention is simply to stop certain behaviors from developing. Prevention programming for at-risk youth applies this theory but in a somewhat more comprehensive manner.

Effective prevention programs directed at at-risk youth are generally viewed as multidisciplinary and are developed on the basis of the knowledge and expertise of several publics. For example, a prevention program directed at alcohol and drug abuse might involve not only school personnel (teachers, counselors, administrators) but also parents, students, community leaders, religious leaders, police, and representatives from various human service organizations. A multidisciplinary approach ensures the widest range of expertise, involvement of those most likely to be affected by the program, and a commitment from the community in making the program work. It enhances the physical and financial resources of the proposed program and alerts young people to the fact that this is not just a school-based program but one that has the backing of both their parents and the community. Because the program has prevention as its purpose, as opposed to crisis management, the following are emphasized: providing information on alcohol and drug use, redesigning environments to remove the availability of alcohol and drugs, changing existing policies and procedures within the educational system to enhance the prevention of alcohol and drug use, changing parenting styles and rules and regulations within the home to better accommodate the needs of the young person, designing alternative activities for young people that do not include alcohol and drug use, and providing peer mentoring systems to allow young people to learn from each other. These are just examples. One of the key factors in prevention program development is individualizing the programs to better meet the unique needs of the targeted population, the school, and the community.

According to Conyne (1994), many of the identified problems of at-risk youth are preventable. What we need are well-designed programs that take into consideration such factors as (a) knowledge and understanding of the concepts that define prevention; (b) local assessments to define the target population; (c) information regarding existing programs, both local and national; and (d) multiple strategies for implementing the program. This process is best done through a team composed of many individuals representing a broad spectrum of the community. Such a broadened base not only expands the knowledge and skill base of the program but also ensures financial and personal commitment from the many publics affected by the program, including students, parents, school personnel, and members of the community (Fagan, Brooke-Weiss, Cady, & Hawkins, 2009; Harpine, Nitza, & Coyne, 2010). Once the program is designed, it can be piloted and then restructured as needed. When the team is satisfied that the program is ready, formal implementation can take place. Evaluation is continual, and the program is revised as necessary. A more in-depth discussion of prevention is found in Chapter 2, and each of the chapters that follow present prevention programming with a problem-specific focus.

Crisis Management

Although crisis management is not the main thrust of this book, it is important to understand the basic differences between prevention and crisis management. Whereas prevention programs have as one of their basic goals reducing the at-risk potential for youth, crisis management programs have as their basic goals eliminating existing at-risk behaviors and providing new behaviors, coping skills, and knowledge that will keep the at-risk behaviors from reoccurring. In the first, we attempt to stop something before it begins (primary prevention), and in the second, we attempt to stop something from continuing (secondary and tertiary prevention). Underlying the development of either secondary or tertiary prevention programs is the fact that many of the behaviors discussed in this chapter are currently present in a large percentage of youth; thus, steps need to be taken to change or remediate these behaviors. It is too late to prevent these behaviors from developing; they are already present. Therefore, programs are designed to eliminate or reduce the behaviors that have placed the individual at risk. In so doing, programs that may be aimed at either individuals or groups of individuals identify the problematic behavior(s), identify the individual(s) operating within this behavioral pattern, design programs based on current knowledge or select existing programs that have proved to be effective, implement strategies, and then evaluate the results of the implementation (Beautrais, 2005).

Similarities between programmatic aspects of primary prevention and secondary and tertiary prevention are obvious. Differences also exist. Secondary and tertiary prevention often occur in a structured setting, such as a treatment center, mental health clinic, or school counseling office. In these settings, counseling/therapy is provided to address specific problem behaviors and varies according

Sidebar 1.6 ■ Finding Balance in the Crisis-Management Paradigm

It is important, regardless of your personal positioning on the prevention–crisis-management paradigm, to realize that both aspects of this paradigm not only are necessary but also provide direction and guidance in working with at-risk youth. It is difficult not to see the benefits that prevention programming would have on stopping at-risk behaviors from developing. On the other hand, on the basis of the startling statistics presented by the Children's Defense Fund (2011), crisis management is needed to aid in the elimination of existing at-risk behaviors. What steps do you see as important in finding an effective balance between these two positions?

■ ■ ■

to the identified problem behaviors, the theoretical orientation of the counselor/therapist, the institution's or organization's policies, the parameters of insurance reimbursement, and the willingness of the individual to take part in the process. Secondary and tertiary prevention are often of a more immediate nature than primary prevention because of the severity of the presenting at-risk behavior. Programs aimed at preventing youth from developing suicidal behaviors do not have the same immediacy as programs developed to deal with youth who have attempted suicide. Primary prevention programs tend to deal with healthy individuals or those with the potential for at-risk behaviors, whereas secondary and tertiary prevention programs tend to deal with individuals who have moved from healthy lifestyles to unhealthy lifestyles. A final difference is that primary prevention programs tend to be group or population based, whereas secondary and tertiary prevention programs focus more on the individual and his or her place in the larger group. Similarities and differences among these differing levels of prevention will become clearer in the chapters that follow.

Summary

This chapter has provided a working definition of at-risk youth, information pertaining to the causal factors and behaviors that are descriptive of this population, factors of resilience, and general information related to the similarities and differences between prevention and crisis management. Such information could have helped our hypothetical teacher, John Patron. It could have provided some foundational material to aid him in better understanding the various parameters that surround the students in his classroom. It could have provided him with directives as he began to seek out information regarding what is currently being done to develop approaches to prevention, community resources that could be utilized by the school, and insight into factors of resilience. If John had the opportunity to read this book, he could be in a much better place in terms of answering the many questions raised at the meeting. For those who share some of John's concerns, have questions similar to John's, and feel the need to know more about the areas of at-risk youth and prevention, this book can be of great assistance. The true benefit of the knowledge gained will be not only better service for those youth who have a potential for developing at-risk behavior but also better preparation for dealing with those youth whose behaviors currently place them at risk.

Useful Websites

At-Risk Students—Wikipedia, the Free Encyclopedia
   http://en.wikipedia.org/wiki/At-risk_students
Children's Defense Fund
   http://www.childrensdefense.org/
National Center for Educational Statistics
   http://nces.ed.gov/
National Coalition for the Homeless
   http://www.nationalhomeless.org/
National Dropout Prevention Center/Network
   http://www.dropoutprevention.org/
National Institute of Mental Health
   http://www.nimh.nih.gov/index.shtml

References

Adams, C. M. (2006). The consequences of witnessing family violence on children and implications for family counselors. *Family Journal, 14,* 334–341.

Bagdi, A., & Pfister, I. K. (2006). Childhood stressors and coping actions: A comparison of children and parents' perspectives. *Child and Youth Care Forum, 35,* 21–40.

Barber, L. W., & McClellan, M. C. (1987). Looking at America's dropouts. *Phi Delta Kappan, 69,* 264–267.

Bazargan, M., & West, K. (2006). Correlates to remain sexually inactive among underserved Hispanic and African American high school students (control of teen pregnancy). *Journal of School Health, 76,* 25–33.

Beaumont, P. J. V. (2002). Clinical presentation of anorexia nervosa and bulimia nervosa. In C. G. Fairburn & K. D. Brownell (Eds.), *Eating disorders and obesity* (pp. 162–170). New York, NY: Guilford Press.

Beautrais, A. L. (2005). National strategies for the reduction and prevention of suicide. *Crisis, 26,* 1–3.

Beekhoven, S., & Dekkers, H. (2005). Early schools leaving in the lower vocational track: Triangulation of qualitative and quantitative data. *Adolescence, 40,* 197–210.

Bernard, B. (2004). *Resiliency: What we have learned.* San Francisco, CA: WestEd.

Blake, B. J., & Bentov, L. (2001). Geographical mapping of unmarried teen births and selected sociodemographic variables. *Public Health Nursing, 18,* 33–39.

Bohon, C., Garber, J., & Horowitz, J. L. (2007) Predicting school dropout and adolescent sexual behavior in offspring of depressed and non-depressed mothers. *Journal of the American Academy of Child and Adolescent Psychiatry, 46,* 15–24.

Brook, J. S., Brook, D. W., & Phal, K. (2006). The developmental context for adolescent substance abuse intervention. In H. A. Liddle & C. L. Rowe (Eds.), *Adolescent substance abuse: Research and clinical advances* (pp. 25–51). Cambridge, England: Cambridge University Press.

Brooks, K., Schiraldi, V., & Ziedenberg, J. (2000). *School house hype: Two years later.* Washington, DC: Justice Policy Institute.

Burrow-Sanchez, J. (2006). Understanding adolescent substance abuse: Prevalence, risk factors, and clinical implications. *Journal of Counseling & Development, 84,* 283–290.

Capuzzi, D., & Gross, D. R. (2008). *Youth at risk: A prevention resource for counselors, teachers, and parents* (5th ed.). Alexandria, VA: American Counseling Association.

Children's Defense Fund. (2011). *Every day in America.* Retrieved from http://www.childrensdefensefund.org/child-research-data-publications/each-day-in-america.html

Coldwell, J., Pike, A., & Dunn, J. (2006). Household chaos: Links with parenting and child behavior. *Journal of Child Psychology and Psychiatry, 47,* 1116–1122.

Conrath, J. (1988). A new deal for at-risk students. *NAASP Bulletin, 14,* 36–39.

Conyne, R. K. (1994). Preventive counseling. *Counseling and Human Development, 27,* 21–28.

Cosden, M. (2001). Risk and resilience for substance abuse among adolescents and adults with L.D. *Journal of Learning Disabilities, 34,* 352–359.

Davis, T. (2013). School counseling. In D. Capuzzi & D. R. Gross (Eds.), *Introduction to the counseling profession* (6th ed., pp. 445–470). New York, NY: Routledge.

Deater-Deckard, K., Ivy, L., & Smith, J. (2006). Resilience in gene–environment transactions. In S. Goldstein & R. Brooks (Eds.), *Handbook of resilience in children* (pp. 49–64). New York, NY: Springer Science+Business Media.

Derzon, J. (2006). How effective are school based violence prevention programs in preventing and reducing violence and other antisocial behaviors? A metaanalysis. In S. Jimerson & M. Furlong (Eds.), *The handbook of school violence and school safety* (pp. 429–441). Mahwah, NJ: Erlbaum.

Dykeman, C. (2008). The impact of dysfunctional family dynamics on children and adolescents. In D. Capuzzi & D. R. Gross (Eds.), *Youth at risk: A prevention resource for counselors, teachers, and parents* (5th ed., pp. 71–95). Alexandria, VA: American Counseling Association.

Dynarski, M., & Gleason, P. (2002). How can we help? What we have learned from recent federal dropout prevention evaluations. *Journal of Education for Students Placed at Risk, 7,* 43–69.

Ekstrom, R. R., Goertz, M. E., Pollack, J. M., & Rock, D. A. (1986). Who drops out of school and why: Findings from a national study. *Teachers College Record, 87,* 356–373.

Fagan, A. A., Brooke-Weiss, B., Cady, R., & Hawkins, J. D. (2009). If at first you don't succeed . . . keep trying: Strategies to enhance coalition/school partnerships to implement school-based prevention programming. *The Australian and New Zealand Journal of Criminology, 42,* 387–405.

Felner, R. D. (2006). Poverty in childhood and adolescence. In S. Goldstein & R. Brooks (Eds.), *Handbook of resilience in children* (pp. 125–148). New York, NY: Springer Science+Business Media.

Fine, M. (1986). Why urban adolescents drop into and out of public high school. *Teachers College Record, 87,* 393–409.

Finn, A. (2008). Death in the classroom: Violence in schools. In D. Capuzzi & D. R. Gross (Eds.), *Youth at risk: A prevention resource for counselors, teachers, and parents* (5th ed., pp. 383–405). Alexandria, VA: American Counseling Association.

Finn, A., & Remley, T. P. (2002). Prevention of school violence: A school and community response. In D. Rea & J. Bergin (Eds.), *Safeguarding our youth: Successful school and community programs* (pp. 19–27). New York, NY: McGraw-Hill.

Flowers, L. R., & Hermann, M. A. (2008). "This isn't the place for me": School dropout. In D. Capuzzi & D. R. Gross (Eds.), *Youth at risk: A prevention resource for counselors, teachers, and parents* (5th ed., pp. 457–478). Alexandria, VA: American Counseling Association.

Friesen, B. J., & Brennan, E. (2005). Strengthening families and communities: System building for resilience. In M. Ungar (Ed.), *Handbook for working with children and youth: Pathways to resilience across cultures and contexts* (pp. 295–312). Thousand Oaks, CA: Sage.

Gaffney, D. A. (2006). The aftermath of disaster: Children in crisis. *Journal of Clinical Psychology: In Session, 62,* 1001–1016.

Gagliardi-Blea, C. J., Weber, D. J., Rofkahr, C., & Robinson-Kurpius, S. E. (2008). "I can't live without it": Adolescent substance abuse. In D. Capuzzi & D. R. Gross (Eds.), *Youth at risk: A prevention resource for counselors, teachers, and parents* (5th ed., pp. 407–434). Alexandria, VA: American Counseling Association.

Garnier, H. E., Stein, J. A., & Jacobs, J. K. (1997). The process of dropping out of high school: A 19-year perspective. *American Educational Research Journal, 34,* 395–419.

Goldstein, S., & Brooks, R. B. (2006). *Handbook of resilience in children*. New York, NY: Springer Science+Business Media.

Haber, M. G., & Toro, P. A. (2004). Homelessness among families, children and adolescents: An ecological–developmental perspective. *Clinical Child and Family Psychology Review, 7*, 123–164.

Haley, M., & Sherwood-Hawes, A. (2004). Children having children: Teenage pregnancy and parenthood. In D. Capuzzi & D. R. Gross (Eds.), *Youth at risk: A prevention resource for counselors, teachers, and parents* (4th ed., pp. 211–242). Alexandria, VA: American Counseling Association.

Haley, M., & Vasquez, J. (2008). A future in jeopardy: Sexuality issues in adolescence. In D. Capuzzi & D. R. Gross (Eds.), *Youth at risk: A prevention resource for counselors, teachers, and parents* (5th ed., pp. 281–315). Alexandria, VA: American Counseling Association.

Hamilton, B. E., Martin, J. A., & Ventura, S. J. (2012). Births: Preliminary data for 2011. *National Vital Statistics Report, 61*, Table 2.

Hamrin, V., & Scahill, L. (2005). Selective serotonin reuptake inhibitors for children and adolescents with major depression: Current controversies and recommendations. *Issues in Mental Health Nursing, 26*, 433–450.

Harpine, E. C., Nitza, A., & Coyne, R. (2010). Prevention groups: Today and tomorrow. *Group Dynamics: Theory, Research, and Practice, 14*, 268–280.

Houseknecht, S. K., & Hango, D.W. (2006). The impact of marital conflict and disruption on children's health. *Youth and Society, 38*, 58–89.

Inaba, D. S., & Cohen, W. (2000). *Uppers, downers, and all arounders: Physical and mental effects of psychoactive drugs*. Ashland, OR: CNS Publications.

Ingersoll, G., & Orr, D. (1988). Adolescents at risk. *Counseling and Human Development, 20*, 1–8.

Jimerson, S. R., Anderson, G. E., & Whipple, A. D. (2002). Winning the battle and losing the war: Examining the relation between grade retention and dropping out of school. *Psychology in the Schools, 39*, 441–457.

Jones, T. L., & Prinz, R. J. (2005). Potential roles of parental self-efficacy in parent–child adjustment: A review. *Clinical Psychological Review, 25*, 341–363.

Kaplan, H. B. (2006). Understanding the concept of resilience. In S. Goldstein & R. Brooks (Eds.), *Handbook of resilience in children* (pp. 39–48). New York, NY: Springer Science+Business Media.

Kushman, J. W., Sieber, C., & Heariold-Kinney, P. (2000). This isn't the place for me: School dropout. In D. Capuzzi & D. R. Gross (Eds.), *Youth at risk: A prevention resource guide for counselors, teachers, and parents* (3rd ed., pp. 353–381). Alexandria, VA: American Counseling Association.

Lewis, R. E. (2008). Resilience: Individual, family, school, and community perspectives. In D. Capuzzi & D. R. Gross (Eds.), *Youth at risk: A prevention resource guide for counselors, teachers, and parents* (5th ed., pp. 39–68). Alexandria, VA: American Counseling Association.

Maples, M. F., Packman, J., Abney, P., Daugherty, R. F., Casey, J., & Pirtie, L. (2005). Suicide by teenagers in middle school: A postvention team approach. *Journal of Counseling & Development, 83*, 397–405.

Marshall, K. (2004). Resilience research and practice: National Resilience Resource Center bridging the gap. In H. C. Waxman, Y. N. Padron, & J. P. Gray (Eds.), *Educational resiliency: Student, teacher and school perspectives* (pp. 63–86). Greenwich, CT: Information Age.

McWhirter, J. J., McWhirter, B. T., McWhirter, A. M., & McWhirter, E. H. (2007). *At risk youth: A comprehensive response* (4th ed.). Pacific Grove, CA: Brooks/Cole.

Meggert, S. S. (2008). "Who cares what I think": Problems of low self-esteem. In D. Capuzzi & D. R. Gross (Eds.), *Youth at risk: A prevention resource for counselors, teachers, and parents* (5th ed., pp. 97–125). Alexandria, VA: American Counseling Association.

Minga, T. (1988). States and the "at-risk" issues: Said aware but still "failing." *Education Week, 8*, 1–16.

National Center for Education Statistics. (2012). *Dropout rates in the United States: 2011*. Retrieved from http://nces.ed.gov/fastfacts/display.asp?ID=16

National Coalition for the Homeless. (2009). *How many people experience homelessness?* Retrieved from http://www.nationalhomeless.org/factsheets/how_many.html.

National Institute of Mental Health. (2007). *Suicide facts*. Retrieved December 1, 2012, from http://www.nimh.nih.gov/learn/publications/suicide-in-the-u.s.-statistics-and-prevention

Paulu, N. (1987). *Dealing with dropouts: The urban superintendents' call to action*. Washington, DC: U.S. Department of Education, Office of Educational Research and Improvement.

Placier, M. L. (1993). The semantics of policy making: The case of "at risk." *Educational Evaluation and Policy Analysis, 15*, 380.

Reschly, A. L., & Christenson, S. L. (2006). School completion. In G. G. Bear & K. M. Mike (Eds.), *Children's needs III: Development, prevention, and intervention* (pp. 103–113). Washington, DC: National Association of School Psychologists.

Ross, D. (2003). *Childhood bullying, teasing, and violence: What school personnel, other professionals, and parents can do* (2nd ed.). Alexandria, VA: American Counseling Association.

Rumberger, R. W. (1993). Chicano dropouts: A review of research and policy issues. In R. Valencia (Ed.), *Chicano school failure and success: Research and policy agendas for the 1990's* (pp. 64–89). London, England: Falmer Press.

Stevens, P., & Griffin, J. (2001). Youth high-risk behaviors: Survey and results. *Journal of Addictions & Offender Counseling, 22*, 31–47.

Stormont, M. (2007). *Fostering resilience in young children vulnerable for failure: Strategies for K–3*. Columbus, OH: Pearson/Merrill/Prentice Hall.

Stormont, M. A., & McCathren, R. B. (2008). Nowhere to turn: Homeless youth. In D. Capuzzi & D. R. Gross (Eds.), *Youth at risk: A prevention resource for counselors, teachers, and parents* (5th ed., pp. 435–455). Alexandria, VA: American Counseling Association.

Unger, M. (2004). *Nurturing hidden resilience in troubled youth*. Toronto, Ontario, Canada: University of Toronto Press.

Unger, M. (Ed.). (2005). *Handbook for working with children and youth: Pathways to resilience across cultures and contexts*. Thousand Oaks, CA: Sage.

Vaillant, G. E. (2002). *Aging well: Surprising guideposts to a happier life from the landmark Harvard study of adult development*. Boston, MA: Little, Brown.

Von Ransom, K. M., & Robinson, K. E. (2006). Who is providing what type of psychotherapy to eating disorder clients? A survey. *International Journal of Eating Disorders, 39*, 27–34.

Werner, E. E. (2006). What can we learn about resilience from large-scale longitudinal studies? In S. Goldstein & R. Brooks (Eds.), *Handbook of resilience in children* (pp. 91–106). New York, NY: Springer Science+Business Media.

Werner, E. E., & Smith, R. S. (2001). *Journeys from childhood to midlife: Risk, resilience and recovery*. Ithaca, NY: Cornell University Press.

White, S. W., & Kelly, F. D. (2010). The school counselor's role in school dropout prevention. *Journal of Counseling & Development, 88*, 227–235.

Wright, K. S., & Blanks, E. E. (2008). The secret and all-consuming obsessions: Eating disorders. In D. Capuzzi & D. R. Gross (Eds.), *Youth at risk: A prevention resource for counselors, teachers, and parents* (5th ed., pp. 203–247). Alexandria, VA: American Counseling Association.

Wright, M. O., & Masten, A. S. (2006). Resilience processes in development. In S. Goldstein & R. Brooks (Eds.), *Handbook of resilience in children* (pp. 17–38). New York, NY: Springer Science+Business Media.

Chapter 2

Prevention: An Overview

David Capuzzi and Douglas R. Gross

The number of children and adolescents who engage in behaviors (e.g., unprotected sex, substance use and abuse, abnormal eating patterns, suicide attempts) and are exposed to environmental factors (e.g., abuse, violence, homelessness) that place them at risk for adverse mental and physical health consequences is increasing at alarming rates (Hovell, Blumberg, Liles, Powell, & Morrison, 2001; Kazdin, 1993; Popenhagen & Qualley, 1998; Reddy & Richardson, 2006). In addition, many children and adolescents are experiencing serious psychological and emotional impairment. Because the impairments that youth experience can persist and increase in severity across the life span, the importance of early prevention and intervention efforts has increased in significance.

One way of emphasizing the significance and importance of early prevention efforts is by looking at examples of some of the problems that characterize contemporary residents of the United States:

- There are 30 million individuals over the age of 16 (or 14% of the adult population in the United States) who do not read well enough to understand a newspaper article written at the eighth-grade level. An additional 63 million read at the fifth-grade reading level or lower (Literacy Mid-South, 2011).
- Approximately 20% of the population (or 45 million adults) have been identified as experiencing some type of mental disturbance, but in 2010 only 39% of these 45 million American adults received mental health services (NAMI Advocate, 2012).
- The number of youth dropping out of school each year is approximately 25% of those enrolled in K–12 settings.

- The leading causes of morbidity and mortality among youth and young adults in the United States are related to six categories of priority health-risk behaviors: (a) behaviors that contribute to unintentional injuries and violence; (b) tobacco use; (c) alcohol and other drug use; (d) sexual behaviors that contribute to unintended pregnancy and sexually transmitted diseases, including HIV infection; (e) unhealthy dietary behaviors; and (f) physical inactivity (Centers for Disease Control and Prevention, 2012b).
- It's estimated that each year in the United States, 1 in every 750 infants is born with a pattern of physical, developmental, and functional problems referred to as fetal alcohol syndrome, while another 40,000 are born with fetal alcohol effects (KidsHealth, 2012).
- Even though consumption of alcohol by persons under the age of 21 is illegal, youth aged 12 to 20 years drink 11% of all alcohol consumed in the United States. More than 90% of this alcohol is consumed during episodes of binge drinking. Underage drinkers consume more drinks per drinking occasion than adult drinkers. In 2010, there were approximately 189,000 emergency room visits by patients under the age of 21 for injuries and other conditions linked to alcohol (Centers for Disease Control and Prevention, 2012a).
- Adolescent suicide ranks second or third in most reports of the leading causes of death in the 11- to 24-year-old age group (American Foundation for Suicide Prevention, 2012).
- First marriages end in divorce 50% of the time, and 50%–75% of child mental health referrals are for children affected by divorce (American Psychological Association, 2012).
- Increasing numbers of women are physically assaulted by intimate male partners. Every 9 seconds in the United States a woman is assaulted or beaten. Domestic violence is the leading cause of injury to women—more than car accidents, muggings, and rapes combined. Studies suggest that up to 10 million children witness some form of domestic violence annually. Nearly one in five teenage girls who have been in a relationship said a boyfriend threatened violence or self-harm if presented with a breakup. Every day in the United States, more than three women are murdered by their husbands or boyfriends (Domestic Violence Statistics, 2012).

Dryfoos (1997) summarized data supplied by the U.S. Census Bureau, the Centers for Disease Control and Prevention, the U.S. Department of Justice, and the National Center for Education Statistics with respect to the prevalence of at-risk behaviors of the 14- to 17-year-old population. The data indicate that 25% of all the young people in this age range are behind in grade, and 5% have already dropped out. Between 18% and 48% are involved in some form of substance abuse, and 53% are sexually active. More than 9% have been adjudicated as delinquents, 22% carry some form of weapon, and 21% have frequently been truant. About 25% of this population report that they have been preoccupied with suicidal thoughts, and 9% report that they have made suicide attempts. Similar data have been reported by Astor, Meyer, Benbenishty, Marachi, and Rosemond (2005); Collins et al. (2002); Fetro, Coyle, and Pham (2001); and King (2001).

The National Center for Education Statistics (Chapman, Laird, & Kewal Remani, 2010) reemphasized the importance and significance of early prevention efforts by emphasizing the impact of school dropout on income and future employment, with the following statistics:

- The median income for persons ages 18 through 67 who had not completed high school was roughly $23,000 in 2008.
- In comparison, the median income of persons ages 18 through 67 who had completed their education with at least a high school diploma, including a General Educational Development certificate, was approximately $42,000 in 2008. Over the course of a person's lifetime, this difference translates into a loss of approximately $630,000 in income for a person who did not complete high school.
- Among adults ages 25 and older, a lower percentage of dropouts are in the labor force compared with adults who earned a high school credential.
- Among adults in the labor force, a higher percentage of dropouts are unemployed compared with adults who earned a high school credential.
- Dropouts ages 25 or older report being in worse health than adults who are not dropouts, regardless of income. Dropouts also make up disproportionately higher percentages of the nation's prison and death row inmates.
- Comparing those who drop out of high school with those who complete high school, the average high school dropout is associated with costs to the economy of approximately $240,000 over his or her lifetime in terms of lower tax contributions, higher reliance on Medicaid and Medicare, higher rates of criminal activity, and higher reliance on welfare.

The cost associated with these examples in terms of economics is staggering. Approximately $273 billion was spent in 1990 in treatment and social services associated with alcohol abuse, drug abuse, and mental illness (Horner & McElhaney, 1993). These costs do not include those associated with teenage pregnancy, AIDS, eating disorders, suicide, homelessness, and school dropout (Astor et al., 2005; Reddy & Richardson, 2006). When these additional areas are taken into consideration, the estimated figure increases to incomprehensible levels. As significant as these dollar amounts are, however, they do not include the immeasurable costs associated with human loss and suffering and the concomitant issues related to grief and loss.

In the wake of the need for counseling and therapy created by conditions in the North American culture, the availability of counselors, social workers, psychiatric nurses, psychologists, and psychiatrists pales by contrast (Coker & Dixon-Saxon, 2013; Conyne, 1994). Mandates connected with managed care and the understaff-

Sidebar 2.1 ■ Mental Illness in the United States

Some experts estimate that approximately one in four adults suffer from a diagnosable mental disorder. Of those individuals, about 6%, or 17 million people, suffer from what is considered a serious mental illness. However, only about 15% of adults in the United States seek some kind of mental health treatment. One can only speculate about why more adults do not seek assistance for mental health issues. The stigma attached to mental health counseling, lack of health insurance, apprehension about becoming involved in the process of counseling, time constraints, and so forth could all be reasons for such reluctance.

■ ■ ■

ing of social service agencies further compound the difficulties experienced by children, adolescents, and adults in need of assistance from the professionally prepared, licensed helper.

Prevention is based on a different way to help than that associated with prevalent diagnostic/prescriptive approaches. Prevention is not focused on dysfunction and associated remediation; it is focused on a proactive approach designed to empower the individual, change systemic variables, and forestall the development of dysfunction. Prevention is also based on awareness of the risk factors that researchers have identified as the most common antecedents of at-risk behaviors (Dryfoos, 1997; Hallfors et al., 2006):

1. Parents' ability to provide nurturing and support is closely connected to a child's ability to mature and develop. Parents who are unable to parent in ways that convey a sense of nurturing and support create barriers to optimal development.
2. The schooling experience is a significant precursor to maturation and development. Poor grades, deficits in basic skills, low academic expectations, and repeated school discipline problems are predictors of involvement in at-risk behavior.
3. Peer influences are strong determinants of youth behavior during the middle school years and sometimes earlier. Youth who engage in high-risk behaviors lack the ability to resist joining their friends in experimenting with drugs, sex, and other delinquent behavior.
4. Young people who are depressed or have conduct disorders (e.g., engaging in multiple problem behaviors such as truancy, stealing, cheating, running away, arson, cruelty to animals, unusually early sexual intercourse, and excessive fighting prior to the age of 15) are extremely vulnerable to making choices that are far from responsible and productive.
5. Life in a low-income family and an impoverished neighborhood also increases the probability of at-risk behavior because economically disadvantaged youth often lack access to quality education and safe environments.
6. Race and ethnicity are also factors affecting youth's vulnerability—not because of race and ethnicity alone, but because African American, Hispanic, and Native American youth may be at a disadvantage economically and live in poorer, less safe neighborhoods.

In 2012, the National Dropout Prevention Center published an extensive list of situations that put youth at risk. That list was subdivided into the following categories related to school, student, community, and family:

School Related
- conflict between home/school culture
- ineffective discipline system
- lack of adequate counseling
- negative school climate
- lack of relevant curriculum
- passive instructional strategies
- inappropriate use of technology
- disregard for student learning styles

- retentions and suspensions
- low expectations
- lack of language instruction

Student Related
- poor school attitude
- low ability level
- attendance/truancy issues
- behavior/discipline problems
- pregnancy
- drug abuse
- poor peer relationships
- nonparticipation
- friends have dropped out
- illness/disability
- low self-esteem/self-efficacy

Community Related
- lack of community support services or response
- lack of community support for schools
- high incidences of criminal activities
- lack of school/community linkages

Family Related
- low socioeconomic status
- dysfunctional home life
- no parental involvement
- low parental expectations
- non-English-speaking home
- ineffective parenting/abuse
- high mobility

Defining Qualities of Prevention

As noted by the American Academy of Pediatrics (2004); Conyne (1994); Dryfoos (1997); Gilliland and James (1993); Janosik (1984); Kadish, Glaser, Calhoun, and Ginter (2001); and Reddy and Richardson (2006), prevention efforts focus on averting human dysfunction and promoting healthy functioning. The emphasis in prevention is on enhancing optimal functioning or well-being in psychological and

Sidebar 2.2 ■ Age and the Impact of Risk and Protective Factors

It is interesting to note (National Institute on Drug Abuse, 2011) that the potential impact of specific risk and protective factors changes with age. For example, risk factors within the family have a greater impact on a younger child, whereas association with drug-abusing peers may be a more significant risk factor for an adolescent. In addition, early intervention with risk factors (e.g., aggressive behavior and poor self-control) often has a greater impact than later intervention by changing a child's life path (trajectory) away from problems and toward positive behaviors.

■ ■ ■

social domains and on developing competencies. This emphasis is in contrast to an emphasis on the identification and diagnosis of various disorders or maladaptive behavioral patterns in individuals and the provision of treatment to lessen impairment (Christensen, 2013; Kazdin, 1993). Prevention efforts are characterized by a number of defining qualities, outlined below.

1. Prevention efforts are proactive. Prevention initiatives address individual and systemic strengths and further develop those strengths so that dysfunction either does not develop or does not manifest itself to the point that impairment occurs. This process contrasts with reactive approaches that are designed to intervene after problems have developed (Brooks, 2006; King, 2001; National Institute on Drug Abuse, 2011).

2. Prevention efforts focus on functional people and those who are at risk. As noted by Conyne (1994), prevention services (e.g., classroom guidance, individual or small-group counseling) focus on those who are healthy and coping well so that strengths may be identified and enhanced and additional skills can be learned. Prevention efforts are also directed at those known to be at risk, such as children of divorce, children of alcoholics, or the homeless. The purpose is to provide proactive intervention so that future difficulties are avoided (Bosworth, Espelage, DuBay, & Daytner, 2000).

3. Prevention efforts are cumulative and transferable. When professionals help others through prevention, every effort is made to point out relationships and to assist clients to master a hierarchy of skills. For example, elementary-age children who have participated in groups designed to enhance self-esteem may, at a later date, feel good enough about themselves to participate in assertiveness training. The ability to use assertiveness skills may be useful in the context of refusing drugs; these same skills may prevent a youth from being victimized in some other situation.

4. Prevention efforts are used to reduce incidence (Astor et al., 2005; Conyne, 1994; King, 2001). Prevention activities are used before the fact so that problems do not develop. They may also be used to reduce the incidence of a new dysfunction.

5. Prevention efforts promote peer helping. When elementary, middle school, and high school youth learn to enhance communication, assertiveness, problem solving, and other related abilities, they are better able to help peers, encourage friends to seek professional assistance, and participate in supervised peer-helper programs. In many instances, the power of a member of the peer group outdistances that of a concerned adult in terms of providing encouragement, support, and straightforward feedback (Dryfoos, 1997; King, 2001; National Institute on Drug Abuse, 2011).

6. Prevention efforts can be population based, individually based, or group based. Many prevention efforts are focused on at-risk populations (e.g., information and discussion about the HIV virus or hepatitis B may be shared with sexually active adolescents, or victims of abuse may be assisted so that they do not develop lifelong dysfunctional patterns). Prevention may also be focused entirely on an individual so that suicidal preoccupation can be eliminated or depression can be overcome. When larger populations are reached through prevention programming, it is possible to affect the life space of large numbers of people (Conyne, 1994; National Institute on Drug Abuse, 2011; Reddy & Richardson, 2006).

7. Prevention efforts can be used early in the life span. We know that children who are homeless or who have been physically or sexually abused may develop traits and self-concepts that put them at risk during adolescence and adulthood. Early prevention efforts can effect changes in self-esteem, behavior, feelings, and thinking so that these children are not at risk for substance abuse, prostitution, depression, and suicide at a later time (Brooks, 2006; Buckley, 2000; Dryfoos, 1997; National Institute on Drug Abuse, 2011; Reddy & Richardson, 2006).

8. Prevention efforts target more than a single system. Because each person must simultaneously interact in a variety of environments, practitioners do not emphasize one system to the exclusion of others. Healthy individuals must learn to cope with the demands of several systems on a daily basis (Dryfoos, 1997; Fagan, Brooke-Weiss, Cady, & Hawkins, 2009; King, 2001; McGowan, 2006; National Institute on Drug Abuse, 2011).

9. Prevention efforts are sensitive to the needs of diverse populations. No constellation of services or approach to prevention can make an equal impact on all groups. Diverse populations present unique challenges; what one population finds acceptable may be totally incompatible with the needs of another. Practitioners must be sensitive to the traditions, needs, and differences presented by subcultures in North America (Brown & Simpson, 2000; Conyne, 1994; Dryfoos, 1997; Kitts, 2005; Shaughnessy, Doshi, & Jones, 2004).

10. Prevention efforts are collaborative. As noted by Conyne (1994), prevention efforts can be complex and must be conducted in concert with professionals from a number of disciplines. For example, a counselor working with an adolescent who is depressed may need the assistance of a psychiatrist or nurse practitioner if medication is needed along with counseling to control a body-chemistry-related bipolar pattern of depression. Often the expertise needed to assist an individual, a family, or a larger population may require input and teaming among professionals from several disciplines.

11. Prevention efforts are applicable in more than one context. Faculty and staff in a school setting, for example, may seek the assistance of someone who can provide staff development, train a crisis team, and provide input on a written crisis management plan. Such efforts may initially be focused on substance use and abuse prevention or suicide prevention. After the adults connected with a particular school or school district have been prepared with respect to one particular at-risk population, they can usually apply the same principles and process to providing prevention services to another at-risk group (Harpine, Nitza, & Conyne, 2010).

12. Prevention efforts are empowering. Empowerment should be the primary goal of all prevention efforts (Brooks, 2006; Conyne, 1994). This empowerment should apply not only to the recipients of prevention efforts but also to the providers of prevention services. When those receiving assistance build on strengths and learn new coping skills, they feel better about themselves and their ability to make responsible, healthy decisions. As professionals increase their ability to enrich the lives of others, they, too, feel productive, competent, and capable of impacting change.

13. Prevention efforts involve parents. Inviting parents to be in responsible roles in their children's schools, such as paid or volunteer classroom aides or voting members of school reorganization initiatives, results in more positive outcomes for children and adolescents. Establishment of parent centers in schools for parents and youth for whom English is a second language or for whom assistance with health and social services, transportation, child care, or meals is needed has been found to be effective (Brooks, 2006; Dryfoos, 1997; National Institute on Drug Abuse, 2011; Reddy & Richardson, 2006).

Sidebar 2.3 ■ Family Bonding and Prevention

Family bonding is really crucial to the relationship between parents and children. Family bonding can be strengthened by the provision of skills training for parents on topics such as supporting children, parent–child communication, and parental involvement. Sometimes parents do not realize that parental monitoring and supervision are critical aspects of prevention. These skills can also be enhanced by education on rule setting, techniques for monitoring activities, praise for appropriate behavior, and consistent discipline that enforces defined family rules.

■ ■ ■

14. *Prevention efforts make connections to the world of work.* Many at-risk youth have little exposure to the world of work and may not have adult role models who are consistently employed. When these youth are exposed to curricula that provide career information, skills training, and opportunities for volunteer or paid work experience, their involvement in at-risk behaviors decreases (Dryfoos, 1997).

15. *Prevention efforts include social and life-skills training.* Improving social, decision-making, and assertiveness skills leads to more positive outcomes (Harpine et al., 2010). Research also demonstrates that consistency of participant involvement and opportunity for "booster" sessions are required to maintain long-term effects (Beautrais, 2005; Dryfoos, 1997).

16. *Prevention efforts include in-service training for both faculty and staff.* Prevention efforts rarely succeed unless time and money are committed to the in-service training necessary to provide the adults in the school with the insight, skills, and motivation needed to successfully implement initiatives aimed at aspects of systemic reform.

17. *Prevention efforts include the presence of dedicated adults.* Successful prevention programs are usually the result of the efforts of adult role models who have a great deal of empathy and provide high levels of support for young people who have risk factors in their lives that predispose them to engaging in at-risk behaviors. It is very difficult to implement new programs and policies in a school in which the faculty and staff are not receptive to new ways of enhancing the school climate and are unreceptive to the needs of youth who may be quite different from themselves.

18. *Prevention programs should enhance protective factors and reverse or reduce risk factors.* The most effective programs combine efforts to enhance qualities and circumstances that make engagement in at-risk behaviors less likely at the same time efforts to reduce risk factors are initiated (National Institute on Drug Abuse, 2011).

Approaches to Prevention

A number of experts in contemporary prevention strategies have identified prevention as primary, secondary, or tertiary (Buckley, 2000; Hadge, 1992; Janosik, 1984; King, 2001; McWhirter, McWhirter, McWhirter, & McWhirter, 1998, 2007; Roberts, 1991). As practitioners consider prevention strategies for possible implementation with an individual, a family, a school, or a community, it is important to be able to assess needs and identify strategies in relation to whether these strategies can be categorized as primary, secondary, or tertiary.

Primary Prevention

Primary prevention involves proactive planning of strategies and activities to keep specific problems or crises from developing in the first place (Gilliland &

James, 1993). In primary prevention, the purpose is to reduce the incidence of future problems by reinforcing internal coping ability, modifying external variables, or both. Primary prevention provides assistance prior to the development of problems through counseling, teaching, or other services that emphasize anticipatory planning. Through anticipatory planning, individuals of all ages are given the opportunity to select and practice behaviors that are helpful in both present and future circumstances.

Examples of primary prevention include parent education programs to prevent child neglect and abuse and educational programs on university campuses to prevent sexual harassment, date rape, or violation of affirmative action guidelines. School programs for teenage boys and girls regarding the consequences of teenage pregnancies, the impact of school dropout, or the importance of effective communication skills are additional examples of primary prevention. Entire communities might also benefit from primary prevention efforts. For example, a series of mental health education seminars might be offered, free of charge, to residents of a community and might be collaboratively planned by representatives from the local schools, mental health services, and business sectors. Television and radio journalists might provide coverage of the services offered by women's and children's shelters or local crisis hotlines. Whatever the emphasis, the focus is always on preventing future and, more often than not, long-term pain or impairment.

Chapter 3 of this edition of our text presents valuable, additional information on primary prevention from a resilience point of view. This information provides an additional perspective that may prove helpful to those whose practice focus is working with children and adolescents.

Secondary Prevention

Secondary prevention consists of early intervention with people in crisis for the purpose of restoring equilibrium as soon as possible and reducing the impact of the distress. During periods of crisis, people are aware that the situation is out of control, and they may feel helpless. Unless secondary prevention is made available, a crisis may escalate to the point that it may be difficult to contain or consequences may be irreversible. For example, a suicidal adolescent who does not obtain assistance may attempt suicide, survive, and be left with lifelong physical impairment and emotional turmoil that overlay the traits and characteristics that precipitated the suicidal crisis in the first place. When individuals, families, schools, or communities recognize the parameters connected with a crisis situation, they may be quite motivated and extremely receptive to secondary prevention efforts.

Examples of secondary prevention include support groups for students who are experiencing the grief and loss associated with the unexpected death of a peer, school and community collaborative efforts to provide child care and alternative education opportunities for teenage parents, residential or outpatient treatment for teenagers who abuse alcohol, or counseling services established to stop battering or other violent behavior. During the secondary prevention process, emphasis should be placed on individual, family, school, and community resources and abilities. Preoccupation with defeat and negative consequences seldom results in the management of a particular crisis situation and the reestablishment of equilibrium.

It is important to note, at this juncture, that more and more school districts are writing *tragedy response plans* for the purpose of planning and coordinating efforts of school personnel who are presented with a sudden crisis situation. The reason for doing so is to prevent the systemic chaos and resultant negative impact on individuals and groups on a school campus at the time an unanticipated crisis occurs. These tragedy response plans usually delineate not only the roles of members of the crisis team but also the roles of all other school personnel as well as the roles of individuals or groups in the community that the school may need to call on in the midst of a crisis. Developing plans in advance has a number of advantages, including the opportunity to have such plans evaluated by experts in crisis management and by the school or district's legal team in advance so that modifications and additions can be made.

Tragedy response plans usually outline crisis responses to natural disasters (earthquakes, tornadoes, release of airborne toxins, and so forth), fire, death, accidents, child abduction, violence, and other events that need to be addressed immediately and may not have been anticipated. These plans are usually quite comprehensive and include guidelines for evacuating and transporting students, contacting parents, responding to journalists' inquiries, and working with police and disaster relief workers from the community, among others. Many school districts are beginning to publish their plans on the Internet, and we encourage school or community groups that are working on tragedy response plans to read what other school and community groups have developed and to contact representatives from schools that have experience in this area. Making such contacts can provide opportunities for collaborative sharing and evaluation and can eliminate the necessity to start from scratch.

Tertiary Prevention

Tertiary crisis prevention attempts to reduce the amount of residual impairment that follows the resolution of some crisis. Adolescents who complete residential or outpatient programs for substance abuse may benefit through participation in weekly support groups, facilitated by a professional, for the purpose of providing the reinforcement and support needed to prevent relapse. These same adolescents may need to participate concurrently in individual counseling or therapy to address the unmet needs that led to the use and abuse of a substance in the first place, because emotional development and coping skills are usually arrested about the time substance use begins. Victims of sexual abuse may participate in either group or individual (or both) counseling or therapy long after the abuse has ceased for the purpose of repairing damaged self-esteem and rebuilding the capacity to trust and share intimacy with significant others.

As emphasized by Janosik (1984), crisis in contemporary society is so prevalent that it is not possible for all those experiencing crisis to access the help of professionals. It is possible, however, to identify factors that place individuals, families, schools, and communities at risk. Thus, it is of paramount importance to reduce emotional pain, residual impairment, and cost to society as a whole through judicious use of prevention, whether primary, secondary, or tertiary in nature.

Types of Primary Prevention

The youth of today are faced with coping amidst a society that is more populated, more connected by advanced communication technology, and more complex with respect to a variety of psychosocial stressors. This sixth edition of *Youth at Risk* places more emphasis on prevention with respect to causative factors (such as low self-esteem, stress, depression) and a number of at-risk behaviors (such as drug abuse, unprotected sex, eating disorders, suicidal preoccupation, gang membership). The chapters that follow Chapter 3 highlight secondary and tertiary prevention efforts. This chapter provides information on primary prevention efforts based on the types described by McWhirter et al. (1998, 2007) and further addressed by Buckley (2000), Collins et al. (2002), Hovell et al. (2001), Kadish et al. (2001), and Watts (2000). These primary prevention efforts include developing life skills, enhancing interpersonal communication, learning strategies for cognitive change, achieving self-management and self-control, and coping with stress.

Developing Life Skills

Life skills can be defined as the ability to make use of personal resources for the purpose of expressing needs and positively influencing the environment. Such skills influence the formation of relationships and friendships, nonviolent methods of conflict resolution, and communication with adults (Beautrais, 2005; McWhirter et al., 1998, 2007). Developing life skills can be accomplished through education and training in life skills, school peer mediation, peer tutoring, and peer facilitation.

Education and training in life skills involve developing and incorporating instructional modules into the curriculum at elementary, middle, and high school levels. Also involved is the collaborative input of a variety of professionals (counselors, nurses, physicians, social workers, psychologists, physical educators, and classroom teachers) for the purpose of teaching skills needed by most individuals on a day-to-day basis (Spaeth, Weichold, Friedrich-Schiller, & Wiesner, 2010). The format for teaching any targeted skill should, ideally, contain the following components: teach, model, role-play, provide feedback, and assign homework. Almost any skill can be taught within this paradigm, and the fact that implementation is most often effected in the classroom means that entire populations can be accessed so that more and more young people can master skills that can help them avoid future problems.

School peer mediation, peer tutoring, and peer facilitation all involve training and supervising students to perform interpersonal helping tasks. School peer mediation requires trained peer mediators who work in partnerships with other students for the purpose of facilitating problem solving between disputing students. As noted by McWhirter et al. (1998, 2007), peer mediation ensures that both peer mediators and peer disputants increase experience with critical thinking, problem solving, and self-discipline.

Peer tutors are students who teach other students in both formal and informal learning situations. Peer tutoring can provide a cost-effective means of meeting individual needs, developing better ownership of the value of the educational experience, and enhancing self-esteem and motivation.

Peer facilitation, sometimes called peer helping, is a process in which students are trained to listen, paraphrase, support, and provide feedback to other students in the school (Walker, Ashby, Hoskins, & Greene, 2009). Peer facilitation is an effective way to empower children and adolescents and to provide adjunct support to the professional counselor or other human services specialist.

Enhancing Interpersonal Communication

Interpersonal communication skills are primary factors in the development of mutually beneficial relationships. Most programs designed to enhance interpersonal

Sidebar 2.4 ■ Peer Helping Programs and Prevention

Peer helping programs are key components of most prevention programs because youth usually pay close attention to interaction and input from peers. Youth involved in peer helping programs, however, must be carefully screened and consistently supervised by a professional member of the prevention team. Supervision and training must be provided at least once a week, and often it is necessary to provide supervision more than once a week. Because providing adequate supervision is time consuming, sometimes schools and agencies are reluctant to create a peer helping component as part of a prevention program even though studies have shown how effective peer helping programs can be.

■ ■ ■

communication skills offer training in verbal and nonverbal communication, creation of constructive friendships, avoidance of misunderstanding, and the development of long-term relationships with significant others (Brooks, 2006; McWhirter et al., 1998, 2007). Lack of ability to communicate well with others can lead to lowered self-esteem, isolation, and the development of future at-risk behaviors. Assertiveness training and resistance and refusal training are often important components of training in interpersonal communication (Milller, Eckert, & Mazza, 2009).

Assertiveness training is most often accomplished in the context of small groups. It can include providing assistance with how to express positive and negative feelings; how to initiate, maintain, and end conversations; and how to set limits. Nonverbal communication is an important component of assertiveness training because the manner in which something is communicated—body language, eye contact, personal distancing, and voice tone—can influence the message as much as the content of the message itself.

Resistance and refusal training is provided to help children and adolescents resist peer pressure or other negative social influences. Students are taught to label and recognize various forms of pressure and to develop behaviors that can help them resist such pressure and influence. Both assertiveness training and resistance and refusal training provide numerous modeling, role-play, feedback, and reinforcement opportunities during the process of acquiring such interpersonal communication skills so that new behaviors are more likely to be used in day-to-day interactions with peers.

Learning Strategies for Cognitive Change

Because cognition mediates both behavior and affect, cognitive restructuring can be an effective primary prevention strategy. Techniques used in problem solving and decision making, self-management and self-control, and cognitive restructuring are among the primary prevention strategies that can be taught to children and adolescents.

All young people have the potential to problem solve and make decisions. At times, however, the emotional components connected with a particular problem, the egocentric focus commonly associated with the early years of human growth and development, and the lack of experience with systematically approaching problem-solving situations provide barriers to effective problem solving and decision making (Beautrais, 2005; McWhirter et al., 1998, 2007). Instruction can be provided, however, in each step of the problem-solving and decision-making process. Teaching children and adolescents how to resolve problematic situations can help them enhance self-esteem, overcome feelings of being helpless, and promote a generalized sense of empowerment.

Calling their model the DECIDE model, McWhirter et al. (1998, 2007) suggested that the following components be taught:

1. *Define the problem.* The problem is defined as clearly as possible and is stated as a goal to be achieved. This goal is assessed by asking the following questions: Does it meet the underlying needs? If it is attained, does it help the individual achieve satisfaction?
2. *Examine variables.* The specifics of the total situation are examined. Background issues and environmental factors are considered, so it may be necessary to gather and appraise additional information. It is particularly important to identify the feelings and thoughts of the youth at this step. Oftentimes earlier maladaptive responses must be modified. In both this step and Step 1, questions and suggestions from other students in the classroom or the group are useful.
3. *Consider alternatives.* Various means of solving the problem are considered. The strengths and weaknesses of each possibility are evaluated. Again, the teacher or counselor may call for brainstorming to generate ideas from other students about alternatives and strategies.
4. *Isolate a plan.* The alternatives are gradually narrowed down until what seems like the best response or solution remains. A plan for carrying out this alternative is prepared, and the potential consequences are considered in more detail.
5. *Do action steps.* After a plan is decided on, action must be taken to implement it. Thus, youngsters are systematically encouraged to follow through on the necessary steps to carry out their plan. They perform the behaviors that make up the solution plan.
6. *Evaluate effects.* Finally, youngsters need to evaluate the effectiveness of the solution. It is important to teach them to look for effects in their thoughts and feelings. They analyze and evaluate the outcome, review the decision, and, if necessary, develop another plan to achieve their goal.

McWhirter et al. reported that this model is effective for teaching problem solving and decision making.

Achieving Self-Management and Self-Control

Self-management means that self-control has been achieved. It implies that individuals can develop the ability to control, to a great extent, their thoughts, feelings, and behaviors. Teaching children and adolescents the techniques of self-management and self-control can result in outcomes similar to those connected with teaching problem solving and decision making: enhanced self-esteem, reduced feelings of being helpless, and a sense of empowerment. Teaching self-management and self-control involves teaching children and adolescents self-assessment, self-monitoring, and self-reinforcement (McWhirter et al., 1998, 2007). Self-assessment means that the individual learns to evaluate his or her own behaviors against a standard that has personal meaning to determine whether the behavior is adequate. Self-monitoring requires the individual to observe his or her own behavior and record it. Record keeping may involve notation of contingencies in the environment prior to and immediately following the behavior. Self-reinforcement involves supplying one's own consequences for a given behavior (e.g., self-praise, buying something of personal significance). Generally, children and adolescents who master the techniques of self-management and self-control feel energized, motivated, and positive about themselves.

Coping With Stress

The term *coping with stress* is particularly significant in contemporary society. There are so many potential stressors encountered on a day-to-day basis that it behooves the adults in society to teach children and adolescents as much as possible about stress and stress management. It is an important primary prevention strategy. Chapter 7, "Stress and Trauma: Coping in Today's Society," addresses this topic fully through discussion and analysis of perspectives on stress, including stimulus-oriented views, response-oriented views, stress as a transaction between person and environment, life event stressors, daily stress, home and family stress, school stress, and developmental stress.

Planning Prevention Programs

Laudatory prevention efforts of schools and communities have failed because planning efforts have not included important steps or because a group of concerned adults has moved to the implementation stage and shortchanged the entire planning process. The following steps, which are based on our experience in a variety of school and community settings, will help ensure success:

1. Read the research on prevention programs. There are excellent reviews and monographs on approaches to prevention (American Academy of Pediatrics, 2004; Astor et al., 2005; Collins et al., 2002; Dryfoos, 1997; Gager & Elias, 1997; Goldston, Yager, Heinicke, & Pynoos, 1990; Kadish et al., 2001; Reddy & Richardson, 2006; Romano, 1997; Weisberg, Caplan, & Harwood, 1991). Often practitioners who are anxious to implement programs and services do not take the time to learn about and build on the successes and failures of others. On the basis of numerous outcome studies, a number of generalizations can be made:

- Prevention programs directed to the early years (e.g., pre- and postnatal parents and children during preschool years) can reduce factors that increase risk for maladaptive behaviors. Most of these efforts are focused on primary prevention and reduce the incidence of dysfunction in childhood and adolescence (Lally, Mangione, & Honig, 1988; National Institute on Drug Abuse, 2011; Reddy & Richardson, 2006).
- Prevention programs that involve parents, connect to the real world of work, incorporate social and life-skills training, incorporate staff development, and involve dedicated role-model adults seem to have the most lasting and positive impact (Brooks, 2006; Dryfoos, 1997; National Institute on Drug Abuse, 2011).
- School-based programs targeting adolescents have improved prosocial competence and decreased at-risk behaviors (such as the behaviors discussed in Part 3 of this book; Schinke, Botvin, & Orlandi, 1991; Schneider, Attili, Nadel, & Weisberg, 1989).

- Broad-based programs aimed at several causative factors or at-risk behaviors seem to be the most successful because youth at risk usually present with a number of conditions (Astor et al., 2005; Caplan & Weisberg, 1989).
- Occasionally programs have not been effective or have made problems escalate (Bangert-Drowns, 1988). Finding out why could be extremely important to practitioners prior to implementing any prevention effort (Collins et al., 2002).

2. Assess needs. Sometimes the professional helper fails to target the right population; the best combination of causative factors; or the at-risk behaviors of most concern to children, adolescents, and their families. It is important to touch base with the population being served prior to doing much planning. Children and adolescents, families, school faculty and staff, and components of the community (e.g., hospitals, businesses, churches, social service agencies) should be asked about their view of factors creating risk, problematic behaviors, and skill deficits. Prevention programming should always be designed to address needs and concerns identified by recipients of future services.

3. Meet with administrators, elected officials, and business owners. Prevention efforts take time, commitment, and money to implement. Numerous prevention programs have met with failure because planners failed to obtain the input and support of those in positions to reinforce efforts and keep programs and services funded and in place on a long-term basis. Getting this input is a critical step in planning for program support.

4. Establish a broad-based planning group. Educators, parents, youth, administrators, mental health professionals, physicians, nurses, and police should all be included in planning efforts for prevention programming. The more interdisciplinary and representative the group, the richer the input. The best prevention efforts have been based on the collaborative teaming of members of the community to be served (National Institute on Drug Abuse, 2011).

5. Target the population, the causative factors, or the at-risk behaviors. Often, planning groups are too ambitious with respect to goals and expectations. There is always more to be accomplished than can be realized with respect to a given prevention program. It is important to use the results of a needs assessment to target initial efforts so that initiatives are well planned and supported by adequate resources. Once a focus has been established, findings of research conducted relative to similar populations, risk factors, or at-risk groups should be used so that problems can be circumvented and past successful practices can be put into operation.

Sidebar 2.5 ■ Prevention Programming and Community Resources

There are countless descriptions of prevention programs as well as outcome studies emphasizing the need to approach prevention from a broad base of stakeholders so that a school or agency is not attempting to deliver the program independent of support and input from the community. Planning a prevention program should actually be done using community input because doing so often precipitates support, resources, and funding that a school, school district, or agency could not provide on its own. Working with numerous "voices" in the planning process is often a demanding task and requires strong leadership, patience, and openness to divergent viewpoints and input.

■ ■ ■

6. Identify existing prevention programs and resources. Sometimes planning groups recreate programs, services, or resources that already exist and could be built on or used as adjuncts to newly created programs. It is important to identify existing prevention programs and assess them in terms of whether they offer primary, secondary, or tertiary prevention. Planning groups can then determine how to focus new initiatives (i.e., primary, secondary, or tertiary) and do a better job of effectively utilizing newly committed funding and resources.

7. Carefully describe policies and procedures. Before implementing a new program, it is extremely important to draft a description of all policies and procedures to be followed. This step ensures that everyone involved in the program can be clear about roles and responsibilities. A written description also provides an opportunity for input, revision, and refinement. Program descriptions can (and should) be checked in advance of implementation for legal and ethical implications.

8. Plan variations for diversity. For many young people, minority status is associated with low socioeconomic status; poor living conditions; fragmented families; and a variety of critical cultural, ethnic, and racial differences. All human service specialists must be flexible about making adaptations in prevention programming in a way that shows sensitivity and respect for diversity. Variations for diversity are addressed throughout this edition of *Youth at Risk*.

9. Plan staff development. Whether prevention programming is centered in school or community settings, all staff need to be educated, supervised, and prepared in advance of program implementation. Adults working on behalf of children and adolescents need to be carefully prepared and provided with opportunities to have their questions answered and their concerns addressed.

10. Make sure adjunct services and referral options have been identified. Those working on behalf of children and adolescents often need the assistance of other medical and social service professionals. Identifying adjunct services and referral options and acting as a liaison with employees in those settings, in advance, should never be overlooked.

11. Plan evaluation procedures prior to program implementation. Practitioners often neglect the evaluative component of prevention programming efforts. Evaluation procedures should be preplanned, and data collection should be an integral part of efforts on behalf of youth. Data can be used to modify and improve the services offered and can provide justification for continued funding and commitment of other needed resources.

Summary

Our overview of prevention has provided introductory material highlighting the problems that underscore the need for escalation of prevention efforts; defined the qualities of prevention programming; described the differences among primary, secondary, and tertiary prevention and noted the need for additional primary prevention programs; and suggested guidelines and steps for prevention programming. We hope that this information provides an enriched perspective with which to approach the material in the chapters that follow. The context of this chapter is reflective of our belief that more emphasis needs to be placed on proactive prevention efforts so that, as time passes, individuals, families, schools, and communities can lessen the amount of time and energy directed toward remediation and containment of impairment and dysfunction.

Useful Websites

American Association of Suicidology
   http://www.suicidology.org
American Foundation for Suicide Prevention
   http://www.afsp.org
Inspire USA Foundation
   http://www.reachout.com
National Association of School Psychologists
   http://www.nasponline.org
National Suicide Prevention Lifeline
   http://www.suicidepreventionlifeline.org
Suicide and Suicide Prevention
   http://suicidehotlines.com

References

American Academy of Pediatrics. (2004). Policy statement: School-based mental health services. *Pediatrics, 113,* 1839–1845.

American Foundation for Suicide Prevention. (2012). *Facts and figures.* Retrieved from http://www.afsp.org/index.cfm?fuseaction=home.viewpage&page_id=050fea9f-b064-4092-b1135c3a70de1fda

American Psychological Association. (2012). *Marriage and divorce.* Retrieved from http://www.apa.org/topics/divorce/index.aspx

Astor, R. A., Meyer, H. A., Benbenishty, R., Marachi, R., & Rosemond, M. (2005). School safety interventions: Best practices and programs. *Children and Schools, 27,* 17–32.

Bangert-Drowns, R. L. (1988). The effects of school-based substance abuse education: A meta-analysis. *Journal of Drug Education, 18,* 243–264.

Beautrais, A. L. (2005). National strategies for the reduction and prevention of suicide. *Crisis, 26,* 1–3.

Bosworth, K., Espelage, D., DuBay, T., & Daytner, G. (2000). Preliminary evaluation of a multimedia violence prevention program for adolescents. *American Journal of Health Behavior, 24,* 268–280.

Brooks, J. E. (2006). Strengthening resilience in children and youths: Maximizing opportunities through the schools. *Children and Schools, 28,* 69–76.

Brown, E. J., & Simpson, E. M. (2000). Comprehensive STD/HIV prevention education targeting US adolescents: Review of an ethical dilemma and proposed ethical framework. *Nursing Ethics, 7,* 339–349.

Buckley, M. A. (2000). Cognitive–developmental considerations in violence prevention and intervention. *Professional School Counseling, 4,* 60–70.

Caplan, M. Z., & Weisberg, R. P. (1989). Promoting social competence in early adolescence: Developmental considerations. In B. H. Schneider, G. Attili, J. Nadel, & R. P. Weisberg (Eds.), *Social competence in developmental perspective* (pp. 371–385). Norwell, MA: Kluwer Academic.

Centers for Disease Control and Prevention. (2012a). *Alcohol and public health.* Retrieved from http://www.cdc.gov/alcohol/fact-sheets/underage-drinking.htm

Centers for Disease Control and Prevention. (2012b). *Youth risk behavior surveillance—United States, 2011.* Retrieved from http://www.cdc.gov/mmwr/preview/mmwrhtml/ss6104a1.htm

Chapman, C., Laird, J., & Kewal Remani, A. (2010). *Trends in high school dropout and completion rates in the United States: 1972–2008 compendium.* Washington, DC: U.S. Department of Education, National Center for Education Statistics, Institute of Education Sciences.

Christensen, E. (2013). Diagnosis and treatment planning. In D. Capuzzi & D. R. Gross (Eds.), *Introduction to the counseling profession* (6th ed., pp. 313–336). New York, NY: Routledge.

Coker, J. K., & Dixon-Saxon, S. (2013). Counseling in clinical mental health and private practice settings. In D. Capuzzi & D. R. Gross (Eds.), *Introduction to the counseling profession* (6th ed., pp. 396–419). New York, NY: Routledge.

Collins, J., Robin, L., Wooley, S., Fenley, D., Hunt, P., & Taylor, J. (2002). Programs-that-work: CDC's guide to effective programs that reduce health-risk behaviors of youth. *Journal of School Health, 72,* 93–99.

Conyne, R. K. (1994). Preventative counseling. *Counseling and Human Development, 27,* 1–10.

Domestic Violence Statistics. (2012). *Domestic violence statistics.* Retrieved from http://domesticviolencestatistics.org/domestic-violence-statistics/

Dryfoos, J. D. (1997). Adolescents at risk: Shaping programs to fit the need. *Journal of Negro Education, 65,* 5–18.

Fagan, A. A., Brooke-Weiss, B., Cady, R., & Hawkins, J. D. (2009). If at first you don't succeed . . . keep trying: Strategies to enhance coalition/school partnerships to implement school-based prevention programming. *The Australian and New Zealand Journal of Criminology, 42,* 387–405.

Fetro, J. V., Coyle, K. K., & Pham, P. (2001). Health-risk behaviors among middle school students in a large majority–minority school district. *Journal of School Health, 71,* 30–37.

Gager, P. J., & Elias, M. J. (1997). Implementing prevention programs in high-risk environments: Application of the resiliency paradigm. *American Journal of Orthopsychiatry, 67,* 363–373.

Gilliland, B. E., & James, R. K. (1993). *Crisis intervention strategies.* Pacific Grove, CA: Brooks/Cole.

Goldston, S. E., Yager, J., Heinicke, C. M., & Pynoos, R. S. (Eds.). (1990). *Preventing mental health disturbances in childhood.* Washington, DC: American Psychiatric Association.

Hadge, C. (1992). *School-based prevention and intervention program: Clearinghouse fact sheet* (Report No. CG 025 63 1). Piscataway, NJ: Rutgers University, Center of Alcohol Studies. (ERIC Document Reproduction Service No. ED372329)

Hallfors, D., Brodish, P. H., Khatapoush, S., Samchez, V., Cho, H., & Steckler, A. (2006). Feasibility of screening adolescents for suicide risk in "real world" high school settings. *American Journal of Public Health, 96,* 282–287.

Harpine, E. C., Nitza, A., & Conyne, R. (2010). Prevention groups: Today and tomorrow. *Group Dynamics: Theory, Research, and Practice, 14,* 268–280.

Horner, J., & McElhaney, S. (1993). Building fences. *American Counselor, 2,* 17–21, 30.

Hovell, M. F., Blumberg, E. J., Liles, S., Powell, L., & Morrison, T. C. (2001). Training AIDS and anger prevention social skills in at-risk adolescents. *Journal of Counseling & Development, 79,* 347–355.

Janosik, E. H. (1984). *Crisis counseling: A contemporary approach.* Monterey, CA: Wadsworth Health Sciences.

Kadish, T. E., Glaser, B. A., Calhoun, G. B., & Ginter, E. J. (2001). Identifying the developmental strengths of juvenile offenders: Assessing four life-skills dimensions. *Journal of Addictions & Offender Counseling, 21,* 85–95.

Kazdin, A. E. (1993). Adolescent mental health: Prevention and treatment programs. *American Psychologist, 48,* 127–141.

KidsHealth. (2012). *Fetal alcohol syndrome.* Retrieved from http://kidshealth.org/parent/medical/brain/fas.html

King, K. A. (2001). Developing a comprehensive school suicide prevention program. *Journal of School Health, 71,* 132–137.

Kitts, R. L. (2005). Gay adolescents and suicide: Understanding the association. *Adolescence, 40,* 621–628.

Lally, R., Mangione, P. L., & Honig, A. S. (1988). The Syracuse University Family Development Research Program: Long-range impact on an early intervention with low-income children and their families. In D. Powell (Ed.), *Parent education as early childhood intervention: Emerging directions in theory, research, and practice* (pp. 79–104). Norwood, NJ: Ablex.

Literacy Mid-South. (2011). *Literacy facts.* Retrieved from http://www.literacymidsouth. org/resources/literacy-statistics/

McGowan, M. (2006). Assessing "risk" versus promoting resilience. *Therapy Today, 17,* 27–28.

McWhirter, J. J., McWhirter, B. T., McWhirter, A. M., & McWhirter, E. H. (1998). *At-risk youth: A comprehensive response* (2nd ed.). Pacific Grove, CA: Brooks/Cole.

McWhirter, J. J., McWhirter, B. T., McWhirter, E. H., & McWhirter, R. J. (2007). *At risk youth: A comprehensive response* (4th ed.). Pacific Grove, CA: Brooks/Cole.

Miller, D. N., Eckert, T. L., & Mazza, J. J. (2009). Suicide prevention programs in the schools: A review and public health perspective. *School Psychology Review, 38,* 168–188.

NAMI Advocate. (2012). *Survey finds many living with mental illness go without treatment.* Retrieved from http://www.nami.org/ADVTemplate.cfm?Section=2012&Template=/ContentManagement/ContentDisplay.cfm&ContentID=133572

National Dropout Prevention Center. (2012). *Situations that put youth at risk.* Retrieved from http://www.dropoutprevention.org/statistics/situations-that-put-youth-at-risk

National Institute on Drug Abuse. (2011). *Drug facts: Lessons from prevention research.* Retrieved from http://www.drugabuse.gov/publications/drugfacts/lessons-prevention-research

Popenhagen, M. P., & Qualley, R. M. (1998). Adolescent suicide: Detection, intervention, and prevention. *Professional School Counseling, 1,* 30–36.

Reddy, L. A., & Richardson, L. (2006). School-based prevention and intervention programs for children with emotional disturbance. *Education and Treatment of Children, 29,* 379–404.

Roberts, A. R. (Ed.). (1991). *Contemporary perspectives on crisis intervention and prevention.* Englewood Cliffs, NJ: Rutgers University Center of Alcohol Studies.

Romano, J. L. (1997). School personnel training for the prevention of tobacco, alcohol, and other drug use: Issues and outcomes. *Journal of Drug Education, 27,* 245–258.

Shaughnessy, L., Doshi, S. R., & Jones, S. E. (2004). Attempted suicide and associated health risk behaviors among Native American high school students. *Journal of School Health, 74,* 177–182.

Schinke, S. P., Botvin, G. J., & Orlandi, M. A. (1991). *Substance abuse in children and adolescents: Evaluation and intervention.* Newbury Park, CA: Sage.

Schneider, B. H., Attili, G., Nadel, J., & Weisberg, R. P. (Eds.). (1989). *Social competence in developmental perspective.* Norwell, MA: Kluwer Academic.

Spaeth, M., Weichold, K., Friedrich-Schiller, R. K. S., & Wiesner, M. (2010). Examining the differential effectiveness of a life skills program (IPSY) on alcohol use trajectories in early adolescence. *Journal of Consulting and Clinical Psychology, 78,* 334–348.

Walker, R. L., Ashby, J., Hoskins, O. D., & Greene, F. N. (2009). Peer-support suicide prevention in a non-metropolitan U.S. community. *Adolescence, 44,* 335–346.

Watts, G. F., Sr. (2000). Attitude toward sexual intercourse and relationship with peer and parental communication. *American Journal of Health Studies, 16,* 156–163.

Weisberg, R. P., Caplan, M., & Harwood, L. (1991). Promoting competent young people in competence-enhancing environments: A systems-based perspective on primary prevention. *Journal of Consulting and Clinical Psychology, 55,* 542–549.

Resilience: Individual, Family, School, and Community Perspectives

Rolla E. Lewis*

The literature on resilience provides an alternative view that sees youth at promise rather than at risk and offers counselors, teachers, and parents positive and viable resources for promoting the well-being of youth. The models, methods, and data emerging from education, prevention, and counseling fields about resilience do not represent a singular point of view, however. There is diversity that results in debate and controversies about resilience, but there is agreement that the family of phenomena referred to as resilience challenges the negative assumptions found in deficit-focused models. Resilience results from good outcomes in spite of exposure to risk. There is no denial that risk exists. The issue becomes one of creating healthy systems that invite youth to participate in meaningful activities rather than repairing individuals who have been overcome and damaged by risks.

This chapter looks at resilience literature and practices not to synthesize but rather to call attention to different pathways counseling and teaching professions can follow to construct healthy systems and climates that support positive youth development. In addition, this chapter calls for creating collaborative efforts between professionals and community members to help all youth grow toward their greatest potential in just and caring communities. The resilience literature cited in this chapter refers to the evolving multidisciplinary research and practices that have emerged from the fields of prevention, counseling, education, social work, and youth development (Benard, 2004; Benard & Slade, 2009; Goldstein & Brooks, 2006; Luthar, Cicchetti, & Becker, 2000a, 2000b; Masten, 2001; Masten, Cutuli, Herbers, & Reed, 2009; Masten, Herbers, Cutuli, & Lafavor, 2008; Rutter, 2012; Ungar, 2012). Although a

---

*The author wishes to thank Dr. Christopher A. Sink for the resources regarding spirituality, religion, and resilience.

discussion of this is beyond the scope of this chapter, the resilience and wellness constructs have much in common (Goldstein & Brooks, 2006; Myers & Sweeney, 2005; Prilleltensky & Prilleltensky, 2005, 2006). This chapter concentrates on how the resilience literature moves primary prevention perspective and practices away from short-term, individual interventions and toward comprehensive, collaborative, and multidisciplinary interventions designed to foster positive youth development in the school and beyond into the community (Benard, 2004; Benard & Slade, 2009; Brooks, 2006; Lewis, 2011a; Luthar et al., 2000a; Masten, 2001; Ungar, 2012). In this current edition of *Youth at Risk*, Capuzzi and Gross emphasize both the enhancement of protective factors and the reduction of risk factors. In many ways, the resilience literature offers school counselors one pathway back to and forward from the counseling profession's roots in human development and education as well as back to and forward from the assumption that growth and development are human imperatives. In following the development pathway, this chapter is guided by key research, effective practices, and professional possibilities.

1. *Key research.* Key research points to resilience as an evolving construct that is understood in multiple ways (Benard, 2004; Kaplan, 2006; Lewis, 2011a; Luthar et al., 2000a, 2000b; Masten, 2001; Masten et al., 2008; Rutter, 2012; Ungar, 2012; Werner, 1989, 1998; Werner & Smith, 1982, 1992, 2001; Wright & Masten, 2006). A notable body of resilience research and practice has at its heart the radical notion that "resilience is a capacity all youth have for healthy development and successful learning" (Benard, 2004, p. 4). Such a view shifts the professional perspective to see youth as having the developmental resources and self-righting capacities they need to navigate through life. Counselors, teachers, and parents are in a position to help youth realize these abilities, but core providers must perceive their own self-righting capacities if they are going to help youth understand their own health. In other words, to promote the health of youth at risk, helpers are advised to recognize their own resilience and health.

   Most of the practices found in this chapter begin with the assumption that resilience is a self-righting capacity fostered transactionally in the presence of certain environmental supports. Resilience is an end product of buffering processes that do not eliminate risk (Werner & Smith, 2001). Thus, risk should be considered in broader socially constructed and ecologically embedded contexts whereby poverty, racism, and injustice are rooted in social practices and cultural contexts. Resilience can then be viewed as a dynamic process associated with global factors like affiliation with caring adults within supportive communities. Metaphorically, youth are like diverse seeds with great potential, like acorns with the capacity to become oak trees but dependent on adequate ecological variables such as soil, water, and sun. Resilience practices can guide school counselors, teachers, and parents to appreciate the true meaning of education (*educare*, a Latin word, means to lead out rather than put in) by advocating for environments where all youth draw out their own self-righting and learning capacities under the mentorship of caring adults.

2. *Effective practices.* What makes counseling practice effective? The effective practices fostering resilience described in this chapter point to fostering posi-

tive relationships within supportive systems, helping clients tap strengths within themselves, and recognizing that alternative stories are available in every situation (Lewis, 2011a, 2011b, 2014; Winslade & Monk, 2007; Winslade & Williams, 2012). Fostering resilience has less to do with technique and more to do with taking a positive and affirming stance with others. Coupled with taking a positive and affirming stance, it is vital for counselors, especially those working in the schools, to develop research agendas to determine what works in their schools and to use the results to help all students achieve their personal/social, academic, and career potential (Whiston, 2002).

3. *Professional possibilities*. Practices promoting resilience can guide school counselors and teachers in their efforts to foster success for all students' personal, social, academic, and career development. Years ago, Masten (1994) pointed out, "Fostering resilience is an attempt to deflect a developmental pathway in a more positive direction" (p. 21). Schools and communities offer numerous possibilities for helping youth recognize their self-righting capacities and for shifting school systems to support youth in defining their life trajectories along positive pathways. Pathways that include instilling a sense of hope and recognizing students' self-righting capabilities are fundamental. As Werner and Smith (1992) concluded in their seminal 40-year longitudinal study, "The central component in the lives of the resilient individuals . . . which contributed to their effective coping in adulthood appeared to be a confidence that the odds can be surmounted. Some of the luckier ones developed such hopefulness early in their lives, in contact with caring adults" (p. 207). Others had to wait, but more often than not, it was their belief in themselves and someone else's belief in them that made the difference.

Begin by being an ally to youth. Believe in the capacity of youth to contribute to their communities. Allies see youth as resources, and professional efforts can open pathways for youth to perceive their own ability to spring back from adversity, to realize their own self-righting capacities, to understand their own ability to learn, and to fulfill their own power to engage passionately in meaningful activities. Teachers and counselors model these capacities by showing how learning to live is partly about an individual's ability to get up after he or she has been knocked down, to have heart, gumption, determination, and compassion. Youth and adults experience the world in different ways. Life can be rocky at any developmental or life stage; life demands participation and engagement. Learning to learn is related to individuals' ability to learn from difficulties and failures and from their capacity to struggle with uncertainty and let solutions and deeper wisdom emerge (Claxton, 1997, 1999). Learning to learn is also concerned with helping all students develop competencies and finding adults who will nurture capabilities in meaningful contexts (Brooks, 2006). Learning to work is connected to individuals' ability to adjust to the ongoing and continual changes in their livelihoods as students and adults. More important, learning to work is connected to finding one's capacity to be passionate about the work one chooses to do and doing things one finds meaningful. Promoting resilience begins with wellness and with the perspective that youth have both resources and adults who advocate for providing opportunities for youth to find healthy pathways to learn to live, learn to learn, and learn to work.

Resilience Defined

Given the diversity within the resilience literature, this chapter defines resilience as a dynamic developmental process of healthy human development growing out of nurturing relationships that support social, academic, and vocational competence and the self-righting capacity to spring back from exposure to adversity and other environmental stressors. Resilience is a relational self-righting capacity. It does not occur in a social vacuum, and it may emerge at different developmental stages. More often than not, resilience entails having a positive relationship with a caring teacher or an adult mentor (Werner & Smith, 2001). Global factors associated with resilience include possessing cognitive and self-regulation skills, having positive views of self and the motivation to be effective, and connecting with competent and caring adults (Masten, 2001).

Luthar et al. (2000a) pointed out that although resilience is a dynamic process, it is frequently misrepresented as a narrow trait that makes some youth "have what it takes" to overcome the odds whereas others "do not have" those special qualities. According to Masten (2001), "Resilience does not come from rare and special qualities, but from the everyday magic of the ordinary, normative human resources in the minds, brains, and bodies of children, in their families and relationships, and in their communities" (p. 235). Resilience is not extraordinary; it is the power of the ordinary. Helping all youth tap this power of the ordinary is the fundamental challenge facing all adults who care about kids. The key here is that positive relationships that nurture, challenge, and provide meaningful opportunities are central (Lewis, 2011a). It is easier to teach health, well-being, and ecological connectedness if it is known or embodied in one's own life (Goleman, Bennett, & Barlow, 2012). In order to foster healthy human development, teachers and counselors must recognize their own capacity for health, well-being, and resilience. They must recognize the positive relationships that nurtured, challenged, and provided meaningful opportunities in their own lives.

Because diverse professional fields contribute to the evolving resilience literature, there are a variety of perspectives about resilience that lead to misunderstandings (Kaplan, 2006). On the one hand, as Masten (1994) pointed out, "Studies of resilience suggest that nature has provided powerful protective mechanisms for human development. . . .When adversity is relieved and basic human needs are restored, then resilience has a chance to emerge. Rekindling hope may be an important spark for resilience processes to begin their restorative work" (pp. 20–21). On the other hand, one of McWhirter, McWhirter, McWhirter, and McWhirter's (1998) concerns is that "the justice system has used the term resiliency to help punish offenders—contending that a violent and abrasive upbringing provides no explanation for violent behavior because some youth who grow up in the same type of environment do not engage in violence" (p. 80). Such practices by those in the justice system totally misunderstand the research and practices emerging from resilience literature. As made clear by Werner (1998), "As long as the balance between stressful events and protective factors is favorable, successful adaptation is possible even for youngsters who live in 'high risk' conditions. However, when stressful life events outweigh the protective factors in a child's life, even the most resilient individual can develop problems" (p. 8).

As diverse as it is, the resilience literature does not support institutionalizing ways to blame individuals in need of help, creating policies that fail to support children and families, or spending more money trying to fix serious coping problems rather than promoting prevention (Werner & Smith, 2001). Ineffective practices are contrary to the assumptions guiding the resilience practices cited in this chapter. The imperative for growth and development unfolds naturally when certain environmental attributes are evident. These attributes are evident when individuals are encouraged to tap their own resilience; foster resilience in others; and collaborate with others to create systemic approaches to fostering relationships, connection, and learning power in others (Lewis, 2011a).

Resilience: Factors, Perspectives, and Practices

There are multiple factors influencing the developmental trajectories of youth and many explanations for the difficulties youth face (Lewis, 2011a; Luthar et al., 2000a; Masten & Obradovic, 2006; Resnick et al., 1998; Ungar, 2012; Wright & Masten, 2006). Merely identifying risks and causal factors does not work to help youth develop in positive ways. Benard (2004) and Ungar (2012) showed that identifying risks does not translate into strategies for reducing those risks. This section explores how resilience promotion efforts viewed in broader social contexts help children spring back from deprivation and adversity and more fully realize their potential. Rather than attempting to capture the scope of the literature and prevention efforts, I highlight in this section the key longitudinal resilience research that reveals the self-righting capacity in people when structures of support are present for them. Seminal research conducted by Emmy E. Werner and her colleagues described protective factors within youth, the family, and the community (Werner, 1989, 1998, 2006; Werner & Smith, 1982, 1992, 2001). I also examine additional research that profiles qualities of resilient youth and three protective factors that enhance student resilience in the schools (Benard, 2004; Benard & Slade, 2009).

Emmy E. Werner: The Mother of Resilience

The life span, cross-cultural studies conducted by Emmy E. Werner and her colleagues concluded that resilience is the natural human capacity for self-righting

Sidebar 3.1 ■ Promoting Healthy Development in the United States

On December 14, 2012, a gunman killed 26 people, including 20 children, in a massacre at Sandy Hook Elementary School in Newtown, Connecticut. On December 16, President Barack Obama spoke at a prayer vigil in honor of the victims, where he said,

> This is our first task—caring for our children. It's our first job. If we don't get that right, we don't get anything right. That's how, as a society, we will be judged. And by that measure, can we truly say, as a nation, that we are meeting our obligations? Can we honestly say that we're doing enough to keep our children—all of them— safe from harm? Can we claim, as a nation, that we're all together there, letting them know that they are loved, and teaching them to love in return? Can we say that we're truly doing enough to give all the children of this country the chance they deserve to live out their lives in happiness and with purpose? I've been reflecting on this the last few days, and if we're honest with ourselves, the answer is no. We're not doing enough. (Obama, 2012)

What do you think?

■ ■ ■

(Werner, 1989; Werner & Smith, 1982, 1992, 2001). Werner and Smith's (1992) transactional–ecological model of human development posits that people are active, self-righting organisms continuously adapting to their environment. All people have an imperative for growth and development. The researchers' prospective, developmental, and longitudinal design was used to assess how youth at various stages of development grow in high-risk conditions and respond to risk factors (Werner & Smith, 1982, 1992, 2001). The results led researchers to conclude that it was unusual for more than half their cohort to develop serious disabilities or persistent problems, even among children exposed to potent risk factors. The results also showed that most delinquent youth do not develop into career criminals (Werner & Smith, 1992, 2001).

Their prospective, developmental, and longitudinal research design changed how they discerned the individuals being studied over time; they anticipated endemic failure and ended up bearing witness to human resilience. Their shift in perspective needs explanation. The prospective design is different from the retrospective design. Researchers using prospective designs study groups of youth over time, whereas researchers using retrospective designs are more likely to investigate risk factors linked to the history of a person with identified difficulties. Prospective designs offer researchers different possibilities in describing youth who grow up in high-risk environments, whereas retrospective designs focus either on events that led to pathology or on interventions that are devised to diminish pathology. Longitudinal research offers an alternative way of understanding and learning about human capacities over time. In other words, how did things work out in the long run?

The results led to a hopeful and optimistic view that needs to be explained in the context of research, commentary, and life stories supporting inborn, self-righting capacities. Werner and colleagues' research (Werner, 1989; Werner, Bierman, & French, 1971; Werner & Smith, 1977, 1982, 1992, 2001) extended more than 40 years and found protective factors within youth, families, and communities. Beginning with the entire population of 698 youth born in 1955, the study on Kauai, Hawaii, followed 505 individuals from the prenatal stage to the adult stage of development. Data were collected from cohort members in the prenatal period, at birth, and at ages 1, 2, 10, 18, 32, and 40. By birth, one third of the group was considered at risk because of four or more factors: significant poverty, being reared by parents with little formal education, moderate to severe perinatal stress, family discord, divorce, alcoholism, or mental retardation. One third of these high-risk youth did not develop difficulties as a result of the exposure to risk, and another one third rebounded as they reached adulthood to become competent adults (Werner & Smith, 1992, 2001).

Werner and Smith (1992) found that resilience is not something that is fixed and concrete but a quality that is enhanced by protective buffers that appear to transcend ethnic, social class, and geographical boundaries. Individual variability had to be taken into account, but the majority of resilient youth in the Kauai study had a variety of internal or external protective factors. Those youth who overcame the odds were described as resilient, and as Werner and Smith (1992) pointed out, "they began to perceive themselves as movers of their destiny rather than as pawns in a power game played by outsiders" (p. 21).

The vast majority of delinquent youth in the study did not become adult career criminals. The majority of chronic criminals from the study cohort consisted of a small group who had averaged four or more arrests before reaching 18 years of age. Those who did become persistent offenders needed remedial educational help (usually with reading) prior to age 10, were considered troublemakers by their fifth-grade teachers and by their parents, and had grown up in homes in which significant caregivers were absent for extended periods of time during adolescence (Werner & Smith, 1992). The researchers asserted that youth "exposed to adversities in early childhood are not predestined to grow into adults with failed marriages, criminal records, or psychiatric disorders. At each developmental stage, there is an opportunity for protective factors (personal competencies and sources of support) to counterbalance the negative weight exerted by adverse experiences" (Werner & Smith, 1992, p. 171). So-called second chance opportunities were usually found at major life transitions. Such opportunities enabled high-risk individuals to rebound and are frequently found in adult education programs, military service, active participation in a church community, or a supportive friend or spouse.

Werner and Smith (1992) asserted that the protective factors within the individual, family, and community have a more profound impact on the lives of youth than risk factors. They concluded that the protective factors

> appear to transcend ethnic, social class, geographical, and historical boundaries. Most of all, they offer a more optimistic outlook than the perspective that can be gleaned from the literature on the negative consequences of perinatal trauma, caregiving deficits, and chronic poverty. They provide us with a corrective lens—an awareness of the self-righting tendencies that move children toward normal adult development under all but the most persistent adverse circumstances. (Werner & Smith, 1992, p. 202)

Counselors, teachers, parents, and other core providers can foster the protective buffers that support positive life trajectories for youth in which competence, confidence, and ability to care for others will flourish if those helpers believe in youth. According to Werner and Smith (1992), "The life stories of the resilient youngsters now grown into adulthood teach us that competence, confidence, and caring can flourish, even under adverse circumstances, if children encounter persons who provide them with the secure basis for the development of trust, autonomy, and initiative" (p. 209).

Kitashima (1997), a youth from the Kauai study, embodies this point in sharing what made a difference in her life growing up in a high-risk household. Kitashima found caring and supportive people in school to be significant contributors to her success. At the same time, she found some professionals in the school made her a target of racism and put-downs. She described a time when her fifth-grade math teacher told her, "You are a good-for-nothing Hawaiian and will never amount to anything." In contrast, her school principal told her, "You are Hawaiian, and you can be anything you choose to be" (Kitashima, 1997, p. 34). At age 16, when she became pregnant and had a child, another school principal supported her desire to stay in school. As with many youth from the Kauai study, the protective factors counterbalanced the risks, and Kitashima went on to become a successful adult.

Besides support from her principal, one factor having a profound impact on her resilience was her faith in something greater than herself. Her faith led Kitashima (1997) to conclude, "Treasures exist in each one of our children—be they our own or somebody else's—and we need to be patient until they realize their promise. . . . Never give up on kids" (p. 36). Kitashima's guiding beliefs and comments open a larger question that focuses on the connection between resilience and spirituality, religion, and matters of philosophical meaning. There is a growing body of research that shows that spirituality and religion enhance resilience and have positive effects on psychological outcomes for adolescents; in addition, they help adolescents adjust to mental health problems, and they enhance psychological well-being and academic learning (Kim & Esquivel, 2011; Yonker, Schnabelrauch, & DeHaan, 2012). The research about how spirituality, religion, and philosophical meaning enhance resilience should cause counselors and teachers to reflect on their role in promoting such conversations in their schools. School professionals work in positions where they must wrestle with complex issues and cannot ignore broad concerns about religion, spirituality, or philosophical meaning—nor can they proselytize particular positions or beliefs. They can promote dialogues about what adds life and well-being to their communities. Counselors and teachers thinking about philosophy, religion, or spirituality can recognize and appreciate the issues raised and how core beliefs can foster resilience. Kitashima's story certainly speaks to the need to believe in all children and, equally, the moral obligation to stand up for all youth.

Changing Perspectives and Practices

Early research regarding resilience concentrated on understanding the personal qualities found in resilient individuals. As research has evolved, resilience has been acknowledged to derive from factors outside of the youth and to be the result of underlying protective processes rather than individual protective factors (Luthar et al., 2000a, 2000b). There is interplay between the self-righting qualities inherent in individuals and the protective processes in families and communities fostering resilience. Benard's (2004) review of the resilience research revealed that when personal and environmental protective processes support healthy development systemically they enhance the self-righting qualities inherent in individuals.

The transactional–ecological model of human development asserts that personality and individual outcomes result from transactional processes interacting between and among self, agency, and other environmental influences (Benard, 2004). Successful prevention interventions must focus on enhancing and creating positive environmental contexts that support individuals, families, and communities. The individual traits that enhance positive environmental contexts include social competence, problem-solving skills, autonomy, and a sense of purpose and belief in a bright future. These resilience traits and protective factors support the self-righting tendencies within the person. Youth with a positive sense of well-being demonstrated the following (Benard, 2004):

Sidebar 3.2 ■ Wrestling With Complex Issues

This chapter contends that professionals cannot ignore broad concerns about religion, spirituality, or philosophical meaning, nor can they proselytize particular positions or beliefs. What can you do to promote dialogues about what adds life significance and well-being to your community? Does your local high school offer comparative religion or philosophy as content courses? Why? Why not? How does viewing religion as a human construction liberate or constrain such conversations?

■ ■ ■

- *social competence:* responsiveness, flexibility, empathy and caring, communication skills, and a sense of humor;
- *problem-solving skills:* ability to think abstractly and reflectively, planning skills, and flexibility;
- *autonomy:* internal locus of control, sense of power, self-discipline, and adaptive distancing; and
- *sense of purpose and future:* healthy expectations, goal-directedness, success orientation, educational aspirations, persistence, hopefulness, hardiness, belief in a bright or compelling future, and a sense of coherence or meaning.

Environmental protective factors were also needed. Environmental characteristics or protective factors that support positive youth development include the following:

- *Caring relationships:* Having a connection with at least one caring person is the single most important factor in fostering resilience in youth. Relationships noted for stable care, affection, attention, intergenerational social networks, and a basic sense of trust foster climates of care and support.
- *High expectations:* When adults have high expectations for youth, it means they see youth's strengths and assets more than problems and deficits; in addition, they recognize the potential for maturity, responsibility, self-discipline, and common sense in youth. Resilience is also fostered when adults provide youth with structure, order, clear expectations, and cultural traditions; when they value youth; and when they promote youth's social and academic success.
- *Opportunities to participate and contribute:* These opportunities grow naturally from relationships that are based on caring and high expectations (Benard, 2004). Participation connects youth to other people, to interests, and to valuing life itself. Meaningful participation means that youth are valued participants; have socially and economically useful tasks; and have responsibilities for decision making, planning, and helping others.

Benard (2004) indicated that prevention efforts must focus on believing in young "people's innate resilience and developmental wisdom" (p. 113). Such a focus shifts the perspective from risk to resilience, a shift that occurs by focusing on strengths in youth and caregivers. Thus, the focus is on helping "caregivers of our youth recognize their own resilient nature" (Benard, 2004, p. 114). Resilience practices build on strengths. Professionals, such as school counselors, are challenged to create supportive systems and work as partners in collaborating to help young people draw on the power to help themselves (Galassi & Akos, 2007; Lewis, 2014; Winslade & Monk, 2007; Winslade & Williams, 2012). Seeing people as inherently possessing power shifts the professional role away from authority, expert, and director to that of becoming an ally working with others who have resources, expertise in their own lives, and the capacity to recognize their own well-being.

Problems are defined as external to the person. Narrative counselors (Winslade & Monk, 2007) state that the person is not the problem; the problem is the problem. To begin solving problems, professionals are challenged to enter into dialogues with individuals, families, and communities who are seeking assistance to address concerns such as conflict and violence (Winslade & Williams, 2012). The next section explores problems influencing professional and personal discourses; ways to develop dialogues; and how understanding resilience as transactional processes informs professional discourses related to risk, racism, poverty, and career development.

Discourses of Risk, Racism, Poverty, and Careers

Like fish in water, people and cultures exist in language. We are biological, social, and psychological beings embedded in discourses that describe our ecosocial experience, understanding, and actions. Such discourses are culturally and ecologically embedded and define the taken-for-granted world in which we exist. Those being helped and those helping exist in complex networks found in multiple bioregional, community, cultural, familial, and personal contexts that are described in various discourses, including discourses of disorder (Bowers, 2000, 2001; Capra, 2002; Gergen & McNamee, 2000; Lewis, 2011a, 2014). Thus, professionals are challenged to reflect critically on the discourses that shape their own taken-for-granted assumptions about the world, education, social situations, and their professional roles (Atkinson & Claxton, 2000; Lewis, 2014; Lott, 2002; Winslade & Monk, 2007). Reflecting on discourses defining the taken-for-granted world forces professionals to recognize a need to come as partners into dialogues shaping courses of action taken in systems, such as schools, or as helpers working with others who may exist in separate cultural discourses.

Looking at discourse patterns allows a number of professional possibilities, but this chapter focuses on two things. First, exploring discourse patterns enables counselors to understand how both clients and professionals are shaped by a variety of discourses in their lives. Numerous discourses shape the way they experience the world and the language registers they use at home, school, work, and so on to describe that experience to multiple audiences. For instance, the middle class use formal-register discourse patterns that go straight to the point, whereas among many poor and underrepresented people casual-register discourse patterns go around and around. The formal-register discourse pattern is valued more in school and in middle-class venues and leads to the categorization of groups of people into upper and lower strata, thus allowing those with the valued discourse patterns to maintain their power and ability to "maneuver in the society they control" (Lott, 2002, p. 101). "Power, defined as access to resources, enables the group

Sidebar 3.3 ■ Restorative Justice in Schools

Lee Copenhagen (2012) is a school counselor at Tennyson High School in Hayward, California; he advocates for restorative justice (RJ) as an alternative to traditional punishments. Although Lee affirms the notion of responsibility and accountability, some adults are concerned that RJ fails to punish enough. Lee has integrated the notion of circle conversations (Winslade & Williams, 2012) as a way to offer alternative paths for conflict resolution and restoring relationships between and among students as well as staff and students. Circle conversations allow every voice to be heard, to be responsible, and to be accountable. What are some possibilities for you to use circle conversations in your own family, household, classroom, or school? Is it possible to hold others responsible and accountable without traditional punishments? What do you think works best in a diverse community?

■ ■ ■

with greatest access to set the rules, frame the discourse, and name and describe those with less power" (Lott, 2002, p. 101).

Second, understanding discourses opens the opportunity for teachers and counselors to launch themselves out beyond their taken-for-granted world by listening to learn and by hearing people as experts of their own experiences. Understanding multiple discourses opens opportunities to develop collaborative dialogues between and among people in specific contexts at specific points in time. Everyone sees, experiences, and tells stories about the world from certain perspectives and uses language in different ways, and counselors and teachers are challenged to enter into collaborative dialogues, to describe power, and to invite the less powerful to access tools to fully participate. Such a stance moves the image away from that of the helping expert who is above the client and who is charged with removing the problem from the client and instead places the image on two people side-by-side, with both viewing the problem together, knocking the problem out of the way, or working together to resolve it.

Risk Discourse

The discourse regarding troubled families, schools, and communities binds problems to individuals composing those families, schools, and communities that are at risk. An alternative discourse would not place the problem in people; rather, problems would be described as interactive processes constructed in specific ecosocial locations. Benard (1994) pointed out, "Labeling youths, their families, and their communities as at risk means we are acting on stereotypes, on unquestioned assumptions about who people really are. . . . In contrast, resilience research focuses on learning . . . individual stories and truths, on studying the individual variation within groups having risk status" (p. 4). Fostering resilience means recognizing social ecology and the discourses that we participate in because risk factors rarely occur in isolation (Ungar, 2012).

Swadener and Lubeck (1995), who seemed unfamiliar with the resilience literature, stated that describing youth "at risk" creates an "ideology of risk, which has embedded in it interpretations of children's deficiencies or likelihood of failure due to environmental, as well as individual variables. The problem of locating pathology in the victim is the most objectionable tenet of much of the dominant rhetoric of risk" (p. 18). In other words, describing youth as at risk creates political consequences that result in the victims of social injustice being blamed for the results of that injustice. For Swadener and Lubeck, the need to confront structural injustices is lost when professional conversations and actions focus on fixing youth at risk. According to Fine (1995),

> "Youth at risk" is an ideological and historical construction. While numbers and their skewed class and racial distributions are intolerable, and the academic and economic consequences are severe, we must remember that today more students graduate from high school than was true fifteen years ago. . . . Fundamentally, the notion of 'risk' keeps us from being broadly, radically, and structurally creative about transforming schools and social conditions for all of today and tomorrow's youth. (p. 90)

Although Swadener and Lubeck (1995) and Fine (1995) did not locate themselves in the counseling profession or even in prevention work, such perspectives should prompt counselors, teachers, parents, and others to pause and think. By taking advantage of the deconstruction of the at-risk construct, counselors and teachers can critically reflect on their own practice and open up possibilities for different kinds of professional practice to help youth move beyond victim-focused identities (Jennings, 2001).

Doing Something About It

Counselors can offer alternative discourses. On the one hand, there are immense social and ecological challenges confronting humanity, and young people continually pay the price for cultural denial (Lewis, 2011a). On the other hand, counselors can participate in discourses that build on the traditions that foster resilience, emphasize health and competence, and communicate hope to and faith in youth.

Racism Discourse

Lewis (2011b) shared how people's lives are woven into stories that illustrate racism's toxic effects in counselors' personal and professional lives. Professionals and those they serve are woven into a racist social fabric. Euro-American counselors and African American counselors experience the world in different ways; one might walk down the street sensing that there is no racism in the United States, whereas the other might experience racist remarks or more subtle forms of marginalization while walking down the same street. As Kitashima's (1997) account (mentioned earlier) demonstrates, racism infects both individual and environmental attributes fostering resilience; most counselors and teachers recognize that not every youth has the personal and environmental attributes Kitashima had when faced with racism at school. Youth need allies to advocate for safe space and equity.

Counselors, teachers, parents, and other core providers are challenged to understand how dominant discourses affect how their clients' stories are heard, understood, and responded to. Counselors, themselves, have to know stereotypes, their privilege, and the cultural context in which they meet others, and they must be able to listen deeply to the story of others without judgment if they are to engage in profoundly human conversations. They should also recognize how diversity and biracialism have positive impacts on individuals and communities (Sirikantraporn, 2012) and how the academic achievement gap hurts diverse youth but also endangers the economic future of the United States (McKinsey & Company, 2009). There are numerous ways for viewing the world and how power, privilege, and disadvantage do not have to be deemed as absolute and fixed.

Doing Something About It

In the above example of the two counseling professionals, if the African American described feeling marginalized by some experience on the street or at a conference, the Euro-American might be curious about the colleague's experience and listen to learn from the experience being described. There are separate realities that open themselves up to being shared and experiences that simply have to be understood. A Chinese American graduate student described an incident in Portland, Oregon, where he was told, "Why don't you go back to where you came from?" Having been born in the United States, he was where he came from—a country where racism is woven into the social fabric. When he conveyed his story to the predominantly Euro-American class, the group recognized that such comments are not part of their day-to-day experience—their White privilege shields them from such day-to-day hostility—but their responsibility is to make their community safe for all. Rather than merely saying "Thanks for sharing," the Euro-American students were challenged to describe ways they could take hold of the loom and weave stories that recognize and appreciate diversity as well as the need to advocate for the basic right for all people to be able to walk safely in their communities (Lewis, 2011b). A diverse community is a resilient community.

Poverty Discourse

While recognizing that there are multiple dimensions to poverty besides having financial need, the poverty discourse reveals social distancing (Lott, 2002; Ungar, 2012). Look at poverty and children. In the United States, 22% of all children are poor. By race, the breakdown is as follows: 18.7% (over 16.4 million) of White non-Hispanic children, 39.1% (over 4.0 million) of Black children, and 35.0% (over 6.1 million) of Hispanic children are poor (Children's Defense Fund, 2012). All poor children experience various forms of social distancing, and all need multiple resources for overcoming poverty.

Those who are not poor distance themselves from the poor in a variety of ways that result in excluding, separating, devaluing, discounting, and discriminating (Lott, 2002). Such discrimination allows for the conscious and unconscious marginalization of the poor as expendable, and it results in undeserving individuals who are viewed as uneducated, unmotivated, lazy, unpleasant, angry, and stupid. As an individual problem, poverty can be described as resulting from behaviors rather than from the social and economic structures perpetuating poverty. For instance, schools perpetuate classism; the most profound memories a group of low-income women could recall about school were those of being treated with disdain and not being encouraged by teachers and school officials (Lott, 2002). Lott asserted that the middle-class discourse blames the poor for their position and maintains social policies that maintain distance from the poor. Class distancing includes within-race status groupings as well; for instance, some upper strata Whites distance themselves from poor Whites by referring to them derogatorily as "White trash," "hillbillies," and so on.

Doing Something About It

As important as financial resources are, poverty involves more than mere financial resources. Other resources include emotional, mental, spiritual, and physical support systems; relationship/role models; and knowledge of hidden rules. Understanding the hidden rules is one area that helps professionals foster collaborative dialogues with children, parents, and families. As mentioned earlier, middle-class formal-register discourse patterns are different from the casual-register discourse patterns frequently used by the poor. In accounting for events, those students, families, and communities who use casual-register discourse patterns tell their stories in different, less direct ways. It is important to listen to, learn from, and appreciate the richness found in the casual-register discourse patterns. At the same time, it is important to recognize that formal-register discourse patterns are given status by those in power in such settings as schools and some places of employment. For counselors and teachers, their understanding of the formal-register discourse pattern is a privilege. Counselors and teachers need to enter into collaborative dialogues with students, parents, and community members who use casual-register discourse patterns to let them in on a secret: Learning the formal-register discourse pattern is one pathway for access to education and entrance into certain careers. I am not advocating imposing middle-class values and forcing formal-register discourse patterns on all students; rather, I mean that teachers and counselors can respectfully provide access to the resources necessary to enter into contexts that require a certain way of speaking. Fostering resilience requires having flexibility; working with individuals, families, and communities to make choices; and helping them to access and develop multiple resources to address their poverty.

Careers Discourse

A meaningful careers dialogue begins with hopes and dreams. Parents, counselors, and teachers need to see that hope emerges from finding passion for work and meaning embedded in those activities one chooses to do. Encouraging passion and meaningful participation can serve as guides when teachers, counselors, and parents collaborate their efforts in designing developmental comprehensive counseling and guidance programs that focus on helping youth to become aware of, to explore, and to make decisions about possible career pathways (Herring, 1998).

Yet, it is crucial for teachers, counselors, and parents to recognize that embedded in any careers discourse are assumptions about the nature of work, career opportunities, corporate power, political power, social comparisons, material accumulation, consumerism, leisure, and so on (Bowers, 2000, 2001; Lewis, 2011a; Schor, 1992, 1998). Today's youth are developing career pathways during a historic period when the world and its diverse nations grapple with finite resources, such as oil; communities face business upheaval, such as jobs being outsourced to other countries; and individuals confront career uncertainty, such as being laid off when businesses downsize. Given the changing nature of the world in which we live, fostering passion, hope, and career resilience is crucial to offer alternative discourses that empower youth with a sense of their competence and capacity to make it in an uncertain world (Lewis, 2011a).

Doing Something About It

Maintaining hope and passion is a challenge facing both adults and youth, and youth need models for finding passion and meaning in the activities in which they engage. First, start with fundamental questions: Why are we doing this? What are we trying to accomplish? Second, find role models who can show students how to maintain passion and find meaning in what they do. One model is the Edible Schoolyard concept that found root at Martin Luther King Jr. Middle School in Berkeley, California—a project that grew out of a relationship between nationally recognized chef Alice Waters of Chez Panisse Restaurant and the school principal (Capra, 2002; Goleman et al., 2012; Spretnak, 2011; Williams & Brown, 2012). The project also involves the Berkeley-based Center for Ecoliteracy and its cofounder, Fritof Capra (2002), who argued that resilient communities are ecologically and socially diverse communities that extend learning beyond the classroom. Those involved with the Edible Schoolyard see the project as an opportunity to integrate natural and human systems, as well as for youth to learn that life is about social and ecological connections, changes, and challenges (see http://www.ecoliteracy.org/about-us/what-we-do).

The Edible Schoolyard integrates middle school classroom learning and competence, relationships developed among students and adults, and processes involved in growing and preparing food they will eat at school; in other words, the project is guided by a tradition that teaches the head, the heart, and the hand. If the plants get eaten by pests, students must use their heads to find out what happened, have heart not to be discouraged, and use their hands for replanting and maintaining viable solutions for controlling the pests. Thus, the students learn to work together to get up after they are knocked down and to find the resources necessary to overcome real-life problems. Students also learn that work is related to community practices that foster passion and hope. Obviously, when it comes to weeding, there might not be much passion, but when it comes to learning how to grow, prepare, serve, and share food, there is the hope that the results will taste good and be appreciated by others in the school community. By taking on a number of roles and responsibilities that result from participating in processes that range from mulching the soil to planting the seed to clearing the table in projects like the Edible Schoolyard, middle school students are taught fundamental skills related to career and life success. Fostering resilience means exposing youth to different career discourses, providing youth with the resources and opportunities to make connections, helping them to get back up after getting knocked down, experiencing competence in context, and making work-related adjustments in an ever-changing world.

Approaches to Fostering Resilience

This section discusses approaches that exemplify resilience practices. The approaches were selected because they illustrate how resilience practices support processes that begin with believing in individuals, families, schools, and communities. Each approach shows how fostering resilience is a collaborative process that is respectful of multicultural perspectives and hopeful about engaging youth as resources. Each approach shows the importance that significant relationships develop over time and include just hanging around, listening to another person's story, struggling with difficult tasks, and being alive in the moment with another person. Because a caring adult is the single consistent known factor fostering resilience found across the resilience literature (Benard, 2004; Goldstein & Brooks, 2006; Lewis, 2011a; Ungar, 2012), these approaches describe ways caring adults can foster relationships with youth.

Structured Narrative

Youth have abundant opportunities to create stories of success or stories of woe. Because schools are one of those places where youth create stories regarding their abilities to learn to live, to learn to learn, and to learn to work, much of this section focuses on a written counseling intervention that can be adapted in different school contexts. The structured narrative intervention described here was developed in an effort to address the cold efficiencies necessitated from school counselor-to-student ratios that had been as high as over 900 to 1 in the school in which the study took place.

The writing intervention was designed to help individual students cultivate positive stories about their possibilities for renewal and redirection and to provide

57

normally anonymous students with voices during the critical transition into high school (Lewis, 1999). Students had space to tell their stories and knew someone would take time to "listen" to every story by reading them. As a written approach, structured prompts help students to clarify or redefine personal narratives and to see possibilities for living with greater hope and power (Lewis, 1999, 2002; Roberson & Weston, 2011).

As an intervention, the structured narrative grows out of a tradition that uses narrative and writing in counseling (L'Abate, 1992; Lewis, 1999, 2002). The nature of narrative is nonnormative and can be optimistic because every person has numerous possibilities for describing any experience. Structured narrative lessons may be used in a number of ways, from lessons designed to enhance the transition into high school to lessons created to enhance the mindful practice required by graduate students in the teaching and counseling professions. Such lessons orient individuals to requirements defined by organizations such as schools or prompt individuals to explore narrative possibilities that entering the teaching and counseling professions provide. The lessons may also be used to assess individuals who might need additional help in developing their writing skills, making connections with caring adults, or reaching personal and professional goals.

"A Write Way," consisting of six structured narrative lessons, was used to help youth during their transition into high school (Lewis, 1999; Roberson & Weston, 2011). The prompts are formatted on a page to limit the length of responses, to make responding more attractive to reluctant writers, and to focus respondents on time-limited tasks. The prompts must be adapted to local needs and range from closed-ended questions to short essays that provide opportunities for creative responses. For instance, in a study focusing on youth transitioning into high school, youth were asked the closed-ended question: "Do you plan to graduate from high school? Yes or no." They were also given the prompt: "Describe a time when you were a positive leader or participant at home, school, or elsewhere" (Roberson & Weston, 2011). The study concluded that creating structures helps students understand high expectations, but caring and supportive face-to-face relationships are equally important in helping students succeed (Lewis, 1999; Roberson & Weston, 2011).

One purpose of A Write Way lessons was to help youth see possibilities for viewing or rewriting their school story in a positive way by assisting them to become oriented to the organizational demands of the school, document their own perspective about learning, and open them up to see more possibilities for living and learning in themselves. Prompts were designed to explore developmental possibilities and not leap to conclusions about themselves as learners or as people because drawing conclusions too quickly might close off possibilities for discovering the world and themselves anew (Roberson & Weston, 2011).

Structured narratives assist individuals in seeing that their life trajectories are not set by the stars or fate: People can change their life stories by discovering the possibilities inherent in coexisting alternative stories, and the vast majority of youth do become successful adults. Structured narratives attempt to give youth greater agency in describing their lives and are especially useful when youth see their life stories in the context of other life stories. In the end, stories supporting positive relationships or overcoming the odds are critical to children, and these stories encourage students to take action in constructing more satisfying personal stories about their experiences. Resilience is fostered by taking action developing one's own ever-changing story and by listening to the success stories of others. The structured narrative and other active approaches facilitate youth in becoming agents in their own life narratives, and reflective approaches like bibliotherapy facilitate youth in valuing the stories of others (Boyd, 2009). Stories can focus on individual youth in organizational contexts, but what is frequently called for is to change the beliefs guiding the organization.

Resilience and Youth With Disabilities

In addition to enhanced schoolwide protective processes, youth with disabilities may require specific interventions, such as multidisciplinary and multimodal teams that address the needs of the whole person. Counselors may be designated on those teams as strengths advocates and can play an important role by looking for the student's strengths. In fact, individualized educational programs can identify and maximize strengths without eliminating the need to detect and accommodate weaknesses that add to risk, and remediation efforts can be directed toward building up youth competence (Mather & Ofiesh, 2006).

"Children with ADHD [attention-deficit/hyperactivity disorder] exhibit many characteristics attributed to creativity and giftedness," according to Gregg (1996, p. 6). These children need help with their social skills, but more important, they need the unconditional support of at least one "prosocial adult who believes in the child" (Gregg, 1996, p. 6). Three conditions must be present to help foster resilience in youth with disabilities: (a) an opportunity for bonding to take place; (b) increased academic skills, social skills, and self-esteem to assist youth in successful bonding; and (c) the recognition and reinforcement of accomplishments in a consistent and systematic manner (Gregg, 1996).

One responsible and caring adult—teacher, counselor, administrator, relative, or other core provider—can help a youth with a disability to become more prosocial. Providing disabled youth with coaches or mentors is one way to help them initiate the bonding relationship. Supporting all facets of each youth's education, from art to athletics to reading, helps the student to find and express possible talents and encourages him or her to work effectively with others. Developing creative "alternatives to suspension and expulsion—like community service—for all but the most serious offences, to keep from further isolating and alienating"

Sidebar 3.4 ■ Action Research

Action research is asserted to be a crucial tool for closing the achievement gap and for promoting positive program outcomes and continuous improvement (Rowell, 2005, 2006). Roberson and Weston (2011) were graduate school counselors-in-training at California State University, East Bay, when they designed transition lessons to help ninth graders understand basic high school graduation requirements, school rules, and college eligibility requirements. Their real work started by looking at the available data and choosing one thing to improve at their school. In the course of their work, they realized that another challenge was defining a baseline concern with a department or a school and following the collective efforts to improve the situation for at least 3 years (Lewis, 2014). What concerns you at your school or organization? What data could you look at in your school or community? What is one thing you could work on to improve within the remaining timeframe for this year? Who could mentor you? Who could be your allies?

■ ■ ■

youth enables them to remain attached to the school culture (Gregg, 1996, p. 9). Helping youth find something meaningful to do at school is critical to their future success. Besides the critical skill of reading (there is a high correlation between reading and income), youth must be encouraged to develop a passion for what they do.

In a similar vein, Brooks (1997) said it is vital to identify and reinforce a youth's strengths, because "every person possesses at least one small 'island of competence,' one that is, or has the potential to be, a source of pride and accomplishment" (p. 391). Teachers who are taught to show personal interest in youth by spending a few extra moments or writing words of encouragement on papers or in notes foster resilience in youth. Adults working with youth must constantly balance care and support with high expectations, maintaining a delicate balance between being too loose and holding too tightly to the agenda at hand. Adults must strive to blend positive warmth, nurturance, acceptance, and humor with meaningful, measurable, and realistic expectations. To foster resilience, schools must be places where youth experience a growing sense of competence and meaningful participation (Benard & Slade, 2009; Lewis, 2011a).

Adaptations for Diversity

Diversity is integral to resilience theory and practice because listening deeply to the experience of others opens up possibilities for relationships grounded in understanding and compassion (Lewis, 2011b). Each section in this chapter has raised concerns that call on counselors, teachers, parents, and others to become aware of their personal and professional discourse, to wrestle with the scourge of racism and poverty, and to listen deeply to the stories of their clients. Illustrated below, in an intervention integrating special needs and culturally appropriate practice, is an approach that sees the strengths in clients, that recognizes the self-righting capacities in all people, and that understands that resilience approaches are ultimately about empowerment.

Macfarlane (1998) developed an approach for Maori special education students in New Zealand that used culturally appropriate practice. "In New Zealand it is the dominant culture that provides the guidelines for conventional and special education, as well as the majority of professionals determining 'who is the problem'" (Macfarlane, 1998, p. 2). Like underrepresented youth in the United States, Maori youth frequently find themselves alienated from school. Macfarlane's (1998) bicultural approach began with a meeting, or what the Maori refer to as *hui*, during which school officials and Maori youth could "speak with each other about difficult things in a way that avoids sliding back into the dynamics that gave rise to the problems in the first place" (p. 3). By moving away from punitive and judgmental discourse, the *hui* was designed to promote culturally appropriate alternatives to suspension-based community partnerships with the school. The conference was embedded in a culturally appropriate discourse that drew on Maori culture and values, such as the four principles of consensus, reconciliation, examination, and harmony. The conference started by saying in Maori and English, "I am who I am. You are who you are. Let us move together in tandem" (Macfarlane, 1998, p. 11). The youngsters were introduced to a new school discourse that placed their values

Sidebar 3.5 ■ Cultivating Resilience

The Hauora is a Maori philosophy of health and well-being. The four dimensions of Hauora are as follows: (a) health, or physical well-being; (b) self-confidence, or mental and emotional well-being; (c) self-esteem, or social well-being; and (d) personal beliefs, or spiritual well-being. Some advocate for the inclusion of a fifth dimension of Hauora: connection to the land, or ecological well-being. Like many things in cultural and spiritual communities, the debate continues among the Maori, but the notion of Hauora has been integrated into many primary and secondary schools in New Zealand to help children understand how integral fitness and well-being are in fully living life. How does your community or school promote fitness and well-being? How does your own life philosophy align with the Hauora five dimensions? How does your life philosophy differ? How do you cultivate your own health and well-being? How do you advocate for fitness and well-being in your community? How do you stand with the youth having difficulties in your community?

■ ■ ■

and culture central to finding solutions to the problems being faced at school. The youth experienced discourse in school that embedded Maori students' success and well-being. It is an approach that does not leave youth out on their own but calls on adults and youth to move together in tandem. To foster resilience within all youth, we need to create systems that support the well-being of all youth (Lewis, 2011a, 2014).

Summary

The resilience literature offers counselors, teachers, parents, and other core providers a path back to their roots in education and development that takes into account ecological contexts. Resilience research supports an optimistic, longitudinal view of the person and offers a proactive approach for enhancing human development. Most radically, resilience adherents see people as having innate self-righting capacities for changing their life trajectories, a landscape that defines risks in ecological contexts rather than in people, and an outlook that asks people to slow down enough to listen deeply to the stories embedded in everyday lives. Resilience-promoting interventions are primarily systemic; link individual, family, school, and community; and require counselors, teachers, parents, and others to consider the ground they stand on.

At the very least, fostering resilience in the schools is vital to the well-being of youth. Counselors, teachers, parents, and others can look to prevention and practices designed to foster resilience to help youth learn to live, learn to learn, and learn to work (Goldstein & Brooks, 2006; Lewis, 2014; Ungar, 2012). Lewis (1999) offered a tool for helping students make successful transitions at predictable developmental points, such as the move from middle to high school, and pointed youth toward developing more empowering learning stories. Gregg (1996) and Brooks (1997, 2006) reminded counselors, teachers, parents, and others that every youth has a gift, or an "island of competence," that can be tapped if one looks. Indeed, the resilience literature calls on counselors, teachers, parents, and others to see that all people have the innate capacity for self-righting and well-being and need support to tap it.

Useful Websites

Building Learning Power (BLP)
   http://www.buildinglearningpower.co.uk/
California Safe and Supportive Schools
   http://californias3.wested.org/
Center for Ecoliteracy
   http://www.ecoliteracy.org/
CESCal Flashlight Builder
   http://www.cescal.org/flashlight.cfm
The Collaborative for Academic, Social, and Emotional Learning (CASEL)
   http://www.casel.org/home/index.php
Greater Good Center
   http://greatergood.berkeley.edu/
International Resilience Project
   www.resilienceproject.org
Resilience: Building a World of Resilient Communities
   http://www.resilience.org/
UCLA School Mental Health Project
   http://smhp.psych.ucla.edu/
University of San Diego Action Research Center
   http://www.sandiego.edu/soles/centers-and-research/action-research/index.php
WestEd
   http://www.wested.org/cs/chks/print/docs/hks_resilience.html

References

Atkinson, T., & Claxton, G. (2000). *The intuitive practitioner: On the value of not always knowing what one is doing*. Philadelphia, PA: Open University Press.

Benard, B. (1994, December). *Applications of resilience: Possibilities and promise*. Paper presented at the Conference of the Role of Resilience in Drug Abuse, Alcohol Abuse, and Mental Illness, Washington, DC.

Benard, B. (2004). *Resiliency: What we have learned*. San Francisco, CA: WestEd.

Benard, B., & Slade, S. (2009). Listening to students: Moving resilience research to youth development practice and school connectedness. In R. Gilman, E. S. Huebner, & M. J. Furlong (Eds.), *Handbook of positive psychology in schools* (pp. 353–369). New York, NY: Routledge.

Bowers, C. A. (2000). *Let them eat data: How computers affect education, cultural diversity, and the prospects of ecological sustainability*. Athens: University of Georgia Press.

Bowers, C. A. (2001). *Educating for eco-justice and community*. Athens: University of Georgia Press.

Boyd, B. (2009). *On the origin of stories: Evolution, cognition, and fiction*. Cambridge, MA: Belknap Press.

Brooks, R. B. (1997). A personal journey: From pessimism and accusation to hope and resilience. *Journal of Child Neurology, 12*, 387–396.

Brooks, R. B. (2006). The power of parenting. In S. Goldstein & R. Brooks (Eds.), *Handbook of resilience in children* (pp. 297–314). New York, NY: Springer Science+Business Media.

Capra, F. (2002). *The hidden connections: Integrating the biological, cognitive, and social dimensions of life into a science of sustainability*. New York, NY: Doubleday.

Children's Defense Fund. (2012). *The state of America's children handbook, 2012.* Retrieved from http://www.childrensdefense.org/child-research-data-publications/data/soac-2012-handbook.html

Claxton, G. (1997). *Hare brain, tortoise mind: Why intelligence increases when you think less.* London, England: Fourth Estate.

Claxton, G. (1999). *Wise up: The challenge of lifelong learning.* New York, NY: Bloomsbury.

Copenhagen, L. (2012, October). *Restorative discipline in schools: An introduction to restorative justice based alternatives for school discipline* [Staff development PowerPoint]. Hayward, CA: Tennyson High School.

Fine, M. (1995). The politics of who's "at risk." In B. B. Swadener & S. Lubeck (Eds.), *Children and families "at promise": Deconstructing the discourse of risk* (pp. 76–94). Albany: State University of New York Press.

Galassi, J. P., & Akos, P. (2007). *Strengths-based school counseling: Promoting student development and achievement.* Mahwah, NJ: Erlbaum.

Gergen, K. J., & McNamee, S. (2000). From disordering discourse to transformative dialogue. In R. A. Neimeyer & J. D. Raskin (Eds.), *Constructions of disorder: Meaning-making frameworks for psychotherapy* (pp. 333–349). Washington, DC: American Psychological Association.

Goldstein, S., & Brooks, R. B. (2006). *Handbook of resilience in children.* New York, NY: Springer Science+Business Media.

Goleman, D., Bennett, L., & Barlow, Z. (2012). *Ecoliterate: How educators are cultivating emotional, social, and ecological intelligence.* San Francisco, CA: Jossey-Bass.

Gregg, S. (1996). *Preventing antisocial behavior in disabled and at-risk students: Policy briefs.* Charleston, WV: Appalachia Educational Laboratory.

Herring, R. D. (1998). *Career counseling in schools: Multicultural and developmental perspectives.* Alexandria, VA: American Counseling Association.

Jennings, R. G. (2001). Transformation of "at-risk" identity: Parental involvement and resiliency promotion. In L. Ramirez & O. Gallardo (Eds.), *Portraits of teachers in multicultural settings: A critical literacy approach* (pp. 153–165). Needham Heights, MA: Allyn & Bacon.

Kaplan, H. B. (2006). Understanding the concept of resilience. In S. Goldstein & R. Brooks (Eds.), *Handbook of resilience in children* (pp. 39–48). New York, NY: Springer Science+Business Media.

Kim, S., & Esquivel, G. B. (2011). Adolescent spirituality and resilience: Theory, research, and educational practices. *Psychology in the Schools, 48,* 755–765.

Kitashima, M. (1997). Lessons from my life: No more "children at risk". . . all children are "at promise." *Resiliency in Action, 2,* 30–36.

L'Abate, L. (1992). *Programmed writing: A paratherapeutic approach for intervention with individuals, couples, and families.* Pacific Grove, CA: Brooks/Cole.

Lewis, R. E. (1999). A Write Way: Fostering resiliency during transitions. *Journal of Humanistic Education and Development, 37,* 200–211.

Lewis, R. E. (2002). The structure narrative exercise. In G. McAuliffe & K. Eriksen (Eds.), *Teaching strategies for constructivist and developmental counselor education* (pp. 55–58). Westport, CT: Bergin & Garvey.

Lewis, R. E. (2011a). Ecohumanism: Integrating humanism with resilience theory. In M. Scholl, A. McGowan, & J. T. Hansen (Eds.), *Humanistic perspectives on contemporary counseling issues* (pp. 191–214). Philadelphia, PA: Routledge.

Lewis, R. E. (2011b). What is the color of your heart? Personalizing humanism. In R. Borunda (Ed.), *What is the color of your heart? A humanist approach to diversity* (pp. 149–165). Dubuque, IA: Kendall/Hunt.

Lewis, R. E. (2014). *Promoting relational wellness and learning power in schools: An ecological approach.* Manuscript submitted for publication.

Lott, B. (2002). Cognitive and behavioral distancing from the poor. *American Psychologist, 57,* 100–110.

Luthar, S. S., Cicchetti, D., & Becker, B. (2000a). The construct of resilience: A critical evaluation and guidelines for future work. *Child Development, 71*, 543–562.

Luthar, S. S., Cicchetti, D., & Becker, B. (2000b). Research on resilience: Response to commentaries. *Child Development, 71*, 573–575.

Macfarlane, A. H. (1998, November). *Hui: A process for conferencing in schools.* Paper presented at the Western Association for Counselor Education and Supervision Conference, Seattle, WA.

Masten, A. S. (1994). Resilience in individual development: Successful adaptation despite risk and adversity. In M. C. Wang & E. W. Gordon (Eds.), *Educational resilience in inner-city America: Challenges and prospects* (pp. 3–25). Hillsdale, NJ: Erlbaum.

Masten, A. S. (2001). Ordinary magic: Resilience processes in development. *American Psychologist, 56*, 227–238.

Masten, A. S., Cutuli, J. J., Herbers, J. E., & Reed, M. J. (2009). Resilience in development. In S. J. Lopez & C. R. Snyder (Eds.), *Oxford handbook of positive psychology* (pp. 117–131). New York, NY: Oxford University Press.

Masten, A. S., Herbers, J. E., Cutuli, J. J., & Lafavor, T. L. (2008). Promoting competence and resilience in the school context. *Professional School Counseling, 12*, 76–84.

Masten, A. S., & Obradovic, J. (2006). Competence and resilience in development. In B. M. Lester, A. S. Masten, & B. McEwen (Eds.), *Resilience in children* (pp. 13–27). Boston, MA: Blackwell.

Mather, N., & Ofiesh, N. (2006). Resilience in children with learning disabilities. In S. Goldstein & R. Brooks (Eds.), *Handbook of resilience in children* (pp. 239–256). New York, NY: Springer Science+Business Media.

McKinsey & Company. (2009). *The economic impact of the achievement gap in America's schools: Summary of findings.* Retrieved from http://mckinseyonsociety.com/downloads/reports/Education/achievement_gap_report.pdf

McWhirter, J. J., McWhirter, B. T., McWhirter, A. M., & McWhirter, E. H. (1998). *At-risk youth: A comprehensive response—For counselors, teachers, psychologists, and human service professionals.* Pacific Grove, CA: Brooks/Cole.

Myers, J. E., & Sweeney, T. J. (Eds.). (2005). *Counseling for wellness: Theory, research, and practice.* Alexandria, VA: American Counseling Association.

Obama, B. (2012). *Transcript: President Obama at Sandy Hook prayer vigil.* Retrieved from http://www.npr.org/2012/12/16/167412995/transcript-president-obama-at-sandy-hook-prayer-vigil

Prilleltensky, I., & Prilleltensky, O. (2005). Beyond resilience: Blending wellness and liberation in the helping professions. In M. Ungar (Ed.), *Handbook for working with children and youth: Pathways to resilience across cultures and contexts* (pp. 89–104). Thousand Oaks, CA: Sage.

Prilleltensky, I., & Prilleltensky, O. (2006). *Promoting well-being: Linking personal, organizational, and community change.* Hoboken, NJ: Wiley.

Resnick, M. D., Bearman, P. S., Blum, R. W., Bauman, K. E., Harris, K. M., Jones, J., . . . Udry, J. R. (1998). Protecting adolescents from harm: Findings from the National Longitudinal Study on Adolescent Health. *Journal of the American Medical Association, 278*, 823–832.

Roberson, G., & Weston, M. (2011, May). *A Write Way: Transitional guidance curriculum.* Paper presented at SOLES Action Research Conference, San Diego, CA.

Rowell, L. (2005). Collaborative action research and school counselors. *Professional School Counseling, 9*, 28–36.

Rowell, L. (2006). Action research and school counseling: Closing the gap between research and practice. *Professional School Counseling, 9*, 376–384.

Rutter, M. (2012). Resilience: Causal pathways and social ecology. In M. Ungar (Ed.), *The social ecology of resilience: A handbook of theory and practice* (pp. 33–42). New York, NY: Springer.

Schor, J. B. (1992). *The overworked American: The unexpected decline of leisure*. New York, NY: Basic Books.

Schor, J. B. (1998). *The overspent American: Why we want what we don't need*. New York, NY: Harper Perennial.

Sirikantraporn, S. (2012, November 19). Biculturalism as a protective factor: An exploratory study on resilience and the bicultural level of acculturation among Southeast Asian American youth who have witnessed domestic violence. *Asian American Journal of Psychology.* Advance online publication. doi:10.1037/a0030433

Spretnak, C. (2011). *Relational reality: New discoveries of interrelatedness that are transforming the modern world*. Topsham, ME: Green Horizons Books.

Swadener, B. B., & Lubeck, S. (Eds.). (1995). *Children and families "at promise": Deconstructing the discourse of risk*. Albany: State University of New York Press.

Ungar, M. (Ed.). (2012). *The social ecology of resilience: A handbook of theory and practice*. New York, NY: Springer.

Werner, E. E. (1989). Children of the garden island. *Scientific American, 260,* 106–111.

Werner, E. E. (1998). Resilience and the life-span perspective: What we have learned—so far. *Resiliency in Action, 3,* 1, 3, 7–9.

Werner, E. E. (2006). What can we learn about resilience from large-scale longitudinal studies? In S. Goldstein & R. Brooks (Eds.), *Handbook of resilience in children* (pp. 91–106). New York, NY: Springer Science+Business Media.

Werner, E. E., Bierman, J. M., & French, F. E. (1971). *The children of Kauai*. Honolulu: University of Hawaii Press.

Werner, E. E., & Smith, R. S. (1977). *Kauai's children come of age*. Honolulu: University of Hawaii Press.

Werner, E. E., & Smith, R. S. (1982). *Vulnerable but invincible: A longitudinal study of resilient children and youth*. New York, NY: McGraw-Hill.

Werner, E. E., & Smith, R. S. (1992). *Overcoming the odds: High risk children from birth to adulthood*. Ithaca, NY: Cornell University Press.

Werner, E. E., & Smith, R. S. (2001). *Journeys from childhood to midlife: Risk, resilience, and recovery*. Ithaca, NY: Cornell University Press.

Whiston, S. C. (2002). Response to the past, present and future of school counseling: Raising some issues. *Professional School Counseling, 5,* 148–155.

Williams, D. R., & Brown, J. D. (2012). *Learning gardens and sustainability education: Bringing life to school and schools to life*. New York, NY: Routledge.

Winslade, J., & Monk, G. (2007). *Narrative counseling in schools: Powerful and brief* (2nd ed.). Thousand Oaks, CA: Corwin Press.

Winslade, J., & Williams, M. (2012). *Safe and peaceful schools: Addressing conflict and eliminating violence*. Thousand Oaks, CA: Corwin Press.

Wright, M. O., & Masten, A. S. (2006). Resilience processes in development. In S. Goldstein & R. Brooks (Eds.), *Handbook of resilience in children* (pp. 17–38). New York, NY: Springer Science+Business Media.

Yonker, J. E., Schnabelrauch, C. A., & DeHaan, L. G. (2012). The relationship between spirituality and religiosity on psychological outcomes in adolescents and emerging adults: A meta-analytic review. *Journal of Adolescence, 35,* 299–314.

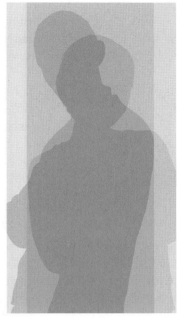

PART 2

Examining the Problem

Building on the foundational information in Part 1, the four chapters that compose Part 2 provide the reader with current and comprehensive information regarding the factors generally considered to be causal to the development of at-risk behaviors. It is important to keep in mind that it is impossible to draw a direct cause–effect relationship between any one of the four factors identified and any of the 11 issues and/or behaviors identified in Part 3 of this text. Authors in Part 2 understand this and caution their readers to view these causal factors as both cumulative and cyclical. This perspective enhances the awareness that, taken separately, any one of these causal dimensions enhances the likelihood of at-riskness in youth. When viewed from a cumulative and cyclical perspective, the development of at-risk behaviors is almost inevitable.

Chapter 4, "The Impact of Dysfunctional Family Dynamics on Children and Adolescents," spells out the various gradations of family dysfunctionality and couples this with case examples to enhance the reader's understanding. The author elaborates on five causal factors within the family dynamic that enhance the possibility of at-riskness in youth. In this presentation, the following areas are discussed: at-risk adults parenting, parental conflict, family denial, parentification of children, and serious illness and disability within the family. Again, case examples highlight these explanations. After presenting information on the incidence and impact of abuse and neglect, the chapter ends with a discussion of prevention approaches and adaptations to diversity aimed at ameliorating the identified causal factors.

Chapter 5, "'Who Cares What I Think?': Problems of Low Self Esteem," touches upon a causal factor that permeates any discussion of at-risk behaviors. The information in this chapter includes not only definitions and indicators of low self-esteem but also causal factors from parental, social, psychological, physical, environmental, and cultural perspectives. Prevention approaches are presented from individual, family, school, community, and global perspectives. The case examples such as TeenPATH, Stars I and II, YMCA Teen Services, and Red Eagle Soaring provide a realistic application of the approaches described. The chapter ends with adaptations for diversity.

Chapter 6, "Identifying and Preventing Mood Disorders in Children and Adolescents," approaches the topic by illuminating the complex issues of both definition and diagnosis. The chapter focuses on major mood disorders, particularly major depressive disorder and bipolar I affective disorder, in child and adolescent populations and emphasizes the hallmarks of the disorders, diagnostic issues, and quandaries that exist with definitions. Prevention issues from an individual, family, school, and community perspective are presented and illustrated with the cases of Anna and Robert. The chapter concludes with a discussion of adaptations for diversity.

Chapter 7, "Stress and Trauma: Coping in Today's Society," begins by presenting the confusion surrounding the definition of stress and delineates the following perspectives on stress and traumatic stress: (a) stimulus-oriented views, (b) response-oriented views, and (d) stress as a transaction between the person and the environment. From this foundation, the authors present 15 factors that may have a causal relationship with the development of at-risk behaviors. Approaches to prevention from individual, family, school, and community perspectives are presented with case illustrations of Sonia and Jamal. A discussion of adaptations for diversity concludes the chapter.

Chapter 4

The Impact of Dysfunctional Family Dynamics on Children and Adolescents

Cass Dykeman

In their influential work on high-risk youth in schools, Pianta and Walsh (1996) defined the term *at-risk status* as the likelihood that a given youth will attain a specific outcome given certain conditions. The specific outcomes of concern for this book are presented in Chapter 1. This chapter explores dysfunctional family dynamics as the certain condition. Why look at the family dynamics of at-risk youth? Because ample evidence exists that family dynamics play a major role in problem behaviors in youth (Szapocznik & Prado, 2007).

The level of dysfunction in families can vary widely. Moreover, severity of at-risk status runs parallel to severity of family dysfunction. Thus, in this chapter I define the multilevel nature of family dysfunction and explore the causal factors. Then I examine prevention at the individual, family, school, and community levels. Finally, adaptations for diversity are addressed.

Problem Definition

When examining the level of dysfunction in family dynamics, it is possible to classify families at either the moderate dysfunction level or the severe dysfunction level. This classification is important because severity level determines the appropriate interventions to be used. This section defines the distinctions between the moderate and severe levels of dysfunction to enable the reader to better understand family dynamics when planning work with youth and parents.

Moderate Dysfunction

In families at the moderate dysfunction level, each parent presents an appropriate image to the outside world. Hence, it is difficult to believe that there may be severe problems with one of the children. However, below the surface and hidden from community views are problems that the family is not willing to reveal. The at-risk youth becomes the not-so-popular messenger, letting the community know that the family has secrets and is not perfect. The advantage of working with families at the moderate dysfunction level is that the adults are competent in dealing with the basic aspects of life (e.g., working, providing food).

Severe Dysfunction

In the family at the severe dysfunction level, one or more adults may exhibit many at-risk behaviors, such as substance abuse. In work with severely dysfunctional families, adults may often be found to be functioning at a less capable level than their children. This collapse of adult–child differentiation in functioning limits the extent to which one can effectively intervene in the life of an at-risk child.

Causal Factors

Before working with at-risk youth, one must understand how dysfunctional family dynamics can lead to destructive behavioral patterns in youth. Dysfunctional family dynamics create a noxious emotional atmosphere for at-risk youth. Such an atmosphere produces severe personal stress and emotional upheaval. Moreover, this highly charged emotional atmosphere causes the at-risk youth to accommodate his or her behavior in such a way as to reduce the internal stress and upheaval. Accommodating the stress and upheaval creates problem behaviors, such as poor school performance, depression, anorexia, loss of control, and myriad other at-risk behaviors. This section first examines specific family factors that lead to these problem behaviors. Then the level and impact of abuse, neglect, and poverty are considered.

Specific Family Factors

Several specific family factors contribute to youth at-riskness. These factors include at-risk adults who become parents, parental conflict, family denial, parentification of children, and serious illness and disability.

At-Risk Adults Parenting

We can gain critical insight on the direction and depth of the problems exhibited by an at-risk youth through cultivating an awareness of the problems of the youth's parents. The problematic behaviors of the at-risk youth and his or her at-risk parents may differ, but the end goal of these separate behaviors typically runs parallel.

One final note of importance needs to be mentioned. The transmission of at-risk tendencies from parent to child is much easier to see in families at the severe dysfunction level. Families at the moderate level generally possess the skills to hide problems. The at-risk behaviors in youth from families at this level can appear to exist without cause. However, rarely does an at-risk youth emerge sui generis (i.e., self-generated). While keeping mindful that exceptions do exist, one should always seek to understand the underlying family aspects of a youth's at-risk behavior. Otherwise, work with at-risk youth may never amount to more than the bandaging of symptoms.

Parental Conflict

If parents are having difficulty processing conflict between them, the situation is likely to deteriorate into communication problems between the parents. This

Sidebar 4.1 ■ Case Study: At-Risk Parenting

Bob Adams was a 45-year-old father of two who had been married for 24 years to Tern. Both were professional people with highly responsible jobs. Bob had a severe drinking problem that had affected the family for years. In addition, Bob had been consistently impervious to suggestions that he address his problem. Bob and Tern's two daughters, ages 17 and 19, were both high achievers in high school. Despite Bob's problems, the Adamses appeared as a picture-perfect family to other members of the community. However, the family's underlying dysfunction emerged when the oldest daughter Mary left for college.

Although initially excited to go off to college, Mary soon found herself consumed with worries about her family; she had always been the one to smooth over conflicts between her parents. She found that these worries left her little time for peers or academics. She returned home after passing only one course during the fall quarter.

After being home for the entire year, she applied to another college and went off to school once again. Needless to say, she could not stay at the new college either, returning home after only a few weeks. At about this time, Bob had a severe alcoholic episode, having to be brought home in a taxi one evening because of his drunkenness. He fought with his wife and destroyed the house before being hospitalized for several days. He checked out of the hospital before treatment was completed and against medical advice.

Mary's reaction to all of the confusion in her life was to take a bottle of pills. Her attempt at suicide was a cry for help, one that almost cost Mary her life. In trying to fix her parents and their marriage, she became unable to manage her own life.

This case demonstrates several important points. First, the father's severe drinking problem both produced and directed his daughter's at-risk behavior. Second, by never getting her life together, Mary avoided leaving home and abandoning her parents, for whom and to whom she felt responsible. As many family counselors would conclude, Mary rescued the marriage and family by putting herself at risk. Thus, if a counselor attempted to work with Mary's suicidal feelings independent of her family role as the rescuer, the counseling would be doomed to fail.

■ ■ ■

problem also extends to communication problems between parents and children. Secrets begin to exist between the parents. In the conflict between parents, children often become the emotional pawns in the intensified atmosphere of the home. Moreover, a direct relationship exists between both verbal and nonverbal parental conflict and at-risk behavior in children (Sturge-Apple, Skibo, & Davies, 2012).

Conflict between parents also leads to power struggles in parenting children. Each parent attempts to structure his or her relationship with the child as an individual instead of as a member of the marital unit. Loyalty issues are pressed onto the child. For example, a teenager comes home after curfew and is grounded for a week by the father. However, after 2 days the mother allows the teenager to visit friends but says, "Don't tell Dad!" This pattern of deceit between parents empowers the at-risk youth in two ways. First, the youth learns not to follow rules, and second, the youth learns to be deceitful. As family functioning begins to deteriorate, the youth will begin to demonstrate increasingly maladaptive behavior (Sourander et al., 2006).

The brief example in Sidebar 4.2 illustrates four important points about the struggles faced by at-risk youth. First, it is difficult to discipline a youth having severe difficulties without complete cooperation between the parents. One parent undercutting the effectiveness of the other makes it impossible to bring about change in the family and creates a situation in which the youth can become at risk. Second, loyalty issues

Sidebar 4.2 ■ Case Study: Parental Conflict

James Cooper was a 10-year-old fourth grader who was in frequent difficulties at school and in the community. His teacher reported him to be an aggressive, high-energy boy with a low attention span. However, his level of inappropriate conduct was never very severe until the day he assaulted another student on the playground during recess. The student he assaulted had to go to the emergency room for four stitches. At that time, James's parents were forced to enter counseling to assist him with his anger management program. Completion of this anger management program was the main prerequisite for the school district's lifting of James's suspension. In the family counseling part of the anger management program, it was immediately evident that Mr. and Mrs. Cooper had a very long history of marital and parental discord. Mr. Cooper was upset with Mrs. Cooper over numerous issues, which included an affair, overspending, poor discipline of the children, and meddling in-laws. Both Mr. and Mrs. Cooper reported that their fighting had escalated recently. Given the parents' marital trauma, the assault incident can be viewed as the inevitable act of a high-energy, aggressive boy who needed to create a major problem to bring his parents back together.

■ ■ ■

between family members can create severe problems if the loyalty lines are inappropriately drawn (Visher & Visher, 1996). A youth who is dependent on one parent can become angry with the other parent and attempt various at-risk behaviors. In other words, Parent A will fight Parent B through the at-risk behavior of their children.

Third, a youth's temperament will shape the at-risk behaviors the youth uses to heal family trauma. For example, an aggressive youth may choose fighting, whereas a depressed youth may choose a self-destructive act such as a suicide attempt. Fourth, parental conflict can lead to divorce. To oversimplify a difficult and complex problem, let us say that a divorce happens when two people fail to communicate and resolve conflicts. Following divorce, if a youth exhibits at-risk behaviors, it usually takes a significant problem to force the parents to face the gravity of the issues. Amato and Cheadle (2005) reported that parental conflict after divorce is a significant problem for children—a problem because youth give voice to their concerns over parental conflict through at-risk behaviors.

Family Denial

Denial is the defense mechanism whereby problems and their intensity are ignored or redirected. Denial is acted out in two ways within families. The first way denial is enacted is by burying one's head in the sand, that is, ignoring the reality of the situation. The second way denial is enacted is by finger pointing (i.e., blaming other people or events for one's problems). Both methods of using denial lead to youth becoming at risk.

Parentification of Children

One dysfunctional pattern of family dynamics that begins in the early years of childhood is parentification of children. This pattern occurs when parents give responsibilities and privileges to younger children that would be more appropriate for older children or adults. Young children, by their actions and requests, maintain the control of the household and frequently dictate the mood of the entire family. Parents, fearful of disrupting the family calm, refrain from effective discipline techniques. Thus, the children gain control of the family.

Parentified children are placed in situations in which they are given the power to make decisions that belong with the parents. The parents, by giving the power to the child, abdicate their responsibility for protecting the child from potentially dangerous situations.

This parentification is a common by-product of divorce. As the conflict between divorcing parents escalates, more and more self-care is left with the child. In addition, some very young children are even expected to carry the burden for maintaining the well-being of the parents during the separation and divorce process. Life is fine as long as the child is behaving, giving attention to the parents, and causing no apparent difficulty. The burden can become intense as the child grows and matures. It is very tiring to always be happy, provide love for a parent, care for other children, and be adultlike. In these cases, the parents often report that the child has never been a difficulty but rather has been the ideal child who always took care of everything.

Children and youth want to be in control of the decisions that affect their lives and will take every opportunity to gather more power. Parents must be encouraged to involve their children in the decision-making process but be reminded that involvement is different from making a final decision. Final decisions belong to the parents, not the children. When the child makes the choices alone, at-risk status is inevitable.

Serious Illness and Disability Within the Family

Serious illness and disability can catapult a family into a trauma response and affect their ability to maintain healthy coping. Consider an example in which the father has a newly diagnosed heart condition but denies his symptoms to his family. He might fear his role as the provider would be questioned. If the parents are unable to discuss the issue with each other or with the children, the family members are left more vulnerable to fears and fantasies about how bad the situation is. As secrecy or even dishonesty or deceit increases, these families become more at risk and sensitive at home, work, or school.

Kazak, Christakis, Alderfer, and Coiro (1994) discussed the impact of illness in families. They suggested that (a) family members tend to overreact to simple problems; (b) parents are protective of the children; and (c) in general, the entire family is acutely sensitive. In an attempt to cope with this sensitivity, the family will focus on less serious problems and concerns. Thus, denial becomes a major risk aspect. This denial can be considered dysfunctional. However, it can also be understood as an expected part of the reaction to trauma (Riolli & Savicki, 2010).

Typically, families will go through a series of stages in coping with the shock of the diagnosis of an illness, disability, hospitalizations, and treatment. There is a movement from defensive coping strategies such as denial or anger toward more functional ways of coping. The families at greatest risk are those unable to move toward the last stage. They remain mired in defensive coping patterns that affect all members in negative ways.

The family faced with an illness or disability must handle many emotionally charged issues. Because there is relatively little support in the medical setting for such issues, multidisciplinary teams that include counselors and appropriate referral are critical. In most instances, problematic family issues that existed before the medical crisis are exaggerated during the trauma of illness, loss of function, surgery, and other medical interventions. Fortunately, diagnosis and medical intervention also provide an opportunity for change. In states of crisis and trauma, otherwise rigid or resistant families may be responsive to psychosocial resources. In this way, the danger of the illness can provide new opportunities for change in the communication and coping systems within the family.

Sidebar 4.3 ■ Case Study: Serious Illness Within the Family

Jeff Stone was a 7-year-old brought to the Riverbend Children's Medical Center for rehabilitation surgery. The surgery was for a hand deformed at birth that left it shrunken and twisted. All Stone family members referred to this appendage as the "paw." When Jeff experienced anxiety about reconstructive surgery, the Stones were unable to discuss the hand with him, because this issue had been avoided from the time of Jeff's birth. Mr. and Mrs. Stone felt tremendous guilt over their boy's disability. The consulting counselor to the surgery unit met with the family to develop an initial assessment of the boy's view of the situation. Because it is often easier to draw a problem than to discuss it, using art materials is an effective method for assessment and offers a rich symbolic view of the patient's experience of hospitalization and trauma (Appleton, 2001). The counselor suggested that Jeff draw a person. Jeff drew an image of a teddy bear with a deformed paw. During the family interactions, the counselor also observed the defensive nature of the family coping.

After the initial assessment, the counselor worked to create a plan that would increase family communication and address denial. Specifically, the counselor invented a game called "Secrets." In this game, the family members examined the names they gave things that bothered them at home, school, or work. While playing the game, Mrs. Stone was able to disclose that the "paw" was her way to avoid discussing the boy's disability or embarrassing him or the other family members. Mrs. Stone hoped that the reference to a "paw" was easier on Jeff and the family. When this issue arose, the father and siblings spoke of the "paw" disparagingly. With the intern's assistance, Jeff was able to share his feelings of inferiority in the family and of feeling like a nonperson (or stuffed bear). Through these disclosures, it was clear no one in the family was comfortable with the term "paw."

In follow-up counseling, medical staff members were accessed for a discussion about the diagnosis and plans for rehabilitation of Jeff's weak hand. The counselor discussed the ways the hospital team might help the family to discuss the disability openly during medical and counseling interventions. In this way, the multidisciplinary team of doctors, nurses, physical therapists, counselor, and intern shared methods to encourage the family to practice more open communication during and after the surgery process. This support proved effective, and the Stones began to learn a new way to cope with difficult issues by discussing them together and with others.

■ ■ ■

Incidence Levels and Impact of Abuse and Neglect

Atrocities of violence against children are among the most difficult to discuss. However, abuse is a historical problem that does not go away. In fact, as professionals are trained to understand and report abuse, the number of reported cases has risen dramatically. A consideration of the incidence of abuse and neglect will help us recognize those children who are at the highest risk for maltreatment.

In 1973, the Child Abuse Prevention and Treatment Act (Public Law 93-247) defined the legal responsibilities of health care providers encountering child abuse or neglect. Intervention can be social, legal, medical, or any combination of the aforementioned. Congress defined child abuse and neglect as the physical and mental injury, sexual abuse, negligent treatment, or maltreatment of a child under age 18 by a person who is responsible for the child's welfare under circumstances that indicate the child's health or welfare is thereby harmed or threatened. Every state now has within its statutes a legal definition of abuse.

The U.S. Congress mandated periodic reports documenting the levels of child abuse (i.e., physically abused, sexually abused, and emotionally abused) and neglect (i.e., physically neglected, emotionally neglected, and educationally neglected) in this country. This report is called the National Incidence Study of Child Abuse and Neglect (NIS). Professionals across a spectrum of schools and agencies act as sentinels and gather data about maltreatment (*maltreatment* being the term used to collectively refer to abuse and neglect). In this way, the NIS estimates provide a more complete measure of the scope of child abuse and neglect known to community professionals that may not be included in official statistics. The most recent NIS study is NIS-4 (Sedlak et al., 2010). The NIS-4 maltreatment statistics I report follow the NIS Endangerment Standard rather than the more restrictive NIS Harm Standard. The NIS Endangerment Standard includes all the cases reported in the NIS Harm Standard as well as child abuse and neglect incidents made known from a wider variety of sources.

The NIS-4 researchers reported that an estimated 2.9 million children (or 1 child in 25) in the United States were abused or neglected during the latest NIS study period. The NIS-4 study also detailed the families in which child maltreatment occurred most often. We will first examine some individual characteristics related to child maltreatment (i.e., age, gender, and race/ethnicity) and then turn to an examination of family characteristics (i.e., socioeconomic status, family structure, and metropolitan status of county of residence).

Individual Factors Related to Child Maltreatment

Child's age. The NIS-4 reported that child maltreatment is generally invariant across age categories (i.e., 0–2, 3–5, 6–8, 9–11, 12–14, and 15–17). The one exception is that the rate for aged 6–8 (42 per 1,000) was statistically greater than that for aged 15–17 (29 per 1,000). However, the lower incidence of maltreatment reported in young children might reflect underreporting of these children. As children mature, they are involved with an increasing number of community professionals who can observe them and make appropriate investigations. They may also be better able to escape, retaliate, or ask for help.

Child's gender. With one exception, there was no difference between genders in terms of rate of maltreatment. The exception was for sexual abuse. Girls experienced sexual abuse at a rate 3.8 times higher than boys. Because serious injury can accompany sexual abuse, this accounts for a higher injury rate among girls as well.

Child's race/ethnicity. The NIS-4 examined child maltreatment differences between White, Black, and Latino groups (other groups were excluded because of insufficient data for extensive analysis). Overall, Black children experienced a maltreatment rate of 50 per 1,000. This rate was statistically higher than the rates for White children (29 per 1,000) and Latino children (30 per 1,000). In terms of specific categories of maltreatment, two findings stood out. First, Black children experienced a higher rate of physical abuse (10 per 1,000) compared with White children (5 per 1,000) and Latino children (6 per 1,000). Second, Black children (5 per 1,000) and White children (4 per 1,000) experienced a higher rate of emotional abuse compared with Latino children (2 per 1,000).

Family Factors Related to Child Maltreatment

Socioeconomic status (SES). Children in low SES families (i.e., annual household income of less than $15,000) are five times more likely to suffer some form of maltreatment than children not in low SES families. In terms of specific maltreatment categories, the greatest difference between the low and not low SES groups was in the area of physical neglect. Children in low SES households were eight times more likely to experience physical neglect. In terms of parental employment, children with no parent working were three times more likely to experience maltreatment than children who had at least one parent working.

Family structure. The NIS-4 used six non-overlapping categories to explore the relationship between family structure and maltreatment. These categories were as follows:

1. Living with two married biological parents
2. Living with two married parents and at least one was not a biological parent
3. Living with two unmarried parents (biological or legal parental relationship)
4. Living with one parent who had an unmarried partner (not the child's parent) in the household (OP-UM)
5. Living with one parent who had no partner in the household
6. Living with no parent

The highest rate of maltreatment occurred in the OP-UM category. Children in this category are eight times more likely to experience maltreatment than children living with two married biological parents. In terms of specific maltreatment categories, children in the OP-UM category experience physical abuse at a rate of 10 times and sexual abuse at a rate of 17 times the rates of children residing with two married biological parents. Figure 4.1 contains the rates for all six family structure categories.

Metropolitan status of county of residence. In every maltreatment category, rural children experienced higher rates (68 per 1,000 overall) than their urban counterparts (31 per 1,000 overall). More than any other statistic, this one reveals the higher at-risk status of rural youth.

Impact

Abuse is an issue of control and power, whether it is perpetrated within or outside of the family. The impact of physical and sexual abuse is directly related to intensity, the amount of coercion, and the level of conflict involved. Webb and Terr (1999) distinguished between two kinds of trauma. A single traumatic event in an otherwise normal life is called Type I trauma, and the effects of prolonged and repeated trauma are called Type II trauma. Within families, children are more likely to suffer Type II trauma and endure repeated and anticipated pain, violence, and chaos. The Type II syndrome, according to Webb and Terr, includes coping mechanisms of denial, psychological numbing, self-hypnosis, dissociation, and extreme shifts between rage and passivity.

When observing children suspected of being maltreated, one needs to understand the form their trauma and symptoms take. According to Gil (1996), children will exhibit the impact of abuse and neglect through either internalized or externalized behaviors. Children who cope through internalized behavior negotiate the pain by themselves. They are likely to avoid interaction and appear depressed, joyless, phobic, hypervigilant, and regressed. Given the stress of coping without help, these children manifest physical symptoms, including sleep disorders and somatic problems (e.g., headaches and stomachaches). In addition, they withdraw emotionally and may appear overly compliant. In more severe

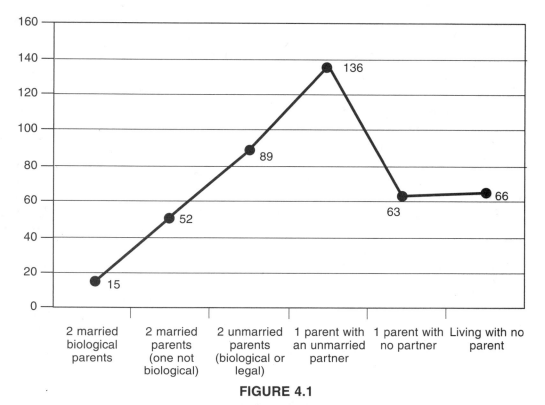

FIGURE 4.1

Rate Per 1,000 of Child Maltreatment by Family Structure

Note. Adapted from *Fourth National Incidence Study of Child Abuse and Neglect (NIS-4): Report to Congress*, by A. J. Sedlak, J. Mettenburg, M. Basena, I. Petta, K. McPherson, A. Greene, and S. Li, 2010, Washington, DC: U.S. Department of Health and Human Services, Administration for Children and Families. Adapted with permission.

cases they disassociate, self-mutilate, and become suicidal. They are also likely to use drugs to numb both the physical and emotional pain of abuse. Conversely, children who cope through externalized behavior direct their pain outward and toward others. They express emotions that are often hostile, provocative, and violent. They may kill or torture animals, destroy property through fire settings, and exhibit sexualized behaviors. However, the effects are not, for the most part, multigenerational.

Physical abuse effects. Physically abused children have deficits in gross motor development, speech, and language. The impact of physical abuse includes psychic trauma, chaos, rejection, deprivation, distorted parental perceptions, and unrealistic expectations. Further disruptions of family life occur with hospitalizations, separation, foster placement, and frequent home changes.

At a minimum, children hurt by others suffer an impaired capacity to enjoy life. When the abuse is more extreme, psychiatric symptoms will appear (e.g., enuresis, hyperactivity, and bizarre behavior). In school, abused children who exhibit more internalized behaviors will present learning problems, compulsiveness, hypervigilance, and suicidal tendencies. Children who cope with abuse through more externalized behaviors are oppositional. Typically, these children have problems managing aggressive behavior and cannot establish relationships with other children (Wang, Deater-Deckard, Petrill, & Thompson, 2012).

Sexual abuse effects. The impact of child sexual abuse can be measured along a continuum from neutral to very negative (Friedrich, 2002). At its extreme, the effects of sexual abuse manifest in dissociation. The term *dissociation* refers to "a disruption of and/or discontinuity in the normal, subjective integration of one or more aspects of psychological functioning, including—but not limited to—memory, identity, consciousness, perception, and motor control" (Spiegel et al., 2011, p. E19). Dissociation occurs when the child is exposed to overwhelming events that result in extreme feelings of helplessness. In the traumatic situation, the child attempts to cope by dissociating the self from the act being perpetrated. This dissociation becomes part of the child's development and results in long-term difficulties. In this way, internalized behaviors such as eating disorders, substance abuse, and depression can be understood as behavioral readouts of dissociation. Externalized behaviors accompanying sexual abuse include school difficulties, anger, running away, delinquency, and sexualized behaviors.

Sexualized behavior is an externalized behavior that is shaped by sexual experiences, feelings, and attitudes that occur in the abuse process (Finkelhor, 1984). Early and manipulated exposure to sex may result in a child's excessive or preoccupying interest in it. There is a difference between normal sexual curiosity and sexualization. Unlike other children, the sexualized child exhibits behaviors in the following domains: (a) boundary problems (e.g., hugs adults he or she doesn't know well), (b) displaying private parts (e.g., shows private parts to adults), (c) sexual interest (e.g., talks in a flirty way), (d) sexual intrusiveness (e.g., touches other people's private parts), and (e) sexual knowledge (e.g., pretends that dolls/stuffed animals are having sex; Merrick, Litrownik, Everson, & Cox, 2008). This lack of inhibition can extend to play, art, and conversations that are imitative of adult sexual relationships.

The sexualized child is clearly at risk for developmentally inappropriate sexual behavior as well as pregnancy, sexually transmitted diseases, and prostitution. Thus, it is critical for the professional to understand and differentiate what is normal sexual development in children from behaviors that indicate trauma.

Neglect effects. The dynamics of neglect differ markedly from those of physical or sexual abuse. The main difference is the attention received from the parents. The attention associated with abuse is inappropriate, excessive, harsh, and damaging, but the parent is still involved with the child. Neglecting parents do the opposite. For example, they fail to stimulate or interact on an emotional or a physical level. In extreme cases, it is as though the parent does not know the child exists.

The effects of child neglect and deprivation occur across all levels of development, including social, affective, physical, emotional, behavioral, and cognitive. We can expect to see internalized behaviors, including a lack of affect (feelings), social detachment, and impaired empathy, as well as externalized behaviors, including violence and delinquency. Neglected youth can be identified by behaviors that convey low self-esteem, a negative worldview, and internalized or externalized anxieties or aggressions. Because of the lack of nurturance, there is typically poor intellectual development, developmental disabilities, and developmental delays. In addition, neglected children are seriously bereft of personal or family resources for care.

Stress resistance. Some abused and neglected children appear relatively less traumatized than others. Garbarino, Guttman, and Seeley (1986) proposed the concept of "stress-resistant children" who become prosocial and competent despite harsh or even hostile upbringing. It is speculated that these children receive compensatory psychological nurturance and sustenance. This nurturance may come from home, school professionals, neighbors, or family friends. Perhaps the experience of even minimal care enables the child to cope better and to develop social competence. With a basis of social competence, the child's view of the world and his or her role within it remain more positive. In a time when counseling is reduced to a bare minimum of contact with at-risk youth, school professionals might examine what is the good-enough intervention to promote the natural adaptability of young people. For a further examination of methods that are designed to increase the natural adaptability and resilience of children, see Chapter 3 in this volume.

Continuing Effects/Youth Sex Offenders

Only 1% of sexual abuse victims are known to enter the victim–offender cycle (Ogloff, Cutajar, Mann, & Mullen, 2012). Still, that rate is eight times greater than the rate for the general population (Ogloff et al., 2012). Thus, counselors should be aware of and prepared to prevent the victim–offender cycle from occurring.

What distinguishes those who enter the victim–offender cycle from other victims? Lambie, Seymour, Lee, and Adams (2002) reported that when compared with a whole population of sexual abuse victims, those who enter this cycle were more likely to have (a) fantasized and masturbated about the abuse, (b) reported deriving pleasure from the abuse, (c) had infrequent social contact with peers, and (d) lacked family and nonfamily support during childhood.

What do the homes of youth sex offenders look like? With these youth, Concepcion (2004) noted the presence of (a) broken families, (b) substance abuse, (c) multigenerational abuse, (d) high rates of poverty, (e) witnessing of domestic violence by children, (f) lack of positive anger management, (g) blurred privacy boundaries, and (h) denial of responsibility by family members.

What do the youth sex offenders look like? Let us examine three articles on this topic. Oxnam and Vess (2006) found that youth sex offenders fell into one of three distinct personality groups: antisocial, inadequate, and normal. They noted that members of the antisocial group tend to act out in an aggressive and unpredictable manner, with a propensity to dominate and abuse others' rights. They described the inadequate group as youth who are chronically insecure and avoidant of interpersonal contact. Finally, they found a group with no distinguishing personality features that they labeled normal. Richardson (2005) studied the interpersonal schemas of youth sex offenders. He found three maladaptive schemas prominent in these youth: emotional inhibition, social isolation/alienation, and mistrust/abuse. Farr, Brown, and Beckett (2004) studied both the ability to empathize and the masculinity levels in youth sex offenders. They found youth sex offenders far less able to empathize than a comparison nonoffender group of youth. In terms of masculinity, two subscales of the measure they used differentiated youth sex offenders from nonoffenders. These subscales were (a) callous sexual attitudes toward females and (b) adversarial attitudes toward females and sexual minorities. The youth sex offenders scored far higher on both subscales.

One theme emphasized by many of the authors cited in this subsection was the need for family-based interventions for youth sex offenders. It is amazing that little research has been done on family-based interventions for youth sex offenders. One promising approach is the use of multifamily group therapy. A detailed description of this approach to treating youth sex offenders appears in Nahum and Brewer (2004). The reported benefits of this approach included economical use of clinician resources, family-to-family transfer of knowledge and mentoring, community-based resourcefulness, and accelerated catalyzing of emotions.

Approaches to Prevention

The preceding section reviewed a number of dysfunctional family situations and some of the youth at-risk behaviors that could flow from such family situations. The impact of physical and sexual abuse on youth was also explored. However, when faced with at-risk youth, professionals need more than knowledge; they need to be armed with practical ways to help these youth. Such arming is the goal of this section.

Pianta and Walsh (1996) posited that three forms of prevention operate in work with at-risk youth: primary prevention, secondary prevention, and tertiary prevention. An example of primary prevention is Washington State's HIV/AIDS Education Law (RCW 28A.230.020). This law mandates that all students in all common schools receive HIV/AIDS prevention education each year. The law represents primary prevention because it is directed to all students before the period when at-risk behaviors (e.g., intravenous drug use) begin. A transition-to-middle-school support group for students with low grades is an example of secondary prevention because it is directed at a specific population before it obtains at-risk status (e.g., school dropout). An example of tertiary prevention is a school-based aftercare group for students who have recently returned from a stay at a drug rehabilitation center. The goal of tertiary prevention is to remediate students who have already obtained an at-risk status.

With the forms of prevention defined, attention now turns to the levels of prevention: individual, family, school, and community.

Individual Level

Counseling

Individual counseling can be a secondary or tertiary prevention activity. Counselors who work with at-risk youth must exemplify the importance of well-defined rules and responsibilities. In working with the at-risk youth, the counselor must be sure to follow the rules of the counseling process. Just as the at-risk youth attempts to alter the rules in other settings for personal gain, the youth will attempt to have the counselor alter and ignore the rules of the counseling process.

For example, the youth may have a simple request, such as asking the counselor to write an excuse that would allow him or her to miss a class at school or be permitted to miss detention. Other, more critical violations of the rules may be requests for emergency appointments late at night or over the weekend. One counselor from a rural district spent 6 hours with a youth along a country road following a phone call requesting her help. It was considerate of the counselor but also very risky and ethically questionable. The youth did not follow the rules of counseling—attending the counseling session in the appropriate location. One way to decrease the at-risk behavior is to define up front the role of the counselor and the rules of the counseling process.

Another aspect of prevention within the individual counseling process is determining the severity of the at-risk youth's actions and interactions. Whether the youth is abusing alcohol, is pregnant, or is a runaway, the counselor needs to determine the extent of danger to the well-being of the youth. The prudent counselor takes few chances with an at-risk youth. Risk taking on the part of the counselor is ill advised because these youth tend to be impulsive in their actions and prone to hurting themselves physically.

In determining severity, the counselor needs to be highly aware of the concept of duty to warn. This is prevention of the highest order. At the initiation of counseling, both the at-risk youth and the family are informed that any suspicious or questionable behaviors will be reported. Both confidentiality and at-risk status are clearly defined early in the process, reinforcing the professional's responsibility to follow the rules.

If there are questions about the level of severity of the youth's behavior, professionals need to follow a cautious route and involve the parents. Following the rules may mean having a crisis team available to give the youth the appropriate treatment, including the possibility of hospitalization. If the youth is suicidal, a coordinated professional effort may need to be used to resolve the problem. The sooner the at-risk youth is involved in treatment, the greater the opportunity for successful resolution and prevention of problems.

In principle, the counselor should always involve a family in at-risk prevention planning. However, there are situations in which individual counseling with an at-risk student should be emphasized over family counseling. These situations include when (a) the relationship between the parents is questionable, (b) parenting skills are almost nonexistent, (c) one parent is an alcoholic, and (d) the parents are frequently absent from the home.

When the emphasis is on individual counseling, even more responsibility is on the counselor to follow the rules. To treat effectively the myriad difficulties of an at-risk youth, the professional must maintain a high level of confidence. Treating the at-risk youth can be a substantial test of a counselor's self-confidence. Thus, appropriate attention to the counselor's own self-care against stress and anxiety is warranted. This self-care is the best antidote to counselor burnout.

Abuse Prevention

Providing care. It is critical that professionals who work with the difficult issues of child abuse and neglect are trained in the specifics of these issues. Hurt children evoke complex responses in caregivers. At some point, the most skilled practitioner wants to rescue the child from trauma. Therefore, a support system and professional contact base are essential in this work. Also, specific resources for reporting, dealing with legal issues, finding safe housing, and locating community support services are necessary for effective interventions to occur.

Clarification of roles, empowerment, and the stages of intervention. Given the issues of coercion in child abuse, it is particularly important for the counselor to form a noncompetitive working alliance with at-risk youth (de la Peña, Friedlander, Escudero, & Heatherington, 2012). This alliance is critical because abused and neglected children have poor and often brutalized experiences with trust and intimacy. When hearing the story, the young person must understand that he or she is a survivor, not merely a victim. Furthermore, the young person needs to know that he or she carries no responsibility for the abuse.

At the first stages of intervention, the counselor can work to develop small steps of self-care, plans for safety, and other support resources. The young person must be told at the outset that the counselor must report the threat of harm to self or others. Depending on the severity of the abuse or neglect, the later stages of counseling will direct the young person toward self-care and independence. In this way, the counselor can help the young person toward the future. This process cannot be rushed, and the length of time it takes will depend on the young person's internal, familial, and other support resources. As gains are made in a transfer of learning to the world outside counseling, prevention and education become important. Mutual support is critical and can reinforce affective awareness and empowerment.

Empowerment also occurs through mastery. As seen in other developmental sequences, children develop a sense of mastery by practicing. Nonverbal processes give an outlet for raw emotion and a place to practice or work through the trauma impact.

Family Level

The Family Role of the At-Risk Youth

When an at-risk youth is identified, much attention is often given directly to the youth without commensurate attention to the entire family. This inattention is unfortunate because at-risk behavior is simply a behavioral readout of family dysfunction. In other words, the youth's at-risk behavior is not sui generis but rather the acting out of a script provided by the family system.

One common script is that of the identified patient. The family of the at-risk youth asserts that all in the family is well except for the at-risk youth. In truth, the at-risk youth's behaviors are merely the symptoms of family dysfunction. The greater the difficulties demonstrated by the youth, the larger the number of issues that need attention within the family. It is inappropriate to assume that the identified problem child is the only family member with mental health needs or the only family member who may be at risk.

Impact of Malevolent Family Dynamics

Once a youth demonstrates at-risk behaviors, family dynamics play a significant role in whether the at-risk behaviors will escalate or decline. If the dysfunctional aspects of the family dynamics are not identified, discussed, and changed, the behaviors of the at-risk youth will continue to escalate (Hooven, Nurius, Logan-Greene, & Thompson, 2012). Thus, involvement of the family is vital to prevent at-risk behaviors from escalating.

Families and Chance of At-Risk Behavior

The involvement of the family of the at-risk youth in assessment, diagnosis, and treatment planning is essential. The counselor provides a model of behavior to the parents, and the parents provide a wealth of information, spoken or unspoken, to the counselor. Many counselors wonder which family members should be involved in the counseling process. It is important to consider all members of the household as potential participants in the work with at-risk youth.

Frequently, one of the most effective means to bring about change in youth is couples counseling for the parents. If the parents can commit to working on their relationship (along with being willing to learn different parenting approaches with their children), the chances of successfully assisting an at-risk youth increase

Sidebar 4.4 ■ Personal Reflection and Integration

At-risk youth commonly present with chaotic, strife-torn families. Consider the following questions about your experience with your family of origin:

1. What word would best characterize interpersonal relations within your family of origin?
2. What role(s) did you play within the structure of your family of origin?
3. How did your family of origin respond to any trauma that members experienced?

Given your answers to these questions, what countertransference reactions do you anticipate wrestling with when working with at-risk youth embedded in chaotic, strife-torn families?

■ ■ ■

significantly. However, as demonstrated throughout the case studies, there frequently is much disarray in the relationship between the parents. Such disarray makes it understandable why the youth may be having emotional difficulty. Also, parents provide an inappropriate model for the developing youth when they work too much, drink too much, or allow their lives to be out of control (Coldwell, Pike, & Dunn, 2006). Once parents can be taught to reorient and redirect some of their energies, the positive changes in youth are absolutely astounding. Therefore, parent counseling along with family counseling can produce remarkable changes in dysfunctional family structures.

Family counseling must be part of the intervention and prevention plan for at-risk youth. In working with the family, the counselor must maintain a neutral position and avoid a position of being on someone's side. The youth and the parents will attempt to enlist the counselor's support in their efforts to maintain the dysfunctional family system. A youth or parent may call the counselor on the phone, bring damaging evidence to the session to demonstrate someone's problems, or ask for additional sessions—all of these situations represent some of the influence peddling family members try. It is important to remember that the goal is not to fix the at-risk youth but rather to support the development of a new and functional family interaction system.

Postabuse Family Intervention

The critical issue for children not removed from their families is monitoring the risk factors for the child and his or her parents. Any postabuse plan must assess and ensure a safe environment by evaluating parental abuse proneness, the vulnerability of the child, and environmental stresses that trigger abuse (Green, 1988). The counselor will also need to assess the family's level of coping and complexity. At-risk families are typically ones with multiple problems, poor ability to cope with stress, and few resources for help internally or in the community. Therefore, it is important for the counselor to devise realistic goals. Postabuse counseling will be a process of mediating the need for the family members to express their feelings versus the need for safety from punishment or retaliation at home for this behavior. Self-help groups such as Parents Anonymous may be helpful to families as well (see http://www.parentsanonymous.org).

School Level

Preservice/In-Service Needs

School counselors and teachers are the frontline soldiers in the war against at-risk behaviors. To be capable soldiers, school counselors and teachers need to possess adequate knowledge in the following areas: parent consultation, referral and networking, and professional comportment.

Parent consultation. All school professionals need to be comfortable with the principle of parent consultation. If a school professional does not contact parents regarding at-risk behaviors, the professional is maintaining too much responsibility for the at-risk youth. Parents need to be encouraged to take responsibility for their at-risk children and to become actively involved in the prevention process as soon as possible.

An effective consultation with the parents can assist the family in understanding the necessary steps of the helping process. It is important for the school professional making the initial contact with the family to understand the critical nature of his or her role. It is essential to provide the family with a clear understanding of the helping process. The initial consultation should be used to encourage and assist the family in receiving the most effective services possible. If the initial consultation is a positive experience, more than likely the family will be ready to pursue the necessary steps of the treatment process.

Referral and networking. Another necessary knowledge area for school counselors and teachers is referral and networking. If school professionals cannot provide the at-risk youth with appropriate services, they must refer the at-risk youth and the family to an appropriate agency, institution, or private practitioner. Frequently, someone such as a school counselor identifies the at-risk youth, but the services required for treatment are offered elsewhere. Thus, schools must link their efforts for at-risk youth with the efforts of local agencies, practitioners, and hospitals.

Maintaining a comprehensive referral network of helping professionals is probably one of the most important aspects of prevention as well as a major responsibility for school professionals treating at-risk youth. The network should include both medical and nonmedical mental health service providers. Specifically, referral sources need to include psychiatrists, drug and alcohol counselors, mental health counselors, clinical psychologists, marriage and family specialists, and clergy. School professionals treating at-risk youth must have a thorough knowledge of the variability and comprehensiveness of various services in the community.

Professional comportment. Critical to proper professional comportment is knowledge on how to act in an ethical and legal manner when working with at-risk youth. One key ethical and legal concern in working with at-risk youth is the issue of confidentiality. Too often school professionals maintain confidentiality without considering the ramifications to the youth as well as to themselves. Being direct and upfront with the youth about the types of information and behavior that are treated in a confidential manner versus those to be reported to the parents helps avoid potential problems later.

School counselors and teachers often serve as the primary connection between at-risk youth and their families. Thus, it is essential for school professionals to possess knowledge of parental consultation, referral and networking, and proper professional comportment. Using professional colleagues for support and consultation, making effective and necessary referrals of particularly difficult cases, and seeking personal counseling when the stress becomes too great are some ways a school counselor or teacher can maintain a high level of self-confidence and effectiveness.

Curriculum-based interventions. When people think of school counselors working with at-risk youth, they usually think of school counselors performing secondary and tertiary prevention activities. For example, they may think of school counselors facilitating support groups or conducting individual counseling. However, school counselors have an important role to play in the primary prevention of at-risk status in youth.

In 1997, the American School Counselor Association published national standards for school counseling programs. The model program contained K–12 guidance curriculum goals in three areas: personal/social development, career development, and academic development. Lapan, Gysbers, and Sun (1997) found that full implementation of a guidance program serves as a powerful antidote to at-risk status. Students in schools with a more fully implemented guidance program reported that (a) they earned higher grades, (b) their education better prepared them for the future, (c) their school made more career information available to them, and (d) their school had a more positive climate. School guidance programs are not the sole domain of counselors. In fact, because of their small numbers, the main role of the school counselor in the guidance program is that of facilitator. The key deliverer of the curricular parts of the guidance program is the teacher. Thus, the student outcomes just noted are possible only if school counselors and teachers work in concert.

School counselors are not the only educational professionals with a curriculum that serves as an at-risk primary prevention activity. Family and consumer sciences teachers have also published a national curriculum. This curriculum aims to help young people develop the social skills and decision-making skills that can serve as a protection against at-risk behaviors. In addition, this curriculum contains standards on parent training for youth. There is no better example of primary prevention activity than giving people parenting skills before they become parents! Thus, national curricula exist in the United States that directly address the skill deficits that can lead to an at-risk status for youth. Such curricula have been shown scientifically to be efficacious. Unfortunately, there is no single curriculum that is universal in U.S. schools.

Mentoring programs. To prevent the development of at-risk behaviors, the child may need to find other role models and mentors in his or her own day-to-day experiences. At-risk youth sometimes find their own ability to develop appropriate roles and responsibilities from interactions with peers, schoolteachers, neighbors, and other community leaders. For at-risk youth to change their pattern of behavior means that they need to see an alternative way of life.

Physical and sexual abuse education for children. The NIS-4 report (Sedlak et al., 2010) stressed that schools play a central role in identifying and helping abused and neglected young people. School professionals are the frontline observers who form relationships of care with young people. Rencken (1989) advocated three axes of prevention for abuse that are useful at the school and community levels: empowerment, sex education, and gender equity. The first axis includes teaching assertiveness and the ability to say no from a foundation of self-esteem, responsibility, and age-appropriate control. The second axis is sex education to remediate ignorance for young people and their families. The third axis is a discussion of gender role differences between males and females in society and the development of equitable power arrangements.

It is clear that physically abused and neglected children are not always helped, even with reporting. Child protection agencies and the court system are already seriously overworked. Often they are unable to follow up on cases except where there is threat of fatality. To address this problem, grassroots support systems are being developed. Schools and mental health agencies are teaming together to develop individualized and tailored care that uses the natural support systems in communities to help protect children. These support systems include safe places for children to go after school, neighborhood police stations, child mentorship, and after-school activities such as tutoring and gym nights. Schools can become a place to provide support to at-risk youth and their families. Grants and donations of time and money are typically used by schools and agencies to develop these support resources.

Community Level

Parent Education

A powerful prevention activity is parent education. Both schools and community agencies can sponsor such an activity for minimal cost. If only one activity could be selected to prevent at-risk status in youth, it should be parent education. Nothing provides more bang for the buck.

Two parent education activities that have solid research support are Systematic Training for Effective Parenting (STEP) and parent monitoring. It is important to note that these activities can be easily sponsored and led not only by school personnel but also by local community agencies or churches. Neither is the kind of fancy, complex activity that garners media attention. Rather, they are doable, proven at-risk prevention activities that can make a difference in the lives of youth and their parents. As such, they merit the considerations of anyone looking for ways to address the at-risk youth problems they encounter in their workplace or in their community.

STEP program. STEP is a widely used parent education program (see http://www.cfchildren.org/second-step.aspx). The STEP program curriculum presents parents with practical ideas that are based on Adlerian psychology. There are a wide variety of STEP modules, including those for parents of young children, parents of teens, Christian parents, and Latino parents. Although it is designed for the average parent, there is even evidence of STEP's effectiveness with parents who have previously abused their children (Fennell & Fishel, 1998).

The STEP program is well laid out, with clear lesson plans and appropriate participant activities. A person who has had some previous training in developmental psychology and in communication skills would do an excellent job of facilitating STEP training. There is also extensive training available.

Parent monitoring. Although it may sound like an incredibly simplistic solution, extensive research supports the idea that at-risk behaviors can be decreased by increasing the parental monitoring of youth (Metzger, Ice, & Cottrell, 2012). Thus, parental monitoring can be taught in order to lower at-risk status. Murray, Kelder, Parcel, and Orpinas (1998) identified four skills that are essential in building competent monitoring in parents:

1. Parents will ask their child where he or she is going.
2. Parents will obtain a list of telephone numbers of their child's friends.
3. Parents will call parents of their child's friends.
4. Parents will visit their child's school.

Learning objectives are identified for each skill. For example, one of the learning objectives for the second skill is "parents will be able to recognize most of their child's friends on the street and know their names" (Murray et al., 1998, p. 50).

Community Capacity Building

At-risk behaviors of youth do not wreak havoc in just families and schools. The social and economic costs of such behaviors affect every community. Thus, building the capacity of communities to prevent at-risk behaviors benefits all citizens. Given the central role of schools in most communities, school personnel can be key instigators in prompting a community to focus on at-risk prevention. In terms of community-wide prevention efforts, school personnel should work toward two goals: education on family dynamics and community-wide networking.

Education on family dynamics. One key community prevention goal is educating the general public about the variation in family structures and individual differences. It is still difficult for many local institutions such as churches, hospitals, and other community organizations to make allowances for the various family structures, such as blended families, single-parent families, interracial families, and dual-career families. Moreover, if at-risk youth are to find surrogate role models in the community, it is important for the potential role models to understand the dysfunctional and nontraditional aspects of family life in the current culture.

Community-wide networking. Another key community prevention goal is the successful networking of school personnel with other professionals in the community who serve at-risk youth. These professionals include private practice counselors, community agency counselors, probation officers, law enforcement officers, and pediatricians. This networking is necessary given the multifaceted nature of at-risk status in youth. For example, substance abuse may lead to both academic and health problems. Given this complexity, school professionals must have an effective network of other professionals to offer the youth and the family the best services possible. The network should include knowledge of runaway shelters, crisis intervention teams, support groups, hospitals, and outpatient services.

Adaptations for Diversity

At present, persons of color represent 45% of the U.S. population under age 18 (U.S. Department of Health and Human Services, 2011). Thus, no counselor can hope to be effective with at-risk youth and their families without knowing how to adapt for diversity. Why should counselors care about diversity beyond simple demographics? Because there is strong evidence that the inability to adapt for diversity leads to unilateral client termination (Owen, Imel, Adelson, & Rodolfa,

---

Sidebar 4.5 ■ Personal Reflection and Integration

No effective counselor is an island. Thus, consider the following questions:

1. What are the two most important community partners in your work with dysfunctional families and why?
2. As you think about your professional life moving forward, what are two resources in the community you wish to cultivate to better help you in your work with dysfunctional families and why?

■ ■ ■

2012). Also, counseling for at-risk youth without a family component leads to decreased functioning in families of color (Szapocznik & Prado, 2007). Fortunately, there is guidance for counselors on how to adapt family treatment for at-risk youth of color: specifically, the groundbreaking work done by José Szapocznik. His approach is known as brief structural family therapy (BSFT).

BSFT was originally developed by Szapocznik in the 1970s to treat at-risk youth within the Cuban American community of Miami. Szapocznik chose a family-based approach in order to align with this community's valuing of family connectedness over individual autonomy. Over time, researchers have examined the effectiveness of BSFT with at-risk youth from a variety of Latino communities as well with African American youth and Asian youth. A large body of evidence shows that BSFT is highly effective in treating at-risk youth of color and their families (Szapocznik, Schwartz, Muir, & Brown, 2012).

As opposed to treatment as usual (TAU) with at-risk youth, BSFT focuses "on diagnosing family interactional patterns and restructuring (i.e., changing) the family interactions associated with the adolescent's problem behaviors" (Szapocznik et al., 2012, p. 135). While using a family-based approach to treat at-risk youth from family-centric cultures seems obvious and is evidence-based, TAU approaches (e.g., individual counseling, adolescent group counseling) continue to dominate. The effective counselor selects interventions that privilege the client's worldview over his or her own. For counselors wanting more detail about BSFT, there is a full-text manual that can be downloaded for free at http://archives.drugabuse.gov/pdf/Manual5.pdf.

Summary

This chapter has provided an overview of how dysfunctional family dynamics both precede and fuel at-risk behavior. In addition, the chapter provides some ideas about how to best provide a program of prevention to assist at-risk youth and their families. Several points need to be emphasized for those charged with working with at-risk youth.

First, there is no more difficult population to serve than at-risk youth. They tend to be more professionally demanding, emotionally draining, and behaviorally unpredictable than youth in general. Professionals assigned to work with this population must learn to be direct and honest with the youth as well as his or her family. As mentioned in the discussion of prevention, these same professionals must learn to follow the rules in serving these youth.

Sidebar 4.6 ■ Personal Reflection and Integration

José Szapocznik's work makes it clear that adapting to diversity is critical to success in the treatment of at-risk youth of color and their families. Thus, ask yourself the following questions:

1. What adaptations to TAU have I found effective in working with at-risk youth of color and their families and why?
2. Which BSFT ideas and techniques would I like to add to my counselor tool belt and why?

■ ■ ■

Second, the at-risk family is a special entity and needs tremendous amounts of attention to keep it functioning without tragedy. A professional working with an at-risk individual has to always be aware of the remaining family members to make sure that another member does not manifest a severe behavioral difficulty. Consultation with other important adults surrounding the family members is necessary to effectively work with the at-risk family. This is a responsible approach for counselors working with any family and is particularly important when these community persons reflect the culture of the family that is different from the counselor's own cultural background or identity.

Finally, treating at-risk youth mandates that professionals be involved with families and community agencies. There is no place in work with at-risk youth for the professional Lone Ranger. The biggest mistake made by caring professionals is to assume too much individual responsibility for the at-risk youth and his or her family. Find a support system to assist in the treatment process, and be sure to have a support system available for you. Maintaining physical energy and emotional balance is as important as any decision the professional can make. The following websites provide additional information relating to the chapter topics.

Useful Websites

Committee for Children's Second Step
  http://www.cfchildren.org/second-step.aspx
National Institute on Drug Abuse (BSFT full-text manual download)
  http://archives.drugabuse.gov/pdf/Manual5.pdf
U.S. Government's Children, Youth, and Families at Risk (CYFAR) Program
  http://www.csrees.usda.gov/nea/family/cyfar/cyfar.html
U.S. Government's National Clearinghouse on Families and Youth
  http://ncfy.acf.hhs.gov/category/tags/risk-youth

References

Amato, P. R., & Cheadle, J. (2005). The long reach of divorce: Divorce and child well-being across three generations. *Journal of Marriage and Family, 67,* 191–206. doi:10.1111/j.0022-2445.2005.00014.x

Appleton, V. B. (2001). Avenues of hope: Art therapy and the resolution of trauma. *Art Therapy: Journal of the American Art Therapy Association, 18,* 6–13. doi:10.1080/07421656.2001.10129454

Coldwell, J., Pike, A., & Dunn, J. (2006). Household chaos: Links with parenting and child behaviour. *Journal of Child Psychology and Psychiatry, 47,* 1116–1122. doi:10.1111/j.1469-7610.2006.01655.x

Concepcion, J. I. (2004). Understanding preadolescent sexual offenders. *The Florida Bar Journal, 78,* 30–37. Retrieved from http://www.floridabar.org/DIVCOM/JN/JN-Journal01.nsf

de la Peña, C. M., Friedlander, M. L., Escudero, V., & Heatherington, L. (2012). How do therapists ally with adolescents in family therapy? An examination of relational control communication in early sessions. *Journal of Counseling Psychology, 59,* 339–351. doi:10.1037/a0028063

Farr, C., Brown, J., & Beckett, R. (2004). Ability to empathize and masculinity levels: Comparing male adolescent sex offenders with a normative sample of non-offending adolescents. *Psychology, Crime and Law, 10,* 155–167. doi:10.1080/10683160310001597153

Fennell, D. C., & Fishel, A. H. (1998). Parent education: An evaluation of STEP on abusive parents' perceptions and potential abuse. *Journal of Child and Adolescent Psychiatric Nursing, 11,* 107–121. doi:10.1111/j.1744-6171.1998.tb00022.x

Finkelhor, D. (1984). *Child sexual abuse.* New York, NY: Free Press.

Friedrich, W. M. (2002). *Psychological assessment of sexually abused children and their families.* New York, NY: Sage.

Garbarino, J., Guttman, E., & Seeley, J. W. (1986). *The psychologically battered child.* San Francisco, CA: Jossey-Bass.

Gil, E. (1996). *Treating abused adolescents.* New York, NY: Guilford Press.

Green, A. H. (1988). The abused child and adolescent. In C. J. Kestenbaum & D. J. Williams (Eds.), *Handbook of clinical assessment of children and adolescents* (Vol. 2, pp. 841–863). New York: New York University Press.

Hooven, C., Nurius, P. S., Logan-Greene, P., & Thompson, E. A. (2012). Childhood violence exposure: Cumulative and specific effects on adult mental health. *Journal of Family Violence, 27,* 511–522. doi:10.1007/s10896-012-9438-0

Kazak, A. E., Christakis, D., Alderfer, M., & Coiro, M. J. (1994). Young adolescent cancer survivors and their parents: Adjustment, learning problems, gender. *Journal of Family Psychology, 8,* 74–84. doi:10.1037/0893-3200.8.1.74

Lambie, I., Seymour, F., Lee, A., & Adams, P. (2002). Resiliency in the victim–offender cycle in male sexual abuse. *Sexual Abuse: A Journal of Research and Treatment, 14,* 31–48. doi:10.1023/A:1013077426928

Lapan, R., Gysbers, N. C., & Sun, Y. (1997). The impact of more fully implemented guidance programs on the school experiences of high school students: A statewide evaluation study. *Journal of Counseling & Development, 75,* 292–302. doi:10.1002/j.1556-6676.1997.tb02344.x

Merrick, M. T., Litrownik, A. J., Everson, M. D., & Cox, C. E. (2008). Beyond sexual abuse: The impact of other maltreatment experiences on sexualized behaviors. *Child Maltreatment, 13,* 122–132. doi:10.1177/1077559507306715

Metzger, A., Ice, C., & Cottrell, L. (2012). But I trust my teen: Parents' attitudes and response to a parental monitoring intervention. *AIDS Research and Treatment.* Advance online publication. doi:10.1155/2012/396163

Murray, N., Kelder, S., Parcel, G., & Orpinas, P. (1998). Development of an intervention map for a parent education intervention to prevent violence among Hispanic middle school parents. *Journal of School Health, 68,* 46–53. doi:10.1111/j.1746-1561.1998.tb07189.x

Nahum, D., & Brewer, M. M. (2004). The use of multi-family group therapy for sexually abusive youth. *Journal of Child Sexual Abuse, 13,* 215–243. doi:10.1300/J070v13n03_11

Ogloff, J. R. P., Cutajar, M. C., Mann, E., & Mullen, P. (2012). Child sexual abuse and subsequent offending and victimisation: A 45 year follow-up study. *Trends and Issues in Crime and Criminal Justice, 440,* 1–6. Retrieved from http://www.aic.gov.au/publications/current%20series/tandi/421-440/tandi440.html

Owen, J., Imel, Z., Adelson, J., & Rodolfa, E. (2012). "No-show": Therapist racial/ethnic disparities in client unilateral termination. *Journal of Counseling Psychology, 59,* 314–320. doi:10.1037/a0027091

Oxnam, P., & Vess, J. (2006). A personality-based typology of adolescent sexual offenders using the Millon Adolescent Clinical Inventory. *New Zealand Journal of Psychology, 35,* 36–44. Retrieved from http://hdl.handle.net/10536/DRO/DU:30019518

Pianta, R. C., & Walsh, D. J. (1996). *High-risk children in schools.* New York, NY: Routledge.

Rencken, R. H. (1989). *Intervention strategies for sexual abuse.* Alexandria, VA: American Counseling Association.

Richardson, G. (2005). Early maladaptive schemas in a sample of British adolescent sexual abusers: Implications for therapy. *Journal of Sexual Aggression, 11,* 259–276. doi:10.1080/13552600500402419

Riolli, L., & Savicki, V. (2010). Coping effectiveness and coping diversity under traumatic stress. *International Journal of Stress Management, 17,* 97–113. doi:10.1037/a0018041

Sedlak, A. J., Mettenburg, J., Basena, M., Petta, I., McPherson, K., Greene, A., & Li, S. (2010). *Fourth National Incidence Study of Child Abuse and Neglect (NIS–4): Report to Congress.* Washington, DC: U.S. Department of Health and Human Services, Administration for Children and Families.

Sourander, A., Pihlakoski, L., Aromaa, M., Rautava, P., Helenius, H., & Sillanpää, M. (2006). Early predictors of parent- and self-reported perceived global psychological difficulties among adolescents. *Social Psychiatry and Psychiatric Epidemiology, 41,* 173–182. doi:10.1007/s00127-005-0013-3

Spiegel, D., Loewenstein, R. J., Lewis-Fernández, R., Sar, V., Simeon, D., Vermetten, E., . . . Dell, P. F. (2011). Dissociative disorders in *DSM-5. Depression and Anxiety, 28,* E17–E45. doi:10.1002/da.20923

Sturge-Apple, M. L., Skibo, M. A., & Davies, P. T. (2012). Impact of parental conflict and emotional abuse on children and families. *Partner Abuse, 3,* 379–400. doi:10.1891/1946-6560.3.3.379

Szapocznik, J., & Prado, G. (2007). Negative effects on family functioning from psychosocial treatments: A recommendation for expanded safety monitoring. *Journal of Family Psychology, 21,* 468–478. doi:10.1037/0893-3200.21.3.468

Szapocznik, J., Schwartz, S. J., Muir, J. A., & Brown, C. H. (2012). Brief strategic family therapy. *Couple and Family Psychology: Research and Practice, 1,* 134–145. doi:10.1037/a0029002

U.S. Department of Health and Human Services, Health Resources and Services Administration, Maternal and Child Health Bureau. (2011). *Child health USA 2011.* Rockville, MD: U.S. Department of Health and Human Services.

Visher, E. B., & Visher, J. S. (1996). *Therapy with stepfamilies.* New York, NY: Brunner/Mazel.

Wang, Z., Deater-Deckard, K., Petrill, S. A., & Thompson, L. A. (2012). Externalizing problems, attention regulation, and household chaos: A longitudinal behavioral genetic study. *Development and Psychopathology, 1,* 1–15. doi:10.1017/S0954579412000351

Webb, N. B., & Terr, L. (1999). *Play therapy with children in crisis.* New York, NY: Guilford Press.

Chapter 5

"Who Cares What I Think?": Problems of Low Self-Esteem

Sandra S. Meggert

As counselors, we observe many adolescents in pain. We see many with negative attitudes or low self-esteem and suspect there are many more. Many researchers believe that one of the major causes of deviant or potentially destructive behavior is low self-esteem (Hazler, Carney, & Granger, 2006; Kaplan, 1975; Maternal and Child Health Branch, Hawaii State Department of Health, 1991). A review of the literature supports the belief that negative self-esteem affects behavior in negative or destructive ways (Aronson & Mettee, 1968; Burrow-Sanchez, 2006; Graf, 1971; Kaplan, 1975; Kaplan, Martin, & Johnson, 1986; Lorr & Wunderlich, 1986; Weinburg, 2001). Kaplan (1976) stated that poor self-esteem or "negative self-attitudes increase the probability of later adoption of each of a range of different types of deviant responses" (p. 788). Low self-esteem is a critical factor in at-risk behavior. Eskilson, Wiley, Meuhlbauer, and Dodder (1986) reported that adolescents who feel excessive demands to succeed academically are apt to disclose involvement in deviant activities, to have low self-esteem, and to feel inadequate and unable to fulfill their families' aspirations for them. Aronson and Mettee (1968) used college students as participants in a study on dishonesty and hypothesized that students with "low self-esteem are more prone to commit immoral acts" (p. 126). Results showed that 87% of the students with induced low self-esteem cheated on a test as compared with 60% of the neutral group and 40% of the induced high self-esteem group. In a similar study, Graf (1971) reported that 40% of those with induced low self-esteem, 17% of the neutral group, and 14% of the group with induced high self-esteem engaged in dishonest behavior.

Kaplan's (1976) theory suggests that low self-esteem influences a person to adopt delinquent or other behaviors that are deviant from the norm. The theory identifies two routes that negative self-attitudes may take to influence deviant behavior. One is that these attitudes make conformity to membership group patterns painful or distressing, the other is "by influencing the person's need to seek alternatives to the disvalued normative patterns in order to satisfy the self-esteem motive" (p. 788). The Maternal and Child Health Branch of the Hawaii State Department of Health (1991) collected data on adolescent health in Hawaii and found that adolescents with low self-esteem were more likely to exhibit high-risk behaviors than were their peers with high self-esteem.

The results of a study of adolescents at risk for compulsive overeating (Marston, Jacobs, Singer, Widaman, & Little, 1988) showed that students designated at risk perceived their life quality as poor, and the authors hypothesized that this meant the students were getting along poorly with the person to whom they felt closest. Because esteem is closely tied to perceived evaluations from significant others, the quality of significant relationships is a crucial ingredient of self-esteem. The research findings of Yanish and Battle (1985) supported the importance of significant others to adolescents. They found depression in adolescents to be more strongly affected by the relationship with parents than with peers. Masche's (2000) longitudinal study of 54 intact families tentatively concluded that the self-concept of adolescents was influenced by the quality of both the parent–adolescent and marital relationships. A longitudinal study by Cohen, Burt, and Bjorck (1987) indicated that low self-esteem and depression, an indicator of low self-esteem, are positive predictors of controllable negative events, for example, expulsion from school. Portes and Zady (2000) studied cultural differences in self-esteem and adaptation of Spanish-speaking second-generation adolescents. They concluded that parent–child conflicts and depression were common predictors of self-esteem for this population and noted this was similar to samples from the dominant culture labeled *mainstream*. Hazler and Mellin (2004) noted there are symptoms of depression in adolescents that differ from those in adults, and these must be addressed. Drawing on the work of Moreau (1996), Mufson and Moreau (1997), and Stanard (2000), they identified these symptoms as "excessive boredom, substance abuse, family problems, insubordination, symptoms of conduct disorder, and eating disorders" (Hazler & Mellin, 2004, p. 19) and explained that with adolescents, the stages of depression are "followed by stages of improved functioning which reflect the more episodic nature of adolescent depressive disorders" (p. 19). They focused on depression in adolescent females and described specific issues important to work on in this population: the "internal feeling of belonging and the external knowledge of interactions and conflicts with others that cause social isolation or loneliness and require specific interpersonal, culturally appropriate approaches to treatment for adolescent females" (p. 22). The most observable symptoms of depression with female adolescents are "eating disorders, dissatisfaction with one's body, and weight loss" (p. 20), which are also symptoms of low self-esteem.

Simmons, Burgeson, Carlton-Ford, and Blyth (1987) stated that young people who encounter several important life events at the same time they are adjusting to the changes of adolescence are expected to be at greater risk than those who have longer periods of time to adjust to adolescence. Findings in this study showed that girls suffer loss of self-esteem, and both boys and girls show declines in grade point average and participation in extracurricular activities. For girls, each subsequent life change brings more difficulty with coping. Simmons et al. suggested that, in terms of self-esteem, this group of young adolescents does better if one aspect of their life is comfortable. If this goal is accomplished, then the timing and pacing of major changes are of primary importance. Kelly, Lynch, Donovan, and Clark (2001) found that low self-esteem and family dysfunction in adolescent girls diagnosed with at least one mental disorder were found to be predictors of suicidal ideations.

As discussed in the many preceding examples, adolescents who exhibit signs of low self-esteem may be considered at risk for adopting or experimenting with deviant or potentially destructive behaviors. These young people may or may not be responding to life situations with deviant behaviors currently. However, when the signs indicate low self-esteem, interventions designed to improve self-esteem are important to help these youth avoid at-risk behaviors.

This chapter examines low self-esteem as one of the primary causes of the at-risk behaviors just described and delineates strategies and programs to prevent low levels of self-esteem. Self-esteem is defined in relation to at-risk youth, and behavioral descriptions frequently linked to low self-esteem are discussed. The chapter also presents causal factors that influence the development of self-esteem as well as prevention strategies that can be used by parents, individual, schools, and communities to make young people feel like valued and significant participants in making their environment a satisfying, safe, and rewarding place. A case study describes a successful experimental program with at-risk students that has brought about changes that reflect improved levels of self-esteem.

Definitions of Self-Esteem

Self-esteem refers to subjective evaluations of worth. These value judgments develop through personal success or failure experiences, interactions with others, maturation, heredity, and social learning and are formulated from an individual's perspective. Kaplan (1975, 2006) discussed the self-esteem motive as being an individual's need to optimize positive feelings about self while reducing negative feelings. It is the process of increasing feelings of self-respect, approval, worth, and esteem. When the balance is on the negative side, a person is said to feel self-rejection, self-derogation, and, in many cases, self-hate.

Self-esteem is also a function of perceived evaluation by significant others. Mack and Ablon (1983) believed that no human is ever totally independent of the evaluation of others, and everyone retains "to some degree, a dependence upon connectedness with others for validation of our worth" (p. 10). A person's self-evaluation is referred to as self-esteem (Robison-Awana, Kehle, & Jenson, 1986) and is influenced by the individual's feelings of competence and efficacy. Carlock (1999) summed up various definitions compiled from Cantor and Bernay (1992), McDowell (1984), and Satir (1981) and described self-esteem as follows:

> How you feel about yourself, how highly you regard yourself. That degree of regard is based on your sense of how lovable and special you believe you are, how wanted you feel and your sense of belonging, how special or unique you believe you are, how competent you feel and how well you fulfill your potential, how willing you are to take risks and face challenges and how able you are to set goals, make choices, and fulfill your goals and dreams. (p. 5)

Guindon (2002) described self-esteem as being both "general (global) and selective (specific or situation)" (p. 206) and pointed out the ambiguity or uncertainty this may cause when selecting appropriate interventions to build self-esteem. She maintained a client may have positive general self-esteem but have low self-esteem in a specific area depending on the situation and expectations. She provided the following definitions:

1. *Self-esteem.* The attitudinal, evaluative component of the self; the affective judgments placed on the self-concept consisting of feelings of worth and acceptance that are developed and maintained as a consequence of awareness of competence, sense of achievement, and feedback from the external world.
2. *Global self-esteem.* An overall estimate of general self-worth, a level of self or respect for oneself, a trait or tendency relatively stable and enduring, composed of all subordinate traits and characteristics within the self.
3. *Selective self-esteem.* An evaluation of specific and constituent traits or qualities or both within the self, at times situationally variable and transitory, that are weighted and combined into an overall evaluation of self, or global self-esteem. (p. 207)

Guindon emphasized that using these definitions can help the counselor design interventions focused on the specific areas of self-esteem that need improvement. She explained that working on the specific areas of self-esteem that need improvement may ultimately affect the global self-esteem.

Two other terms are sometimes used interchangeably with self-esteem: self-concept and self-acceptance. *Self-concept* refers to the perception individuals have about their personal attributes and the roles they fulfill. Some of these perceptions are accurate, and some are not. According to Beane and Lipka (1980), people receive feedback about the roles they play and internalize information about the character and quality of their role performance: "Self-concept refers to the valuative assessment of those descriptions" (p. 3). For example, individuals have an academic self-concept, a social self-concept, or a physical appearance self-concept. Elliott (1988) maintained that anyone with low self-esteem has an unstable self-concept. The term *self-acceptance* pertains to the degree to which people are comfortable with their self-concept (Frey & Carlock, 1984).

For purposes of this discussion, *self-esteem* is defined as the pattern of beliefs an individual has about self-worth. It is the subjective part of self-concept, the evaluation of self and behaviors based on an individual's perceptions of personal experiences and feedback from significant others. It is expressed in feelings of power or helplessness—called *efficacy*—or in beliefs about personal control.

Indicators of Low Self-Esteem

Beliefs about self develop as a result of perceptions and evaluations of success and failure experiences. In this process, an individual forms some beliefs about personal control (internal vs. external) and personal effectiveness (self-efficacy).

Sidebar 5.1 ■ Self-Awareness: The Need for Counselors' Self-Awareness of Personal Self-Esteem Issues

On a scale of 1–5, rate your current level of self-esteem. What are the factors contributing to your response?

■ ■ ■

Locus of control refers to a person's belief about outcomes. Locus of control is the conviction that success or failure at a task is internally determined by one's own actions or ability, or that the outcome is due to external influences such as luck, fate, or chance. According to D. S. Johnson (1981), "Internal attributions for success are associated with higher levels of self-esteem," and low self-concept "was predicted independently and significantly by internal attribution for failure and external attribution for success" (p. 174). Abramson, Seligman, and Teasdale (1978) suggested that low-achieving students ascribe any failures to internal causes and all successes to external causes. Personal effectiveness—or *self-efficacy*, as defined by Benoit and Mitchell (1987)—has four essential elements: awareness of required behavior to bring about success, expectation that this behavior will be successful, belief that there is a relationship between behavior and outcome and that this behavior will have an impact, and belief that the outcome will provide something valued.

Evidence supports the fact that an individual with low self-esteem does most likely believe in luck (external control) rather than ability (internal control) to achieve success. However, failure is attributed to personal shortcomings (internal control). Because self-esteem judges whether such an individual can, in fact, succeed at a given task, the lack of belief in self makes it likely that someone with low self-esteem will also exhibit feelings of helplessness or powerlessness, in other words, low levels of self-efficacy. In this case, a possible defense might be to deny that the outcome of the behavior has any value and to withdraw or drop out.

Individuals with low self-esteem often find it necessary to develop defenses. People who have low self-esteem hurt. To avoid this hurt, their tendency is either to shun experiences they believe will bring additional pain or to change these experiences in some way. They erect barriers or defenses. At times, they may be hostile, critical, or suspicious of others or lack identification with others. Sometimes retreating defenses are exhibited when a person avoids coming to grips with problems or denies reality (Kaplan, 1975, 2006). A person might retreat into an "I don't care" stance or simply resist trying. It is too much of a risk for someone with feelings of poor self-worth to be exposed to additional hurt or situations in which failure is expected.

People with low self-esteem may be distractible, timid, shy, withdrawn, inhibited, anxious, and less academically able and may have a narrow range of interests (see, e.g., Domino & Blumberg, 1987). They are more likely to daydream and to want to find jobs in which they have little or no supervision and in which there are minimal amounts of competition. From their perspectives, an ideal situation is one in which they have no supervision because then no one can confirm their failure. Generally, they express the idea that they do not really want to get ahead in life. This expressed preference could be because they will not place themselves in a position in which they expect to fail, which is also a defense.

Individuals with low self-esteem have few coping strategies. They often feel a lack of control over life events. They do not feel connected and have few, if any, expectations of future success. They lack a sense of belonging. It is possible that dropping out is a defensive way of demonstrating some power, self-defeating though it may be. Chapman and Mullis (1999) studied the connection between coping strategies and self-esteem in adolescents. Their data showed that adolescents who had lower self-esteem and boys used more avoidance coping strategies compared with girls, who typically used spiritual and social support.

Low self-esteem can cause emotional distress as well. Many individuals who question their worth are sad, lethargic, tense, anxious, and angry. Some of these feelings stem from concurrent feelings of helplessness and powerlessness. Physically, they may exhibit sleeplessness, headaches, or nightmares. McGee and Williams (2000) found that levels of global self-esteem predicted reports of suicidal ideation, problem eating, and multiple compromising behaviors by adolescents in New Zealand.

Those who have low self-esteem are generally dissatisfied with themselves and their lives, are contemptuous of self, and have low levels of self-respect. Typically, they are fearful of new experiences and have a poor physical appearance and a low energy level. Apologizing, criticizing others, showing an interest in material things, and bragging are all indicators of low self-esteem.

Causal Factors

Parental, individual, social, psychological, physical, environmental, and cultural influences affect self-esteem. They all contribute to the development of self-esteem to the extent that each or all of these are valued or devalued by significant others who provide feedback. This feedback is both verbal and nonverbal, overt and covert, and it dramatically affects how adolescents see themselves.

Parental Influences on Self-Esteem

Frey and Carlock (1984) identified a representative list of "psychological pathogens" to self-esteem (pp. 25–31). Many of these are associated with parental influences. These pathogens may persist throughout life and, if so, may consistently keep self-esteem low unless someone or something intervenes. Among the pathogens they identified and the problems that might arise when these are present during childhood are the following:

- *Expecting perfection.* Nobody has achieved this state of perfection yet, but many people try. A burden of always trying to be perfect throughout childhood guarantees failure. Those who set idealistic or unrealistic goals for themselves are constantly frustrated, critical, and impatient with themselves and others, always trying harder and never quite feeling successful. Negative self-evaluations, which are formulated by the young person from perceptions of adult reactions, deeply affect his or her feelings about self. Unless a person learns to set realistic goals and acknowledge small steps along the way, self-esteem remains low because the person never feels adequate.

Sidebar 5.2 ■ Case Study: The Impact of Feedback on Self-Concept Development

Jennifer has just graduated from college and applied and was interviewed for her first job. Days after the interview she received a call from the human resources director and was told that of the ten people who were interviewed, she was the only one who did not cry during the interview. What do you think were the dynamics going on for the other nine job seekers? If one of the nine was a client of yours, how would you work with that person? What do you think was going on during the interview?

■ ■ ■

- *Inconsistency and failure to set limits.* Although some people believe consistency is a myth, children often search for consistency and limits, apparently seeking the security that structure and predictability provide. When such structure is missing, the result is anger, insecurity, and hostility.
- *Failure to give positive feedback.* Many parents and significant others assume that children know that positive behavior is appreciated and only respond to negative or improper behavior. Being constantly reminded or punished when behavior is inappropriate and seldom being appreciated when behavior is appropriate create feelings of inadequacy and inferiority.
- *Failure to listen.* Failing to listen to a child indicates a lack of respect and communicates that the child or what the child is trying to communicate is not important. When this feeling is carried through childhood, it fosters additional feelings of inferiority and inadequacy that are sometimes expressed in anger or hostility.
- *Rejection.* Consistent rejection critically affects an individual's self-esteem. The rejected child's basic needs are not being met, in some cases deliberately. The child may view death, divorce, severe illness, or disregard for the child as rejection, with the ensuing feelings of inadequacy, guilt, self-hate, or self-rejection.
- *Being a maladjusted role model.* Children who model their behavior after an adult who is maladjusted often end up disliking themselves because of those behaviors. Their self-esteem is greatly diminished in such cases.
- *Failure to help children adapt.* Societal and cultural values are being questioned more now than ever before. It is difficult for children to feel adequate in a society in which values are shifting or unclear. It becomes even more difficult when children try to adapt to a different culture and then experience conflict in values.
- *Forcing children into a pattern.* Sometimes parents try to fit children into certain behaviors or patterns that may restrict their unique development or be beyond their capacity. This practice is sometimes called living vicariously, and it creates frustration, feelings of worthlessness, and feelings of inadequacy in both parent and child.
- *Allowing and supporting procrastination.* Believing that one does not have the self-discipline necessary to complete a task contributes to poor self-esteem. The longer the child procrastinates, the more the feelings of inadequacy and worthlessness multiply. Concurrently, there is a loss of self-respect.

Frey and Carlock (1984) listed several additional pathogens and observed that "one can be the recipient of several of these dynamics" (p. 31). Each of these, or a combination of several, is detrimental to a child's self-esteem.

Parents have a significant impact on the self-esteem of their children. Parental attitudes and behaviors have been shown to affect children (Appleton & Dykeman, 2004; Lord, Eccles, & McCarthy, 1994). A study by Lord et al. (1994) that focused on the number of divorces and remarriages and the child's subsequent adjustment found some evidence of a "negative linear relationship" between these variables. Buri and Dickinson (1994) reported that although parental authority was predictive of self-esteem, these behaviors were less important than overgeneralization, particularly in female adolescents. The authors described overgeneralization as the inclination for a person to view a failure as an indication of his or her general inadequacy.

Sidebar 5.3 ■ Case Study: Working With a Client Who Believes He or She Must Be Perfect

In working with a child who strives and expects to be perfect, constantly worries about grades, is anxious and frustrated with his or her progress, and is losing sleep over this concern, what do you do?

■ ■ ■

A consequence of the dynamics just described is that young people today feel unimportant or even irrelevant in their families (Glenn & Nelson, 1989). Many believe that they are important only when they are doing what someone else wants them to do. Glenn and Nelson speculated that this is one impetus for early sexual involvement. Sex becomes a strategy to make young people believe themselves to be significant in the eyes of someone else. For girls, the irony is that if she has a child, she is automatically treated as an adult when, in fact, there are now two children.

The need to feel significant is also a powerful motivator to become a gang member. News stories frequently report the initiation rites to join a gang. Some young people want so badly to belong that they lose their lives during the initiation process.

Note that many of the pathogens identified are behaviors found in extremely inexperienced parents who may use the child to satisfy personal needs not previously filled. The child will not feel valued, may be confused, and most likely will develop low self-esteem. The cycle will remain unbroken unless there is some type of intervention.

Using self-esteem and psychosocial competence as indicators, Sim (2000) studied the role of parental regard on Singaporean adolescents' psychosocial competence. Results indicated adolescents' regard for parents was positively related to self-esteem and negatively associated with antisocial susceptibility. Regard for parents was also found to mediate the relationship between parental monitoring and antisocial susceptibility.

Individual Influences on Self-Esteem

People learn about themselves as they interact with their environment and receive feedback on how well or how poorly they do things. Young children learn about their capabilities and their limits or strengths from others and form beliefs about their own competence. If a child receives negative feedback consistently, he or she will learn to believe in his or her own inferiority. This belief, in turn, could affect attitudes and outlook on life and leave the child with a sense of not "fitting in" or not belonging and being powerless.

These beliefs about self are powerful and form a lens through which a person views the world (Ayduk, Gyurak, & Luerssen, 2009). This view will have an influence on the experiences the individual chooses to undertake and probably outcomes as well. Building self-esteem includes a measure of being realistic about one's abilities. When most feedback is negative, a child's view of his or her competence often becomes unrealistic, and the child makes choices based on what he or she believes to be true about self. Carlock (1999) stated that "it is important for young children not just to learn specific skills and behaviors but to acquire an overall belief in their ability to affect their world" (p. 291).

Social Influences on Self-Esteem

A basic assumption in social psychology is that self-concepts are heavily influenced by social contexts (Bachman & O'Malley, 1986). Each of us has a long history of dependency in infancy and childhood during which we need to receive positive responses from adults. We are motivated to behave in ways that increase the likelihood of receiving these positive responses. As children, we internalize adult standards in this manner, and we attempt to regulate our own behavior and react with positive or negative self-feelings at the perceived evaluations/reactions of significant adults (Kaplan, 1976, 2006).

Kaplan (1976) further noted that low self-esteem is thought to be caused by self-perceptions that either one's behavior or characteristics do not meet personal standards valued by the social system, by self-perceptions that one is not valued positively or perhaps is even valued negatively by significant others, or that one might not have developed "normatively acceptable coping mechanisms" that could protect one from the effect of "self-perceptions of failure or rejection by others" (p. 790). A person with a history of being devalued is most likely to have low self-esteem. This low self-esteem can be said to evolve from two sources: (a) an individual's history of negative self-evaluation and perception and (b) perceptions of highly valued others in the environment responding to the individual with less than positive attitudes (Kaplan, 1975). An individual is more likely to value the attitudes of those persons "who were associated with need gratification or deprivation" (p. 37).

Society imposes strong gender-based role behaviors that continue their impact on self-esteem long after adolescence (Hoffman, Hattie, & Borders, 2005). A study by Burnett, Anderson, and Heppner (1995) demonstrated that masculine bias is still strong in the United States. *Masculinity*, defined as having high levels of traditional masculine behaviors (such as competitiveness, decisiveness, and independence) as opposed to feminine characteristics (such as focus on relationships and nurturing), has been shown to be "significantly correlated with self-esteem for both men and women, but individual femininity was not significantly related to self-esteem in either sex" (Burnett et al., 1995, p. 325).

Even though masculine behaviors are clearly valued in the United States, they are not generally characteristic of at-risk youth (Benenson & Heath, 2006). If they are evident in some, they are not generally evident in socially acceptable ways. For example, aggressiveness and rebelliousness might substitute for competitiveness and independence. Enns (1992) stated that "there is some evidence that the socialization process is even more stringent for men than it is for women, and that boys and men experience higher costs for straying from traditional gender roles than do girls and women" (p. 11). There is the possibility that absence of masculine skills in boys, and to some extent girls, has the potential of contributing to low self-esteem. Bower (1993) reported that development of self-esteem in males and females is different because of societal pressures that dictate male and female role behaviors. Some research has also indicated that teenage girls have lower self-esteem than teenage boys (Dwyer, 1993). A *U.S. News & World Report* article surveyed research regarding the self-esteem of adolescent girls (Saltzman, 1994). After examining several research studies, Saltzman concluded that social science has no conclusive answers and that parents have to assess and address the needs of their daughters individually.

Many social changes are high-risk changes. As young people are alienated from society and practice more violent methods to feel significant and powerful, many die or become incapacitated. Wars are fought on TV, and children feel threatened. Technology has changed the world of work, and many parents or parental figures are unemployed. Divorce is common, and homes are broken. Values are lost. Young people hear of others their own age dying from the variety of perils to which they are exposed. Many of them believe that they will live short lives. No one has prepared them for the choices they have to make.

Psychological Influences on Self-Esteem

Mack and Ablon (1983) wrote that it is "questionable, indeed, whether human beings can deeply experience positive self-worth except as the result of a relationship" (p. 9). Everyone knows two basic truths about the self. One is that the self is alone and private, and the other is "that one is a real self only to the extent that caring and reaching beyond the self continue" (Yankelovich, 1981, p. 240). Therefore, an important psychological determinant of self-esteem is the individual's feelings about the level of success within relationships.

The whole notion of connectedness or belonging to someone is central to the development of self-esteem. Belonging to a family, a culture, a community, or a school provides a connection to aid in sustaining a sense of worth (Preckel & Brull, 2010). Lacking such a feeling, a person is likely to feel not valued and retreat into a defensive posture to protect the self from the pain of feeling isolated, hopeless, worthless, and unconnected. According to Mack and Alblon (1983), "Virtually all maladaptive defensive patterns in childhood, adolescence, and adult life have at least one major purpose, protection of the pain associated with lowered self-esteem" (p. 38).

Television has become a psychological determinant of self-esteem (Glenn & Nelson, 1989). Young people receive messages about the society in which they live in a passive manner. They do not have to participate to learn. In the past, people learned about functioning in society while they were actively involved in living and working. The learning might be trial and error, role modeling, or direct teaching, but individuals were active. Glenn and Nelson referred to this as on-the-job training. Today, with the use of television, children's reality becomes distorted. Within a short time, they see problems solved through miracles, violence, various medications, sex, and drinking. According to Glenn and Nelson (1989), young people learn the following:

1. In productive and desirable social interactions, drinking or substance abuse is necessary.
2. Pain, fatigue, listlessness, and boredom are all dispelled through self-medication.
3. Indiscriminate or uninvolved sexual encounters are appropriate ways to communicate.
4. Problems can be resolved instantly through manipulation, violence, and breaking the law.

Sidebar 5.4 ■ Self-Awareness: How Do Gender Messages Affect Us?

What are some gender-based messages you heard in your early environments? How do these messages affect your life today?

■ ■ ■

5. Deferred gratification, hard work, and personal initiative are unacceptable, and drinking and self-medication can help a person avoid these stresses. Any stressful situation can be alleviated by using specific products and/or services. (pp. 42–43)

These "truisms" are further complicated by some parents who foster the belief that most material possessions can be obtained in ways other than hard work. So because things come easy, there is no respect for possessions and no positive messages about the purpose of life. It is easy to speculate that if no active role modeling or teaching of healthier, more productive attitudes dispute these claims, young people may feel alienated, angry, and confused. When they use these same behaviors that work on television to solve their problems, they get into trouble. The nonacceptance of their behaviors confirms their sense of worthlessness and insignificance. The only way they can feel any sense of worth is when they are with others who feel and think as they do.

Physical Influences on Self-Esteem

Inherited physical characteristics, such as physique, appearance, and disabilities, also may influence self-esteem. The physical attributes that an individual has inherited can affect others' perceptions and behavior. Others may respond negatively to an individual's disabled condition or physical appearance, thus affecting that individual's self-esteem, even though the individual's initial self-perception may not have been negative.

Others' reactions are also influenced by maturational rates. Adults treat children differently at differing maturation levels. Children who reach physical, social, or emotional maturity early are quite often treated as adults and develop positive self-esteem. Those who mature later and continue to be treated as children tend to develop low self-esteem. Even when this latter group matures, they often maintain old self-perceptions and the corresponding low self-esteem. Maturation also affects mastery of developmental tasks. Social disapproval, maladjustment, and increased difficulty in mastering higher level developmental tasks are all possible results of delayed maturation (Frey & Carlock, 1984).

Environmental Influences on Self-Esteem

It is difficult to define the effect environment plays in the development of low self-esteem. A person learns values and has needs satisfied within the environment through social interaction with significant others, and if needs are not met and the expressions of beliefs and values meet with disapproval within the environment, self-esteem is likely to be damaged.

An additional aspect of environment has to do with the groups within the environment with which the person identifies. Each member of a group is evaluated by every other member. If the group is significant to an individual, these evaluations affect self-esteem. For example, if a person's perception is one of not being valued by the group, low self-esteem is probable. Esteem is related to one's rank in a group rather than the rank of the group compared with other groups (Rosenberg, 1965).

As the U.S. population has moved from rural to city areas, the environment in which children had built-in networks and role models has diminished and, in many cases, been lost. In the past, grandparents, aunts, uncles, cousins, neighbors, and friends were available to help educate and advise young people, and that was a given. In the absence of such an array of support, young people have turned to their peers for guidance and approval. In doing so, they use peer norms, created out of lack of experience, for evaluating behavior rather than the collective experience and wisdom of a network of adult role models (Glenn & Nelson, 1989).

Parents have also suffered a loss of support. In most cases, the parents have no network of relatives nearby to assist in parenting, they have to depend on themselves to make the right choices, and they have no experience being parents. Because both parents usually work, they parent part-time. In single-parent families, even part-time parenting is shared with other stresses involved in survival. So now there are time factors as well as inexperienced parents as well as the challenges presented to children in today's world. It becomes easier to see why parents use the same stress reducers as their children.

Approaches to Prevention

The pervasive distress and too frequent demise of our young people seem to be out of control. Jason et al. (1993) reported that in Chicago schools, "more than 40% of children do not graduate high school" (p. 69). They believed that the problems leading to dropout often begin in the elementary schools. It is clear that some interventions and prevention strategies targeting low self-esteem must be integrated into every level of the community. Smith and Sandhu (2004) concurred, noting that interventions must occur at an early age on multiple levels. Klindera and Menderwald (2001) explored the idea of youth being actively involved in planning programs for this at-risk population. They made a strong argument that this involvement would yield new ideas that reflect the interests of this age group. They speculated that at-risk youth will more readily accept and participate in programs that they were involved in planning and that allow them to share the responsibility for the implementation. They outlined specific guidelines to make this partnership work: convenient meeting times, easily accessible meeting places, food or funds for food, and willingness to change existing rules and policies (p. 6).

In this section, specific approaches for individuals, parents, schools, and communities are discussed. No one segment of the population is solely responsible for providing prevention. All groups should overlap, and building and maintaining high levels of self-esteem should become an integral part of the total community structure. Although parents are charged with the initial environment for the child, they, too, are part of a community and have need of resources from the community. A global approach that could be used by the entire community is described at the end of this next section.

Individual

Self-esteem develops as a result of interaction with and feedback from others. It is doubtful whether an individual can build self-esteem in a vacuum. If the feedback, either verbal or nonverbal, is negative the individual internalizes negative feelings about self and has poor feelings of worth. If feedback is positive and the individual feels successful, self-esteem is enhanced. An individual who feels valued and worthwhile has high self-esteem and responds to others in a manner that communicates this level of self-esteem.

It is difficult, perhaps impossible, for someone suffering from low self-esteem to undertake a prevention program alone. Most of the feedback that builds or destroys self-esteem comes either directly or indirectly from others. An individual is influenced by role models and can be encouraged to learn skills and attitudes that will lead to successful experiences. As self-esteem is raised, a person may seek out avenues that will bring more success.

Volunteering, learning to be assertive, learning to cope with anger and conflict constructively, attending workshops and special classes to learn life skills, and entering programs that are specifically designed for young people are all ways an individual can build self-esteem. In each of these possibilities, external guidance is often necessary for a person with low self-esteem.

Family

The environment in which a child is raised has a significant impact on the child's self-esteem (Barber, Chadwick, & Orter, 1992; Benard & Marshall, 2001; Blake & Slate, 1993; Cerezo & Frias, 1994; M. Harvey & Byrd, 1998; Shek, 1997). Historically, children were born into an intact family, and that was the primary environment in which the child learned about being an adult. Today, families vary in structure. Households in which both parents work outside the home are common. Single parenting, stepparenting, joint parenting, parenting by someone other than the biological parent, and homelessness have altered family structures and added to the pressures young people face as they grow into adulthood. Many who find themselves in parenting roles have no idea how to accomplish this and fall back on personal experience. They feel the loss of assistance and experience that an extended family provides, so they parent as they were parented, as best as they can remember. They may have low self-esteem as a result of their own childhood experiences and perpetuate their own feelings of low self-worth in their children. Their own parental role models may not have had the wisdom of the extended family experience either, and this lack of parenting skills continues from one generation to the next. Sharaf, Thompson, and Walsh (2009) studied the significance of self-esteem and family support in protecting against adolescent suicide risk. They found the "process of resiliency, with intrapersonal (self-esteem) and interpersonal (family support) forces interacting to counteract suicide vulnerability. Self-esteem mitigates suicide risk among adolescents" (p. 165).

In terms of prevention, steps must be taken to teach parents how to parent. Recognizing and admitting the need to learn parenting is a primary step in the process of building self-esteem. Sensitivity to cultural norms for parenting is essential in approaching parents. Today's parents have access to parenting classes and special support groups to help them learn to work with their children. These groups are sponsored by school specialists as well as churches and agencies in the community. Joining a class or support group serves a dual purpose. The parents learn skills at the same time that they are increasing their network of support. Getting to know neighbors is another excellent way to extend the support network and can serve as a means to check perceptions of neighborhood situations.

Citing the work of Patterson, Reid, and Dishion (1992) and of Reid, Patterson, and Snyder (2002), Smith and Sandhu (2004) described a program that "teaches parents prosocial behaviors, alternatives to aggression as a discipline strategy, and problem-solving skills. In addition, parents are taught to nurture and communicate effectively with children, to establish and negotiate family rules and consequences, and to reward prosocial behavior" (p. 288). This curriculum has been successful in "reducing family conflict and increasing a sense of family unity. Long-term effects include a stronger sense of connectedness among family members with a greater likelihood of positive social interactions" (p. 288). Another program prepares parents to be emotional coaches, who, rather than ignoring or discouraging negative emotional reactions such as anger or unhappiness, view the enactment of such emotions as opportunities for the child to develop a deeper understanding of self and others, particularly regarding these potentially troubling feelings (Gottman & DeClair, 1997; Gottman, Katz, & Hooven, 1996).

From a multicultural perspective, parents must understand their own needs for success, status, and control as these needs relate to their child-rearing practices. They must be able to put these needs aside and respond to each child as a unique person and to recognize and accept the contributions their children make in the family. There may have to be conscious efforts made to include each child and to discover ways in which each child can successfully contribute to the well-being of the family. Taking out the garbage can become significant if a child understands that his or her contribution is important to the family. When a parent asks a child for assistance with a task or project, one that cannot be done alone, the child learns that his or her contribution is an integral part in the task completion. In this case, it is essential that the child understands his or her help is not gratuitous but essential. For example, if the family pet has a thorn in a paw, it is difficult for one person to hold the animal, examine or probe the paw, and extract the thorn. It is much easier if someone else holds the animal. Asking for the child's assistance, and pointing out that this task is difficult or impossible for one person to do alone, validates the value of the child's contribution.

Another way to prevent low self-esteem is to allow children to do what they can do and not do it for them. Often adults, who can do things faster or better, become impatient and complete tasks for the children. Doing so indicates a lack of respect for the child and gives negative messages about the child's abilities and worth. These negative messages are both overt and covert and have a powerful effect on self-esteem. Though it may be difficult, allowing a child to complete a task more slowly and in a different manner or to make a mistake brings greater opportunities for learning. Using the mistake as a teachable moment is of greater value than scolding, punishing, or doing it for them.

Spending time with the child, talking or playing, gives positive messages about the child's importance. Letting children know that they are valued is critical in building self-esteem. Ironically, this is often the most difficult prevention technique; it takes time and is the first date to be canceled when schedules get tight. During regularly scheduled time together, bonds are cemented, relationships are nurtured, and both parent and child feel important. In using this strategy, parents must listen carefully, suspend judgment, and be accepting of the child's point of view. Children will discuss serious topics if they believe what they say will be heard and valued. They also learn from the role modeling.

Many families hold regularly scheduled meetings to discuss family matters. These meetings are used to resolve conflicts, plan outings, make decisions about the household, test out new ideas, and involve the whole family in a variety of discussions. Again, these meetings should not be canceled except with solid reasons.

If meetings are canceled too often, their usefulness diminishes. The interesting effect of using preventive measures is that the parents' or parental figures' self-esteem grows as well. When parent–child interactions are positive and productive, both participants feel valued.

School

Everyone needs to feel connected to others and to feel supported and accepted. Drawing on the work of Elias et al. (1994) and of Eron, Gentry, and Schlegel (1994), Smith and Sandhu (2004) noted children who are "well liked by peers are happier at school, better adjusted both psychologically and emotionally, and considerably less likely to engage in aggressive and violent behaviors" (Elias et al., 1994, p. 289). Because every child has the opportunity to attend school, this is an ideal place to continue the low-self-esteem prevention programs. Hamachek (1995) noted that school performance and "self-attitudes" (i.e., self-esteem) are interactive. D. W. Johnson, Johnson, and Taylor (1993) reported higher levels of self-esteem achievement and cohesion in fifth graders who participated in cooperative learning environments. Strategies for improving school performance cannot be developed without attending to methods to "help students feel better about themselves". Educators have long been aware of the need for students to feel good about themselves and what they can do (Leflot, Onghena & Colpin, 2010). Many schools have peer-tutoring or lower-grade-tutoring programs, peer helpers, and student aides. In such tutoring programs, students are paired with students for teaching or coaching. The tutored students are either peers or, in many cases, younger students in elementary schools. Peer helper programs train selected young people in listening skills and have them talk with and listen to their peers. Student aides assist teachers and office staff. Some of these programs tend to exclude the high-risk populations.

In school, students labeled as high risk are frequently referred to the counselor, who can work on self-esteem issues with students individually or in groups. Lemoire and Chen (2005) believed the conditions that are present in a person-centered approach to counseling are important when one is working with individuals with low self-esteem, specifically lesbian, gay, bisexual, and transgender (LGBT) adolescents. Unconditional positive regard, acceptance, and empathy combine to provide a safe environment and appear to "hold some promise in addressing the psychological distresses of LGBT adolescents" (Lemoire & Chen, 2005, p. 148). Although the researchers identified a specific group of adolescents, their reasoning seems applicable to a broader range of students, as they noted, "The counseling process highlights and strengthens a positive sense of self by allowing the client the firsthand experience of self-exploration and self-understanding" (p. 149). Burrow-Sanchez (2006) agreed. He described motivational interviewing, which uses person-centered counseling strategies, as an effective method to reduce a "client's ambivalence toward change while increasing his or her motivation to engage in the behavior-change process" (p. 286). The counselor supports client behaviors that are congruent with the desired changes and uses reflection, reframing, and active listening to make the client feel understood and accepted.

Guindon (2002) suggested that if counselors understand the definitions of self-esteem (global or selective), they can select the type of intervention best suited to the clients' needs at the time and will understand that if the need is for global self-esteem, it may not be readily changeable. However, as with "mountains made of teaspoons of dirt, global self-esteem is made up of numerous facets of selective self-esteem which can be addressed individually and ultimately affect the whole or global self-esteem" (Guindon, 2002, p. 207). Shechtman (2002) placed low-performing children in one of two groups: one group received concentrated academic help and the other group received therapy. After 6 months, those who received therapy showed improvements in "grades, self-esteem, social status, and self-control" (p. 295). These improvements were still present at follow-up. The recommendation was that more therapy groups are needed in schools.

Myers, Sweeney, and Witmer (2000) developed a model for wellness that has been used successfully in many contexts with "young-to-older adults." Their Wheel of Wellness includes six life tasks—spirituality, self-direction, work, leisure, love, and friendship (p. 253)—and identifies a sense of worth as one of the 12 subtasks under self-direction. Using this wheel, professionals can assess an individual on 16 characteristics of wellness, either formally or informally, and design an individualized program to improve or enhance any deficiencies.

Reasoner (1994) described several programs that have been successful in improving self-esteem and reducing crime and violence. A Florida high school program that focused on positive adviser–advisee relationships reported that, within 3 weeks, grade point averages and attendance, both indicators of levels of self-esteem, improved (Testerman, 1996). Still another study (McCormick & Wold, 1993) found positive changes in the self-concept of gifted and talented female students who had exhibited underachievement in science and math after exposure to a program describing nontraditional career choices.

Hains (1994) reported on the effectiveness of a cognitive stress management program that showed high school participants made significant improvement in anxiety, self-esteem, depression, and anger. In another cognitive restructuring program, participants were exposed to either a computer-based program that targeted irrational beliefs or a relaxation training program. Those participating in the computer-based program improved self-esteem (Horan, 1996).

A mediation intervention program was piloted at a middle school in Georgia, and results indicated a decrease in suspensions, an improvement in school morale, and an increase in both requests for peer mediation and the belief that it works (Thompson, 1996). Edmondson and White (1998) found significant improvement in the self-esteem of students who participated in both a tutorial and a counseling program. Conclusions drawn from a 3-year longitudinal study of urban children in Georgia stressed the importance of both early and developmentally specific interventions (Spencer, 1991). Kraizer (1990) discussed skills that children need to possess in order to master the stresses of development. She identified a list of life skills essential to successful passage into adolescence, then she advocated early and continuing intervention to prevent development of inappropriate behaviors.

Because schools are community institutions and have the most contact with children, and because many services were available to families but delivery was fragmented or crisis oriented, the West Virginia Education Association and Appalachia Educational Laboratory (1993) surveyed the existing school–community partnerships in that state. In this survey process, the researchers gathered information about problems inherent in school-linked services and about additional school-linked service possibilities. With these data, the research team developed profiles for each of these social service programs and made recommendations for changes at the school, district, and policymaking levels.

Bernard Haldane (1989) developed the Dependable Strengths Articulation Process in 1948, initially for use with returning military personnel who wanted to change careers after World War II. The program has evolved and is being used with high school students in Washington State (Forester, 2004). The Dependable Strengths Assessment Training (DSAT) encouraged students "to articulate their strengths and use those strengths when making their most important plans" (p. 1). Participants in a 2002 DSAT training workshop adopted the assessment with middle school, junior, and senior high school students with success. Using a pre-scribed set of activities, students are directed to identify strengths, get feedback from peers about strengths, prioritize them, test them for reliability, and use them when making plans. Although there were no formal data gathered from these experiences using DSAT, users indicated students were more positive and more successful in school (conversations with participants, June 17–21, 2002, University of Washington, Seattle).

One of the warning signs of adolescent suicide is low self-esteem. Maples et al. (2005) identified the need for suicide prevention and intervention programs for schools. They advocated for forming partnerships among schools, community, and families to educate everyone to the warning signs and interventions for prevention. Simpson (1999, p. 28) noted several strategies that have worked successfully in several educational settings:

- *School gatekeeper training:* in-service training for school staff on identifying students at risk for suicide and where to refer them for help.
- *Community gatekeeper training:* training similar to school gatekeeper training but designed for parents, recreation staff, and other community members.
- *General suicide education:* school-based program for students geared to help them identify the warning signs of suicide and to build self-esteem and coping skills.
- *Screening programs:* programs to identify high-risk youth for targeted assistance.
- *Peer support programs:* programs to foster peer relationships, competency development, and social skills among high-risk youth.
- *Crisis centers and hotlines:* emergency counseling for those who may be suicidal.
- *Means restrict:* activities designed to restrict student access to firearms, drugs, and other means of committing suicide.

With such a program in place, at-risk students can be targeted, and strategies to help them build self-esteem and provide support and connection to their community can be implemented with the hope of ultimately preventing suicide. Writing after a middle school student committed suicide, Maples et al. (2005) suggested a postvention program needs to be in place as well to help everyone deal with the aftermath of a suicide. They advocated a team approach developed by Roberts, Lepkowski, and Davidson (1998) that includes counselors, administrators, parents, and teachers. The program, called TEAM, has four components: developing a team (T), establishing procedures (E), arranging supports (A), and monitoring progress (M). The authors recommended that this approach along with appropriate training be in place before any crisis occurs. Further recommendations include the following by the West Virginia Education Association and Appalachia Educational Laboratory (1993):

School and District-Level Recommendations
- The responsibilities of schools should include serving as a focal point to connect families with health and social service providers.
- The mission of the school should include health and social services provision.
- Educational focus should be on prevention and early intervention.
- Schools should provide training to staff to teach them to work effectively with health and social service problems of students.
- Research and evaluation should be undertaken regularly to assess program success and recommend any needed improvements.
- Districts should establish foundations whose funds would be used to develop programs to benefit children and families. Independent sources would donate these funds. (p. 36)

Policy Recommendations
- Funding for programs for at-risk populations should be provided for in the budget, which would serve to standardize school-linked programs. These programs should be protected from budget cuts.
- Early intervention and prevention programs should be given priority.
- Operational procedures of schools and service providers should be examined and changed if these procedures interfere with effective delivery of services. (p. 37)

The recommendations reflect the belief that no one group or institution is totally responsible for bringing health and social services to those community members who need them. The philosophy is that the entire community must work as a team, with the school being the common link between service providers and families.

Jones and Watson (1990) studied high-risk students in higher education. Several of their findings can be considered for earlier educational experiences as well. Recommended prevention programs and strategies include the following:

- Market the benefits of persistent, positive student behaviors.
- Provide career information beginning at an early age. Encourage goal identification.
- Use low-achieving college students to tutor K–12 students. This raises the self-esteem of each participant.
- Encourage and market counseling services as part of the curriculum. Involve teachers in the referral process.
- Provide in-class programs designed to teach positive attitudes and skills that would include acceptance of others, such as high-risk students.
- Use peer advisers.
- Enlist school organizations to develop programs to assist fellow students.
- Provide educational programs to teach teachers how to teach. Provide opportunities for teachers to learn alternative teaching techniques and ways to empower students.

- Evaluate testing materials to see that the needs of high-risk students are being assessed effectively.
- Develop orientation programs addressing the needs of high-risk populations.
- Acknowledge school personnel who work with high-risk students by reducing class loads.
- Develop methods to assure high-risk students an in-school support system. Using local businesses, provide opportunities for high-risk students to do visits, internships, or part-time work in the community. Many schools invite business people into the classroom to work with students.
- Provide programs for teachers and school personnel to examine their attitudes toward minorities, women, and other high-risk populations. (pp. 85–88)

Community

If we accept the philosophy that at-risk students and families and the school are all part of the total community, any of the just-listed strategies can be offered throughout the community and sponsored by any business or agency. The following are examples of programs that have been developed in a major metropolitan area that may be similar to programs available in other areas.

Zimmerman, Ramirez-Valles, and Maton (1999) suggested that interventions within a community should focus on involving youth in action groups—for example, voluntary and neighborhood committees, church groups (p. 747)—that may serve as a buffer from risks they encounter.

The Outdoor Adventure Group

A program designed for adolescents with mental illness is a possible intervention program with at-risk youth. The Outdoor Adventure Group uses a group as a main intervention tool for change with mentally ill adolescents. The group members participate in suitable and developmental risk-taking tasks that are similar to tasks they might encounter in their everyday lives. The goal is that they acquire skills that can be generalized to their life outside of the group. "Each activity is carefully planned, prescribed, and managed to accommodate the specific needs of the learner. The curriculum involves a series of incremental challenges in difficulty during which the participants must rely on one another to persevere. A cooperative rather than a competitive learning environment is established to develop group cohesiveness, and unique problem-solving situations are introduced"(Schell, Cotton, & Luxmoore, 2012, p. 409). The 8- to 10-week program consists of once-a-week meetings (full day) and a culminating three-day and two-night weekend camp. Each meeting is attended by two clinicians and two staff members from Out Doors, Inc. Results in the research group showed significant increases in self-esteem, whereas in the control group self-esteem remained relatively stable. Feedback from partici-

---

Sidebar 5.5 ■ Self-Awareness: Searching for Prevention Programs in Your Community

As you think about your community, what are some programs available for youth who are at risk? Begin developing a list. Are there any programs of particular interest to you for volunteer work?

■ ■ ■

pants identified self-improvement and social skills development as major changes, along with self-esteem, mastery, and achievement of personal goals set at the beginning of the program.

YMCA (1994) Teen Services
- *County Youth Initiative* provides opportunities for leadership training, public speaking, project planning and delivery of community services, and employment.
- *Earth Service Corps* provides opportunities for environmental education and action, leadership development, and project planning and implementation.
- *The Manifesto Newspaper* provides an opportunity, through a youth-produced countywide newspaper, for teenagers to share their ideas and creativity with members of the community.
- *Y-Zone* provides a safe, alternative environment for youth to participate in activities and special events on a weekend night. This program has expanded in adjacent communities to being available both weekend nights.
- *Youth Employment* sponsors a youth-run espresso cart at a local YMCA. The youth are hired and trained before they begin working this cart.

Central Area Youth Association (1992)
- *TeenPATH (Teen Parent Assistance and Transitional Housing Program)* provides assistance to homeless or near-homeless teen parents under the age of 18. The program's goal is to provide assistance to teen parents to break out of the poverty cycle. Through TeenPATH, stable, safe housing is found. In return, the teen parents are required to complete high school, get work training and/or employment, and be responsible parents.
- *Mentorship* assigns role models who offer companionship, guidance, and support and who help empower participants to be free of gang and drug involvement.
- *STARS (Special Tutor for At-Risk Students)* provides one-on-one tutorial services to at-risk students in Grades K–8. Tutors are available both in school and after school in churches, libraries, and community centers.
- *Sports Program* provides adult role models who focus on team work, mental health, physical health, and individual and group responsibilities.
- *4-H Challenge* teaches participants, particularly minority males, coping skills, communication skills, problem-solving skills, and decision-making skills.
- *Introduction to Challenge* places youth in support groups and introduces the rules, concepts, and benefits of the Challenge program.
- *Boot Camp/National Guard* introduces youth to orderly, disciplined environments and provides opportunities for building self-esteem.
- *Job Power* allows youth to explore assets and liabilities with regard to employment.
- *Ropes Course* provides outdoor activities to help adult and youth participants learn and develop problem-solving, goal-setting, and communication skills while experiencing total commitment.
- *I'll Take Charge* provides opportunities for youth to take responsibility for their choices.

- *Self-Determined Projects* allow members to determine, with guidance, their own projects that might not be available otherwise.
- *Multimedia* teaches students techniques and technology involved in video production while exposing them to drama, music, and arts.
- *Job Readiness* helps youth to create contacts without turn-downs, teaches them job interviewing skills, and brings the community together to help youth become productive, responsible members of society.
- *Elite Boxing* provides a meaningful outlet for physically aggressive youth in a positive, acceptable manner.
- *BALANCE (Beautiful, Ambitious Ladies Able to Negotiate With Commitment to Self-Esteem and Excellence)* provides weekly support groups for young women, through which substance abuse education and services are provided.

STARS I and II

Two community-based programs for African American youth, STARS I and II, target at-risk youth in two age groups (ages 6–10 years for STARS I and 11–17 years for STARS II) and their parents or guardians. In STARS I, "sessions [are] focused on cultural legacy family communication, the role of the extended family, and decision making" (Dabrowski, Avery, Gyger, & Emshoff, 1993, p. 4). The program for the older children focuses on providing drug education, increasing the children's assertiveness, teaching them how to resist peer pressure, raising their self-esteem, and improving their family communication. Program outcomes showed improvement in all areas for both adults and the children.

Other Community Programs

Nassar-McMillan and Cashwell (1997) offered adventure-based counseling as an intervention to foster self-esteem. Kennison (1996) described a similar wilderness program for youth with diagnosed attention-deficit/hyperactivity disorder in which activities are built to address the characteristic behaviors of this population. Another special population program, Camp Elsewhere, provided a program for adolescent females with eating disorders, who reported the program had a positive impact on them (Tonkin, 1997). According to participants, a university-sponsored, 2-week residential leadership education program for adolescent girls positively affected self-confidence (Taylor & Rosselli, 1997).

The HAWK Federation focuses on issues unique to Black adolescent males and is rooted in African traditions. Initial reports indicate that those who participated in the program improved their academic achievement (Nobles, 1989). Delgado (1997) described a substance abuse program for Puerto Rican teenagers. Another program with a cultural focus is MAAT Center for Human and Organizational Enhancement, Inc., a rites-of-passage program for Egyptian adolescents (A. R. Harvey & Coleman, 1997).

Additional community programs include providing volunteer chore services; training to become volunteers; volunteering in social service agencies, churches, and community agencies; and participating in community projects sponsored by individual clubs and organizations, for example, Junior Chamber of Commerce and Boys and Girls Clubs. Many of these programs offer training and provide built-in support and networking sources.

A Global Approach to Prevention

Glenn and Nelson (1989, pp. 48–49) identified seven tools that are critical to the parenting process and building of self-esteem. These tools can also be used in schools, in the community, and by individuals. The authors noted that they discovered these tools, which are basic to survival in times of change, while they were studying failure, not success. These tools, referred to by the authors as the "significant seven," include the following:

- perceptions of personal capabilities,
- perceptions of personal significance,
- perceptions of personal power or influence over life,
- intrapersonal skills,
- interpersonal skills,
- systemic skills, and
- judgmental skills.

Perception, as described by Glenn and Nelson (1989), is "the conclusion we reach after we have had time to reflect on that experience" (p. 51). Perception guides our attitudes and behaviors, and as we mature, we become more and more creatures of perception. Perceptions include four components: "The experience, what we interpret as significant about the experience, why it is important, and how we generalize the experience" (p. 55). Because perceptions change as we mature and because they are unique to each individual, it is important that the four components reflect the perceiver's point of view. Even if an experience is shared, perceptions of the experience differ for each person. It is significant to each person in different ways, it is important to each person for different reasons, and the experience is generalized individually. In terms of building self-esteem, the learner must see the personal importance and value of an experience for himself or herself. As teachers or role models, we have to suspend our own perceptions, judgments, and beliefs and genuinely and respectfully listen to the learner's perspective.

In teaching the first tool and helping young people develop a strong idea about their personal capabilities, there are some critical behaviors we have to give up (Glenn & Nelson, 1989). We must give up assuming that we know how someone else will react in situations and acting as if that were true. We no longer need to rescue or explain, expect attainment of perfection, or dominate and control. Instead, we must learn to listen and hear individual perceptions; check out assumptions; be open to, accepting, and respectful of a young person's thoughts and feelings; and be encouraging and celebrate successes. These changes in adult behaviors will help young people begin to feel valued and respected in the community.

As noted earlier, in the past each family member used to feel that his or her contributions were essential to the family's maintenance and survival. For the most part, this reality has been lost. What has not been lost is the need to be needed. The individual's perception of personal significance is of primary importance. To develop this second tool, we must find ways to acknowledge each individual's personal worth, to help the person see that the family is richer because this person is contributing his or her uniqueness. This goal can be accomplished by listening, understanding, and accepting another's perspective; by soliciting ideas and perceptions from young people; by having frequent personal contact; and by providing a loving, warm family climate.

The third tool, the individual's belief in his or her ability to influence life, refers to the earlier discussion of internal versus external locus of control. Adults can help children build this internal power by establishing firm boundaries for behavior. One of the purposes for maladaptive behavior is to see if limits are real. If an adult cares enough to set limits and to adhere to them, the child learns that he or she is valued and loved and knows the parameters within which to make decisions about behavior. At the same time, he or she also learns about the natural or logical consequences of stepping outside of these parameters. Children will learn from their mistakes if allowed to do so. They will build a belief system that says they have influence over their world. As already noted, adults have to be good listeners so there can be continued discussions with the child as he or she matures and encounters new decision-making opportunities.

Intrapersonal skills, the fourth tool, refers to an individual being able to understand and express feelings and to exercise self-control and self-discipline (Glenn & Nelson, 1989). As a child learns to make decisions within established boundaries, in new situations he or she can consider available responses and choose appropriately. The parent who does not allow the child to make a decision and does it for the child is a primary interference here. A better intervention is to provide a list of alternatives, discuss with the child the consequences of each action (from the child's perspective), and allow the child to decide.

Interpersonal skills, the fifth tool, refers to those skills that allow people to communicate with each other. The extent to which a young person learns these skills is closely related to how well the child gets along with others. Adults can teach these skills through modeling and talking with children.

The systemic and judgmental skills, identified by Glenn and Nelson (1989) as the sixth and seventh tools, are not always specifically taught. They are based on, composed of, and the result of earlier lessons learned. To understand how the system in which we live works is to become aware of the connection between what we do and the result of our actions. By becoming aware of cause and effect, we learn to predict outcomes and are able to set attainable, realistic goals. We learn to be flexible and to take responsibility for our actions because we know the possible outcomes or consequences. For children to learn and increase these skills, adults must provide information about behavior in a caring, respectful climate. Helping an individual to develop good judgment skills requires adults to allow the person most affected by the decision to make it, to provide opportunities for young people to make decisions and experience the consequences, and to collaborate with them during the process. As part of the learning process, we also need to help them evaluate their decisions.

Adaptations for Diversity

Self-esteem develops within the cultural environment in which an individual lives (Hales, 1990; McCarthy & Holliday, 2004). Culture defines how roles will be played by members. One's success or failure in fulfilling cultural role expectations influences self-esteem. Success brings with it a feeling of belonging to a group, of being an important contributing member of that culture, and of feeling good about self. Failure, of course, brings the opposite.

A problem occurs when at-risk youth belong to a nondominant culture and are faced with living in another culture, one with new or different expectations. Conflict is inevitable. A person who is respected for specific behaviors in one culture and chastised or punished for the same behavior in another culture could easily develop lowered self-esteem. Evidence of this is seen in at-risk youth today. Brentro, Brokenleg, and Van Bockern (1990) suggested a feeling of competence is one aspect essential to the development of self-esteem, and in the above scenario an individual may not feel competent.

Okech and Harrington (2002) advocated addressing an African American's Black consciousness and described Black consciousness as "an individual's beliefs or attitudes about his or her self, own race, and the White majority vis-à-vis the Black experience" (p. 214). They stated the person's level of Black consciousness is significantly related to the individual's self-esteem and agreed with Whaley (1993) that cultural identity or Black consciousness, rather than self-esteem, should be the focus of interventions for African American students. According to Phinney (1992), continuing to identify with one's own culture as well as with the main culture is an important component of high self-esteem. Problems arise if the cultural or national group is not esteemed by other cultures or nations. Those identifying with the original culture or group may suffer low self-esteem. It becomes difficult when minorities identify with their own culture, are accepted and develop positive feelings of worth and belonging within that culture, but then do not receive the same positive responses in the new culture. Ishiyama (1995) referred to this phenomena as *cultural dislocation.* This dislocation is particularly painful when the culture of origin does not appear to be valued in the new culture and the beliefs and values of the two cultures are divergent. We see this occurring with minorities when they experience difficulty assimilating another culture's values.

Moore, Madison-Colmore, and Moore (2003) advocated the use of an Afrocentric approach to treat adolescent youth for substance abuse. This approach is defined as a "belief that everyone has a specific culture and history that are the focal points from which they derive a sense of past and future" (Anderson, 1993, p. 221). African Americans value "collectivity, sharing, and spirituality . . . unity of things and the importance of both vertical and horizontal relationships" (p. 221). When these values are not present, individuals feel alienated. The Afrocentric approach to adolescent treatment for substance abuse uses a strengths-based approach that includes focus on interpersonal relationships and existing survival methods existing in this culture. The church, peer groups, and gangs are primary organizations for youth and are already existing entities where constructive intervention can occur. The authors described programs for at-risk youth offered through the church. Programs focus on cultural values as well as on developing a strength-based treatment plan and a commitment to work. They include multiple relevant assignments that include building a support system and finding a mentor.

The MAAT Center for Human and Organizational Enhancement, Inc., has developed a program called the Africentric Youth and Family Rites of Passage Program. The goal of the program is the empowerment of African American male adolescents at risk for exhibiting delinquent behaviors (A. R. Harvey & Hill, 2004, p. 65). The 9-month program has "an Afrocentric orientation, and teaches African American adolescent males and their families how to build character, self-esteem, and unity as a family, a community, and a race." The program uses a "psychosocial

Africentric approach," which includes the principles of "responsibility, reciprocity, respect, restraint, reason, reconciliation, interconnectedness, interdependence, inclusivity, participation, patience, perseverance, sharing, sacrifice, spirituality, cooperation, discipline, and unconditional love" (p. 67). The at-risk youth had statistically significant gains in self-esteem and knowledge about drug use, and the program also had positive effects on the parents and guardians of the participants.

A study by McMahon, Felix, and Nagarajan (2011), investigated the impact of environmental stressors and social support on global self-worth. The study showed that the most frequently named source of support for African American youth was women, most often mothers (p. 259). The authors concluded parental support is particularly key in developing global self-worth in African American youth.

Another issue was highlighted in a recent discussion with immigrants to the state of Washington (personal communication, 2000). Conflicts have emerged between those children who were born and lived in another country and culture before emigrating with their parents and those who were born in the United States after the move. Members of the same family are conflicted, some wanting to retain what is known and familiar and some wanting to "fit in" and not be associated with the "old" culture. Whatever the resolution of the conflict, it will be a direct threat to self-esteem.

Sheets (1995) and Washington (1989) discussed the impact of school culture on self-esteem. Describing different ethnic cultures, they both agreed that teaching and programs that are culturally appropriate can help minorities maintain a positive level of self-esteem and self-validation.

To add to any existing conflicts between dual cultures, norms, and values, Kumamoto (1997) explained that people's views of self and culture are changing because of the massive changes in the world today. The changing—or perhaps conflicting—guidelines for roles for everyone, regardless of culture, affect members of both the dominant and the minority cultures. With the resulting confusion, the success or failure in adapting to new ways of acting and interacting creates an additional assault on self-esteem.

In previous generations young people had roles to play that confirmed their value as important contributors to the welfare of the family and community. Thus, they played a meaningful role in their community, one that ensured the transfer of cultural beliefs and values (Glenn & Nelson, 1989). In contemporary society, with single-parent families and population mobility, that situation is less likely to occur. Changes in society have provided more passive ways for values to be transmitted to the young. Roles that are depicted in the media often do not reflect appropriate cultural beliefs and values, and many young people do not have multiple adult role models who can correct inappropriate perceptions of behaviors and beliefs illustrated in the media.

Sidebar 5.6 ■ Case Study: How Do You Help Kevin?

Kevin, a 13-year-old African American male, is displaying drug abuse symptoms (e.g., lack of attention, agitation, failing grades, and weight loss) and has entered an outpatient treatment program at his church. His counselor used the strengths-based approach and while building rapport discovered Kevin had a reading learning disability and loves music and swimming. Kevin does not know if he wants to go to college.

■ ■ ■

Case Study: Red Eagle Soaring

Red Eagle Soaring (RES) is a Native American youth theater program in Seattle, Washington. It "offers Seattle urban Native youths ages 11–19 contemporary theatre integrated with the traditional performing arts that define the Native culture—drumming, singing, and storytelling" (RES, 2013, para. 1). Many students in this program are homeless. The program offers after-school drama classes in the fall, a 2-week performing arts intensive in the summer, and a touring spring play that travels to tribal settings, schools, and conferences to perform. The program "celebrates the Native American culture and fosters community interconnectedness." Native teens are provided a "learning community that openly and explicitly supports and encourages academic achievement, artistic expression, spiritual awareness, physical well-being, and social capital" (RES, 2013, para. 1). In a YouTube video, students describe how they have changed as a result of this experience. They stress the positive: making friends, connecting with their culture, improving self-esteem, being empowered, and learning ways to stay healthy. In one of their original plays, as seen on YouTube, they act out a scenario to show the negative effects of smoking (see www.youtube.com/watch?v=DfPGLRMwsdA).

Summary

In our society, young people daily exhibit deviant behaviors. There is mounting evidence that there are many more adolescents demonstrating characteristics that are understood to be at risk. These young people are considered at risk because unless they are helped to succeed, they will become part of the deviant subculture. Research has shown that there is a connection between how a person feels about himself or herself and how that person acts (Kaplan, 1975, 2006; Kaplan et al., 1986; Marston et al., 1988). Self-esteem is an issue that must be confronted as a cause of at-risk behaviors.

This chapter has identified specific symptoms of low self-esteem; factors that influence self-esteem; and prevention programs and strategies for parents, individuals, schools, and communities. The activities and programs designed to be used with at-risk youth are not extensive. We must look within our own communities to discover available and successful youth programs. Additional information and resources may also be found in popular magazines (Corbett in *Essence*, 1995; Cordes in *Parenting*, 1994; Herman in *Utne Reader*, 1992; McMahon in *Cosmopolitan*, 1994; McMillan, Singh, & Simonetta in *Education Digest*, 1995; and Tafel in *McCalls*, 1992). Carlock's book *Enhancing Self-Esteem* (1999) identifies many publications and educational audiotapes and videotapes that focus on building self-esteem. The goal is to reach all adolescents, particularly those at risk, and give them a chance to succeed and feel worthwhile.

Useful Websites

Ask.com
    www.ask.com/Self-Esteem+Definition
Dr. Nathaniel Branden
    http://www.nathanielbranden.com/discussions/children/nurturing-self-esteem-in-young-people/
KidsHealth
    http://kidshealth.org/parent/emotions/feelings/self_esteem.html

Meanstinks.com
www.meanstinks.com
Mind for Better Mental Health
http://www.mind.org.uk/mental_health_a-z/8061_how_to_increase_your_self-esteem
Psychology Today
www.psychologytoday.com/basics/self-esteem
TeensHealth
http://kidshealth.org/teen/your_mind/emotions/self_esteem.html
http://selfesteem.tpronline.org

References

Abramson, L. Y., Seligman, M. E. P., & Teasdale, J. D. (1978). Learned helplessness in humans: Critique and reformulation. *Journal of Abnormal Psychology, 87*, 49–74.

Anderson, T. (1993). *Introduction to African American studies: Cultural concepts and theory.* Dubuque, IA: Kendall/Hunt.

Appleton, V., & Dykeman, C. (2004). The impact of dysfunctional family dynamics on children and adolescents. In D. Capuzzi & D. R. Gross (Eds.), *Youth at risk: A prevention resource for counselors, teachers, and parents* (4th ed., pp. 69–92). Alexandria, VA: American Counseling Association.

Aronson, M., & Mettee, S. (1968). Dishonest behavior as a function of differential levels of induced self-esteem. *Journal of Personality and Social Psychology, 9*, 121–127.

Ayduk, O., Gyurak, A., & Luerssen, A. (2009). Rejection sensitivity moderates the impact of rejection on self-concept clarity. *Personality & Social Psychology Bulletin, 35*, 1467–1474.

Bachman, J. G., & O'Malley, P. M. (1986). The frog's pond revisited (again). *Journal of Personality and Social Psychology, 50*, 35–46.

Barber, B. K., Chadwick, B. A., & Orter, R. (1992). Parental behaviors and adolescent self-esteem in the United States. *Journal of Marriage and Family Therapy, 54*, 128–141.

Beane, J. A., & Lipka, R. P (1980). Self-concept and self-esteem. A construct differentiation. *Child Study Journal, 10*, 1–6.

Benard, B., & Marshall, K. (2001). *Competence and resilience research: Lessons for prevention.* Minneapolis: University of Minnesota, National Resilience Resource Center and the Center for the Application of Prevention Technologies. Retrieved from http://www.cce.umm.edu/pdfs/NRRC/capt_pdf/protective.pdf

Benenson, J. F., & Heath, A. (2006). Boys withdraw more in one-to-one interactions, whereas girls withdraw more in groups. *Developmental Psychology, 42*, 272–282.

Benoit, R. B., & Mitchell, L. K. (1987). Self-efficacy: Its nature and promise as an approach to dealing with high school dropout among minorities. *CACD Journal, 8*, 31–38.

Blake, P. C., & Slate, J. R. (1993). A preliminary investigation into the relationship between adolescent self-esteem and parental verbal interaction. *The School Counselor, 41*, 81–85.

Bower, B. (1993). Gender paths wind toward self-esteem: Gender differences in self-esteem development. *Science News, 143*, 308.

Brentro, L. K., Brokenleg, M., & Van Bockern, S. (1990). *Reclaiming youth at-risk: Our hope for the future.* Bloomington, IN: National Education Service.

Buri, J. R., & Dickinson, K. A. (1994, May). *Comparison of familial and cognitive factors associated with male and female self-esteem.* Paper presented at the annual meeting of the Midwestern Psychological Association, Chicago, IL.

Burnett, J. W., Anderson, W. P., & Heppner, P. P. (1995). Gender roles and self-esteem: A consideration of environmental factors. *Journal of Counseling & Development, 73*, 323–326.

Burrow-Sanchez, J. J. (2006). Understanding adolescent substance abuse: Prevalence, risk factors, and clinical implications. *Journal of Counseling & Development, 84,* 283–290.

Cantor, D., & Bernay, T. (1992). *Women in power: The secrets of leadership.* Boston, MA: Houghton Mifflin.

Carlock, C. J. (Ed.). (1999). *Enhancing self-esteem.* Philadelphia, PA: Accelerated Development.

Central Area Youth Association. (1992). *A history and overview* [Paper and brochures]. (Available from CAYA, 119 23rd Ave., Seattle, WA 98122)

Cerezo, M., & Frias, D. (1994, November). Emotional and cognitive adjustment in abused children. *Child Abuse & Neglect, 18,* 23–32.

Chapman, P. L., & Mullis, R. L. (1999). Adolescent coping strategies and self-esteem. *Child Study Journal, 29,* 69–77.

Cohen, L. H., Burt, C. E., & Bjorck, J. P. (1987). Life stress and adjustment: Effect on life events experienced by young adolescents and their parents. *Developmental Psychology, 23,* 583–592.

Corbett, C. (1995, February). The winner within: A hands-on guide to healthy self-esteem. *Essence, 26,* 56–70.

Cordes, H. (1994, March). Resources: Groups, books, magazines, and other tools for building girls' self-esteem. *Parenting, 8,* 96.

Dabrowski, R. M., Avery, M. E., Gyger, R. L., & Emshoff, J. G. (1993, March). *Community based, family-focused prevention of youth substance use.* Paper presented at the Southeastern Psychological Association, Atlanta, GA.

Delgado, M. (1997). Strengths-based practice with Puerto Rican adolescents: Lessons from a substance abuse prevention project. *Social Work in Education, 19,* 101–112.

Domino, G., & Blumberg, E. (1987). An application of Gough's conceptual model to a measure of adolescent self-esteem. *Journal of Youth and Adolescence, 16,* 87–90.

Dwyer, V. (1993). Eye of the beholder: Young women have self-image problems. *Maclean's, 106,* 46–47.

Edmondson, J. H., & White, J. (1998). A tutorial and counseling program: Helping students at risk of dropping out of school. *Professional School Counseling, 1,* 43–47.

Elias, M. J. K., Weissberg, R. P., Hawkins, J. D., Perry, C. L., Zins, J. E., Dodge, K. A., . . . Garmezy, N. (1994). The school-based promotion of social competence: Theory, research, practice, and policy. In R. J. Hagerty, N. Garmezy, M. Rutter, & L. Sherrod (Eds.), *Stress, risk and resilience in children and adolescence: Processes, mechanisms, and interventions* (pp. 269–315). New York, NY: Cambridge University Press.

Elliott, G. C. (1988). Gender differences in self-consistency: Evidence from an investigation of self-concept structure. *Journal of Youth and Adolescence, 17,* 41–57.

Enns, C. (1992). Self-esteem groups: A synthesis of consciousness-raising and assertiveness training. *Journal of Counseling & Development, 71,* 7–13.

Eron, L. D., Gentry, J. H., & Schlegel, P. (Eds.). (1994). *Reason to hope: A psychosocial perspective on violence and youth.* Washington, DC: American Psychological Association.

Eskilson, A., Wiley, G., Meuhlbauer, G., & Dodder, L. (1986). Parental pressure, self-esteem, and adolescent reported deviance: Bending the twig too far. *Adolescence, 21,* 501–515.

Forester, J. R. (2004). Your best plans must use your best strengths. In S. Mygatt-Wakefield (Ed.), *Unfocused kids: Innovative practices to help students focus on their plans after high school; a resource for educators* (pp. 383–394). Greensboro, NC: ERIC/CAPS and the American Counseling Association.

Frey, D., & Carlock, C. J. (1984). *Enhancing self-esteem.* Muncie, IN: Accelerated Development.

Glenn, H. S., & Nelson, J. (1989). *Raising self-reliant children in a self-indulgent world.* Rocklin, CA: Prima.

Gottman, J., & DeClair, J. (1997). *The heart of parenting: Raising an emotionally intelligent child.* New York, NY: Simon & Schuster.

Gottman, J., Katz, L., & Hooven, C. (1996). *Meta-emotion: How families communicate emotionally, links to child peer relations and other developmental outcomes.* Mahwah, NJ: Erlbaum.

Graf, R. C. (1971). Induced self-esteem as a determinant of behavior. *Journal of Social Psychology, 85,* 213–217.

Guindon, M. H. (2002). Toward accountability in the use of the self-esteem construct. *Journal of Counseling & Development, 80,* 204–214.

Hains, A. A. (1994). The effectiveness of a school-based, cognitive–behavioral stress management program with adolescents reporting high and low levels of emotional arousal. *School Counselor, 42,* 114–125.

Haldane, B. (1989, March). *The dependable strengths articulation process: How it works.* Paper presented at the annual convention of the American Association for Counseling and Development, Boston, MA.

Hales, S. (1990, Winter). Valuing the self: Understanding the nature of self-esteem. *The Saybrook Perspective,* 3–17.

Hamachek, D. (1995). Self-concept and school achievement: Interaction dynamics and a tool for assessing the self-concept component. *Journal of Counseling & Development, 73,* 419–425.

Harvey, A. R., & Coleman, A. A. (1997). An Afrocentric program for African American males in the juvenile justice system. *Child Welfare, 76,* 197–211.

Harvey, A. R., & Hill, R. B. (2004, January). Africentric youth and family rites of passage program: Promoting resilience among at-risk African American youths. *Social Work, 49*(1), 65–74.

Harvey, M., & Byrd, M. (1998). The relationship between perceptions of self-esteem, patterns of familial attachment and family environment during early and late phases of adolescence. *International Journal of Adolescence and Youth, 7,* 93–111.

Hazler, R. J., Carney, J. V., & Granger, D. A. (2006). Integrating biological measures into the study of bullying. *Journal of Counseling & Development, 84,* 298–307.

Hazler, R. J., & Mellin, E. A. (2004). The developmental origins and treatment needs of female adolescents with depression. *Journal of Counseling & Development, 82,* 18–24.

Herman, E. (1992, January/February). Are politics and therapy compatible? A lesson from the self-esteem movement. *Utne Reader,* 97–100.

Hoffman, R. M., Hattie, J. A., & Borders, D. (2005). Personal definitions of masculinity and femininity as an aspect of gender self-concept. *Journal of Humanistic Counseling, Education and Development, 44,* 66–75.

Horan, J. J. (1996). Effects of computer-based cognitive restructuring on rationally mediated self-esteem. *Journal of Counseling Psychology, 43,* 371–375.

Ishiyama, F. I. (1995). Culturally dislocated clients: Self-validation and cultural conflict issues and counseling implications. *Canadian Journal of Counseling, 29,* 262–273.

Jason, L. A., Weine, A. M., Johnson, J. H., Danner, K. E., Kurasaki, K. S., & Warren-Sohlberg, L. (1993). The school transition project: A comprehensive preventative intervention. *Journal of Emotional and Behavioral Disorders, 1,* 65–70.

Johnson, D. S. (1981). Naturally acquired learned helplessness: The relationship of school failure to achievement behavior, attributions, and self-concept. *Journal of Educational Psychology, 73,* 174–180.

Johnson, D. W., Johnson, R. T., & Taylor, B. (1993). Impact of cooperative and individualistic learning on high-ability students' achievement, self-esteem, and social acceptance. *Journal of Social Psychology, 133,* 839–844.

Jones, D. J., & Watson, B. C. (1990). *High-risk students and higher education.* Washington, DC: George Washington University, Clearinghouse on Higher Education.

Kaplan, H. B. (1975). *Self-attitudes and deviant behavior.* Pacific Palisades, CA: Goodyear.

Kaplan, H. B. (1976). Self-attitude and deviant response. *Social Forces, 54,* 788–801.

Kaplan, H. B. (2006). Understanding the concept of resilience. In S. Goldstein & R. Books (Eds.), *Handbook of resilience in children* (pp. 39–48). New York, NY: Springer Science+Business Media.

Kaplan, H. B., Martin, S. S., & Johnson, R. J. (1986). Self-rejection and the explanation of deviance: Specification of the structure among latent constructs. *American Journal of Sociology, 92,* 384–411.

Kelly, T. M., Lynch, K. G., Donovan, J. E., & Clark, D. B. (2001). Alcohol use disorders and risk factor interactions for adolescent suicidal ideation and attempts. *Suicide and Life-Threatening Behavior, 32,* 181–193.

Kennison, J. A. (1996). Therapy in the mountains. In *Proceedings of the 1995 International Conference on Outdoor Recreation and Education.* Boise, ID: Association of Outdoor Recreation and Education.

Klindera, K., & Menderwald, J. (2001). *Youth development is a good prevention strategy.* Retrieved from Advocates for Youth website: http://www.advocatesforyouth.org/publications/550?task=view

Kraizer, S. (1990). Skills for living: The requirement of the 90s. In *Critical issues in prevention of child abuse and neglect: Adolescent parenting life skills for children* (pp. 131–139). Austin, TX: Children's Trust Fund of Texas.

Kumamoto, C. C. (1997, March). *Unison in variety, congeniality in difference: Sifting beyond the multicultural sieve.* Paper presented at the annual meeting of the Conference on College Composition and Communication, Phoenix, AZ.

Leflot, G., Onghena, P., & Colpin, H. (2010). Teacher–child interactions: Relations with children's self-concept in second grade. *Infant and Child Development, 19,* 385–405.

Lemoire, S. J., & Chen, C. P. (2005). Applying person-centered counseling to sexual minority adolescents. *Journal of Counseling & Development, 83,* 146–154.

Lord, S., Eccles, J. S., & McCarthy, K. A. (1994). Surviving the junior high school transition: Family processes and self-perceptions as protective and risk factors. *Journal of Early Adolescence, 14,* 162–199.

Lorr, M., & Wunderlich, R. A. (1986). Two objective measures of self-esteem. *Journal of Personality Assessment, 50,* 18–23.

Mack, J. E., & Ablon, S. L. (Eds.). (1983). *The development and sustenance of self-esteem in childhood.* New York, NY: International Universities Press.

Maples, M. F., Packman, J., Abney, P., Daugherty, R. F., Casey, J. A., & Pirtle, L. (2005). Suicide by teenagers in middle school: A postvention team approach. *Journal of Counseling & Development, 83,* 397–405.

Marston, A. R., Jacobs, D. F., Singer, R. D., Widaman, K. F., & Little, T. D. (1988). Characteristics of adolescents at risk for compulsive overeating on a brief screening test. *Adolescence, 23,* 59–72.

Masche, J. G. (2000, March/April). *Does a happy marriage make positive parent–adolescent relationships and self-satisfied children?* Paper presented at the biennial meeting of the Society for Research on Adolescence, Chicago, IL.

Maternal and Child Health Branch, Hawaii State Department of Health. (1991). *Adolescent health in Hawaii: The Adolescent Health Network's teen health advisor report.* Rockville, MD: Health Resources and Services Administration.

McCarthy, J., & Holliday, E. L. (2004). Help-seeking and counseling within a traditional male gender role: An examination from a multicultural perspective. *Journal of Counseling & Development, 82,* 25–30.

McCormick, M. E., & Wold, J. S. (1993). Programs for gifted girls. *Roeper Review, 16,* 85–88.

McDowell, J. (1984). *Building your self-image.* Wheaton, IL: Living Books.

McGee, R., & Williams, T. (2000). Does low self-esteem predict health compromising behaviors among adolescents? *Journal of Adolescence, 23,* 569–582.

McMahon, S. (1994, August). Let us now praise me. *Cosmopolitan, 217,* 68.

McMahon, S. D., Felix, E. D., & Nagarajan, T. (2011). Social support and neighborhood stressors among African American youth: Networks and relations to self-worth. *Journal of Family Studies, 20,* 255–262.

McMillan, J. H., Singh, J., & Simonetta, L. G. (1995). Self-oriented self-esteem self-destructs. *Education Digest, 60,* 9–12.

Moore, S. E., Madison-Colmore, O., & Moore, J. L. (2003). An Afrocentric approach to substance abuse treatment with adolescent African American males: Two case examples. *The Western Journal of Black Studies, 27,* 219–230.

Moreau, D. (1996). Depression in the young. In J. A. Sechzer, S. N. Pfafflin, F. L. Denmark, A. Griffin, & S. J. Blumenthal (Eds.), *Women in mental health* (pp. 31–44). New York, NY: New York Academy of Sciences.

Mufson, L., & Moreau, D. (1997). Depressive disorders. In R. T. Ammerman & M. Hersen (Eds.), *Handbook of prevention and treatment with children and adolescents* (pp. 403–430). New York, NY: Wiley.

Myers, J. E., Sweeney, T. J., & Witmer, J. M. (2000). The Wheel of Wellness counseling for wellness: A holistic model for treatment planning. *Journal of Counseling & Development, 78,* 251–266.

Nassar-McMillan, S. C., & Cashwell, C. S. (1997). Building self-esteem of children and adolescents through adventure based counseling. *Journal of Humanistic Education and Development, 36,* 59–67.

Nobles, W. W. (1989, July 25). *The HAWK Federation and the development of Black adolescent males: Toward a solution to the crises of America's young Black men.* Testimony before the Select Committee on Children, Youth, and Families. U.S. House of Representatives, 101st Cong., 1st sess., Washington, DC.

Okech, A. P., & Harrington, R. (2002). The relationships among Black consciousness, self-esteem, and academic self-efficacy in African American men. *The Journal of Psychology, 137,* 214–224.

Patterson, G. R., Reid, J. B., & Dishion, T. J. (1992). *Antisocial boys: A social interactional approach* (Vol. 4). Eugene, OR: Castalia.

Phinney, J. S. (1992). Acculturation attitudes and self-esteem among high school and college students. *Youth and Society, 23,* 299–312.

Portes, P. R., & Zady, M. F. (2000, April). *Cultural differences in the self-esteem and adaptation of Spanish-speaking second generation adolescents.* Paper presented at the annual meeting of the American Educational Research Association, New Orleans, LA.

Preckel, F., & Brull, M. (2010). The benefits of being a big fish in a big pond: Contrast and assimilation effects on academic self-concept. *Learning and Individual Differences, 20,* 522–531.

Reasoner, R. W. (1994). *Self-esteem as an antidote to crime and violence.* Port Ludlow, WA: National Council for Self-Esteem.

Red Eagle Soaring. (2013). *About.* Retrieved from http://redeaglesoaring.org/about-2

Reid, J. B., Patterson, G. R., & Snyder, J. (2002). *Antisocial behavior in children and adolescents: A developmental analysis and model for intervention.* Washington, DC: American Psychological Association.

Roberts, R., Lepkowski, W., & Davidson, K. (1998). Dealing with the aftermath of a student suicide: A T.E.A.M. approach. *NAASP Bulletin, 82,* 53–59.

Robison-Awana, P., Kehle, T. J., & Jenson, W. R. (1986). But what about smart girls? Adolescent self-esteem and sex role perceptions as a function of academic achievement. *Journal of Educational Psychology, 78,* 179–183.

Rosenberg, M. (1965). *Society and the adolescent self-image.* Princeton, NJ: Princeton University Press.

Saltzman, A. (1994). Schooled in failure? Fact or myth—teachers favor boys; girls respond by withdrawing. *U.S. News & World Report, 117,* 88–93.

Satir, V. (1981, June). Paper presented at the AVANTA Process Community Conference, Park City, UT.

Schell, L., Cotton, S., & Luxmoore, M. (2012). Outdoor adventure for young people with a mental illness. *Early Intervention in Psychiatry, 7,* 407–414.

Sharaf, A. Y., Thompson, E. A., & Walsh, E. (2009). Protective effects of self-esteem and family support on suicide risk behaviors among at-risk adolescents. *Journal of Child and Adolescent Psychiatric Nursing, 22*(3), 160–168.

Shectman, Z. (2002). Child group psychotherapy in the school at the threshold of a new millennium. *Journal of Counseling & Development, 80,* 293–299.

Sheets, R. H. (1995). From remedial to gifted: Effects of culturally centered pedagogy. *Theory Into Practice, 34,* 186–193.

Shek, D. T. L. (1997). Family environment and adolescent psychological well-being, school adjustment and problem behavior: A pioneer study in a Chinese context. *Journal of Genetic Psychology, 153,* 113–128.

Sim, T. N. (2000). Adolescent psychological competence: The importance of role and regard for parents. *Journal of Research on Adolescence, 10,* 49–64.

Simmons, R. C., Burgeson, R., Carlton-Ford, S., & Blyth, D. A. (1987). Impact of cumulative change in early adolescence. *Child Development, 58,* 1220–1234.

Simpson, M. (1999). Student suicide: Who's liable? *NEA Today, 17,* 25–29.

Smith, D. C., & Sandhu, D. S. (2004). Toward a positive perspective on violence prevention in schools: Building connections. *Journal of Counseling & Development, 83,* 287–293.

Spencer, M. B. (1991). *Adolescent African American male self-esteem: Suggestions for mentoring program content* (Mentoring Program Structures for Young Minority Males conference paper series). Washington, DC: Urban Institute.

Stanard, R. P. (2000). Assessment and treatment of adolescent depression and suicidality. *Journal of Mental Health Counseling, 22,* 204–217.

Tafel, R. (1992, June). How your self-esteem affects your child's. *McCalls, 119,* 40–42.

Taylor, E. L., & Rosselli, H. (1997, March). *The effect of a single gender leadership program on young women.* Paper presented at the annual meeting of the American Educational Research Association, Chicago, IL.

Testerman, J. (1996). Holding at-risk students. *Phi Delta Kappan, 77,* 364–365.

Thompson, S. M. (1996). Peer mediation: A peaceful solution. *School Counselor, 44,* 151–154.

Tonkin, R. S. (1997). Evaluation of a summer camp for adolescents with eating disorders. *Journal of Adolescent Health, 20,* 412–413.

Washington, E. D. (1989). A componential theory of culture and its implications for African-American identity. *Equity and Excellence, 24,* 24–30.

Weinburg, N. Z. (2001). Risk factors for adolescent substance abuse. *Journal of Learning Disabilities, 34,* 343–351.

West Virginia Education Association and Appalachia Educational Laboratory. (1993). *Schools as community social-service centers: West Virginia programs and possibilities.* (Available from Appalachia Educational Laboratory, PO Box 1348, Charleston, WV 25325)

Whaley, A. L. (1993). Self-esteem, cultural identity, and psychosocial adjustment in African American children. *Journal of Black Psychology, 19,* 406–422.

Yanish, D. L., & Battle, J. (1985). Relationship between self-esteem, depression, and alcohol consumption among adolescents. *Psychological Reports, 57,* 331–334.

Yankelovich, Y. D. (1981). *New rules: Search for self-fulfillment in a world turned upside down.* New York, NY: Random House.

YMCA. (1994). *YMCA teen services* [Flyer]. Seattle, WA: Author.

Zimmerman, M. A., Ramirez-Valles, J., & Maton, K. L. (1999). Resilience among urban African American male adolescents: A study of the protective effects of sociopolitical control on their mental health. *American Journal of Community Psychology, 27,* 733–751.

Chapter 6

Identifying and Preventing Mood Disorders in Children and Adolescents

Marilyn J. Powell and Colleen R. Logan

Mood disorders during childhood and adolescence significantly affect families, schools, communities, and, of course, individual children's lives. The most predominantly diagnosed mood disorders during childhood and adolescence are major depressive disorder (MDD) and bipolar I affective disorder (De Santis & Ekegren, 2003). Prevalence estimates for these disorders in youth populations vary. The National Institute of Mental Health (NIMH; 2003) has documented that 6% of children between the ages of 9 and 17 are affected by MDD (NIMH, 2003). Brent and Maalouf (2009) noted a prevalence rate for depression in children of 1%–2% prior to adolescence with an increase to 3%–8% during the teen years. The prevalence of bipolar I affective disorder (bipolar I disorder) in children is more difficult to estimate given the controversy in the field with respect to how symptoms of mania manifest in youth (Bradfield, 2010). In fact, the American Academy of Child and Adolescent Psychiatry cautions against the use of this diagnosis in children under 6 years of age (McClellan, Kowatch, & Findling, 2007). Bipolar I disorder is much more commonly diagnosed in adolescence, and, thus, the prevalence of bipolar I disorder in teens was estimated by McClellan et al. (2007) at approximately 1% of the adolescent population. For many adolescents, bipolar I disorder begins with a depressive episode, with mania appearing later in the course of the illness, which, of course, further complicates prevalence statistics (Leboyer, Paillere-Martinot, & Bellivier, 2005). Although, the signs and symptoms associated with bipolar II disorder include vacillating *hypo*manic and depressive episodes, bipolar II remains underresearched and less well documented within child and adolescent populations; thus, this diagnosis is particularly controversial within this age group (Pfeifer, Kowatch, & DelBello, 2010). Given that these disorders have high correlations with family discord, suicide attempts, alcohol and drug use, and academic un-derachievement—and that they tend to persist into adulthood—identifying, un-derstanding, and preventing these disorders are essential tasks for professional counselors working with youth (Bradfield, 2010; McWhirter & Walters, 2008[1]).

This chapter focuses on major mood disorders—MDD and bipolar I disorder—in children and adolescents. First we review diagnostic issues these disorders present in child and adolescent populations, with the caveat that at present the guide for diagnosis is the *Diagnostic and Statistical Manual of Mental Disorders* (4th ed., text rev.; *DSM-IV-TR*; American Psychiatric Association, 2000). However, the fifth edition of this publication, the *DSM-5*, is scheduled for release in May of 2013 at this writing. Thus, we use the *DSM-IV-TR* to guide the diagnostic discussion in this chapter, as proposed changes in the *DSM-5* are, according to the American Psychiatric Association website (American Psychiatric Association, *DSM-5* Development Group, 2013), under review and revision; therefore, discussion of previews in the popular media or previously published versions would be purely speculative at this juncture. However, although accurate and thorough diagnosis is critical, this chapter is not meant to instruct counselors on specific diagnostic processes in determining whether an individual child or adolescent is experiencing MDD or bipolar I disorder. Rather, we focus on hallmarks of the disorders; diagnostic issues and quandaries that will remain constant regardless of any revisions to the *DSM*; prevention efforts for individuals, families, schools, and communities; and, finally, considerations of diversity when working with children and adolescents at risk for or experiencing MDD or bipolar I disorder.

Causal Factors

Mood disorders are found in the *DSM-IV-TR* (American Psychiatric Association, 2000) in four areas: mood disorders, bipolar disorders, mood disorders due to a general medical condition, and adjustment disorders with depressed mood or mixed emotional features. In a prior edition of this chapter, McWhirter and Walters (2008) reviewed the list of possible mood disorders, such as (a) depressive disorders, including MDD, that are characterized by one or more major depressive episodes but without mania; and (b) dysthymic disorder, a mood disturbance without the severity required for the diagnosis of MDD but present for at least 2 years in a way that impacts the life of the individual across social, occupational, and relational dimensions. Bipolar I and II affective disorder along with cyclothymia make up the bipolar disorders listed in the *DSM-IV-TR*. And mood disorders due to medical conditions are resultant of physical processes directly caused by a particular disease or as a result of a particular treatment (e.g., a brain tumor affecting emotional response or resultant mood complications of chemotherapy; *DSM-IV-TR*). Seasonal affective disorder is also listed as a diagnostic possibility related to the amount, frequency, and duration of natural light that can affect mood regulation and stability. Again, as noted by McWhirter and Walters (2008), some of these conditions can co-occur, further challenging the accuracy of the diagnostic picture when one is working with children and youth.

Symptom presentation differences between children and adults in terms of diagnostic signs and symptoms are addressed in the *DSM-IV-TR*. In particular, as

---

[1]The authors express their appreciation for the contributions made by McWhirter and Walters in the fifth edition of this text.

noted by McWhirter and Walters (2008): Children may not gain as much weight as expected rather than losing weight when depressed; irritability may be a more clinically prevalent and significant sign of depression for children than traditionally observed "depressed mood" in adults; and young children may have more somatic complaints and disruptive behavior disorders co-occurring with depression and bipolar symptoms than adults do (Fava et al., 2010). These differences are critical to accurate diagnosis, and it is of note that this is not an exhaustive list. Professional counselors working with children need to become conversant and educated in how mood disorders, or symptoms of a possible disorder, may manifest differently or be misdiagnosed, particularly given that so much of the diagnostic literature focuses on adult presentation of these symptoms.

In their prior version of this chapter, McWhirter and Walters (2008) also astutely commented on the complications of diagnosing bipolar disorder in children. In particular, McWhirter and Walters cited evidence from Sanchez, Hagino, Weller, and Weller (1999) that there may be a low rate of occurrence of mania in the patterns required for the diagnosis of bipolar disorder coupled with the reality that many symptoms of mania in children (disruptive behavior, difficulty sustaining attention, impulsivity, irritability, and overactivity as well as moodiness) may overlap, as stated earlier, with other disorders typically emerging in childhood, such as oppositional defiant disorder (ODD), conduct disorder (CD), attention-deficit/hyperactivity disorder (ADHD), and posttraumatic stress disorder (PTSD; *DSM-IV-TR*). Thus, the task of the professional counselor is made that much more difficult given that mood disorders in children, as outlined earlier, are significantly prevalent and yet often difficult to distinguish from learning and/or behavioral disorders.

The continuum of mood issues for children and adolescents spans developmental concerns and adjustment disorders as well as major mental disorders, including MDD and bipolar I disorder. Complicating the diagnostic picture of mood disorders in children and adolescents are the often comorbid disorders also significantly found in childhood and adolescence, including but not limited to PTSD (Steinbuchel, Wilens, Adamson, & Sgambati, 2009), ADHD (Faraone, Glatt, & Tsuang, 2003), ODD, and CD (Bradfield, 2010; Soutullo et al., 2005; Steinbuchel et al., 2009). These concomitant disorders can include overlapping symptoms including but not limited to irritability, mood dysregulation and lability, aggressiveness and angry outbursts, excessive sensitivity, fearfulness and withdrawal from others, and rapidly shifting emotional states (*DSM-IV-TR*). In addition, although the symptoms of these disorders may overlap—which can cause differential diagnostic confusion—there is also, unfortunately, no rule preventing a child from experiencing two or more major mental disorders in a co-occurring fashion, that is, clearly meeting all diagnostic criteria for multiple disorders. Many childhood disorders, such as PTSD, have strong environmental components, and the variability of the environment coupled with the complexities of development and reactivity of children at different ages and stages make children especially vulnerable to dysfunction, particularly when safety, support, and secure attachments with loving adults are not readily available.

With regard to overlapping symptoms, irritability, for example, is a hallmark symptom of both depression and bipolar disorders in children and adolescents (Fava et al., 2010). Irritability may also be a sign of other mental disorders, such as ADHD, CD, and PTSD to name just a few. An experienced counselor can also attest to the notion that irritability is possibly indicative of normal developmental stages and their resultant challenges, such as family conflict or adjustments, school dilemmas, and normative events that occur in the healthy developmental trajectory. All of these factors, along with the sometimes challenging prospect of obtaining a clear symptom picture from child and adolescent clients moving through complicated developmental stages and tasks, make the identification of such syndromes a particularly difficult, while meaningful and important, task. It is, therefore, incumbent upon the professional counselor to carefully sort through all of the hypothetical sources of a child's irritability (including family history), ascertain whether it is a change from previous behavior, and carefully assess how long and in what settings it is occurring while also attending to all of the other factors that relate to this particular symptom. It is no small task and one that must be approached carefully and methodically in order to understand and appreciate the full diagnostic picture.

In fact, this multidimensional symptom example highlights the extraordinary complexity of accurately diagnosing children and adolescents with major mental disorders, particularly mood disorders. Although irritability, in our example, may be a symptom indicative of many possible psychiatric disorders, professional counselors need to keep in mind that most symptoms have a range of severity that informs the diagnostic process. A child may seem irritable because of a parent–child conflict developing out of a systemic inability to traverse the challenges of emerging adolescence. Or, the child or adolescent may have experienced a recent trauma, or even a negative social event, that parents may not be aware of and thus may not be able to put into context. In addition, professional counselors must also remember that to diagnose a major mental disorder in the current *DSM-IV-TR* system, there needs to be observed impairment in social, educational, and personal functioning as well as across multiple environments in many cases and certainly for the prescribed period of time. These extra-symptom caveats serve to help counseling professionals assess the level of severity and the depth of the impact of any symptoms that might be present in order to determine the additional likelihood of a major mood disorder, but these disorders may be overlooked in assessment and treatment models that are less well attuned to contextual and environmental factors. As a result, professional counselors are in a unique position to keep these multidimensional and multicontextual factors at the forefront of discussions with parents, teachers, and other mental health or health care professionals.

As noted in the introduction to this chapter, also complicating the diagnostic picture is the advent of the fifth edition of the *Diagnostic and Statistical Manual of Mental Disorders* in the spring of 2013. Readers may go to www.DSM5.org to find information about this manual's publication and diagnostic category

---

Sidebar 6.1 ■ *DSM-5* Use

The *DSM-5* was released in spring 2013. This version completely replaced the *DSM-IV-TR* and significantly changed as well as replaced a number of diagnostic categories. What is your plan to ensure that you are fully prepared and well-versed in the diagnostic manual? What types of and how many training sessions will you attend? What will be your primary source of information regarding this critically important change?

■ ■ ■

Sidebar 6.2 ■ Case Study: How Do You Help Anna?

Anna is 12 years old. She has a lot of friends and typically does well in school. This fall, however, her grades started slipping and she was often seen spending time alone. Her teachers report that they rarely see her smiling anymore, and, in fact, she often is teary or on the brink of tears. Her parents also report that Anna is acting differently lately. As soon as she comes home from school, she goes to her room and gets in bed. She sleeps until dinner and then after homework she goes back to sleep again. And it is difficult to get her out of bed on the weekends. Anna's mother wonders if Anna is depressed. Although depression seems likely in Anna's case, are there other potential reasons for Anna's behavior? How would you investigate and contextualize the situation with Anna? How would you communicate with her teachers? Her parents?

■ ■ ■

and system changes, to look at press releases, and to read information about the controversy concerning speculated shifts in criteria or categories; also available at the website is information on the manual's history, process, and reasons for revision. Professional counselors need to be especially attuned to possible diagnostic category changes, prevalence and incidence rates of disorders, and other updates. Continuing education and further training are essential in order to remain current in terms of this diagnostic system as well as any changes from previous versions.

However, just as important as learning the revised diagnostic criteria as conceptualized by the American Psychiatric Association, counselors also must hold firm to the contextual view of human concerns and conditions, not losing the expertise inherent within the counseling profession to carefully consider family and community context, to keep in mind diversity issues, to evaluate new or contradictory research findings, and to carefully evaluate ever-evolving constructs when applying the system of diagnosis and conceptualizations of child and adolescent disorders. Diagnostic labels can help in many ways when applied holistically and ethically: giving a name to something heretofore mysterious, troubling, and isolating; helping to formulate a successful treatment plan; and, perhaps even more important, helping families and treatment systems to understand what is indeed happening and, as a result, creating the ability to dialogue about the issues and concerns. However, when labels are applied hastily, inaccurately, without adequate understanding, or within the sometimes myopic and symptom-only focus of the medical model, the child or adolescent in question can be lost to the label, which unwittingly perpetuates bias, stigma, reduction of potential, and hopelessness that can severely and negatively impact the developmental trajectory of a child. Counselor, educate thyself and do no harm.

Although mood disorders—depression and bipolar disorders, in particular—are well documented to have genetic components, there is no way to factor out the environmental stressors that either act as precursors to the development of a diagnosable disorder or make the genetic predisposition a reality. For example, childhood trauma has emerged as one of the major risk factors for developing a mood disorder, primarily MDD. Exposure to trauma in childhood is, unfortunately, a typical experience for many individuals. Breslau, Lucia, and Alvarado (2006) noted that 40%–76% of children will experience at least one traumatic event by the age of 17. PTSD, the constellation of symptoms including those of intrusion

Sidebar 6.3 ■ Case Study: How Do You Help Robert?

Robert is enrolled in a very prestigious elementary school. The majority of the students do very well in school, and there are very few reported concerns. Robert, however, is an enigma to the school counselor. One minute he is sad and sullen, and the next minute he is exploding with energy and unable to sit down and focus on his schoolwork. He earns average grades, but his behavior is all over the place. The teachers are very frustrated, as they are used to being able to contain behavior in their classrooms. In a staff meeting on Friday, his teacher blurted out that he acted like he was bipolar or something like that. The school counselor made a note to contact his parents and recommend they take him to a therapist for treatment and medication. Are there any other possible explanations for Robert's behavior? Taking into account the context of the situation, what steps would you take to assess and address Robert's behavior?

■ ■ ■

(e.g., hypervigilance, flashbacks, nightmares) and avoidance (e.g., withdrawal, isolation, and avoidance of cues that prompt memories of the trauma), can also resemble other anxiety disorders, mood disorders, conduct disorders, and, in some cases, psychotic disorders. In addition, there is evidence that alcohol disorders in adolescents are often comorbid with PTSD and depressive disorders (Steinbuchel et al., 2009); in our clinical experience, this often is a chicken-and-egg situation, as the professional counselor has to sort through whether the trauma led to depression and subsequent substance abuse, or whether early substance abuse increased the likelihood of trauma resulting in depression. In summary, however, it is clear in the research literature that trauma and mood disorder often occur hand in hand. Preventing childhood trauma, strengthening communities and families to coordinate supportive and rapid intervention when trauma occurs, and promoting resilience-developing activities and resources in schools and homes are all important advocacy opportunities for counseling professionals.

Aside from trauma, other stressful events are often associated with the development of mood disorders in children. Some examples of these types of stressful events include parent–child conflict, family conflict, divorce or estrangement of co-parents, and inconsistent parenting environments where children are left inadequately supervised or do not develop internal regulatory mechanisms and a strong sense of self. In addition, peer and sibling conflict, when severe and left unchecked, can also increase risk for mood disorders in children and adolescents, particularly when there is a genetic vulnerability present as well (Brent & Maalouf, 2009; Ong & Caron, 2008). The stability of the family with respect to resources can also play a role in the development of mood disorders in children; for example,

Sidebar 6.4 ■ Advocating for Children and Youth

Professional counselors are uniquely positioned to serve as advocates for children and youth. Advocacy efforts typically require collaboration and cooperation. How do you see yourself serving on a multidisciplinary team composed of social workers, psychologists, and perhaps even psychiatrists? How do you see yourself contributing to discussions centered around assessment and diagnosis? Do you feel that you are adequately prepared to participate in this type of discussion? If not, what steps will you take to educate yourself?

■ ■ ■

loss of employment can result in changing living situations and economic status. Homelessness and poverty can also have a significant negative impact on the mental health of children (Brent & Maalouf, 2009). Finally, death and loss or chronic illness can also disrupt development and contribute to a mood disorder when not addressed and supported in an affirmative way as the child copes with the event. Counselors must inquire about social history in just as conscientiously a manner as they do medical and developmental history in order to determine if any of these additional vulnerabilities are present when a mood disorder is suspected in a child or adolescent (Brent & Maalouf, 2009).

Environmental challenges or conflict situations affect children in different ways, but, intuitively, stress and mood disturbance, particularly when not addressed and/or buffered by support, certainly increase the risk for developing a more severe depressive experience or manifesting a genetic vulnerability in the form of a major mental illness such as major depression or bipolar disorder. Moreover, children and adolescents with depressed parents are particularly at risk for mood disorders themselves for a variety of reasons, both environmental and genetic (Brent & Maalouf, 2009). A genetic history of depression contributes to greater risk, as does an environment where one or more parent is depressed and there is high emotionality associated with the onset and protraction of depressed episodes (Brent & Maalouf, 2009).

Youth who struggle in school either socially or academically may also be at risk for mood disorders. Students with bipolar disorder often have significant challenges in school (Weinberg & Rehmet, 1983). Learning differences and ADHD often co-occur and are risk factors for the development of mood disorders. Interventions to support the child to succeed and to support the family and help them to understand the symptoms in productive and positive ways are essential to ameliorate the effects of these combination disorders (Barkley, 2005). Difficult and unstable peer relationships and the prevalence of bullying, in person and online, are on the rise despite best efforts to create antibullying programs and interventions (Gay, Lesbian & Straight Education Network [GLSEN], 2011). One cannot underestimate the impact of verbal and physical harassment, as it is often the genesis of dysfunctional relationships in the school environment. And, given that children spend most of their waking hours at school, it is not an issue that can be taken lightly.

Suicide is also a significant risk, particularly for adolescents with bipolar I disorder or MDD (Brent & Maalouf, 2009). Assessment of ideation, access to means, and plan for method of suicide must be assessed any time a counselor has an indication of suicide risk. Co-occurring substance abuse can also increase risk and is, as noted earlier, often present in tandem with mood disorders in teens (Brent & Maalouf, 2009). Prevention in school settings is discussed at length later in this chapter, and there are few places better suited for proactive prevention initiatives and early identification of developing childhood issues—including risk or presentation of mood disorders—than the school milieu. School counselors must work proactively in prevention mode, however, rather than simply reacting to issues that occur; this is a tall order when resources are scarce and needs are many.

Prevention

Individual

As noted earlier, mood disorders are thought to have significant genetic components; however, this does not render prevention irrelevant. As discussed earlier in this chapter, when a biological family history is positive for these kinds of severe conditions, children may also be at risk of developing the disorders. In addition, the literature supports a link between trauma and the development of major depression and bipolar disorder. Thus, providing opportunities for children at risk for major mood disorders to develop resilience and solid coping skills is important. This goal can be accomplished through working on developing positive worldviews, increasing communication skills, and learning how to manage feelings. Early intervention, when trauma has occurred, is particularly important and may ameliorate symptoms and prevent the development of more severe forms of these disorders.

Given this combination of genetic and environmental factors, as well as the stigma associated with seeking help and the often prohibitive cost of accessing treatment, children and youth with major mood disorders can often go untreated or be misdiagnosed as exhibiting behavioral problems rather than suffering from mental illness. Professional counselors need to astutely and critically assess the entire context within which the child or adolescent resides and not rush toward a hasty diagnosis. In addition, professional counselors are called to serve as advocates working to develop resources to understand the complexities associated with childhood mood disorders and advocating for changes where they can occur in order to give youth a smoother developmental trajectory. It is important for counselors to pay particular attention to the potential for mood disorders, especially where there is trauma and/or significant family system stress and when there is a family history of mood disorders.

Family

As stated earlier in this chapter, it is understood that a family history of mood disorders can contribute to an increased risk of mood disorder vulnerability in children. In addition, researchers at the University of Montreal (2011) found that children with depressed mothers had enlarged amygdalae, the part of the brain that is linked to emotional responses, compared with children who did not have exposure to depressed parents. Thus, it is thought that children who are raised by mothers struggling with depression, in particular, have particular difficulty with having basic needs met and thus develop a heightened sense of reactivity and sensitivity to situations that are unfamiliar. Counselors can help assess and identify familial history of mood disorders and, thus, be proactive and identify the early signs of a mood disorder in children. Of critical importance is early intervention with depressed parents, particularly mothers, in community settings, helping them get treatment and understand the impact of their depression on their children. Enhanced parent training and education about bonding and responding to children's needs while also addressing their needs for treatment can help a parent arrest the negative impact that the mental illness has on themselves and their families.

When the adults in the family struggle, the children are often negatively affected. Counselors can be attuned to histories of trauma among family members, noting symptoms that may have developed or gone untreated after such an event, and can advocate for or provide, where appropriate, preventive psychoeducation about how trauma, loss, death, severe illness, and so forth may affect the family, even over a long period. Often, when parents are prepared for negative potential reactions and if they are aware of the possible effects of traumatic life events, they

Sidebar 6.5 ■ Working With a Mother and Daughter

Imagine you are working as a counselor in private practice. A mother comes to see you because she is concerned about her 10-year-old daughter. She tells you that her daughter has mood swings that are becoming intolerable. One minute she's happy, and the next minute she's sad. Her mother shares with you that she is exasperated with her daughter and just wants you to "fix her." How would you work with the mother to address her concerns? What questions might you ask that would give you more information about family history and the context for your client's concerns? Would you ask to meet with the daughter alone, meet with the mother and daughter together, or both?

■ ■ ■

become more understanding of their experience as well as the need to assist their children proactively to possibly prevent the development of additional decline in emotional or mental health functions. Counselors are particularly well positioned in any work with children and families to reinforce the strengths of the system and help the family develop resilience and coping strategies. For example, counselors can help families improve their communication skills, build stronger interpersonal and familial relationships, and gain an increased understanding and awareness of the signs associated with potential mood disorders versus normative development milestones. Counselors are particularly adept at skills analysis and coaching and can provide vulnerable families with tools to help them weather stressful situations, reshape interfamilial relationships, and support children as they navigate the pitfalls of growth and development. The goal is to help families find strength-enhancing ways to possibly inoculate the children against developing mood disorders that exist, at least in part, in response to environmental factors. This goal is, again, particularly important where there may be a genetic or biological predisposition to such disorders.

School

According to Meadus (2007), mood disorders among children and adolescents are more persistent than previously thought and have numerous negative associated features, including impaired social, academic, and vocational relationships; illicit substance use; and increased risk of suicide. Within the school milieu, school counselors can use the following prevention techniques: (a) help train our youth to become resilient and flexible, as with families in the above section, and help them cope appropriately in variable social settings; (b) provide antibullying programs, education, and support; (c) promote awareness of suicide risk and develop suicide prevention strategies; and (d) ensure a culture of respectful interactions, peer mediation, and valuation of the emotional health of all children. School counselors have unique opportunities to observe children, help them learn life skills, assist them in naming and remembering their strengths when faced with challenges, and help them build solid social networks with peers. Schools must be emotionally safe, not just physically safe, although that is critical as well. Emotional safety in the school environment helps prevent depression, in particular, as children develop a sense of self-worth and accomplishment that can buffer or offset the trials and tribulations of childhood and adolescence that sometimes lead to depression and suicidal ideation or suicide attempts. For students with genetic vulnerabilities, even when depression and symptoms of bipolar disorder are present, having an affirmative educational environment is essential in preventing either further severity or worsening symptoms.

It is of note that behaviors and other signs of depression may differ in children, and school counselors can train teachers and other school personnel to be on alert for symptoms such as irritability and angry outbursts that may be more indicative of depression in children than what is typically seen in adults and understood in the general community. Slowing down a rush to judgment that a child is unruly or "bad," oppositional/defiant, or conduct disordered to examine the possibility of a mental illness such as MDD or bipolar disorder is essential. Also, educating school personnel about the co-occurring nature of depression, bipolar symptoms, ADHD, learning differences, conduct disorders, and oppositional–defiant behavior can lead to better awareness and to the prevention of severity. That is, if the symptoms can be addressed early and with appropriate supports, there may be a better outcome than would be present if this complicated diagnostic picture is misunderstood or disregarded. School counselors should consult with school psychologists and other educational professionals to get a full picture of the whole child and his or her social, peer, educational, and familial context. Also, it is critical to carry out an early and accurate diagnostic review of students at risk for learning and attention disorders, because those disorders have symptoms that can overlap with or co-occur with major mood disorders. School counselors can communicate often with parents regarding behaviors of concern, keep a solid community referral list, and actively offer assistance where warranted. Recognition and identification are essential, as is taking the time to assess the entire situation and not just jumping to what seems like the obvious diagnosis. The school counselor is the key to bringing all stakeholders together for the benefit of the child.

Community

Counselors can also play a significant role when it comes to developing resources in the community. Researchers at the Search Institute (Scales, Benson, Roehlkeppartain, Sullivan, & Mannes, 2001) suggested a number of ways to create strengths-based communities that include not only engaging parents in efforts to support, help, and guide our youth but also incorporating adults from all aspects of the community, such as business owners, spiritual and/or religious representatives, as well as civic leaders. It is this type of proactive community engagement that can help children and youth develop resiliency and coping skills. It also means listening to the input of our children and youth and including them in decision-making processes. A commitment to the active collaboration of the community—such as

Sidebar 6.6 ■ Addressing the Suicidal Ideations of a 10th Grader

Imagine that you were working as a school counselor and a 10th-grade girl shared with you that she was lesbian. She sobs and tells you that all of the kids are making fun of her and teasing her mercilessly. She tells you that she often doesn't want to go to school so that she doesn't have to face the torment and harassment anymore. She admits that sometimes she even wishes she were dead. How would you respond to her? Would you feel compelled to tell her parents that she thinks she is a lesbian? How would you address her thoughts of suicide?

■ ■ ■

schools; congregations; businesses; and youth, human service, and health care organizations—can help create an asset-building culture that contributes fully to young people's healthy development.

Adaptations for Diversity

As described earlier, the diagnostic picture for mood disorders in children and adolescents is complicated. Developmental challenge periods can result in symptoms that mimic symptoms related to a disorder; different human temperaments introduce additional confounding noise into the equation; and childhood and adolescent reactivity to family, school, and peer environments must also factor into a solid diagnostic review. It is also incumbent upon counselors and therapists to become intimately familiar with the racial, gender, ethnic, and other minority status of children and adolescent populations they serve in order to avoid the diagnostic and treatment bias inherent and well documented in these populations. For example, girls are 2 times more likely to be diagnosed with depression than boys. Boys are 3 times more likely to be diagnosed with ADHD than girls (Barkley, 2005). Although genuine gender differences, including but not limited to hormonal and pubertal development, are important considerations, there are also social and environmental concerns as a counselor attempts to develop a clear conceptualization of the potential mood disorder. For example, it is documented that depressed boys may exhibit different symptoms of the disorder than girls: Boys' depression may manifest in less "socially acceptable" or "gender specific" ways (Meadus, 2007).

The fact that racial and ethnic minority children and adolescents are more frequently diagnosed with schizophrenia and CD or ODD has many potential etiological and social factors that must be considered when diagnosing an individual child within his or her context and examining the signs and symptoms potentially indicative of a major mental disorder (NIMH, 2003). Working within systems predisposed to identifying disorders rapidly, as is often required—and often without care to contextual, developmental, and racial/ethnic considerations—is a rich ground for advocacy and education, the areas of community intervention and prevention uniquely suited for the counseling profession.

Issues of sexual minority status may also arise during this developmental time period, particularly around puberty or post-puberty. Youth identifying as gay, lesbian, bisexual, transgender, or queer may be presented for diagnosis and review of "disorder" by parents, faith communities, and schools as the community or systems involved attempt to determine what is "wrong" with the child. We do not yet have solid systems and responses in place to assist sexual minority or questioning youth to explore and determine where they lie on the continuum of sexual expression in ways that are safe, affirmative, and supportive of whatever identification develops for the child. Sexual minority youth are more likely than their heterosexual counterparts to exhibit symptoms of depression and are also more likely to be bullied in school (GLSEN, 2011). They are also more likely than children and adolescents not questioning their sexual orientation or gender identity to attempt or commit suicide (Centers for Disease Control and Prevention, 2011). Given that these risk factors are not inherent in these adolescents or their developing identity and orientation, but rather stem from societal and internalized homoprejudice, it is incumbent on the counseling community to stand at the forefront of this issue and create safe, affirmative systems and spaces for these youth to address these unique differences that are not always seen but certainly are felt. Affirmative assessment processes, bullying prevention programs, and treatment of any mood disruption that occurs with or develops into a diagnosable disorder attributable to environmental stressors must be rooted within services for youth and adolescents who contend with this particular developmental challenge along with all of the other conundrums adolescence has to offer.

Summary

Depression and bipolar disorders are significant and complicated mental health problems among children and adolescents. Mood disorders manifest differently in adolescence and especially in childhood than they do in adulthood. They have been linked to other risk factors, such as suicide, school attrition, substance use, and delinquency, further augmenting the difficulty in accurately diagnosing the problem and in recommending and implementing effective intervention. Current research supports several treatment approaches as being equally successful in remitting depression and other mood disorders. Future research should continue to examine the active ingredients in depression prevention and intervention to improve efficacy as well as further our understanding of depression among children and adolescents. In light of effective medications for treating adult depression, but less effective results with youth, pharmacological research for mood disorders in children and youth is especially recommended.

What is very clear is that depression and other affective problems can have a catastrophic effect on children and adolescents and on those around them. Parents, counselors, teachers, and other school personnel who play primary roles in the lives of children and adolescents must be especially aware of and responsive to the symptoms, causes, and problems associated with depression. Recognizing and responding quickly to depression and to its root causes are especially important in avoiding the potentially devastating effects of this disorder on the young people with whom we live and work.

Useful Websites

American Counseling Association
   www.counseling.org
American Psychological Association
   www.apa.org
American School Counselor Association
   www.schoolcounselor.org
National Association of School Psychologists
   www.nasponline.org
National Institute of Mental Health
   www.nimh.nih.gov
National Youth Network
   www.nationalyouth.com

References

American Psychiatric Association. (2000). *Diagnostic and statistical manual of mental disorders* (4th ed., text rev.). Washington, DC: Author.

American Psychiatric Association, *DSM-5* Development Group. (2013). *Diagnostic and statistical manual of mental disorders* (5th ed.) Retrieved from http://www.dsm5.org/Pages/Default/aspx

Barkley, R. A. (2005). *Taking charge of ADHD: The complete, authoritative guide for parents* (Rev. ed.). New York, NY: Guilford Press.

Bradfield, B. C. (2010). Bipolar mood disorder in children and adolescents: In search of theoretic, therapeutic and diagnostic clarity. *South African Journal of Psychology, 40*, 241–249.

Brent, D. A., & Maalouf, F. T. (2009). Pediatric depression: Is there evidence to improve evidence-based treatments? *The Journal of Child Psychology and Psychiatry, 50*, 143–152.

Breslau, N., Lucia, V. C., & Alvarado, G. F. (2006). Intelligence and other predisposing factors in exposure to trauma and posttraumatic disorder. *Archives of General Psychiatry, 63*, 1238–1245.

Centers for Disease Control and Prevention. (2011). *Sexual identity, sex of sexual contacts and health risk-behaviors among students in grades 9–12.* Retrieved from http://cdc.gov/mmwr/pdf/ss/ss60e0606.pdf

De Santis, J. P., & Ekegren, K. (Eds.). (2003, January–March). Advocating for mental health services for children with depressive disorders. *The Journal for Specialists in Pediatric Nursing, 8*, 38–40.

Faraone, S. V., Glatt, S. J., & Tsuang, M. T. (2003). The genetics of pediatric-onset bipolar disorder. *Biological Psychiatry, 53*, 970–977.

Fava, M., Hwang, I., Rush, A. J., Sampson, N., Walters, E. E., & Kessler, R. C. (2010). The importance of irritability as a symptom of major depressive disorder: Results from the National Comorbidity Survey Replication. *Molecular Psychiatry, 15*, 856–867.

Gay, Lesbian & Straight Education Network. (2011). *2011 National School Climate Survey: LGBT youth face pervasive, but decreasing levels of harassment.* Retrieved from http://www.glsen.org/cgi-bin/iowa/all/news/record/2897.html

Leboyer, M., Paillere-Martinot, H. C., & Bellivier, F. (2005). Age at onset in bipolar affective disorders: A review. *Bipolar Disorders, 2*, 111–118.

McClellan, J., Kowatch, R., & Findling, R. L. (2007). Work Group on Quality Issues. Practice parameter for the assessment and treatment of children and adolescents with bipolar disorder. *Journal of American Academic Child Adolescent Psychiatry, 46*, 107–125.

McWhirter, B. T., & Walters, K. P. (2008). Preventing and treating mood disorders in children and adolescents. In D. Capuzzi & D. Gross (Eds.), *Youth at risk: A prevention resource for counselors, teachers and parents* (5th ed., pp. 127–153). Alexandria, VA: American Counseling Association.

Meadus, R. J. (2007). Adolescents coping with mood disorder: A grounded theory study. *Journal of Psychiatric and Mental Health Nursing, 14*, 209–217.

National Institute of Mental Health. (2003). *Breaking ground and breaking through: The strategic plan for mood disorders research* (U.S. Department of Health and Human Services, National Institutes of Health, Publication No. 0507-B-05). Retrieved from http://www.nimh.nih.gov

Ong, H. S., & Caron, A. (2008). Family-based psychoeducation for children and adolescents with mood disorders. *Journal of Family Studies, 17*, 809–822.

Pfeifer, J. C., Kowatch, R. A., & DelBello, M. P. (2010). Pharmacotherapy of bipolar disorders in children and adolescents: Recent progress. *CNS Drugs, 24*, 575–593.

Sanchez, L., Hagino, O., Weller, E., & Weller, R. (1999). Bipolarity in children. *Psychiatric Clinics of North America, 22*, 629–648.

Scales, P. S., Benson, P. L., Roehlkeppartain, N. R., Sullivan, T. K., & Mannes, M. (2001). The role of the neighborhood and the community in building developmental assets for children and youth: A national study of social norms among American adults. *Journal of Community Psychology, 29*, 703–727.

Soutullo, C. A., Chang, K. D., Díez-Suárez, A., Figueroa-Quintana, A., Escamilla-Canales, I., Rapado-Castro, M., & Ortuno, F. (2005). Bipolar disorder in children and adolescents: International perspective on epidemiology and phenomenology. *Bipolar Disorders, 7*, 497–506.

Steinbuchel, P. H., Wilens, T. E., Adamson, J. J., & Sgambati, S. (2009). Posttraumatic stress disorder and substance abuse disorder in adolescent bipolar disorder. *Bipolar Disorders, 11*, 196–204.

University of Montreal. (2011). Children of depressed mothers have a different brain: MRI scans show their children have an enlarged amygdale. *Science Daily*. Retrieved from http://www.sciencedaily.com/releases/2011/08/110815152041.htm

Weinberg, W. A., & Rehmet, A. (1983). Childhood affective disorder and school problems. In D. P. Cantwell & G. P. Carlson (Eds.), *Affective disorder in childhood and adolescence: An update* (pp. 109–128). Jamaica, NY: Spectrum.

Chapter 7

Stress and Trauma: Coping in Today's Society

Savitri V. Dixon-Saxon and J. Kelly Coker*

In December 2012, a heavily armed young man walked into an elementary school in a small town in Connecticut. He proceeded to shoot 20 children, all between 6 and 7 years old, and six adults before taking his own life. This shocking and devastating event captured the attention of the nation and the world. It sparked many debates about gun control, mental health issues, and school safety. One additional aftermath of this tragedy has been the impact on the children, both those who attended the school where the event occurred and those around the country who may have developed fears and anxiety related to being safe at school. The question arises: How do we help children cope with both everyday stressors and stress brought about by extreme trauma?

There is an increasing interest in the role trauma (extreme stress) and posttraumatic stress play in at-risk behaviors and mental health problems of youth (Berthold, 2000; Kilpatrick & Williams, 1998; Lahad, Shacham, & Niv, 2000; Parson, 1995). The society in which we live is characterized by conflicting social and economic demands, multiple other demands on our time, and an increasingly complex and ever-changing world of work. As a result, coping with stress has become synonymous with modern adult life. What is interesting, however, is that the image of a carefree childhood void of stress and trauma has dominated our cultural view of youth for most of this century. Since the mid-1980s, however, there has been an increasing awareness not only that children and adolescents experience stress and trauma (Bagdi & Pfister, 2006; Dinicola, 1996; Humphrey, 1988; La Greca, Silverman, Vernberg, & Roberts, 2002; McMahon, Grant, Compas, Thurm, & Ey, 2003; Osofsky et al., 2004), but also that in complex fashions yet to be understood, the numerous

---

*The authors wish to acknowledge the work Jane Rheineck and Russell D. Miars did on the fifth edition version of this chapter.

stresses and trauma youth actually do experience are linked to the alarming rise in at-risk behavioral difficulties many youth display (Gottlieb, 1991; K. J. Kim, Conger, Elder, & Lorenz, 2003; Raghavan & Kingston, 2006; Wilburn & Smith, 2005).

Problem Definition

There is no uniformly agreed-upon definition of the stress concept by researchers. Until recently, an additional complication in understanding stress in youth has been that most research has been conducted exclusively with adults (Johnson, 1986; Lazarus, 1991, 1999; Sherr, Bergenstrom, & McCann, 1999). Several authors (Dise-Lewis, 1988; Humphrey, 1988; Kruczek & Salsman, 2006; Sandler, Wolchik, MacKinnon, Ayers, & Roosa, 1997) are quite clear that stress in youth should be regarded as distinct from stress in adults. Kruczek and Salsman reported that a child's age and developmental level impact the response to and recovery from stress and trauma and should be accounted for in both assessment and treatment.

This chapter examines what is currently known about human stress, trauma, and coping processes in general, giving special attention to causes and prevention of stress in youth. The chapter first reviews the predominant ways stress and trauma have been conceptualized over the past three decades and then concentrates on causal factors (the sources of stress and trauma), with consideration of how developmental stages interact with the experience of stress and the coping strategies used by youth when faced with stress and trauma. The chapter next addresses approaches to prevention of stress and trauma from individual, family, school, and community perspectives. It concludes with a brief consideration of stress and trauma from a cultural perspective. In this chapter the term *children* refers to youth preschool to age 10 whereas *adolescents* refers to youth ages 11 to 19. As used here, the term *youth* is inclusive of preschool to age 19.

Perspectives on Stress and Traumatic Stress

The stress concept has historically been conceptualized from three major perspectives: stimulus-oriented views, response-oriented views, and stress as a transaction between person and environment (Johnson, 1986). These three perspectives do not include the special attention that is given in the research literature to trauma and posttraumatic stress. For this reason, trauma and posttraumatic stress are included below as a fourth perspective on the stress concept.

Stimulus-Oriented Views

With the stimulus-oriented perspective, the focus is on stress as a specific stimulus: "Stress is seen as resulting from experiencing any of a number of situations that are noxious or threatening or that place excessive demands on the individual" (Johnson, 1986, p. 16). Research that has defined stress from a life-events perspective (e.g., divorce, death in the family) falls under this view. This perspective, when used alone, is limiting in that it cannot account for why some individuals experience potential stressors negatively while others experience the same stressor as a positive challenge (Johnson, 1986; Undergraff & Taylor, 2000). The ability to cope with stimulus-oriented stressors is a key component in understanding how young people approach stressful events in their lives. A recent study conducted by Abaied and Rudolph (2011) examined maternal influences on youth responses to peer stress. Peer relationships, particularly as young people move into adolescence, become a potential stimulus for experiencing stress. Although interpersonal stress is discussed in more detail later in the chapter, the experience of navigating sometimes complex social relationships can be seen as a stimulus-oriented stressor. Abaied and Rudolph (2011) examined how mothers can mitigate young people's stress experiences related to peer socialization through two dimensions: engagement versus disengagement and effortful versus involuntary responses to stress. Results of correlation and multiple regression analyses indicated that maternal coping strategies do affect how young people approach peer-related stress. To be specific, when mothers promote purposeful engagement when dealing with a stressful situation, they instill a sense in their child that she or he is capable of dealing with stressful peer interactions effectively. Conversely, when mothers suggest that their children deny or avoid peer problems, they foster a maladaptive response to stress (Abaied & Rudolph, 2011). Understanding the potential stimuli that can lead to a stress response (either positive or negative) can be an important part of helping children and adolescents understand how to cope with their stress response.

Response-Oriented Views

Up until the 1960s, stress was almost exclusively defined from a stimulus perspective. Embedded in this framework was an engineering analogy of stress in which an external force created a strain on the object and deformed it in proportion to the pressure of the stressor (Lazarus, 1993b). After several decades of work on the stress concept, Hans Selye (1974, 1993) asserted that stress is the organism's physiological response to external stressors. Selye's (1974, 1993) work popularized a physiological version of the engineering analogy by conceiving stress as having three distinct phases: alarm, resistance, and exhaustion. This sequence was termed the *General Adaptation Syndrome* (GAS) and refers to the "manifestations of stress in the whole body" (Selye, 1974, p. 139).

In the alarm reaction phase, the organism responds with a series of complex biochemical alterations, such as increased breathing and blood sugar release through the discharge of hormones preparing the body for fight or flight (Selye, 1993). Because a state of alarm cannot be maintained continuously, a second phase, the stage of resistance, ensues. If the stressor continues to impinge on the organism, its limited adaptational energy is focused more singularly on further resisting the threat presented by the stressor. Unfortunately, when the organism's adaptational energy is focused on selected stressors in an ongoing fashion, it leaves itself vulnerable to other ensuing stressors (Ivancevich & Matteson, 1980). This biological stress syndrome (Selye, 1974, 1993) is how numerous stress studies have successfully linked various stressors with the onset of psychiatric (Rabkin, 1993) and somatic (Creed, 1993; Holmes & Rahe, 1967; Selye, 1993) disease processes.

The final phase is the stage of exhaustion. Selye (1993) emphasized that the body is limited in the amount of adaptational energy available to withstand stress. Once the adaptational energy has been expended, significant efforts at restoration must follow. If the body cannot engage in replenishment and restore itself to the level of resistance, a phase of burnout (Pines, 1993) may occur. Most adults have had some experience with burnout in terms of their involvement with work, career, or other prolonged life events. We tend to forget, however, that because of the incredible energy that youngsters expend in multiple spheres of activity, they also, by their very developmental nature, are equally vulnerable to burnout (Youngs, 1985).

According to Katz, Sprang, and Cooke (2012), the stress response in children and adolescents is significantly affected by the exhaustion phase outlined in the cycle above. Children and adolescents who have difficulty regulating the body's systems at a time of stress experience *allostatic load*, which is a chronic dysregulation of physiological systems (Katz et al., 2012). This dysregulation represents a physical experience of stress in children and adolescents. A high external stress burden that leads to an allostatic load state has been correlated with several issues, including eating disordered behavior, violence, and adolescent alcohol use. Stressors that have been associated with allostatic load in children might include physical crowding in the home, exposure to excessive noise, poor housing quality, or current or prior episodes of living in poverty. An increase in healthy behaviors, such as increased exercise and eating well, has been shown to reduce allostatic load in children. An interesting finding is that maternal responsiveness also has a positive impact on a young person's ability to better regulate physical systems in the body, similar to findings identified in the study by Abaied and Rudolph (2011).

Stress as a Transaction Between Person and Environment

The view that stress is a transaction between person and environment was most fully developed by Lazarus (Lazarus & Folkman, 1984). Of significance with this perspective are the following: how the person views the stressfulness of the environmental event; whether the event is seen as threatening or nonthreatening, desirable or undesirable, controllable or uncontrollable; and if the person believes coping resources are readily available for dealing with the events. Lazarus and Folkman (1984) offered their definition of stress: "Psychological stress is a particular relationship between the person and the environment that is appraised by the person as taxing or exceeding his or her resources and endangering his or her well-being" (p. 19). The emphasis in this definition is on the psychological processes (cognitive and mediational variables) in the person's experience of stress.

Lazarus has argued that stress should be seen as a subset of emotion (Lazarus, 1993b, 1999). This view is adopted for two reasons. First, knowing that a person is experiencing either "emotions resulting from harms, losses and threats" (anger, anxiety, fear) or "emotions resulting from benefits" (joy, pride) in response to stress is very useful and says a lot more about how a troubled person–environment relationship is being coped with than when the subjective experience of emotion is omitted. As Houston (1987) has noted, "An event cannot be regarded as a stressor without reference to the affective response it elicits" (p. 379). Second, the more striking issue in understanding stress is the person's various coping responses to stressors, not just the body's physiological response and adaptation to stress.

A recent study examined the transactional relationship between depression and stress within the peer domain (Agoston & Rudolph, 2011). The researchers examined two different adaptation to stress responses in a population of adolescents: effortful versus involuntary. When adolescents intentionally strive to address stress with peers in a positive way, they experience fewer maladaptive stress responses. Prior to this research, few studies had examined the bidirectional linkages between depression and responses to stress in adolescents. Results of the correlation and path analyses supported the hypothesis that maladaptive responses to peer stress predict depression and that depression predicts maladaptive responses to peer stress. Some gender differences were found, suggesting that girls experience less depression with more effortful engagement to deal with peer stressors but that depression is a stronger predictor of maladaptive stress responses in boys (Agoston & Rudolph, 2011). The transactional model of stress suggests that paying attention to all components of a stress experience is key in understanding both the causes and impact of stressful experiences.

Causal Factors

It is exceedingly difficult to pinpoint exact causal factors relating stress to certain emotional or behavioral outcomes (Johnson, 1986). Part of the difficulty is that it is now known that the experiences of stress and traumatic stress are determined by personality characteristics and contextual factors (Allen, 1995; Peterson, Kennedy, & Sullivan, 1991) and are compounded even further by the idiosyncratic range of individual response variation around any one given source of stress (Lazarus, 1991, 1993b). This situation is particularly true for children and adolescents as developmental changes interact with stressors to produce varied outcomes in coping responses (Compas & Phares, 1991; Kruczek & Salsman, 2006).

Life-Event Stressors

Life-event stressors have a significant impact on youth, particularly adolescents. Life events are a greater predictor of adolescent depression than depressed mood (Sanchez, Lambert, & Ialongo, 2011). However, it is important to remember that youth's responses to life-event stressors vary by the severity of life events and the biological, social, and environmental circumstances of the individual. Certain life conditions—like poverty, sleep and food deprivation, predispositions for mental illness, levels of self-esteem and self-concept, and an environment of a high-stress family or community—make children more vulnerable to the adverse effects of stress than others (Terzian, Moore, & Nguyen, 2010).

The challenge for practitioners is to determine how significant the life-event stressors are for the individual child. Two validated instruments used to identify stress in children and adolescents are two self-reports: the Perceived Stress Scale, which is used to measure the child's perception of stressful events; and Coddington's Life Events Scale for Adolescents, which is used to identify positive and negative stressful events (Terzian et al., 2010).

Traumatic Stress

According to Cohen and Collens (2012), each of us develops a way of thinking or schemas that include beliefs and expectations about people, ourselves, and the world; as a result of those schemas, we have expectations of how people will behave

Sidebar 7.1 ■ Self-Awareness—Causes of Stress

Think about experiences in your own life where you've experienced a negative stress response. What do you think the causes were? What was the stimulus that led to your stress? What was your physiological response? Finally, what else accompanied your feeling of stress (i.e., other negative or positive emotions, impact on relationships or environment, and so forth)? When working with children and adolescents, it is important to think about all of the mitigating factors that accompany their experience of stress.

■ ■ ■

and what the environment will be like. We are able to accommodate new information to these schemas even if it does not match our schema or expectation. However, certain life events totally undermine our expectations of people and the environment and alter who we are, who other people are to us, or what our environment is like (Cohen & Collens, 2012). These stressful or traumatic events can result in trauma or even posttraumatic stress disorder (PTSD). Some of those events are death, rape, physical violence, war, torture, mental abuse, sexual abuse, and natural disasters. Any one of these experiences can result in trauma or PTSD (Kearney, Wechsler, Kaur, & Lemos-Miller, 2010). The most extreme and disruptive stressors youth face are traumatic events that result from some human action, such as violence, or a natural disaster. The defining characteristics of trauma are that the event is perceived as a potential threat to survival and that on a subjective level the event is experienced as uncontrollable or unpredictable (American Psychiatric Association, 2000; Friedman & Marsella, 1996). Therefore, it becomes imperative that mental health professionals understand and can distinguish the difference between normal developmental coping skills and those that impair the healthy developmental process. Traumatic stress from any of these sources differs from challenging or painful stress in that an acute or chronic posttraumatic stress condition results when normal coping resources are ineffective or depleted (Hobfoll, Dunahoo, & Monnier, 1995).

The key to whether a traumatic event leads to a posttraumatic stress condition is based on a complex matrix of preexisting genetic factors (proneness to anxiety), developmental factors (disruption of attachment), and coping style (resilience) that interact with the following: length of exposure to the traumatic experience; the perceived intensity of the traumatic experience; and posttrauma factors such as quickness of treatment intervention, strength of the person's social support (especially family), and overall coping resources. When extreme or negative levels of these factors converge in one person's experience and coping fails, the clinical syndrome of PTSD is the likely outcome. PTSD can be acute or chronic, and as a diagnosable psychiatric condition it includes symptoms of intrusive reexperiencing (flashbacks), emotional avoidance to avoid the trauma-based memories, hyperarousal (generalized anxiety, insomnia, irritability), internalizing (turning feelings inward), or externalizing (acting out; American Psychiatric Association, 2000; Goodman, Miller, & West-Olatunji, 2012). PTSD requires clinical diagnosis and intervention at the individual and family level, as the condition rarely resolves on its own (Allen, 1995) and may actually induce secondary traumatic stress in spouses, children, and other family members (Steinberg, 1998).

PTSD symptoms may be acute (less than 3 months duration) or chronic (more than 3 months), and for some traumas (war-related, rape) the disorder can occur and/or recur weeks, months, or even years after exposure to the traumatic event (American Psychiatric Association, 2000; Carty, O'Donnell, & Creamer, 2006; Freedy & Donkervoet, 1995; Voelker, 2005). It is common for people with PTSD to have dreams, memories, and physical distress when exposed to the stimulus. Children, in particular, are likely to have dreams that are difficult for them to explain, so they may play in ways to reenact the trauma (Kearney et al., 2010). In addition, they may exhibit problems sleeping and may have separation anxiety (Modrowski, Miller, Howell, & Graham-Bermann, 2012). Young children with limited verbal capabilities are likely to demonstrate fear, aggression, and agitation. The greatest challenge in identifying traumatic stress and PTSD in children, however, is that the

Sidebar 7.2 ■ Case Study: Trauma and Young Children

Sonia is 2-and-a-half years old and witnessed her father beat and shoot her mother. Although her mother survived the gunshot, Sonia was left alone with her bleeding unconscious mother when her father fled from the home, leaving Sonia's mother Julia for dead. Sonia and her siblings had witnessed their mother's abuse at the hands of their father frequently. However, Sonia was the only one around when Julia was shot. Fortunately a neighbor heard the gunshot and saw Sonia's father flee. The neighbor reports that when she arrived at the home, Sonia was standing over her mother, touching her face trying to wake her up. Sonia and her siblings have been living with their maternal grandmother, who is trying to care for the children while she also tends to her own daughter as much as possible. Because the other children are school-aged, Sonia must accompany her grandmother to the hospital to visit her mother. Sonia is always happy to see her mother and she seems happy most of the time, but she screams in the middle of the night, never completely waking up. She never talks about what she saw, and her grandmother is unclear about what Sonia saw or what she understands but doesn't want to ask Sonia too many questions. What support would be appropriate for a child this age?

■ ■ ■

behaviors are so similar to the behaviors common to other disorders like depression, anxiety, and oppositional defiant disorder (Kearney et al., 2010).

Natural Disasters

In addition to causing financial losses, natural disasters affect children's personal growth and development. Some of the potentially devastating costs include missed school; a decrease in academic function; missed social opportunities; and exposure to life stressors such as divorce, domestic violence, and substance abuse (La Greca et al., 2002).

A very recent natural disaster was Superstorm Sandy, which hit the U.S. East Coast in late 2012. This massive storm was responsible for at least 125 deaths in the United States and over $62 billion in damage. It is the second costliest storm to date in the United States, after Hurricane Katrina (Associated Press, 2012). Given how recent this event is to the writing of this chapter, there is little to no research examining the impact on experiences of stress and trauma it had among those affected. We can look, however, to research that has been done examining the impact of serious natural disasters, such as Hurricane Katrina, on experiences of trauma and stress in children and adolescents.

Hurricane Katrina has been identified as the most devastating natural disaster in U.S. history (Weisler, Barbee, & Townsend, 2006), and as such it caused an unprecedented need for mental health care that may take years to measure (Voelker, 2005). A survey conducted by Dr. Ronald Kessler (2006) of the Harvard Medical School has indicated that the prevalence of serious mental health concerns after Hurricane Katrina rose from 6.1% to 11.3%, while moderate to mild mental health problems increased from 9.7% to 19.9%. Factors that set Katrina apart from other natural disasters included the (a) vast expanse of geographic destruction, (b) displacement of thousands of people, and (c) intense civil unrest (Voelker, 2005). In a survey conducted by the Centers for Disease Control and Prevention, approximately 44% of the children victimized by Hurricane Katrina, as reported by their caregivers, had symptoms of new mental health problems that included depression, anxiety, and sleep disturbances (Weisler et al., 2006).

More recent research is beginning to look at a synergistic effect of exposure to natural disasters. Events such as Hurricane Katrina do not always occur as singular events; people who live in the Gulf Coast region of the country can expect exposure to multiple natural disasters in their lifetimes. According to Salloum, Carter, Burch, Garfinkel, and Overstreet (2011), more information is needed about how multiple exposures to traumatic events such as natural disasters can affect children and adolescents' development of posttraumatic stress. These researchers examined the cumulative effect of exposure to Hurricane Katrina, Hurricane Gustav, and community violence on posttraumatic stress and depressive symptoms in school-aged children. The interesting question for research was whether exposure to previous natural disasters and community violence would amplify the impact of exposure to Hurricane Gustav, or if past exposure would supersede any impact Gustav might have had on emotional health.

Salloum and his colleagues (2011) found that prior exposure to natural disasters or community violence did amplify symptoms of PTSD in children exposed to the threat of Hurricane Gustav, but when children had prior exposure to both natural disasters and community violence, this cumulative exposure had a mitigating impact and there was not as high of a PTSD reaction to Gustav exposure. Participants who had no previous exposure to either natural disasters or community violence did not experience significant PTSD symptoms with their exposure to Gustav.

These results highlight the importance of understanding the cumulative effect of exposure to trauma-inducing events on children's overall mental health and well-being. Hurricane Gustav, fortunately, was a near miss and did not have the devastating impact that Hurricane Katrina did just a year earlier. For those children who experienced a PTSD reaction to Gustav, this storm served as a trauma reminder: These children were having an anniversary reaction based on their experiences with Katrina.

There is sufficient evidence that psychological debriefing and psychoeducational programming are beneficial in response to natural disasters (Kruczek & Salsman, 2006). These researchers suggested that the most effective format of intervention with children and adolescents is group work that includes caregivers and teachers. If symptoms of acute stress or PTSD are present, Kruczek and Salsman recommend cognitive–behavioral interventions, either in an individual or group environment, to help them manage their symptoms. As with all levels of intervention, caregivers' involvement in this stage can also facilitate and stabilize adaptive coping skills. In addition, Mohay and Forbes (2009) have suggested five basic principles of providing psychological first aid. These principles are as follows: "(1) promote a sense of safety, (2) promote calming, (3) promote a sense of self and collective efficacy, (4) promote connectiveness and (5) promote hope" (p. 187).

Sidebar 7.3 ■ Self-Awareness After a Disaster

Natural and man-made disasters are an unfortunate reality for many children and adolescents. Imagine you are a counselor working with the American Red Cross in response to a natural disaster that displaced many families and caused many injuries. What do you feel are the primary issues to address with the youngest victims of the disaster? How might you implement Mohay and Forbes's (2009) five basic principles of providing psychological first aid?

■ ■ ■

Home and Family Stress

Home and family are important contexts for understanding stress in children and adolescents and represent a large portion of the types of stressors youth experience (Humphrey, 1988). Numerous studies have identified significant relationships between the extent of parental stress and levels of child distress (Compas & Phares, 1991; Jones & Prinz, 2005; Low & Stocker, 2005; Steinberg, 1998). Discussions of chronic illness, child maltreatment, divorce and marital dissolution, family economic problems, and adolescent–parent conflict are considered to illustrate how home and family stress can be strong sources of stress for many youth.

Chronic Illness

One of the results of today's medical advances is that people, in general, live much longer with chronic illness. Although these advancements certainly have positive benefits, such as improved quality of life for people with chronic illness, it is important to acknowledge the impact a family member's chronic illness has on developing children. When a family member has a chronic illness, that person's illness can become the central focus of a family. As a result, growing children sometimes experience unintended neglect (Vanderwerp, 2011).

Of course, the source of the stress is different depending on the relationship between the chronically ill person and the child. For example, when the family member with the chronic illness is a sibling, the healthy sibling may experience unintended neglect or, at least, perceive that he or she is neglected (Vanderwerp, 2011). When the chronically ill person is a parent, children may isolate themselves and experience such significant stress as a result of worrying about a parent that they, themselves, start to complain of physical symptoms like headaches and other body aches (Sieh, Meijer, Oort, Visser-Meily, & Van der Leij, 2010). Many of these children have the added stress and responsibility of caregiving for their chronically ill parents. It is estimated that 1.3 million youth in the United States are caregivers, making them even more vulnerable to experiencing academic difficulty and school dropout and being socially isolated from their peers. In addition, these children oftentimes have the added fear of being taken away from their parents (Berger, 2012). Of course the experience of chronic illness is moderated by the age of the child, the support of other caregivers and adults, a child's sex, and the child's socioeconomic status.

Child and Family Abuse

Youth maltreatment or child abuse is a significant cause of stress and other physical and emotional health problems. *Maltreatment* is the term used to describe the abusive, threatening, or damaging acts committed against another. Although there is no precise understanding of the prevalence of youth maltreatment, there are estimates that of children in Western countries like the United States, the United Kingdom, Australia, and Canada, 4%–16% experience physical abuse, 5%–10% experience sexual abuse, about 10% experience psychological abuse, and 1%–15% are victims of neglect (Kearney et al., 2010). Regrettably, less than 5% of youth receive official services for these issues (Kearney et al., 2010). Youth with marginalized identities because of race, socioeconomic status, or ethnicity experience maltreatment at the hands of parents, guardians, or caretakers at a

Sidebar 7.4 ■ Case Study: Children, Caregiving, and Stress

As an outpatient therapist, you have been working with 9-year-old Jamal for over a year. Jamal's mother has full-blown AIDS, but she has been reasonably healthy for about the last 6 months. Jamal, however, tells you often that he worries about his mother's health, particularly now that she has to take care of his incarcerated sister's six children, who range in age from 3 to 14. The children were supposed to be in the care of their father, but he is away often trying to work a series of unstable jobs. Jamal does his best to help his mother out as much as possible, but he does not get along with his older nephews who are 12 and 14 because they play really rough with him and sometimes beat him up. Jamal is a very sweet boy and tries really hard to please, but lately he has been complaining of headaches and stomachaches, and his mother informed you that he is not performing as well in school as he has in the past. Considering the profile presented of Jamal, what interventions might help him cope with his current stressors?

■ ■ ■

much higher rate than other groups; in addition, young children under the age of 4 are more likely to be victims than other children. Typically, the stress youth experience from the abuse is not expressed as such but, rather, is expressed through a wide range of posttraumatic-linked emotional and behavior difficulties, such as anger, apathy, delinquency (Scheeringa, Wright, Hunt, & Zeanah, 2006; Stoddard et al., 2006; Widom, 1991), school problems, shame, or eating disorders. Family violence and abuse can also be a cause of stress. Witnessing intimate partner violence at home is a significant source of stress for children; however, social support can certainly serve as a mediator to this and other traumatic experiences (Kearney et al., 2010).

Divorce and Marital Dissolution

It is estimated that about 50% of marriages in the United States end in divorce. However, in recent years there has been a slowdown in the number of couples seeking a divorce, primarily because of factors like the increase of two-income family households, the growing rate of couples who marry later in life, and the economic recession (Milstead, 2012). About 13% of the people in the United States are divorced or separated, and most of those households have children under the age of 18 (Dillman Taylor, Purswell, Lindo, Jayne, & Fernando, 2011). Given the high incidence of divorce, researchers have expanded their concern about the effects of divorce; rather than focusing on divorce as a singular life event readjustment, they now focus on the chronic effects of divorce on children's mental, emotional, social, and academic development (Houseknecht & Hango, 2006; Kalter, 1987; McMahon et al., 2003; Wertlieb, 1991). The antecedents (emotional conflict and diminished support) and aftermath of divorce are now considered as more inclusive aspects of the actual stress youth experience from marital dissolution (Arnold & Carnahan, 1990). These researchers have also summarized a number of studies that showed an interaction between sex, age, time of divorce in the youth's life, and the stress of readjustment. In general, boys appear to experience the stress of divorce more intensely at the elementary level, whereas girls at this age fare about as well as those in intact families. Later, however, adolescent girls of divorcing parents show significantly increasing problems with self-esteem and, later still, in heterosexual relationships—which subsequently affects their parenting styles and increases their children's stress levels (Nair & Murray, 2005). Much of the research about divorce and its impact on youth describes the social, psychological, and academic difficulties these youth experience (H. Kim, 2011); however, responses vary by family, and children from homes with high conflict prior to divorce often improve in these areas after a divorce. Overall, one of the better ways to understand divorce as a source of stress for youth is to recognize the significant loss/change in access to parents the experience usually represents. Diminished access to parents can significantly reduce the felt social support youth receive from parents at times when they may critically need it. Oftentimes, parents in the midst of adjusting to changes in their financial resources, changes in their social relationships, and the resulting emotional distress and changes in responsibility are not aware of the long-term impact on youth (Moses, 2013). It is only when parents are free from the trauma themselves that they can provide a positive influence on their children's adjustment to divorce (Taylor, 2004). As noted further in the section on prevention approaches, for a variety of life events and chronic stressors, social support plays a critical role in buffering the negative effects of stress (Gottlieb & Wagner, 1991; Taylor, 2004).

Economic and Occupational Stress

No discussion of home and family stress is complete without mentioning the chronic and often devastating effects of economic stress in the family (Committee for Economic Development, 2002; McMahon et al., 2003).

Economic Stress

According to the National Center for Children in Poverty, about 39% of children in the United States live in poverty (National Center for Children in Poverty, 2012). The family stress model asserts that the parents' or caregivers' experience of economic stress, as well as the behaviors and attitudes that result from that stress, impacts the emotional health of children (Conger et al., 2002). According to the family economic stress model, parenting practices, financial pressure, and parents' and adults' responses all influence the impact economic stress has on children's stress and mental health (Solantaus, Leinonen, & Punamäki, 2004). Conger et al. (2002) maintained the same assertion, that the impact of poverty and economic hardship on children is reflective of the emotional and behavioral responses to poverty and economic hardship of parents.

Sidebar 7.5 ■ Case Study: Intersecting Stress Factors

Your 13-year-old niece is visiting you and your family for a weekend and you notice that the sweet little girl you have always known has become this sulking, sullen, distant person. Your attempts to engage her are met with one-word responses and very little eye contact. If you did not recognize the people who dropped her off as your own sister and brother-in-law, you would think a perfect stranger was in your house. You are aware that her parents have been having financial difficulties and your niece, who was a competitive gymnast, has had to suspend her gymnastics training. She had been training at the same gym for 4 hours every day since she was 5, and many of her friends were also gymnasts. As an informed counselor or therapist, what recommendations would you make to her parents about how to support Olivia right now?

■ ■ ■

Occupational Stress

In addition to economic stress, parents' work can also result in occupational stress. Occupational stress in adults has been associated with a number of health and psychological adjustment variables (Ahola et al., 2006; Holt, 1993; Wang, 2006) that contribute to the overall level of stress in the family. The dual roles of career and parent—especially for women, but increasingly for men as well (Zunker, 2002)—create stress in the form of daily hassles, such as child care arrangements, and strain in the parenting role. Regardless of a parent's occupation, suffering a job loss, undergoing a career change, and being a displaced worker are all stresses deriving from economic change and uncertainty and from the stress inherent in the rapid change to a technology and service-based economy (Zunker, 2002).

Military Families

Youth whose parents serve in the military also experience stress associated with deployments, extended trainings, and family relocation. Over 1.2 million school-aged children are involved in relocating military families each year. Oftentimes these children are in homes where there is little or no extended family support, and during deployments, children are often affected by caregiver stress of the non-military family member. Another stressor military families experience is reintegration of a deployed parent after the deployment is over. This reintegration results in significant changes, and sometimes loss, for children of military parents because family roles change and the non-military parent or caregiver may shift significant time and attention to the returning partner (Lowe, Adams, Browne, & Hinkle, 2012).

Homelessness

At the time of this publication, families in the United States are still experiencing the devastating effects of a serious economic recession. According to Isaacs and Lovell (2010), one in nine children, about 8.1 million, have an unemployed parent. In addition, it is estimated that there are 1.7 million homeless youth in America (National Coalition for the Homeless, 2008). Homeless youth have disproportionately high rates of exposure to at least one form of victimization. This increased rate, coupled with a higher incidence of previous abuse or victimization among this group, creates a condition whereby trauma incidents and related PTSD symptoms are perpetuated (Bender, Ferguson, Thompson, Komlo, & Pollio, 2010). In a study of both trauma experiences and incidences of PTSD among a sample of homeless youth in three cities, Bender and her colleagues found that 57% of the youth surveyed had experienced at least one trauma event, and 24% met criteria for PTSD as laid out in the *Diagnostic and Statistical Manual of Mental Disorders* (4th ed.; American Psychiatric Association, 1994). This number is significantly higher than what was found in a sample of non-homeless youth who had experienced a trauma event (15%; Bender et al., 2010). Greater inter-city transience (youth who are more likely to be "on the move") was also correlated with higher incidence rates of trauma events and PTSD. Implications of this study include the need for increased resources and referral sources for addressing trauma among homeless youth. We also suggest that homeless youth who frequent shelters or agencies should be routinely screened and subsequently treated for PTSD.

School Stress

All aspects of the school experience challenge youth to adapt to the stresses of the educational process. Sears and Milburn (1990, p. 225) listed 25 common school-age stressors. These stressors include anxiety about going to school, changing schools, being competitive (including fear of failure and fear of success), experiencing conflict with teachers, failing an exam, worrying about taking tests, and enduring peer teasing. Anxiety can also be elevated when children fear for their safety at school, either because of threats related to bullying or concerns about tragic events such as the Sandy Hook and Columbine shootings occurring at their schools.

Positive Assets

Childhood in general and the school experience specifically seem to have grown in complexity and potential challenges. According to Byrne, Thomas, Burchell, Olive, and Mirabito (2011), school problems are one of the most consistent causes of childhood stress. School problems are such a central part of experiences of almost all youth that a positive school experience has been associated with the development of resiliency and positive development assets (Search Institute, 2003). The Search Institute has conducted numerous studies examining factors that contribute to positive mental health and social developmental among children and adolescents. The 40 developmental assets they have identified include both external assets, such as having a caring school environment and having parents involved in schooling, and internal assets, such as having a commitment to learning (including achievement motivation), feeling a bond with the school, and doing homework (Search Institute, 2003).

Negative Assets

Conversely, a lack of engagement in school, a lack of perceived support in the school environment, and a lack of parent involvement in school activities are all potential contributors to increased problem behaviors, depression, and stress (Search Institute, 2003).

Sexual Identity/Gender Expression

Although supportive peer relationships assist in minimizing stress-related responses for all youth, they appear to be particularly important for sexual minorities (Diamond & Lucas, 2004).

Cox and her colleagues examined how young lesbian, gay, and bisexual (LGB) youth deal with coming out as affected by the social stress model (Cox, Dewaele, Van Houtte, & Vincke, 2011). The social minority theory suggests that people from more stigmatized categories experience additional stress and negative life events. One stress-inducing dichotomy specific to LGB youth is coming out or not coming out. Disclosure of sexual orientation to family members is accompanied by crisis (although this is often temporary). Not coming out and continued concealment of sexual orientation is often accompanied by a sense of isolation and lack of social support. Both decisions, therefore, can result in continued distress.

Cox et al. (2011) measured the coming-out experience among LGB adolescents as it related to their experience of positive growth and subsequent learning, referred to as "stress-related growth" in the study. Adolescents who established a connection with a local LGB community experienced more stress-related growth than adolescents who experienced support from parents during the coming-out process. Although the coming-out process was still stressful for these adolescents, the enhanced support they received provided them with more opportunities for learning and growth rather than increasing their levels of depression and anxiety (Cox et al., 2011).

Gender Differences

According to Sontag and Graber (2010), there are gender differences in stress and coping that either emerge or are noticeable in adolescence. Although both groups experience an increase in interpersonal stress between preadolescence and adolescence, girls tend to experience greater levels of stress than boys. Girls tend to be more relational and dependent on interpersonal relationships; thus, perceived failures or challenges in those relationships result in increases in anxiety and depression. By the same token, girls are more likely to seek social support as a coping strategy to deal with stress.

Gender socialization has emerged as a significant variable in the experience of stress in youth (Burton, Stice, & Seeley, 2004; Gore & Colten, 1991; Tolin & Foa, 2006). Some of the conclusions emerging from the literature in this area are extremely relevant to our understanding of the sources of stress in youth, particularly in older adolescents. For example, Peterson et al. (1991) concluded from a number of studies that although in early adolescence there is only one gender divergence (for body image, with girls showing a decline), by late adolescence there is marked gender divergence across all measures of self and negative affect, with girls becoming markedly more depressed as adolescence proceeds. The available evidence suggests that girls "amplify" negative moods as a form of coping with developmental stressors, whereas boys are "more likely to distract themselves from a depressed mood" (Peterson et al., 1991, p. 105). Thus, girls' coping responses to stress change along gender lines during adolescence (suggesting they become more vulnerable to various stressors), but boys' coping responses appear to remain the same. Paradoxically, girls' coping responses to developmental stress in adolescence may set a lifelong pattern of coping with stress with depressive affect. In a similar manner, the pattern of boys' coping may be protective for gender-based functioning in instrumental and achievement spheres, but it may also be quite maladaptive for future interpersonal relationships requiring emotional intimacy (Peterson et al., 1991).

Interpersonal Stress

Interpersonal relationships increasingly become a source of stress for youth as they progress from childhood to early adolescence and through late adolescence. This finding appears to be true for both girls and boys, but adolescent girls tend to demonstrate greater interpersonal sensitivity and, consequently, greater interpersonal stress than boys (Rizzo, Daley, & Gunderson, 2006). Furthermore, Compas and Wagner (1991) noted that when stressful life events occur in adolescents' lives, they are likely to be "directly related to others in their social networks, especially their parents" (p. 75). In a study that directly examined adolescent–parent conflict, Smetana, Yau, Restrepo, and Braeges (1991) found that conflict, although stressful, provides a context for debates over the extent of adolescents' developing autonomy and thus serves an adaptive function. However, when the interaction style between parent and adolescent is negative (i.e., devaluing or judging), adolescent development is inhibited (causing further intrapersonal stress and interpersonal conflict). Another interesting significant finding was that adolescent–parent conflict is greater in married than divorced families, and children and adolescents who have had to deal with the stress of parental divorce may actually increase their coping competence and resilience to future life stress (Smetana et al., 1991). Finally, Compas and Wagner (1991) noted that interpersonal stress shows a reliable developmental variation: In junior high, negative family interaction is the predominant source of interpersonal stress, whereas by senior high conformity and concerns about acceptance by the peer group are the dominant interpersonal stressors. Stress arising from dependency on the peer group subsides by later adolescence, and with entry into college, academic events become the predominant source of stress.

Approaches to Prevention

Both primary and secondary prevention strategies are important in reducing stress in youth. Primary prevention consists of attempts to minimize youth's vulnerability to stress or to actually prevent its occurrence, whereas secondary prevention consists of teaching vulnerable youth the therapeutic coping skills they need to know (Lazarus, 1991). Tertiary prevention consists of clinical treatment of stress and post-traumatic stress after the damage has occurred; although such tertiary prevention is not actually preventive in an absolute sense, such interventions can prevent the exacerbation of traumatic stress as well as lessen the secondary traumatic stress experienced by family members of the traumatized individual (Steinberg, 1998).

Because so many stressors of youth (especially in children) are outside of their control and related to situations with parents, other family members, teachers, or socioeconomic conditions (Ryan-Wenger, 1992; Salmon & Bryant, 2002), it is particularly relevant to approach the prevention of stress in youth from a systemic perspective. At the same time, many life and traumatic stressors are unavoidable for youth or stem from normal developmental challenges. In this overview of approaches to prevention in the individual, family, school, and community, consideration is given to possible systemic prevention of stress as well as various coping and protective factors that appear to buffer the effects of stress and trauma in youth.

Individual

As already noted, secondary prevention of stress consists of teaching therapeutic stress and coping skills to the individual in hopes that the negative effects of stress will not escalate. This skills education may be done either in a remedial fashion once the need for stress reduction has been identified or more broadly and in advance through coping skills training (Elias, 1989; Sandler et al., 1997). With respect to coping, researchers have identified conceptual frameworks that relate to the present discussion of coping effectiveness in the individual as a preventive measure against stress (Carlson & Dalenberg, 2000; Ebata & Moos, 1991). The approach/avoidance coping model (Lazarus & Folkman, 1984) distinguishes between active approach-oriented coping (toward threat) versus passive or avoidance-oriented coping (away from threat). Approach coping includes efforts to change ways of thinking about a problem (stressor) as well as behavioral attempts to resolve or address the problem. Avoidant coping includes cognitive attempts to deny or minimize threat and behavioral attempts to avoid or get away from the problem. Research has shown that adolescents who use more approach coping than avoidance coping are better adjusted and less distressed (Ebata & Moos, 1991). Furthermore, Ebata and Moos (1991) concluded that adolescents who show a pattern of avoidance coping may be at greater risk for poorer adjustment to subsequent life stressors and crises. Through coping skills training, adolescents can be shown the positive value of approach coping and be encouraged to engage in approach coping behavior when faced with life events and developmental stressors.

An additional way to think about stress prevention for the individual from a coping perspective is highlighted by the problem-focused/emotion-focused distinction (Lazarus, 1993a, 1999). In this framework, coping efforts can be focused on modifying the stressor itself (problem-focused coping) or on attempts to regulate the emotional responses that accompany the stressor (emotion-focused coping). Ebata and Moos (1991) reported research that suggests that adolescents who used more problem-focused coping with interpersonal stressors (i.e., talking with the other person) reported fewer stressful emotional and behavioral reactions than those who used emotion-focused strategies, such as ignoring the situation or yelling at the other person. Ebata and Moos (1991) summarized several studies that examined the relationship between family and peer support, active coping strategies, and substance use in adolescents. In general, adolescents who used active behavioral and cognitive coping and sought adult support showed less substance use, whereas those adolescents who relied more on peers and acting out to cope showed more substance use (Ebata & Moos, 1991). Other authors (e.g., Gottlieb, 1991; Hendron, 1990) have also noted that attachment, support, and guidance from at least one adult figure (teacher, coach, parent, school counselor) in an adolescent's life can buffer the effects of stress and facilitate approach and problem-focused coping.

Family

A direct way in which the family plays a role in the prevention of stress in youth is through the family's function as an informal social support network (Sandler et al., 1997; Willis, 1987). This idea has also been advanced for posttraumatic stress reactions (Dinicola, 1996). Although the caregivers of traumatized youth may also be at risk for developing secondary traumatic stress reactions (Steinberg, 1998), research still indicates that family support may be the most important buffer in mitigating the effect of trauma (Gaffney, 2006; Wasserstein & La Greca, 1998), whereas the absence of family support can have a detrimental effect on traumatized youth. Dimensions of family support that appear to make a real difference in buffering the negative effects of stress are as follows: esteem support (e.g., emotional and confidant support), informational support (e.g., problem-solving steps), motivational support (e.g., encouragement), and instrumental support (e.g., material aid such as money). In contrast, one of the reasons child abuse is so likely to have posttraumatic stress features is that the various forms of family support are so lacking in the abusive family. Other family factors that appear to be protective of stress in youth were noted by Kimchi and Schaffner (1990) and include such dimensions as adequate rule setting and structure, family cohesion, lower parental conflicts, open communication, warmth toward the child, and patience in parenting style. As noted earlier, the family can be a powerful source of stress in youth; likewise, it can be a powerful buffer to stress when functioning effectively.

School

Gottlieb (1991) emphasized the benefits of social support interventions. Because inclusion, acceptance, and approval from one's peer group are so important in adolescence, peer counseling programs in schools can materially increase the social support adolescents feel. Humphrey (1988) also suggested that stress from academic competition needs to be offset by an increased emphasis on cooperative learning experiences. With such added peer/social support, the stressful aspects of school and the challenges of developmental changes can be minimized.

Klingman (2001) also developed a five-step approach to school-based intervention for large-scale traumatic events. The first step, *anticipatory guidance*, is to prepare schools for a large-scale event prior to any event occurring. This process involves developing disaster plans and emergency procedures and collaborating with community agencies. The second step, *primary preventive interventions*, includes programs integrated into schools that have already experienced large-scale events. Some of these programs include psychological debriefing and psychoeducational services. *Early indicated preventive interventions* describes the third step. Interventions at this level may involve such activities as mass screenings to identify those children who are exhibiting acute stress symptoms. Those identified in the third step then move to the fourth step: *indicated prevention programming*. Interventions at the fourth step involve providing the identified students with counseling in order to explore their traumatic events, to begin developing coping skills, and to assist in preventing PTSD. The final step, *tertiary preventive interventions*, consists of programs designed to prevent relapse for those students who already have PTSD.

School personnel can be especially helpful because the schools are often the first point of contact for children. They can be instrumental in identifying students who demonstrate impairments in multiple areas (e.g., social, family, and academics) and collaborate with appropriate outside agencies. Teachers, in particular, are often the frontline helpers in students' lives. Although counselors and psychologists often have special training to address issues of trauma and crisis among school children, teachers are sometimes lacking in skills related to responding to experiences of traumatic stress and trauma. Gelkopf and Berger (2009) tested a classroom-based stress prevention model called ERASE-Stress on school-aged youth in the Middle East. Their goal was to test the efficacy of a teacher-led stress prevention program with children and adolescents who were currently not experiencing symptoms of trauma-related stress but who were living in areas where violence and terrorism did exist and occur. ERASE-Stress is a 12-session psychoeducational program aimed at reducing and preventing posttraumatic stress reactions. The focus is more on resilience than on coping strategies. Gelkopf and Berger randomly assigned seventh- and eighth-grade classes of homeroom teachers who were trained in delivering the program. Students in the experimental group received all 12 sessions delivered by their homeroom teacher, and the control classroom received no intervention. All subjects completed questionnaires designed to measure their exposure to traumatic events, symptoms of PTSD, somatic complaints, and levels of depression. All instruments were administered pre- and postintervention. Results indicated that the ERASE-Stress program was effective in reducing stress-related symptoms among seventh- and eighth-grade students exposed to varying levels of terrorism (Gelkopf & Berger, 2009).

Another ancillary finding of this study was that the teachers, themselves, also seemed to benefit from receiving training in the program and delivering the program. Teachers who live in areas exposed to violence are likely to develop similar trauma-related symptoms of stress, anxiety, and depression. The involvement in a stress-reduction program for students provided the teachers with an opportunity to develop their own strategies for reducing trauma-related stress.

Community

Mental health professions in community agencies and private practice settings also provide prevention and intervention services to children and their families related to trauma and stress. Unfortunately, children and adolescents are subject to exposure to potentially traumatic events at a rate of about 60% (Berkowitz, Stover, & Marans, 2011). Community-based mental health providers can work with children, adolescents, and their families to mitigate the effects of maltreatment, victimization, injury, and other traumatic events. Berkowitz and his colleagues described a secondary prevention program called the Child and Family Traumatic Stress Intervention (CFTSI) for use with children and their family members who have been exposed to or directly experienced a traumatic event (Berkowitz et al., 2011). The CFTSI is a four-session intervention designed to prevent the development of chronic PTSD after exposure to a traumatic event. Across the four sessions, the mental health provider meets with the caregiver alone, the child alone, and the caregiver and child together. Both caregiver and child complete instruments designed to measure PTSD symptoms, mood, and trauma history. The program includes a combination of teaching relaxation techniques, providing psychoeducation about responses to trauma, normalizing and acknowledging feelings associated with traumatic events, and teaching and practicing coping strategies.

In an examination of the CFTSI's efficacy, Berkowitz and his colleagues found that children who received the program were 65% less likely to develop symptoms of PTSD than those children who did not. In addition, participants in the program were significantly less likely to experience avoidance or to reexperience the traumatic event.

Community-based mental health providers who are equipped with empirically validated prevention and intervention strategies are able to support children and adolescents who are exposed to traumatic events and are at risk for experiencing PTSD and other trauma- and stress-related symptoms.

Clearly, violence and exposure to violence is a reality many children live with. The stress associated with violence in the schools can be another important target of community prevention. The threat of violence in schools affects nearly all students, and the fear that results can inhibit a sense of industry, achievement, and self-confidence (Christie & Toomey, 1990). Furthermore, posttraumatic reactions and PTSD are likely for those in immediate proximity to a violent crime at school or a school shooting. Given that schools are embedded in the larger community, the stress of violence must be prevented by community-based programs. Because much of the violence in schools may be related to the problems of drugs and gangs in and around schools (in the inner city and suburbs alike), school–community prevention strategies that address these issues reduce an aspect of chronic stress in youth.

In addition, the community can play a preventive role in reducing stress in youth by publicly supporting the continuing efforts of schools to integrate psychosocial education and other at-risk intervention programs into the schools (see Elias, 1989). McWhirter, McWhirter, McWhirter, and McWhirter (1994) identified "five Cs of competency" that distinguish high- and low-risk youth: *critical* school (academic) competencies; *concept* of self and self-esteem; *communication* with others; *coping* ability; and *control* over decision making, delay of gratification, and purpose in life. Adults in the community can help prevent stress in youth by teaching and valuing these coping competencies that are so necessary to deal with a rapidly changing world.

Adaptations for Diversity

Considering stress, traumatic stress, and coping from an ethnocultural perspective is the most recent development in the stress field (deVries, 1996; Marsella, Friedman, Gerrity, & Scurfield, 1996; Nader, Dubrow, & Stamm, 1999). Cross-cultural applicability is an important question and begins with whether the stress concept (including posttraumatic stress) validly applies to children, adolescents, and adults from other cultures (deVries, 1996). On the basis of the available research, Marsella et al. (1996) concluded that PTSD is a valid and clinically meaningful diagnosis in non-Western cultures. These authors cautioned, however, that in most cases there are culture-specific responses to trauma not captured in the universal aspects of the diagnosis. In a similar manner, deVries (1996) and Perren-Klinger (2000) supported the concept that traumatic stress is valid cross-culturally, but they added that a person's unique culture or ethnic subculture may offer protective responses to stress that are integrated into the culture's existing framework for handling problems and illnesses, including stress/traumatic stress.

From the same perspective, Gonzales and Kim (1997) indicated that the available literature on stress, coping, and the overall mental health of youth also requires specific consideration of cultural factors. Hispanic and African American children and adolescents appear to be at an increased risk for PTSD and are less likely to show a decrease in symptoms over time (Kruczek & Salsman, 2006). Poverty and social oppression, especially in urban environments, are likely to exacerbate the risk of traumatic events that may lead to PTSD (Kruczek & Salsman, 2006). In addition to all the life stress and coping adaptation concepts outlined in the literature, working with ethnic minority youth requires consideration of their "cultural ecology," which includes the stress-related variables of socioeconomic status, neighborhood context, migration/acculturation, and ethnic/racial discrimination.

Sidebar 7.6 ■ Self-Awareness—School and Community Approaches to Prevention

Consider the setting in which you work. If you are a school-based provider, what are specific stress prevention efforts you see in place at your school? What are the primary causes of stress among students, and what is needed to address these causes? If you are a community-based provider, what does your agency or organization do to prevent stress among your child and adolescent clients? What are additional actions that could be taken to enhance efforts to address stress among this population?

■ ■ ■

Summary

In this chapter, stress has been discussed from three perspectives: a stimulus-oriented view, response-oriented view, and person–environment transaction view. In addition, trauma and posttraumatic stress are considered to be examples of extreme stress that significantly challenge one's ability to cope. Recent research and theory emphasize the person–environment transactional model in which both the perception of stress and coping responses to stress play an active role in the stress phenomenon (including traumatic stress). Only since the mid-1980s has research focused specifically on stress and coping in youth, and only in the past two decades has a fuller appreciation of trauma and posttraumatic stress in youth, especially ethnocultural considerations, emerged in the literature. Causal factors for stress and trauma in youth are multiple and varied and are complexly interwoven with the developmental challenges of childhood and adolescence. Life events, daily hassles, traumatic stress, family stress, child abuse, divorce, economic factors, school stress, and developmental challenges are all causal factors for stress in youth. This chapter has considered approaches to prevention across individual, family, school, and community from a larger systems perspective as well as from individual coping skills and social support factors that are preventive of stress in youth. Important ethnocultural factors have been highlighted as they relate to the cross-cultural validity of posttraumatic stress and stress and coping in ethnic minority youth.

Useful Websites

American Association of Caregiving Youth
    www.aacy.org
American School Counselor Association
    www.schoolcounselor.org
National Center for Children in Poverty
    www.nccp.org
National Child Traumatic Stress Network
    www.nctsn.org
Sesame Street Hurricane Toolkit
    www.sesamestreet.org/parents/topicsandactivities/toolkits/hurricane
Stress Free Kids
    www.stressfreekids.com

References

Abaied, J. L., & Rudolph, K. D. (2011). Maternal influences on youth responses to peer stress. *Developmental Psychology, 47*, 1776–1785.

Agoston, A. M., & Rudolph, K. D. (2011). Transactional associations between youths' responses to peer stress and depression: The moderating roles of sex and stress exposure. *Journal of Abnormal Child Psychology, 39*, 159–171.

Ahola, K., Honkonen, T., Kivimäki, M., Virtanen, M., Isometsä, E., Aromaa, A., & Lönnqvist, J. (2006). Contribution of burnout to the association between job strain and depression: The health 2000 study. *Journal of Occupational & Environmental Medicine, 48*, 1023–1030.

Allen, J. G. (1995). *Coping with trauma: A guide to self-understanding.* Washington, DC: American Psychiatric Press.

American Psychiatric Association. (1994). *Diagnostic and statistical manual of mental disorders* (4th ed.). Washington, DC: Author.

American Psychiatric Association. (2000). *Diagnostic and statistical manual of mental disorders* (4th ed., text rev.). Washington, DC: Author.

Arnold, L. E., & Carnahan, J. A. (1990). Child divorce stress. In L. E. Arnold (Ed.), *Childhood stress* (pp. 373–403). New York, NY: Wiley.

Associated Press. (2012). Superstorm Sandy death damage and magnitude: What we know one month later. *Huffington Post Online.* Retrieved from http://www.huffingtonpost.com/2012/11/29/superstorm-hurricane-sandy-deaths-2012_n_2209217.html

Bagdi, A., & Pfister, I. K. (2006). Childhood stressors and coping actions: A comparison of children and parents' perspectives. *Child & Youth Care Forum, 35,* 21–40.

Bender, K., Ferguson, K., Thompson, S., Komlo, C., & Pollio, D. (2010). Factors associated with trauma and posttraumatic stress disorder among homeless youth in three U.S. cities: The importance of transience. *Journal of Traumatic Stress, 23,* 161–168.

Berger, D. (2012, May). *Help for a "hidden population" of caregiving kids.* Retrieved from http://www.cnn.com/2012/05/17/health/cnnheroes-siskowski-youth-caregivers/index.html

Berkowitz, S. J., Stover, C. S., & Marans, S. R. (2011). The child and family traumatic stress intervention: Secondary prevention for youth at risk of developing PTSD. *Journal of Child Psychology and Psychiatry, 52,* 676–685.

Berthold, S. M. (2000). War traumas and community violence: Psychological, behavioral, and academic outcomes among Khmer. *Journal of Multicultural Social Work, 8,* 15–46.

Burton, E., Stice, E., & Seeley, J. R. (2004). A prospective test of the stress-buffering model of depression in adolescent girls: No support once again. *Journal of Consulting & Clinical Psychology, 72,* 689–697.

Byrne, D. G., Thomas, K. A., Burchell, J. L., Olive, L. S., & Mirabito, N. S. (2011). Stressor experience in primary school-aged children: Development of a scale to assess profiles of exposure and effects on psychological well-being. *International Journal of Stress Management, 18,* 88–111.

Carlson, E. B., & Dalenberg, C. J. (2000). A conceptual framework for the impact of traumatic experiences. *Trauma, Violence & Abuse, 1,* 4–29.

Carty, J., O'Donnell, M. L., & Creamer, M. (2006). Delayed-onset PTSD: A prospective study of injury survivors. *Journal of Affective Disorders, 90,* 257–261.

Christie, D. J., & Toomey, B. G. (1990). The stress of violence: School, community, and world. In L. E. Arnold (Ed.), *Childhood stress* (pp. 297–323). New York, NY: Wiley.

Cohen, K., & Collens, P. (2012). The impact of trauma work on trauma workers: A metasynthesis on vicarious trauma and vicarious posttraumatic growth. *Psychological Trauma: Theory, Research, Practice, and Policy.* Advance online publication. doi:10.1037/a0030388

Committee for Economic Development. (2002). *Preschool for all: Investing in a productive and just society.* New York, NY: Author.

Compas, B. E., & Phares, V. (1991). Stress during childhood and adolescence: Sources of risk and vulnerability. In E. M. Cummings, A. L. Greene, & K. H. Karraker (Eds.), *Life-span developmental psychology: Perspectives on stress and coping* (pp. 111–129). Hillsdale, NJ: Erlbaum.

Compas, B. E., & Wagner, B. M. (1991). Psychosocial stress during adolescence: Intrapersonal and interpersonal processes. In M. E. Colten & S. Gore (Eds.), *Adolescent stress: Causes and consequences* (pp. 67–85). New York, NY: Aldine de Gruyter.

Conger, R. D., Wallace, L., Sun, Y., Simons, R. L., McLoyd, V. C., & Brody, G. H. (2002). Economic pressure in African American families: A replication and extension of the family stress model. *Developmental Psychology, 38,* 179–193. doi:10.1037/0012-1649.38.2.179

Cox, N., Dewaele, A., Van Houtte, M., & Vincke, J. (2011). Stress-related growth, coming out, and internalized homonegativity in lesbian, gay, and bisexual youth: An examination of stress-related growth within the minority stress model. *Journal of Homosexuality, 58,* 117–137.

Creed, F. (1993). Stress and psychosomatic disorders. In L. Goldberger & S. Breznitz (Eds.), *Handbook of stress: Theoretical and clinical aspects* (pp. 496–510). New York, NY: Free Press.

deVries, M. W. (1996). Trauma in cultural perspective. In B. A. van der Kolk, A. C. McFarlane, & L. Weissaeth (Eds.), *Traumatic stress: The effects of overwhelming experience on mind, body, and society* (pp. 398–413). New York, NY: Guilford Press.

Diamond, L. M., & Lucas, S. (2004). Sexual-minority and heterosexual youths' peer relationships: Experiences, expectations, and implications for well-being. *Journal of Research on Adolescence, 14*, 313–340.

Dillman Taylor, D., Purswell, K., Lindo, N., Jayne, K., & Fernando, D. (2011). The impact of child parent relationship therapy on child behavior and parent–child relationships: An examination of parental divorce. *International Journal of Play Therapy, 20*, 124–137. doi:10.1037/a0024469

Dinicola, V. F. (1996). Ethnocultural aspects of PTSD and related disorders among children and adolescents. In A. J. Marsella, M. J. Friedman, E. T. Gerrity, & R. M. Scurfield (Eds.), *Ethnocultural aspects of posttraumatic stress disorder* (pp. 389–414). Washington, DC: American Psychological Association.

Dise-Lewis, J. E. (1988). The life events coping inventory: An assessment of stress in children. *Psychosomatic Medicine, 50*, 484–489.

Ebata, A. T., & Moos, R. H. (1991). Coping and adjustment in distressed and healthy adolescents. *Journal of Applied Developmental Psychology, 12*, 33–54.

Elias, M. J. (1989). Schools as a source of stress to children: An analysis of causal and ameliorative influences. *Journal of School Psychology, 27*, 393–407.

Freedy, J. R., & Donkervoet, J. C. (1995). Traumatic stress: An overview of the field. In J. R. Freedy & S. E. Hobfoll (Eds.), *Traumatic stress: From theory to practice* (pp. 3–28). New York, NY: Plenum.

Friedman, M. J., & Marsella, A. J. (1996). Posttraumatic stress disorder: An overview of the concept. In A. J. Marsella, M. J. Friedman, E. T. Gerrity, & R. M. Scurfield (Eds.), *Ethnocultural aspects of posttraumatic stress disorder: Issues, research, and clinical applications* (pp. 11–32). Washington, DC: American Psychological Association.

Gaffney, D. A. (2006). The aftermath of disaster: Children in crisis. *Journal of Clinical Psychology: In Session, 62*, 1001–1016.

Gelkopf, M., & Berger, R. (2009). A school-based teacher-mediated prevention program (ERASE-Stress) for reducing terror-related traumatic reactions in Israeli youth: A quasi-randomized controlled trial. *The Journal of Child Psychology and Psychiatry, 50*, 962–971.

Gonzales, N. A., & Kim, L. S. (1997). Stress and coping in an ethnic minority context: Children's cultural ecologies. In S. A. Wolchik & I. N. Sandler (Eds.), *Handbook of children's coping: Linking theory and intervention* (pp. 481–511). New York, NY: Plenum.

Goodman, R. D., Miller, M., & West-Olatunji, C. A. (2012). Traumatic stress, socioeconomic status, and academic achievement among primary school students. *Psychological Trauma: Theory, Research, Practice, and Policy, 4*, 252–259. doi:10.1037/a0024912

Gore, S., & Colten, M. E. (1991). Adolescent stress, social relationships, and mental health. In M. E. Colten & S. Gore (Eds.), *Adolescent stress: Causes and consequences* (pp. 1–14). New York, NY: Aldine de Gruyter.

Gottlieb, B. H. (1991). Social support in adolescence. In M. E. Colten & S. Gore (Eds.), *Adolescent stress: Causes and consequences* (pp. 281–306). New York, NY: Aldine de Gruyter.

Gottlieb, B. H., & Wagner, F. (1991). Stress and support processes in close relationships. In J. Eckenrode (Ed.), *The social context of coping* (pp. 165–188). New York, NY: Plenum Press.

Hendron, R. L. (1990). Stress in adolescence. In L. E. Arnold (Ed.), *Childhood stress* (pp. 247–264). New York, NY: Wiley.

Hobfoll, S. E., Dunahoo, C. A., & Monnier, J. (1995). Conservation of resources and traumatic stress. In J. R. Freedy & S. E. Hobfoll (Eds.), *Traumatic stress: From theory to practice* (pp. 49–72). New York, NY: Plenum Press.

Holmes, T. H., & Rahe, R. H. (1967). The social readjustment rating scale. *Journal of Psychosomatic Research, 11,* 213–218.

Holt, R. R. (1993). Occupational stress. In L. Goldberger & S. Breznitz (Eds.), *Handbook of stress: Theoretical and clinical aspects* (pp. 342–367). New York, NY: Free Press.

Houseknecht, S. K., & Hango, D. W. (2006). The impact of marital conflict and disruption on children's health. *Youth & Society, 38,* 58–89.

Houston, K. B. (1987). Stress and coping. In C. R. Snyder & C. E. Ford (Eds.), *Coping with negative life events* (pp. 373–399). New York, NY: Plenum Press.

Humphrey, J. H. (1988). *Children and stress.* New York, NY: AMS Press.

Isaacs, J. B., & Lovell, P. (2010). *Families of the recession: Unemployed parents and their children.* Retrieved from http://www.brookings.edu/research/papers/2010/01/14-families-recession-isaacs

Ivancevich, J. M., & Matteson, M. T. (1980). *Stress and work: A managerial perspective.* Glenview, IL: Scott, Foresman.

Johnson, J. H. (1986). *Life events as stressors in childhood and adolescence.* Beverly Hills, CA: Sage.

Jones, T. L., & Prinz, R.J. (2005). Potential roles of parental self-efficacy in parent–child adjustment: A review. *Clinical Psychology Review, 25,* 341–363.

Kalter, N. (1987). Long-term effects of divorce on children: A developmental vulnerability model. *American Journal of Orthopsychiatry, 57,* 587–599.

Katz, D. A., Sprang, G., & Cooke, C. (2012). The cost of chronic stress in childhood: Understanding and applying the concept of allostatic load. *Psychodynamic Psychiatry, 40,* 469–480.

Kearney, C., Wechsler, A., Kaur, H., & Lemos-Miller, A. (2010). Posttraumatic stress disorder in maltreated youth: A review of contemporary research and thought. *Clinical Child & Family Psychology Review, 13,* 46–76. doi:10.1007/s10567-009-0061-4

Kessler, R. C. (2006). Katrina spawned mental disorders but not thoughts of suicide. *Bulletin of the World Health Organization.* Abstract retrieved from http://www.psychiatric-times.com/article/showArticle.jhtml?articleID=192500417

Kilpatrick, K. L., & Williams, L. M. (1998). Potential mediators of posttraumatic stress disorder in child witnesses to domestic violence. *Child Abuse and Neglect, 22,* 310–330.

Kim, H. (2011). Consequences of parental divorce for child development. *American Sociological Review, 76,* 487–511. doi:10.1177/0003122411407748

Kim, K. J., Conger, R. D., Elder, G. H., & Lorenz, F. O. (2003). Reciprocal influences between stressful life events and adolescent internalizing and externalizing problems. *Child Development, 74,* 127–143.

Kimchi, J., & Schaffner, B. (1990). Childhood protective factors and stress risk. In L. E. Arnold (Ed.), *Childhood stress* (pp. 475–500). New York, NY: Wiley.

Klingman, A. (2001). Prevention of anxiety disorders: The case of posttraumatic stress disorder. In W. K. Silverman & P. D. A. Treffers (Eds.), *Anxiety disorders in children and adolescents: Research, assessment and interventions* (pp. 368–391). Cambridge, England: Cambridge University Press.

Kruczek, T., & Salsman, J. (2006). Prevention and treatment of posttraumatic stress disorder in the school setting. *Psychology in the School, 43,* 461–470.

La Greca, A. M., Silverman, W. K., Vernberg, E. M., & Roberts, M. C. (2002). *Helping children cope with disasters and terrorism.* Washington, DC: American Psychological Association.

Lahad, S., Shacham, Y., & Niv, S. (2000). Coping and community resources in children facing disaster. In A. Shalev, R. Yelhuda, & A. C. McFarlane (Eds.), *International handbook of human response to trauma* (pp. 389–395). New York, NY: Plenum.

Lazarus, R. S. (1991). *Emotion and adaptation.* New York, NY: Oxford University Press.

Lazarus, R. S. (1993a). Coping theory and research: Past, present, and future. *Psychosomatic Medicine, 55,* 234–247.

Lazarus, R. S. (1993b). Why we should think of stress as a subset of emotion. In L. Gold-berger & S. Breznitz (Eds.), *Handbook of stress: Theoretical and clinical aspects* (pp. 21–39). New York, NY: Free Press.

Lazarus, R. S. (1999). *Stress and emotion: A new synthesis.* New York, NY: Springer.

Lazarus, R. S., & Folkman, S. (1984). *Stress, appraisal, and coping.* New York, NY: Springer.

Low, S. M., & Stocker, C. (2005). Family functioning and children's adjustment: Associa-tions among parents' depressed mood, marital hostility, parent–child hostility, and chil-dren's adjustment. *Journal of Family Psychology, 19,* 394–403.

Lowe, K. N., Adams, K. S., Browne, B. L., & Hinkle, K. T. (2012). Impact of military de-ployment on family relationships. *Journal of Family Studies, 18,* 17–27. doi:10.5172/jfs.2012.18.1.17

Marsella, A. S., Friedman, M. J., Gerrity, E. T., & Scurfield, R. M. (1996). Ethnocultural aspects of PTSD: Some closing thoughts. In A. J. Marsella, M. J. Friedman, E. T. Gerrity, & R. M. Scurfield (Eds.), *Ethnocultural aspects of posttraumatic stress disorder: Issues, research, and clinical applications* (pp. 529–538). Washington, DC: American Psychological Association.

McMahon, S. D., Grant, K. E., Compas, B. E., Thurm, A. E., & Ey, S. (2003). Stress and psy-chopathology in children and adolescents: Is there evidence of specificity? *Journal of Child Psychology and Psychiatry, 44,* 107–133.

McWhirter, J. J., McWhirter, B. T., McWhirter, A. M., & McWhirter, E. H. (1994). High- and low-risk characteristics of youth: The five Cs of competency. *Elementary School Guidance & Counseling, 28,* 188–196.

Milstead, D. (2012, May). *As two-income family model matures, divorce rate falls.* Retrieved from http://www.cnbc.com/id/46797203/As_TwoIncome_Family_Model_Matures_Divorce_Rate_Falls

Modrowski, C. A., Miller, L. E., Howell, K. H., & Graham-Bermann, S. A. (2012). Consis-tency of trauma symptoms at home and in therapy for preschool children exposed to intimate partner violence. *Psychological Trauma: Theory, Research, Practice, and Policy.* Advance online publication. doi:10.1037/a0027167

Mohay, H., & Forbes, N. (2009). Reducing the risk of posttraumatic stress disorder in children following natural disasters. *Australian Journal of Guidance and Counselling, 19,* 179–195.

Moses, M. (2013). Helping children endure divorce. *Tennessee Bar Journal, 49,* 34–38.

Nader, K., Dubrow, N., & Stamm, B. H. (Eds.). (1999). *Honoring difference: Cultural issues in the treatment of trauma and loss.* Philadelphia, PA: Brunner/Mazel.

Nair, H., & Murray, A. D. (2005). Predictors of attachment security in preschool children from intact and divorced families. *Journal of Genetic Psychology, 166,* 245–263.

National Center for Children in Poverty. (2012). *Ten important questions about child poverty and family economic hardship.* Retrieved from http://www.nccp.org/faq.html#question5

National Coalition for the Homeless. (2008). *Homeless youth.* Retrieved from http://www.nationalhomeless.org/factsheets/youth.html

Osofsky, J. D., Rovaris, M., Hammer, J. H., Dickson, A., Freeman, N., & Aucoin, K. (2004). Working with police to help children exposed to violence. *Journal of Community Psychol-ogy, 32,* 593–606.

Parson, E. R. (1995). Post-traumatic stress and coping in an inner-city child: Traumatic witnessing of interparental violence and murder. *Psychoanalytic Study of the Child, 50,* 135–147.

Perren-Klinger, G. (2000). The integration of traumatic experiences: Culture and resources. In J. M. Violnati & D. Patton (Eds.), *Posttraumatic stress intervention: Challenges, issues, and perspectives* (pp. 43–64). Springfield, IL: Charles C Thomas.

Peterson, A. C., Kennedy, R. E., & Sullivan, P. (1991). Coping with adolescence. In M. E. Colten & S. Gore (Eds.), *Adolescent stress: Causes and consequences* (pp. 93–110). New York, NY: Aldine de Gruyter.

Pines, A. M. (1993). Burnout. In L. Goldberger & S. Breznitz (Eds.), *Handbook of stress: Theoretical and clinical aspects* (pp. 386–402). New York, NY: Free Press.

Rabkin, J. G. (1993). Stress and psychiatric disorders. In L. Goldberger & S. Breznitz (Eds.), *Handbook of stress: Theoretical and clinical aspects* (pp. 477–495). New York, NY: Free Press.

Raghavan, C., & Kingston, S. (2006). Child sexual abuse and posttraumatic stress disorder: The role of age at first use of substances and lifetime traumatic events. *Journal of Traumatic Stress, 19*, 269–278.

Rizzo, C., Daley, S., & Gunderson, B. (2006). Interpersonal sensitivity, romantic stress, and the prediction of depression: A study of inner-city, minority adolescent girls. *Journal of Youth & Adolescence, 35*, 444–453. doi:10.1007/s10964-006-9047-4

Ryan-Wenger, N. M. (1992). A taxonomy of children's coping strategies: A step toward theory development. *American Journal of Orthopsychiatry, 62*, 256–263.

Salloum, A., Carter, P., Burch, B., Garfinkel, A., & Overstreet, S. (2011). Impact of exposure to community violence, Hurricane Katrina, and Hurricane Gustav on posttraumatic stress and depressive symptoms among school age children. *Anxiety, Stress & Coping, 24*, 27–42. doi:10.1080/10615801003703193

Salmon, K., & Bryant, R. A. (2002). Posttraumatic stress disorder in children: The influence of developmental factors. *Clinical Psychology Review, 22*, 163–188.

Sanchez, Y. M., Lambert, S. F., & Ialongo, N. S. (2011). Adverse life events and depressive symptoms in African American youth: The role of control-related beliefs. *Depression Research & Treatment.* doi:10.1155/2011/871843

Sandler, I .N., Wolchik, S. A., MacKinnon, D., Ayers, T. S., & Roosa, M. W. (1997). Developing linkages between theory and intervention in stress and coping processes. In S. A. Wolchik & I. N. Sandler (Eds.), *Handbook of children's coping: Linking theory and intervention* (pp. 3–40). New York, NY: Plenum.

Scheeringa, M. S., Wright, M. J., Hunt, J. P., & Zeanah, C. H. (2006). Factors affecting the diagnosis and prediction of PTSD symptomology in children and adolescents. *American Journal of Psychiatry, 163*, 644–651.

Search Institute. (2003). *40 developmental assets for middle childhood (ages 8–12).* Minneapolis, MN: Author. Retrieved from http://www.search-institute.org

Sears, S. J., & Milburn, J. (1990). School age stress. In L. E. Arnold (Ed.), *Childhood stress* (pp. 223–246). New York, NY: Wiley.

Selye, H. (1974). *Stress without distress.* New York, NY: Lippincott.

Selye, H. (1993). History of the stress concept. In L. Goldberger & S. Breznitz (Eds.), *Handbook of stress: Theoretical and clinical aspects* (pp. 7–17). New York, NY: Free Press.

Sherr, L., Bergenstrom, A., & McCann, E. (1999). An audit of a school based counselling provision for emotional and behavioural difficulties in primary school children. *Counselling Psychology Quarterly, 12*, 271–285.

Sieh, D. S., Meijer, A. M., Oort, F. J., Visser-Meily, J. A., & Van der Leij, D. V. (2010). Problem behavior in children of chronically ill parents: A meta-analysis. *Clinical Child & Family Psychology Review, 13*, 384–397. doi:10.1007/s10567-010-0074-z

Smetana, J. G., Yau, J., Restrepo, A., & Braeges, J. L. (1991). Conflict and adaptation in adolescence: Adolescent–parent conflict. In M. E. Colten & S. Gore (Eds.), *Adolescent stress: Causes and consequences* (pp. 43–65). New York, NY: Aldine de Gruyter.

Solantaus, T., Leinonen, J., & Punamäki, R. (2004). Children's mental health in times of economic recession: Replication and extension of the family economic stress model in Finland. *Developmental Psychology, 40*, 412–429. doi:10.1037/0012-1649.40.3.412

Sontag, L. M., & Graber, J. A. (2010). Coping with perceived peer stress: Gender-specific and common pathways to symptoms of psychopathology. *Developmental Psychology, 46*, 1605–1620. doi:10.1037/a0020617

Steinberg, A. (1998). Understanding the secondary traumatic stress of children. In C. R. Figley (Ed.), *Burnout in families: The systemic costs of caring* (pp. 29–46). New York, NY: CRC Press.

Stoddard, F. J., Ronfeldt, H., Kagan, J., Drake, J. E., Snidman, N., Murphy, J. M., . . . Sheridan, R. L. (2006). Young burned children: The course of acute stress and physiological and behavioral responses. *American Journal of Psychiatry, 163,* 1084–1090.

Taylor, R. J. (2004). Therapeutic intervention of trauma and stress brought on by divorce. *Journal of Divorce & Remarriage, 41,* 129–135.

Terzian, M., Moore, K. A., & Nguyen, H. N. (2010, October). *Assessing stress in children and youth: A guide for out-of-school time program practitioners.* Retrieved from http://www.childtrends.org/Files/Child_Trends-2010_10_05_RB_AssessingStress.pdf

Tolin, D. F., & Foa, E. B. (2006). Sex differences in trauma and posttraumatic stress disorder: A quantitative review of 25 years of research. *Psychological Bulletin, 132,* 959–992.

Undergraff, J. A., & Taylor, S. E. (2000). From vulnerability to growth: Positive and negative effects of stressful life events. In J. H. Harvey & E. D. Miller (Eds.), *Loss and trauma: General and close relationship perspectives* (pp. 3–28). Philadelphia, PA: Brunner-Routledge.

Vanderwerp, L. S. (2011). *Siblings and illness: A study of how children are differentially impacted by the chronic illness of a sibling.* Retrieved from http://www.google.com/search?q=children%27s+stress+when++sibling+or+family+member+is+chronically+ill&rls=com.microsoft:en-us:IE-SearchBox&ie=UTF-8&oe=UTF-8&sourceid=ie7&rlz=1I7NDKB_enUS512

Voelker, R. (2005). Katrina's impact on mental health likely to last years. *Journal of the American Medical Association, 294,* 1599–1600.

Wang, J. L. (2006). Perceived work stress, imbalance between work and family/personal lives, mental disorders. *Social Psychiatry & Psychiatric Epidemiology, 41,* 541–548.

Wasserstein, S. B., & La Greca, A. M. (1998). Hurricane Andrew: Parent conflict as a moderator of children's adjustment. *Hispanic Journal of Behavioral Sciences, 20,* 212–224.

Weisler, R. H., Barbee, J. G., IV, & Townsend, M. H. (2006). Mental health and recovery in the Gulf Coast after Hurricane Katrina and Rita. *Journal of the American Medical Association, 296,* 585–588.

Wertlieb, D. (1991). Children and divorce: Stress and coping in developmental perspective. In J. Eckenrode (Ed.), *The social context of coping* (pp. 31–54). New York, NY: Plenum Press.

Widom, C. S. (1991). Childhood victimization: Risk factors for delinquency. In M. E. Colten & S. Gore (Eds.), *Adolescent stress: Causes and consequences* (pp. 201–221). New York, NY: Aldine de Gruyter.

Wilburn, V. R., & Smith, D. E. (2005). Stress, self-esteem, and suicidal ideation in late adolescents. *Adolescence, 40,* 33–45.

Willis, T. A. (1987). Help-seeking as a coping mechanism. In C. R. Snyder & C. E. Ford (Eds.), *Coping with negative life events* (pp. 19–50). New York, NY: Plenum Press.

Youngs, B. (1985). *Stress in children.* New York, NY: Arbor House.

Zunker, V. G. (2002). *Career counseling: Applied concepts of life planning.* Pacific Grove, CA: Brooks/Cole.

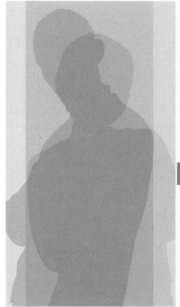

PART 3

Working With Youth at Risk: Prevention and Intervention

In the previous two sections, the topic of youth at risk was introduced and the causes were examined. In Part 3, the text addresses issues and/or behaviors most often identified as placing youth at risk. All of the chapters in this part of the text contain the following subtopics: an introduction, problem identification, a case study, approaches to prevention, intervention strategies, adaptations for diversity, and a summary. Authors discuss both prevention and intervention from individual, family, school, and community perspectives. In this way the reader is able to obtain a comprehensive and comparative overview of the material in each chapter.

Chapter 8, "'Who Am I?' Unique Issues for Multiracial Youth" is revised for this sixth edition. It emphasizes multiracial youth, racially and ethnically diverse families, and immigrant youth and families. Within these contexts, academic and behavioral problems, self-esteem, education and career goals, language and communication, and parentification are presented in terms of at-riskness in youth. Attention is also given to culturally appropriate intervention and prevention approaches. Biracial and multicultural models are presented together with the case study of Simone.

Chapter 9, "The Secret and All-Consuming Obsessions: Eating Disorders," provides excellent introductory material with respect to the impact of the media, gender socialization, and body image on youth at risk for eating disorders. Risk factors such as gender, age, socioeconomic status, family characteristics, and identification with socialized norms are also discussed. Such background information, along with a thorough discussion of definitions, symptoms, and etiology, creates the context for the case study of Marissa and the subsequent presentation of approaches to prevention and intervention. The chapter includes an extremely current and well-done subsection on diversity issues, including those faced by African American, Latina, Native American, Asian, and non-Western women, men, gay and lesbian individuals, transgender and transsexual individuals, and athletes.

The adolescent at risk for suicide has become an increasing concern for schools and communities throughout the United States. Between 1960 and 1988 the adolescent suicide rate rose by 200% compared with an increase in the general population of approximately 17%. According to some experts, one teenager attempts suicide every 90 seconds and one completes the act of suicide every 90 minutes. Chapter 10, "'I Don't Want to Live': The Adolescent at Risk for Suicidal Behavior," presents information all professionals and all parents should know if prevention and intervention efforts are to succeed. Discussions of ethnic and gender differences, methods, risk and protective factors, precipitants, myths, and profiles provide the groundwork for the subsequent case study, prevention, intervention, and diversity material. An adolescent who is suicidal is communicating the fact that he or she is experiencing difficulty problem solving, sustaining self-esteem, managing stress, and expressing feelings. It is important for all of us to respond in constructive, safe, informed ways when working with this very vulnerable adolescent population.

Chapter 11, "A Future in Jeopardy: Sexuality Issues in Adolescence," focuses on prevention, intervention, and current research around important topics of teen sexuality that put teens at risk for negative outcomes, such as teen pregnancy, AIDS and other sexually transmitted diseases, and rape and date rape. In each of these areas, the authors spell out prevention and intervention approaches from an individual, family, school, and community perspective. Individual risk factors are also set forth as these relate to both rape and date rape and sexual predators. The chapter includes the case study of Julia and concludes with adaptations for diversity.

Chapter 12, "'I Am Somebody': Gang Membership," examines the youth gang phenomenon, its historical significance, and the development of gang activities. The chapter looks at present-day gang involvement, including major gangs and their distribution; factors for gang involvement; gang characteristics; gang member characteristics; females in gangs; and ethnic gang involvement, including Asian gangs, African American gangs, Hispanic gangs, and White supremacist gangs. The discussion in Chapter 12 includes an examination of views as to why gangs form, risk factors for gang involvement, and statistics that set the stage for understanding gangs and their impact upon society. The case of Christopher profiles a young man involved in gangs; the profile provides a way of understanding the reality of those factors shaping the choices and lives of our youth. From the information about gang organization, risks, and statistics, the focus shifts to an understanding of diversity and gang involvement, prevention approaches, and strategies for intervention.

Chapter 13, "'It Takes a Village': Advocating for Sexual Minority Youth," discusses efforts to protect sexual minority youth from the risks associated with minority stress and prevention and intervention when they have symptoms from this stress, ranging from depression to self-harm. The authors provide the reader with current data related not only to the number of "sexual minority" youth but also to the myriad of factors that place these individuals at risk. Using the case of Emma, the authors take the reader through prevention and intervention strategies from an individual, family, school, and community perspective. These strategies include, but are not limited to, guidelines for program development, risk factors, and advice for "coming out." The chapter concludes with an excellent section on adaptations for diversity.

Chapter 14, "Death in the Classroom: Violence in Schools," is an excellent chapter that addresses the recent escalation of violence in schools. This is a particularly timely chapter given the fact that we are hearing and reading more and more about school violence and its consequences. The author defines the problem and presents aspects of prevention and intervention from individual, family, school, and community perspectives. Several current intervention and prevention programs used by schools and communities are presented. The author uses the case of Thurston High School and Kip to illustrate significant points within the chapter. The chapter concludes with adaptations for diversity.

Adolescent substance abuse often results in harm to youth, their families, communities, and society as a whole. According to the National Institute on Drug Abuse for Teens (2013), drug and alcohol abuse contribute to the deaths of more than 120,000 Americans and cost taxpayers more than $143 billion every year in preventable health care costs, lost productivity, automobile crashes, law enforcement, and crime. Alcohol use is associated with over half of all murders and rapes in the United States and is a factor in 40% of all violent crimes. As the author of Chapter 15 points out, this is not a problem limited to adults. Significant percentages of youth and adolescents are experimenting with and becoming regular users of chemical substances, particularly alcohol, nicotine, marijuana, inhalants, and methamphetamines as well as engaging in the non-medical use of prescription-type pain relievers, tranquilizers, stimulants, and sedatives. Chapter 15, "'Escaping Reality': Adolescent Substance Abuse," focuses on providing information not only on current drugs of choice and their human impact but also on intervention and prevention strategies dealing with this impact aimed at the individual, family, school, and community. These strategies are highlighted in the cases of Tim and Daniel. Adaptations for diversity close out the chapter.

"Nowhere to Turn: The Young Face of Homelessness," is the title of Chapter 16. Families with small children now represent approximately 40% of the homeless population. The National Center on Family Homelessness (2011) reports that up to 1.6 million children are homeless in the United States each year. This translates to one in 45 children. From the most recent statistics available, it is clear that the faces of the homeless have changed drastically since the days of the White male alcoholic, or "skid row bum." Forty percent of the homeless are families, and 25% are children. Homeless children's differences in appearance, behavior, and ability demand tolerance and flexibility from teachers and school administrators. This chapter describes the problem of homelessness for two specific groups: children living with their families and youth living alone. The authors define the problem, the characteristics for both groups, and specific contributing factors for homelessness for each group. Strategies for prevention and intervention are presented from individual, family, school, and community perspectives. A family case study and the case of Latisha are used by the authors to illustrate major points. Adaptations for cultural diversity close the chapter.

Chapter 17 is "'This Isn't the Place for Me': School Dropout." The placement of this chapter toward the end of the book is fitting because the problem of the school dropout involves many of the personal, family, and social issues discussed in previous chapters. The authors define the problem and follow this definition with discussions on ethnicity; socioeconomic status; and a school, family, and peer perspective. Early warning signs, underlying causes, and clinical and systemic approaches to prevention and intervention are presented and supplemented with the cases of Charles and Michelle. Adaptations for diversity conclude this informative and cutting-edge chapter.

Our text concludes with a brand new chapter, "A Nation at Risk: Bullying Among Children and Adolescents," that examines bullying and highlights the definition, prevalence, impact, and mental health factors associated with bullying. Issues such as gender; race–ethnicity; age; disability status; and lesbian, gay, bisexual, and transgender youth are also presented as these relate to the impact of bullying. Using the case of Conner, the author sets forth prevention and intervention strategies for the individual, family, school, and community. The chapter concludes with a strong section on adaptations for diversity.

References

National Center on Family Homelessness. (2011). *The characteristics and needs of families experiencing homelessness.* Retrieved from http://www.familyhomelessness.org/media/306.pdf

National Institute on Drug Abuse for Teens. (2013). *Prescription drug abuse.* Retrieved from http://www.teens.drugabuse.gov/facts/facts_rx1.php

Chapter 8

"Who Am I?": Unique Issues for Multiracial Youth

Laura R. Haddock and Jeannie Falkner

The U.S. population has witnessed considerable social, cultural, and demographic changes in recent decades. For centuries, the United States has attracted people from all over the world who are searching for their share of the American dream. Beginning as early as the 1600s with the *Mayflower*, U.S. history is full of stories of immigration. As a result, the United States is filled with a mosaic of races and nationalities. Youth of racial and ethnic minorities, including those of color, immigrant youth, and biracial youth, experience a variety of internal and external challenges. There are numerous unique characteristics, potential problems, and social needs for those with mixed cultural heritage. These challenges are related to a need to define identities in a society that is often harsh in response to social dimensions outside of the mainstream. Considerable attention must be focused on providing counseling services to racial and ethnic minority youth and those with combined heritage. Some issues that are pertinent to working with these populations include racial and ethnic identity development, isolation, career dreams, and academic and behavioral concerns (Harris, 2002; Herring, 1992; Moss & Davis, 2008). A counselor's multicultural knowledge, awareness, and skills in working with people from diverse backgrounds are critical to effective counseling. It is clear from research that racial and ethnic minorities are more vulnerable to social, emotional, and academic problems and that limited support systems are available to racial and ethnic minority youth (Esquivel & Keitel, 1990; Moss & Davis, 2008). This chapter addresses stressors encountered by these minority youth and issues pertinent to counseling. A case study is provided as well as suggestions for prevention and intervention strategies.

Problem Definition

Who Is the Multiracial Youth?

Although any attempt to explain the dynamics of growing up in a particular racial or ethnic group risks the loss of the uniqueness of the individual, counselors must nevertheless strive to appreciate the complexity of racially and culturally diverse families. Every individual is born into and influenced by his or her cultural context, which includes existing beliefs, values, rules, roles, and family practices (Sue & Sue, 2012). Nationality, culture, and society exert significant influence on our perceptions, influencing our values, painting our view of the world, and texturing our responses to experience. Individuals cannot hold themselves apart from some form of cultural influence. No one is culture free. Today we stand on the threshold of a new kind of person: a person who is socially, cognitively, and emotionally a product of the interweaving of cultures in the twenty-first century.

Racial identity, more specifically, refers to a collective identity based on perceived membership in a group that shares cultural traditions and racial group membership (Phelps, Taylor, & Gerard, 2001). In 2011, 36.6% of all people in the United States were racial and ethnic minority individuals (U.S. Census Bureau, 2011). However, a growing segment of the population of the United States claims to be of multiple heritages, which creates unique needs for those who do not have a clearly defined ethnicity but do have a need to articulate a defining race (Gibbs, 2003, p. 322).

According to Felbeck (2010), more than 7 million people in the United States identify as being more than one race. The U.S. Census Bureau is now projecting that minorities will outnumber White people of European descent in the United States by the year 2042 (Mixed Heritage Center, n.d.). This date could be an over-estimation, as biracial and multiracial children often have been identified with a parent of color, which has resulted in people of mixed heritages frequently being ignored or neglected, being forced to choose one heritage to the exclusion of others (Harris, 2002; Phelps et al., 2001; Sue & Sue, 2012).

Biracial and Multiracial Youth in Context: A Sociocultural Perspective

A sociocultural perspective highlights that, to a greater or lesser extent, racial and ethnic minority youth undergo a socialization that includes learning to adapt to the external pressures of the dominant culture. Poverty, unemployment, exposure to crime and violence, discrimination, and inadequate health care are just some of the environmental issues facing minority youth (Orton, 1996). These contextualized factors compound the difficulties for multiracial minority youth as they strive to adapt to their environment. The youth of today have a view of the world that profoundly transcends indigenous culture and develops from the complex social, political, economic, and educational interactions of our time. The various conceptions of an "international," "transcultural," "multicultural," or "intercultural" individual have each been used with varying degrees of explanatory or descriptive utility. Essentially, they all attempt to define someone whose horizons extend significantly beyond his or her own culture.

Though it is a sad commentary on a world that shows so much progress, social ostracism and racism continue to be direct external stressors to many interracial couples and their children. As late as 1945, over half of the states in the United States had active laws that banned interracial marriages. Only in 1967 did the Supreme Court formally ban states from prohibiting interracial marriages. The stigma attached to the family becomes a silent barrier for the couple and their children as they attempt to establish their place in the American social order.

To add to the difficulty of acceptance within a society whose dominant culture has only relatively recently sanctioned multiracial marriages, the biracial child is often raised in a number of nontraditional family compositions, including single parents, never-married parents, and stepfamilies. Although the numbers of such nontraditional families are increasing, the stigma of not conforming to the traditional family norm mirrors a larger societal belief that nonnuclear families are unstable and represent declining "family values" (Hill, 1999; Orton, 1996). In addition, counselors will find that trends related to the terms *biracial* have shifted. Historically, the term *biracial* gave primary consideration to Black and White races, which is not surprising considering the historical significance of racial issues such as segregation. However, current literature uses the term when referring to any individual with "parents who represent two distinct racial ancestries" (Moss & Davis, 2008, p. 219).

Causal Factors

When outside prejudices and values are internalized by the minority youth, this negative internalization can lead to problems of identity (Bracey, Bamaca, & Umana-Taylor, 2004; Herring, 1995; Martin, 2008; Miville, Koonce, Darlington, & Whitlock, 2000). Racial and ethnic minority youth are faced with constant cultural messages from a monoracial society. The limited numbers of multiracial and culturally diverse families in the media and children's books offer few role models with whom the youth can identify (Turner, 2011). It comes as no surprise, Martin (2008) suggests, that media plays an influential role in promoting both positive and negative racial images. TV captures the viewer and influences the ways viewers see themselves in the context of the world around them. Positive images promote

---

Sidebar 8.1 ■ Can You Guess the Racial Identity of Your Favorite Celebrity?

Media is a powerful social force and may help shape societal attitudes. From the 1959 remake of *Imitation to Life* to *Guess Who's Coming to Dinner* in 1967, which portrayed a positive representation of the controversial subject of interracial marriage at a time when interracial marriage remained illegal in 17 states, the media has challenged our preconceived notions of race.

As you watch your favorite TV show, movie, or performer, notice how race, interracial relationships, and the multiracial individual are portrayed. To help you get started, we have provided the following quiz.

Can you guess the racial identity of the following popular multiracial celebrities?

1. Halle Berry: Film
2. Lea Michele: TV star of *Glee*
3. Rihanna: Singer
4. Mariah Carey: Singer
5. President Barack Hussein Obama II
6. Kim Kardashian: Reality TV star
7. Bruno Mars: Singer
8. Taylor Daniel Lautner: Film

■ ■ ■

self-pride, whereas negative stereotypes reinforce a disruption of positive racial identity. A recent hopeful trend shows popular media increasingly showcasing positive multiracial personalities in the spotlight.

Nevertheless, limited research has been focused on multiracial children and youth; the research that has been done has focused primarily on the offspring of African American and Euro-American relationships (Nishimura, 1995; Mixed Heritage Center, n.d.). Previous research focused primarily on the negative features of multiracial marriages, which corroborated cultural stereotypes of multiracial and ethnic minorities as experiencing low self-esteem, experiencing feelings of inferiority, and being social or occupational failures (Felbeck, 2010; Herring, 1992). So how can counselors combat deeply rooted stereotypes and assumptions, keep with the counseling profession's strengths-based approach, promote client advocacy, and conduct research that highlights the resilience and strengths of minority youth and their families?

Community Acceptance of Racial and Ethnic Minorities

The concept of community includes the geographical location of one's residence and the ethnic composition of one's neighborhood. This sense of community extends beyond the geographical restriction and encompasses the rules and roles prescribed for its members. When an individual matches the racial and ethnic roles prescribed by the community, this sense of community provides a structure of support networks that can buffer the individual from the demands of daily life (Swartz-Kulstad & Martin, 1999).

Difficulties can arise when youth move into a neighborhood where social stratification occurs among racial and economic lines. When such divisions and community norms are juxtaposed with those of the individual, psychological distress can distort self-evaluations of personal competence and result in failure to engage in supportive interpersonal relationships (Sandhu, Portes, & McPhee, 1996).

But how can you determine what the rules and roles are when one of the greatest challenges facing biracial youth in America is finding a comfortable descriptive term? In our society, the name individuals choose to identify their ethnic heritage has taken on significant importance. Endless forms—be it birth certificate, school registration, driver's license, voter's card, or census form—require selecting a descriptive identity, and more often than not, the choices include singular cultures and "other." Add to this the inability to check more than one racial identity on most demographic surveys (which, until 2000, included the U.S. Census), and cultural isolation is perpetuated. This situation does little to strengthen a teen's sense of identity or confidence. Racial identity indicators are not simply neutral descriptions; they are often interpreted as symbols of relationships with parents, families, and ancestors and are commonly associated with feelings of attachment and loss (DaCosta, 2007).

Racially and Ethnically Diverse Families

The role of ethnicity in the life of the multiracial youth is affected by the immediate environment as well as by the historical and sociopolitical context (Herring, 1992; Moss & Davis, 2008). The most immediate influence in the socialization of children is that of the family. The family is considered a major organizing force in an individual's life, and nuclear and extended family members have been found to

Sidebar 8.2 ■ Other? Is That My Only Option?

Jonas is a popular high school senior. He is the son of Michael and Zandra, who are very supportive of his academic and athletic success. Jonas recently won his district long jump event and is completing the paperwork to travel to the regional competition. One of the necessary application forms asks that he identify his race. Jonas stares at the options: African American, Hispanic, White/Caucasian, Asian, or Native American. He sighs, glances at his African American mother, thinks of his Caucasian father, and checks "other."

As you read this scenario, note your reaction to Jonas and his situation.

1. How do you think Jonas might feel about choosing one race to identify his multicultural heritage?
2. How do you think his parents might feel?
3. What thoughts came to mind?
4. What feelings did you experience?
5. If you were to counsel Jonas and/or his family, what racial identity issues might you need to address?

■ ■ ■

be the primary source of psychological support for an individual's ethnocultural background (Akutsu, Snowden, & Organista, 1996; Caldwell, Rafferty, Reischl, DeLoney, & Brooks, 2010; Swartz-Kulstad & Martin, 1999).

For the multiracial family, identifying ethnicity can prove to be a formidable task, as two or more heritages must be integrated into a composite that reduces dissonance for the children as they assimilate their cultural uniqueness. The greater the difference between spouses or partners in cultural background, the more difficulty the family has been found to have in the transmission of a cultural heritage (Herring, 1992; McGoldrick, 2005). Interracial couples often react to each other as "though the other's behaviors were a personal attack rather than just a difference rooted in ethnicity" (Herring, 1992, p. 123). When the marital stress is unresolved, children may feel they are to blame for their parents' problems. Under such circumstances, the multiracial child may feel quite isolated and find little support from his or her parents.

It is important for counselors to appreciate the possible existence of antagonism between racial and ethnic groups in the context of the multiracial minority family. A social system that maintains the myth of monoracialism tends to assign the multiracial person the heritage of the least desirable racial status (Root, 1996). For the children to internalize the positive cultural heritages, the parents must first address the differences and be open to communication about their children's socialization process. As parents face the difficulties of conflict among community, family, social, and intergenerational roles, parents must also attempt to help the child develop healthy adaptations.

Because of the historical context of oppression, multiracial youth with an African American parent face an additional challenge. Children from interracial marriages between Asian Americans and Euro-Americans are more likely to be considered multiracial, whereas children who have an African American parent are often considered Black (Root, 1996; Sue & Sue, 2012). When one parent of the biracial child is African American, the biracial youth may face a disregard of the non-African American heritage and be labeled as Black regardless of the racial identity he or she

Sidebar 8.3 ■ Couples Are Not Exempt From Stereotypes

One thing to keep in mind is that just because racial minorities become a couple, it does not mean that they are immune to racism. Take the parents of Simone, a case study you will find a little later in the chapter. Tyrone, an African American man, may have romanced the Mexican American woman, all the while entertaining stereotypes. The family of the Mexican American woman Isabella could object to her relationship with an African American man. Counselors must remember that when people enter a relationship from different racial backgrounds, it is necessary to learn as much as possible about the other's culture and to confront stereotypes. Educating relatives may also be necessary to reduce resistance and encourage them to respect your mate. It's necessary for individuals in such couples to navigate not just mainstream American culture and the culture of their parents but their significant other's culture as well. They must identify how best to pass down their cultural heritage to their children, while respecting their mate's culture.

■ ■ ■

embraces. One critical step in developing cultural competence is to avoid making assumptions and labeling heritage on the basis of appearance. To emphasize this point, let's take a moment to review the answers to the celebrity racial identity quiz!

As mentioned earlier in this chapter, a social bias against nontraditional family structure is also a risk factor for the multiracial youth. In particular, the role of the nonresident African American father has been a source of controversy. Counselors, social workers, and other mental health professionals will do well to examine their own biases and make a special effort to use the positive protective influences these fathers can provide for their children. Coley and Medeiros (2007) found that these nonresidential fathers contributed to positive child outcomes when there was a positive engagement between father and child. In particular, parental monitoring, parental involvement, and parent–child communication are associated with a decreased frequency of risky behaviors (Caldwell et al., 2010). Although much of the research has focused on nonresidential African American fathers and their sons, the positive outcomes may provide direction for enhancing the relationship between nonresidential fathers and daughters as well. Coming up you will find several suggestions for enhancing a protective relationship and promoting positive socialization for biracial youth whose family consists of a nonresidential African American father. Finally, contrary to popular belief, research indicates that "many nonresident African American fathers are willing and able to participate in a family intervention aimed at assisting their children" (Caldwell et al., 2010, p. 33).

Sidebar 8.4 ■ Celebrity Identities Revealed

Answers to the racial identity quiz

1. African American father and English mother
2. Sephardic Jewish Spanish father and Italian Catholic mother
3. Afro-Bajan, Irish, and Afro-Guyanese
4. Irish, Afro-Venezuelan
5. Kenyan and Caucasian American
6. Turkish Armenian, Russian Armenian, Scottish, English, and Dutch
7. Puerto Rican and Filipino
8. French, Dutch, German, and Native American Ottawa and Potawatomi

■ ■ ■

Immigrant Youth and Families

In addition to the issues of identity faced by racial and ethnic minority youth, one or more family members may be an immigrant to the United States. U.S. immigrants represent a large number of school-age children and youth. Of these, those with Asian and Hispanic backgrounds represent the largest groups of recent immigrants (Constantine, Erickson, Banks, & Timberlake, 1998; Marotta & Garcia, 2003; Olatunji, 2005).

First-generation immigrant families face multiple adjustments to their new culture. Acculturation is a socialization process that involves adapting to a new culture as a result of changes in cultural attitudes, values, and behaviors (Robinson, 2012). Acculturation requires the immigrant to negotiate this transition to improve his or her life conditions in a manner that is congruous with the new environment. Acculturation is multifaceted and involves cognitive, behavioral, and self-identification that occur through contact over an extended period of time (Kopala, Esquivel, & Baptiste, 1994). Predisposing variables such as age, language proficiency, education, previous contact, family structure, and cultural similarity all influence the acculturation process.

Assimilation describes those people who do not desire to maintain their cultural identities and instead identify and associate with the new environmental culture (Robinson, 2012). Historically, immigrants of European heritage have assimilated more easily into the mainstream culture than immigrants whose heritages are noticeably different.

Immigrant families and youth experience physical, social, and cultural changes that may result in physical or mental disorders (Kopala et al., 1994). These families may have limited support systems and be reluctant to use the professional support systems that may be available. Language barriers and the demands and challenges associated with living in a new country may overwhelm immigrant family members and create additional psychological concerns for the family. Current immigration patterns consist primarily of Asian and Latin Americans, who have not been so easily assimilated into a predominantly Eurocentric culture. Latinos are expected to make up 29% of the population by 2050 (pewhispanic.org); thus, counselors can expect to work with Latino youth and their families in multiple settings.

Academic and Behavioral Problems of Racial and Ethnic Minority Youth

Although many racial and minority youth will adapt with resilience to the multiple challenges faced, some will experience academic and behavioral problems that require intervention. Racial and ethnic identity issues will not generally be the presenting problem in a school setting. Students instead will be referred for reasons that include poor academic achievement, off-task behavior, poor social skills, social isolation, negative attitudes, aggressive behavior toward parents, sadness and depression, interfamilial conflicts, or acting-out behaviors (Herring, 1992, 1995; Orton, 1996).

Because the cultural context of the U.S. school system is primarily Caucasian middle class, behaviors that are adaptive according to a child's culture may appear maladaptive within the school context (Aaroe & Nelson, 2000; Esquivel & Keitel, 1990; Malott, Alessandria, Kirkpatrick, & Carandang, 2009). The chance for accurate assessment may be at risk as the number of school children from culturally and linguistically diverse backgrounds is increasing while the number of culturally diverse teachers is declining (Aaroe & Nelson, 2000). Any assessment of academic and behavioral concerns must address the problems associated with cross-cultural linguistic equivalences and differential attention to, interpretation of, and tolerance for adolescent behaviors (Lau et al., 2004).

Research shows that whereas parents from different cultural backgrounds found commonality in identifying negative classroom behaviors and interpersonal school survival adaptations, teachers were significantly dissimilar in their responses (Aaroe & Nelson, 2000). Teachers, in fact, were found to exhibit a lower tolerance and more narrowly defined standard for classroom behavior. This finding may be a factor in the overrepresentation of minority youth in programs for emotionally and behaviorally troubled youth.

Nevertheless, the difficulties faced by minority youth in interactions with their environment must be considered, because cultural variables can be a contributing factor in attempts to adapt to their environment (Malott et al., 2009; Swartz-Kulstad & Martin, 1999). The Latino population is a youthful one, with Latinos making up 19%, or nearly one out of five, of the K–12 school community (Pew Hispanic Center, 2005). Latino teens tend to begin their families early through teen pregnancy, often living in a multigenerational home sharing parenting and financial responsibilities. However, this situation places the young Latino family at risk for unemployment and a lack of career opportunities. School counselors have the responsibility to address unequal academic achievement and dropout rates for the minority youth while embracing cultural family structures that may be outside of the mainstream.

Regardless of the competent functioning in their culture of origin, culturally diverse youth and their families risk being judged as deficient relative to the educational norms and cultural differences in a new educational setting (Maital, 2000).

Ethnic Identity and Self-Esteem

Erikson's (1968) concept of identity formation has been primary to counselors' understanding of identity and refers to the self in relation to one's relationship with others. The peer group is one venue from which youth view themselves in relation to others. Group self-esteem focuses on one's feeling about being a member of a racial or ethnic group.

Cultures vary in their orientation toward identity. Some cultural groups value independence and emphasize individualism, whereas other cultures place identity clearly within the family constellation. The minority youth who is at odds with dominant cultural values may have difficulty in balancing the need to be seen as an individual against the value to place the family above self.

As minority youth seek a group in which they can find acceptance, the reality of social marginality may be a cogent perspective from which to view this struggle (Nishimura, 1995). The need for acceptance and validation of their ethnic identity becomes paramount, as ethnic identity has been found to be a significant predictor of wellness for minority adolescents (Rayle, 2004). According to Phinney (1989, as cited in Nishimura, 1995), "Adolescents who explore and are clear regarding the meaning of their ethnicity, show higher scores in the areas of self-evaluation, sense of mastery, social and peer interactions, and family relations than adolescents who have not explored their ethnicity" (p. 53).

Failure to explore one's identity may lead to loneliness or acting out as a form of protest in being pressured to fit into someone else's vision of who the youth should be (Herring, 1992). When the education system does not meet the needs of the racial minority youth, academic disidentification may occur. *Disidentification* is the "lack of a significant relation between a student's view of his or her academic abilities in comparison to peers (i.e., academic self-concept) and the student's academic outcomes (i.e., grade point average)" (Cokley, McClain, Jones, & Johnson, 2011, p. 55). Thus, disidentification puts the education system at odds with the youth whose self-esteem is not rewarded by academic achievement.

In contrast, academically oriented minority youth may be left to resolve the dissonance by removing themselves from their peer group norms, resulting in further social isolation and a loss of possible support systems. Some African American students have been found to adopt behaviors and attitudes that enhance their academic successes but distance them from their culture, often resulting in symptoms of depression, anxiety, and a loss of racial identity (Arroyo & Zigler, 1995; Ohrt, Lambie, & Leva, 2009).

Sexuality and gender identity are often played out during adolescence. Gender identity development includes a comprehensive assessment of one's self, including feelings of intrinsic worth, competence, sexuality, and self-approval (Robinson, 1993). The special needs of multiracial youth must be recognized, as these youth are often rejected by both majority and minority peer groups because their physical appearance is unusual, their family background is unorthodox, and they feel torn between two competing set of norms and values (Herring, 1992).

Physical beauty and gender roles are often defined within ethnic and cultural values and beliefs. Especially for female minority youth, pressure to emulate White women's norms of beauty can result in these girls viewing their diverse cultural gender identities from a deficit perspective. For the youth from multiracial and multiethnic families, gender role conflicts between conflicting parental values and societal norms may be overwhelming. Pressure to conform to community roles and behaviors can create feelings of living a dual life, resulting in psychological pain and distress for the minority youth (Kelch-Oliver & Leslie, 2006; Swartz-Kulstad & Martin, 1999).

Finally, socioeconomic class, race, culture, and gender combine to intensify issues of powerlessness and rejection experiences by the multiracial youth (Robinson, 1993). Further difficulties can occur when racial and minority youth move into a neighborhood where social stratification occurs along divided racial and socioeconomic lines. Immigrants living in low-income urban areas have been found to experience more loneliness, anxiety, and isolation than their ethnic peers of suburban environments (Esquivel & Keitel, 1990).

Education and Career Goals

One area of concern for the multiracial minority youth can be the discrepancy between the minority child's cultural values and those encouraged in the U.S. school system. Racial bias and stereotyping may affect the educational and career choices of minority youth. For example, some cultures emphasize cooperation rather than competition, the latter of which is prominent in the U.S. educational system. Minority youth also experience inordinately high dropout rates from school (Constantine et al., 1998; Olatunji, 2005).

Many minority youth have had few opportunities to develop motivation for careers that require high educational attainment, are high status, and may be financially rewarding (Constantine et al., 1998). Without the opportunity to create a vision for the future in which education is relevant to career path and financial rewards, the minority youth is left to repeat educational and career choices that lead to employment in low-status, low-paying, and racially stereotypical occupations. These factors, including socialization experiences, perceptions of career barriers, and discrimination, contribute to education and career barriers for some minority youth (Constantine et al., 1998).

In contrast, those individuals whose culture emphasizes education and immigrants who immigrated for educational purposes will adapt more rapidly than others whose educational goals are less valued. Having a family that is supportive of education and achievement and associating with an achievement-oriented peer group are factors that enhance academic success (Constantine & Gushue, 2003).

Language and Communication

When minority children and youth experience difficulties in functioning in the academic setting, it is often attributable to differences in language and communication styles. Miscommunication can lead to disrupted interpersonal relations and can play a key role in difficulties in successful adaptation to the academic environment (Swartz-Kulstad & Martin, 1999). For effective communication, both parties must be able to send and receive verbal and nonverbal messages appropriately and accurately (Sue & Sue, 2012). Differences in tone, context, and verbal and nonverbal style can easily be misinterpreted, creating hostility and suspicion. The counselor will need to be sensitive to differences in language and style and help the families of the multiracial youth negotiate the many intricate facets of family communication.

Minority youth run the risk of receiving culturally biased educational and mental health assessments when communication styles and interpersonal behaviors differ from those of the dominant culture (Leidy, Guerra, & Toro, 2012). Some minority students may lack familiarity with the social and educational norms that exist within the U.S. school system. For example, in classes where verbal expressiveness is encouraged and teachers expect their students to ask questions and enter freely into discussions, a minority youth whose culture values implicit aspects of communication and deference to authority may be seen as resistant or withdrawn.

Language is a critical component of communication for the child in the educational system. The need to consider linguistic differences and language barriers in education and counseling is imperative. For immigrant children and youth, problems may initially stem from fears of needing to speak standard English in a group situation. This fear is reflected in bilingual immigrant children who exhibit a high incidence of "elective mutism" (Kopala et al., 1994).

Even when a child has learned a new language, it may take 3–5 years to learn those aspects of language related to cognitive and academic functioning. Often these children achieve at lower levels compared with their monolingual counterparts, particularly in the area of reading and language arts. This problem is exacerbated for the student who may have limited exposure to formal learning experiences in his or her native country. Many adolescents who immigrate to the United States lack literacy skills because they never or seldom attended school. As a result, they experience higher levels of academic failure and lowered self-esteem.

The Role of Technology

As we explore inter- and intrapersonal relationships across cultures, we would be remiss not to consider the impact of technology on the access to and dynamics of such relationships. The world today is filled with a patchwork of technology that has made possible simultaneous interpersonal and intercultural communication. Clearly this technology has profound implications for cross-cultural relationships. Innovations including social media, online dating, smart phones, and e-mail have brought people everywhere into potential contact. Barely a city or village exists that is more than a day or two from anyplace else, and almost everywhere people have computer access. Bus lines, railroads, highways, and airports have created linkages within and between local, regional, national, and international levels of human organization. The impact is enormous. Human connections through communication have made possible the exchange of goods, products, and services as well as the more significant exchange of thoughts, beliefs, and ideas. Accompanying the growth of human communication has been the erosion of barriers that have, throughout history, separated people geographically, linguistically, and culturally. Thus, the potential for cultural identities to merge and mingle is greater than ever.

Parentification in Immigrant Families

In examining the relationship between youth and parents in the multiracial and multiethnic family, a postmodern constructionist perspective can be useful as a caution against ascribing family dysfunction on the basis of Eurocentric family values. Intergenerational roles must be viewed within the racial and ethnic makeup of the family and its members. Adolescents who belong to a family whose culture emphasizes collective identity achievement and family responsibility may be at odds with an academic environment that promotes individual goals and views academic achievement as paramount to success in adulthood. Nevertheless, the caretaking of parents by children has been identified as problematic in a variety of family constellations. Such parent–child role reversals can cause significant behavioral and emotional problems, especially as the child approaches adolescence (Chase, 1999; Leidy et al., 2012). When children acculturate faster than their parents, the natural balance of power is reversed and the protective family structure is disrupted.

Challenges also arise as immigrant families may fear deportation, which causes them to avoid authority figures, including school counselors and mental health professionals. Counselors will need to stay attuned to changes in immigration laws and provide outreach to communities who may be affected by these changes.

Development and Role of Biracial and Multiracial Identity Models

The process for successful identity formation is paramount in the understanding of human behavior as individuals achieve integration of physical, social, and cognitive factors into a sense of self-hood, self-worth, and emotional security. Racial and ethnic identity development models provide practitioners with a framework for understanding the psychological development of ethnic minorities as they exist with the majority population (Aldarondo, 2001).

Several models of biracial identity development have been proposed and can provide a framework from which to examine the development of one's racial identity. W. E. Cross's (1995) model for African American racial identity, Kerwin and Ponterotto's (2009) racial identity model, Root's (1996) identity model, and Poston's (1990) biracial identity model all provide a theoretical foundation for case conceptualization and practice with the multiracial youth.

W. E. Cross's original 1971 hierarchical model of racial identity for African Americans has been updated to include a component of the individual's race salience as well as empirically supported stage revisions. Although the subsequent revisions by Cross may cause some confusion if one is comparing earlier models with more recent ones, the model continues to find prominence in multicultural perspectives of identity formation.

Kerwin and Ponterotto's (2009) biracial model contains seven stages and is based on empirical research that builds on previous models of biracial identity development. This nonlinear, nondirectional model provides a dynamic process through which to examine racial identity. In a similar manner, Root's (1996) model differs from the more prescriptive paradigms in that more flexibility is allowed within the process, identifying four specific paths from which successful multiracial identify formation may proceed.

Poston's (1990) model attests that any model based on integrating only one racial identity is not salient to biracial identity. Poston's model incorporates the uniqueness of biracial identity formation and can be helpful in highlighting the unique experience of the biracial youth.

Continued development of racial identity models will enhance the promotion of counseling that is sensitive to the unique experiences of the multiracial youth. Each model addresses coping mechanisms on a continuum that prepare the minority group member for managing racial oppression in the larger society (Brinson, 1996). The facilitation of positive socialization is the ultimate goal and is considered paramount for the minority youth.

Case Study

Simone is the 14-year-old daughter of Isabella and Tyrone. Isabella was born in the United States to parents who emigrated from Mexico to seek work and better economic opportunities. Tyrone was raised by his single African American mother, who worked as an administrative assistant at a local community college. Isabella and Tyrone met during high school, where they attended a large urban school whose student body was composed of Hispanic, African American, and a few Caucasian and Asian students.

Isabella became pregnant with their daughter, Simone, during her junior year at age 16. Tyrone was a popular senior, age 17, and preparing for graduation at the time Isabella became pregnant. Isabella's parents were disappointed, but they assumed that Tyrone and Isabella would be married and raise Simone. However, Tyrone received a football scholarship to the community college where his mother worked, and while he remained in contact with Isabella and Simone, he and Isabella never married.

Simone grew up living with her mother, Isabella, and her grandparents. Isabella's two younger brothers also lived in the household. When Simone was an infant, Isabella worked a number of jobs as a sales associate while her mother cared for Simone. The family enjoyed a close relationship, and Simone was given special attention by the whole family as the only grandchild. Simone grew into a happy child who loved school and had many friends. She grew up being fully aware of who her father is although she did not spend a great deal of time with him. When visiting her father, Simone routinely spent the night with Tyrone's mother and Tyrone would typically take them to dinner when Simone was visiting.

Simone is fluent in Spanish and English, as her maternal grandparents' primary language was Spanish, but she is frequently questioned at school about speaking Spanish, as she has dark curly hair and her father's dark complexion. She is repeatedly labeled as African American although her facial features reflect her Latino heritage. She does get frustrated with her curly, frizzy hair and "wishes I had mom's silky long hair." Isabella and Simone's neighborhood has remained an economically stable working-class community over the years with a number of multigenerational Hispanic households. Isabella enjoys celebrating El Día de los Muertos and Día de la Virgen de Guadalupe with her family and neighbors. Simone is especially looking forward to turning 15 next year and being honored with her Quinceañera, a traditional Mexican celebration of her womanhood.

Simone also spends some weekends and holidays with Tyrone's mother. On these occasions Simone, Tyrone's mother, and occasionally Tyrone attend the Baptist church where Simone enjoys singing in the choir. Lately Tyrone's mother has encouraged Simone to join the church and be baptized. Tyrone's mother has commented to Simone that "those voodoo" rituals in the Catholic Church are not really Christian and has questioned Simone about why she would want to be a part of those "strange" Mexican ceremonies since she was born in America.

Simone, now in the 10th grade, has recently begun to develop from a lanky teen to a curvy full-figured woman. Older boys have begun to take notice of her at her new high school, and she is spending less time on her studies and more time talking and texting with friends. As a result, her grades have fallen significantly, and without improvement she is at risk to fail this year. Consequently, her mother, uncles, and grandparents incessantly question her about her school performance. Simone does not feel the freedom to be honest about her grades and is routinely dishonest or avoids answering about homework assignments and hides her graded papers if they are not scores she believes will meet her family's expectations.

Simone recently asked her mother if she could attend the homecoming football game with her new girlfriends. Isabella and her grandparents insisted she could attend only if her two uncles went with her, not only to protect her but because one of Simone's friends is known to smoke cigarettes and another friend has a reputation of being "loose" with boys. Isabella was horrified and cried that she would get her father to take her, as he understood football and, "He won't make me sit with him! In fact, he's cool! He gets to stand on the sideline with the coaches!"

Simone has been referred for counseling, as her family is concerned that she is "headed down a dangerous path."

A Culturally Appropriate Approach

Simone is exploring who she is, questioning authority, shifting who her friends are, and not maximizing her academic abilities. She is feeling alienated from her family and academically inferior to her peers. She is also experiencing considerable discomfort with her physical appearance.

The growing diversity of the U.S. population suggests that an increased understanding of cultural factors is required for counselors to be culturally competent practitioners. The Association for Multicultural Counseling and Development (AMCD) has established multicultural competencies for counselors (Arredondo et al., 1996). Research supports the concept that racial and ethnic minority children have higher degrees of problems associated with racial identity development, social marginality, isolation, sexuality conflicts, career dreams, and academic and behavioral concerns (Akos & Ellis, 2008; Harris, 2002). All people have culture, and one's culture can and does affect an individual's ability to adapt to his or her environment. As Swartz-Kulstad and Martin (1999) noted, "Adaptation difficulties typically produce concerns that further affect the individual's functioning" (p. 281). Counselors must be prepared to incorporate cultural factors into their conceptualization of the concerns and the treatment process.

Cultural Considerations

To provide more effective cross-cultural counseling, counselors must be aware of their communication style, their counseling style, and the expectations of their clients. A large repertoire of verbal and nonverbal behaviors will be beneficial (Schoen, 2005). Counselors are in need of ever-present awareness of challenges and limitations. Things like generational or gender differences between clients and counselors can create resistance. Many teens look at any adult with suspicion. Racial differences can be met with outright animosity. Such barriers may be mediated by action-oriented and artistic therapies. For example, concrete activities such as art projects could allow Simone to express her worldview and engage in self-discovery of subconscious themes, emotions, or beliefs.

Deliberate selection of counseling styles and approaches must harmonize with an appropriate communication style to enhance outcomes. In taking a culturally sensitive approach, counselors need to know and respect the traditional values of the particular ethnic group with whom they are working. For example, because traditional Hispanic values suggest a preference for self-control in counseling sessions, clients can experience greater comfort when the focus of the session is on the expression of thoughts rather than feelings (Schoen, 2005). This need is consistent with the value of the counselor maintaining an unassuming manner.

It is also possible that clients may not trust the counselor because of race. Quality counseling is predicated on trust. Mistrust affects the counseling dynamic negatively. If the client is unable to trust the counselor, the working alliance will not be formed and the true benefits of counseling will be unrealized. Sue and Sue (2012) reminded the counselor to view behaviors of clients who are culturally different from themselves in a nonjudgmental manner and avoid personalizing hostilities as the relationship evolves (p. 129). The counselor's cultural competence may be put to the test. Although sometimes uncomfortable, an honest conversation between the counselor and the client about how race may be affecting the therapeutic relationship can be very helpful. Counselors can seek supervision regarding specific approaches, but being self-aware, recognizing your own discomfort, and being proactive in addressing the issue is the key to growth.

Finally, the counselor might ignore the client's strengths if they do not mirror the dominant culture's strengths (Spanierman, 2002). The counseling process will

Sidebar 8.5 ■ Cultural Competence Quiz

The Multicultural Counseling Competencies identify a need for competence related to Counselor Awareness of Own Cultural Values and Biases, Counselor Awareness of Worldview, and Culturally Appropriate Intervention Strategies. Within each area, there are competencies that represent attitudes and beliefs, knowledge, and skills (Arredondo et al., 1996). For example, the three competencies of Counselor Awareness of Worldview would challenge you to address the following related to Simone:

1. Identify any issues of acculturation/assimilation of her Mexican immigrant family that you consider relevant to Simone's racial identity.
2. Do you consider her desire to go to the ballgame with friends without her parents or adult supervision an issue of mainstream adolescent development or a rejection of her Latino familismo heritage?
3. How would your assessment of her behavior influence your counseling goals?

■ ■ ■

benefit if the counselor attends to the client's strengths, even if they are different from those that are valued by the dominant culture. As Schoen (2005) noted, "Realistically, being culturally responsive does not imply a comprehensive knowledge of each culture; rather, it means conveying an interest and respect for other cultures, evidencing an eagerness to learn about other cultures, and appreciating the particular heritage of the client" (p. 256).

Acculturation Considerations

The norms, values, and assumptions of the dominant culture may be affecting Simone in a variety of ways. For example, stereotypes of Hispanic or African American cultures and specifically biracial individuals may be negatively affecting how others view her and the expectations they have of her. In addition, these negative stereotypes may become internalized and affect how Simone perceives herself (Kopala et al., 1994). Because there are few role models with whom Simone can identify, Simone may feel that her particular expression of self is not valued. It is likely that this sense of devaluation, in the larger culture, will affect Simone's view of herself and her academic achievement. This situation is further complicated by the mixed messages that Simone receives from her family members regarding social freedom and religion.

In consideration of all of these factors, counseling for this young woman should be prudently planned. Because Simone expresses at least minimal concern related to educational achievement, an opportunity to discuss nonthreatening issues may be pursued. The influence of parental expectations should be included in these discussions. When trust and comfort are established, more sensitive issues may be gradually introduced. Self-concept, racial identity, sexuality, and peer relationships are all areas of potential exploration.

Contextual and Historical Considerations

On an individual level, the counselor should first focus on and value Simone's unique strengths. Simone is a young woman with a great deal to offer, and the counselor should try and build on her positive qualities to increase her self-esteem. Next, it will be important to explore with Simone the reasons for her feelings of insecurity across all levels. How Simone feels about herself, what messages she is receiving from her family and her peers, and the meaning she derives from these messages are all important areas to cover. Once this exploration is concluded, Simone could benefit from exploring her sense of identity related to racial identity development. This exploration might also include investigating her thoughts, feelings, and desires with regard to her social network and the struggles she is experiencing while attempting to fit in with her peers.

It will be necessary for Simone and the counselor to explore Simone's environment and for the counselor to recommend strategies to help Simone cope with this environment. The counselor must become an advocate for Simone against racism. In addition, it seems important to examine her various reference group identities (e.g., African American, Hispanic, female, spiritual) and to understand how these affect her worldview and her decisions. At this time, the counselor may want to explore Simone's family (immediate and extended) to obtain a more complete picture of Simone's presenting concerns. It may be helpful for the counselor to understand the family's reaction to Simone's physical changes, altered peer group, and social interests. To do this, the counselor and Simone may construct a genogram so that they can obtain a deeper understanding of Simone's development in the context of important family variables. This genogram would be particularly useful if Simone focuses on the multicultural aspects to incorporate contextual factors that may be influencing her choices (Schoen, 2005). By understanding the role the family has on her current choices, Simone may feel better able to accept or reject these choices for herself.

Simone is currently fearful of social isolation or rejection. It will be helpful for the counselor to work with Simone to assist her in understanding that her self-perception is related to how she receives and internalizes the messages from her peers (Kelch-Oliver & Leslie, 2006; Spanierman, 2002). For example, if she is experiencing discrimination related to her appearance and receiving the message that she is inadequate, it is likely that she is internalizing this message. This internalization further isolates her from developing personal relationships or strengthening her self-concept. It is important that the counselor attempt to validate and acknowledge that these feelings are real and warranted. Normalizing Simone's experience will assist in increasing her self-efficacy, which in turn has the potential to result in increased academic confidence, improved social relationships, and greater self-acceptance.

Because many people in Simone's life hold high expectations for her future, Simone is experiencing tremendous pressure. She seems to believe that she must be a high achiever to win approval. Simone's perceptions are being greatly influenced by the prevailing norms and values society holds about achievement (Hook & Ashton, 2002). She seems to be operating from the dominant culture's definition of success that is perpetuated by her parents; thus, she is driven by the concept that to be successful, a person must have distinguished, individual achievements in public domains. Therefore, accomplishments that are frequently important to women, such as making connections to others, may not be seen as achievements by others.

To add to the difficulty, Simone must deal with the fact that expectations held by individuals for themselves and those held by others for them may not agree with broader social stereotypes. She will struggle with the contradiction between the familial expectation that she will accomplish great things and the societal perceptions of what achievements are appropriate for her. Because these two beliefs are generally contradictory, this struggle is present at a variety of levels (Hook & Ashton, 2002).

Approaches to Prevention

When considering the potential symptoms that a racial or ethnic minority youth might be at risk of experiencing, it becomes especially important to examine what could prevent the onset of these struggles. There is opportunity for protective features to be present on an individual, family, school, and community level. "Prevention efforts that support and maximize protective factors while reducing risk factors are more likely to be successful" (McWhirter, McWhirter, McWhirter, & McWhirter, 2007, p. 235). The relationship between prevention and treatment interventions is critical, and prevention efforts are implemented as interventions. In addition, counselors understand that opportunities exist for youth to participate in prevention efforts even if some of the minority youth are already struggling with issues. To be precise, counselors can offer the program to youth who are at risk for symptom development as well as those already experiencing some level of symptoms. The assumption is that the service will be helpful to all of the youth.

Individual

Because every youth is different, each with a unique personality and character traits, counselors must find a way to respond to and support each individual. When considering the risk for racial and ethnic minorities, education on issues such as responsibility and self-discipline, hope, optimism, and communication skills has the potential to be of great benefit for youth facing such risks as poverty, psychosocial and environmental stressors, or dysfunctional family dynamics.

The socialization and developmental processes of racial and ethnic minority youth can be considerably more complicated that those of racial majority children (Herring, 1995). Counselors must develop prevention and intervention efforts that take into account the developmental level of the youth, language, learning style, cultural considerations, and the appropriateness of the method for the particular problem.

Family

Because of the impact of factors within the home on a child's identity development, prevention efforts focused on involving parents and families are critical (Lane, Gresham, & O'Shaughnessy, 2002). Biological and developmental factors, family factors, and ineffective parenting all have the potential to contribute to a child's academic and social–emotional problems. Current data suggest that factors are intertwined and thus have an impact on the youth collective (Swartz-Kulstad & Martin, 1999).

The earliest prevention efforts could focus on prenatal and health care programs. Beginning in utero, parents are afforded an opportunity to bond with their children, encouraging stability and support. During infancy, efforts that promote interaction, consistency, and communication assist in building a strong foundation of parental bonding. The counselor can begin the task of facilitating a narrative that integrates both parents' racial and ethnic parenting styles and rituals into the newly formed family. Ultimately, parent training programs counteract parent and family risk factors by offering parents opportunities to learn effective discipline methods and supportive parenting that promotes a positive racial identity, thereby reducing risk factors for the multiracial child.

School

A number of factors contribute to a child's potential success in minimizing the impact of the factors that place him or her at risk. These protective factors include a strong support network of primary and extended family, teachers, mentors, counselors, and other competent, committed adults (Hauser, 1999; Rak & Patterson, 1996). School counselors in particular have a unique opportunity to promote success in youth. The access given school counselors places them in a position to be one of these competent adults who can create a committed support network for the youth they serve (Constantine & Gushue, 2003).

School-based programs have the opportunity to address multiple risk factors in youth, families, and schools as well as build links between these three areas (Rayle, 2004). School-based programs are more accessible to families and can potentially avoid the stigma associated with services offered in traditional mental health settings. School-based programs also remove some of the practical and social barriers to treatment access, such as lack of transportation or financial resources.

Prevention in school begins with comprehensive preschools, compensatory programs, and before- and after-school programs (McWhirter et al., 2007). Additional protective factors for racially diverse youth include the following: providing teachers and parents with resources, such as a reading list to help families understand biracial issues; inviting multiracial community role models as speakers; and creating an open dialogue among students, teachers, and administrators on the value of cultural diversity.

Community

Prevention efforts that encompass the community and larger society generally involve family members, school personnel, and communities. A need exists to provide social support and coordinated programs that enable community members to assist young people. Prevention efforts strengthen existing support for families in the school and in community organizations that work with the schools. Empowering young people and helping them to develop plans for social action is a preventive approach on the individual level. At the community level, these efforts serve as a broader approach to treatment. The target here is not individuals or even groups of individuals but the norms, structures, and practices of organizations, communities, society, and the nation.

Intervention Strategies

Individual

Individual counselors must implement strategies for responding to the needs of at-risk youth. A multifaceted approach should begin with the counselor's self-assessment of any biases the counselor may have in counseling multiracial youth. Page (2003) found several counselor concerns, including a lack of training and discomfort with racial identity issues. Counselors also reported a lack of real-world experiences with this group. As the number of biracial and multiracial youth grows, understanding their experience becomes paramount (Kelch-Oliver & Leslie, 2006).

The counselor will want to pay close attention to the phenomenological experience, including clients' perceptions of and attitudes toward their racial identity and that of their peers (Akos & Ellis, 2008). By using a developmental racial identity framework, the counselor has a context within which to promote continued self-acceptance and self-efficacy. Self-esteem and ethnic identity are dynamic: Multiracial students with higher self-esteem are also more likely to engage in positive racial identity (Bracey et al., 2004). What is vitally important is that youth are invited into the counseling process, that their experiences are validated, and that they are presumed to be knowledgeable about what is important to them. Even when youth are unable to articulate or even acknowledge a problem, letting them know that their opinions and feelings are important and they are expected to influence the direction of their counseling can lay the groundwork for successful change.

Although particular techniques for interventions may vary in response to the ages of the youth or the presenting problem, the counselor–client relationship should be vibrant, characterized by a shared definition of the problem. The counselor should remain sensitive to the multiracial context of what otherwise may appear to be a generalized adolescent problem while not assuming that every issue is one of racial identity. For example, name calling that falls in the genre of bullying for the multiracial teen may have meaning targeted at the youth's racial identity. The counselor should remain aware of terms such as "Oreo," "wigger," "mulatto," "half-caste," "mongrel," "cross-breed," and "mutt" that may be used in reference to the youth at risk and should actively promote awareness and a no-tolerance policy for such behavior. The counselor can provide cultural diversity days and help integrate art and music that highlight heritages of biracial artists to provide positive role models for the biracial youth (Moss & Davis, 2008).

Considering the context allows youth an opportunity to understand what has shaped their thoughts, feelings, and behaviors. This context may include racial identity, family dynamics, school dynamics, and community dynamics (Moss & Davis, 2008; Nishimura, 1995).

Addressing the intersections of gender, class, race, and culture allows counselors to explore psychosocial identity formation (Akos & Ellis, 2008; Robinson, 1993). If counselors acknowledge the role of racial identity, including how race serves to maintain or exacerbate the problems, youth have an opportunity to examine internalized messages and determine options for change. Vernon (2004) noted, "Counseling for empowerment implies that young people have the capacity to change, grow, act, and shape their environment despite contextual limitations" (p. 326). When a counselor teaches youth how to advocate for themselves and how to enact

Sidebar 8.6 ■ Exploring the Layers of Simone's Identity

Let's expand the cultural context for our case study. Simone's father, Tyrone, is an African American who graduated from the university and works as a college recruiter. He is often seen as a role model who is frequently invited to the join the coaches on the field during home games. Simone's mother, Isabella, is concerned Tyrone will not monitor Simone's activities, especially around the older boys. Isabella wants her brothers, Simone's uncles, to chaperone Simone at the game. Tyrone became angry with Isabella and her family: "You are all trying to get up in my business again. Leave that girl alone for a change. She can't do anything without your whole family in tow!"

1. How might you conceptualize this conflict through a multicultural lens?
2. Which of the AMCD guidelines resonate with you for this case?

■ ■ ■

positive social change strategies to advance acceptance of themselves and others like them, it can be a powerful intervention that enhances self-efficacy—and, thus, self-esteem—and it can broaden youth's knowledge of and sensitivity to issues specific to the multiracial experience.

Coping skills training allows counselors an opportunity to assist at-risk youth in dealing with situations that cause conflict and tension. All young people feel fear, disappointment, or anger at one time or another. How they cope with these situations is indicative of their adjustment. The greater the difficulty coping with stress, the greater the risk for establishing unhealthy coping patterns. Ultimately, ineffective strategies like withdrawal, acting out, or denial may emerge. Racial and ethnic minority youth then risk developing anxiety or depression, which may lead to learning problems, poor communication, negative self-talk, conduct problems, or academic underachievement (Esquivel & Keitel, 1990). Fortunately, a number of programs have proved to be effective in enhancing children's skills for coping with stress, anxiety, or depression. For example, the FRIENDS program trains children and their parents to handle stress and anxiety while fostering increased peer social support (Shortt, Barrett, & Fox, 2001).

Overall, a culturally competent counselor should be able to relate to racial and ethnic minority youth and have knowledge of cultural and class factors. Counselors are cautioned against a compartmentalized approach to cultural competency, for example, where one only addresses diversity on "cultural" holidays, such as placing singular focus on Black History Month, rather than using a holistic approach to education. In addition, culturally skilled counselors routinely become involved with minority individuals outside the counseling setting (e.g., community events, social and political functions, celebrations, friendships, neighborhood groups, and so forth) so that their perspective of minorities is richer than academic or helping in nature.

Developing multicultural competence is a lifelong learning endeavor. The novice counselor is reminded to first adhere to the Multicultural Counseling Competencies (Arredondo et al., 1996) and to be proactive in engaging in racially diverse experiences and training. As the ethnic and racial makeup of the population continues to become more diverse, we counselors will need to expand our interventions to meet the needs of a culturally rich client population.

Family

The nature of the family structure has been forced to shift in response to the ever-changing social and economic conditions. Because of the increases in diverse family structures, immigrant families, and multiracial families, more families are called on to deal with stressors related to racial and ethnic conflicts. Even normal developmental issues can be difficult to deal with, but family distress can emerge when cultural minority issues are added to the mix. McWhirter et al. (2007) noted that "working with the entire family is often the optimal approach for dealing with young people at risk for drop out, substance abuse, pregnancy, delinquency, suicide or other problems" (p. 304).

Parent interventions help parents respond effectively to normal behavior and emotional problems so that these problems do not escalate. Parents gain knowledge of how to provide support for their children's cognitive, social, and emotional growth. Parent training programs can also assist parents with interacting successfully with teachers and advocating for their children's social and academic development. Family training may focus on such issues as communication and problem-solving skills. Ideally, the support offered to the parents will not only enhance fundamental parenting skills but also facilitate parent support, decrease the sense of isolation, and provide strategies to cope with stressful life events. It is most effective if parents are trained to recognize and cope with the signs of risk before the youth's behavior becomes completely unmanageable. Training in behavior management, the implementation of rewards and consequences, and help with communication skills can be particularly effective with younger children (Kim & Lyons, 2003). Because expectations regarding child behavior and accepted methods of discipline are frequently defined by culture, cultural appropriateness is critical to the success of parent training programs. The counselor is best served by getting acquainted with the family and understanding the family traditions, ideals, uniqueness, and traditions.

Highlighting positive family cultural and racial norms by acknowledging and reinforcing traditions serves to provide a positive environment for multiracial youth to explore their racial identity. For example, having the parents of the multiracial youth openly discuss the differences in parenting styles and advocating for a respectful dialogue and exploration of the commonalities build a framework for positive biracial parenting skills. One adjunct to family counseling is family support groups. Not only do these groups offer education for parents, but they also provide an opportunity for parents to build relationships with other parents in similar circumstances or who have handled similar problems. Parent support groups afford parents opportunities to express their concerns and learn what has or has not worked for other parents in similar circumstances. Such support groups are often available through community resources.

School

Without a doubt, emphasis on academic success is critical for school counselors of racial and ethnic minority children. As Dupper and Poertner (1997) observed, "Education, which increases a youth's skills and employment opportunities, is an important route" (p. 415) for a youth to take to counteract the potential consequences of the identified risks. School counselors may address the academic, personal, and career needs of the students they serve (American School Counselor Association, 2004). With an at-risk population such as racial and ethnic minority youth, the school counselor becomes an essential force in providing opportunities that facilitate self-esteem and subsequent academic success.

In an effort to reach the youth, counselors may seek access via the family (Dupper & Poertner, 1997). Such collaboration may be difficult to achieve, as parents may fear cultural insensitivity, condescending school personnel, or accusations of being responsible for their children's difficulties. Conversely, teachers may believe that parents will not respect their expertise, will not participate, or will hold their children's teachers responsible for their problems. These reservations all too often materialize, and the common goal of serving the youth is not enough to overcome the barriers. "Rather, multicultural competence, communication, skills, time, resources, empathy and patience are also required" (McWhirter et al., 2007, p. 244).

Because poverty is common among racial and ethnic minorities, there may be diminished focus on the day-to-day needs of the present to meet the basic survival needs of housing and nutrition. These families may be less likely to see the relevance in education if it offers no immediate impact on the families' well-being and there is a lack of resources to connect education to long-term consequences and career potential (T. L. Cross & Burney, 2005). If the lack of emphasis on education is present, the role of the school counselor is often to educate families about the role of education in advancing the lives of youth. Families in repressed economic circumstances are not always aware that education can actually mediate negative outcomes such as delinquency and ongoing poverty.

In addition to educating families, the school counselor may be in a position to educate faculty and staff about the role and impact of racial and ethnic identity development on youth. Counselors can work with faculty to assist them in understanding a student's absences or a seeming lack of ambition in an otherwise academically competent student (T. L. Cross & Burney, 2005). School counselors often have regular opportunities to serve as advocates for youth and their families. Providing valuable information to the people involved in the lives of racial and ethnic minority youth is one form of such advocacy.

Another focal point for school counselors is the role of education. Racial and ethnic minority youth may not enter the academic realm with the middle-class standards and aspirations espoused by a school system. While school systems may predict students who will pursue a secondary education and then enter into a skilled workforce or postsecondary institution, a primary role of the school counselor is college and career preparatory activities (T. L. Cross & Burney, 2005). With racial and ethnic minority youth, this role is even more vital because many of these individuals may lack role models related to completing a high school education, pursuing higher education, or considering associated career opportunities. Often school counselors find themselves serving as the only voice of high expectation related to postsecondary academic opportunities (Gillespie & Starkey, 2006). Continued awareness of the cultural position of education within the household is critical because it may outweigh the norms of the student's peer groups resulting from profound social and familial pressure.

Finally, the school counselor is afforded the opportunity to assist in the development and implementation of wraparound services that include community, family, health, social services, and educational perspectives. This multidisciplinary approach offers comprehensive involvement with the at-risk youth and distributes the weight of managing these students' needs, which would be difficult for the school counselor to accomplish independently (Bryan, 2005). The involvement of committed networks of supportive and influential adults in the lives of racial and ethnic minority youth serves as a significant strength in preventing negative effects and providing children with the greatest potential for success.

Community

When considering what makes up a community, it becomes obvious that it could be composed of many groups, such as family, peers, neighborhoods, or church groups. For ethnic and minority youth, a connection with their community is important to foster a sense of belonging. The community also has an opportunity to offer tools for healthy development, such as role modeling, encouragement, and provision of basic needs.

Racial and ethnic minority youth often lack a sense of community with any other groups in their environment or belong to communities that undermine their resources and abilities (Vernon, 2004). Counselors have the opportunity to promote the building of community and aid youth in accessing or nurturing existing communities. Community programs that promote positive social interactions, build communication skills, and foster a shared sense of identity are especially helpful to this end (Sinclair, Hurley, Evelo, Christenson, & Thurlow, 2002). Prevention efforts within the community could focus on improving socioeconomic conditions, expanding opportunities for adequate housing, assisting parents in accessing child care and job opportunities, and assisting families in integrating into community norms (Lane et al., 2002; McWhirter et al., 2007; Vernon, 2004).

Promoting a sense of community can be fostered through participation in clubs or organizations with a particular theme, such as a sports team, volunteer groups, scouts, or Boys and Girls Clubs of America. It is critical for counselors to assist children in accessing community resources and building the skills needed for drawing the community's support, as youth who are already experiencing a sense of isolation may not feel comfortable initiating participation in such activities.

Adaptations for Diversity

> Perhaps travel cannot prevent bigotry, but by demonstrating that all peoples cry, laugh, eat, worry, and die, it can introduce the idea that if we try and understand each other, we may even become friends.
> —Maya Angelou

There is no one model or pattern for conducting counseling with racial and ethnic minority youth. The approach depends on the problems, the conditions surrounding them, and the counselor's theoretical orientation. The following proactive activities enhance multicultural sensitivity and demonstrate commitment to diversity (Brinson, 1996; Herring, 1992; Montague, 1996; Vernon, 2004).

1. Attempt to identify and understand the issues from the worldview of the client. Practice examining how your life might be different if you were a member of a minority culture. If you are a member of a minority culture, try to consider how you may have oppressed others.
2. Be comfortable acknowledging and exploring the client's cultural differences. Be open to durable and significant relationships with members of minority cultures. Do not wait to be invited; take some initiative.
3. Identify and embrace the existence of strengths for a culturally diverse family and attempt to incorporate these strengths into coping skills.
4. Be aware of how the client identifies himself or herself racially. Engage in a conversation about how this decision was made.
5. Promote sensitivity through the use of insightful, nonjudgmental interventions and techniques that clarify the client's view and culturally determined perceptions about reality.
6. Read texts, watch movies, and attend theaters that feature characters and themes from other cultures.
7. Prior to working with a new cultural group, consider the assumptions, bias, stereotypes, and negative concepts you may hold against the group. Also consider the assumptions, bias, stereotypes, and negative concepts that could be held against the group you identify yourself as a member of.

8. Create your own cultural genogram and use it as a source of connection with members of cultures different from your own. Consider visible and invisible identities.
9. Learn a second language and find venues to practice your new language to facilitate its use within your practice.
10. Find a colleague who can serve as a confidant and consultant with expertise in multicultural issues. Consult honestly and often.

Summary

The many societal changes reflected in the demographic growth and diversification of the United States have greatly influenced the counseling profession. Counseling professionals must realize that culture cannot be ignored—it is an influential aspect of the counseling experience. The growth in the number of racial and ethnic minorities has altered the balance with the majority culture. What is unique to our time is a fundamental change in the structure and process of identity. The identity of the "multicultural," far from being frozen in a social character, is more fluid and mobile, more susceptible to change, more open to variation. It is an identity based not on a "belongingness," which implies either owning or being owned by culture, but on a style of self-consciousness that is capable of negotiating ever new formations of reality. In this sense the multicultural person is a radical departure from the kinds of identities found in both traditional and mass societies. He or she is neither totally a part of nor totally apart from his or her culture; instead, he or she lives on the boundary. Because of these changes, counselors need to explore their own sense of racial and ethnic identity and to increase their level of training with regard to working with cultural minorities.

Sensitivity to acculturation considerations and a foundation of knowledge regarding culturally appropriate interventions help shape culturally competent counselors. Counselors must learn to consider cultural impact within individual, familial, school, and community contexts. Doing so offers the greatest opportunity for successful counseling with racial and ethnic minority youth. The following websites provide additional information relating to the chapter topics.

Useful Websites

Association for Multicultural Counseling and Development Multicultural Counseling Competencies
http://www.counseling.org/Resources/Competencies/Multcultural_Competencies.pdf
Mixed Heritage Center
http://www.mixedheritagecenter.org/index.php?option=com_content&task=view&id=1475&Itemid=29
Multiracialidentity.com
http://multiracialidentity.com/
Race: The Power of Illusion Quiz
(take this quiz to see if you can match the person with his or her race)
http://www.pbs.org/race/002_SortingPeople/002_00-home.htm
U.S. Census Bureau State and County Facts
http://quickfacts.census.gov/qfd/states/00000.html

References

Aaroe, L., & Nelson, J. R. (2000). A comparative analysis of teachers', Caucasian parents', and Hispanic parents' views of problematic school survival behaviors. *Education and Treatment of Children, 23*, 314–324.

Akos, P., & Ellis, C. M. (2008). Racial identity development in middle school: A case for school counselor individual and system intervention. *Journal of Counseling & Development, 86*, 26–33. doi:10.1002/j.1556-6678.2008.tb00622.x

Akutsu, P. D., Snowden, L. R., & Organista, K. C. (1996). Referral patterns in ethnic-specific and mainstream programs for minorities and Whites. *Journal of Counseling Psychology, 43*, 56–64.

Aldarondo, F. (2001). Racial and ethnic identity models and their application: Counseling biracial individuals. *Journal of Mental Health Counseling, 23*, 238–256.

American School Counselor Association. (2004). *Position statement: Cultural diversity. The professional school counselor and cultural diversity.* Retrieved from http://www.school-counselor.org/content.asp?contentid=249

Arredondo, P., Toporek, M. S., Brown, S., Jones, J., Locke, D. C., Sanchez, J., & Stadler, H. (1996). Operationalization of the Multicultural Counseling Competencies. *Journal of Multicultural Counseling and Development, 24*, 42–78. doi:10.1002/j.2161-1912.1996.tb00288.x

Arroyo, C. G., & Zigler, E. (1995). Racial identity, academic achievement, and the psychological well-being of economically disadvantaged adolescents. *Journal of Personality and Social Psychology, 69*, 903–914.

Bracey, J., Bamaca, M. Y., & Umana-Taylor, A. J. (2004). Examining ethnic identity and self-esteem among biracial and monoracial adolescents. *Journal of Youth and Adolescents, 33*, 123–132.

Brinson, J. (1996). Cultural sensitivity for counselors: Our challenge for the twenty-first century. *Journal of Humanistic Education and Development, 34*, 195–207.

Bryan, J. (2005). Fostering educational resilience and achievement in urban schools through school–family–community partnerships. *Professional School Counseling, 8*, 219–227.

Caldwell, C. H., Rafferty, J., Reischl, T. M., DeLoney, H., & Brooks, C. L. (2010). Enhancing parenting skills among nonresident African American fathers as a strategy for preventing youth risky behaviors. *American Journal of Community Psychology 45*, 17–35. doi:10.1007/s10464-009-9290-4

Chase, N. D. (1999). Parentification: An overview of theory, research, and societal issues. In N. D. Chase (Ed.), *Burdened children: Theory, research, and treatment of parentification* (pp. 3–33). Thousand Oaks, CA: Sage.

Cokley, K., McClain, S., Jones, M., & Johnson, S. (2011). A preliminary investigation of academic disidentification, racial identity, and academic achievement among African American adolescents. *The High School Journal, 95*, 54–68.

Coley, R. L., & Medeiros, B. L. (2007). Reciprocal longitudinal relations between nonresident father involvement and adolescent delinquency. *Child Development, 78*, 132–147.

Constantine, M. G., Erickson, C. D., Banks, R. W., & Timberlake, T. L. (1998). Challenges to the career development of urban racial and ethnic minority youth: Implications for vocational intervention. *Journal of Multicultural Counseling and Development, 26*, 82–95.

Constantine, M., & Gushue, G. (2003). School counselors' tolerance attitudes and racism attitudes as predictors of their multicultural case conceptualization of an immigrant student. *Journal of Counseling & Development, 81*, 185–191.

Cross, T. L., & Burney, V. H. (2005). High ability, rural, and poor: Lessons from Project Aspire and implications for school counselors. *Journal of Secondary Gifted Education, 16*, 148–156.

Cross, W. E. (1995). The psychology of nigrescence: Revising the Cross model. In J. Ponterotto, M. Casas, L. Suzuki, & C. Alexander (Eds.), *Handbook of multicultural counseling* (pp. 93–122). Thousand Oaks, CA: Sage.

DaCosta, K. (2007). *Making multiracials: State, family and market in the redrawing of the color line.* Palo Alto, CA: Stanford University Press.

Dupper, D. R., & Poertner, J. (1997). Public schools and the revitalization of impoverished communities: School-linked, family resource centers. *Social Work, 42,* 415–422.

Erikson, E. H. (1968). *Identity, youth, and crisis.* New York, NY: Norton.

Esquivel, G., & Keitel, M. (1990). Counseling immigrant children in the schools. *Elementary School Guidance and Counseling, 24,* 213–218.

Felbeck, K. (2010). *Mixed: Portraits of multiracial kids.* San Francisco, CA: Chronicle Books.

Gibbs, J. T. (2003). Biracial adolescents. In J. T. Gibbs & L. N. Huang (Eds.), *Children of color* (2nd ed., pp. 322–350). San Francisco, CA: Jossey-Bass.

Gillespie, A., & Starkey, D. S. (2006). The role of the rural school counselor in preparing high school students for college. *Delta Education Journal, 3,* 24–28.

Harris, H. (2002). School counselor's perceptions of biracial children: A pilot study. *Professional School Counseling, 6,* 120–130.

Hauser, S. T. (1999). Understanding resilient outcomes: Adolescent. *Journal of Research on Adolescence, 9,* 1–24.

Herring, R. (1992). Biracial children: An increasing concern for elementary and middle school counselors. *Elementary School Guidance and Counseling, 27,* 123–131.

Herring, R. (1995). Developing biracial identity: A review of the increasing dilemma. *Journal of Multicultural Counseling and Development, 23,* 29–39.

Hill, S. (1999). *African American children: Socialization and development in families.* Thousand Oaks, CA: Sage.

Hook, M., & Ashton, K. (2002). Transcending a double bind: The case of Jenna. *The Career Development Quarterly, 50,* 321–325.

Kelch-Oliver, K., & Leslie, L.A. (2006). Biracial females' reflections on racial identity development in adolescence. *Journal of Feminist Family Therapy, 18,* 53–75. doi:10.1300/J086v18n04_03

Kerwin, C., & Ponterotto, J. G. (2009). Biracial identity development: Research and practice. In J. Ponterotto, M. Casas, L. Suzuki, & C. Alexander (Eds.), *Handbook of multicultural counseling* (2nd ed., pp. 199–217). Thousand Oaks, CA: Sage.

Kim, B., & Lyons, H. (2003). Experiential activities and multicultural competence training. *Journal of Counseling & Development, 81,* 400–408.

Kopala, M., Esquivel, G., & Baptiste, L. (1994). Counseling approaches for immigrant children: Facilitating the acculturative process. *School Counselor, 41,* 352–360.

Lane, K. L., Gresham, F. M., & O'Shaughnessy, T. E. (2002). *Interventions for children with or at risk for emotional and behavioral disorders.* Boston, MA: Allyn & Bacon.

Lau, A. S., Garland, A. F., Yeh, M., McCabe, K. M., Wood, P. A., & Hough, R. L. (2004). Race/ethnicity and inter-informant agreement in assessing adolescent psychopathology. *Journal of Emotional and Behavioral Disorders, 12,* 145–156.

Leidy, M. S., Guerra, N. G., & Toro, R. I. (2012). Positive parenting, family cohesion, and child social competence among immigrant Latino families. *Journal of the Latina/o Psychological Association, 1,* 3–13. doi:10.1037/2168-1678.1.S.3

Maital, S. L. (2000). Reciprocal distancing: A systems model of interpersonal processes in cross-cultural consultation. *School Psychology Review, 29,* 389–401.

Malott, K. M., Alessandria, K. P., Kirkpatrick, M., & Carandang, J. (2009). Ethnic labeling in Mexican-origin youth: A qualitative assessment. *Professional School Counseling, 12,* 352–364. doi:10.5330/PSC.n.2010-12.352

Marotta, S., & Garcia, J. (2003). Latinos in the United States in 2000. *Hispanic Journal of Behavioral Sciences, 25,* 13–34.

Martin, M. D. (2008). Television media as a potential negative factor in racial identity development of African American youth. *Academic Psychiatry, 32,* 338–342. Retrieved from http://ap.psychiatryonline.org

McGoldrick, M. (2005). Ethnicity and family therapy: An overview. In M. McGoldrick, J. K. Pearce, & J. Giordana (Eds.), *Ethnicity and family therapy* (3rd ed., pp. 3–30). New York, NY: Guilford Press.

McWhirter, J., McWhirter, B., McWhirter, E., & McWhirter, R. (2007). *At risk youth: A comprehensive response for counselors, teachers, psychologists, and human service professionals* (4th ed.). Belmont, CA: Thompson Brooks/Cole.

Miville, M. L., Koonce, D., Darlington, P., & Whitlock, B. (2000). Exploring the relationships between racial/cultural identity and ego identity among African Americans and Mexican Americans. *Journal of Multicultural Counseling and Development, 28,* 208–224. doi:10.1002/j.2161-1912.2000.tb00616.x

Mixed Heritage Center. (n.d.). *U.S. minorities to become majority in 2042: Date is eight years sooner than previous estimates from U.S. Census Bureau.* Retrieved from http://www.mixedheritagecenter. org/index.php?option=com_content&task=view&id=1483&Itemid=29

Montague, J. (1996). Counseling families from diverse cultures: A nondeficit approach. *Journal of Multicultural Counseling and Development, 24,* 37–40.

Moss, R. C., & Davis, D. (2008). Counseling biracial students: A review of issues and interventions. *Journal of Multicultural Counseling and Development, 36,* 219–230.

Nishimura, N. (1995). Addressing the needs of biracial children: An issue for counselors in a multicultural school environment. *School Counselor, 43,* 52–57.

Ohrt, J. H., Lambie, G. W., & Leva, K. P. (2009). Supporting Latino and African-American students in advanced placement courses: A school counseling program's approach. *Professional School Counseling, 13,* 59–63. doi:10.5330/PSC.n.2010-13.59

Olatunji, A. N. (2005). Dropping out of high school among Mexican-origin youths: Is early work experience a factor? *Harvard Educational Review, 75,* 286–305.

Orton, G. L. (1996). *Strategies for counseling with children and their parents.* Pacific Grove, CA: Brooks/Cole.

Page, M. N. (2003). Reactions in the field: Interviews with helping professionals who work with biracial children and adolescents. *Dissertation Abstracts International, 63,* 3959.

Pew Hispanic Center. (2005). *Hispanics: A people in motion.* Retrieved March 20, 2008, from http://pewhispanic.org/files/reports/40.pdf

Phelps, R. E., Taylor, J. D., & Gerard, P. A. (2001). Cultural mistrust, ethnic identity, racial identity, and self-esteem among ethnically diverse Black university students. *Journal of Counseling & Development, 79,* 209–217.

Poston, W. S. C. (1990). The biracial identity developmental model: A needed addition. *Journal of Counseling & Development, 69,* 152–155.

Rak, C., & Patterson, L. (1996). Promoting resilience in at-risk children. *Journal of Counseling & Development, 74,* 368–373.

Rayle, A. (2004). Counseling adolescents toward wellness: The roles of ethnic identity, acculturation, and mattering. *Professional School Counseling, 8,* 81–90.

Robinson, T. (1993). The intersections of gender, class, race and culture: On seeing clients whole. *Journal of Multicultural Counseling and Development, 21,* 50–58.

Robinson, T. L. (2012). *The convergence of race, ethnicity, and gender* (4th ed.). Upper Saddle River, NJ: Pearson Education.

Root, M. P. P. (1996). *The multiracial experience.* Thousand Oaks, CA: Sage.

Sandhu, D. S., Portes, P. R., & McPhee, S. A. (1996). Assessing cultural adaptation: Psychometric properties of the Cultural Adaptation Pain Scale. *Journal of Multicultural Counseling and Development, 24,* 15–25.

Schoen, A. (2005). Culturally sensitive counseling for Asian Americans/Pacific Islanders. *Journal of Instructional Psychology, 32,* 253–258.

Shortt, H., Barrett, P., & Fox, T. (2001). Evaluating the FRIENDS program: A cognitive–behavioral group treatment for anxious children and their parents. *Journal of Clinical Psychology, 30,* 525–235.

Sinclair, M., Hurley, C., Evelo, D., Christenson, S., & Thurlow, M. (2002). Making connections that keep students coming to school. In B. Algozzine & P. Kay (Eds.), *Preventing problem behaviors: A handbook of successful prevention strategies* (pp. 162–182). Thousand Oaks, CA: Sage.

Spanierman, L. B. (2002). Academic self-efficacy within a culture of modern racism: The case of Benita. *The Career Development Quarterly, 50,* 331–334.

Sue, D. W., & Sue, D. (2012). *Counseling the culturally diverse* (6th ed.). New York, NY: Wiley.

Swartz-Kulstad, J., & Martin, W. (1999). Impact of culture and context on psychosocial adaptation: The cultural and contextual guide process. *Journal of Counseling & Development, 77,* 281–294.

Turner, M. (2011). *The impact of multicultural literature in education: A review of the importance, noted research, and bibliography of culturally diverse children's literature* (Unpublished master's thesis). Peabody College, Vanderbilt University, Nashville, TN.

U.S. Census Bureau. (2011). *State and county quick facts.* Retrieved from http://quickfacts.census.gov/qfd/states/00000.html

Vernon, A. (2004). *Counseling children and adolescents* (3rd ed.). Denver, CO: Love.

Chapter 9

The Secret and All-Consuming Obsessions: Eating Disorders

Meredith J. Drew, Ann M. Ordway, and Mark D. Stauffer*

Through media, food is presented in advertisements of colorful, enticing, and over-sized portions of appetizing options. We are encouraged to "super-size it" and are offered choices that are available at all hours of the day and night. Food is marketed as a panacea promising to fill an existential gap, serving a need beyond sustenance, nutrition, and togetherness at the table. This pressure informs individuals but also families. Children and youth learn about family relationships and rituals that, for better or for worse, are reinforced around the table, where food is often the center-piece and the meal is the highlight of the gathering. Truly, food can be a comfort when we are ill; when we are sad; when we are angry, lonely, or wish to celebrate.

A conflict emerges, however, as advertisers promise fulfillment through feasting on less healthy foods, while conversely pressing viewers to be ultrathin and unre-alistically fit. This body image pursuit emphasizes control and discipline over self-indulgence. The idealized body type that is portrayed in advertising is naturally possessed by only 5% of American women (Jhally, Kilbourne, & Media Education Foundation, 2002). By age 6, girls especially start to express concerns about their own weight or shape, and 40%–60% of elementary school girls (ages 6–12) are concerned about their weight or about becoming too fat (Smolak, 2011). With such conflicting messages, it is no wonder that eating disorders are prevalent. Indeed, women who are exposed to "thin-ideal" television programs (i.e., ones that por-tray primarily thin, attractive actors) have higher rates of eating disorder symp-toms (Bissel & Zhou, 2004). Though the etiology of eating disorders is not merely the result of societal messaging, such societal messages may, nonetheless, be en-couraging exaggerated, if not epidemic, levels of disordered eating.

*We wish to note the work completed by Kimberly Wright and Elva Banks in the fifth edition of this chapter. Thanks also to Christine Reilly for her research assistance.

An estimated 25 million people in the United States and 70 million people worldwide suffer from eating disorders (National Institute of Mental Health [NIMH], 2011). The rate of new cases of eating disorders has been increasing since the 1950s (Hudson, Hiripi, Pope, & Kessler, 2007; Striegel-Moore & Franko, 2003; Wade, Keski-Rahkonen, & Hudson, 2011). The increase in diagnosed eating disorders may be attributed to real increases in disorder, but it also may reflect clinical recognition of previously unacknowledged eating disorders. For example, men's eating disorders and binge eating disorders may have been underdiagnosed (S. White, Reynolds-Malear, & Cordero, 2011).

Research has highlighted the serious consequences of eating disorders. A review of nearly 50 years of research confirms that anorexia nervosa (AN) has the highest mortality rate of any psychiatric disorder (Arcelus, Mitchell, Wales, & Nielsen, 2011). In addition, more information about the comorbity of psychiatric disorders and eating disorders is emerging. For example, one study found that as many as 64% of individuals with bulimia nervosa reported three or more psychiatric disorders (Hudson et al., 2007). Comorbity with addictions is also of concern, as those who are diagnosed with an eating disorder are 4 times more likely to be diagnosed with an alcohol or substance abuse disorder than the general population (Harrop & Marlatt, 2010). Eating disorders also affect a person's general functioning and quality of life. Many who suffer from an eating disorder have compounding and resultant relationship, financial, and productivity struggles.

Despite the pervasiveness and the health and mortality risks, eating disorders go untreated. In a large U.S. nationwide study of 3,252 female (58%) and 2,315 male (42%) high school students, "the proportion of symptomatic students who had never received treatment was 83% to 95% of boys and 83% to 86% of girls," depending on the symptom type (Austin et al., 2008, p. 4). To add to concerns, funding to combat disordered eating remains low. For example, the National Institutes of Health (2011) reported that research dollars spent on Alzheimer's disease averaged $88 per affected individual, schizophrenia averaged $81 per affected individual, and autism averaged $44 per affected individual. It was reported that for eating disorders, the average amount of research dollars per affected individual was just $0.93 (National Institutes of Health, 2011).

Eating disorders continue to plague many individuals regardless of gender, ethnicity, or cultural factors. There are many components that contribute to understanding an eating disorder and how to provide prevention methods or intervention strategies. This chapter provides an in-depth examination of the history of eating disorders and the diagnosis, symptoms, and definitions of each eating disorder. A detailed case study applies prevention and intervention techniques to demonstrate the application of evidence-based practices in the field of eating disorders. Prevention and intervention strategies approach eating disorders from the individual family, school, and community perspectives to provide a comprehensive analysis for how to address the disorder in essential environments. Because eating disorders have the highest mortality rate of any other mental health disorder, understanding the diagnosis and how to work with this at-risk population is essential.

Risk Factors

New research has been able to highlight risk factors and individual susceptibility for eating disorders. Although all individuals have some level of risk, specific populations face additional challenges.

Sidebar 9.1 ■ Self-Awareness: Media Influence on Body Image

Watch television for an hour, read a popular magazine, or surf the Internet. Keep a record each time you come across a sexual image or an image that depicts a male or female in an idealized or perfect body image. What are some of the messages conveyed by these images? To what degree do you think such images contribute toward body dissatisfaction in both men and women? How are your own thoughts about your appearance influenced by your exposure to images in the media?

■ ■ ■

Gender

Until recently, eating disorders were thought to be a female disorder. Although female gender does still remain a risk factor for developing an eating disorder (Garner & Keiper, 2010), eating disorders and body image struggles affect both genders. In general, mainstream television viewing has been found to be related to poorer body image (Schooler, Ward, Merriwether, & Caruthers, 2004). The visual images of the media become the reference point against which both men and women measure themselves. The greater the discrepancy between the visual image and the real image, the greater the dissatisfaction in one's own appearance. In one study of American elementary school girls who read magazines, 69% said that the pictures influenced their concept of the ideal body shape and 47% said the pictures made them want to lose weight (Martin, 2010). In another study of 173 college men, Baird and Grieve (2006) found that men who viewed male models in men's magazines reported increased body dissatisfaction. It is clear that overly focusing on weight and body type has a direct impact on youth and disordered eating. It is estimated that over half of teenage girls and one third of teenage boys use unhealthy methods to control their weight (Neumark-Sztainer, 2005).

Though both adolescent girls and boys may be susceptible, disordered eating may manifest differently by gender. Disordered eating may be attributed to the cultural desire for females to be thin and for males to be muscular, which is supported by Ousley, Cordero, and White (2008), who found that college males were as concerned as college females regarding tone and shape. Males who, through participation in athletics, are exposed to restrictive eating practices (as frequently occurs in wrestling) appear to be at greater risk. Currently, men are identifying more muscular shapes as the ideal and holding the belief that women also prefer more muscular men than they actually endorse (Grieve, Newton, Kelley, Miller, & Kerr, 2005). Moreover, sexual orientation issues are prevalent in males with eating disorder issues, but the relationship of sexual orientation to the existence of eating disorders has not been fully examined in the literature and is therefore not fully understood. However, males present with approximately 5% to 10% of the cases of AN and bulimia nervosa (BN), whereas females present with the larger majority of the total presenting cases (Costin, 2007). When examining youth in a large-scale multinational study—one that drew from a base of 35,000 student responses from 270 public, private, and parochial schools—Austin et al. (2008) estimated that in the United States, "almost 1 in 4 girls and 1 in 10 boys reported at least 1 disordered eating or weight control symptom serious enough to warrant further evaluation by a health professional" (p. 4).

Even with the large number of individuals who suffer from an eating disorder, the numbers are still believed to be underreported for both genders because of non-disclosure, lack of recognition of the disorder, or diagnosis of other psychiatric disorders masking this disease (Stice, 2002). It is likely that many cases of anorexia or bulimia among males go unreported for several reasons: (a) Men are reluctant to admit symptoms of a "female disorder," (b) eating large quantities of food is not considered abnormal by adolescent boys and young men, and (c) clinicians are less likely to explore eating disorder symptoms among males because those symptoms are not always as obvious (Costin, 2007). Even considering the potential underreporting among men, women are at higher risk for developing anorexia or bulimia.

Age

Adolescence is a high-risk period for the development of eating disorders. The most frequent period for the emergence of anorexia and bulimia is between the ages 14 and 18, but atypical onset patterns exist. The onset of eating disorder symptoms and fixations on thinness, however, are becoming more common among even young children, who are taught at a young age to consider weight and appearance. In a similar manner, there has been an increase in eating disorders among middle-aged and older women, who respond to age-related body changes with obsessive dieting and efforts to return to or maintain an unrealistic ideal body image (Costin, 2007).

Race and Ethnicity

Anorexia and bulimia have historically been associated with upper-middle-class White female populations; however, the risk and prevalence of these are increasing for minority groups (Striegel-Moore & Smolak, 2002). Findings from the National Eating Disorder Screening Program (NEDSP; Austin et al., 2008), the Youth Risk Behavior Surveillance System (Centers for Disease Control and Prevention, 2005), as well as the Commonwealth Fund Survey (Neumark-Sztainer & Hannan, 2001) all suggest that there is little difference among girls when examining eating disorder symptoms across ethnic groups. In the same NEDSP study, White boys, in most symptom categories, reported lower rates than other ethnic groups (Austin et al., 2008). Culture may also influence the prevalence of specific eating disorder symptoms. For example, binge eating and obesity are more prevalent than other eating disorders in African American and Native American groups (Costin, 2007). Though some preliminary research exists, significant additional research is needed.

Socioeconomic Status

Historically, women with anorexia and bulimia have most frequently come from the middle to upper-middle socioeconomic class (Soh, Touyz, & Surgenor, 2006). This pattern is not consistent, however, especially among youth with upwardly mobile aspirations, such as first-generation college students and recent U.S. immigrants. DeLeel, Hughes, Miller, Hipwell, and Theodore (2009) surveyed 581 9- and 10-year-old girls to determine if differences exist by race or socioeconomic status. The girls from the minority group presented with greater evidence of eating disturbances, thus challenging the previous notion that eating disorders predominantly affected financially secure White females (DeLeel et al., 2009). To further investigate the change in socioeconomic status, Davey, Jones, and Harris (2011) examined high school students in Australia who attended either a unisex school or a coed school to determine if differences existed in eating disorder attitudes, gender composition, and socioeconomic level. However, the influences of environmental factors were reinforced, not socioeconomic status. The students in the unisex school were at greater risk for developing an eating disorder because of gender pressures, not socioeconomic level (Davey et al., 2011).

Family Characteristics and Influences

Despite variations in researchers' opinions as to the specific role family plays in the emergence of eating disorders, there is a clear consensus that familial influence is prevalent (Costin, 2007; Perosa & Perosa, 2010). Families of eating disordered individuals have a higher rate of affective disorders, alcoholism, and maladaptive family relationships (McGrane & Carr, 2002; Vandereycken, 2002). Some researchers have also linked the development of eating disorders to parent–child relationships and attachment (Latzer, Hochdorf, Bachar, & Canetti, 2002), whereas others have considered the relationship between family interaction and individuation (Fishman, 2006). Women with eating disorders have been found to have had higher rates of childhood separation anxiety and insecure attachment in adulthood (Troisi, Massaroni, & Cuzzolaro, 2005). Research has supported the position of family theorists that eating disorders are a response or adaptation to coping with a maladaptive family (Vandereycken, 2002). Paradoxically an "eating disorder, for all of the problems it causes, is an effort to cope, communicate, defend against, and even solve other problems" (Costin, 2007, p. 78). Others suggest that the etiology of eating disorders is rooted in the early eating experiences (e.g., breastfeeding, control of first solid foods) of children within the family (Fisher, Sinton, & Birch, 2009). Parental commentary that is critical of a child's weight-based appearance is likely to influence self-image and potentially increase the risk for restrictive food intake or other disordered eating patterns (see chapter case study).

Problem Identification: Definitions, Symptoms, and Etiology

Until May 2013, BN and AN were specified in the *Diagnostic and Statistical Manual of Mental Disorders* (4th ed., text rev.; *DSM-IV-TR*; American Psychiatric Association, 2000) along with the heterogeneous, catch-all category of Eating Disorder Not Otherwise Specified (EDNOS). As a consequence of the heterogeneous nature of this category, EDNOS has been the most common eating disorder diagnosis, because it included disordered syndromes of binge eating and purging and other subthreshold disordered eating not under the BN categories (Smink, van Hoeken, & Hoak, 2012). In 2013, the newly revised fifth edition of the *DSM* entails a specified Binge Eating Disorder (BED; American Psychiatric Association, 2013). In the *DSM-5*, the

---

Sidebar 9.2 ■ Self-Awareness: Incorporating Risk Factors With Your Population

Eating disorders affect people from all walks of life. Although it is true that some may never display signs, it is also true that others are predisposed to eating disorders. As you reflect on the population and environment you currently work in, what are the identifiable risk factors? What has research demonstrated that will help support your work as a counselor? How might the environment that your population is a part of contribute to the development of an eating disorder?

■ ■ ■

category EDNOS has been changed to Feeding and Eating Disorders Not Elsewhere Classified (FED-NEC) and includes subthreshold BN and atypical AN as well as subthreshold BED and purging disorder (PD). This section covers prevalent and emerging definitions, symptoms, and etiology of disordered eating. Readers should note that most research discussed in this chapter is based on fourth edition criteria because those studies were conducted prior to the *DSM-5* launch. For this reason, we provide material related to criteria for *DSM-IV* and *DSM-5*.

Anorexia Nervosa (AN)

The prevalence of AN (typically referred to as anorexia) is 1 in 100 girls and young women (American Psychiatric Association, 2005). Approximately 90% of the cases of AN are female, although male cases are on the rise; despite this rising rate, there is still limited information regarding diagnosis or treatment of males (Darcy et al., 2012). Cases with restrictive eating disturbances that do not meet all of the criteria for AN are more common. Onset is most likely to occur in adolescence and early adulthood, but cases of earlier and later onset have been reported. Anorexia is a constellation of symptoms: extreme drive for thinness, fear of becoming fat, perfectionist tendencies, and low self-esteem (American Psychiatric Association, 2005).

The diagnostic criteria presented in the *DSM-IV-TR* allow for specificity in diagnosis and include the critical elements of anorexia outlined below. One key change in the new *DSM-5* criteria is that *amenorrhea*, or lack of menstruation, has been removed from the criteria (Stice, Rohde, Shaw, & Marti 2012). The diagnostic criteria for AN are as follows:

- refusal to maintain body weight at or above a minimally normal weight for age and height (e.g., weight is 15% less than the normal healthy weight expected for one's height);
- intense fear of gaining weight or becoming fat, even though one is underweight; and
- disturbance in the way in which one's body weight or shape is experienced, undue influence of body weight or shape on self-evaluation, or denial of the seriousness of the current low body weight.

Furthermore, the *DSM–5* specifies two types of anorexia:

- *Restricting type:* During the current episode of AN, the person has not regularly engaged in binge eating or purging behavior (i.e., self-induced vomiting or the misuse of laxatives, diuretics, or enemas).
- *Binge eating/purging type:* During the current episode of AN, the person has regularly engaged in binge eating or purging behavior (i.e., self-induced vomiting or the misuse of laxatives, diuretics, or enemas).

Specify:

- In partial remission: Full criteria of AN has been previously met, but refusal to maintain body weight has not been met for sustained periods, yet intense fear and disturbance in way of body weight or shape is experienced is still met.
- In full remission: Full criteria of AN has been previously met, none of the criteria has been met for a sustained period of time.

Specify current severity:

- Mild: Body mass index (BMI) ≥ 17 kg/m²
- Moderate: BMI 16–16.99 kg/m²
- Severe: BMI 15–15.99 kg/m²
- Extreme: BMI < 15 kg/m²

One of the first noticeable symptoms of anorexia is a preoccupation with food, particularly a focus on the fat, carbohydrate, and calorie content of food. At the onset of developing anorexia, an adolescent woman, for example, may restrict herself to a so-called healthy diet or exercise more than usual. Slowly, her list of forbidden foods may grow as her actual intake diminishes. As the disorder progresses, she may remove herself from social dining situations, and as her weight noticeably drops, she may conceal her body and reduce time with friends. Soon, cognitive functions dull, decision making becomes difficult, and food control is obsessive. As is common with anorexia, she is at risk and may develop other psychiatric disorders, such as depression, anxiety disorders such as panic disorder, or alcohol and other drug problems. There is a markedly elevated risk for obsessive-compulsive disorder (Altman & Shankman, 2009).

As more severe stages of AN develop, the body changes and begins to shut down. Osteoporosis begins; hair and nails become brittle; skin often changes to a yellowish color; and severe constipation, low blood pressure, or low body temperature are present (American Psychiatric Association, 2005). The body begins to create lanugo—soft hair that covers the body to keep it warm—in response to the changing body temperature. Kidneys begin to fail because of dehydration; the heart muscle begins to change, placing the person at greater risk for a heart attack; and muscle loss occurs, creating a weaker body more susceptible to fainting.

AN Etiology

Psychoanalytic theorists postulate that anorexia serves as a defense against maturation. Fears about becoming a woman and developing sexually inspire attempts to control her body and prevent the inevitable; in addition, some theorists posit that anorexia may be caused by a lack of attachment developed in early childhood (Ross & Green, 2011). Developmentalists view anorexia as an adaptive tool used to combat great anxiety about developmental crises, such as increased expectations and responsibilities associated with maturation (Bryant-Waugh, 2006). Sociocultural theorists claim that it is the striving for perfection in appearance as a visible hallmark of success that motivates the woman with anorexia (Kashubeck-West & Tagger, 2013). Learning theory is related to this sociocultural explanation in that initial weight loss is met with praise and positive reinforcement. As the anorexic becomes emaciated, the initial positive attention received from others turns to concern that may be positively reinforcing as well. Internal reinforcement operates simultaneously as the anorexic prides herself on her self-control. The control issue escalates as she resists others' attempts to feed her and refuses external intervention. Negative reinforcement maintains the pattern as the fear of food and fat provides the incentive for avoiding food (Zucker, Herzog, Moskowich, Merwin, & Lin, 2011). Family theorists hypothesize that the behavior is a means of gaining control and independence from a critical and controlling parent. Food and the body become the areas in which the anorexic can exert control and feel autonomous (Eisler, Lock, & Le Grange, 2011). Biological theories suggest that some individuals have a biological, genetic predisposition to developing anorexia. This vulnerability can then be triggered by environmental or developmental stressors (Racine, Root, Klump, & Bulik, 2011). It is most reasonable to propose a multietiological perspective that incorporates several theoretical considerations while recognizing that no single etiological course can apply to each case; a combination of genetic, environmental, personality, and risk factors may all contribute to the development and diagnosis of AN.

Bulimia Nervosa (BN)

Prevalence estimates for BN (also known as bulimia) vary, but approximately 3% of the population will be diagnosed (National Alliance on Mental Illness [NAMI], 2013). Prevalence-related statistics may be low because most teenage girls with bulimia do not seek treatment (Austin et al., 2008; Hudson et al., 2007). A study that was conducted with 1,100 participants surprisingly found that men accounted for 25% of bulimia cases (Hudson et al., 2007), which is consistent with the increase in hospitalizations for bulimia (Zhao & Encinosa, 2009). Despite these considerable statistics, a great number of people exhibit bulimic symptoms without meeting the complete diagnostic criteria. As with anorexia, the typical onset of bulimia is during adolescence and early adulthood.

BN is a disorder characterized by cyclical periods of binge eating followed by purging behavior (vomiting, laxative use, diuretic use, or excessive exercising). Many individuals engage in purging behavior without a binge precursor. Approximately 35%–57% of adolescent girls engage in crash dieting, fasting, self-induced vomiting, diet pill use, or laxative use (Boutelle, Neumark-Sztainer, Story, & Resnick, 2002). Overweight girls are more likely than normal weight girls to engage in such extreme dieting (Neumark-Sztainer & Hannan, 2001; Wertheim, Paxton, & Blaney, 2009). Girls who frequently diet are 12 times as likely to binge as girls who don't diet (Neumark-Sztainer, 2005).

The diagnostic criteria of the *DSM-IV-TR* specified two types of bulimia: purging type and non-purging type. The *DSM-5* no longer includes these two types. The criteria are as follows:

1. Recurrent episodes of binge eating in which an episode is characterized by both of the following:

   - Eating, in a discrete period of time (e.g., within any 2-hour period), an amount of food that is definitely larger than most people would eat during a similar period of time and under similar circumstances.
   - Lack of control over eating during the episode (e.g., a feeling that one cannot stop eating or control how much one is eating).

2. Diagnosis includes all of the following:

   - Recurrent inappropriate compensatory behavior to prevent weight gain, such as self-induced vomiting; misuse of laxatives, diuretics, enemas, or other medications; fasting; or excessive exercise.
   - The binge eating and inappropriate compensatory behavior both occur, on average, at least once a week for 3 months.
   - Self-evaluation is unduly influenced by body shape and weight.
   - The disturbance does not occur exclusively during episodes of AN.

Specify:

- In partial remission: After full criteria for BN were previously met, some but not all of the criteria have been met for a sustained period of time.
- In full remission: After full criteria for BN were previously met, none of the criteria have been met for a sustained period of time.

Specify:

- Mild: 1–3 average episodes of inappropriate compensatory behaviors per week.
- Moderate: 4–7 average episodes of inappropriate compensatory behaviors per week.
- Severe: 8–13 average episodes of inappropriate compensatory behaviors per week.
- Extreme: 14 or more average episodes of inappropriate compensatory behaviors per week.

Perhaps the first identifiable symptom of bulimia is an occasional binge eating episode. The episode may be in response to feeling a need to nurture oneself with food or to indulge oneself following a period of dieting or restricted food intake. However, the reinforcement of the binge (feeling soothed, reducing anxiety) often leads to repeated binges. In a recent study of 496 girls, diagnostic progression for BN and BED (i.e., from subthreshold to threshold) suggested an escalation mechanism related to binge eating (Stice et al., 2012). Various factors affect escalation. For example, the fear of weight gain is often the impetus for later purging behavior, and the unexpected relief a purge can provide may create new impetus. As with addictive processes, the cycle escalates from an occasional episode to a daily habit.

Binge behavior can be ritualistic for the individual and can take place at any point in his or her day. It does not always follow a specific pattern, although because individuals with bulimia are at risk for additional psychiatric disorders, there may be additional factors to consider in regard to their binging behavior. Ninety-four percent of individuals who have bulimia are also diagnosed with another psychiatric disorder, and 64% of individuals with bulimia may be diagnosed with up to three psychiatric disorders (Hudson et al., 2007). Those who are diagnosed with bulimia are more likely also to be diagnosed with another eating disorder (NAMI, 2013).

A woman, for example, with bulimia may withdraw most noticeably from meals where she will be observed and will become very anxious if prevented from purging. As the disorder progresses, the bulimic's body image becomes more distorted, her sense of being out of control is less tolerable, and she exhibits mood changes. As she exerts more effort into "controlling" her food intake, she increases her sense of deprivation and sets the scenario for future binges. Each day presents a new opportunity to "be good," which translates into significant restricting. The binge/purge cycle increasingly becomes a means of managing all painful emotions, and her awareness of her feelings becomes muted. Although her weight will likely remain stable, fluctuating within 5 pounds, she will begin to look less physically well. Her face and neck may appear swollen, and she may develop a burst blood vessel in the eye from the force of vomiting. She may find additional means of purging, including laxative abuse, excessive exercise, or diuretics.

Etiology of BN

There is no consensus on the etiology of bulimia, and it appears that there may be many avenues to onset, but a combination of genetic and environmental factors are involved. Family history of eating disorders or other mental illness, traumatic events (e.g., sexual abuse), or life stressors (e.g., being bullied at school) can increase the risk (NAMI, 2013). The etiology of bulimia is being viewed as multidimensional. Investigations of the biological factors in eating disorders have found that eating disorders tend to be more common among biological relatives, and there is an increased concordance in monozygotic twins (Bulik, 2002). Another biological factor is the correlation between bulimia and affective disorders, particularly depression. The affective instability typically appears prior to the onset of bulimia and suggests a biological vulnerability to bulimic symptoms (NAMI, 2013). Research has supported the position of family theorists that eating disorders are a response or adaptation to coping with a maladaptive family (Vandereycken, 2002). The inability of the individual to identify internal states is seen as a developmental deficit resulting from the parent's inability to respond to the child in a manner that allows the child to internalize her own awareness (Franko, Thompson, Bauserman, Affenito, & Striegel-Moore, 2008). Contributing personality factors are low self-esteem, feelings of ineffectiveness, sensitivity to rejection, and compliance with others. Sociocultural factors include the changing gender roles in the dominant culture, the increased pressure for thinness, and the use of the pursuit of thinness as a means of adaptation and social acceptability (Kashubeck-West & Tagger, 2013).

Binge Eating Disorder (BED)

Research has estimated that approximately 2.8% of adults suffer from BED (Hudson et al., 2007). BED is characterized by binge eating (eating a large amount of food in a short period of time) with the absence of regular inappropriate compensatory behaviors (e.g., vomiting) that are characteristic of BN. Generally, individuals who engage in BED may be of normal weight or overweight and may also struggle with obesity because of high food intake without elimination (e.g., purging, excessive exercise, laxative use). Comorbity rates are similar to bulimia, with 79% of individuals diagnosed reporting an additional psychiatric disorder and 49% reporting three or more additional psychiatric disorders (Hudson et al., 2007). Although there are many consistencies among those with BED, a typical progression is difficult to describe because it develops in more varied ways.

The criteria for BED (American Psychiatric Association, 2000, 2013) include the following:

Recurrent episodes of binge eating in which an episode is characterized by both of the following:

- Eating, in a discrete period of time (e.g., within any 2-hour period), an amount of food that is definitely larger than most people would eat in a similar period of time under similar circumstances.
- Lack of control over eating during the episode (e.g., a feeling that one cannot stop or control what or how much one is eating).

The binge eating episodes are associated with three (or more) of the following:

- eating much more rapidly than usual,
- eating until feeling uncomfortably full,
- eating large amounts of food when not feeling physically hungry,
- eating alone because of being embarrassed by how much one is eating, and
- feeling disgusted with oneself, depressed, or very guilty after overeating.

In addition, a diagnosis of BED is characterized by the following:

- Marked distress regarding binge eating is present.
- Binge eating occurs at least once a week for 3 months. Binge eating is not associated with the use of inappropriate compensatory behaviors as in BN and does not occur exclusively during the course of BN or AN.

Specify:

- In partial remission: After full criteria for BED were previously met, binge eating occurs at an average frequency of less than one episode per week for a sustained period of time.
- In full remission: After full criteria for BED were previously met, none of the criteria have been met for a sustained period of time.

Specify:

- Mild: 1–3 binge eating episodes per week.
- Moderate: 4–7 binge eating episodes per week.
- Severe: 8–13 binge eating episodes per week.
- Extreme: 14 or more binge eating episodes per week.

Etiology of BED

As with anorexia and bulimia, there is disagreement about the etiology of BED. There is some similarity in the etiology of BED and that of bulimia. Developmentalists note that the passage through adolescence into adulthood stresses coping skills beyond the person's capacity (Bryant-Waugh, 2006). A family-based model suggests that factors in the home influence adolescent and adult eating patterns. Individuals who as children were subjected to so-called control food rules (e.g., "You can have ice cream if you finish your homework") were found to engage in more binge eating as adults (Puhl & Schwartz, 2003). Other family risk factors include severe childhood obesity, family overeating, inadequate parenting, family discord, and high parental demands (Striegel-Moore et al., 2005). A conditioning model, based on learning theory, suggests that the comfort derived from food gradually reinforces a pattern of self-soothing that relies on food (Williamson, White, York-Crowe, & Stewart, 2004). An addictions model contends that the processes for binge eating are similar to those of an alcohol/drug addiction; thus, using addiction models with these individuals could support treatment (Barry, Clarke, & Petry, 2009).

Pearson, Combs, Zapolski, and Smith (2012) conducted a longitudinal study with 1,906 children in middle school. The study began in the spring of fifth grade for students, and then measures were taken again during the fall of sixth grade and the spring of sixth grade. The researchers used a combination of surveys regarding pubertal development, eating disorder examination, eating expectancy, and negative urgency behavior to determine if risk for developing BED emerges during this time of development. The researchers found that the negative urgency of these participants—defined as a personality trait whereby one acts rashly when distressed—predicted an increase in eating to alleviate the negative feeling, which then predicted an increase in BED. The implications of this study highlight the importance of addressing coping skills for children and adolescents at an early age to reduce risk for disordered eating. Addressing the shame, guilt, and distress about the binge eating may prove difficult because it often leads individuals to engage in additional binge eating (NIMH, 2011). In addition, BED in late childhood or early adolescence can be understood from biological, personality, and psychosocial learning perspectives (Pearson et al., 2012).

Other Specified Feeding or Eating Disorder

The category Other Specified Feeding or Eating Disorder includes atypical AN, BN of low frequency and/or limited duration, BED of low frequency and/or limited duration, purging disorder (PD), and night eating syndrome. This diagnosis should be used in presentations in which symptom characteristics of feeding and eating disorders that cause clinically significant distress or impairment in social, occupational, or other important areas of functioning predominate but do not meet full criteria for any of the disorders in the feeding and eating disorders diagnostic class. The specific reason follows the "other" diagnosis, such as:

- Atypical AN: All of the criteria for AN are met except that, despite significant weight loss, the individual's current weight is in the normal range.
- PD: The individual is of normal body weight but regularly uses inappropriate compensatory behavior after eating small amounts of food (e.g., self-induced vomiting after two cookies).
- Night eating syndrome: Recurrent episodes of night eating by eating after awakened or consuming excessive foods after evening meals. There is awareness and recall of the night eating.
- Unspecified Feeding or Eating Disorder which is categorized by insufficient information to specify reasons for a specific diagnosis, yet symptoms are characteristic of feeding and eating disorders causing significant distress and impair social, occupation, and other important areas of functioning but do not meet full criteria for any of the disorders in the feeding and eating disorders diagnostic class.

Case Study

Marissa is a Caucasian female whose struggle with an eating disorder manifested during her sophomore year of high school. She experimented with binging and purging on and off during eighth grade and her freshman year of high school. Marissa usually refrained from eating altogether as a preferred alternative to purging. Marissa mastered the art of moving food around on her plate to make it appear as though she was eating. She began emptying packets of artificial sweetener on her tongue to dissolve and ingest for energy. Such practice continued until a nearly emaciated Marissa collapsed at school and was rushed to a local emergency room. She was discovered to be severely underweight (approximately 105 pounds at 5' 8", body mass index = 16.0), and she had an irregular heartbeat and irregular breathing patterns. Marissa was admitted to an inpatient treatment facility for adolescents with eating disorders, where she remained for over 9 consecutive months.

Marissa is the older of two girls. Her parents divorced when she was 6 years old, following an acrimonious custody litigation in which her mother, Lisa, was initially awarded custody of her and her sister, Danielle. Lisa was always highly critical of Marissa, telling her that she took after her father's side and she would always have to watch her weight. Marissa recalled Lisa calling her names such as "Pudge," "Lardo," and "Bubble Butt" from when she was small. Lisa also opined that if Marissa did not maintain a slim figure (like Lisa's) she would never have boys interested in her. Furthermore, Lisa appeared to favor Danielle, who was built like Lisa. In the context of many psychological evaluations, Lisa was diagnosed with borderline personality disorder.

There were ongoing problems between Marissa's parents; specifically, Lisa regularly made false allegations toward the father and interfered with parenting time. Ultimately, when Marissa and Danielle were 10 and 8, respectively, custody was transferred to their father. However, Lisa continued to make false allegations against the girls' father, triggering investigations by Child Protective Services and additional psychological evaluations. As Marissa approached adolescence, she showed signs of low self-esteem and an obsession with her weight, her appearance, and exercise. She received low to moderate grades in school and did not show any interest in improving. Marissa indicated that she wanted to be a hairstylist when she grew up.

Following her hospitalization, Marissa reentered high school as a junior, having not attended school her sophomore year. She immediately began to fail all of her classes. Her parents blamed each other, and Marissa quickly relapsed. Through the assistance of counselors, Marissa quit school, with her parents' consent, at the age of 16. She quickly obtained her General Educational Development certificate and enrolled in cosmetology school, where she began to excel. The parenting schedule was modified to allow Marissa to make her own arrangements as to when and under what circumstances she would see her mother. She continued to reside with her father and sister.

Approaches to Prevention

Successful primary prevention curtails the development of eating disorders in unaffected individuals. Secondary prevention detects early warning signs of eating disorders and encourages treatment for those in the early stages of the disorders. Ultimately prevention efforts are to be aimed at all aspects of society: individual,

Sidebar 9.3 ■ Case Study: Creating Your Own Approach

Clients will present with a variety of symptoms and may be limited in the information that they share with us as counselors. Upon first meeting Marissa, are there signs that may have led to an earlier detection of an eating disorder? If so, how would you begin addressing these concerns? If you feel that there aren't, where would you begin working? Create a treatment plan with specific goals that would reflect your initial stage of work with Marissa as a client.

■ ■ ■

family, school, and community. Prevention efforts are geared toward the risk factors associated with eating disorders, not necessarily eating disorders in general (Neumark-Sztainer, 2011). Levine and Smolak (2006) identified the risk factors as body dissatisfaction, weight concerns, internalization of thin ideal, dieting behaviors, media influences, peer teasing, and unhealthy weight controls (p. 101).

Individual

Educational programming is the most common approach to preventing eating disorders at the individual level, especially with high-risk individuals and after early detection of symptoms. In the case of Marissa, high-risk factors were prevalent. Her low self-esteem was intensified by her mother's critical comments. Feelings of inadequacy and lack of motivation and her obsession with her weight, appearance, and exercise made her more susceptible to an eating disorder.

Prevention programs aimed at high-risk groups might have helped Marissa to identify her problems earlier. One important task is to empower young, developing women, especially when identity and self-esteem are tenuous. To combat *lookism* and *weightism*, high school programs increase media literacy and critical thinking to dispel the media myths about women for greater bodily acceptance (Levine & Murnen, 2009). In addition to programming, secondary prevention focuses on warning signs and confrontation skills. Friends and family members take an active role in identifying and communicating about disordered eating. There are programs that educate teachers, parents, and school personnel staff on the signs of disordered eating, so that individuals showing risk factors and early warning signs can be helped immediately (Russel-Mayhew, Arthur, & Ewashen, 2007).

Family

The role of the family in preventing eating disorders and disordered eating is crucial and has received strong research support (Neumark-Sztainer, 2011). Families who eat dinner together on a regular basis reduce the risk for eating disorders and also have children and adolescents who have higher dietary intake, higher levels of psychosocial well-being, greater academic success, and lower levels of substance abuse (Neumark-Sztainer, Larson, Fulkerson, Eisenberg, & Story, 2010). Although family influence can be positive, it can also encourage eating disorders. Families that criticize regarding weight, focus on thin idealization, and have a history of eating disorders pose additional risks for children to suffer from an eating disorder (Neumark-Sztainer, 2011).

Avoiding the maladaptive dynamics that contribute to eating pathology would be prudent for family members. Family environments in which eating disorders flourish tend to be controlling, emotionally neglectful, and conflictual. In the case study of Marissa, the constant conflict between her parents placed her in the middle. It caused disruption to her life as custody changed. When families place a strong emphasis on appearance (how each member looks) and on appearances (how they are judged by others), they tend to plant these values in their children.

Prevention efforts aimed at families have resulted in specific strategies that prevent the onset of eating disorders. Loth, Neumark-Sztainer, and Croll (2009) conducted 27 semi-structured interviews with individuals receiving treatment for eating disorders. These interviews resulted in eight recommendations for parents to prevent eating disorders with their children.

1. Enhance parent support.
2. Decrease weight and body talk.
3. Provide a supportive home food environment.
4. Model healthy eating habits and physical activity patterns.
5. Help children build self-esteem beyond looks and physical appearance.
6. Encourage appropriate expression of feeling and use of coping mechanisms.
7. Increase parental understanding of eating disorder signs and symptoms.
8. Gain support in dealing appropriately with struggles as a parent.

The goal of alleviating the entrenched battles over food within the family allows the family to address the emotional needs of all family members so that healthy functioning is restored. The family can also model an acceptance of making mistakes, including a tolerance of human mistakes made by others, the parents, and the children. Tolerance is also warranted with regard to appearance. Parents who support healthy maturation, separation, and individuation essentially engage in preventive practices (Perosa & Perosa, 2010). Researchers emphasize the need to actively address the changing relationship between parent and child throughout adolescence. Because family therapy to implement corrective measures has proven effective for the treatment of eating disorders (especially with young adolescents under certain circumstances, but not as much with those over the age of 18), it stands to reason that the family has a critical role in prevention and would benefit substantially from pre-illness education (Perosa & Perosa, 2010).

How could Lisa, Marissa's mother, have helped prevent Marissa's eating disorder by addressing her own psychological struggles? With this help, could she have reduced derogatory name calling, recognized Marissa's low self-esteem, and maintained custody of her daughters? In addition, with increased parental awareness, would Marissa's parents have seen the signs of an eating disorder, the early indicators? Communication was not open in Marissa's family, specifically around feelings and emotions. How does closed communication affect engagement with a struggling adolescent? It is important to note that Marissa began showing signs of improvement and consistent progress when she was given some control regarding the relationship with her mother.

School

Middle and high school personnel must spearhead prevention efforts and the early detection of eating disorders among adolescents. Because children, particularly girls, are showing evidence of weight preoccupation and disturbed body image at younger ages, this is also true in elementary school (Smolak, 2011). Signs indicating risk of eating disorders emerge by fifth grade among students who are distressed (Pearson et al., 2012).

As schools create prevention programs, many do not have a primary focus of eating disorders but look to integrate this topic with additional harmful behaviors that children may be engaging in (Neumark-Sztainer, 2011). Although school counselors may not be specifically trained in eating disorders, they are aware of the signs and symptoms and have access to resources to support the child and family. School counselors should also be trained in prevention programs for at-risk youth. For example, *Body Project*, a selective dissonance-based eating disorder prevention program, has shown support at the high school level when counselors recruit

Sidebar 9.4 ■ Case Study: Using School Prevention Resources

Marissa spent much of her time at school or with her family. During this time, nobody from either environment noticed the change in Marissa, which ultimately led to her fainting and hospitalization as a direct result of her eating disorder. The lack of awareness in this case is unfortunately not an anomaly. Many who suffer from an eating disorder hide it from those with whom they are close or who they fear may find out. As a counselor, what would you do to support adolescents who may be struggling with an eating disorder? What would your ideal prevention program be composed of? Now, how could you begin to implement aspects of your program, combining them with prevention efforts that already exist in your work?

■ ■ ■

youth with body image concerns to critique the thin ideal in written, verbal, and behavioral exercises (Stice, Mazotti, Weibel, & Agras, 2000). Most prevention programs target the student, which is needed, but it is also important to educate the teachers and staff (Neumark-Sztainer, 2011). After all, they are the eyes and ears of the school! School counselors should provide an in-service training for staff on the signs and symptoms of eating disorders and how to get help when these signs are observed. Providing specific training to teachers who specialize in health, physical education, and science as well as to athletic coaches would demonstrate how to model discussions regarding body satisfaction (Neumark-Sztainer, 2011).

Programs that target the whole school and provide outreach to the larger community are highly effective. In one whole-school, wellness-based eating disorder program that targeted 1,095 elementary and middle school students, 114 parents, and 92 teachers, self-concept, eating attitudes, and behaviors were positively affected by participation (Russel-Mayhew et al., 2007). Each group participated in a different age-appropriate program: Elementary students saw a puppet show, middle school students saw a dramatic/comical play, parents received in-service training regarding prevention strategies, and teachers received in-service training regarding creating a more body-positive environment. Though research has found one-time programs, in general, to be less effective, the study demonstrated that the involvement of teachers and parents may create a more effective response.

In the case of Marissa, a wellness program introduced to her at the elementary or middle school level might have prevented her eating disorder. Because the parental conflict promoted uncomfortable feelings, she did not reach out to the school counselor, but should someone have recognized she was in trouble? What prevented Marissa's teachers from recognizing the signs of her body mass at critical levels? If her parents had participated in a wellness program that was suggested, would they have recognized behaviors in themselves that needed to change to support their daughters? When Marissa returned to school after her treatment, she relapsed quickly. How could the environment have supported her on return? It is important to note that after Marissa's relapse, counselors were able to assist her in creating a program that would support her efforts for success.

Community

At present, community prevention of eating disorders is minimal. Studies have measured a decrease in disordered behavior by participants when media was reduced and community prevention programs educated participants regarding the idealized images (Levine & Murnen, 2009). It is also difficult to implement community prevention strategies, as there are limits to community access in comparison to school-wide programs. Researchers are becoming more creative in prevention efforts, for example, by turning to Internet-based prevention programs. Beintner, Jacobi, and Taylor (2012) studied *StudentBodies*, which is an interactive Internet program that has been shown to effectively reduce risk factors and decrease the onset of eating disorders. Like *StudentBodies*, there are many organizational sources online that provide resources to anyone who can access the Internet; unfortunately, though, just providing the information to communities is not enough (Neumark-Sztainer, 2011).

Intervention Strategies

Given the enormity of the challenge in preventing eating disorders, the majority of theorizing and research has been in the area of intervention and treatment of eating disorders.

Individual

Individual interventions vary depending on the theoretical approach used in conceptualization. Psychoanalytic, cognitive–behavioral, developmental, and feminist counselors may approach the treatment of eating disorders in different ways; however, there are some central unifying principles. Regardless of counseling orientation, an initial consideration is the medical stability of the client. Consultation with a physician is essential during the assessment phase. The medical complications arising from anorexia, bulimia, and binge eating are dangerous; thus, it is imperative to monitor the client's physical condition.

A medical evaluation of blood pressure, heart rate, and body temperature will help determine the extent of the client's physical danger. Further laboratory tests are necessary to evaluate vulnerable physical conditions, including electrolyte levels, estrogen and cholesterol levels, liver and thyroid functioning, and cardiac functioning. A medical evaluation should be a component of treatment with all eating disordered clients as a precaution.

A second consideration is the need for nutritional restabilization. Without adequate nutrition, counseling will be less effective because of the cognitive and affective disturbances that result from starvation and/or binging. For those with anorexia or bulimia, the quality of the nutritional state is highly compromised as a result of the eating pathology. For the anorexic, the nutritional goal is a restoration of body weight. For the bulimic, the goal is a restabilization of the nutritional process. For the binge eater, the goal is regulation of the caloric intake. Consultation with a nutritionist skilled at restoration among the population is a useful adjunct to treatment but must be done skillfully, as the client may be fearful of these interventions. Therefore, except in the most severe cases, delaying the introduction of nutritional counseling may improve the client's acceptance of the intervention.

Counseling Approaches

Once a therapeutic relationship is built through support and trust, individual counseling will proceed on the basis of the therapeutic orientation. An integrative approach may be best suited to the multidimensional nature of eating disorders. Treatment should address the behavioral, cognitive, affective, and interpersonal disturbances as they apply to each client. Individual counseling should be tailored to meet each client's needs (Stewart & Willamson, 2004). Initial steps in counseling may include helping the client manage affect in more appropriate ways and introducing alternative coping mechanisms that can instill hope that change is possible. Many of the counseling goals surround psychoeducation, including addressing nutrition, exercise, and physical health. Goals also address both the psychological concerns that led to the development of an eating disorder as well as the family issues that may contribute (Levine & Murnen, 2009). Once these initial goals have been addressed, which could take an extended period of time, counseling moves toward maintenance of healthy weight and habits as well as relapse prevention.

Group counseling has also been used successfully with eating disordered clients. Although some research has warned about using a group counseling model because of contagious behaviors, imitation, or competition, there is still a need to further evaluate the validity of these concerns (Vandereycken, 2011). The use of group counseling in conjunction with individual counseling allows clients to reduce the isolation and shame of their disorders. Groups can be effective venues for developing interpersonal skills and challenging dysfunctional thoughts and behaviors (Nevonen & Broberg, 2006). Mindfulness training groups have seen success with this population, specifically after meals when anxiety is often at its highest (Levine & Murnen, 2009). Psychoeducational groups, recovery skills groups, body image groups, decision-making groups, discharge planning groups, relapse prevention groups, and creative groups have been used with this population, working toward a specific goal.

Pharmacological treatment, especially for bulimia, has gained favor in recent years (American Psychiatric Association, 2000). The use of antidepressant medication may have some merit in treating secondary conditions, such as depression or obsessive-compulsive disorder (Levine & Murnen, 2009). A review of the literature suggests that antidepressant medication is most effective when combined with cognitive–behavioral counseling for bulimia and BED (Grilo, Masheb, & Crosby, 2012). Research has shown predominantly negative results when medication is introduced for anorexia because of compliance issues, nutritional defects, and factors intrinsic to anorexia. Further clinical trials may be needed to evaluate the effectiveness of medication (Crow, Mitchell, Roerig, & Steffen, 2009).

Inpatient treatment is warranted in clients with anorexia or bulimia who are experiencing dangerously low weights. Inpatient treatment is comprehensive and

Sidebar 9.5 ■ Case Study: How Do You Help Marissa?

Marissa is not unique in her struggle with an eating disorder and her struggles academically and within her home environment. Even with prevention efforts in place, many still suffer. Therefore intervention is crucial and needs to be a combination of key elements that affect each individual. What would you do to address intervention efforts, in addition to what was suggested in the chapter? Are there elements that you feel would support her treatment and reduce her risk of relapse prevention? Create a relapse prevention plan that would address Marissa's triggers, coping skills, and continued needs that would help support her growth to move forward.

■ ■ ■

includes multiple phases. The main reasons a client would be admitted to an inpatient program are having a low weight, being unable to make progress in an outpatient program, and having a higher risk for suicidal and other behaviors (Levine & Smolak, 2006). A program specifically designed for eating disorder treatment is more effective than a general psychiatric inpatient center.

The structured environment of an inpatient setting often helps to reduce the anxiety of the client with an eating disorder. The treatment protocol will differ, however, depending on the disorder. Inpatient treatment is generally composed of multiple phases that end with the maintenance stage that the client continues in outpatient treatment. Inpatient programs focus on feeding and weight gain while also using broader psychosocial interventions; when possible, it is also recommended that the client continue outpatient treatment for a minimum of 12 months following hospitalization (Long, Fitzgerald, & Hollin, 2012). Although treatment may vary slightly, there is a common counseling plan. One recent treatment plan used technology with this population: Supportive text messages were used as a follow-up with clients discharged from inpatient treatment, and researchers found that this tool enhanced treatment outcome after discharge (Bauer, Kordy, Okon, & Meermann, 2012). Because the risk of relapse is high, this tool was used to help support the client and act as a reminder of his or her goals.

Internet Resources

The rise of the Internet as a source of information has brought the eating disorder community both questions and answers. There are over 27,000 Internet sites pertaining to eating disorders (Shafran, 2002). Many of these provide helpful information to individuals who might otherwise be too ashamed to seek help. Yet the information on the Internet can vary in accuracy, and some sites actively promote unhealthy behavior (e.g., pro-anorexia sites). Ensuring the validity of the information is impossible; however, national association or governmental mental health sites are more likely to provide current and accurate information or referrals. One of the potentially beneficial aspects of the Internet is the ability for those with eating disorders to gain social support through chat rooms and self-help meetings online. For those unwilling to attend a live support group, these contacts can provide understanding and comfort. Treatment options are available online.

Family

When feasible, family counseling can be a powerful component of treatment for the adolescent or young adult client (Lock & Le Grange, 2005). In addition to addressing the distress created in the family by the eating disorder, family counseling can intervene in any dysfunctional interpersonal relationships. Common issues in these families are enmeshment, overprotection, hostility, and rigidity (Vandereycken, 2002). The length of time in family counseling varies for each family, but the goals generally address communication, support, distorted thinking, responsibility, and reestablishment of boundaries (Levine & Murnen, 2009). Family therapy is considered by some to be among the most effective treatments for eating disorders, and despite differences in specific diagnoses, some universal principles in family counseling for clients with eating disorders have been prescribed.

Common issues to be addressed in family counseling often include strengthening boundaries between parents and children, dealing with family and parental conflict in healthy ways, and openly dealing with other disorders affecting the family (Loth et al., 2009). Reducing the family's focus on food, weight, and appearance is often an immediate goal of the process, then the focus moves to learning healthy expressions of emotions to resolve past issues (Suisman et al., 2012). Particularly for younger clients, who will return to their home environment, family counseling is considered an important piece of the treatment process. In the case of Marissa, her relationship with her mother needs special attention to begin to move forward. The negative comments, conflict with Marissa's father, comparison to her sister, and her mother's own psychological issues have pushed Marissa toward her eating disorder.

School

Although few school counselors are trained in the treatment of eating disorders, it may be up to the school to first identify disturbed eating patterns. School personnel should be aware of eating disorder signs and symptoms and be prepared to encourage students suspected of disturbances to seek counseling. Resources and referrals that are available to the students seeking treatment should be current. Specialized training may be needed for staff and counselors to understand their role in prevention or intervention (Russel-Mayhew et al., 2007). Some school settings offer support groups for eating disorders, depending on the training of a school counselor. Referrals to eating disorder experts are made, while the school supports the student and program. In the case of Marissa, the school counselor recognized her relapse and helped connect her to the support services that she needed.

Community

Community interventions are minimal. Perhaps because of the perceived rarity of these disorders, wide-scale community interventions are not practiced. Another possibility for the lack of community-level intervention is the inherent challenge of the societal standards of beauty and appearance. In order to affect the community, the media and standards of beauty would have to change. Review of the literature that exists will reveal an increase in eating disorders among populations that previously had not been affected (Levine & Murnen, 2009). This increase may eventually lead to society-wide interventions to combat the perceptions of thin idealization and the dangers that follow these unrealistic goals.

Adaptations for Diversity

Ethnicity and Women

One important consideration, given the impact of the media on eating disorders, is to what extent White-oriented media affects people of color. This issue is of particular concern because few non-White women are featured in the media, and those depicted often have physical characteristics that are similar to the White standard of beauty. Findings from recent research in this area seem to vary on the basis of the ethnic group under investigation. Schooler et al. (2004), for example, found that the viewing of mainstream television had a significant effect on the body image of White women but no effect on the body image of African American women. Schooler et al. pointed to social comparison theory as an explanation for this, stating that African American women may be less likely to compare them-

Sidebar 9.6 ■ Self-Awareness: Cultural Consideration

The existence of an eating disorder is often viewed differently depending upon race and ethnicity. According to Keel (2005), the same scenario, including pattern of food intake and exercise regime over the course of 5 days, was viewed differently by college students when the subject was described as an African American or Hispanic female rather than as a White female. What are some stereotypes that accompany body image within different cultures? What factors influence interpretation of the images of two women of similar height and build such that an African American woman is viewed as "curvy" and "voluptuous" and a White woman as "overweight" or "obese"?

■ ■ ■

selves with White women portrayed by mainstream media because there is no point of comparison. Whereas White women tend to view thinness as an ideal, African American women appear to embrace an ideal that includes an image of voluptuousness, with more curves (Costin, 2007).

Another important consideration when addressing the eating behaviors of women of color is the impact of changes in socioeconomic status. Because eating disorders have been related to socioeconomic status, the increasing status of non-White populations in the United States may serve to increase their vulnerability to eating disorders (Soh et al., 2006). As discussed by Hsu (1987), as African Americans become more upwardly mobile, they may be more likely to adopt more traditional White, middle-class values and the related disorders as well. For example, as African Americans more commonly live biculturally, an internalized devaluing of their own race can occur. This devaluation can result in greater acceptance of White standards.

Although eating disorder behaviors may be increasing among people of color, the typical help-seeking patterns and underutilization of mental health services by people of color may continue to obscure the prevalence of the disorders among these groups (Cachelin & Striegel-Moore, 2006). Such rates may be further obscured by the tendency of clinicians to inadequately assess and refer people of color for eating disorder concerns (Becker, Franko, Speck, & Herzog, 2003; Walcott, Pratt, & Patel, 2003).

Multiple studies have identified strong similarities between ethnic groups with regard to eating behaviors. One study compared eating and psychological pathology between White and minority women and found that there were no differences in eating disorder symptomatology between the two groups. Unfortunately, little can be gleaned from these findings given the considerable within-group differences among the minority group (Striegel-Moore & Smolak, 2002). Findings from one ethnic sample cannot necessarily be generalized to another, and non-Whites cannot be adequately investigated as if they are a single group. Still, other better defined studies have also found strong similarities between ethnic groups. Shaw, Ramirez, Trost, Randall, and Stice (2004) found that in a sample of 785 Latino, Asian, African American, and Caucasian participants, there were no differences between ethnic groups among measures of eating disorder behaviors, bulimic modeling, restrained eating, emotionality, or self-esteem. The only difference found was that Caucasians and Asians had significantly smaller thin ideals compared with Latinos or African Americans. In a similar manner, in a study of 427 African Americans, Latinas, and Caucasians, M. A. White and Grilo (2005) found no differences in the binge eating behaviors of these participants. Differences were found only with regard to body image dissatisfaction and dietary restraint. To be specific, Caucasians demonstrated more body image dissatisfaction and dietary restraint than other ethnicities.

O'Neill's (2003) meta-analysis of 18 studies considering differences in the prevalence of eating disorder behavior among African American and Caucasian females also found only minimal differences between these groups. In this study, Caucasian women were found to have slightly higher rates of eating disorders in general but with only a small effect size. No differences in the prevalence of bulimia or binge eating were found. In addition, a large survey of female subscribers (9,971 women) to *Consumer Reports* found that there were no differences among the White, African American, Hispanic, Native American, and Asian American women with respect to reported binge eating behavior (Le Grange, Stone, & Brownell, 1998). Black women were reported to purge more than the other groups, and Asian American women more frequently endorsed exercise as weight control. This sample was identified as being above the median U.S. income level, which likely skewed the results, but it may suggest that socioeconomic status level remains an important variable.

Other studies have indicated greater differences in the eating pathology of groups of ethnically diverse participants. A study by Bisaga et al. (2005) of 1,445 high school girls found that Hispanic and non-Hispanic White girls had significantly higher levels of eating disorder symptoms than African American and Caribbean girls. Correlations were also found between early dieting and eating disorder symptoms among Caucasian, Caribbean, and mixed-descent girls. In addition, a second study of African American and White female college athletes found that White female athletes had more disturbed eating behaviors, lower self-esteem, higher drives for thinness, and more body dissatisfaction than African American female athletes.

A clear difficulty in interpreting the eating disorder research with ethnic minorities is that the variety of measures and samples makes drawing firm conclusions a challenge. However, there has been some consistency with regard to body image and thin ideals. Multiple studies have indicated that White and Asian women have higher body dissatisfaction and smaller thin ideals than African American or Latina women do (Aruguete, DeBord, Yates, & Edman, 2005; Mack et al., 2004; M. A. White & Grilo, 2005).

Another study with a large ethnically diverse sample (17,159 White, Black, Asian American, Native American, and Hispanic adolescent females) found that among all ethnic groups, body dissatisfaction and perceptions of being overweight were correlated with restricting, purging, and binge eating (French et al., 1997). The researchers concluded that overall, the non-White groups have a lower prevalence of dieting and weight concerns, but the "ethnic subculture does not appear to protect against the broader sociocultural factors that foster body dissatisfaction among adolescent females" (p. 315). It may be, as these authors suggested, that the discrepancies between studies are due to the within-group cultural differences of the ethnic groups. Such inconsistencies make it challenging to draw conclusions about eating disorders within non-White groups.

Males

Risk factors for men include athletic involvement (especially in sports with a physical appearance orientation, such as wrestling or body building), history of obesity, and homosexuality (Austin, Nelson, Birkett, Calzo, & Everett, 2013; Cogan, 2009; Weltzin et al., 2005).

- White men tend to report less "drive for thinness" and are more likely to endorse a "drive for fitness," or muscle dysmorphia, which includes preoccupation with appearance, anxiety about body image, hiding one's own body, and compulsive preoccupation with food and exercise (Aruguete et al., 2005; Kashubeck-West, Mintz, & Weigold, 2005; Maida & Armstrong, 2005). A recent review of the literature suggests a worldwide prevalence of up to 100,000 males suffering from muscle dysmorphia (Leone, Sedory, & Gray, 2005).
- Like females, males with eating disorders develop hormone irregularities as their testosterone levels drop, and they typically report less sexual interest. These men are at even greater risk than women for osteopenia and osteoporosis and have lower bone density levels (Anderson, Watson, & Schlechte, 2000).
- Men are less likely to develop anorexia, but those who do tend to have a similar course of the disorder. A recent study by Crisp et al. (2006) indicated that men were significantly more likely to be vegetarian and abuse alcohol and to have family backgrounds involving more frequent severe psychopathology, more parental overprotectiveness, and enmeshment.
- Bulimic attitudes have been associated with immediate feelings of anger in men but anger suppression in women (Meyer et al., 2005).
- Of all the eating disorders, men are most likely to develop binge eating disorders (American Psychiatric Association, 2000).

Gay, Lesbian, Bisexual, and Transgender Individuals

Recent research has begun to challenge prior findings that anorexia and bulimia were more common among gay men but less likely among lesbian women. Feminist values and greater appreciation for the female form have been considered to be protective factors for lesbian women, whereas the emphasis on appearance in the gay male subculture has been considered a risk factor. However, the distinctions may be blurring as more lesbian women and heterosexual men express dissatisfaction with their bodies.

- Lesbian women (ages 18–24) were found to have minimal body dissatisfaction and were less likely to cut down on foods or engage in weight control behaviors compared with heterosexual women, which is consistent with the belief that lesbians resist the cultural focus of beauty and women (Polimeni, Austin, & Kavanagh, 2009).
- As with previous studies, heterosexual girls have been found to be more preoccupied with looking like female media portrayals, more likely to diet, and more likely to be dissatisfied with their bodies than lesbian/bisexual girls. Gay/bisexual boys were more likely to binge and were more preoccupied with looking like male media portrayals than heterosexual boys (Austin et al., 2013).
- Adolescent male and female sexual minorities of all ethnic groups are at substantially greater risk for disordered weight-control behaviors. Across ethnicity groups, one in three lesbian/bisexual girls engaged in disordered weight-control behaviors compared with fewer than one in 10 heterosexual girls; across ethnicity groups, one in five gay and bisexual boys reported disordered weight-control behaviors compared with one in 20 heterosexual boys (Austin et al., 2013).
- Gay men (age 18–24) indicated feeling pressured to have a muscular ideal body type by media influences, specifically magazines and environments, such as clubs and bars, where competition is present (Morgan & Arcelus, 2009).

- For male-to-female transsexuals, eating disorders may suppress their libido and allow for more correspondence with female ideals of attractiveness. For female-to-male transsexuals, eating disorders, particularly anorexia, may suppress secondary sexual characteristics such as breasts and menstruation (Hepp & Milos, 2002).

Athletes

James is a 19-year-old Caucasian male attending a small private local university as a junior. He is visibly thin, and his face appears drawn. He is a good student—intelligent, participatory, and thorough. Yet he is very fatigued and fears he will not be able to maintain his good grades. James has a secret. For years, he has suffered with BN, which has gone undiagnosed because he is male. In high school, James was on the wrestling team. Though an excellent wrestler, his natural weight teetered between two categories: the higher category often included young men who were bigger and stronger than James. When James wrestled in the lower weight category, he would excel. Hence, James's coach assigned him to the lower weight category, requiring James to maintain a weight of approximately 5 pounds less than what would be a healthy weight for his height. To do so, James began fasting for up to 48 hours before a wrestling meet. After the meet, James would indulge in all of the foods he most enjoyed. This process caused James to regain some of the weight, creating a vicious cycle. James determined that the best thing to do was to purge—this way, he could enjoy his favorite foods, fill up, and yet never gain weight. Once a coach from another team was in the men's room right before a meet and just after James finished purging. The coach asked James if he was okay, and James said he was just nervous. James was afraid to admit he was binging and purging because only girls do that. James didn't want anyone to think he was gay.

Despite anecdotal data, evidence suggests that athletes are not, as a group, at greater risk for developing eating disorders, particularly anorexia and bulimia (Kirk, Singh, & Getz, 2001). However, athletic coaches need special training to identify eating disorders in their athletes because they are frequently involved in early identification (Cogan, 2009). Because coaches and sports play a central role in many athletes' lives, it is important that the message sent does not encourage an eating disorder. Papathomas and Lavallee (2006) conducted an in-depth interview of an elite athlete who developed bulimia. Because being an athlete was his only identity and his eating disorder was directly linked to this sport, he had to leave the sport. The sport furthered his desire to maintain the desired physique, and he also had a personality geared toward perfectionism (Papathomas & Lavallee, 2006). The potential that sports may increase the likelihood of a lifelong eating disorder is implied by this case. In fact, studies have found more eating disorder symptoms in female nonathletes than in female collegiate athletes (Gutgesell, Moreau, & Thompson, 2003; Reinking & Alexander, 2005). Certain sport groups may, however, produce an increased vulnerability for developing eating disorder symptoms:

- Among females, lean-sport athletes (e.g., swimming, cross-country) had higher scores on body dissatisfaction than non-lean-sport athletes (e.g., basketball, volleyball, field hockey, softball; Reinking & Alexander, 2005).

- Different sports have been found to be more vulnerable to different types of eating pathology. Higher drive for thinness scores were found among participants in swimming, basketball, and gymnastics. Gymnasts and wrestlers had significantly higher purging scores and were more likely to restrict their intake. Cross-country runners had significantly higher binging scores than other athletes.

- Leone et al. (2005) warned that men involved in strength-related sports such as football, wrestling, and body building may also be at higher risk for developing muscle dysmorphia because of these sports' strong focus on the body and on obtaining muscle mass.

- White female athletes were found to have lower self-esteem, higher drive for thinness, more body dissatisfaction, and more disturbed eating patterns than African American female athletes, African American male athletes, or White male athletes (Engel et al., 2003).

- Eating disorders in the athletic community can be obscured. The personality traits associated with eating disordered individuals (perfectionism, competitiveness, emphasis on achievement) are common in athletics (Waldrop, 2005) but less likely to be identified as problematic. Fostered by the athletic culture, these traits can be precursors to eating pathology that goes unrecognized because athletes seem to have a purpose for their efforts (exercise as purging goes unnoticed) and tend to present with higher levels of self-esteem (Cogan, 2009).

Summary

It is clear that eating disorders reflect an interaction of social, interpersonal, intrapersonal, and physical variables. The societal ideal for people, especially women, to be thin and attractive promotes greater pressure for females with regard to appearance and causes an increase in risk over that experienced by males. There has been an identification of general risk factors associated with AN, BN, and BED; yet, eating disorders may affect individuals who do not identify with these categories. Most individuals who suffer from an eating disorder do not progress to the level of requiring hospitalizations or inpatient treatment but suffer from psychological and medical consequences of the disorder.

Prevention and intervention efforts are aimed at the individual, family, school, and community. Ultimately a combination of these efforts is needed to begin to reduce the occurrence of eating disorders. Programs in prevention and intervention offer a multidisciplinary approach that incorporates individual counseling, group counseling, family counseling, psychoeducational training, and other alternative methods. Unique to this mental illness is the need for medical evaluations because of the risk associated with the complications of the disorders. Unfortunately, recovery from an eating disorder is often a slow process, and the relapse rate is high. There is no one cause of eating disorders, and there may be a combination of influences that drive an individual who may already have a tendency toward developing this disorder. Early prevention efforts have had some success, and early identification of a developing eating disorder is crucial in beginning to fight this deadly disorder. The following websites provide additional information relating to the chapter topics.

Useful Websites

Binge Eating Disorder Association
www.bedaonline.com
Eating Disorders Coalition for Research, Policy & Action
www.eatingdisorderscoalition.org
National Alliance on Mental Illness
www.nami.org
National Association for Anorexia Nervosa and Associated Disorders, Inc.
www.anad.org
National Association for Eating Disorders
www.nationaleatingdisorders.org
National Institute of Mental Health
www.nimh.nih.gov/index.shtml

References

Altman, S. E., & Shankman, S. A. (2009). What is the association between obsessive–compulsive disorder and eating disorders? *Clinical Psychology Review, 29,* 638–646.

American Psychiatric Association. (2000). *Diagnostic and statistical manual of mental disorders* (4th ed., text rev.). Washington, DC: Author.

American Psychiatric Association. (2005). *Eating disorders.* Retrieved from www.healthyminds.org

American Psychiatric Association. (2013). *Diagnostic and statistical manual of mental disorders* (5th ed.). Washington, DC: Author.

Anderson, A. E., Watson, T., & Schlechte, J. (2000). Osteoporosis and osteopenia in men with eating disorders. *Lancet, 355,* 1967–1968.

Arcelus, J., Mitchell, A. J., Wales, J., & Nielsen, S. (2011). Mortality rates in patients with anorexia nervosa and other eating disorders. *Archives of General Psychiatry, 68,* 724–731.

Aruguete, M. S., DeBord, K. A., Yates, A., & Edman, J. (2005). Ethnic and gender differences in eating attitudes among Black and White college students. *Eating Behaviors, 6,* 328–336.

Austin, S. B., Nelson, L. A., Birkett, M. A., Calzo, J. P., & Everett, B. (2013). Eating disorder symptoms and obesity at the intersections of gender, ethnicity, and sexual orientation in U.S. high school students. *American Journal of Public Health, 103,* 16–22.

Austin, S. B., Ziyadeh, N. J., Forman, S., Prokop, L. A., Keliher, A., & Jacobs, D. (2008). Screening high school students for eating disorders: Results of a national initiative. *Prevention of Chronic Disease, 5.* Retrieved from http://www.cdc.gov/pcd/issues/2008/oct/07_0164.htm

Baird, A., & Grieve, F. (2006). Exposure of male models in advertisements leads to a decrease in men's body satisfaction. *North American Journal of Psychology, 8,* 115–122.

Barry, D., Clarke, M., & Petry, N.M. (2009). Obesity and its relationship to addictions: Is overeating a form of addictive behavior? *American Journal on Addictions, 18,* 439–451.

Bauer, S., Kordy, H., Okon, E., & Meermann, R. (2012). Technology-enhanced maintenance of treatment gains in eating disorders: Efficacy of an intervention delivered via text messaging. *Journal of Consulting & Counseling Psychology, 80,* 700–706.

Becker, A. E., Franko, D. L., Speck, A., & Herzog, D.B. (2003). Ethnicity and differential access to care for eating disorder symptoms. *International Journal of Eating Disorders, 33,* 205–212.

Beintner, I., Jacobi, C., & Taylor, C. B. (2012). Effects of an Internet-based prevention programme for eating disorders in the USA and Germany—A meta-analytic review. *European Eating Disorders Review, 20,* 1–8.

Bisaga, K., Whitaker, A., Davies, M., Chuang, S., Feldman, J., & Walsh, B. T. (2005). Eating disorder and depressive symptoms in urban high school girls from different ethnic backgrounds. *Journal of Development and Behavioral Pediatrics, 26,* 257–266.

Bissel, K. L., & Zhou, P. (2004). Must see TV or ESPN: Entertainment and sports media exposure and body-image distortion in college women. *Journal of Communication, 54,* 5–21.

Boutelle, K., Neumark-Sztainer, D., Story, M., & Resnick, M. (2002). Weight control behaviors among obese, overweight, and nonoverweight adolescents. *Journal of Pediatric Psychology, 27,* 531–540.

Bryant-Waugh, R. (2006). Pathways to recovery: Promoting change within a developmental-systemic framework. *Clinical Child Psychology and Psychiatry, 11,* 213–224.

Bulik, D. (2002). Eating disorders in adolescents and young adults. *Child and Adolescent Psychiatric Clinics of North America, 11,* 201–218.

Cachelin, F. M., & Striegel-Moore, R. H. (2006). Help seeking and barriers to treatment in a community sample of Mexican American and European American women with eating disorders. *International Journal of Eating Disorders, 39,* 154–161.

Centers for Disease Control and Prevention. (2005). *Youth risk behavior surveillance system.* Atlanta, GA: Author.

Cogan, K. D. (2009). Eating disorders. In K. F. Hays (Ed.), *Performance psychology in action: A casebook for working with athletes, performing artists, business leaders, and professionals in high-risk occupations* (pp. 183–202). Washington, DC: American Psychological Association.

Costin, C. (2007). *The eating disorder sourcebook: A comprehensive guide to the causes, treatments, and preventions of eating disorders.* New York, NY: McGraw-Hill.

Crisp, A., Gowers, S., Joughin, N., McClellen, L., Rooney, B., Nielsen, S., . . . Hartman, D. (2006). Anorexia nervosa in males: Similarities and differences to anorexia nervosa in females. *European Eating Disorders Review, 14,* 163–167.

Crow, S. J., Mitchell, J. E., Roerig, J. D., & Steffen, K. (2009). What potential role is there for medication treatment in anorexia nervosa? *International Journal of Eating Disorders, 42,* 1–8.

Darcy, A. M., Doyle, A. C., Lock, J., Peebles, R., Doyle, P., & Le Grange, D. (2012). The eating disorders examination in adolescent males with anorexia nervosa: How does it compare to adolescent females? *The International Journal of Eating Disorders, 45,* 110–114.

Davey, Z., Jones, M., & Harris, L. (2011). A comparison of eating disorder symptomology, role concerns, figure preference, and social comparison between women who have attended single sex and coeducational schools. *Sex Roles, 65,* 751–759.

DeLeel, M. L., Hughes, T. L., Miller, J. A., Hipwell, A., & Theodore, L. A. (2009). Prevalence of eating disturbance and body image dissatisfaction in young girls: An examination of the variance across racial and socioeconomic groups. *Psychology in the Schools, 46,* 767–775.

Eisler, I., Lock, J., & Le Grange, D. (2011). Family-based treatments for adolescents with anorexia nervosa: Single-family and multifamily approaches. In D. Le Grange & J. Lock (Eds.), *Eating disorders in children and adolescents: A clinical handbook* (pp. 150–174). New York, NY: Guilford Press.

Engel, S. G., Johnson, C., Powers, P., Crosby, R. D., Wonderlich, S. A., Wittrock, D. A., & Mitchell, J. E. (2003). Predictors of disordered eating in a sample of elite Division I college athletes. *Eating Behaviors, 4,* 333–343.

Fisher, J. O., Sinton, M. M., & Birch, L. L. (2009). Early parental influence and risk for the emergence of disordered eating. In L. Smolak & J. K. Thompson (Eds.), *Body image, eating disorders, and obesity in youth: Assessment, prevention, and treatment* (2nd ed., pp. 17–33). Washington, DC: American Psychological Association.

Fishman, H. C. (2006). Juvenile anorexia nervosa: Family therapy's natural niche. *Journal of Marital & Family Therapy, 32,* 505–514.

Franko, D. L., Thompson, D., Bauserman, R., Affenito, S. G., & Striegel-Moore, R. H. (2008). What's love got to do with it? Family cohesion and healthy eating behaviors in adolescent girls. *International Journal of Eating Disorders, 41,* 360–367.

French, S. A., Story, M., Neumark-Sztainer, D., Downes, B., Resnick, M., & Blum, R. (1997). Ethnic differences in psychosocial and health behavior correlates of dieting, purging, and binge eating in a population-based sample of adolescent females. *International Journal of Eating Disorders, 22,* 315–322.

Garner, D. M., & Keiper, C. D. (2010). Eating disorders. *Mexican Journal of Eating Disorders, 1,* 1–26.

Grieve, F. G., Newton, C. C., Kelley, L., Miller, J., & Kerr, N. A. (2005). The preferred male body shapes of college men and women. *Individual Differences Research, 3,* 188–192.

Grilo, S. M., Masheb, R. M., & Crosby, R. D. (2012). Predictors and moderators of response to cognitive–behavioral therapy and medication for the treatment of binge eating disorder. *Journal of Consulting & Clinical Psychology, 80,* 897–906.

Gutgesell, M. E., Moreau, K. L., & Thompson, D. (2003). Weight concerns, problem eating behaviors and problem drinking behaviors in female collegiate athletes. *Journal of Athletic Training, 38,* 62–66.

Harrop, E. N., & Marlatt, G. A. (2010). The comorbidity of substance use disorders and eating disorders in women: Prevalence, etiology, and treatment. *Addictive Behaviors, 35,* 392–398.

Hepp, U., & Milos, G. (2002). Gender identity disorder and eating disorders. *International Journal of Eating Disorders, 32,* 473–478.

Hsu, L. K. G. (1987). Are eating disorders becoming more common in Blacks? *International Journal of Eating Disorders, 6,* 113–125.

Hudson, J. I., Hiripi, E., Pope, H. G., & Kessler, R. C. (2007). The prevalence and correlates of eating disorders in the national comorbidity survey replication. *Biological Psychiatry, 61,* 348–358.

Jhally, S., Kilbourne, J., & Media Education Foundation. (2002). *Killing us softly 3: Advertising's image of women.* Northampton, MA: Media Education Foundation.

Kashubeck-West, S., Mintz, L. B., & Weigold, I. (2005). Separating the effects of gender and weight loss desire on body satisfaction and disordered eating behaviors. *Sex Roles, 53,* 505–518.

Kashubeck-West, S., & Tagger, L. (2013). Feminist multicultural perspectives on body image and eating disorders. In C. Zerbe-Enns & W. Nutt Williams (Eds.), *The Oxford handbook of feminist multicultural counseling psychology* (pp. 392–412). New York, NY: Oxford University Press.

Keel, P. K. (2005). *Eating disorders.* Upper Saddle River, NJ: Pearson/Prentice Hall.

Kirk, G., Singh, K., & Getz, H. (2001). Risk of eating disorders among female college athletes and nonathletes. *Journal of College Counseling, 4,* 122–132.

Latzer, Y., Hochdorf, Z., Bachar, E., & Canetti, L. (2002). Attachment style and family functioning as discriminating factors in eating disorders. *Contemporary Family Therapy, 24,* 581–599.

Le Grange, D., Stone, A. A., & Brownell, K. D. (1998). Eating disturbances in White and minority female dieters. *International Journal of Eating Disorders, 24,* 395–403.

Leone, J. E., Sedory, E. J., & Gray, K. A. (2005). Recognition and treatment of muscle dysmorphia and related body image disorders. *Journal of Athletic Training, 40,* 352–359.

Levine, M. P., & Murnen, S. K. (2009). "Everybody knows that mass media are/are not (pick one) a cause of eating disorders." A critical review of evidence for a causal link between media, negative body image, and disordered eating in females. *Journal of Social & Cultural Psychology, 28,* 9–42.

Levine, M. P., & Smolak, L. (2006). *The prevention of eating problems and eating disorders: Theory, research, and practice.* Mahwah, NJ: Erlbaum.

Lock, J., & Le Grange, D. (2005). Family based treatment of eating disorders. *International Journal of Eating Disorders, 37,* 564–567.

Long, C. G., Fitzgerald, K., & Hollin, C. R. (2012). Treatment of chronic anorexia nervosa: A 4-year follow-up of adults patients treated in an acute inpatient setting. *Clinical Psychology and Psychotherapy, 19,* 1–13.

Loth, K. A., Neumark-Sztainer, D., & Croll, J. K. (2009). Informing family approaches to eating disorder prevention: Perspectives of those who have been there. *International Journal of Eating Disorders, 42,* 146–152.

Mack, K. A., Anderson, L., Galuska, D., Zablotsky, D., Holtzman, D., & Ahluwalia, I. (2004). Health and sociodemographic factors associated with body weight and weight objectives for women: 2000 behavioral risk factor surveillance system. *Journal of Women's Health, 13,* 1019–1032. doi:10.1089/jwh.2004.13.1019

Maida, D. M., & Armstrong, S. L. (2005). The classification of muscle dysmorphia. *International Journal of Men's Health, 4,* 73–91.

Martin, J. B. (2010). The development of ideal body image perceptions in the United States. *Nutrition Today, 45,* 98–100.

McGrane, D., & Carr, A. (2002). Young women at risk for eating disorders: Perceived family dysfunction and parental psychological problems. *Contemporary Family Therapy, 24,* 385–398.

Meyer, C., Leung, N., Waller, G., Perkins, S., Paice, N., & Mitchell, J. (2005). Anger and bulimic psychopathology: Gender differences in a nonclinical group. *International Journal of Eating Disorders, 37,* 69–71.

Morgan, J. F., & Arcelus, J. (2009). Body image in gay and straight men: A qualitative study. *European Eating Disorders Review, 17,* 435–443.

National Alliance on Mental Illness. (2013). *Bulimia nervosa fact sheet.* Retrieved from http://www.nami.org/factsheets/bulimia_factsheet.pdf

National Institute of Mental Health. (2011). *Eating disorders.* Retrieved from http://www.nimh.nih.gov/health/publications/eating-disorders/complete-index.shtml

National Institutes of Health. (2011). *Estimates of funding for various research, condition, and disease categories (RCDC)* [Data set]. Retrieved from report.nih.gov/rcdc/categories/

Neumark-Sztainer, D. (2005). Can we simultaneously work towards prevention of obesity and eating disorders in children and adolescents? *International Journal of Eating Disorders, 38,* 220–227.

Neumark-Sztainer, D. (2011). Prevention of eating disorders in children and adolescents. In D. Le Grange & J. Lock (Eds.), *Eating disorders in children and adolescents: A clinical handbook* (pp. 421–439). New York, NY: Guilford Press.

Neumark-Sztainer, D., & Hannan, P. (2001). Weight-related behaviors among adolescent girls and boys: A national survey. *Archives of Pediatric and Adolescent Medicine, 154,* 569–577.

Neumark-Sztainer, D., Larson, L. I., Fulkerson, J. A., Eisenberg, M. E., & Story, M. (2010). Family meals and adolescents: What have we learned from Project EAT (eating among teens). *Public Health Nutrition, 13,* 1113–1121.

Nevonen, L., & Broberg, A. G. (2006). A comparison of sequenced individual and group psychotherapy for patients with bulimia nervosa. *International Journal of Eating Disorders, 39,* 117–127.

O'Neill, S. K. (2003). African American women and eating disturbances: A meta analysis. *Journal of Black Psychology, 29,* 3–16.

Ousley, L., Cordero, E. D., & White, S. (2008). Eating disorders and body image of undergraduate men. *Journal of American College Health, 56,* 617–621.

Papathomas, A., & Lavallee, D. (2006). A life history and analysis of a male athlete with an eating disorder. *Journal of Loss & Trauma, 11,* 143–179.

Pearson, C. M., Combs, J. L., Zapolski, T. C. B., & Smith, G. T. (2012). A longitudinal transactional risk model for early eating disorder onset. *Journal of Abnormal Psychology, 121,* 707–718.

Perosa, L. M., & Perosa, S. L. (2010). Age differences in family factors associated with eating disorders. *Annals of the American Psychotherapy Association, 2010,* 78–81. Retrieved from http://www.americanpsychotherapy.com

Polimeni, A., Austin, B., & Kavanagh, A.M. (2009). Sexual orientation and weight, body image, and weight control practices among young Australian women. *Journal of Women's Health, 18,* 355–362.

Puhl, R. M., & Schwartz, M. B. (2003). If you are good you can have a cookie: How memories of childhood food rules link to adult eating behaviors. *Eating Behaviors, 4,* 283–293.

Racine, S. E., Root, T. L., Klump, K. L., & Bulik, C. M. (2011). Environmental and genetic risk factors for eating disorders: A developmental perspective. In D. Le Grange & J. Lock (Eds.), *Eating disorders in children and adolescents: A clinical handbook* (pp. 25–33). New York, NY: Guilford Press.

Reinking, M. F., & Alexander, L. E. (2005). Prevalence of disordered eating behaviors in undergraduate female collegiate athletes and nonathletes. *Journal of Athletic Training, 40,* 47–51.

Ross, J. A., & Green, C. (2011). Inside the experience of anorexia nervosa: A narrative thematic analysis. *Counseling and Psychotherapy Research, 11,* 112–119.

Russel-Mayhew, S., Arthur, N., & Ewashen, C. (2007). Targeting students, teachers, and parents in a wellness-based prevention program in schools. *Eating Disorders, 15,* 159–181.

Schooler, D., Ward, L. M., Merriwether, A., & Caruthers, A. (2004). Who's that girl: Television's role in the body image development of young White and Black women. *Psychology of Women Quarterly, 28,* 38–47.

Shafran, R. (2002). Eating disorders and the Internet. In C. G. Fairburn & K. D. Brownell (Eds.), *Eating disorders and obesity* (pp. 362–366). New York, NY: Guilford Press.

Shaw, H., Ramirez, S., Trost, A., Randall, P., & Stice, E. (2004). Body image and eating disturbances across ethnic groups: More similarities than differences. *Psychology of Addictive Behaviors, 18,* 12–18.

Smink, F. R. E., van Hoeken, D., & Hoak, H. S. (2012). Epidemiology of eating disorders: Incidence, prevalence, and mortality rates. *Current Psychiatric Reports, 14,* 406–414. doi:10.1007/s11920-012-0282-y

Smolak, L. (2011). Body image development in childhood. In T. Cash & L. Smolak (Eds.), *Body image: A handbook of science, practice, and prevention* (2nd ed.). New York, NY: Guilford Press.

Soh, N. L., Touyz, S. W., & Surgenor, L. J. (2006). Eating and body image disturbances across cultures: A review. *European Eating Disorders Review, 14,* 56–65.

Stewart, T. M., & Williamson, D. A. (2004). Multidisciplinary treatment of eating disorders—Part 2: Primary goals and content of treatment. *Behavior Modification, 28,* 831–835.

Stice, E. (2002). Sociocultural influences on body image and eating disturbance. In C. G. Fairburn & K. D. Brownell (Eds.), *Eating disorders and obesity* (pp. 103–107). New York, NY: Guilford Press.

Stice, E., Mazotti, L., Weibel, D., & Agras, W. S. (2000). Dissonance prevention program decreases thin-ideal internalization, body dissatisfaction, dieting, negative affect, and bulimic symptoms: A preliminary experiment. *International Journal of Eating Disorders, 27,* 206–217.

Stice, E., Rohde, P., Shaw, H., & Marti, C. N. (2012). Efficacy trial of a selective prevention program targeting both eating disorders and obesity among female college students: 1- and 2-year follow-up effects. *Journal of Consulting and Clinical Psychology, 81,* 183–189. doi:10.1037/a0031235

Striegel-Moore, R. H., Fairburn, C. G., Wilfley, D. E., Pike, K. M., Dohm, F. A., & Kraemer, H. C. (2005). Toward an understanding of risk factors for binge eating disorder in Black and White women: A community-based case-control study. *Psychological Medicine, 35,* 907–917.

Striegel-Moore, R. H., & Franko D. L. (2003). Epidemiology of binge eating disorder. *International Journal of Eating Disorders, 34,* S19–S29.

Striegel-Moore, R., & Smolak, L. (2002). Gender, ethnicity, and eating disorders. In C. G. Fairburn & K. D. Brownell (Eds.), *Eating disorders and obesity* (pp. 251–255). New York, NY: Guilford Press.

Suisman, J. L., O'Connor, S. M., Sperry, S., Thompson, J. K., Keel, P. K., Burt, S. A., . . . Klump, K. L. (2012). Genetic and environmental influences on thin ideal internalization. *International Journal of Eating Disorders, 45,* 1–7.

Troisi, A., Massaroni, P., & Cuzzolaro, M. (2005). Early separation anxiety and adult attachment style in women with eating disorders. *British Journal of Clinical Psychology, 44,* 89–97.

Vandereycken, W. (2002). Families of patients with eating disorders. In C. G. Fairburn & K. D. Brownell (Eds.), *Eating disorders and obesity* (pp. 215–220). New York, NY: Guilford Press.

Vandereycken, W. (2011). Can eating disorders become "contagious" in group therapy and specialized care? *European Eating Disorders Review, 19,* 289–295.

Wade, T. D., Keski-Rahkonen, A., & Hudson J. (2011). Epidemiology of eating disorders. In M. Tsuang & M. Tohen (Eds.), *Textbook in psychiatric epidemiology* (3rd ed., pp. 343–360). New York, NY: Wiley.

Walcott, D. D., Pratt, H. D., & Patel, D. (2003). Adolescents and eating disorders: Gender, racial, ethnic, sociocultural and socioeconomic issues. *Journal of Adolescent Research, 18,* 223–243.

Waldrop, J. (2005). Early identification and intervention for female athlete triad. *Journal of Pediatric Health Care, 19,* 213–220.

Weltzin, T. E., Weisensel, N., Franczyk, D., Burnett, K., Klitz, C., & Bean, P. (2005). Eating disorders in men: Update. *Journal of Men's Health and Gender, 2,* 186–193.

Wertheim, E., Paxton, S., & Blaney, S. (2009). Body image in girls. In L. Smolak & J. K. Thompson (Eds.), *Body image, eating disorders, and obesity in youth: Assessment, prevention, and treatment* (2nd ed., pp. 47–76). Washington, DC: American Psychological Association.

White, M. A., & Grilo, C. M. (2005). Ethnic differences in the prediction of eating and body image disturbances among female adolescent psychiatric inpatients. *International Journal of Eating Disorders, 38,* 78–84.

White, S., Reynolds-Malear, J. B., & Cordero, E. (2011). Disordered eating and the use of unhealthy weight control methods in college students: 1995, 2002, and 2008. *Eating Disorders, 19,* 323–334.

Williamson, D. A., White, M. A., York-Crowe, E., & Stewart, T. M. (2004). Cognitive–behavioral theories of eating disorders. *Behavior Modification, 28,* 711–738.

Zhao, Y., & Encinosa, W. (2009). *Hospitalizations for eating disorders from 1999–2006* (HCUP Statistical Brief No. 70). Rockville, MD: Agency for Healthcare, Research, and Quality. Retrieved from http://www.hcup-us.ahrq.gov/reports/statbriefs/sb70.pdf

Zucker, N. L., Herzog, D., Moskowich, A., Merwin, R., & Lin, T. (2011). Incorporating dispositional traits into the treatment of anorexia nervosa. In R. A. H. Adan & W. H. Kaye (Eds.), *Behavioral neurobiology of eating disorders* (pp. 289–314). Berlin, Germany: Springer.

Chapter 10

"I Don't Want to Live": The Adolescent at Risk for Suicidal Behavior

David Capuzzi and Douglas R. Gross

The adolescent at risk for suicidal preoccupation and behavior has become an increasing concern for schools and communities throughout the United States. Between 1960 and 1988, the suicide rate among adolescents increased much more dramatically than it did in the general population (King, 2001a). The adolescent suicide rate rose by 200% compared with an increase in the general population of approximately 17% (Garland & Zigler, 1993). Much of the current literature (Coy, 1995; Kostenuik & Ratnapalan, 2010; Zenere & Lazarus, 1997) ranks suicide, following accidents, as the second or third leading cause of death for youth in the United States.

The topic of adolescent suicide has been a major focus for newspaper features, television specials, and legislative initiatives as the problem of adolescent suicide has reached epidemic proportions (Hafen & Frandsen, 1986; Kolves, 2010), and this age group is now at the highest risk of suicide in one third of all countries (Cox et al., 2012). In 1999, Surgeon General David Satcher made urgent recommendations to the public regarding suicide, stating that "the country is facing an average of 85 suicides and 2,000 attempts per day" (p. 1). In 2000, there were nearly 4,000 adolescent suicides recorded, accounting for 15% of deaths for young people between the ages of 15 and 24 (National Center for Health Statistics, 2002). Such data provide the basis for ranking suicide as the third leading cause of death among the 11–24 age group (American Academy of Pediatrics, 2004; National Institute of Mental Health, 2002). According to the Centers for Disease Control and Prevention's (2000) surveillance data from 1999, 19.3% of high school students had seriously considered attempting suicide, 14.5% had made plans to attempt suicide, and 8.3% had made more than one suicide attempt during the 12-month period prior to the survey. Because teachers in typical U.S. high school classrooms can expect to have at least one young man and two young women who attempt suicide

(King, 2000; King, Strunk, & Sorter, 2011), counselors, teachers, and parents are becoming more and more concerned about their responsibilities (Maples et al., 2005; Wyman et al., 2010). Many states are requiring that schools include guidelines for suicide prevention, crisis management, and postvention in their written tragedy response plans.

The adolescent at risk for suicidal behavior continues to be of increasing concern. Recently, there have been high-profile cases in the news about teenagers who have taken their lives as result of bullying via the Internet. This chapter provides the reader with background information, including statistics, ethnic and gender differences, methods, and precipitants. A discussion of risk and protective factors, myths, and the suicidal profile provides the prelude to a description of individual, family, school, and community approaches to prevention and intervention strategies.

Problem Definition

Ethnic and Gender Differences

The suicide rate is higher among adolescent males than among females, although adolescent females attempt 3 to 4 times as often as adolescent males (Webb, 2009). Caucasian and Native American adolescent males complete suicide more often than any other ethnic group (Balis & Postolache, 2008; Canetto & Sakinofsky, 1998; Judge & Billick, 2004; Metha, Weber, & Webb, 1998; Price, Dake, & Kucharewski, 2001). A number of theories to explain the differences in rates between genders and races have been proposed, but no clear answers have been found. As early as 1954, Henry and Short provided an explanation based on a reciprocal model of suicide and homicide, which suggested that some groups were seen as more likely to express frustration and aggression inwardly, whereas others were more likely to express it outwardly. Empirical data, however, do not support this reciprocal relationship. Some models used to explain racial differences in suicide have suggested that the extreme stress and discrimination that confront African Americans in the United States help to create protective factors, such as extended networks of social support (Balis & Postolache, 2008), that lower the risk and keep the suicide rates for African American adolescents lower than those of Caucasian adolescents (Borowsky, Ireland, & Resnick, 2001; Bush, 1976; Gibbs, 1988). It is important to note, however, that despite the overall pattern suggested by the data, during the period between 1980 and 1994, the suicide rates for African American adolescent males showed a 320% increase in the 10–14 age group and a 196% increase in the 15–19 age group (Balis & Postolache, 2008; Lyon et al., 2000; Metha et al., 1998; Rutter & Behrendt, 2004).

Sidebar 10.1 ■ Suicide and Public Awareness

It is interesting to note that some experts rank suicide as the third leading cause of death in the adolescent population and others rank suicide as the second leading cause. Ten years ago, almost all the literature on the topic of youth suicide ranked it as the third leading cause. Many believe that in the past there was reluctance, and often shame, connected with labeling a death as a suicide. We believe that in recent years schools, community agencies, parent groups, and so forth have been doing a better job of creating public awareness of this problem and that there is less reluctance to classify suicide deaths as such.

■ ■ ■

Native Americans have the highest adolescent suicide rates of any ethnic group in the United States (Balis & Postolache, 2008; Committee on Adolescence, 2000; Cox et al., 2012; Shaughnessy, Doshi, & Jones, 2004). There is considerable variability across tribes: The Navajo, for example, have suicide rates close to the national average of 11 to 13 per 100,000 of the population, whereas some Apache groups have rates as high as 43 per 100,000 (Berlin, 1987). The high suicide rates in the Native American population have been associated with factors such as alcoholism and substance abuse, unemployment, availability of firearms, and child abuse and neglect (Berman & Jobes, 1991). In general, less traditional tribes have higher rates of suicide than do more traditional tribes (Wyche, Obolensky, & Glood, 1990). Suicide rates for both Asian American and Hispanic American adolescents continue to be lower than those for African and Native American youth even though the 1980–1994 time period bore witness to much higher rates than previously recorded (Hallfors et al., 2006; Metha et al., 1998). Some studies show, however, that suicide rates for Hispanic Latina girls are higher than those of Latino boys, all Caucasian adolescents, and all African American adolescents (Balis & Postolache, 2008); the reasons for this are unclear.

Methods

The use of firearms outranks all other methods of completed suicides; firearms are now being used by both genders (Balis & Postolache, 2008; Pickens, 2011). Studies in the United States show that availability of guns increases the risk of adolescent suicide (Brent et al., 1993; Committee on Adolescence, 2000). The second most common method is hanging, and the third most common is gassing. Males use firearms and hanging more often than do females, but females use gassing and ingestion more often than do males for completed suicides (Berman & Jobes, 1991). The most common method used by suicide attempters is ingestion or overdose.

Risk Factors

As noted by Garland and Zigler (1993) and Shaffer and Craft (1999), the search for the etiology of suicide spans many areas of study (Kostenuik & Ratnapalan, 2010; Orbach, 2001). Risk factors that have been studied include neurotransmitter imbalances and genetic predictors, psychiatric disorders, poor self-efficacy and problem-solving skills, sexual or physical abuse, concerns over sexual identity or orientation, availability of firearms, substance abuse, violent rock music, divorce in families, unemployment and labor strikes, loss, disability, giftedness, and phases of the moon. It is important to note that almost all adolescent suicide victims have experienced some form of psychiatric illness (Beautrais, 2005; King et al., 2011). The most prevalent psychiatric disorders among completed adolescent suicides seem to be affective disorders (King et al., 2011), conduct disorder or antisocial personality disorder, and substance abuse (Shaffer, 1988; Shaffer & Craft, 1999). Among affective disorders, particular attention should be paid to bipolar illness and depressive disorder (see this volume, Chapter 6), with comorbidity such as attention-deficit disorder, conduct disorder, or substance abuse (Rohde, Lewinsohn, & Seeley, 1991).

The suicide of a family member or a close friend of the family can also be a risk factor for adolescent suicide; prior attempts also escalate risk (Cox et al., 2012; Judge & Billick, 2004). An adolescent experiencing a physical illness that is chronic or terminal can also be at higher risk (Capuzzi, 1994; Kostenuik & Ratnapalan, 2010). Many researchers have studied cognitive and coping style factors, such as generalized feelings of hopelessness and poor interpersonal problem-solving skills (Beautrais, 2005; Spaeth, Weichold, Silbereisen, & Wiesner, 2010), as risk factors for adolescent suicide (Garland & Zigler, 1993). High neuroticism and low extraversion, high impulsiveness, low self-esteem, and an external locus of control have also been studied and can be used to predict risk (Beautrais, Joyce, & Mulder, 1999). Alcohol and drug abuse, the breakup of a relationship, school difficulties or failure, social isolation, a friend who committed suicide (Cox et al., 2012), chronic levels of community violence (Pickens, 2011), and availability of lethal methods have also been studied and identified as risk factors (Hallfors et al., 2006; Price et al., 2001).

The best single predictor of death by suicide seems to be a previous suicide attempt (Hallfors et al., 2006; King, 2000; Shaffer, Garland, Gould, Fisher, & Trautman, 1988). Some studies indicate that as many as 40% of attempters will make additional suicide attempts, and as many as 10%–14% of these individuals will complete suicide (Diekstra, 1989).

Protective Factors

Although there is a plethora of research on risk factors for suicide, there is not as much on protective factors. One might assume that in conjunction with any of the risk factors discussed above, not having that factor would be considered protective. This is probably true in many cases, and that may be why there is not as much research for this aspect of suicidality. One important fact that has come out of the research within the last 10 years is that it may be more effective to increase the protective factors in a suicidal client's life than it is to try to reduce the number of risk factors (Haley, 2004). Although a client may have several risk factors, having some protective factors may reduce the risk of a suicide attempt. Increasing protective factors has been effective even in cases where one cannot eliminate the risk or where the risk is ill defined (Haley, 2004). In a well-done overview of the literature (Haley, 2004), the protective factors discussed below were found to be essential and important. Haley's findings have also been supported by Balis and Postolache (2008); Harpine, Nitza, and Conyne (2010); and Sale, Weil, and Kryah (2012).

Social network/external support. Having a strong network of social support can minimize conditions of suicidality. Having people to turn to, to discuss problems with, and to get feedback regarding the reality of a situation can be immensely

---

Sidebar 10.2 ■ Addressing Risk and Protective Factors

The debate about whether to concentrate on decreasing risk factors or on enhancing protective factors when counseling with suicidal or potentially suicidal youth has not been resolved. On the basis of our experience, and given what we know about the benefits of multifaceted efforts to create effective prevention and intervention programs, it seems best to develop a counseling or treatment plan that addresses both risk and protective factors when working with children and adolescents at risk for suicide. If there are risk factors that cannot be changed or eliminated, a combination of enhancing the client's ability to strengthen or make better use of protective factors as well as minimize the risk factors that can be addressed usually has more impact than focusing only on risk factors or only on protective factors.

■ ■ ■

helpful. Having a social network is seen as protective for adolescents and youth; those adolescents who are connected to their families and have a good network of friends are less likely to make a suicide attempt. The implications for counselors are that it is important to assess for a client's connectedness with others. Just as social isolation is a risk factor, social connectedness is a protective factor. One intervention in a suicidal client's life might be to encourage him or her to become more connected with others. Counselors should also understand that the therapeutic relationship becomes even more important as a means of social connectedness when a client is suicidal.

Reasons for living. This protective factor seems obvious. If one has no sense of purpose or feels there is no future, one is much more likely to make a suicide attempt. Most research conducted on this subject has dealt with the population of adolescents and young adults.

Self-efficacy/self-esteem. What minimal studies have been done looking at self-efficacy as a protective factor have shown that having a sense of personal control over the events of one's life is seen as an important protective factor. *Self-efficacy* can be defined as a perceived ability to cope with problems and to influence positive outcomes. So, rather than feeling hopeless, an individual has a sense of empowerment that things will work out. The individual has confidence he or she can resolve problems, can make things happen for himself or herself, can learn to adjust or cope with difficult situations, and can know that things will get better eventually. This fundamental attitude, in contrast with the hopelessness described by many depressed and suicidal individuals, minimizes that individual's risk that he or she may eventually attempt suicide.

Emotional well-being. Emotional well-being is another protective factor that seems obvious; however, not much research has been done in this area either. In the research that has been conducted, strong associations have been found between emotional well-being and protection from suicide. As suicide is highly correlated with loneliness, depression, and anger, not having these aversive emotions serves as a protective factor.

Problem-solving skills. The ability to effectively solve life's problems may serve as a protective factor. This sense of being "able" may also tie in with issues of self-esteem and self-efficacy.

Gender. As noted in the earlier discussion on risk factors, there are gender differences when it comes to suicide. Current research shows that more females attempt suicide, but more males complete it. There are many postulations as to why this may be so. However, in general, it appears there are different risk factors for males and females, or risk factors and protective factors affect both genders in different ways. Generally, being female is more protective than being male, at least statistically.

Ethnicity. Not being White can also be seen as an element of protection. Non-White ethnic minority adults have approximately half the rate of completed suicide as White individuals.

Religiosity. Several authors have mentioned the role of religion as a protective factor against suicide. It could be that a person's religious faith precludes him or her from engaging in activities that could be considered risk factors for suicide. Another prospective reason is that people who attend church or other places of worship usually have a greater amount of fellowship with a support network. They are less isolated because presumably they attend church at least once per week, if not attending other church activities throughout the week. Generally, too, people with faith have a belief that God will take care of their problems.

Precipitants

Often, completed suicide is precipitated by what, to the adolescent, is interpreted as a shameful or humiliating experience (e.g., failure at school or work, interpersonal conflict with a romantic partner or parent). There is mounting evidence indicating that adolescents who do not cope well with major and minor life events and who do not have family and peer support are more likely to have suicidal ideation (Hallfors et al., 2006; King et al., 2011; Mazza & Reynolds, 1998; Stanard, 2000). The humiliation and frustration experienced by some adolescents struggling with conflicts connected with their sexual orientation may precipitate suicidal behavior (Harry, 1989; Kitts, 2005), although being gay or lesbian, in and of itself, may not be a risk factor for suicide (Blumenthal, 1991; Russell & Joyner, 2001). Hoberman and Garfinkel (1988) found the most common precipitant of suicide in a sample of 229 youth suicides to be an argument with a boyfriend, a girlfriend, or a parent (19%) followed by school problems (14%). Other humiliating experiences such as corporal punishment and abuse also serve as precipitants; the experience of sexual or physical assault seems to be a particularly significant risk factor for adolescent women (Hoberman & Garfinkel, 1988).

Understanding the Myths

The biggest problem connected with the topic of adolescents at risk for suicide is the fact that parents, teachers, mental health professionals, and the adolescents themselves are not made aware of a variety of myths and misconceptions as well as the signs and symptoms associated with adolescent suicide (Moskos, Achilles, & Gray, 2004). Because subsequent case study, prevention, and intervention information in this chapter is based on prior awareness of these two areas, the following information about myths and the suicidal profile is pertinent.

It is important to disqualify myths and misconceptions surrounding the topic of adolescent suicide at the beginning of any initiative to provide prevention, crisis management, and postvention services. The following are some of the most commonly cited misconceptions (Capuzzi, 1988, 1994; Capuzzi & Gross, 2008; King, 1999).

Adolescents who talk about suicide never attempt suicide. This is probably one of the most widely believed myths. Suicidal adolescents make attempts (either verbally or nonverbally) to let a friend, parent, or teacher know that life seems to be too difficult to bear. Because a suicide attempt is a cry for help to identify options, other than death, to decrease the pain of living, always take verbal or nonverbal threats seriously. Never assume such threats are only for the purpose of attracting attention or manipulating others. It is better to respond and enlist the aid of a professional than it is to risk the loss of a life.

Suicide happens with no warning. Suicidal adolescents leave numerous hints and warnings about their suicidal ideations and intentions. Clues can be verbal or in the form of suicidal gestures such as taking a few sleeping pills, becoming accident prone, reading stories focused on death and violence, and so on. Quite often, the social support network of the suicidal adolescent is small. As stress escalates and options, other than suicide, seem few, suicidal adolescents may withdraw from an already small circle of friends, making it more difficult for others to notice warning signs.

Most adolescents who attempt suicide fully intend to die. Most suicidal adolescents do not want to end their lives. They feel desperate and ambivalent about whether it would be better to end their lives and, thus, their emotional pain or try to continue living. This confusion is usually communicated through both behavior and verbal communication (both of which are discussed in a subsequent subsection of this chapter).

Adolescents from affluent families attempt or complete suicide more often than adolescents from poor families. This, too, is a myth. Suicide is evenly divided among socioeconomic groups.

Once an adolescent is suicidal, he or she is suicidal forever. Most suicidal adolescents are suicidal for a limited period of time. In our experience, the 24- to 72-hour period around the peak of the crisis is the most dangerous. If counselors and other mental health professionals can monitor such a crisis period and transition the adolescent into long-term counseling/therapy, there is a strong possibility there will never be another suicidal crisis. The more effort that is made to help an adolescent identify stressors and develop problem-solving skills during this post-suicidal crisis period and the more time that passes, the better the prognosis.

If an adolescent attempts suicide and survives, he or she will never make an additional attempt. There is a difference between an adolescent who experiences a suicidal crisis but does not attempt suicide and an adolescent who actually makes an attempt. An adolescent who carries through with an attempt had identified a plan, had access to the means, and maintained a high enough energy level to follow through. He or she may believe that a second or third attempt may be possible. If counseling/therapy has not taken place or has not been successful during the period following an attempt, additional attempts may be made. Most likely, each follow-up attempt will become more lethal.

Adolescents who attempt or complete suicides always leave notes. Only a small percentage of suicidal adolescents leave notes. This is a common myth and one of the reasons why many deaths are classified and reported as accidents by friends, family members, physicians, and investigating officers when suicide has actually taken place.

Most adolescent suicides happen late at night or during the predawn hours. This myth is not true for the simple reason that most suicidal adolescents actually want help. Mid to late morning and mid to late afternoon are the time periods when most attempts are made because a family member or friend is more likely to be around to intervene than would be the case late at night or very early in the morning.

Never use the word suicide *when talking to adolescents because using the word gives some adolescents the idea.* This is simply not true; you cannot put the idea of suicide into the mind of an adolescent who is not suicidal. If an adolescent is suicidal and you use the word, it can help the adolescent verbalize feelings of despair and assist with establishing rapport and trust. If a suicidal adolescent thinks you know he or she is suicidal and realizes you are afraid to approach the subject, it can bring the adolescent closer to the point of making an attempt by contributing to feelings of despair and helplessness.

The most common method for adolescent suicide completion involves drug overdose. Guns are the most frequently used method for completing suicide among adolescents, followed by hanging. The presence of a gun or guns in the home escalates the risk of adolescent suicide approximately five times even if such firearms are kept locked in a cabinet or drawer. Restricting the presence of and access to guns significantly decreases the suicide rate among adolescents.

All adolescents who engage in suicidal behavior are mentally ill. Many adolescents have entertained the thought of suicide, but this does not indicate mental illness. Adolescents who attempt or complete suicide are usually not suffering from a mental disorder but are having a great deal of difficulty coping with life circumstances.

Every adolescent who attempts suicide is depressed. Depression is a common component of the profile of a suicidal adolescent, but depression is not always a component. Many adolescents simply want to escape their present set of circumstances and do not have the problem-solving skills to cope more effectively, lower stress, and work toward a more promising future.

Suicide is hereditary. Although suicide tends to run in families, just as physical and sexual abuse do, and has led to the development of this myth, suicide is not genetically inherited. Members of families do, however, share the same emotional climate because parents model coping and stress management skills as well as high or low levels of self-esteem. The suicide of one family member tends to increase the risk among other family members that suicide will be viewed as an appropriate way to solve a problem or set of problems. In conjunction with this myth, it should be noted that some adolescents are predisposed, because of genetic factors, to depression as a response to life circumstances. Because of the connection between depression and suicide, many have mistakenly come to the belief that suicide can be genetically inherited.

If an adolescent is intent on attempting suicide, there is nothing anyone can do to prevent its occurrence. Two of the most important things a counselor, teacher, or parent can do are to know the risk factors and warning signs connected with adolescent suicide and to know how to respond. It is important for counselors to be prepared to provide preventive and crisis management services and for teachers and parents to know how to facilitate a referral to a qualified professional. Suicide can be prevented in most cases.

Recognizing the Profile

A number of experts believe that about 90% of the adolescents who complete suicide (and lethal first attempts can result in completions) give cues to those around them in advance (Beautrais, 2005; Beautrais et al., 1999; Capuzzi, 1994; Capuzzi & Golden, 1988; Capuzzi & Gross, 2008; Cavaiola & Lavender, 1999; Cohen, 2000; Curran, 1987; Davis, 1983; Fernquist, 2000; Hafen & Frandsen, 1986; Hallfors et al., 2006; Hussain & Vandiver, 1984; Johnson & Maile, 1987; Judge & Billick, 2004; Maples et al., 2005; Mazza & Reynolds, 1998; Rutter & Behrendt, 2004). Whether these cues or hints are limited or numerous will depend on the adolescent, because each adolescent has a unique familial and social history. It is important for adults (and young people as well) to recognize the signs and symptoms to facilitate intervention. A comment such as "I talked with her a few days ago and she was fine—I am so shocked to learn of her death" may mean that no one was aware of the warning signs. One of the essential components of any staff development effort is teaching the profile of the suicidal or potentially suicidal adolescent so that referral and intervention can take place. Behavioral cues, verbal cues, thinking patterns and motivations, and personality traits are the four areas that we describe below.

Behavioral Cues

The following are some behavioral cues that can be possible warning signs of adolescents who are suicidal.

Lack of concern about personal welfare. Some adolescents who are suicidal may not be able to talk about their problems or give verbal hints that they are at risk for attempting suicide. Sometimes such adolescents become unconcerned with their personal safety in the hopes that someone will take notice. Experimenting with medication, accepting dares from friends, reckless driving, carving initials into the skin of forearms, and other behaviors may all be ways of gesturing or letting others know that the adolescent is in pain and does not know how to continue with life if nothing changes.

Changes in social patterns. Relatively unusual or sudden changes in an adolescent's social behavior can provide strong cues that such a young person is feeling desperate. A cooperative teenager may suddenly start breaking the house rules that parents have never had to worry about enforcing. An involved adolescent may begin to withdraw from activities at school or end long-term friendships with school and community-related peers. A stable, easygoing teenager may start arguing with teachers, employers, or other significant adults with whom prior conflict was never experienced. One should note such pattern changes and talk about them with the adolescent who does not seem to be behaving as he or she usually has in the past.

A decline in school achievement. Many times, adolescents who are becoming more and more depressed and preoccupied with suicidal thoughts are unable to devote the time required to complete homework assignments and maintain grades. If such an adolescent has a history of interest in the school experience and has maintained a certain grade point average, loss of interest in academic pursuits can be a strong indication that something is wrong. The key to assessing such a situation is the length of time the decline lasts.

Concentration and clear-thinking difficulties. Suicidal adolescents usually experience marked changes in thinking and logic. As stress and discomfort escalate, logical problem solving and option generation become more difficult. It becomes easier and easier to stay focused on suicide as the only solution as reasoning and thinking become more confused and convoluted. Capuzzi (1988) noted, "It may become more and more obvious that the adolescent's attention span is shorter and that verbal comments bear little relationship to the topic of a conversation" (p. 6).

Altered patterns of eating and sleeping. Sudden increases or decreases in appetite and weight, difficulty with sleeping, or wanting to sleep all the time or all day can all be indicative of increasing preoccupation with suicidal thoughts. These altered patterns can offer strong evidence that something is wrong and that assistance is required.

Attempts to put personal affairs in order or to make amends. Often, once a suicide plan and decision have been reached, adolescents will make last-minute efforts to put their personal affairs in order. These efforts may take a variety of directions: attempts to make amends for a troubled relationship, final touches on a project, reinstatement of an old or neglected friendship, or the giving away of prized possessions (skis, jewelry, DVDs, collections, and so forth).

Use or abuse of alcohol or drugs. Sometimes troubled adolescents use or abuse alcohol or other drugs to lessen their feelings of despair or discontent. Initially, they may feel that the drug enhances their ability to cope and to increase feelings of self-esteem. Unfortunately, the abuse of drugs decreases their ability to communicate accurately and problem solve rationally. Thinking patterns become more skewed, impulse control lessens, and option identification decreases. Rapid onset of involvement with illicit or over-the-counter drugs is indicative of difficulty with relationships, problem solving, and the ability to share feelings and communicate them to others.

Unusual interest in how others are feeling. Suicidal adolescents often express considerable interest in how others are feeling. Because they are in pain but may be unable to express their feelings and ask for help, they may reach out to peers (or adults) who seem to need help with the stresses of daily living. Such responsiveness may become a full-time pastime and serves to lessen preoccupation with self and to become a vehicle for communicating, "I wish you would ask me about my pain" or "Can't you see that I need help too?"

Preoccupation with death and violence themes. Reading books or poetry in which death, violence, or suicide is the predominating theme may be the major interest of an adolescent who is becoming increasingly preoccupied with the possibility of suicide. These adolescents may be undecided about the possibility of choosing death over life and may be working through aspects of such a decision with this type of reading. Other examples of such preoccupation can include listening to music that is violent; playing violent video games; writing short stories focused on death, dying, and loss; drawing or sketching that emphasizes destruction; or watching movies or videos that emphasize destruction to self and others.

Sudden improvement after a period of depression. Suicidal adolescents often fool parents, teachers, and friends by appearing to be dramatically improved, after a period of prolonged depression, in a very short period of time. This improvement can sometimes take place overnight or during a 24-hour period and encourages friends and family to interpret such a change as a positive sign. It is not unusual for a change, such as the one described here, to be the result of a suicide decision and the formulation of a concrete suicide plan on the part of the adolescent at risk. It may mean that the suicide attempt (and the potential of completion) is imminent and that the danger and crisis are peaking. The important point for family and friends to remember is that it is not really logical for a depression to lessen that rapidly. It takes time, effort, and, at times, medical assistance to improve coping skills and lessen feelings of depression, just as it took time (months or years) to develop nonadaptive responses to people and circumstances and feelings of hopelessness.

Sudden or increased promiscuity. It is not unusual for an adolescent to experiment with sex during periods of suicidal preoccupation in an attempt to refocus attention or lessen feelings of isolation. Unfortunately, doing so sometimes complicates circumstances because of an unplanned pregnancy or an escalation of feelings of guilt.

Verbal Cues

As noted by Schneidman, Farbverow, and Litman (1976), verbal statements can provide cues to self-destructive intentions. Such statements should be assessed and considered in relation to behavioral signs and changes in thinking patterns, motivations, and personality traits. There is no universal language or style for communicating suicidal intention. Some adolescents will openly and directly say something like, "I'm going to commit suicide" or "I'm thinking of taking my life." Others will be far less direct and make statements such as, "I'm going home," "I wonder what death is like," "I'm tired," "She'll be sorry for how she has treated me," or "Someday I'll show everyone just how serious I am about some of the things I've said."

The important thing for counselors, parents, teachers, and friends to remember is that when someone says something that could be interpreted in a number of ways, it is always best to ask for clarification. It is not a good idea to make assumptions

Sidebar 10.3 ■ Informing Others of Suicidal Intention

Often, teenagers will discuss their escalating feelings of despair and hopelessness with their friends via the many forms of social media. This method of sharing often is easier than facing a parent, significant adult, or counselor and admitting that they need help and are thinking of self-harm. One of the most important things we can do is teach teenagers to let a counselor and parent (probably in that order since parents often do not want to admit that a child has suicidal thoughts) know, immediately, if a friend discusses or hints at suicide.

■ ■ ■

about what a statement means or to minimize the importance of what is being communicated. Suicidal adolescents often have a long-term history of difficulty with communicating feelings and asking for support. Indirect statements may be made in the hopes that someone will respond with support and interest and provide or facilitate a referral for professional assistance (Capuzzi & Gross, 2008).

Thinking Patterns and Motivations

In addition to the areas previously described, thinking patterns (Gust-Brey & Cross, 1999) and motivations of suicidal adolescents can also be assessed and evaluated. For such an assessment to occur, it is necessary to encourage self-disclosure to learn about changes in an adolescent's cognitive set and distortions of logic and problem-solving ability. As noted by Velkoff and Huberty (1988), the motivations of suicidal adolescents can be understood more readily when suicide is viewed as fulfilling one of three primary functions: (a) an avoidance function that protects the individual from the pain perceived to be associated with a relationship or set of circumstances; (b) a control function that enables an adolescent to believe he or she has gained control of someone or something thought to be out of control, hopeless, or disastrous; and (c) a communication function that lets others know that something is wrong or that too much pain or too many injuries have been accumulated.

Often suicidal adolescents distort their thinking patterns in conjunction with the three functions of avoidance, control, and communication so that suicide becomes the best or only problem-solving option. Such distortions can take a number of directions. All-or-nothing thinking, for example, can enable an adolescent to view a situation in such a polarized way that the only two options seem to be continuing to be miserable and depressed or carrying out a suicide plan; no problem-solving options to cope with or overcome problems may seem possible (Capuzzi, 1988; Capuzzi & Gross, 2008). Identification of a single event that is then applied to all events is another cognitive distortion, that of overgeneralization. Being left out of a party or a trip to the mountains with friends may be used as evidence for being someone no one likes, a loser, or someone who will always be forgotten or left out. "I can't seem to learn the material for this class very easily" becomes "I'm never going to make it through school" or "I'll probably have the same difficulties when I start working full time." Adolescents who are experiencing stress and pain and who are becoming preoccupied with suicidal thoughts often experience more and more cognitive distortions. Such distortions result in self-talk that becomes more and more negative and more and more supportive of one of the following motivations for carrying through with a suicide plan:

- wanting to escape from a situation that seems (or is) intolerable (e.g., sexual abuse, conflict with peers or teachers, pregnancy, and so forth),
- wanting to join someone who has died,
- wanting to attract the attention of family or friends,
- wanting to manipulate someone else,
- wanting to avoid punishment,
- wanting to be punished,
- wanting to control when or how death will occur (an adolescent with a chronic or terminal illness may be motivated in this way),
- wanting to end a conflict that seems unresolvable,
- wanting to punish the survivors, and
- wanting revenge.

Personality Traits

As noted by Capuzzi (1988), it would be ideal if the research on the profile of the suicidal adolescent provided practitioners with such a succinct profile of personality traits that teenagers at risk for suicide could be identified far in advance of any suicidal risk. Adolescents who fit the profile could then be assisted through individual and group counseling and other means. Although no consensus has yet been reached on the usual, typical, or average constellation of personality traits of the suicidal adolescent, researchers have agreed on a number of characteristics that seem to be common to many suicidal adolescents (Orbach, 2001).

Low self-esteem. Several studies have connected low self-esteem with suicide probability (Beautrais et al., 1999; Cull & Gill, 1982; Faigel, 1966; Freese, 1979; King, 1999; King et al., 2011; Price et al., 2001; Stein & Davis, 1982; Stillion, McDowell, & Shamblin, 1984). Our counseling experience as well as the experience of other practitioners seems to substantiate the relationship between low self-esteem and suicide probability (see this volume, Chapter 5). Almost all such clients have issues focused on feelings of low self-worth, and almost all such adolescents have experienced these self-doubts for an extended time period.

Hopelessness/helplessness. Most suicidal adolescents report feeling hopeless and helpless in relation to their circumstances as well as their ability to cope with these circumstances. The research support for verification of what clinicians report is growing (Beautrais et al., 1999; Cull & Gill, 1982; Jacobs, 1971; Kovacs, Beck, & Weissman, 1975; Maples et al., 2005; Peck, 1983; Rutter & Behrendt, 2004; Stanard, 2000). Most practitioners can expect to address this issue with suicidal clients and to identify a long-term history of feeling hopeless and helpless on the part of most clients.

Isolation. Many, if not most, suicidal adolescents tend to develop a small network of social support. They may find it uncomfortable to make new friends; instead, they rely on a small number of friends for support and companionship. (This may be the reason why so often those around a suicide victim state they did not notice anything unusual; the suicidal adolescent may not be in the habit of getting close enough to others so that changes in behavior, outlook, and so on can be noted.) A number of authorities support this observation (Gust-Brey & Cross, 1999; Hafen, 1972; Harpine, Nitza, & Conyne, 2010; Kiev, 1977; Peck, 1983; Sommes, 1984; Stein & Davis, 1982).

High stress. High stress coupled with poor stress management skills seem to be characteristic of the suicidal adolescent. A number of studies have addressed this trait in terms of low frustration tolerance (Cantor, 1976; Kiev, 1977; Stanard, 2000).

Chapter 7 of this text provides a comprehensive overview of stress as a causal factor relating to suicidal and other at-risk behaviors.

Need to act out. Behaviors such as truancy, running away, refusal to cooperate at home or at school, use or abuse of alcohol or other drugs, and experimentation with sex are frequently part of the pattern present in the life of a suicidal adolescent. Such behaviors may be manifestations of depression. Often, adults remain so focused on the troublesome behavior connected with an adolescent's need to act out that underlying depressive episodes may be overlooked.

Need to achieve. Sometimes, adolescents who are suicidal exhibit a pattern of high achievement. This achievement may be focused on getting high grades, being the class clown, accepting the most dares, wearing the best clothes, or any one of numerous other possibilities. In our counseling experience, this emphasis on achievement often is a compensation for feelings of low self-esteem. Readers should be cautioned, however, about jumping to the conclusion that every adolescent who achieves at a high level is suicidal. This trait, along with all of the other traits and characteristics connected with the profile of the suicidal adolescent, must be assessed in the context of other observations.

Poor communication skills. Suicidal adolescents often have a history of experiencing difficulty with expression of thoughts and feelings. Such adolescents may have trouble with identifying and labeling what they are feeling; self-expression seems awkward, if not stressful. It is not unusual to discover that adolescents who have become preoccupied with suicidal thoughts have experienced a series of losses or disappointments that they have never been able to discuss and, understandably, integrate or resolve.

Other-directedness. Most suicidal adolescents are "other-directed" rather than "inner-directed." They are what others have told them they are instead of what they want to be; they value what others have said they should be instead of what they deem to be of personal value and worth. This trait may also be linked to low self-esteem and may lead to feelings of helplessness or inability to control interactions or circumstances around them.

Guilt. Usually connected with feelings of low self-esteem and a need to be other-directed, the guilt experienced by many suicidal adolescents is bothersome and sometimes linked to their wanting to be punished as a motivation for suicide. Some statements common to the guilt-ridden suicidal adolescent might include, "Nothing I do seems to be good enough," "I feel so bad because I disappointed them," or "I should not have made that decision and should have known better."

Depression. Depression is a major element in the total profile of the suicidal adolescent (Beautrais, 2005; Judge & Billick, 2004; Kitts, 2005; Maples et al., 2005; Mazza & Reynolds, 1998). Hafen and Frandsen (1986) pointed out that there are sometimes differences between depression in an adult and depression in an adolescent. Adults are often despondent, tearful, sad, or incapable of functioning as usual. Although adolescents sometimes exhibit these characteristics, they may also respond by expressing anger, being rebellious, skipping school, running away, using and abusing drugs, and so on. Those adults and peers who associate depression only with feelings of sadness and despondency may not recognize depression in adolescents, who mask the depression with behavior that creates discomfort in family and school environments.

It is extremely important for counselors and other professionals who may be working with suicidal adolescents to complete additional coursework or training to learn about the different types of depression. Although resources and guidelines such as those provided by McWhirter and Kigin (1988) and the *Diagnostic and Statistical Manual of Mental Disorders* (American Psychiatric Association, 2013) are readily available to mental health practitioners, case supervision and consultation may be needed to accurately determine the nature of a depressive episode. Frequently, well-meaning practitioners fail to discriminate between depression created by a constellation of factors (negative self-talk, poor problem-solving skills, high stress, and so forth) and depression that is a result of the body chemistry an adolescent inherited at birth. Treatment or counseling plans are different depending on the kind of depression being experienced. Counselors, therapists, and core or crisis team members need to liaison with nurse practitioners and psychiatrists when medical assessment and subsequent medication are appropriate for depression.

In conjunction with the topic of depression as it relates to suicidal ideation, attempts, and completions, it should be noted that pharmacotherapy is often used in conjunction with counseling. Selective serotonin reuptake inhibitors (SSRIs) have been shown to be effective in treating adolescents with depression (Gould, Greenberg, Velting, & Shaffer, 2003). In the last decade, however, there has been controversy over whether SSRIs can induce suicidal behavior. It is thought that, in some instances, symptoms such as anxiety, panic attacks, hostility, hypomania, and self-harming behaviors have developed in response to taking SSRIs (Judge & Billick, 2004). Parents should be cautioned to watch for such symptoms and to immediately notify their child's counselor and prescribing physician, psychiatrist, or nurse practitioner if such symptoms do develop. Chapter 6 of this edition provides invaluable information on the topic of mood disorders in children and adolescents.

Poor problem-solving skills. Most parents notice differences in the problem-solving ability of their children. Some children are more resourceful than others in identification of problem resolution options. Suicidal adolescents seem, in our experience, to have less ability to develop solutions to troublesome situations or uncomfortable relationships. This difficulty in developing solutions may be a reason why suicidal preoccupation can progress from a cognitive focus to an applied plan with little dissonance created by the formulation and consideration of other problem-solving options and decisions.

Case Study

Jim was a 17-year-old high school junior and the son of affluent, well-educated parents. Jim's dad was a successful attorney, and his mom was an assistant superintendent for the local school district. Jim's 15-year-old sister, Janell, was well liked, a cheerleader, and involved in a variety of school and community-related activities. Janell had a beautiful singing voice and frequently accepted prominent roles in school, church, and community musical productions.

Although Jim had a few close friends, he preferred to spend most of his time reading and studying and was a straight A student. He accepted an opportunity to spend most of his junior year traveling and studying in Europe and thought such an experience would provide an excellent educational option as well as time away from his parents. Jim resented the high expectations his parents placed on both him and Janell and felt that his father did not approve of his earlier decision not to participate in varsity sports. Both parents, Jim felt, pressured him to be involved in school and community civic and social organizations; Jim preferred more solitary and intellectual pursuits. Jim felt somewhat self-conscious and awkward in social situations and never felt that he could present himself as well as his sister could, or in a way acceptable to his parents. He felt directed and criticized by both parents and resented the fact that his parents always seemed too busy to listen to him talk about things of importance to him. He really resented his father's lack of approval and felt that no one in his family seemed to understand his point of view.

Jim had experienced periodic episodes of depression, and because he had decided that it was best not to talk with family members about his feelings, he usually tried to keep his sister and his parents from knowing when he felt really down. Jim noticed that his depression was the worst when he was under a lot of stress with respect to completing class assignments and during times that his parents pressured him into social situations. Bob, Jim's best friend, became so concerned about Jim toward the end of the exam period in the spring of their sophomore year that he told Jim's parents. Jim's parents took him to a psychiatrist, who prescribed an antidepressant and recommended weekly therapy. Jim's parents were angry with him, resented the additional expense, and demanded that Jim get better as soon as possible. Janell hoped her friends would not find out because she was in the midst of being nominated for Queen of the Rose Festival and had already been selected as a Rose Festival Princess. Jim did not like the psychiatrist and felt as criticized by him as he did by his parents. He disliked the side effects of the medication, often skipped his weekly therapy session, and could hardly wait to leave home in late August to attend the orientation session at Cambridge prior to the initiation of his travel/study itinerary.

Shortly after Thanksgiving, Jim's parents received a call from Switzerland: Jim had nearly died after an overdose of his medication and was recovering in a hospital in Zurich. Jim was sent home during the first part of December.

Approaches to Prevention

Individual

Individually focused preventive counseling with Jim could have been focused in several ways. Jim could have benefited from a therapeutic relationship that included self-esteem enhancement as part of the treatment plan. If counseling/therapy had been initiated during elementary school years, Jim might not have responded with depression and, to a great extent, isolation and withdrawal from all but a few friends who provided a limited network of social support. Jim might also have been encouraged to share feelings and communicate with his parents. He also would have benefited from assertiveness training to assist him with sending needed messages to his parents at times when his parents were more preoccupied with career-related responsibilities and interests. Jim's counselor/therapist would probably have worked with him to become more aware of stressors and more adept at managing stress or removing stressors from his environment. Possibly, the combination of efforts made by his parents in couples counseling and by Jim in the context of his individual work would have resulted in outcomes very different from those described in the previous case description.

Family

Most suicidal adolescents have developed their at-risk profiles over time beginning during early childhood. In families in which there is more than one child, it is often easy for parents to identify differences in self-esteem, communication skills, stress management, problem solving, and so on. By the time a child is in elementary school, there may be visible indicators or traits that, if no intervention takes place, will result in the child's involvement in one or several at-risk behaviors. It is our opinion that such a child, by the time the middle school or junior high transition occurs, will be vulnerable to becoming pregnant, contracting AIDS, abusing drugs, developing an eating disorder, dropping out of school, or attempting or completing suicide.

Jim's family could have noted his low self-esteem, discomfort with respect to sharing feelings, depression, response to stress, poor stress management skills, and resentment toward them. They might have been able to detect changes in his thinking patterns or fluctuations in day-to-day behaviors had they developed a relationship with him that included more open lines of communication. Jim's parents did not realize that their son experienced even higher levels of stress in conjunction with the European study program and felt compelled to succeed at all costs. Jim also did not anticipate the amount of interchange and collaboration required by the group-living situations he found himself in as he and his peers and teachers traveled from one community to another and had begun to feel less self-assured than ever. Ideally, Jim's parents should have sought counseling assistance for themselves and their son when Jim was in elementary school. A counselor might have done an assessment of possible risk factors connected with Jim's family of origin and the families of his grandparents so that counseling could have compensated for predisposing factors and included an educational component for Jim's parents.

School and Community

There are a number of steps that can be taken to involve both the school and the community in prevention efforts (Baber & Bean, 2009; Biddle, Sekula, Zoucha, & Puskar, 2010; King, 2001b; Pickens, 2011; Sale et al., 2012; Spaeth et al., 2010; Wyman et al., 2010). In general, it is easier to initiate efforts in the school setting than it is in the context of a mental health center, because schools can easily access young people, reach and prepare school faculty and staff, involve parents, and collaborate with mental health professionals from the surrounding community.

A number of steps must be taken to facilitate a successful school–community prevention effort. These steps include collaboration with administrators, faculty/ staff in-service, preparation of crisis teams, awareness of individual and group counseling options, parent education, and classroom presentations. We describe each of these steps in the following subsections.

Collaboration With Administrators

There is a compelling need for prevention, crisis management, and postvention programs for the adolescent suicide problem to be put in place in elementary, middle, and high schools throughout the United States (Metha et al., 1998; Speaker & Petersen, 2000; Zenere & Lazarus, 1997). On the basis of our experience in the process of working with school districts all over the country, one of the biggest mistakes made by counselors, educators, and coordinators of counseling/student services is to initiate programs and services in this area without first obtaining the commitment and support of administrators and others in supervisory positions (Reddy & Richardson, 2006). Too often efforts are initiated and then canceled because little or no negotiation with those in decision-making positions has taken place (Adelman

& Taylor, 2000). Building principals and superintendents must be supportive, otherwise all efforts are destined for failure. Developing understanding of the parameters connected with suicide prevention and intervention must start with the building principal and extend to all faculty and staff in a given building (Adelman & Taylor, 2000; King, 2001b) so that advance understanding of why quick action must take place is developed. During a crisis, schedules must be rearranged, and faculty and staff may be called on to teach an extra class or assist with an initial assessment. Everyone connected with a given building must have advance preparation.

In addition to the groundwork that must be done on the building level, it is also important to effect advance communication and planning on the district level. The superintendent, assistant superintendent, curriculum director, staff development director, student services coordinator, and research and program evaluation specialist, among others, must all commit their support to intervention efforts. When administrators have the opportunity to listen to an overview of proposed efforts and ask questions, a higher level of commitment can be established and efforts can be more easily expedited. The probability of extending proposed programming to all schools in a given district is also increased.

Faculty/Staff In-Service

Because teachers and other faculty and staff usually learn of a student's suicidal preoccupation prior to the situation being brought to the attention of the school counselor or another member of the core or crisis team (assuming such a team exists), *all* faculty and staff must be included in building- or district-level in-service on the topic of adolescent suicide. Teachers, aides, secretaries, administrators, custodians, bus drivers, food service personnel, librarians, and school social workers all come in contact with adolescents at risk for suicide. It is imperative that all such adults be educated about both adolescent suicide and building and district policies and programs for prevention, crisis management, and postvention. There are a growing number of publications that provide excellent guidelines for elements of prevention programming focused on school faculty and staff (Beautrais, 2005; Davidson & Range, 1999; Kirchner, Yoder, Kramer, Lindsey, & Thrush, 2000; Maples et al., 2005; Metha et al., 1998; Reddy & Richardson, 2006; Speaker & Petersen, 2000; Zenere & Lazarus, 1997). When a young person reaches out to a trusted adult, that adult must have a clear understanding and a considerable amount of self-confidence so he or she knows exactly what to say and do as well as what not to say and do.

Many schools and school districts have actually precipitated suicide attempts by not providing for faculty/staff in-service on the topic prior to introducing discussion among student groups. When middle and high school students participate in educational programs on the topic of adolescent suicide, they begin to realize that they, as well as some of their friends, are at risk and they may approach admired adults for assistance. Adults in the school who have no knowledge of what to do and who have not had the opportunity to have their questions answered and their apprehension lowered may be threatened by what a student is sharing and fail to make appropriate comments and decisions. Highly stressed, depressed, suicidal adolescents do not have the perspective to realize that such responses are connected with discomfort on the part of the adult and have little to do with what could be interpreted as disapproval and lack of acceptance. For these adolescents, awkward and minimal responses to suicidal self-disclosure on the part of a trusted adult can be interpreted as the loss of the last link to society and provide additional reinforcement for finalizing a suicide plan.

It is unethical not to prepare school faculty and staff before information on suicide is presented to the students in a school. It could also become the basis for legal action by parents and family members. Much of the content in this chapter can become the basis for necessary in-service efforts.

Preparation of Crisis Teams

Many schools have crisis or core teams composed of faculty, staff, and parents connected with a particular building. These teams often exist in conjunction with a program for the prevention and intervention efforts necessary to cope with the drug problem among the young people in today's schools. Such teams usually consist of some combination of teachers, counselors, parents, social workers, school psychologists, school nurses, and school administrators. Usually these teams have been educated about traits that place adolescents at risk for substance use and abuse and have had supervision and instruction on the use of appropriate communication, diagnostic, and intervention skills necessary to begin the long-term process of recovery from alcoholism and other addictions. With education beyond that which is provided during the faculty/staff in-service discussed previously, as well as additional supervision and evaluation of clinical skills, a core or crisis team can be taught how to facilitate prevention efforts in a school and how to respond to a student already experiencing a suicidal crisis or in need of postvention efforts. In addition, such a team can be expected to write a policy statement that covers all parameters connected with prevention, crisis management, and postvention efforts. Such a policy could be adopted in other schools; in reality, except for specifics connected with a given building, the same policy statement should be adopted and followed throughout a school district. It is important to realize that everyone who is called on to assist a suicidal adolescent must know what to do. Confusion or lack of certainty about a chain of command or procedures about notification of parents can result in delays and interfere with efforts to save a young person's life.

Individual and Group Counseling Options

Prior to providing students with any information about suicide and suicide prevention efforts in a school, arrangements must be made for the individual and group counseling services that will be needed by those students who seek assistance for themselves or their friends. Unless such counseling options are available, any effort at prevention, crisis management, or postvention will be doomed to failure. The necessity of providing counseling services may present a problem to school personnel, particularly on the secondary level, unless there is a commitment on the part of administrators to free counselors from scheduling, hall monitoring, and other duties not related to the emerging role of the counselor of the 21st century. Working with suicidal adolescents requires a long-term commitment on the part of those interested in intervening. No counselor, psychologist, or social worker can undo the life experiences and self-perceptions of a lifetime without providing consistent, intensive opportunities for counseling.

If the school district cannot make a commitment to providing counseling, then arrangements for referral to community agencies and private practitioners must be made. It is important to provide adolescents and their families with a variety of referral possibilities along with information on fee schedules. There may be some question about whether the school district will be liable for the cost of such counseling if the referral is made by the school. (This issue should be explored by whatever legal counsel is retained by the district.) The dilemma, of course, is that unless counseling takes place when a suicidal adolescent has been identified, the probability is high that an attempt or a completion will take place. If the school is aware of a teenager's suicidal preoccupation and does not act in the best interests of such a teenager, families may later bring suit against the district. Counselors in the school and members of the mental health network in the community must pre-plan to work in concert for the benefit and safety of adolescents at risk for suicide.

Parent Education

Parents of students in a school in which a suicide prevention program is to be initiated should be involved in the school's efforts to educate, identify, and assist young people in this respect. Parents have a right to understand why the school is taking such steps and what the components of a schoolwide effort will be (Maples et al., 2005; Reddy & Richardson, 2006). Evening or late-afternoon parent education efforts can be constructive and engender additional support for a school or school district. Parents have the same information needs as faculty and staff with respect to the topic of adolescent suicide. They will be more likely to refer themselves and their children to the school for assistance if they know of the school's interest in adolescent suicide prevention, have had an opportunity to ask questions about their adolescent sons' and daughters' behavior, and have been reassured about the quality and safety of the school's efforts.

Classroom Presentations

There is continuing debate surrounding the safety of adolescent suicide prevention programs that contain an educational component presented to adolescents. This debate is similar to the one that emerged years ago when schools initiated staff development and classroom presentations on the topic of physical and sexual abuse. There are a number of advocates of education and discussion efforts that are focused on students in conjunction with a schoolwide suicide prevention effort (Capuzzi, 1988, 1994; Capuzzi & Golden, 1988; Curran, 1987; Ross,

Sidebar 10.4 ■ Preparing Adults to Intervene

Even though classroom presentations are a needed component of a well-orchestrated suicide prevention program in a school, readers should be cautioned about responding to pressure to go into schools and work only with the students. The key to successful prevention and intervention in a school setting depends on preparing all the adults at the school, who are in contact with students on a day-to-day basis, so that they know what the signs and symptoms of suicide are and how to successfully refer at-risk students to the building counselor. Consultants who are not a permanent part of a school faculty and staff leave after staff development activities conclude. Students who self-refer to an adult in the building or encourage friends they are worried about to talk with someone in the school after participating in a discussion or presentation about suicide do not obtain needed help when they approach an adult who does not know exactly what to say and do because he or she hasn't had any preparation. All adults must know what to do prior to allowing any presentations on the topic because the "consultant" will not be there to assist when needed.

■ ■ ■

1980; Sudak, Ford, & Rushforth, 1984; Zenere & Lazarus, 1997). Providing adolescents with an appropriate forum in which they can receive accurate information, ask questions, and learn about how to obtain help for themselves and their friends does not precipitate suicidal preoccupation or attempts (Capuzzi, 1988, 1994; Capuzzi & Gross, 2008). Because newspaper and television reports of individual and cluster suicides do not usually include adequate education on the topic, and because many films have unrealistically presented or romanticized the act of suicide, it is important for schools to address the problem in a way that provides information and encourages young people to reach out for help before they reach the point of despair.

A carefully prepared and well-presented classroom presentation made by a member of the school's core team (or another presenter who has expertise on the topic) is essential. Such a presentation should include information on causes, myths, and symptoms as well as information about how to obtain help through the school. Under no circumstances should media be used in which adolescents are shown a suicide plan. In addition, on the elementary level, school faculty should not present programs on the topic of suicide prevention; their efforts are better focused on developmental counseling and classroom presentations directed at helping children overcome traits (such as low self-esteem or poor communication skills) that may put them at risk for suicidal behavior at a later time. Although these efforts should be continued through secondary education, middle and high school students are better served through presentations that address adolescent suicide directly. (Middle and high school students almost always have direct or indirect experience with suicide and appreciate the opportunity to obtain information and ask questions.)

Legal Considerations

Prior to discussing intervention strategies in the next section of this chapter, it seems appropriate to comment about some legal aspects of suicide prevention and intervention efforts in schools. In an excellent review of the results of school violence litigation against schools, Hermann and Remley (2000) noted that even though those who are employed by school districts are expected to exert reasonable care to prevent harm to students, the courts have been reluctant to find educators liable for injuries related to violence or self-harm. State law claims usually fail because much of today's school violence (and suicide attempts and completions are components of school violence) results from what can be termed spontaneous acts of violence. This fact should not, however, lull school personnel into a false sense of security or complacency. A growing number of legal opinions have indicated that an unanticipated act of violence can be predictable and, thus, actionable under state law. Therefore, counselors, teachers, administrators, and other members of school staffs can protect themselves, as well as the youth they serve, by writing and implementing suicide prevention, crisis management, and postvention policy and procedures (Remley, 2009). These policy and procedures documents should mandate staff development for all school personnel so that all adults in the school setting recognize risk factors; possible behavioral, verbal, cognitive, and personality indicators; as well as role responsibilities and limitations. What we view as best practices are more likely to be followed if schools take a proactive rather than a reactive stance to this growing epidemic in our country's youth.

Intervention Strategies

Individual and Family

There are times when adolescents at risk for suicide are not identified until a crisis state has been reached. In such circumstances, it is important for all concerned to initiate action for the purpose of assessing lethality and determining appropriate follow-up. Because many professionals who are not counselors lack experience with adolescents who are in the midst of a personal crisis, the following guidelines may prove helpful. Note that these guidelines can be read in the context of working with Jim. The assumption that one would have to make, however, is that all the adults traveling with Jim and his peers would have participated in staff development efforts and the group would have included a counselor or other professional who could have assessed suicidal risk. An additional assumption is that families would be supportive of the use of these guidelines, either because they realized that the situation had escalated beyond their capacity to handle the situation or because they had participated in a school-sponsored presentation to the community on the topic of adolescent suicide prevention and intervention.

1. *Remember the meaning of the term* crisis management. When thinking of crisis management, it is important to understand the meaning of the word *crisis* as well as the word *management*. The word *crisis* means that the situation is not usual, normal, or average; circumstances are such that a suicidal adolescent is highly stressed and in considerable emotional discomfort. Adolescents in crisis usually feel vulnerable, hopeless, angry, low in self-esteem, and at a loss for how to cope. The word *management* means that the professional involved must be prepared to apply skills that are different from those required for preventive or postvention counseling. An adolescent in crisis must be assessed, directed, monitored, and guided for the purpose of preventing an act of self-destruction. Because adolescents who are experiencing a suicidal crisis may be quite volatile and impulsive, the need for decisive, rapid decision making on the part of the intervener is extremely important.

2. *Be calm and supportive.* A calm, supportive manner on the part of the intervener conveys respect for the perceptions and internal pain of an adolescent preoccupied with suicidal thoughts. Remember that such an adolescent usually feels hopeless and highly stressed. The demeanor and attitude of the helping person are pivotal in the process of offering assistance.

Sidebar 10.5 ■ Crisis Management Readiness

If there is concern that an adolescent is potentially or definitely suicidal, the counselor must assume a crisis management "stance." This stance means that an assessment of suicidality must be done, and it means the counselor will need to be empathically assertive. Rather than making a statement such as "Would you mind if I . . ." the counselor would need to be comfortable saying "Next I need to . . ." Sometimes counselors discover that they are better at doing preventive counseling so that an adolescent client does not get to the point of suicidal ideation and thinking of a suicide plan. If this is the case, the counselor should avoid doing crisis counseling and risk assessment until such time as he or she develops the comfort level to do so.

■ ■ ■

3. *Be nonjudgmental.* Statements such as "You can't be thinking of suicide, it is against the teachings of your church" or "I had a similar problem when I was your age, and I didn't consider suicide" are totally inappropriate during a crisis situation. An adolescent's perception of a situation is, at least temporarily, reality, and that reality must be respected. The same caution can be applied to the necessity of respecting a suicidal adolescent's expression of feelings, whether these feelings are those of depression, frustration, fear, or helplessness. Judgmental, unaccepting responses and comments only serve to further damage an already impaired sense of self-esteem and decrease willingness to communicate. Adolescents could sink further into depression or increase their resolve to carry through with a suicide plan if others are critical and unwilling to acknowledge what appear, to the adolescent, to be insurmountable obstacles.

4. *Encourage self-disclosure.* The very act of talking about painful emotions and difficult circumstances is the first step in what can become a long-term healing process. A professional helper may be the first person with whom such a suicidal adolescent has shared and trusted in months or even years, and this may be difficult to do simply because of lack of experience with communicating thoughts and feelings. It is important to support and encourage self-disclosure so that an assessment of lethality can be made early in the intervention process.

5. *Acknowledge the reality of suicide as a choice, but do not normalize suicide as a choice.* It is important for practitioners to let adolescents know that they are not alone and isolated with respect to suicidal preoccupation. It is also important to communicate the idea that suicide is a choice, a problem-solving option, and there are other choices and options. It may be difficult to communicate this idea in a way that does not make such an adolescent feel judged or put down. An example of what could be said to an adolescent in crisis is, "It is not unusual for adolescents to be so upset with relationships or circumstances that thoughts of suicide occur more and more frequently; this does not mean that you are weird or a freak. I am really glad you have chosen to talk to me about how you're feeling and what you are thinking. You have made a good choice since, now, you can begin exploring other ways to solve the problems you described."

6. *Listen actively and reinforce positively.* It is important, during the initial stages of the crisis management process, to let the adolescent at risk for suicide know you are listening carefully and really understanding how difficult life has been. Not only will such careful listening and communicating on the part of the professional make it easier for the adolescent to share, but it also will provide the basis for a growing sense of self-respect. Being listened to, heard, and respected are powerful and empowering experiences for anyone who is feeling at a loss for how to cope.

7. *Do not attempt in-depth counseling.* Although it is very important for a suicidal adolescent to begin to overcome feelings of despair and to develop a sense of control as soon as possible, the emotional turmoil and stress experienced during a crisis usually makes in-depth counseling impossible. Developing a plan to begin lessening the sense of crisis an adolescent may be experiencing is extremely important, however, and should be accomplished as soon

as possible. Crisis management necessitates the development of a plan to lessen the crisis; this plan should be shared with the adolescent so that it is clear that circumstances will improve. Counseling/therapy cannot really take place during the height of a suicidal crisis.

8. *Contact another professional.* It is a good idea to enlist the assistance of another professional, trained in crisis management, when an adolescent thought to be at risk for suicide is brought to your attention. School and mental health counselors should ask a colleague to come into the office and assist with assessment. It is always a good idea to have the support of a colleague who understands the dynamics of a suicidal crisis; in addition, the observations made by two professionals are likely to be more comprehensive. Because suicidal adolescents may present a situation that, if misjudged or mismanaged, could result in a subsequent attempt or completion, it is in the best interest of both the professional and the client for professionals to work collaboratively whenever possible. It should also be noted that liability questions are less likely to become issues and professional judgment is less likely to be questioned if assessment of the severity of a suicidal crisis and associated recommendations for crisis management have been made on a collaborative basis. No matter what the circumstances, document all that is done on behalf of the youth through keeping careful case notes.

9. *Ask questions to assess lethality.* A number of dimensions must be explored to assess lethality. This assessment can be accomplished through an interview format (a crisis situation is not conducive to the administration of a written appraisal instrument). The following questions help determine the degree of risk in a suicidal crisis; all of them do not need to be asked if the interview results in the spontaneous disclosure of the information.

- *"What has happened to make life so difficult?"* The more an adolescent describes the circumstances that have contributed to feelings of despair and hopelessness, the better the opportunity for effective crisis management. The process of describing stress-producing interpersonal situations and circumstances may begin to lower feelings of stress and reduce risk. It is not unusual for an adolescent in the midst of a suicidal crisis to describe a multifaceted set of problems with family, peers, school, and drugs, for example. The more problems an adolescent describes as stress-producing and the more complicated the scenario, the higher the lethality or risk.

- *"Are you thinking of suicide?"* Although this may not be the second question asked during an assessment of risk (ask it when you think the timing is right), it is listed here because it is the second most important question to ask. Adolescents who have been preoccupied with suicidal thoughts may experience a sense of relief to know there is someone who is able to discuss suicide in a straightforward manner. Using the word *suicide* will convey that the helping professional is listening and is willing to be involved; using the word will not put the idea of suicide in the mind of a nonsuicidal adolescent. This particular question need not be asked until such time as the assessor has developed the rapport and trust of the adolescent; timing is important in this regard so that relief rather than resistance is experienced on the part of the adolescent.

- *"How long have you been thinking about suicide?"* Adolescents who have been preoccupied with suicide for a period of several weeks are more lethal than those who have only fleeting thoughts. One way to explore several components of this question is to remember the acronym FID: When asking about suicidal thoughts, ask about *frequency*, or how often they occur; *intensity*, or how dysfunctional the preoccupation is making the adolescent ("Can you go on with your daily routine as usual?"); and *duration*, or how long the periods of preoccupation last. An adolescent who reports frequent periods of preoccupation so intense that it is difficult or impossible to go to school, to work, or to see friends, and for increasingly longer periods of time so that periods of preoccupation and dysfunction are merging, is more lethal than an adolescent who describes a different set of circumstances.

- *"Do you have a suicide plan?"* When an adolescent is able to be specific about the method, the time, the place, and who will or will not be nearby, the risk is higher. (If the use of a gun, knife, medication, or other means is described, ask if that item is in a pocket or purse and request that the item be left with you. Never, however, enter into a struggle with an adolescent to remove a firearm. Call the police or local suicide or crisis center.) Most adolescents will cooperate with you by telling you about the plan and allowing you to separate them from the means. Remember, most suicidal adolescents are other-directed; such a trait should be taken advantage of during a crisis management situation. Later, when the crisis has subsided and counseling is initiated, the adolescent's internal locus of control can be strengthened.

- *"Do you know someone who has committed suicide?"* If the answer is yes, the adolescent may be at higher risk, especially if this incident occurred within the family or a close network of friends. Such an adolescent may have come to believe that suicide is a legitimate problem-solving option.

- *"How much do you want to live?"* An adolescent who can provide only a few reasons for wishing to continue with life is at higher risk than an adolescent who can enumerate a number of reasons for continuing to live.

- *"How much do you want to die?"* The response to this question provides the opposite view of the one above. An adolescent who gives a variety of reasons for wishing to die is more lethal than an adolescent who cannot provide justification for ending life. It may be unnecessary to ask this question if the previous question provided adequate data.

- *"What do you think death is like?"* This question can be an excellent tool for assessment purposes. Adolescents who do not seem to realize that death is permanent, that there is no reversal possible, and that they cannot physically return are at higher risk for an actual attempt. Also, adolescents who have the idea that death will be romantic, nurturing, or the solution to current problems are at high risk.

- *"Have you attempted suicide in the past?"* If the answer to this question is yes, then the adolescent is more lethal. Another suicide attempt may occur that could be successful because a previous attempter has the memory of prior efforts, and he or she conceptualized and carried through with a suicide plan. An additional attempt may correct deficits in the original plan and result in death.

- *"How long ago was this previous attempt?"* This question should be asked of any adolescent who answers yes to the previous question. The more recent the previous attempt, the more lethal the adolescent and the more critical the crisis management process.

- *"Have you been feeling depressed?"* Because a high percentage of adolescents who attempt or complete suicide are depressed, this is an important question. Using the acronym FID to remember to ask about frequency, intensity, and duration is also helpful in the context of exploring an adolescent's response to this question. As previously discussed, a determination needs to be made about the existence of clinical depression if such a condition is suspected. Adolescents who report frequent, intense, and lengthy periods of depression resulting in dysfunctional episodes that are becoming closer and closer together or are continuously experienced are at high risk.

- *"Is there anyone to stop you?"* This is an extremely important question. If an adolescent has a difficult time identifying a friend, family member, or significant adult who is worth living for, the probability of a suicide attempt is high. Whoever the adolescent can identify should be specifically named; addresses, phone numbers, and the relationship to the adolescent should also be obtained. (If the adolescent cannot remember phone numbers and addresses, look up the information, together, in a phone book.) In the event it is decided that a suicide watch should be initiated, the people in the adolescent's network can be contacted and asked to participate.

- *"On a scale of 1 to 10, with 1 being low and 10 being high, what is the number that depicts the probability that you will attempt suicide?"* The higher the number, the higher the lethality.

- *"Do you use alcohol or other drugs?"* If the answer to this question is yes, the lethality is higher because use of a substance further distorts cognition and weakens impulse control. An affirmative response should also be followed by an exploration of the degree of drug involvement and identification of specific drugs.

- *"Have you experienced significant losses during the past year or earlier losses you've never discussed?"* Adolescents who have lost friends because of moving, vitality because of illness, their family of origin because of a divorce, or other losses are vulnerable to stress and confusion and are usually at higher risk for attempting or completing suicide if they have been preoccupied with such thoughts.

- *"Have you been concerned, in any way, with your sexuality?"* This may be a difficult question to explore, even briefly, during a peaking suicidal crisis. Generally, adolescents who are, or think they may be, gay or lesbian are at higher risk for suicide. It is quite difficult for adolescents to deal with the issue of sexual orientation because of fear of being ridiculed or rejected. They may have experienced related guilt and stress for a number of years, never daring to discuss their feelings with anyone.

- *"When you think about yourself and the future, what do you visualize?"* A high-risk adolescent will probably have difficulty visualizing a future scenario and will describe feeling too hopeless and depressed to even imagine a future life.

As noted at the beginning of this discussion, it is not necessary to ask all of these questions if the answers to them are shared during the course of the discussion. Also, it is appropriate to ask additional questions after a response to any of the above when it seems to be constructive to do so. It should be noted that the interviewing team must make judgments about the truthfulness of a specific response by considering the response in the total context of the interview.

10. *Make crisis management decisions.* If, as a result of an assessment made by at least two professionals, the adolescent is at risk for suicide, a number of crisis management interventions can be considered. They may be used singularly or in combination; the actual combination will depend on the lethality determination, resources and people available, and professional judgment. It is the responsibility of the professionals involved, however, to develop a crisis management plan to be followed until the crisis subsides and long-term counseling or therapy can be initiated.

- *Notify parent/legal guardians.* Parents of minors must be notified and asked for assistance when an adolescent is determined to be at risk for a suicide attempt. Often, adolescents may attempt to elicit a promise of confidentiality from a school or mental health counselor who learns about suicidal intent. Such confidentiality is not possible; the welfare of the adolescent is the most important consideration, and parents should be contacted as soon as possible.

  Sometimes parents do not believe that their child is suicidal and refuse to leave home or work and meet with their son or daughter and members of the assessment team. At times, parents may be adamant in their demands that the school or mental health professional withdraw their involvement. Although such attitudes are not conducive to the management of a suicidal crisis, they are understandable because parents may respond to such information with denial or anger to mask true emotions and cope with apprehensions that perhaps their child's situation reflects their personal inadequacies as people and parents. Because an adolescent at risk for a suicide attempt cannot be left unmonitored, this provides a dilemma for a school or a mental health agency. Conforming to the wishes of uncooperative parents places the adolescent at even greater risk; thus, steps must be taken despite parental protests. Although some professionals worry about liability issues in such circumstances, liability is higher if such an adolescent is allowed to leave unmonitored and with no provision for follow-up assistance. It may be necessary to refer the youth to protective services for children and families when parents or guardians refuse to cooperate. Schools and mental health centers should confer with legal counsel to understand liability issues and to make sure that the best practices are followed in such circumstances.

- *Consider hospitalization.* Hospitalization can be the option of choice during a suicidal crisis (even if the parents are cooperating) when the risk is high. An adolescent who has not been sleeping or eating, for example, may be totally exhausted or highly agitated. The care and safety that can be offered in a psychiatric unit of a hospital is often needed until the adolescent can experience a lowered level of stress, obtain food and rest, and realize that others consider the circumstances painful and worthy of attention. In many hospital settings, multidisciplinary teams (physicians, psychiatrists, counselors, social workers, nurses, nurse practitioners, teachers) work to individualize a treatment plan and provide for outpatient help as soon as the need for assistance on an inpatient basis subsides.

- *Write contracts.* At times, professionals may decide that developing a contract with the adolescent may be enough to support the adolescent through a period of crisis and into a more positive frame of mind after which the adolescent would be more receptive to long-term counseling or therapy. The adolescent and the counselor should write out, sign, and date such a contract. Other professionals, friends, or family members can also witness and sign the contract.

  Contracts should require the adolescent to:
  a. Agree to stay safe.
  b. Obtain enough food and sleep.
  c. Discard items that could be used in a suicide attempt (guns, weapons, medications, and so forth).
  d. Specify the time span of the contract.
  e. Call a counselor, crisis center, and so on if there is a temptation to break the contract or attempt suicide.
  f. Write down the phone numbers of people to contact if the feeling of crisis escalates.
  g. Specify ways time will be structured (walks, talks, movies, and so forth).

- *Organize suicide watches.* If hospital psychiatric services on an inpatient basis are not available in a given community and those doing the assessment believe the suicide risk is high, a suicide watch should be organized by contacting the individuals that the adolescent has identified in response to the question, "Is there anyone to stop you?" After receiving instruction and orientation from the professional, family members and friends should take turns staying with the adolescent until the crisis has subsided and long-term counseling or therapy has begun. In our opinion, it is never a good idea to depend on a family member alone to carry out a suicide watch; it is usually too difficult for family members to retain perspective. Friends should be contacted and included in a suicide watch even though confidentiality, as discussed earlier, cannot be maintained.

Sidebar 10.6 ■ Limitations of Contract Writing

Contracts are never foolproof and are to be used as adjuncts to other aspects of the crisis management process. It is a good idea to have both the client and the counselor sign a written contract and to print several copies that the client can take home and post in places that he or she will readily see. These contracts serve as a reminder of what has been agreed to as well as the fact that the counselor cares about the client's welfare; they do not guarantee, however, that someone will have the control to avoid carrying through with a suicide plan.

■ ■ ■

- *Refuse to allow the youth to return to school without an assessment by a mental health counselor, psychologist, psychiatrist, or other qualified professional.* An increasing number of school districts are adopting this policy. Although it could be argued that preventing a suicidal youth from returning to school might exacerbate suicidal ideation and intent, this policy increases the probability that the youth will receive mental health counseling and provides the school with support in the process of preventing the youth from engaging in self-harm.

School and Community

When an adolescent has attempted or completed a suicide, it is imperative, particularly in a school setting, to be aware of the impact of such an event on the entire system. Usually, within just a few hours, the fact that an adolescent has attempted or completed suicide has been chronicled through the peer group. This awareness could present a problem to the faculty and staff in a given school building, because not answering questions raised by students can engender the sharing of misinformation or rumors, whereas encouraging open discussion could embarrass an attempter on his or her return.

The following guidelines should prove helpful. Had Jim been in the regular school program when he made his attempt, these guidelines would have been put into effect immediately.

1. The principal of the building in which a student has attempted or completed suicide (even though such an incident most likely occurred off the school campus) should organize a telephone network to notify all faculty and staff that a mandatory meeting will take place before school the next morning. (Prior to the meeting, the principal should confirm the death through the coroner's office or through the student's family.) The principal should share information and answer questions about what happened during such a meeting. In the case of a suicide completion, it is recommended that the principal provide all faculty and staff with an announcement that can be read—in each class rather than over a public address system—so that everyone in the school receives the same information. The announcement should confirm the loss and emphasize the services the school and community will be providing during the day and subsequent days. Details about the circumstances or the family of the deceased should not be given so that confidentiality is maintained in that regard.
2. Faculty and staff should be instructed to answer student questions that spontaneously arise but should be told not to initiate a discussion of suicide in general.
3. Faculty and staff should be told to excuse students from class if they are upset and need to spend time in the office of the building counselor or another member of a core or crisis team.
4. Parents who are upset by the suicidal incident should be directed to a designated individual to have questions answered. Parents should also be provided with options for counseling, whether this counseling is provided by school personnel or the parent is referred to members of the mental health community.

5. At times, newspaper and television journalists contact the school for information about both the attempt or the completion and the school's response to the aftermath. Again, it is important to direct all such inquiries to a designated individual to avoid the problems created by inconsistency or the sharing of inaccurate information.

6. If a suicidal attempt occurs prior to the initiation of prevention and crisis management efforts in a given building, it is not a good idea to immediately initiate classroom mental health education on the topic of suicide even if faculty, staff, and core teams have been prepared and a written policy has been developed. Allow sufficient time to pass to prevent embarrassment to the returning student and his or her family.

7. Be alert to delayed or enhanced grief responses on the part of students prior to the anniversary of a suicide completion. Often students will need the opportunity to participate in a support group with peers or to receive individual counseling prior to and, perhaps, beyond the anniversary date.

8. Do not conduct a memorial service on the school campus after a suicide because doing so may provide reinforcement to other students preoccupied with suicidal ideation. In fact, it is unwise to conduct an on-campus memorial service after a death for any reason—it is difficult to explain why a student who has committed suicide is not being remembered when another student, faculty, or staff has been memorialized previously. Students who wish to attend the off-campus memorial or funeral should be excused. Do the same thing after deaths for other reasons.

9. Early in the sequence of events, as listed above, one or two individuals from the school should contact the family and ask if there is any support they might need that the school can provide. It is a good idea to offer such assistance periodically, as time passes, because so many families are left alone with their grief once the memorial or funeral has taken place.

Adaptations for Diversity

It is important to note that the information contained in the introductory section of this chapter suggests a number of adaptations for diversity, particularly with respect to prevention efforts. Because data suggest that Caucasian adolescent males are the highest risk group for suicide, extra efforts should be made to involve those young men who may be vulnerable in early prevention efforts. Individual and group counseling focused on some of the personality traits described earlier could and should be initiated in the elementary school years. Such early prevention efforts are preferable to waiting until suicidal preoccupation develops and observations about behavior can be observed. Because Native Americans have the highest adolescent suicide rates of any ethnic group in the United States, teachers, counselors, and parents should be alerted to early signs so that efforts can be made to avert the development of at-risk behaviors.

The etiology of suicide is something that all adults should be made aware of so that young people experiencing psychiatric illness, abuse, confusion about sexual identity, chronic or terminal physical illness, and other problems discussed earlier in the chapter can be monitored, supported, and referred for counseling/therapy when needed. Staffing sessions should be routinely conducted in elementary, middle, and high school settings so that young people who may be at risk for suicide attempts or completions can be routinely monitored and assisted. Because we know that adolescents who experience what they interpret as shameful or humiliating experiences with peers and with family members may, at times, be at high risk, these young people should also be the focus of observation and action should the need for prevention or intervention efforts be identified. In general, the more adults can be made aware of both risk factors and the suicidal profile, the earlier and more effective the prevention or intervention efforts can be.

Summary

We believe that individuals who are interested in working with suicidal youth must obtain more extensive information than that provided in this chapter. In addition, such individuals should obtain supervision from professionals qualified to provide such supervision after observing actual assessment interview and counseling/therapy sessions. Generally, neither assessment nor preventive or postvention sessions should be attempted by anyone who has graduated from a graduate program with *less than* a 2-year coursework and practicum/internship requirement. (In the case of counselors, such a graduate program should follow the standard set by the Council for the Accreditation of Counseling and Related Educational Programs.) In addition, membership in the American Association of Suicidology, participation in workshops and conferences focused on the topic of adolescent suicide, and consistent reading of journals such as *Suicide and Life-Threatening Behavior* and other books and journals are imperative.

Readers should also be cautioned not to use the material in this chapter as the sole basis for mental health education on the topic of adolescent suicide prevention or faculty/staff development in schools. This chapter provides an overview and a starting point for professionals. Those without expertise on the topic or graduate preparation as a counselor, social worker, psychologist, psychiatric nurse, or other helping professional will not be able to answer the questions of clients, families, and other professionals from reading a single chapter on this topic. Finally, anyone reading this chapter should be cautioned against initiating an adolescent suicide prevention, crisis management, and postvention program without writing a description of the various components so it can be checked by other professionals (including attorneys) and followed by all those involved in such an initiative.

An adolescent who becomes suicidal is communicating the fact that he or she is experiencing difficulty with problem solving, managing stress, expressing feelings, and so on. It is important for us to respond in constructive, safe, informed ways because the future of our communities (whether local, national, or international) depends on individuals who are positive, functional, and able to cope with the complex demands of life. As research and clinical experience provide additional and more sophisticated information about adolescent suicide, it will be necessary to incorporate this information into prevention, crisis management, and postvention efforts. To abdicate our responsibility to do so would communicate a lack of interest in the youth of today and a lack of concern about the future of society.

Useful Websites

American Association of Suicidology
　　http://www.suicidology.org
American Foundation for Suicide Prevention
　　http://www.afsp.org

Inspire USA Foundation
   http://www.reachout.com
National Association of School Psychologists
   http://www.nasponline.org
National Suicide Prevention Lifeline
   http://www.suicidepreventionlifeline.org
Suicide and Suicide Prevention
   http://suicidehotlines.com

References

Adelman, H. S., & Taylor, L. (2000). Moving prevention from the fringes into the fabric of school improvement. *Journal of Educational and Psychological Consultation, 11*, 7–36.

American Academy of Pediatrics. (2004). Policy statement: School-based mental health services. *Pediatrics, 113*, 1839–1845.

American Psychiatric Association. (2013). *Diagnostic and statistical manual of mental disorders* (5th ed.). Washington, DC: Author.

Baber, K., & Bean, G. (2009). Frameworks: A community-based approach to preventing youth suicide. *Journal of Community Psychology, 37*, 684–696.

Balis, T., & Postolache, T. T. (2008). Ethnic differences in adolescent suicide in the United States. *International Journal of Child Health and Child Health, 1*, 281–296.

Beautrais, A. L. (2005). National strategies for the reduction and prevention of suicide. *Crisis, 26*, 1–3.

Beautrais, A. L., Joyce, P. R., & Mulder, R. T. (1999). Personality traits and cognitive styles as risk factors for serious suicide attempts among young people. *Suicide and Life-Threatening Behavior, 29*, 37–47.

Berlin, I. N. (1987). Suicide among American Indian adolescents: An overview. *Suicide and Life-Threatening Behavior, 17*, 218–232.

Berman, A. L., & Jobes, D. A. (1991). *Adolescent suicide: Assessment and intervention*. Washington, DC: American Psychological Association.

Biddle, V. S., Sekula, L. K., Zoucha, R., & Puskar, K. R. (2010). Identification of suicide risk among rural youth: Implications for the use of HEADSS. *Journal of Pediatric Health Care, 24*, 152–157.

Blumenthal, S. J. (1991). Letter to the editor. *Journal of the American Medical Association, 265*, 2806–2807.

Borowsky, I. W., Ireland, M., & Resnick, M. D. (2001). Adolescent suicide attempts: Risks and protectors. *Pediatrics, 107*, 485–493.

Brent, D. A., Perper, J. A., Moritz, G., Baugher, M., Schweers, J., & Roth, C. (1993). Firearms and adolescent suicide: A community case-control study. *American Journal of Diseases in Children, 147*, 1066–1071.

Bush, J. A. (1976). Suicide and Blacks. *Suicide and Life-Threatening Behavior, 6*, 216–222.

Canetto, S. S., & Sakinofsky, I. (1998). The gender paradox in suicide. *Suicide and Life-Threatening Behavior, 28*, 1–23.

Cantor, P. (1976). Personality characteristics found among youthful female suicide attempters. *Journal of Abnormal Psychology, 85*, 324–329.

Capuzzi, D. (1988). *Counseling and intervention strategies for adolescent suicide prevention* (Contract No. 400-86-0014). Ann Arbor, MI: ERIC Counseling and Personnel Services Clearinghouse.

Capuzzi, D. (1994). *Suicide prevention in the schools: Guidelines for middle and high school settings*. Alexandria, VA: American Counseling Association.

Capuzzi, D., & Golden, L. (Eds.). (1988). *Preventing adolescent suicide*. Muncie, IN: Accelerated Development.

Capuzzi, D., & Gross, D. R. (2008). "I don't want to live": The adolescent at risk for suicidal behavior. In D. Capuzzi & D. R. Gross (Eds.), *Youth at risk: A prevention resource for counselors, teachers, and parents* (5th ed., pp. 249–280). Alexandria, VA: American Counseling Association.

Cavaiola, A. A., & Lavender, N. (1999). Suicidal behavior in chemically dependent adolescents. *Adolescence, 34,* 735–744.

Centers for Disease Control and Prevention. (2000). CDC surveillance summaries. *Morbidity and Mortality Weekly Report, 49,* 10.

Cohen, E. M. (2000). Suicidal ideation among adolescents in relation to recalled exposure to violence. *Current Psychology, 19,* 46–56.

Committee on Adolescence. (2000). Suicide and suicide attempts in adolescence. *Pediatrics, 105,* 871–874.

Cox, G. R., Robinson, J., Williamson, M., Lockley, A., Cheung, Y. T. D., & Pirkis, J. (2012). Suicide clusters in young people: Evidence for the effectiveness of postvention strategies. *Crisis: The Journal of Crisis Intervention and Suicide Prevention, 33,* 208–214.

Coy, D. R. (1995). The need for a school suicide prevention policy. *National Association of Student Services Professionals Bulletin, 79,* 1–9.

Cull, J., & Gill, W. (1982). *Suicide probability scale manual.* Los Angeles, CA: Western Psychological Services.

Curran, D. F. (1987). *Adolescent suicidal behavior.* Washington, DC: Hemisphere.

Davidson, M. W., & Range, L. M. (1999). Are teachers of children and young adolescents responsive to suicide prevention training modules? Yes. *Death Studies, 23,* 61–71.

Davis, P. A. (1983). *Suicidal adolescents.* Springfield, IL: Charles C Thomas.

Diekstra, R. F. (1989). Suicidal behavior in adolescents and young adults: The international picture. *Crisis, 10,* 16–35.

Faigel, H. (1966). Suicide among young persons: A review of its incidence and causes, and methods for its prevention. *Clinical Pediatrics, 5,* 187–190.

Fernquist, R. M. (2000). Problem drinking in the family and youth suicide. *Adolescent Psychology, 35,* 551–558.

Freese, A. (1979). *Adolescent suicide: Mental health challenge.* New York, NY: Public Affairs Committee.

Garland, A. F., & Zigler, E. (1993). Adolescent suicide prevention: Current research and social policy implications. *American Psychologist, 43,* 169–182.

Gibbs, J. T. (1988). Conceptual, methodological, and sociocultural issues in Black youth suicide: Implications for assessment and early intervention. *Suicide and Life-Threatening Behavior, 18,* 73–79.

Gould, M. S., Greenberg, T., Velting, D. M., & Shaffer, D. (2003). Youth suicide risk and preventative interventions: A review of the past 10 years. *Journal of the American Academy of Child and Adolescent Psychiatry, 42,* 386–405.

Gust-Brey, K., & Cross, T. (1999). An examination of the literature base on the suicidal behaviors of gifted students. *Roeper Review, 22,* 28–35.

Hafen, B. Q. (Ed.). (1972). *Self-destructive behavior.* Minneapolis, MN: Burgess.

Hafen, B. Q., & Frandsen, K. J. (1986). *Youth suicide: Depression and loneliness.* Provo, UT: Behavioral Health Associates.

Haley, M. (2004). Risk and protective factors. In D. Capuzzi (Ed.), *Suicide across the life span: Implications for counselors* (pp. 95–138). Alexandria, VA: American Counseling Association.

Hallfors, D., Brodish, P. H., Khatapoush, S., Sanchez, V., Cho, H., & Steckler, A. (2006). Feasibility of screening adolescents for suicide risk in "real world" high school settings. *American Journal of Public Health, 96,* 282–287.

Harpine, E. C., Nitza, A., & Conyne, R. (2010). Prevention groups: Today and tomorrow. *Group Dynamics: Theory, Research, and Practice, 14,* 268–280.

Harry, J. (1989). *Sexual identity issues—Report of the Secretary's Task Force on Youth Suicide: Vol. 2. Risk factors for youth suicide* (DHHS Publication No. ADM 89-1622). Washington, DC: U.S. Government Printing Office.

Henry, A. F., & Short, J. F. (1954). *Suicide and homicide.* Glencoe, IL: Free Press.

Hermann, M. A., & Remley, T. P., Jr. (2000). Guns, violence, and schools: The results of school violence litigation against educators and students shedding more constitutional rights at the school house gate. *Loyola Law Review, 46,* 389–439.

Hoberman, H. M., & Garfinkel, B. D. (1988). Completed suicide in children and adolescents. *Journal of the American Academy of Child and Adolescent Psychiatry, 27,* 688–695.

Hussain, S. A., & Vandiver, K. T. (1984). *Suicide in children and adolescents.* New York, NY: SP Medical and Scientific Books.

Jacobs, J. (1971). *Adolescent suicide.* New York, NY: Wiley-Interscience.

Johnson, S. W., & Maile, L. J. (1987). *Suicide and the schools: A handbook for prevention, intervention, and rehabilitation.* Springfield, IL: Charles C Thomas.

Judge, B., & Billick, S. B. (2004). Suicidality in adolescence: Review and legal considerations. *Behavioral Sciences and the Law, 22,* 681–695.

Kiev, A. (1977). *The suicidal patient.* Chicago, IL: Nelson-Hall.

King, K. A. (1999). Fifteen prevalent myths concerning adolescent suicide. *Journal of School Health, 69,* 159–161.

King, K. A. (2000). Preventing adolescent suicide: Do high school counselors know the risk factors? *Professional School Counseling, 3,* 255–263.

King, K. A. (2001a). Developing a comprehensive school suicide prevention program. *Journal of School Health, 71,* 132–137.

King, K. A. (2001b). Tri-level suicide prevention covers it all. *Education Digest, 67,* 55–61.

King, K. A., Strunk, C. M., & Sorter, M. T. (2011). Preliminary effectiveness of surviving the teens suicide prevention and depression awareness program on adolescents' suicidality and self efficacy in performing help-seeking behaviors. *Journal of School Health, 81,* 581–590. doi:10.1111/j.1746-1561.2011.00630.x

Kirchner, J. E., Yoder, M. C., Kramer, T. L., Lindsey, M. S., & Thrush, C. (2000). Development of an educational program to increase school personnel's awareness about child and adolescent depression. *Education, 121,* 235–246.

Kitts, R. L. (2005). Gay adolescents and suicide: Understanding the association. *Adolescence, 40,* 621–628.

Kolves, K. (2010). Child suicide, family environment, and economic crisis. *Crisis: The Journal of Crisis Intervention and Suicide Prevention, 31,* 115–117. doi:10.1027/0227-5910/a000040

Kostenuik, M., & Ratnapalan, M. (2010). Approach to adolescent suicide prevention. *Canadian Family Physician, 56,* 755–760.

Kovacs, M., Beck, A., & Weissman, A. (1975). The use of suicidal motives in the psychotherapy of attempted suicides. *American Journal of Psychotherapy, 29,* 363–368.

Lyon, M. E., Benoit, M., O'Donnell, R. M., Getson, P. R., Silber, T., & Walsh, T. (2000). Assessing African American adolescents' risk for suicide attempts. *Adolescence, 35,* 121–134.

Maples, M. F., Packman, J., Abney, P., Daugherty, R. F., Casey, J. A., & Pirtle, L. (2005). Suicide by teenagers in middle school: A postvention team approach. *Journal of Counseling & Development, 83,* 397–405.

Mazza, J. J., & Reynolds, W. M. (1998). A longitudinal investigation of depression, hopelessness, social support, and major and minor life events and their relation to suicidal ideation in adolescents. *Suicide and Life-Threatening Behavior, 28,* 358–374.

McWhirter, J. J., & Kigin, T. J. (1988). Depression. In D. Capuzzi & L. Golden (Eds.), *Preventing adolescent suicide* (pp. 149–186). Muncie, IN: Accelerated Development.

Metha, A., Weber, B., & Webb, L. D. (1998). Youth suicide prevention: A survey and analysis of policies and efforts in the 50 states. *Suicide and Life-Threatening Behavior, 28,* 150–164.

Moskos, M. A., Achilles, J., & Gray, D. (2004). Adolescent suicide myths in the United States. *Crisis, 25,* 176–182.

National Center for Health Statistics. (2002). Deaths: Leading causes for 2000. *National Vital Statistics Reports, 50*(16).

National Institute of Mental Health. (2002). *Suicide facts*. Retrieved from http://www.nimh.nih.gov/research/suifact.htm

Orbach, I. (2001). Therapeutic empathy with the suicidal wish: Principles of therapy with suicidal individuals. *American Journal of Psychotherapy, 55*, 166–184.

Peck, D. (1983). The last moments of life: Learning to cope. *Deviant Behavior, 4*, 313–342.

Pickens, J. (2011). Community based participatory research on youth violence prevention. *Journal of Multidisciplinary Research, 3*, 9–23.

Price, J. H., Dake, J. A., & Kucharewski, R. (2001). Assets as predictors of suicide attempts in African American inner-city youths. *American Journal of Health Behavior, 25*, 367–375.

Reddy, L. A., & Richardson, L. (2006). School-based prevention and intervention programs for children with emotional disturbance. *Education and Treatment of Children, 29*, 379–404.

Remley, T. P., Jr. (2009). Legal challenges in counseling suicidal students. In D. Capuzzi, *Suicide prevention in schools* (2nd ed., pp. 71–83). Alexandria, VA: American Counseling Association.

Rohde, P., Lewinsohn, P., & Seeley, J. R. (1991). Comorbidity of unipolar depression: Co-morbidity with other mental disorders in adolescents and adults. *Journal of Abnormal Psychology, 100*, 214–222.

Ross, C. (1980). Mobilizing schools for suicide prevention. *Suicide and Life-Threatening Behavior, 10*, 239–243.

Russell, S. T., & Joyner, K. (2001). Adolescent sexual orientation and suicide risk: Evidence from a natural study. *American Journal of Public Health, 91*, 1276–1281.

Rutter, P. A., & Behrendt, A. E. (2004). Adolescent suicide risk: Four psychosocial factors. *Adolescence, 39*, 295–302.

Sale, E., Weil, V., & Kryah, R. (2012). An exploratory investigation of the Promoting Responsibility Through Education and Prevention (PREP) after school program for African American at-risk elementary school students. *School Social Work Journal, 36*, 56–73.

Satcher, D. (1999). *Remarks at the release of the Surgeon General's call to action to prevent suicide*. Retrieved from http://www.surgeongeneral.gov/library/calltoaction/remarks.htm

Schneidman, E., Farbverow, N., & Litman, R. (1976). *The psychology of suicide*. New York, NY: Jason Aronson.

Shaffer, D. (1988). The epidemiology of teen suicide: An examination of risk factors. *Journal of Clinical Psychiatry, 49*, 36–41.

Shaffer, D., & Craft, L. (1999). Methods of adolescent suicide prevention. *Journal of Clinical Psychiatry, 60*, 70–74.

Shaffer, D., Garland, A., Gould, M., Fisher, P., & Trautman, P. (1988). Preventing teenage suicide: A critical review. *Journal of the American Academy of Child and Adolescent Psychiatry, 27*, 675–687.

Shaughnessy, L., Doshi, S. R., & Jones, S. E. (2004). Attempted suicide and associated health risk behaviors among Native American high school students. *Journal of School Health, 74*, 177–182.

Sommes, B. (1984). The troubled teen: Suicide, drug use, and running away. *Women and Health, 9*, 117–141.

Spaeth, M., Weichold, K., Silbereisen, R. K., & Wiesner, M. (2010). Examining the differential effectiveness of a life skills program (IPSY) on alcohol use trajectories in early adolescence. *Journal of Consulting and Clinical Psychology, 3*, 334–348.

Speaker, K. M., & Petersen, G. J. (2000). School violence and adolescent suicide: Strategies for effective intervention. *Educational Review, 52*, 65–73.

Stanard, R. P. (2000). Assessment and treatment of adolescent suicidality. *Journal of Mental Health Counseling, 22*, 204–217.

Stein, M., & Davis, J. (1982). *Therapies for adolescents*. San Francisco, CA: Jossey-Bass.

Stillion, J., McDowell, E., & Shamblin, J. (1984). The suicide attitude vignette experience: A method for measuring adolescent attitudes toward suicide. *Death Education, 8*, 65–81.

Sudak, H., Ford, A., & Rushforth, N. (1984). Adolescent suicide: An overview. *American Journal of Psychotherapy, 38*, 350–369.

Velkoff, P., & Huberty, T. J. (1988). Thinking patterns and motivation. In D. Capuzzi & L. Golden (Eds.), *Preventing adolescent suicide* (pp. 111–147). Muncie, IN: Accelerated Development.

Webb, L. (2009). Counting girls out: A review of suicide among young substance misusers and gender difference implications in the evaluation of risk. *Drugs: Education, Prevention & Policy, 16*, 103–126. doi:10.1080/096876307018014040

Wyche, K., Obolensky, N., & Glood, E. (1990). American Indian, Black American, and Hispanic American youth. In M. J. Rotheram-Borus, J. Bradley, & N. Obolensky (Eds.), *Planning to live: Evaluating and treating suicidal teens in community settings* (pp. 355–389). Tulsa: University of Oklahoma Press.

Wyman, P. A., Brown, H., LoMurray, M., Schmeelk-Cone, K., Petrova, M., Yu, Q., . . . Wang, W. (2010). Prevention program delivered by adolescent peer leaders in high schools. *American Journal of Public Health, 100*, 1653–1661. doi:2105/AJPH.2009.19002

Zenere, F. J., III, & Lazarus, P. J. (1997). The decline of youth suicidal behavior in an urban, multicultural public school system following the introduction of a suicide prevention and intervention program. *Suicide and Life-Threatening Behavior, 27*, 387–403.

Chapter 11

A Future in Jeopardy: Sexuality Issues in Adolescence

Melinda Haley, Jessica C. Gelgand, and Alberto Ivan Rodriguez

Erik Erikson theorized in his model for psychosocial development that adolescents between the ages of 12 and 18 need to achieve a sense of identity in many areas, such as occupation, sex roles, politics, and religion ("Erik Erikson's Eight Stages," 2006). Therefore, adolescence can be a busy time. It can be a time of exploration, identity formation, and social activity. This is a period when an adolescent is attempting to figure out who he or she is as an entity separate from parents, family, and friends. Adolescents are active in exploring what their values are, what they believe in, and who they want to be as adults.

G. Stanley Hall (1904) once deemed adolescence as a period of "storm and stress," and since then, many have viewed adolescence as a period during which an individual goes through many developmental changes. As a part of this exploration, identity formation, and developmental change, many adolescents will face issues pertaining to teen pregnancy and parenthood, drug and alcohol use, rape and date rape, contraction or prevention of sexually transmitted diseases (STDs), career or college decisions, sexual orientation exploration, as well as many other exciting and daunting tasks associated with growing into adulthood. It can be a confusing time for teens and a time in which they are faced with many choices, especially in the area of sexuality.

This time of adolescent exploration and identity formation may also then include sexual awakening and exploration. Along with this burgeoning awareness of sexuality comes risk and responsibility. This chapter focuses on youth at risk for teen pregnancy, STDs (including HIV/AIDS), and rape and date rape. The following case study might be considered typical of a youth at risk. We ask that you keep the case of Julia in mind as you read through this chapter. As you read about these topics in terms of risk factors, prevention, and intervention strategies, consider how Julia might be helped, or what might need to change in Julia's life, to minimize her risk for potential negative outcomes.

Case Study

Julia is a 16-year-old, White, heterosexual female. She is a junior at a large southwestern high school and is not doing well academically. Julia's mother and father are divorced, and Julia has not seen her father since she was 11 years old. Julia's parents' relationship has been fraught with domestic violence, and Julia is not allowed to see her father. Despite her father's actions toward her mother, Julia really misses her father and wishes he were still around. Julia feels that if her parents really loved her they would work things out. Julia often feels bad about herself and doesn't feel she is really loved by anyone.

Julia became sexually active at age 14 when she lost her virginity to her biggest crush. Soon after the big event, Julia's crush dumped her. Julia was devastated and felt ugly and stupid. These feelings further fueled Julia's beliefs that she is not worthy. She began to date other boys to prove that she was attractive and to find the love she so desperately wanted from someone. She gained a reputation in school as "easy" and now feels isolated from other girls because she gets teased a lot and gets called derogatory names.

About two months ago Julia began to indulge in using alcohol and marijuana with some of her recent boyfriends and male friends. Her recent drug use has further deteriorated her relationship with her mother, who found marijuana in Julia's room. Julia does not feel close to her mother and blames her for the loss of her father.

Julia uses condoms most of the time when she has sex, but not always. She tries to be prepared, but sometimes her preparations fall through. Julia feels loved, wanted, and special while having sex, but she feels used and disgusted with herself afterward. Yet, she cannot seem to say no when a boy she likes wants to have sex with her. Even when she says no, she often doesn't mean it; it is like a game to her. When a boy pursues her, she feels wanted. It will be useful to keep Julia in mind as you read the following sections related to issues facing youth at risk: teen pregnancy, STDs, and rape and date rape.

Teen Pregnancy

Adolescent pregnancy has been, and continues to be, a significant social problem in the United States. However, current estimates suggest that there appears to have been an overall decline in childbirth for women ages 15–19 from 1991 to 2009 (Pazol et al., 2011). Overall, the United States continues to have one of the highest teen pregnancy rates among the developed countries (Weiss, 2010). In 2009, the U.S. pregnancy rate for adolescent girls was estimated at 38 per 1,000 females; by comparison, the rate in France was 10 per 1,000, in Canada it was 14 per 1,000, in Japan it was 4.9 per 1,000, and in the United Kingdom it was 25 per 1,000 (National Campaign to Prevent Teen and Unplanned Pregnancy [NCPTUP], 2012). The data suggest that teenagers in the United States remain at a greater risk for conception than their peers from other industrialized nations.

Findings from epidemiological studies suggest that despite the nationwide decline in teen birth rates, major disparities continue to exist across racial and ethnic subgroups. For example, since 1991, birth rates among Hispanic youth continued to be among the highest in the United States, and currently Hispanic adolescent females between the ages of 15 and 19 have one of the highest birth rates in the country (Basch, 2011). In a study by Basch (2011), 48% of Hispanic teenagers had a first birth before the age of 20 compared with 12% of non-Hispanic Whites. In essence, these findings suggest that for some racial/ethnic groups, teen pregnancy continues to be a major problem.

Teen pregnancy and childbirth continue to be associated with a number of negative effects for young women and their children (Basch, 2011; Centers for Disease Control and Prevention [CDC], Division of Reproductive Health, National Center for Chronic Disease Prevention and Health Promotion, 2012b; Weiss, 2010). Babies born to teen mothers are more likely to be preterm, of low birth weight, at greater risk for serious illness or developmental delays, and at greater risk for dying within the first year compared with babies born to older mothers. Many of these children are also more likely to experience child abuse and neglect (Weiss, 2010). As a result, children born to teen parents have a greater risk of doing poorly in school, engaging in early sexual activity and teen pregnancy, and getting into trouble with the law (Medoff, 2010).

Although teen mothers represent only a small proportion of those who are on welfare, the societal costs of medical care, food and housing, and employment training for teen mothers are estimated at $11 billion per year (NCPTUP, 2011). Compared with their peers, teen mothers have a higher risk of reporting low self-esteem and depression (Patel & Sen, 2012), and less than one third of teen mothers ever finish their high school education (NCPTUP, 2011). Consequently, teen mothers are more likely to experience mental health problems, be unprepared for the job market, and be at a greater risk of raising their children in poverty (Duffy et al., 2012; Patel & Sen, 2012).

Risk Factors

Previous research on the risk factors correlated with teen pregnancy focused on the rate of teen sexual activity, quality of parental supervision, effects of poverty, and childhood trauma (Weiss, 2010). There are numerous factors associated with the current trend in teen pregnancy and childbirth, such as parental relationships, pregnancy intentions, pubertal development, and alcohol and drug use (Kramer & Lancaster, 2010; Medoff, 2010; Sieving et al., 2011). However, given that there is not enough space to fully address this topic, the following is an overview of recent research on teen pregnancy risk factors.

Some studies support the view that adolescent girls who are raised by single parents with low educational attainment and low income are at a high risk of becoming teen mothers (Basch, 2011; Weiss, 2010). These studies suggest that the stress and conflict associated with poverty influence adolescent sexual behavior and risk taking. Yet, other studies suggest that regardless of the socioeconomic factors, the quality of the parental relationship is an important determinant associated with teen pregnancy. In summarizing the research in this area, the NCPTUP (2012) indicated that teens who are not close to their parents are more likely to engage in early sexual activity, are more likely to have multiple sexual partners, and are less likely to use contraception on a consistent basis.

Pregnancy intentions have also been found to predict pregnancy outcomes among teens. For instance, Rosengard, Phillips, Adler, and Ellen (2004) found that adolescent girls who indicated either clear pregnancy intentions (planning and likely) or inconsistent pregnancy intentions (not planning and likely) were more apt to report suspected pregnancies or positive test results compared with those who revealed no intention of getting pregnant (not planning and not likely).

In their study on the pregnancy intentions of teenage boys, Rosengard, Phillips, Adler, and Ellen (2005) reported that a majority of those surveyed had no plans of getting someone pregnant. However, some revealed that they were likely to get their female partner pregnant in the near future.

Another factor related to risky sexual behavior and teen pregnancy is early-onset pubertal development. Girls who mature early are less likely to be prepared for the transition and others' expectations of maturation. These girls are at a higher risk of attracting attention from older males, which in turn increases their risk for engaging in high-risk behaviors (Kramer & Lancaster, 2010; Weiss, 2010). Some studies found that adolescent girls who matured earlier (before the age of 12) were more likely to engage in early-onset substance use and sexual activity (Kramer & Lancaster, 2010; Weiss, 2010).

The association between early alcohol and drug use and risky sexual behaviors has been well documented in the literature. For example, results from Mullany et al.'s (2012) study of Native American youth showed that early illicit drug use predicted future sexually risky behaviors, such as inconsistent contraceptive use, multiple sex partners, and adolescent pregnancy.

On the basis of findings from previous studies, teen pregnancy continues to represent a serious risk to the overall life success of youth. For example, teens who become pregnant are less likely to complete their education, are less prepared for the job market, are at a greater risk of developing mental health problems, and are more likely to live in poverty. In addition, children of teen mothers are at a greater risk for developmental delays, child abuse or neglect, early alcohol or drug use, and problems with the law (Lachance, Burrus, & Scott, 2012; NCPTUP, 2010; Weiss, 2010). As a result, researchers and government officials continue to develop programs aimed at reducing the risk of pregnancy among teenagers. Therefore, the next section of this chapter provides an overview of the current trends in teen pregnancy prevention.

Approaches to Prevention

As mentioned, the U.S. adolescent pregnancy rate remains among the highest in the industrialized world (Shuger, 2012). Thus, prevention efforts are vital to continuing the overall decline in teen pregnancy. During the past years, research on the efficacy of pregnancy prevention programs has become increasingly more advanced. In a review of past research, Lachance et al. (2012) found four different areas in which research within the field has improved: (a) Research has become increasingly sophisticated, (b) sample sizes and calculations of statistical power have increased, (c) researchers have increased the use of experimental designs with random assignment, and (d) researchers have increased the use of more sophisticated statistical techniques. The following subsections discuss the most recent teen pregnancy prevention strategies targeted at the individual, family, school, and community levels.

Individual

In the past, prevention strategies for individuals were geared toward reducing adolescent pregnancies and childbirth through education focused on delaying the initiation of sexual activity (Stanger-Hall & Hall, 2011). These abstinence-only programs suggested that the only effective means of avoiding teen pregnancy was by delaying sexual activity until marriage. Abstinence-only programs typically did not discuss contraception and contraceptive failure. One advantage to these types of programs is that they are diverse. For example, some are religious based whereas others are curriculum oriented, and some last as few as one session whereas others can be 20 sessions in length. To date, few studies have examined the effectiveness of abstinence-only programs.

In one of the few studies to review the efficacy of different types of pregnancy prevention programs, Trenholm and colleagues (2008) found that abstinence-only programs have failed to delay the initiation of sexual activity. In a similar manner, Basch (2011) reported that abstinence-only programs did not significantly alter self-reported rates of intercourse and pregnancy. However, both Trenholm et al. and Basch cautioned that the data concerning the effectiveness of abstinence-only programs are largely inconclusive because of methodological limitations (e.g., small sample sizes, no comparison group, lack of random assignment, participant attrition, and lack of follow-up) and the diversity of abstinence programs (e.g., religious, curriculum, and so forth).

Other current prevention strategies geared toward individuals include the following: sex and contraceptive counseling with adolescents (Falk, Brynhildsen, & Ivarsson, 2009), sex education focused on gender roles (Murphy-Erby, Stauss, Boyas, & Bivens, 2011), and culturally sensitive service providers (e.g., openness and knowledge of the unique aspects of the clients' language, cultural values, community institutions, and experiences of discrimination; Murphy-Erby et al., 2011; Sieving et al., 2011).

Family

Parents play an important role in adolescents' ability to avoid sexual risk-taking behaviors through critical factors, such as degree of family involvement, family structure, parental monitoring, and parent–child communication (CDC, 2012b). Past efforts in the area of family prevention have included enhancement of parenting skills and facilitation of parent–child relationships through improved communication (Pazol et al., 2011).

School

Pregnancy prevention efforts have long been established in U.S. schools. In a recent review of school-based pregnancy prevention programs in the United States, Stanger-Hall and Hall (2011) found that a majority of the programs were abstinence-only programs. However, findings from that study revealed that these types of programs showed only a modest impact in delaying the initiation of sexual

---

Sidebar 11.1 ■ Self-Awareness: Preparing for Having the "Sex" Talk

Intervention strategies that have been shown to have a positive impact on facilitating parent–child communication about sex and enhancing parental skills include the following: (a) giving honest answers about sexual issues, (b) knowing parental values about sexual issues, (c) replacing street slang with correct words, (d) answering questions in an age-appropriate manner, (e) trying not to be judgmental, and (f) practicing answering questions with another adult (NCPTUP, 2012). Imagine you are a counselor, teacher, parent, big sister/big brother, caretaker, or other important adult in an adolescent's life. How would you approach the subject of sex in order to educate the adolescent? Have you ever been in such a situation? How did you prepare? How did you feel going into that conversation? What was the adolescent's reaction to your conversation? If you were to do it over again, what would you do or say differently?

■ ■ ■

activity among youth. In a similar manner, sexual education programs in schools tend to produce a relatively modest impact on delaying teen sex (Trenholm et al., 2008). The following are suggestions for school-based prevention programs: Increase awareness of the importance of school and education, encourage high school graduation and exploration of career interests, learn risks associated with sex and negative consequences of early sexual activity, and promote wellness and healthy life choices among students (Weiss, 2010). Other suggestions include targeting specific goals focused on reducing one or more sexual behaviors that lead to teen pregnancy, building social skills through role-playing and interviewing, and using culturally relevant messages about sexual behavior (Weiss, 2010).

Community

Although the rate of unintended pregnancy and child bearing in the United States has declined over the past 20 years, some of our nation's poorest communities continue to have alarmingly high rates. Youth who live in neighborhoods marked by poverty, high crime, single-parent families, and lower levels of education among residents are more likely to engage in sexual risk-taking behaviors. In addition, there continues to be a dearth of research on the efficacy of community prevention efforts, and there seems to be a lack of uniformity among community prevention programs (Falk et al., 2009; Ott, Rouse, Resseguie, Smith, & Woodcox, 2011).

To address this critical need, Ott and colleagues (2011) and Falk and colleagues (2009) suggested the following guidelines for community pregnancy prevention program curricula: (a) Focus on more than one of the sexual antecedents that lead to unintended teen pregnancy (e.g., sexual beliefs, sexual attitudes, norms, intentions, and self-efficacy); (b) ground the curriculum on a theoretical orientation that has been demonstrated to explain and reduce sexually risky behavior; (c) specify both the risk and protective factors to be modified by curriculum activities; (d) provide both basic and current information about the risks of unprotected sex and contraceptive methods; (e) include activities that address peer pressure; (f) provide modeling and demonstrate effective communication skills (e.g., negotiation and refusal skills); (g) use a variety of teaching methods designed to reach different learning styles; (h) use behavioral goals, teaching methods, and materials appropriate for participants' age, sexual experience, and cultural background; and (i) ensure that sessions last long enough to complete important activities.

Intervention Strategies

The following subsections explore current intervention strategies aimed at reducing harm and disadvantageous outcomes for children and teen parents and preventing future unintended pregnancies.

Individual

Teen pregnancy and childbirth are associated with numerous detrimental outcomes. In an effort to reduce harm and prevent future unwanted pregnancies, intervention efforts at the individual level should include regular obstetric health screenings during pregnancy. Other recent trends in intervention efforts with pregnant teens include nutrition counseling, sex and contraceptive counseling, and brief counseling interventions with teen mothers (Falk et al., 2009; Sieving et al., 2011; Slater, Mitschke, & Douthit, 2011).

Brief counseling, especially during the onset of pregnancy, may help clarify the teen mother's pregnancy and post-pregnancy options. A recommended brief counseling approach to use with pregnant teens is a *motivational interviewing* approach (Sieving et al., 2011). Motivational interviewing is a directive and client-centered approach to counseling that focuses on helping clients explore and resolve ambivalence regarding behavior change. The assumptions behind motivational interviewing are that clients have existing motivation to change and counselors can enhance but not create motivation (Sieving et al., 2011).

For some teen mothers, the decision to keep the baby, give it up for adoption, or have an abortion is a difficult one. The potential value of motivational interviewing is that it may help pregnant teens explore this conflict in an atmosphere characterized by warmth, compassion, and positive regard. Motivational interviewing has been found to reduce the risk of drinking during pregnancy (Sieving et al., 2011). It has also been found to be useful in contraceptive counseling (Falk et al., 2009). In addition, motivational interviewing may be especially helpful in clarifying teen mothers' post-pregnancy options.

Family

Family support has long been understood as an essential component to positive long-term outcomes among teen mothers and their children. One recent trend in family interventions is to help assist parents of pregnant teens to improve their relationships with their children by fostering communication (Weiss, 2010). For example, the Young Parenthood Program was designed to help enhance communication between teen mothers and their parents (Slater et al., 2011). This psychoeducational program focuses on strengthening family communication by providing parents with strategies for discussing sexual issues and behavior. Other family interventions include group psychotherapy, solution-focused therapy with parents of pregnant teens, and strategies to increase fathers' involvement and knowledge of parenting skills (Florsheim, 2012; Sieving et al., 2011).

School

Some suggest that being in school helps reduce the deleterious factors, such as poverty, associated with teen parenthood (Gruber, 2012; Sieving et al., 2011). Simply put, teen parents who finish high school have more options than those who do

---

Sidebar 11.2 ■ Self-Evaluation: Value Conflicts When Working With a Pregnant Teen

The following are suggestions for working with pregnant teens in a school context: (a) Encourage parental support and communication; (b) encourage communication about the teen mother's expectations regarding the baby's father, pregnancy outcomes, and post-pregnancy plans; (c) encourage focus on the mental and physical health of the pregnant teen; (d) adopt a family systems approach; (e) promote resiliency and strengths; and (f) link the teen with community resources (Florsheim, 2012; Gruber, 2012; Sieving et al., 2011). Imagine you are the counselor working with Julia. What values do you hold as an individual that would facilitate working with a pregnant teen? What values do you hold that might conflict with working with a pregnant teen? How does your own sexual history influence your thoughts and feelings regarding this issue? How would you handle this conflict in your values and work with a pregnant teen?

■ ■ ■

not. School-based pregnancy intervention programs differ in their focus, content, length, and methodology. Because of these differences, researchers have found it difficult to systematically evaluate the effectiveness of pregnancy interventions in schools. One of the most common school-based intervention programs is called the Young Parenthood Program (Florsheim, 2012). The primary purpose of this program is to provide an academic environment with medical and social services for teen parents and their children. Although a review of all the different kinds of intervention strategies is beyond the scope of this chapter, some of the recent trends in school-based pregnancy interventions include condom availability programs, service-learning programs focused on increasing the pregnant teens' bond with the school, and peer mentoring programs (Florsheim, 2012; Gruber, 2012; Sieving et al., 2011).

Community

Despite declines in the overall rate of unintended pregnancies among women ages 15–19, the rate in the United States continues to rank in the top 10 among developed countries. As a result, unintended pregnancy and childbirth pose a significant public health concern for policymakers and researchers.

At the macro level, U.S. policymakers have responded to this concern by passing a number of acts targeting teen pregnancy prevention and intervention. Three recent bills aimed at reducing teen pregnancy are (a) the Teen Pregnancy Prevention Initiative FY 2012, (b) the Teen Pregnancy Prevention Program, and (c) the Competitive Abstinence Education Grant Program (NCPTUP, 2012; Stanger-Hall & Hall, 2011).

On the micro level, both state and federal governments provide funding for family planning services and supplies. These clinics are designed to meet the needs of individuals from low-income backgrounds and link them with public health and social services. The Teen Pregnancy Prevention Initiative provides the largest source of funding for such programs (Stanger-Hall & Hall, 2011). In addition to more public funding for prevention programs and resources, some have suggested that better child support enforcement may help curb unintended teen pregnancy and risky sexual behavior (Hehir, 2008; Stanger-Hall & Hall, 2011).

AIDS and Other STDs

Recent estimates suggest that the United States has the highest incidence of STD acquisition in the developed world (McElroy, 2010). The acquisition of STDs is associated with numerous negative outcomes and scores of health problems. For example, some estimates suggest that chlamydia and gonorrhea are the leading causes of major health problems, such as pelvic inflammatory disease, ectopic pregnancy, infertility, and chronic pelvic pain (Hosenfeld et al., 2009).

Sidebar 11.3 ■ Case Study: Risk Factors for Julia

Can you identify the risk factors discussed in this chapter that apply to our youth at risk, Julia? What might you suggest for Julia in terms of prevention efforts and intervention strategies? Take a moment to reflect what you would do if you were Julia's counselor. Continue to think about Julia as we turn our discussion to the next section on sexually transmitted diseases. Is Julia at risk in this domain also?

■ ■ ■

Despite increased efforts to reduce the incidence and mortality of STDs in the United States, each year more than 19 million people contract an STD (Workowski & Berman, 2011). As suggested in the previous section of this chapter, at-risk youth tend to engage in risky sexual behavior, and one possible consequence of risky sexual behavior is the acquisition of STDs such as HIV, chlamydia, and gonorrhea.

Risk Factors

The incidence of sexually risky behavior among adolescents in the United States is high. A teenager gets an STD every 8 seconds (Florida Department of Health, 2012). At least 50% of sexually active adolescents will contract an STD during their lifetime (American Sexual Health Association, 2011). Recent reports by the CDC indicated that adolescents make up 25% of the 475,871 people living with HIV in the United States at present (Reisner et al., 2009). Compared with older adults, persons under the age of 25 are at a higher risk for acquiring STDs (Wildsmith, Schelar, Peterson, & Manlove, 2010), and teens who initiate sex at an earlier age are more likely to have multiple partners and less likely to practice safe sex (Houlihan et al., 2008).

Chlamydia is the most commonly reported STD in the United States, with its highest rates found among adolescents (Tebb, Wibbelsman, Neuhaus, & Shafer, 2009), and statistics show that female adolescents have the highest infection rate for both gonorrhea and chlamydia of women of all ages in the United States (Ott, Harezlak, Ofner, & Fortenberry, 2012). In general, adolescent girls are more vulnerable to STD infection (Fageeh, 2008), and those who have an STD are at a higher risk for developing cervical cancer, becoming infertile, having an ectopic pregnancy, developing pelvic inflammatory disease, and acquiring HIV (Farr, Kraft, Warner, Anderson, & Jamieson, 2009).

Research shows that various risk factors are associated with HIV/STD acquisition in adolescence, including the following: early age of sexual debut, inconsistent or incorrect use of condoms, experimentation with alcohol and other substances, unprotected anal sex, race/ethnicity, sociodemographic conditions, and behavioral issues (Dariotis, Sifakis, Pleck, Astone, & Sonenstein, 2011; Hensel, Fortenberry, & Orr, 2010; Johnson, Scott-Sheldon, Huedo-Medina, & Carey, 2011). Taken together, this information suggests that STDs constitute a significant health problem for U.S. youth. In addition, the economic cost of STDs is shocking. Recent estimates indicate that the annual direct and indirect health care cost for STD treatment is $17 billion in the United States (Secura et al., 2012). The next section provides a brief overview of the current trends in STD prevention.

Approaches to Prevention

Despite continuing efforts to reduce HIV and other STD transmission, the rate of acquisition among U.S. teens is alarmingly high. Currently, the primary focus of HIV and other STD prevention programs is on educating and counseling at-risk people, diagnosing and treating infected people and their sex partners, indentifying infected people who are unlikely to seek treatment, and providing preventive vaccinations (CDC, 2010). Because teens are at greater risk for HIV/STD infection than adults, prevention efforts are especially vital to reducing the incidence of STD transmission in the country. The following subsections provide an overview of the HIV/STD prevention efforts geared toward teens.

Individual

Current STD prevention programs geared toward teens include programs focused on teens abstaining from oral, anal, and vaginal intercourse; choosing low-risk sexual partners; discussing their sexual history with new partners; and having monogamous relationships in addition to programs aimed at teaching teens to consistently use a male latex condom during heterosexual and homosexual intercourse (Akers, Gold, Coyne Beasley, & Corbie Smith, 2012). However, research suggests that teens lack consistency in undertaking these precautions (Akers et al., 2012). To make these programs more effective, some have suggested that cultural factors surrounding the discussion of sex and contraception should be integrated into sexual education prevention curriculum (Kirby, 2011). Sexual education programs that have shown success at increasing safe sex practices have incorporated communication skills training so that adolescents are better equipped at negotiating safe sex practices with their sexual partner (Kirby, 2011).

Finally, in terms of individual prevention counseling, a number of different counseling approaches have been used with clients to educate them about specific strategies that can reduce the risk of HIV/STD transmission. For example, motivational interviewing has been shown to be beneficial in terms of self-efficacy to practice safe sex and is a promising tool that can address various issues associated with risky sexual behaviors (Chariyeva, Golin, Earp, & Suchindran, 2012; Golin et al., 2012).

Family

One of the most critical elements of family prevention of STD transmission among teens is parent–child communication. Parents are quite simply the agents of primary prevention. The messages that parents communicate about sex are critical factors in shaping adolescents' beliefs about sex roles and sexual behaviors. According to Planned Parenthood (2009), the following are guidelines on how parents can approach the topic of safe sex with their teens: (a) Talk calmly about sex, (b) avoid giving a lecture, (c) listen to your teen and answer his or her questions as openly and honestly as possible, (d) discuss the issues of STDs and prevention and different forms of sexuality, and (e) talk about where teens can get access to contraceptives and health care services.

In terms of family prevention programming, program evaluators and researchers may want to consider incorporating cultural beliefs and practices into their curriculum. For instance, when working with Latino adolescents and their families, prevention programs may want to address the influence of *machismo* and *marianismo* on sexual roles and behavior. The concept of *marianismo* refers to characteristics of the Virgin Mary and helps lead to the socialization of Latinas as selfless, virtuous, good daughters who are respectful and obedient to men. In contrast, *machismo* refers to the potency, virility, and strength of the Latino male as the head of the family. Machismo leads to greater acceptance and expectation of Latino adolescent males' premarital sexual behavior. These cultural beliefs may put Latino adolescents at an elevated risk for engaging in early sexual activity without contraception (Lescano, Brown, Raffaelli, & Lima, 2009).

School

Schools have become a critical ally in the effort to increase the likelihood that prevention messages regarding safe sex and the consequences of STDs are received by teens. For the last three decades, schools have implemented numerous HIV and other STD prevention programs. In a recent review conducted for the United Nations looking at 87 sex education programs, results indicated that sex education programs increased students' knowledge of sex and showed modest reductions in risky sexual behavior (Kirby, 2011). Findings from this same review stated that curriculum-based sex and STD/HIV education programs implemented in schools can delay sex, reduce the frequency of sex, reduce the number of partners, increase condom use, increase overall contraceptive use, and reduce unprotected sex (Kirby, 2011).

The review conducted for the United Nations identified the following characteristics of an effective STD prevention curriculum in schools: (a) Establish clear goals in determining the curriculum content, which should include prevention education on HIV, other STDs, and/or unintended pregnancy; (b) focus on risky sexual and protective behaviors that enable students to reach the curriculum goals; (c) address specific situations that lead to unsafe sex practices and how to avoid these and how to get out of them; (d) be clear when teaching behaviors that reduce the risk of STDs or pregnancy; (e) focus on risk and protective factors that influence sexual behaviors and that are capable of change by the curriculum (e.g., knowledge, values, societal norms, skills, attitude); (f) promote active student participation to help students internalize and integrate information; (g) implement various activities designed to change risk and protective factors; (h) provide accurate information about the risks involved in having unprotected sex, and teach students different safe sex practices; (i) talk about perceptions of risk, such as vulnerability to STD acquisition; (j) talk about personal attitudes, family views, and peer norms about sexual intercourse and/or having multiple partners; (k) address individual views and peer norm condom usage and contraception; (l) address personal skills and self-efficacy to use those skills; and (m) cover topics in a logical sequence (Kirby, 2011).

Community

Adolescents within the United States have one of the highest rates of STD transmission in the developed world (Coyle et al., 2009). Consequently, focusing on HIV/STD acquisition is considered one of the major priorities in public health legislation and prevention programming today. The National Institutes of Health (NIH) suggested implementing a three-step program that communities can use for the purpose of preventing STD acquisition. The NIH's community preventive measures include the following: (a) primary prevention methods aimed at stopping the STD before acquisition, for example, efforts to educate the public on STD prevention strategies by using the mass media, such as the Internet, television, radio, and newspapers; (b) secondary prevention practices that focus on research aimed at developing interventions to diagnose and treat STDs more effectively, such as developing strategies that could help increase adherence to STD care practices; and (c) tertiary prevention practices that focus on treating those who have already acquired the disease, for example, providing medical resources to infected people to help alleviate any complications the disease might manifest (Chiaradonna, 2008).

Other prevention suggestions are that teens get more involved in community prevention programs. The CDC (2006) offered the following guidelines for getting more youth participation in community prevention agencies: (a) Take teen involvement seriously, (b) involve teens in the planning and activities of the program's goals, (c) use teens' input when developing messages and marketing campaigns targeting teens, (d) provide teens with the appropriate training and make them an integral part of prevention programming efforts, (e) work with teens to make risky sexual behavior taboo in teen culture, (f) take your program message to places where teens congregate, (g) encourage teens to be your media and community ambassadors, (h) help give teens a voice with policymakers and other community leaders, and (i) offer incentives for teens to work for your organization (e.g., scholarships, stipends, grants).

Intervention Strategies

This section explores recent literature and research findings on individual, family, school, and community interventions for adolescents who have contracted an STD.

Individual

In a summary of individual-level interventions for HIV and other STD transmission, Cohen and Scribner (2000) found that most of these levels of interventions focused on counseling, screening, and treatment. In terms of individual interventions, one of the most vital components of treatment is medication adherence. For some at-risk youth, the task of adhering to a strict treatment regimen may be exceptionally difficult. One intervention that has been shown to affect adherence among other at-risk populations is motivational interviewing. Motivational interviewing has been effective in encouraging treatment adherence, which, in turn, has reduced viral load and risky sexual behaviors in youth who are infected with HIV (Markham, Shegog, Leonard, Bui, & Paul, 2009).

Although abstinence is the surest way of preventing STD infection, the following strategies were recommended for adolescents to protect themselves from contracting an STD: (a) Have a mutually monogamous sexual relationship with an uninfected partner, (b) consistently and correctly use a male latex or female polyurethane condom and topical microbicides, (c) use sterile needles if injecting intravenous drugs, (d) delay having sexual relationships as long as possible, (e) have regular checkups for STDs, (f) learn the symptoms of STDs, (g) avoid having sexual intercourse during menstruation, (h) avoid anal intercourse, (i) avoid douching, and (j) decrease susceptibility to HIV infections by preventing and controlling other STDs ("Sexually Transmitted Disease," 2013).

Family

The importance of family during an adolescent's treatment for HIV or other STDs cannot be overstated. Parents and other family members can be a tremendous source of support for teens who have just found out that they have an STD or for those who are undergoing treatment. Consequently, family intervention strategies usually involve a family systems approach in which the parents, the affected teen, and any siblings are all part of the treatment process. However, one recent trend in family intervention involves couples counseling. Relationship-based counseling has been found to be useful in promoting HIV counseling, testing, and condom use. Relationship-based counseling can be administered either with both partners in session or individually.

Perhaps the most important benefit of couples counseling is that it provides both partners with a safe place to disclose highly personal information that they may not have otherwise shared with each other. Because issues surrounding trust and commitment often influence condom and other contraceptive use in long-term relationships, individuals in these types of relationships are often vulnerable to acquiring STDs. Contemporary couples therapy has shown that it can reduce gender–power imbalances that contribute to condom use and has the ability to increase communication and negotiating skills that can help increase safe sex practices (Pequegnat & Bray, 2012).

School

In general, STDs have disproportionately affected teens in the United States. Consequently, because most teens are enrolled in school long before the initiation of sexual behavior, schools may potentially be effective in reducing teen sexual risk-taking behavior. One study showed that school-based health center screening services is an effective setting for the treatment of chlamydia in young females (Braun & Provost, 2010).

In addition to screening and treatment programs, case management services in schools may be helpful in reducing premature morbidity and mortality among teens who are infected with STDs. For example, various recent research findings have shown that HIV-positive youth who had more contact with case management services showed improved retention of HIV care practices (Wohl et al., 2011).

Lastly, a reality group therapy approach may be effective in modifying behaviors and attitudes related to school dropout in at-risk youth. Reality therapy has been effectively applied to schools, and it has the potential to impact student academic achievement, career decision making, and personal/social issues (D. Mason, Palmer, Duba, & Jill, 2009). Because of its focus on the present, on need fulfillment, and on unique problem-solving approaches, reality therapy may also be effective in working with teens who have contracted HIV or any other STDs.

Community

The CDC's Replicating Effective Programs Plus (REP+) site has a variety of HIV/STD intervention programs that have been tested and proven to work. Community Promise is one intervention that is part of the REP+ package that targets high-risk communities with high rates of STD and HIV infection among youth populations. The community intervention consists of four main components: (a) education of agencies about the targeted community, (b) mobilization of community members to be advocates of prevention messages, (c) creation of role-model stories that illustrate personal accounts of people who have already made positive changes toward reducing risky sexual behavior, and (d) distribution of role-model stories and preventive materials (e.g., condoms, bleach kits) by community advocates (CDC, 2009, 2012a). This community intervention has been proven to increase condom carrying and condom usage with main and non-main sex partners within the intervention community (CDC, 2012a).

"Be proud! Be responsible!" is an effective and cost-efficient intervention program that the CDC has categorized as a "Program That Works" and is an educative and skills-building intervention that is aimed at reducing STD and HIV infection

Sidebar 11.4 ■ Case Study: Julia at Risk for an STD?

In returning to Julia, our youth at risk, what behavior is Julia engaging in that will make it more likely she will contract an STD? If you were the counselor working with Julia, what type of prevention effort or intervention strategy would you want to use? Keep Julia in mind as we turn to another topic for youth at risk, rape and date rape.

■ ■ ■

rates among adolescents (Jemmott, Jemmott, Fong, & Morales, 2010). The program is based on three theories: (a) social-cognitive theory, (b) the theory of reasoned action, and (c) the theory of planned behavior (Jemmott et al., 2010). This program teaches adolescents to be proud of themselves and their community and to practice propriety for the sake of themselves, their community, and their family, and it gives them the proper education and skills that are necessary to protect themselves from STD and HIV infection (Jemmott et al., 2010). Research findings on the effectiveness of "Be proud! Be responsible!" have been consistent with previous studies that indicate that adolescents were more likely to use condoms after the intervention. Other findings regarding "Be proud! Be responsible!" show that adolescents were more likely to report using a condom on their last sexual encounter and to more frequently use condoms (Jemmott et al., 2010).

Rape and Date Rape

Rape and date rape are increasing in the U.S. population. Some say rape is the fastest growing crime in the United States (Kim, 2012). Estimates are that one woman is raped every 2 minutes (Burnett et al., 2009). Although heterosexuals, homosexuals, males, or females can commit rape, sexual assault, and dating violence, it is more common for heterosexual males to be the abuser and heterosexual females to be the victim (Elwood et al., 2011; Klem, 2009). Because of space limitations, the chapter focuses on heterosexual women as the victim of heterosexual sexual violence.

Rape and date rape is an issue concerning all men and women but one that especially affects adolescents. It is estimated that over 3 million children and adolescents are sexually abused in the United States (Danielson et al., 2012). The peak age of victimization for women in the United States is between 16 and 19 years old; the second highest victimization rate occurs among 20- to 24-year-olds (McMahon & Schwartz, 2011). Women of the 16- to 19-year-old age range are more likely to be victims of sexual violence than any other age group (National Center for Victims of Crime, 2012).

Date rape is the most common form of rape in this age group; data suggest that date or acquaintance rape accounts for 54%–66% of all sexual assaults, and date-related violence and sexual assault may be as high as 35% within the adolescent

Sidebar 11.5 ■ Self-Awareness: Evaluating Working With an Accused Perpetrator

Some of the current prevention strategies discussed in the professional literature for individuals include the following: (a) raising the consciousness of individuals regarding the sexual rights of women and the prevalence of date rape; (b) social skills and assertiveness training for women; (c) increasing women's self-efficacy to negotiate for safer sex; (d) shifting men's and women's attitudes concerning traditional sex and gender roles, adversarial sexual beliefs, and rape stereotypes and myths; (e) establishing empathy with rape survivors to increase men's awareness of and sensitivity to rape; (f) focusing on attitudes and beliefs that create a culture whereby dating violence is accepted; (g) increasing the focus on how drugs and alcohol affect dating violence; (h) teaching women self-defense, response, and risk-perception strategies; (i) educating individuals on rape myth acceptance; (j) educating to change rape-supportive beliefs; and (k) increasing awareness about date rape drugs (Ting, 2009; Wilmoth, 2008). Pretend you are a counselor working with a young man who is accused of date rape. Which of the above strategies would you find useful in working with this young man? Which do you feel might not be effective? Why?

■ ■ ■

population (National Center for Victims of Crime, 2012; Nicodemus, 2011). It is estimated that during their teen years, one in five girls and one in 20 boys will be victims of dating violence, and three out of four sexual assaults are perpetrated by someone the victim knows (National Center for Victims of Crime, 2012).

Rape has been defined as "the penetration, no matter how slight, of the vagina or anus with any body part or object, or oral penetration by a sex organ of another person, without the consent of the victim"; *acquaintance rape* is defined as any type of sexual assault in which the victim knows the perpetrator previous to the assault; and *date rape* is a type of acquaintance rape and is not consensual sex between dating partners. *Sexual assault* is any form of sexual contact without consent (kissing, touching, and so forth), including rape (Hansen, O'Byrne, & Rapley, 2010; National Center for Victims of Crime, 2012).

Risk Factors for Women

As with any complex behavior, the factors associated with date rape are also complex. Estimates are that between 12% and 40% of all adolescents have become violent toward their dating partners (Nicodemus, 2011). Research has indicated that there are many associated factors that place adolescent women at increased risk for sexual victimization from a dating partner. Among these are use of alcohol and/or drugs, heavy cigarette use, high levels of consensual sexual activity or many sexual partners, early age of first date, losing virginity at a young age, history of sexual abuse, being socially isolated or having poor peer relationships, problems adjusting to school, poor interpersonal control, low self-esteem, depression, having considered or attempted suicide, emotionality, coming from an abusive home, parental aggression, attitudes and beliefs condoning dating violence, beliefs in rape stereotypes, incidence rate of community and school violence, level of satisfaction in the relationship, seriousness and length of the dating relationship, relationship conflict, and being isolated from others in a dating situation (Elwood et al., 2011; Freeman & Temple, 2010; Zinzow, 2011).

Approaches to Prevention

The literature is bountiful in terms of current prevention efforts to combat adolescent date rape and sexual victimization statistics (Zurbriggen, 2009). Most outreach programs and prevention strategies developed to address the problem of sexual assault and date rape have traditionally focused on changing the behavior of women rather than the behavior of men (McCauley, Ruggiero, Resnick, & Kilpatrick, 2010). However, in recent years this trend has changed, and men are becoming a focus (Hillenbrand-Gunn, Heppner, Mauch, & Park, 2010). The following subsections highlight some of the prevention strategies that are currently being used.

Sidebar 11.6 ■ Case Study: Julia as a Victim?

As a counselor working with Julia, what do you see as potential factors in Julia's life that might put her at risk for sexual abuse from a partner or for being a victim of rape or date rape? How might you try to intervene in Julia's life to try to minimize these risk factors or increase her protective factors? Which of the discussed prevention efforts or intervention strategies do you think are most efficacious in helping Julia at this point in her development? Are there any other warning flags present in the case of Julia that might make her a target of a sexual predator?

■ ■ ■

Individual

Determining empirically supported prevention strategies has been difficult because of the following: lack of published research on prevention programs, lack of comparability between programs, ineffective outcome and program evaluation research, lack of a systematic evaluation of one program over time, and lack of theory in prevention programming. In addition, outcome measures have traditionally focused on attitudes and not on how change in attitudes can change behaviors (Foshee et al., 2009; Zurbriggen, 2009).

Although mixed-gender rape prevention programs have been shown to be effective (Townsend & Campbell, 2008), recent trends have used single-gender groups with success and minimized retraumatization for women who have been abused (Bradley, Yeater, & O'Donohue, 2009; Collings, 2011). Strategies that have seemed to be most effective with men include the following: (a) using nonconfrontational information, with a focus on identifying when consent to have sex is given or not given; (b) building victim empathy; (c) teaching participants how to help women recover from a rape experience; (d) using peer education formats; (e) facilitating a balanced discussion of date rape issues; (f) using multiple sources of persuasion in a presentation (e.g., videos, multiple presenters, readings); (g) conveying presenters as expert, reliable, trustworthy, and credible; (h) adopting programs that are nonconfrontational and that do not focus on all men as being potential rapists; and (i) using the elaboration likelihood model, which posits that lasting attitude and behavior changes come when participants are motivated to hear the message, understand the message, and perceive the message as being relevant to them personally (Collings, 2011; Weisz & Black, 2010).

Also in terms of individual prevention efforts, there are many suggestions women can take to protect themselves and reduce their risk for rape and date rape. These protective measures include the following: (a) Use the "buddy system" and look out for each other, (b) monitor your and your friends' alcohol consumption, (c) do not become intoxicated, (d) keep control over your own drink, (e) drink only from sealed bottles rather than open containers such as punch bowls, and (f) discard any drink that does not look or taste right (Nicodemus, 2011).

Family

Parents are often a teen's greatest protective factor. Building a strong, supportive family whereby each member is valued and heard is one of the best forms of prevention. Parents can help their children avoid being a victim of rape or date rape by talking to their kids about sexual violence and teaching them to say no, modeling what healthy relationships look like, modeling healthy beliefs and behaviors and setting clear standards, keeping the line of communication open and creating a safe place for a teen to come to talk, looking for behavioral cues that a teen may be a victim (e.g., withdrawal and isolation from friends; repeated absences and tardiness at school; visible signs of injuries; and feeling depressed, anxious, or sad), and discussing what sexual harassment is and what a teen should do about it (Tharp et al., 2011; Ting, 2009; Townsend & Campbell, 2008). More information can be found on the websites of the Committee for Children (http://www.cfchildren.org/) and the Center for Prevention of Abuse (http://www.centerforpreventionofabuse.org/).

School

Prevention efforts have been well established on college campuses and have been apparent on high school campuses within the last several years. Many prevention efforts have targeted women and have been focused on challenging rape-supportive attitudes. Some suggestions for school prevention efforts are as follows: (a) Provide psychoeducational material that helps women recognize the warning signs of male aggression and teen dating violence; (b) infuse curriculum with information about rape and assault; (c) challenge societal gender role expectations; and (d) provide information and education about date rape drugs, including composition, effects of abuse, effects of involuntary ingestion and sexual assault, risk of consuming beverages at clubs, and legal issues associated with use and abuse (Ting, 2009; Weisz & Black, 2010).

There is research evidence indicating that rape education and prevention programs are successful on high school and college campuses and help change the mindset and attitudes about rape. These types of programs generally are administered in a single session lasting from 30 minutes to 2 hours (Hillenbrand-Gunn et al., 2010). However, these large, single-session, educational prevention efforts have not been shown to be effective in helping women who have already been victimized or those who have the highest risk for being raped. There is more empirical support for the effectiveness of smaller, single-sex groups (Bradley et al., 2009).

Strategies that have increasing empirical support include the following: (a) rape prevention programs that focus on the dynamics of gender socialization and on how society supports a power differential between men and women; (b) educational programs that discuss dating violence, warning signs, and how to protect oneself; (c) peer-led psychoeducational programs focusing on topics of sexual assault risk reduction, rape culture, how to help a victim, and male responsibility in preventing sexual assault; and (d) same-sex programs rather than mixed-gender groups (Hillenbrand-Gunn et al., 2010; Townsend & Campbell, 2008; Wantland, 2008; Weisz & Black, 2010).

Community

Community prevention strategies have included using better lighting in parking structures and parking lots, trimming shrubbery to improve visibility, developing statutory rape laws, and challenging social norms regarding rape. Community preventions that address the broader context in which sexual violence against females occurs are emerging but are not yet well developed (Tharp et al., 2011; Zurbriggen, 2009).

Other community prevention efforts include a federal mandate that directs every university receiving federal funds to have some kind of rape and sexual assault prevention program on campus. Additional programs include the American Bar Association's National Teen Dating Violence Prevention Initiative, which was created to help develop awareness of teen date rape and its causal factors, and the Violence Against Women Act, which was amended in 2005 by the U.S. Congress to include legal assistance for victims of dating violence (Laney, 2010; Ting, 2009).

Intervention Strategies

Interventions can take place on a variety of levels. Some are aimed at the perpetrators to reduce the number of offenses, and some are aimed at the victims of sexual assault and rape. Most would agree that early intervention in either case is more effective. For example, it has been found that interventions aimed to prevent sexual assault by male perpetrators are more effective when they begin early in the teen years, before females are at greatest risk of sexual violation and before males have developed patterns of sexual aggression. Toward this end, interventions that challenge teen attitudes, knowledge, and norms are essential in intervention efforts (Weisz & Black, 2010).

Many victims of rape or sexual assault never report the crime to authorities or seek help; the number of victims who do not report is estimated to be high. Victims do not report rape or sexual assault because of many barriers, such as guilt or embarrassment (Wolitzky-Taylor et al., 2011). Hence, many victims never receive the help they need either medically or psychologically. Interventions for teens who have been victimized by rape or date rape are important for many reasons. Research findings indicate that many victims of rape do not receive health care and subsequently suffer from a host of physical and psychological issues and can suffer from posttraumatic stress disorder and rape trauma syndrome. Psychological issues are considered to be the most important medical problem for victims of sexual assault (McCauley et al., 2010).

Survivors of rape and date rape may suffer from feelings of self-blame, anger, and powerlessness; have nightmares, issues with trust, lowered self-esteem, suicidal thoughts, self-injurious behaviors, and conduct problems; develop eating disorders; have difficulty having sex with a wanted partner; have dissociative episodes and impaired memory, derealization, depersonalization, social adjustment problems, academic problems, increased somatic complaints, and changes in sleep patterns; increase use of substances; and have constant fear for their own safety (Freeman & Temple, 2010; Smith & Kelly, 2008). This section explores possible interventions for individuals, families, schools, and communities.

Individual

Interventions at the individual level should include crisis care, psychological care, care of physical injuries, treatment of STDs, and treatment for unwanted pregnancy (Jo et al., 2011; Klem, 2009; McMahon & Schwartz, 2011). A baseline urine pregnancy test can be conducted to help the adolescent determine whether pregnancy occurred as a result of the rape or prior to it, and counseling can help a teen decide if she wants to keep her baby (Collings, 2011; Jo et al., 2011).

Psychological therapy, both individual and group, is imperative to help someone overcome sexual trauma. A literature review suggests the following modalities are particularly effective in working with adolescents who have been raped or are victims of sexual predators: cognitive processing therapy, cognitive behavior therapy, art therapy, constructivist bibliotherapy, prolonged exposure therapy, relaxation therapy, eye-movement desensitization and reprocessing, or Foa's treatment for trauma victims. In addition, a treatment focus on anxiety and stress management, development of coping skills, thought stopping, positive imagery, psychoeducation, sexual education, and normalizing has been found effective (Danielson et al., 2012; S. E. Mason & Clemans, 2008; McMahon & Schwartz, 2011; Smith & Kelly, 2008; Vural, Hafızoğlu, Türkmen, Eren, & Büyükuysal, 2012).

The following are other interventions at the individual level: (a) conducting health provider screenings that ask women about intimate partner violence; (b) providing a safe environment for women and adolescents to talk about victimization; and (c) offering in high schools and colleges crisis counseling services that include psychoeducation about rape and trauma to normalize reactions, assist the rape survivor in addressing guilt feelings, and help the survivor to vocalize feelings about the rape (McCauley et al., 2010; Tharp et al., 2011).

Family

For children and adolescents suffering from trauma reactions from sexual assault and rape, behaviorally based interventions are thought to be the best treatment option, as well as including parents and families in the treatment (Smith & Kelly, 2008). Danielson and colleagues (2012) asserted that parent training is essential for the treatment of these children. Parents have a lot of control over their children's environment, behaviors, and feelings of security. When parents and other family members are engaged in treatment, the children and adolescents can get consistent care between home and therapeutic environments. For the same reason, it can also be helpful to include the child or adolescent's teacher(s) in this healing process and ensure that parents or teachers are not reinforcing trauma-related behavior problems. Parents and teachers can be taught to reinforce desirable behaviors with positive social reinforcement and token economies (Danielson et al., 2012; Tharp et al., 2011).

S. E. Mason and Clemans (2008) conducted a focus group with survivors of sexual abuse to learn what helped them survive their sexual abuse. Survivors had this to say: (a) Believe and support them when they say they have been abused, (b) allow them to talk about what happened to them, (c) allow them to talk about their feelings regarding what happened to them, and (d) engage them in group counseling. Many survivors stated group therapy was helpful, presumably because of the universal factors associated with groups (e.g., universality, instillation of hope, imparting information, altruism) and normalizing the trauma reaction.

School

School interventions can be effective under the following conditions: (a) A complete comprehensive assessment has been conducted to ascertain the needs of the adolescent; (b) it has been determined that school-based support is the appropriate, least restrictive level of intervention; (c) the adolescent's parents have given informed consent of all treatment options; (d) the child is experiencing adequate adjustment and academic success with intervention; and (e) consultation, supervision, and referral are readily used by the school psychologist (Ting, 2009; Townsend & Campbell, 2008). As noted above, it can be effective to have teachers be a part of the treatment team in terms of providing correct reinforcement of desired behaviors; assisting the student with symptom management; providing a safe environment; and helping with the coordination of communication among school personnel, family members, and the treatment team (Townsend & Campbell, 2008; Weisz & Black, 2010). Research suggests that trauma-focused, cognitive behavior therapy is the most efficacious and has the most empirical support when working with traumatized adolescents (Walker, Reese, Hughes, & Troskie, 2010).

Community

Interventions for community efforts include (a) providing rape kits for hospitals and emergency rooms; (b) developing specialized medical/examiner programs that train nurses and doctors in the treatment and care of rape victims; (c) passing a federal law that designates funds to have more rape kits analyzed; (d) developing better testing methods to test for the presence of date rape drugs, such as flunitrazepam (Rohypnol), gamma-hydroxybutyrate (GHB), and ketamine; (e) increasing the statute of limitations for prosecuting rapes; (f) developing new colposcopic procedures that allow for better examination of genital trauma; and (g) providing advocates who go to the hospital and advocate and provide support for the victim

(Adamowicz & Kała, 2010; Maier, 2012; Newton & Vandeven, 2010; Patterson & Campbell, 2012).

However, community efforts in these areas are seriously lacking in effectiveness and comprehensiveness. For those who are trained, the rape kits themselves are woefully inadequate. Other problems with community interventions include (a) too many items in the rape kit for professionals to navigate, and many steps of evidence collection often get overlooked, which hinders prosecution efforts; (b) not enough analysts to look at evidence, and rape kits are being stacked up all over the country waiting to be examined; (c) the cost of the rape kit is often a victim's burden to pay; (d) date rape tests are often ineffective or inconclusive; and (e) many health professionals simply do not have time or do not want to provide assessments for rape and assault (Maier, 2012; Patterson & Campbell, 2012; Townsend & Campbell, 2008).

Adaptations for Diversity

As with any issue related to human development, health, or risk factors, there can be vast differences between people who hold different cultural identities or statuses. Throughout this chapter we have tried to highlight some of the differences we have found related to specific risk factors for specific groups as well as note differences in epidemiology, incidence rates, preventions, interventions, and treatments related to teen pregnancy, STDs, and rape and date rape.

Cultural and diversity variables are important to consider for any effort related to prevention, intervention, or treatment. Some of the most profound differences for the issues addressed in this chapter relate mainly to issues of ethnicity, socioeconomic status, family configuration and cohesiveness, and age. However, it is important to note that although we've tried to be as inclusive as possible when discussing the issues presented within this chapter, there are physical constraints placed upon what can be included. Therefore, it behooves the counselor to do a thorough analysis of variables of diversity and how those may affect the client, the issue, and any interventions, preventions, or treatment options used to address teen pregnancy, STDs, and rape and date rape.

Summary

This chapter has focused on prevention, intervention, and current research around important topics of teen sexuality that put teens at risk for negative outcomes such as teen pregnancy, STDs, rape, and date rape. The field of counseling and psychotherapy is advancing in its knowledge of risk and protective factors pertaining to youth in many developmental areas, including teen sexuality.

However, the literature review for this chapter also indicated that more work needs to be done in the areas of program comparability outcomes and program evaluation research; in addition, there is a need for a systematic evaluation of one program over time and for the use of theory in prevention programming. One important trend in the literature is the increased recognition of ethnic and diversity issues in working with teen populations at risk. Different risk factors exist for different diverse populations, and in turn different intervention and prevention strategies are needed to address specific variables and trends within these populations.

The limitation of this chapter is its restricted availability to pursue each current prevention, intervention, and risk factor analysis study because of space constraints. Therefore, we have attempted to give an overview of some of the most current or empirically validated interventions and preventions while trying to personalize the material through the case study of Julia. On the basis of our extensive review of the literature, we also have attempted to highlight areas that need further attention.

There are many young people like Julia in our communities who are at risk for negative outcomes. The case study of Julia just puts one face on the epidemic that is facing our youth today in terms of consequences for their sexual choices (e.g., STDs, pregnancy). We recommend that parents, educators, and counselors working with youth use this chapter as a starting place, not an ending point, in finding more effective ways to help the youth of this nation. The following websites provide additional information relating to the chapter topics.

Useful Websites

American Sexual Health Association
http://www.ashastd.org/std-sti/std-statistics.html
Center for Prevention of Abuse
http://www.centerforpreventionofabuse.org/
Centers for Disease Control and Prevention: Sexually Transmitted Diseases
http://www.cdc.gov/std/
Centers for Disease Control and Prevention: Teen Pregnancy
http://www.cdc.gov/teenpregnancy/
Date Rape
http://www.union.k12.ia.us/ukhs/Students/Sociology/2006/Date%20Rape/date_rape.htm
MedlinePlus Teenage Pregnancy
http://www.nlm.nih.gov/medlineplus/teenagepregnancy.html
National Center for Victims of Crime
http://www.victimsofcrime.org/news-center/reporter-resources/child-sexual-abuse/child-sexual-abuse-statistics
Planned Parenthood: Sexually Transmitted Diseases
http://www.plannedparenthood.org/health-topics/stds-hiv-safer-sex-101.htm

References

Adamowicz, P., & Kała, M. (2010). Simultaneous screening for and determination of 128 date-rape drugs in urine by gas chromatography–electron ionization–mass spectrometry. *Forensic Science International, 198,* 39–45. doi:10.1016/j.forsciint.2010.02.012

Akers, A. Y., Gold, M. A., Coyne Beasley, T., & Corbie Smith, G. (2012). A qualitative study of rural Black adolescents' perspectives on primary STD prevention strategies. *Perspectives on Sexual and Reproductive Health, 44,* 92–99.

American Sexual Health Association. (2011). *STD/STI statistics.* Retrieved from http://www.ashastd.org/std-sti/std-statistics.html

Basch, C. E. (2011). Teen pregnancy and the achievement gap among urban minority youth. *Journal of School Health, 81,* 614–618. doi:10.1111/j.1746-1561.2011.00635.x

Bradley, A. R., Yeater, E. A., & O'Donohue, W. (2009). An evaluation of a mixed-gender sexual assault prevention program. *Journal of Primary Prevention, 30,* 697–715.

Braun, R. A., & Provost, J. M. (2010). Bridging the gap: Using school-based health services to improve chlamydia screening among young women. *Infection, 20,* 22.

Burnett, A., Mattern, J. L., Herakova, L. L., Kahl, D. R., Tobola, C., & Bornsen, S. E. (2009). Communicating/muting date rape: A co-cultural theoretical analysis of communication factors related to rape culture on a college campus. *Journal of Applied Communication Research, 37,* 465–485. doi:10.1080/00909880903233150

Centers for Disease Control and Prevention. (2006, April). Sexually transmitted diseases: Treatment guidelines, 2006. *Morbidity and Mortality Weekly Report, 55*(No. RR-11), 1–100.

Centers for Disease Control and Prevention. (2009). *Community promise.* Retrieved from http://www.cdc.gov/hiv/topics/prev_prog/rep/packages/promise.htm

Centers for Disease Control and Prevention. (2010, December 17). Sexually transmitted disease guidelines. *Morbidity and Mortality Weekly Report, 59*(No. RR-12), 2. Retrieved from http://www.cdc.gov/mmwr/pdf/rr/rr5912.pdf

Centers for Disease Control and Prevention. (2012a). *Community PROMISE: Peers reaching out and modeling intervention strategies for community-level HIV/AIDS risk reduction.* Retrieved from http://www.cdc.gov/hiv/topics/prev_prog/rep/packages/promise.htm

Centers for Disease Control and Prevention, Division of Reproductive Health, National Center for Chronic Disease Prevention and Health Promotion. (2012b). *Parent and guardian resources.* Atlanta, GA: Author.

Chariyeva, Z., Golin, C. E., Earp, J. A., & Suchindran, C. (2012). Does motivational interviewing counseling time influence HIV-positive persons' self-efficacy to practice safer sex? *Patient Education and Counseling, 87,* 101–107.

Chiaradonna, C. (2008). The chlamydia cascade: Enhanced STD prevention strategies for adolescents. *Journal of Pediatric and Adolescent Gynecology, 21,* 233–241.

Cohen, D. A., & Scribner, R. (2000). An STD/HIV prevention/intervention framework. *AIDS Patient Care and STDs, 14,* 37–45.

Collings, S. J. (2011). Professional services for child rape survivors: A child-centered perspective on helpful and harmful experiences. *Journal of Child & Adolescent Mental Health, 23,* 5–15. doi:10.2989/17280583.2011.594244

Coyle, K., Basen Engquist, K., Kirby, D., Parcel, G., Banspach, S., Harrist, R., . . . Weil, M. (2009). Short term impact of safer choices: A multicomponent, school based HIV, other STD, and pregnancy prevention program. *Journal of School Health, 69,* 181–188.

Danielson, C., McCart, M. R., Walsh, K., de Arellano, M. A., White, D., & Resnick, H. S. (2012). Reducing substance use risk and mental health problems among sexually assaulted adolescents: A pilot randomized controlled trial. *Journal of Family Psychology, 26,* 628–635. doi:10.1037/a0028862

Dariotis, J. K., Sifakis, F., Pleck, J. H., Astone, N. M., & Sonenstein, F. L. (2011). Racial and ethnic disparities in sexual risk behaviors and STDs during young men's transition to adulthood. *Perspectives on Sexual and Reproductive Health, 43,* 51–59.

Duffy, J., Prince, M., Johnson, E., Alton, F., Flynn, S., Faye, A., . . . Hinzey, A. (2012). Enhancing teen pregnancy prevention in local communities: Capacity building using the interactive systems framework. *American Journal of Community Psychology, 50,* 370–385. doi:10.1007/s10464-012-9531-9

Elwood, L. S., Smith, D. W., Resnick, H. S., Gudmundsdottir, B., Amstadter, A. B., Hanson, R. F., . . . Kilpatrick, D. G. (2011). Predictors of rape: Findings from the National Survey of Adolescents. *Journal of Traumatic Stress, 24,* 166–173. doi:10.1002/jts.20624

Erik Erikson's eight stages of psychosocial development. (2006). Retrieved from http://web.cortland.edu/andersmd/ERIK/sum.HTML

Fageeh, W. M. (2008). Awareness of sexually transmitted diseases among adolescents in Saudi Arabia. *Journal of King Abdulaziz University of Medical Sciences, 15,* 77–90.

Falk, G., Brynhildsen, J., & Ivarsson, A. (2009). Contraceptive counselling to teenagers at abortion visits: A qualitative content analysis. *European Journal of Contraception & Reproductive Health Care, 14,* 357–364. doi:10.3109/13625180903171815

Farr, S. L., Kraft, J. M., Warner, L., Anderson, J. E., & Jamieson, D. J. (2009). The integration of STD/HIV services with contraceptive services for young women in the United States. *American Journal of Obstetrics and Gynecology, 201,* 142.e1–8.

Florida Department of Health. (2012). *Are you in the dark about STDs?* Retrieved from http://www.doh.state.fl.us/disease_ctrl/std/

Florsheim, P. (2012). Young parenthood program: Supporting positive paternal engagement through coparenting counseling. *American Journal of Public Health, 102,* 1886–1892.

Foshee, V. A., Benefield, T., Suchindran, C., Ennett, S. T., Bauman, K. E., Karriker-Jaffe, K. J., . . . Mathias, J. (2009). The development of four types of adolescent dating abuse and selected demographic correlates. *Journal of Research on Adolescence, 19,* 380–400. doi:10.1111/j.1532-7795.2009.00593.x

Freeman, D., & Temple, J. (2010). Social factors associated with history of sexual assault among ethnically diverse adolescents. *Journal of Family Violence, 25,* 349–356. doi:10.1007/s10896-009-9296-6

Golin, C. E., Earp, J. A., Grodensky, C. A., Patel, S. N., Suchindran, C., Parikh, M., . . . Groves, J. (2012). Longitudinal effects of SafeTalk: A motivational interviewing-based program to improve safer sex practices among people living with HIV/AIDS. *AIDS and Behavior, 16,* 1182–1191.

Gruber, K. J. (2012). A comparative assessment of early adult life status of graduates of the North Carolina adolescent parenting program. *Journal of Child and Adolescent Psychiatric Nursing, 25,* 75–83. doi:10.1111/j.1744-6171.2012.00324.x

Hall, G. S. (1904). *Adolescence.* New York, NY: Appleton.

Hansen, S., O'Byrne, R., & Rapley, M. (2010). Young heterosexual men's use of the miscommunication model in explaining acquaintance rape. *Sexuality Research & Social Policy: A Journal of the NSRC, 7,* 45–49. doi:10.1007/s13178-010-0003-4

Hehir, B. (2008, March 12). Legislation will not solve societal problems. *Nursing Standard, 22,* 28.

Hensel, D. J., Fortenberry, J. D., & Orr, D. P. (2010). Factors associated with event level anal sex and condom use during anal sex among adolescent women. *Journal of Adolescent Health, 46,* 232–237.

Hillenbrand-Gunn, T. L., Heppner, M. J., Mauch, P. A., & Park, H. (2010). Men as allies: The efficacy of a high school rape prevention intervention. *Journal of Counseling and Development, 88,* 43–51.

Hosenfeld, C. B., Workowski, K. A., Berman, S., Zaidi, A., Dyson, J., Mosure, D., . . . Bauer, H. M. (2009). Repeat infection with chlamydia and gonorrhea among females: A systematic review of the literature. *Sexually Transmitted Diseases, 36,* 478–489.

Houlihan, A. E., Gibbons, F. X., Gerrard, M., Yeh, H. C., Reimer, R. A., & Murry, V. M. (2008). Sex and the self: The impact of early sexual onset on the self-concept and subsequent risky behavior of African American adolescents. *The Journal of Early Adolescence, 28,* 70–91.

Jemmott, J. B., III, Jemmott, L. S., Fong, G. T., & Morales, K. H. (2010). Effectiveness of an HIV/STD risk-reduction intervention for adolescents when implemented by community-based organizations: A cluster-randomized controlled trial. *American Journal of Public Health, 100,* 720–726.

Jo, S., Shin, J., Song, K., Kim, J., Hwang, K., & Bhally, H. (2011). Prevalence and correlated factors of sexually transmitted diseases—chlamydia, neisseria, cytomegalovirus—in female rape victims. *Journal of Sexual Medicine, 8,* 2317–2326. doi:10.1111/j.1743-6109.2010.02069.x

Johnson, B. T., Scott-Sheldon, L. A., Huedo-Medina, T. B., & Carey, M. P. (2011). Interventions to reduce sexual risk for human immunodeficiency virus in adolescents: A meta-analysis of trials, 1985–2008. *Archives of Pediatrics & Adolescent Medicine, 165,* 77.

Kim, J. (2012). Taking rape seriously: Rape as slavery. *Harvard Journal of Law & Gender, 35,* 263–310.

Kirby, D. (2011). *Sex education: Access and impact on sexual behavior of young people.* Retrieved from http://www.un.org/esa/population/meetings/egmadolescents/p07_kirby.pdf

Klem, J. C. (2009). Dating violence: Counseling adolescent females from an existential perspective. *Journal of Humanistic Counseling, Education and Development, 48,* 48–64.

Kramer, K. L., & Lancaster, J. B. (2010). Teen motherhood in cross-cultural perspective. *Annals of Human Biology, 37,* 613–628. doi:10.3109/03014460903563434

Lachance, C. R., Burrus, B. B., & Scott, A. (2012). Building an evidence base to inform interventions for pregnant and parenting adolescents: A call for rigorous evaluation. *American Journal of Public Health, 102,* 1826–1832. doi:10.2105/AJPH.2012.300871

Laney, G. P. (2010). Violence Against Women Act: History and federal funding. *Journal of Current Issues in Crime, Law, & Law Enforcement, 3,* 305–321.

Lescano, C. M., Brown, L. K., Raffaelli, M., & Lima, L. A. (2009). Cultural factors and family-based HIV prevention intervention for Latino youth. *Journal of Pediatric Psychology, 34,* 1041–1052.

Maier, S. L. (2012). Sexual assault nurse examiners' perceptions of their relationship with doctors, rape victim advocates, police, and prosecutors. *Journal of Interpersonal Violence, 27,* 1314–1340. doi:10.1177/0886260511425242

Markham, C. M., Shegog, R., Leonard, A. D., Bui, T. C., & Paul, M. E. (2009). + CLICK: Harnessing web-based training to reduce secondary transmission among HIV-positive youth. *AIDS Care, 21,* 622–631.

Mason, D., Palmer, C., Duba, D., & Jill, D. (2009). Using reality therapy in schools: Its potential impact on the effectiveness of the ASCA national model. *International Journal of Reality Therapy, 29,* 5.

Mason, S. E., & Clemans, S. E. (2008). Participatory research for rape survivor groups. *Affilia: Journal of Women & Social Work, 23,* 66–76.

McCauley, J. L., Ruggiero, K. J., Resnick, H. S., & Kilpatrick, D. G. (2010). Incapacitated, forcible, and drug/alcohol-facilitated rape in relation to binge drinking, marijuana use, and illicit drug use: A national survey. *Journal of Traumatic Stress, 23,* 132–140.

McElroy, L. (2010). Sex on the brain: Adolescent psychosocial science and sanctions for risky sex. *New York University Review of Law & Social Change, 34,* 708–759.

McMahon, S., & Schwartz, R. (2011). A review of rape in the social work literature: A call to action. *Affilia: Journal of Women & Social Work, 26,* 250–263. doi:10.1177/0886109911417683

Medoff, M. (2010). The impact of state abortion policies on teen pregnancy rates. *Social Indicators Research, 97,* 177–189. doi:10.1007/s11205-009-9495-9

Mullany, B., Barlow, A., Neault, N., Billy, T., Jones, T., Tortice, I., . . . Walkup, J. (2012). The Family Spirit Trial for American Indian teen mothers and their children: CBPR rationale, design, methods and baseline characteristics. *Prevention Science, 13,* 504–518. doi:10.1007/s11121-012-0277-2

Murphy-Erby, Y., Stauss, K., Boyas, J., & Bivens, V. (2011). Voices of Latino parents and teens: Tailored strategies for parent–child communication related to sex. *Journal of Children & Poverty, 17,* 125–138. doi:10.1080/10796126.2011.531250

National Campaign to Prevent Teen and Unplanned Pregnancy. (2010). *Teen pregnancy and child welfare.* Retrieved from http://www.thenationalcampaign.org/why-it-matters/pdf/child_welfare.pdf

National Campaign to Prevent Teen and Unplanned Pregnancy. (2011). *Fast facts: How is the one in three statistics calculated.* Retrieved from http://www.thenationalcampaign.org/resources/pdf/FastFacts_3in10.pdf

National Campaign to Prevent Teen and Unplanned Pregnancy. (2012). *Teen birth rates: How does the United States compare?* Retrieved from http://www.thenationalcampaign.org/resources/pdf/FastFacts_InternationalComparisons.pdf

National Center for Victims of Crime. (2012). *Child sexual abuse statistics.* Retrieved from http://www.victimsofcrime.org/news-center/reporter-resources/child-sexual-abuse/child-sexual-abuse-statistics

Newton, A., & Vandeven, A. (2010). The role of the medical provider in the evaluation of sexually abused children and adolescents. *Journal of Child Sexual Abuse, 19*, 669–686. doi:10.1080/10538712.2010.523448

Nicodemus, P. A. (2011). Predictors of perpetrating physical date violence among adolescents. *North American Journal of Psychology, 13*, 123–132.

Ott, M. A., Harezlak, J., Ofner, S., & Fortenberry, J. D. (2012). Timing of incident STI relative to sex partner change in young women. *Sexually Transmitted Diseases, 39*, 747–749.

Ott, M. A., Rouse, M., Resseguie, J., Smith, H., & Woodcox, S. (2011). Community-level successes and challenges to implementing adolescent sex education programs. *Maternal & Child Health Journal, 15*, 169–177. doi:10.1007/s10995-010-0574-y

Patel, P. H., & Sen, B. (2012). Teen motherhood and long-term health consequences. *Maternal and Child Health Journal, 16*, 1063–1071. doi:10.1007/s10995-011-0829-2

Patterson, D., & Campbell, R. (2012). The problem of untested sexual assault kits: Why are some kits never submitted to a crime laboratory? *Journal of Interpersonal Violence, 27*, 2259–2275. doi:10.1177/0886260511432155

Pazol, K. K., Warner, L. L., Gavin, L. L., Callaghan, W. M., Spitz, A. M., Anderson, J. E., . . . Kann, L. L. (2011). Vital signs: Teen pregnancy—United States, 1991–2009. *Morbidity & Mortality Weekly Report, 60*, 414–420.

Pequegnat, W., & Bray, J. H. (2012). HIV/STD prevention interventions for couples and families: A review and introduction to the special issue. *Couple and Family Psychology: Research and Practice, 1*, 79.

Planned Parenthood. (2009). *Hey, what do I say? A parent to parent guide on how to talk to children about sexuality*. Retrieved from http://www.plannedparenthood.org/nyc/files/NYC/ParentGuide.pdf

Reisner, S. L., Mimiaga, M. J., Skeer, M., Perkovich, B., Johnson, C. V., & Safren, S. A. (2009). A review of HIV antiretroviral adherence and intervention studies among HIV-infected youth. *Topics in HIV Medicine: A Publication of the International AIDS Society, USA, 17*, 14.

Rosengard, C., Phillips, M. G., Adler, N. E., & Ellen, J. M. (2004). Adolescent pregnancy intentions and pregnancy outcomes: A longitudinal examination. *Journal of Adolescent Health, 35*, 453–461.

Rosengard, C., Phillips, M. G., Adler, N. E., & Ellen, J. M. (2005). Psychosocial correlates of adolescent males' pregnancy intention. *Pediatrics, 116*, 414–419.

Secura, G. M., Desir, F. A., Mullersman, J. L., Madden, T., Allsworth, J. E., & Peipert, J. F. (2012). Predictors of male partner treatment for sexually transmitted infection. *Sexually Transmitted Diseases, 39*, 769–775.

Sexually transmitted disease. (2013). *Johns Hopkins medicine*. Retrieved from http://www.hopkinsmedicine.org/healthlibrary/conditions/mens_health/sexually_transmitted_diseases_85,P00651/

Shuger, L. (2012). Teen pregnancy and high school dropout. *National Campaign to Prevent Teen and Unplanned Pregnancy*. Retrieved from http://www.thenationalcampaign.org/resources/pdf/teen-preg-hs-dropout.pdf

Sieving, R. E., Resnick, M. D., Garwick, A. W., Bearinger, L. H., Beckman, K. J., Oliphant, J. A., . . . Rush, K. R. (2011). A clinic-based, youth development approach to teen pregnancy prevention. *American Journal of Health Behavior, 35*, 346–358.

Slater, H. M., Mitschke, D. B., & Douthit, P. (2011). Understanding qualities of positive relationship dynamics between adolescent parents and their school-based counselors. *Journal of Family Social Work, 14*, 354–368. doi:10.1080/10522158.2011.584301

Smith, A. P., & Kelly, A. B. (2008). An exploratory study of group therapy for sexually abused adolescents and non-offending guardians. *Journal of Child Sexual Abuse, 17*, 101–116.

Stanger-Hall, K. F., & Hall, D. W. (2011). Abstinence-only education and teen pregnancy rates: Why we need comprehensive sex education in the U.S. *Plus ONE, 6,* 1–11. doi:10.1371/journal.pone.0024658

Tebb, K. P., Wibbelsman, C., Neuhaus, J. M., & Shafer, M. A. (2009). Screening for asymptomatic chlamydia infections among sexually active adolescent girls during pediatric urgent care. *Archives of Pediatrics & Adolescent Medicine, 163,* 559.

Tharp, A., Burton, T., Freire, K., Hall, D. M., Harrier, S., Latzman, N. E., . . . Vagi, K. J. (2011). Dating matters: Strategies to promote healthy teen relationships. *Journal of Women's Health, 20,* 1761–1765. doi:10.1089/jwh.2011.3177

Ting, S. (2009). Meta-analysis on dating violence prevention among middle and high schools. *Journal of School Violence, 8,* 328–337. doi:10.1080/15388220903130197

Townsend, S. M., & Campbell, R. (2008). Identifying common practices in community-based rape prevention programs. *Journal of Prevention & Intervention in the Community, 36,* 121–135. doi:10.1080/10852350802022399

Trenholm, C., Devaney, B., Fortson, K., Clark, M., Bridgespan, L., & Wheeler, J. (2008). Impacts of abstinence education on teen sexual activity, risk of pregnancy, and risk of sexually transmitted diseases. *Journal of Policy Analysis and Management, 27,* 255–276.

Vural, P., Hafızoğlu, S., Türkmen, N., Eren, B., & Büyükuysal, Ç. (2012). Perceived parental acceptance/rejection and psychopathology in a group of sexually abused children/adolescents. *Medicinski Glasnik, 9,* 363–369.

Walker, D. F., Reese, J. B., Hughes, J. P., & Troskie, M. J. (2010). Addressing religious and spiritual issues in trauma-focused cognitive behavior therapy for children and adolescents. *Professional Psychology: Research & Practice, 41,* 174–180. doi:10.1037/a0017782

Wantland, R. A. (2008). Our brotherhood and your sister: Building anti-rape community in the fraternity. *Journal of Prevention & Intervention in the Community, 36,* 57–73. doi:10.10803/1085350802022316

Weiss, J. A. (2010). Preventing teen pregnancy by avoiding risk exposure. *American Journal of Health Studies, 25,* 202–210.

Weisz, A. N., & Black, B. M. (2010). Peer education and leadership in dating violence prevention: Strengths and challenges. *Journal of Aggression, Maltreatment, & Trauma, 19,* 641–660. doi:10.1080/10926771.2010.502089

Wildsmith, E., Schelar, E., Peterson, K., & Manlove, J. (2010). *Sexually transmitted diseases among young adults: Prevalence, perceived risk, and risk-taking behaviors. Child trends.* Retrieved from http://www.childtrends.org/Files/Child_Trends-2010_05_01_RB_STD.pdf

Wilmoth, W. S. (2008). Using the tools of crisis intervention and empowerment counseling in the reference interview. *Georgia Library Quarterly, 45,* 9–13.

Wohl, A. R., Garland, W. H., Wu, J., Au, C. W., Boger, A., Dierst-Davies, R., . . . Jordan, W. (2011). A youth-focused case management intervention to engage and retain young gay men of color in HIV care. *AIDS Care, 23,* 988–997.

Wolitzky-Taylor, K. B., Resnick, H. S., McCauley, J. L., Amstadter, A. B., Kilpatrick, D. G., & Ruggiero, K. J. (2011). Is reporting of rape on the rise? A comparison of women with reported versus unreported rape experiences in the national women's study-replication. *Journal of Interpersonal Violence, 26,* 807–832. doi:10.1177/0886260510365869

Workowski, K. A., & Berman, S. M. (2011). Centers for Disease Control and Prevention sexually transmitted disease treatment guidelines. *Clinical Infectious Diseases, 53,* S59–S63.

Zinzow, H. G. (2011). Self-rated health in relation to rape and mental health disorders in a national sample of college women. *Journal of American College Health, 59,* 588–594.

Zurbriggen, E. L. (2009). Understanding and preventing adolescent dating violence: The importance of developmental, sociocultural, and gendered perspectives. *Psychology of Women Quarterly, 33,* 30–33.

Chapter 12

"I Am Somebody": Gang Membership

Lisa Langfuss Aasheim

Youth gangs have been present in history for centuries. Gangs are organizations composed of peers who adopt a common name; share common representational signals of membership, such as clothing color or hand signals to indicate affiliation (Densley, 2012); and engage in criminal activity (National Gang Intelligence Center, 2011).

To fully understand the phenomenon of youth gang membership, it is necessary to examine the history of youth gangs, the appeal of such organizations, the positive and negative consequences of involvement, and the relationship between cultural identification and gang involvement. To prevent gang membership, one needs to become familiar with prevention programs, familial and social system supports as related to prevention, and community involvement in prevention efforts. The solutions to the gang problems in the United States are neither quick nor simple (Wyrick & Howell, 2004), so a thorough understanding of both prevention and intervention strategies is necessary to reduce the individual and societal effects of gang involvement.

Gangs have an enormous impact on society in all parts of the United States. No geographical area, racial or cultural group, or school district is immune to problems that may be traced to some aspect of gang activity. Because the gang problem has become so extensive, approaches to prevent increased gang activity and intervene with existing gang activity need to be undertaken simultaneously. Approaches to prevent gang involvement involve both the gang members and their larger systems, including (but not limited to) families, schools, communities, and law enforcement agencies. A plethora of gang reduction and prevention programs have been introduced in the past decade; however, these programs have been found to be largely ineffective or only mildly effective in reducing and preventing gang membership. Wilson and Chermak (2011) discussed the gap between "promising" strategies and strategies that actually yield positive results and noted that there is still tremendous room for improvement and more effective action. The programs that appear mildly successful may not be as successful as they appear because of the common regression effect that occurs when a program is implemented at a peak activity time (when the gang is more active in both recruitment and violent incidents). The apparent success of an intervention program may simply be the natural decrease in activity levels that occurs with all gangs, because activity and violence levels tend to be cyclical in nature (Klein, 2011). Undoubtedly, much work remains in terms of understanding, preventing, and mediating the impact of gang membership.

This chapter first examines the historical significance and development of gangs and gang activities. Next, the chapter looks at present-day gang involvement, including characteristics of gangs, male and female gang members, and ethnic gangs. A case study profiles the life of Christopher, a young man involved in a gang. The chapter considers approaches to prevention and intervention strategies at individual, family, school, and community levels and concludes with a discussion of adaptations for diversity.

Problem Definition

Youth gangs have been present in the United States for centuries. Their membership levels and violent activities correspond to peak levels of immigration and population shifts, most notably in the early 1800s, 1920s, 1960s, and late 1990s (Johnson & Mulhausen, 2005). During the 1920s cities were becoming industrialized and grew rapidly. Cities such as New York, Boston, and Chicago became urbanized with ever-increasing populations. Large numbers of immigrants from varying cultures flocked to these cities seeking a better life for themselves and their children. They were not accepted into the mainstream culture, which was White, Anglo-Saxon, and Protestant. The immigrant parents typically worked at low-paying jobs that barely allowed them to earn a living while trying to assimilate into the culture; the youth banded together for socialization and protection as they experienced adolescence in an unfamiliar country that was frustrating and alien to them. Dozens of gangs made up of members from similar racial, ethnic, and cultural backgrounds emerged. These gangs provided outlets for marginalized youth to socialize, release aggression, and control territory (Johnson & Mulhausen, 2005). The gangs became destructive and powerful presences in their communities and provided youth with a sense of belonging, importance, and social relevance.

Thrasher (1926), an early investigator of gang activity during the late 1920s, viewed youth gangs as means to socialize young delinquents to organized crime and to turn the youth into "gangsters" as they became adults. The large urban areas were the birthplace of many of the notorious Mafia gangs, and gang wars ensued over territorialism, bookmaking, extortion, gunrunning, and liquor sales. Because southern cities experienced less rapid growth and immigrants did not migrate to the South in as large numbers, economic growth as well as gang growth moved in that region at a slower pace.

During the 1930s and 1940s a change occurred within the overall racial and cultural makeup of gangs. African American, Puerto Rican, and Mexican American gangs began to outnumber the previously predominant White gangs. Areas such as Los Angeles, California, saw a significant increase in the number of African American gang members as African Americans attempted to buy houses outside of the designated Black settlement area (Alonso, 2004). Gang wars escalated with the use of handguns, knives, chains, and other self-made implements. Drug use as well as drug trafficking among gang members increased. Gang conflicts continued through the 1950s and saw a slight decrease during the 1960s, perhaps because of the Vietnam War.

Estimates of gang activity today vary. The Federal Bureau of Investigation's (FBI's) National Gang Intelligence Center released a 2011 report indicating that there are over 1.4 million active gang members in more than 33,000 gangs (National Gang Intelligence Center, 2011). In 2009, there were approximately 1 million gang members, so the figure appears to be quickly on the rise. This increase in membership is attributed to aggressive recruitment strategies and drug trafficking organizations as well as more accessible communication because of social media and more accessible communication tools and techniques.

In recent years, technological and transportation advances have made it easier for gangs to expand their criminal networks while decreasing their visibility. That is, gang members no longer need to flash obvious signs or wear obvious clothing to signify membership as their online presence helps members make their affiliation more clear to other gang members while still staying out of the watchful eye of law enforcement (National Gang Intelligence Center, 2011). Some gangs have joined together to create hybrid gangs, or combinations of multiple gangs, which may confuse law enforcement, and additional gangs have figured out techniques to exist solely online and maintain almost no street presence. Instead, their activities are conducted via cyberspace, and the related crimes are typically also technology-based, such as identity theft and other criminal schemes.

Causal Factors

Risk Factors for Gang Involvement

Researchers remain interested in the five factors known to affect risk of gang involvement: individual, familial, school, peer, and societal/community factors (Sharkey, Shekhtmeyster, Chavez-Lopez, Norris, & Sass, 2011). Some youth are attracted to gangs because they have childhood friends who are members, or because the gang offers a social grouping that serves as a substitute when familial or social structure is absent (Krohn, Ward, Thornberry, Lizotte, & Chu, 2011). Others find gang membership attractive when making a decision between work and education and neither option seems viable. Because working-class youth often are not adequately trained to meet the requirements of middle-class society, gangs are the means of reacting to and making adjustments in their lives to find their own social status and acceptance. Furthermore, gangs have an organizational structure that spells out rules concerning expected levels of aggressive behavior as well as the status and prestige earned as a result of adhering to these rules (Bernard, 1990). Matza (1964) disagreed with the subculture theory, instead viewing adolescents as being suspended between childhood and adulthood and seeing this time as a period of risk for males who are discovering their identities and trying to become aligned with a peer group. Because these youth fear losing status by not being accepted, they are easy targets for gangs that specify a rigid structure of behavior for those who want to become members. More recently, researchers have questioned whether gangs are attractive to youth who are already engaging in delinquent behavior or if the criminal behavior occurs following gang involvement (Bendixen, Endresen, & Olweus, 2006). Individual factors indicating a propensity toward gang involvement may also include low autonomic arousal, early antisocial behaviors, deviant values, and association with peers who engage in deviancy (Hill, Lui, & Hawkins, 2001).

Strain theory states that people who are experiencing poverty end up feeling despair and hopelessness about their ability to achieve the American dream, so they turn toward lucrative criminal activity such as drug sales and crime (Sharkey et al., 2011). Gangs provide the structure and organization in which to find the most economic success while allowing for instant gratification and the pride that comes with a crime well done. So, gang membership is more likely for individuals experiencing poverty, social disorganization, helplessness and hopelessness, and barriers to economic and social advancement. Morales (1992) viewed the family as a crucial factor for putting youth at risk for gang involvement and stated that those families whose structure and functioning have disintegrated and broken down through poverty, alcoholism, drug addiction, chronic illnesses, and incarcerated family members put youth at great risk. Thus, according to Morales, adolescents who are involved with overwhelming family problems seek gang membership as a way to belong and gain recognition and protection. These ideas are further delineated in research by Eitle, Gunkel, and Van Gundy (2004), who stated that differences in exposure to stressful life events are associated with adolescent crime and delinquency; thus, stressful life experiences are a likely contributor to gang involvement. Stressful family life events that may contribute to gang involvement include traumatic events (either repeated or single episodes), criminality in the family, addiction in the family, financial difficulty, family disruption, and attachment issues.

Other factors linked by researchers to gang involvement include prior history of criminal activity and delinquency (Densley, 2012), lower socioeconomic status, ethnic minority status and identity (Gray-Ray & Ray, 1990; Hagadorn, 1991), and problems related to positive parental influence (Ruble & Turner, 2000). Tsunokai (2005) described conditions of so-called multiple marginality as a predictor of gang involvement—that is, youth who are dealing with several factors that keep a youth in the minority, such as (but not limited to) low socioeconomic status, dual-culture conflict, governmental neglect, racism, and discrimination.

The psychosocial control theory, which concerns the factor of delinquency and its relation to gang involvement, has been both influential and supported by research. Internal control was emphasized by Hirschi (1969) as the mechanism for explaining

Sidebar 12.1 ■ Self-Awareness: The Need to Understand the Motivation for Gang Involvement

Counselors must be aware of the factors that make gang involvement appealing if they are to truly empathize with the plight of a gang member. Because counselors must create a warm, empathic workspace for each client, counselors must have an empathic understanding of what gang-affiliated or at-risk clients are experiencing. What are some of the most appealing features of gang membership? How do your own views, values, and privilege help or prevent you from understanding the appeal of gang life?

■ ■ ■

conformity and delinquency, with such factors as poor family relations and failure in school being indicators of increased potential for delinquency. A newer version of the theory (Gottfredson & Hirschi, 1990) presented six factors of adolescents who have high self-control that are thus factors inversely related to delinquency and, consequently, gang membership: (a) ability to defer gratification, (b) stamina to persist in a course of action, (c) ability to be cognitive and verbal, (d) ability to engage in long-term pursuits, (e) ability to perceive the value of cognitive and academic skills, and (f) possession of sensitivity and feelings of altruism toward others.

Many factors for gang involvement already described were supported in a study by Dukes and Martinez (1994) that examined the precursors and consequences associated with gang membership in the United States. These researchers found that the youth in the study who were active gang members shared similar characteristics: They came from poor backgrounds, were living away from their parents, and had low self-esteem and poor psychosocial health. In addition, they were members of ethnic minority groups and also had less resistance to peer pressure.

Gang Recruitment

Recruitment should be conceptualized as a process that occurs over time rather than a single event (Densley, 2012). Gangs typically engage in active and aggressive recruitment strategies to make themselves more attractive to prospective members (FBI, 2012). These strategies involve the use of social influence; social media; threats to property and body; and promises of protection, security, and belonging. Gangs use intimidation and violence, recruitment literature, and manifestos to bring in new members (Densley, 2011). Other times, passive methods lead to new membership. In these instances, members share a natural history with a prospective new member, such as a childhood friendship or familial link. In these cases, new recruits often ask to join the gang and are typically accepted right in.

Trust is a key factor in examining one's goodness of fit to the gang. That is, if the gang does not feel a potential member is trustworthy, the gang cannot accept that new member. To determine trustworthiness, new recruits are often initiated through a violent process in which the recruit is beaten violently (so that the gang can determine the recruit's "toughness"), or the recruit is expected to engage in a visible crime, usually violent in nature (e.g., a drive-by shooting). The gang can then determine whether the recruit has the toughness and allegiance to be trusted as a viable member of the group. Once the recruit has demonstrated the appropriate level of allegiance and trust, he or she qualifies for the benefits afforded by membership.

Gang Characteristics

Gangs, by definition, are organizations that share common characteristics—with leaders, rules, and symbols—and that engage in criminal activities (Spindler & Bouchard, 2011). Although gangs have grown more structurally sophisticated in recent years, the core characteristics common to all gangs remain stable over time. Some characteristics of significant concern are levels and types of violence; types of group activities (illegal and legal); and cultural features involving ethnicity, territory, and leadership. Spergel (1995) defined three major types of delinquent youth culture or gang activity that can be characterized by (a) racket activities, (b) violent conflict, and (c) theft. He further stated that without appropriate analysis of the particular community's gang activity, the intervention into and prevention of these activities will be extremely difficult. Furthermore, Bendixen et al. (2006)

found that gang members had a marked increase in the amount of violent activity they engaged in upon joining a gang, followed by a significant decrease in violent behavior upon leaving the gang.

One study examined the difference between the characteristics of gangs versus groups of delinquents. The researchers (Spindler & Bouchard, 2011) found that gangs had much more organization, including a group name, group leader, clear hierarchy, set meeting locations, distinctive codes or signals, rules, and initiation processes. Furthermore, gang members were more likely than delinquent individuals to deal cannabis and hard drugs, grow cannabis, and be involved in violent and property crimes. Finally, gang members were more likely to engage in cannabis and hard drug use themselves than their counterpart delinquents.

Klein, Maxon, and Miller (1995) studied Chicano and Black gangs in Los Angeles for several decades and concluded that the leadership of these gangs is of paramount importance. However, this leadership is not a position but more a collection of functions, with the gang leader's duties varying with each function, such as fighting, athletics, or girls. Skolnick (1995), in another example, concluded that there are two types of gangs: entrepreneurial and cultural. He proposed that the more a gang is involved in the drug trade, the less it becomes a cultural phenomenon and the more it becomes a business enterprise, which presents great difficulty when intervention strategies are sought to decrease gang activity.

Yablonsky (1997), after a review of the research available on gangs, reached the following conclusions about gang characteristics:

1. Gangs are fiercely involved with their territory, their hood, or barrio and will fight ferociously to protect their turf.
2. There are different levels of participation in gangs, in part attributable to age, and these can be characterized by core or marginal participants.
3. Diverse patterns of leadership exist in gangs.
4. Many gangs are totally and intensely involved in the commerce of drugs.
5. Gangs, in part, are generated by their cultural milieu in response to a society that blocks opportunity to achieve the success goals of the larger society. (p. 184)

Gang Member Characteristics

A typical gang member is usually male, is a poor student or a school dropout, is typically an ethnic minority, and is often economically disadvantaged. He is unemployed and is often unemployable because of a police record, and oftentimes he has not had adequate education or training to gain employment independent of job assistance programs. Gang members tend to develop loyalty to their gang,

---

Sidebar 12.2 ■ Self-Awareness: Redefining a Successful Outcome

Counselors oftentimes define success in counseling as meeting a specific set of treatment goals in a timely manner to the satisfaction of both the client and counselor. However, gang-involved clients may have different ideas of a successful interaction than the counselor does. How will you work with your client to determine what successful treatment is? How will you manage your feelings and beliefs when a client determines that remaining gang-affiliated is the wisest choice for him or her? Which direction will treatment go from there?

■ ■ ■

largely because the gang becomes the means to income, survival, and family and social belonging.

To characterize gang members fully, however, one must understand the six basic gang-role categories described by Yablonsky (2005). The first three categories are active gang roles:

1. *Wannabes:* These are youth from about age 9 to age 13 who aggressively seek roles and status in a gang.
2. *Gangbangers:* These youth are ages 13 to 25 and are already accepted as gang members. This group is considered the core—or soldiers—of a gang and comprises about 80% of members in the contemporary multipurpose violent gang.
3. *Older (or original/veterano) gangsters (OGs):* These youth are usually founders of the gang and have achieved permanent status in their gang. Many OGs are retired or semiretired but continue to maintain the permanent status of OG. Note that *gangster* is a term often used in place of *gang member.*

The following three categories are non-active gang roles:

4. *Gangster groupies:* These are youth who do not typically participate in gang activity but gravitate to and hang out with gang members. They typically act like gangsters and engage in the cultural aspects associated with gang lifestyles (e.g., apparel, music).
5. *Former gangsters:* These individuals were active gang members who "matured out" of gang life. However, they often maintain association with the gang, even if just in the eyes of local law enforcement, and are often accused of or charged with crimes committed by others.
6. *Residents in a G neighborhood:* These individuals are typically young men who reside in a gang-ridden neighborhood. Although they opt not to join a gang, they may be perceived as gang members by law enforcement or others and may find themselves arrested for crimes they did not commit simply by means of proximity.

The general public carries a misconception that all individuals involved with gangs participate to a similar degree. Some gang members are only involved in gang activities in a limited way, whereas others—primarily gangbangers and old gangsters—have daily involvement in gangs. The gangbangers and old gangsters not only are fully committed to their gang but also often live near each other. Generally, the gang serves all their social needs. Marginal gang members are often designated as more active participants if they are seen with other core gang members, dress in a similar manner to those gang members, and are caught in activities associated with certain gangs. Police and other authorities will label such individuals as gang members, sometimes even after the gang affiliation has terminated. For these individuals, shedding the gangster label is almost impossible because law enforcement agencies are slow to believe that a gang member at any level has disaffiliated with the gang. Core gang members are totally involved with the activities of the gang and become vehemently encouraging and supportive of violent behavior. Many gangbangers are swept into a delusionary state of being persecuted by police, other gangs, or anyone who gets in their way. These gang members believe that self-esteem, status in the world, and pleasurable activities are all tied to the gang. They may be easier to recognize because they have 24-hour participation and involvement and live out the paranoid gangster code of ethics and lifestyle. No matter what the level of involvement may be, gang members share the beliefs and values that allow them to behave in ways that will gain them prestige, acceptance, and status in the gang world. Gang members often use graffiti to advertise what gangs control certain regions. These are often elaborate and symbolize various gang codes, slogans, or affiliations.

Because of their involvement with violence and drug use as well as their challenging life histories, gang members are almost always in some way emotionally and psychologically vulnerable. Gang members are involved in criminal activities that involve hurting others directly or indirectly, and many display signs of sociopathy and post-traumatic stress. Many gang members live with heightened anxiety, exaggerated startle responses, and paranoia that others are out to hurt them. These factors contribute to a generally unstable, unpredictable presentation that typically interferes with a gang member's ability to engage with others in a calm, prosocial manner.

While acting out irrational violent behavior, core sociopathic gang members tend to show little social conscience or real concern for others. Sympathy for others is not a primary concern for gangsters. Their only concern is for their own emotional and material comfort. In short, these individuals exhibit the following characteristics: "(a) limited feeling of guilt, (b) few feelings of compassion or empathy for others, (c) behavior which is dominated by egocentrism and satisfying their own goals, and (d) manipulation of others for immediate self gratification" (Yablonsky, 1997, p. 113).

Gang members typically have low self-esteem and a sense of futility about living differently. Their violent behavior serves to allow them some means to stroke their egos and gain power and status. Violence often allows them to become enmeshed in a state of euphoria. They get their highs from the violent, brutal acts that they perpetrate to gain these feelings. Their ability to rationalize away this behavior is a function of gang involvement, and desensitizing oneself to violence is often a key to psychological survival.

Females in Gangs

Traditionally, the literature on gang activities and membership has focused on males. Females were typically defined in terms of their primary role: to provide sexual services to male gang members (Yablonsky, 1997). Male gang members have traditionally viewed females as sex objects to be treated in any way they choose for their own pleasure. These attitudes can be clearly heard in much "gangsta" rap. The attitude toward females in general is one of disdain, with gang members delineating their women as either whores or saints. The whores are only there to be used in any manner gang members choose, whereas the saints are there to mother their children and be idolized.

Many young girls are first introduced to gangs through cultural variables, including neighborhood gang exposure, familial gang involvement, and even television and pro-gang rap music. Girls often turn to gangs and gang members as a way of self-protection from violence, family problems, and mistreatment from other people in their lives (Joe & Chesney-Lind, 1995). Ironically, such gang involvement typically results in an increase of mistreatment and various forms of victimization (Miller, 1998). Girls with interest in gangs and gang members often are brought into the gang for sexual use, prostitution, or violence at the command of gang leaders (Ojeda, 2002).

In recent decades, female gang members have become more independent and liberated and have taken on roles more comparable with those of male gang members (LeBinh, 1997). Serious crime by females has steadily increased over the past two decades (Campbell, 1987, 1992; Spergel, 1992; Taylor, 1993). Research suggests that female gang members now make up to 45% of gang members in some key gangs, and female violent offenses are significantly higher than among non-gang-affiliated males (Esbensen & Carson, 2012). Fishman (1992) noted that females in gangs have become more violent and more oriented to male crime since the 1980s, and Taylor (1993) stated that "female gang members are hard core and deadly" (p. 45). Females in gangs have committed serious crimes, such as drive-by shootings, armed robberies, muggings, and automobile thefts as well as drug dealing (Covey, Menard, & Franzese, 1992; Molidor, 1996). The increased level of violence is often attributed to the availability of guns and other sophisticated weapons.

In one of the few studies of female gang members, Molidor (1996) conducted interviews to learn about criminal behavior as well as the physical, sexual, and psychological abuses the females experienced as gang members. Factors for female gang involvement were found to be similar to those of male gang members, with lack of education and severely dysfunctional family life as major factors. Many young females came from homes and neighborhoods in which alcohol and drug use and distribution were prevalent. Female initiations into gangs were also often severely painful and humiliating. However, once the females were part of a gang, they too felt they belonged to a family and acquired a sense of power.

In a comparative study of females involved in gangs and other adolescent females, Shulmire (1996) collected data focused on family demographics and family relationships, school functioning, psychosocial functioning, and level of contacts with gangs. Among the findings were that (a) mothers of gang-involved females had lower educational levels than mothers of the other females, (b) gang-involved females reported feeling mistreated at home more often than other females, (c) gang-involved females revealed problematic relationships with their fathers, and (d) the friendship patterns and social-structural considerations of gang-involved females were connected to gang membership.

Research has indicated that female gang members tend to engage in less dangerous criminal activity than male gang members, yet they are still involved in considerably more criminal activities than nongang members (Fagan, 1990). Being a female in a gang means being deemed either "off limits" (meaning safe from within-gang crime) or an easy target for criminal acts and victimization (Miller, 1998).

Female gang members are more likely to engage in risky sexual behavior and drug abuse (Kivisto, 2001). A study by Hunt, Joe-Laidler, and MacKenzie (2005) examined

Sidebar 12.3 ■ Self-Awareness: Examining the Helper's Responses to Vicarious Trauma

Vicarious trauma is experienced when a helping professional experiences some trauma response while listening to and empathizing with a client's traumatic tales. As you read the section on female gang members, you likely had some emotional, psychological, and perhaps even physical responses. What were your responses, and what would you do with each of those responses while working with the client? What useful purpose do these responses serve? How might these responses not be helpful?

■ ■ ■

the experience of motherhood for teenagers who had been involved in gangs. This study found that these female gang members who had become mothers decreased the amount of time spent with their gang friends and reduced risky behaviors such as the time they spent on the streets, alcohol and drug consumption, and overall criminality.

Gang membership for females appears to be tied to personal self-esteem; relationships to members of their families of origin; and their environment, school, and neighborhood. If they are to choose an alternative lifestyle, these female gang members will need to have their needs met in these areas. In addition, even though current research into female gang members has revealed that their factors for gang involvement are similar to many of those observed for male gang members, prevention and intervention programs for females in gangs may need to be developed separately from those for males involved in gangs.

Ethnic Gangs

Earlier in this chapter, the concept of multiple marginality was introduced to describe some factors that can make gang involvement appealing. These factors include dual-culture conflict, governmental neglect, racism, and discrimination, among others (Tsunokai, 2005). These factors are often experienced by youth who are not part of the majority culture in the United States. Because gangs are useful in fulfilling the needs that may not be met in the home or by the family, it stands to reason that youth who are disenfranchised on multiple levels would seek involvement with other similar individuals, often those of the same ethnic and cultural identification.

Gang membership tends to reflect the local ethnic population and varies geographically. For example, Asian gangs are found in the Northwest and other locations with significant Asian populations. In Los Angeles, where Hispanics make up the largest minority group, Hispanic gang membership is significant. Any organized response to gang activity must include knowledge of the culture and its influence on members of the gang. The brief descriptions of Asian, African American, Hispanic, and White supremacist gangs that follow illustrate the commonalities and ethnic influences.

Asian Gangs

Many Asian gang members arrived in the United States as minors or young adults. These adolescents and young adults, with little or no support system and often without knowledge of the majority language, are at high risk of associating with gang members of the same race who speak the same language. This bond increases their alienation from the mainstream culture. Because of experiences in their homelands, many Asians do not trust the police and rely on gangs for protection and problem solving. Unemployment and lack of marketable skills make Asian gang members look to extortion, physical assaults, residential robbery, and burglary as means to get money.

According to the National Gang Threat Assessment (FBI, 2012), Asian gangs tend to be highly organized and more likely to commit crimes against individuals who are also Asian. Palmer (1992) described three levels of Asian gangs. A *casual gang* is a group of friends who operate together in committing crime by consensus with no leadership; these members participate in the most violent of crimes. The *informal gang* is headed by a charismatic leader, but gang membership fluctuates and is transient in nature. The *formal gang* has an even more defined administrative structure with a defined chain of command.

Extortion is acknowledged to be the most prevalent form of crime committed by Chinese gang members in particular and is often their primary source of income. Through extortion, the gangs exert their control on the Chinese community. Police estimate that more than 90% of Chinese business owners regularly pay one or more gangs. When retail businesses refuse to pay, their shops may be vandalized, burglarized, or set on fire. Asian gangs were once thought of as being exclusively ethnic Chinese. However, with the migration of Southeast Asians into the United States, gang membership presently includes Cambodian and Vietnamese youth.

Tsunokai's (2005) study of Asian gang members in Southern California revealed perhaps surprising results: Unlike the typical gang member, a significant number of Asian gang members attend college and come from families who earn over $60,000 annually. However, similar to most gang members, these study participants feel that they are, in general, not treated in a just and fair manner in society and that society as a whole is against them.

African American Gangs

African American gangs often exist in neighborhoods where household heads are single females and gang affiliations regularly occur. Gangs tend to form in sets based on a locality. Gang names include surnames, such as Crips or Bloods, with the full name being, for example, the Rolling 70s Crips or the Insane Gangsta Bloods. Black gangs exist in the same territory as other ethnic gangs but typically do not fight across ethnic boundaries. Little formal administrative structure exists (unlike the Asian gangs). Gang members frequently sell crack cocaine and heroin, but it is unusual for gang members to use these drugs. Gang members are typically opposed to authority, and it is common for gang members to recruit their siblings and relatives. Dress and color are important symbols of some types of African American gangs, and gang members may adopt certain items of clothing that are worn in designated colors or in specific ways. For example, members of the Los Angeles–based African American gang the Crips wear blue clothing to display their loyalty. Their rival gang, the Bloods, wears red clothing. Although the colors differ, the articles of clothing that identify an individual as a gang member are often the same. Examples include bandannas, colored shoelaces, or a particular style of trousers. These gangs have their own brand of violence and revenge. Drive-by shootings can result from disagreement over turf, as territorialism is a prime concern (FBI, 2012).

African American youth may be at an increased risk for gang involvement because they have been found more likely than White, Hispanic, or Asian youth to initiate physical fighting and weapon-related violence and are more likely to suffer fatal and non-fatal injuries from physical assaults (Centers for Disease Control and Prevention, 2004; Wright & Fitzpatrick, 2006). In addition, increased exposure to violence correlates positively with an increased frequency of violent behavior as a child (Fitzpatrick, 1997). The intergenerational connectedness inherent to African American culture can be a considerable strength in preventing gang affiliation, yet it can also be a considerable factor in promoting it when youth are exposed to the violence and lifestyle.

Hispanic Gangs

Hispanic gangs were recorded in Southern California in the early 1890s and grew in strength after the Zoot Suit Riots of 1943. These riots involved off-duty military men and Hispanic males who were not involved in World War II because of their immigrant status. The discrimination and prejudice of this incident caused Latinos to band together. Soon the Hispanic criminal element took the opportunity to engage in more unlawful pursuits (Allender, 2001). Hispanic immigrants from various sections of Mexico formed gangs to defend their newly acquired territory. Then, as now, Hispanic gangs form alliances for purposes of strength.

Hispanic gangs are generational and primarily male. Young males are known as PeeWees or Lil Winos. An individual gang member who lives to age 22 becomes a *veterano*. Veteranos act as advisors to younger gang members, and they also hide members, dispose of weapons, and arrange meeting places. Gangs are usually named after the street, housing project, or barrio from which the gang originates. Members identify closely with their neighborhood (or hood), and it is this name they tattoo on themselves and write on walls throughout the city. Gangs are composed of divisions roughly based on age cohort. In a sense, the gang is similar to an army, with the divisions operating with some autonomy while still loyal to the hood. These gangs ostensibly operate to protect the hood but actually are operating to promote prized violent behaviors. The size of the gang roughly correlates to the size of the barrio in which the gang lives. Gangs range in size from 30 members to 300 members. Gang boundaries are dynamic, changing as members move in and out, often in response to a specific situation. For core members, the gang becomes a total institution, much like a commune or a military unit, completely absorbing the individual into the subculture. Core members of the gang interact with one another according to established patterns that are binding to them as gang members and that are clearly identifiable, both by other gang members and by others not involved in the gang. Interaction within the gang is specific and ritualistic in form, with sanctions applied whenever someone does not adapt to the patterned form of behavior. Members from rival gangs challenge each other to test group fidelity and to establish membership.

White Supremacist Groups

White supremacists are often referred to as *skinheads* because of their closely cropped hair or shaved heads. The movement began in England in 1968 and moved formally into the United States in 1984. In 1986, the Skinheads of America formed an alliance with the Aryan Nation, an existing White supremacist organization. This group believes that the White race is superior to all others. They do not believe in mixing the races. Skinheads promote racial hatred and violence by distributing literature targeting people of color, gays, lesbians, and Jews. They seek to intimidate and harass individuals through physical attacks and through racial slurs. Disenfranchised adolescents who are experiencing academic problems or drug and alcohol abuse or who have been physically or sexually abused are especially at risk for involvement in these groups. At-risk youth are recruited through school activities, through literature, and on the Internet. The goal of the gang is to gain superiority and power through intimidation. Gang members dress in military-style clothes, steel-toed boots, and T-shirts with "White Pride" logos. Symbols used by skinheads include the circled swastika, an upside-down two-sided ax, a circled A, and a rifle sight (Palmer, 1992). A 1988 nationwide survey of neo-Nazi skinheads indicated continued membership growth and persistent propensity for engaging in violence—mainly against racial and religious minorities. The gangs are composed overwhelmingly of teenagers, many as young as 13 and 14 years of age. It is alarming to note that the skinheads provide a recruitment pool for other White supremacy groups, such as the Order, the Nationalist Socialist Vanguard, and the White Aryan Resistance.

Case Study

Christopher, a 13-year-old New York youth, lives in Brooklyn's dangerous, gang-infested Bedford Stuyvesant section, one of the oldest Black ghettos in the United States. Christopher lives on the fourth floor of a crumbling tenement with his aunt and cousins, with whom he shares a mattress. His mother, a 31-year-old with a crack cocaine addiction, is in and out of jail and lost custody of Christopher several years ago. His father, with whom he has had little contact except when he was being beaten by him, is also an addict and is in prison for a drug deal "gone bad." Christopher knows his dangerous surroundings and carries a .25 automatic for protection like most of his homeboys. He seldom attends school and is unable to read or write well. He smokes marijuana to relax and drinks heavily. He wears designer jeans, a T-shirt, and a $60 pair of Pumas with starched shoelaces.

By the time Christopher was around 9 or 10 years old, he was exhibiting pregang behaviors in elementary school. He was usually found during recess playing "gangs" with others who were from similar backgrounds. As Christopher grew older, he began to volunteer to do simple errands for local gang members who showed him attention and brief admiration. He often ran money or drugs between members or helped provide a distraction while gang members committed theft and property crimes.

Christopher continued his move toward full gang affiliation through his willingness to do any errand or activity that brought him closer to actual gang members. He isolated himself from any friends who were not interested in gangs and was soon considered a loner. He quit attending school entirely as he saw no use in attending.

As he moved into adolescence, Christopher began to wear the colors of his chosen gang and became involved in wannabe gang behaviors that broke the law and involved violence. The police labeled him as a gang member even though he was still only an apprentice. Christopher was on his way to becoming a full gang member and was invested in reaping the benefits that gang involvement would eventually provide. He was willing to do anything to gain the respect and admiration he believed the full gang members had earned.

Approaches to Prevention

The emergence and spread of gang activity has no geographical boundaries. Although gangs are largely considered to be an urban problem, even rural areas are feeling the impact of some gang activity. Often ganglike activities are perpe-

---

Sidebar 12.4 ■ Case Study: Assessing for and Minimizing Risk Factors

Consider the case of Christopher. What difference would a few invested adults have made if they had taken a personal interest in his life and living conditions, especially early on in his tragic youth? How might you, as a counselor, help minimize the risk factors that Christopher experiences? Name at least five possibilities, then rank order them from most important to least important.

■ ■ ■

trated by gang wannabes instead of hard-core gangsters. The presence of individuals willing to strive for the gang lifestyle in any location sends a message to all. Those who are concerned with trying to reclaim these individuals from gangs and redirect them into socially acceptable lifestyles know that a variety of interventions must be used. It is also clear that even with some successful interventions, the social system that promotes and tolerates injustice and encourages gang activity must be changed. Disintegrated families, drugs, lack of economic opportunities, unacceptable ways to gain social status, and poor social support structures such as schools and community agencies are all areas that need to be addressed. Because the problem is large and spreading, it requires strategies that are undertaken concurrently to make any successful impact. Programs that offer the best hope for success are those that lead these youth back from lives of crime and violence to a society that can offer them an attainable social status as well as social programs that help them to realize the need for change while offering a clear path to follow.

Individual

Individual prevention efforts can begin early through various early childhood prevention programs. The Montreal Preventive Treatment Program uses a multiple-component prevention strategy that addresses several early childhood risk factors for gang involvement (Tremblay, Masse, Pagani, & Vitaro, 1996). One of the key aims of this program is to address and reduce antisocial behavior in boys of low socioeconomic status who demonstrate problematic rule-breaking behavior in kindergarten (Office of Juvenile Justice and Delinquency Prevention, 2000). The boys in the program receive social skills training, and the boys' parents receive an average of 17 training sessions that help them increase prosocial behavior in their children.

The following list of critical ages and activities describes the life span development of gang members and illustrates how early these young gang wannabes begin to develop and how young boys and girls may begin their journey to violence and often death.

Average Age	Activity
8.9 years	First heard anything about gangs
9.2 years	First bullied by someone in a gang
9.2 years	First met someone in a gang
10.4 years	First bullied someone else in school
11.3 years	First fired a pistol or revolver
11.3 years	First saw trauma (killing or injury) from gang violence
12.0 years	First joined the gang
12.0 years	First arrested for a criminal offense
12.3 years	First got his or her own gun
13.0 years	First got a permanent tattoo
16.5 years	Age of typical current gang member
24.1 years	Age they expect to get married
26.1 years	Age they expect to quit the gang
59.5 years	Age they expect to die

Children can make better choices about their behavior when they have adequate information and are given skills to control their behavior. The following points may help youth to know what to do when it concerns gangs:

Sidebar 12.5 ■ Case Study: Treatment Planning for Christopher

A key component of a counselor's job is figuring out which problems are a priority to a client and which problems are less important or not as urgent. Make a list of the problems that Christopher is now experiencing. Rank order the problems from most important to least important. Now, take the three most important problems and decide how you might intervene to help Christopher to discover some additional options beyond what he has already considered.

■ ■ ■

1. Know how gang members recruit others. Wanting to belong may make children accept intimidation by gang members.
2. Know how to respond to gang member invitations to join their gang.
3. Take fears seriously about being around gang members and talk with trusted adults about these fears.
4. Know what your goals are and don't let joining a gang deter you from what it is that you really want out of life.
5. Surround yourself with positive individuals.
6. Use common sense. If being around gang members is uncomfortable, make plans that will keep you safely involved in other activities. (Ezarik, 2002)

Note that even though gang members think they will leave their gang and live until at least 60, the grim reality is that many die very young (Knox, 1998). Imagine the lifestyle Christopher is leading. Given the dangerousness of his surroundings, the availability of guns, and the criminal and drug involvement, it is quite unlikely that he can expect to live beyond a few decades old.

Adults who work with youth like Christopher must find ways to help them meet their needs through means that are both nonviolent and acceptable to the youth being helped. If family or adult mentors are not available, other youth often are ready to assist at-risk youth. Peer helping programs have been developed across the United States, and because these programs involve peer group interaction, they often have more chance of success. Peer pressure, which can negatively affect the choices youth make, can also be a powerful positive prevention tool.

One-to-one mentoring programs have also been developed on the basis of positive role modeling. Youth who are at risk for gang involvement are particularly receptive to the positive effects of being mentored by a successful role model, and research has demonstrated that at-risk minority youth paired with successful role model minorities benefit greatly (Landre, Miller, & Porter, 1997). One such program is Big Brothers/Big Sisters, a well-recognized, long-established program that pairs a child with an adult for the purpose of guidance and friendship. Other programs sponsored by local agencies, community groups, and business and industry are also available in most communities. When at-risk youth experience one-to-one mentoring and interact with a positive mentor similar to themselves, they often become able to look toward a gang-free future.

Family

Parental involvement is a primary antigang tool. Strong families are a major asset. The U.S. Department of Justice indicated that young gang members are less likely to reoffend when their parents and family members are involved in prevention and intervention efforts (Office of Juvenile Justice and Delinquency Prevention, 2000). In cases like Christopher's, the parents are unavailable to provide such support. However, other adults in a youth's life can take on the job of parenting and can gain the respect and trust of that youth, even though they are not the true parent that the child often longs for.

A study of 300 ninth-grade students examined the moderating effects of parental style on adolescent problem behavior and gang involvement (Walker-Barnes & Mason, 2004). The researchers found that higher levels of gang involvement are found in youth whose parent(s) use a coercive, guilt-based form of control along with lower levels of parental behavioral control. In other words, the more active a parent is in moderating the child's behavior, the greater the impact that control will have on reducing gang affiliation and antisocial behavior.

Many antigang programs are in operation across the nation. Those that are successful (a) provide more leisure-time activities with youngsters; (b) support tougher law enforcement against gang activities in the community; (c) increase efforts to dry up sources of gang revenue, such as drugs and narcotics; and (d) increase parental supervision of children, including their activities and their friends (Moore, 1998).

Parents can also fight gangs by improving their parenting skills and taking serious responsibility for their children. According to McCarthy (1998), parents who become effective gang fighters (a) monitor the company their children keep; (b) monitor their children's whereabouts; (c) keep their children busy with positive activities at school, at church, or in organized recreational activities; (d) model good behavior for their children and let them know how they are valued as individuals; (e) spend time with their children and include them in family activities often; and (f) watch for signs of pregang behavior, and at the first sign, intervene quickly and seek help from school, community groups, and law enforcement.

School

Schools are typically expected to provide safety and protection for children. However, youth gang activities are linked with crime problems in both elementary and secondary schools across the United States (Howell & Lynch, 2000). Although not all school violence is gang related, there is enough gang-related violence to cause many schools to adopt a dress code with zero tolerance for gang paraphernalia, such as gold chains, baggy pants, and bandannas. Special drug and gang prevention officers often are seen patrolling the halls of many urban schools. Metal detectors are commonplace, and a sense of being under siege often pervades the school setting. Strong schools, however, are a major asset in blocking gang activity. School is an ideal place to identify and work closely with troubled students such as gang wannabes. School counselors, teachers, and administrators must all take an active role in finding more appropriate ways of dealing with all the issues underlying youth delinquency. Many law enforcement personnel state that in schools teachers are naturally the first line of defense, so it makes sense to provide teachers and administrators with thorough training in how to recognize and contend with gang-related activities. Many teachers are flabbergasted by the kinds of weapons that gang members use as well as their level of commitment to violent behavior. A significant impact is made when jailed gang members agree to come to talk at school about their lives of crime. Because of the increasing number of gangs throughout the United States, there is a need for ongoing training in gang awareness and intervention.

Gang members are often bright and resourceful. They belong to organizations that have elaborate social and organizational structures that must be known and remembered. The systems of codes and symbols of typical gangs attest to the fact that many gang members possess exceptional cognitive abilities. For example, gangs use alphabets that are individualized for their own gang, and they communicate using these alphabets so other gangs or law enforcement will not detect their plans. Gangs are dynamic groups that change over time and are influenced by their environment. For example, some gangs that previously used symbols such as bandannas, hats, or baggy clothes to identify themselves have now gone to more public symbols, such as apparel from the NFL and NBA.

Schools are recognizing and changing their approach to academic accountability. With academic competence also comes a measure of social prestige. This can go a long way in keeping marginal gang wannabes in the mainstream of the school culture (Meeks, Heit, & Page, 1995).

Gang prevention programs must emphasize increasing the self-esteem of at-risk youth. Interventions to build self-esteem rest on the assumption that if a person likes himself or herself, he or she will be less likely to engage in activities that are harmful to self or others (Wilson-Brewer & Jacklin, 1990). Self-esteem enhancement is a long-term process. It must begin with healthy parenting practices, be nourished by the community, and be consistently enhanced by schools through activities that give adolescents a feeling of belonging and accomplishment. Alternative community support systems that enhance self-esteem development should, for example, focus on manhood development, with emphasis on rites-of-passage programs to assist male teens in the move from adolescence into adulthood.

Among effective approaches to prevention that can be used in school settings are two techniques that have been demonstrated to be successful: conflict resolution education and dispute mediation training. One of the first conflict resolution curricula for adolescents was developed by Prothrow-Smith (1987). Participants learn how to communicate in such a way as to not escalate the conflict, to use problem-solving skills, and to maintain self-control through anger management. Conflict resolution education focuses on the use of peers as dispute mediators. Selected students are trained in communication, leadership, problem solving, and assertiveness. In middle schools, peer mediators resolve playground conflicts. In high schools, they may resolve disputes in interpersonal relationships. Teachers, security personnel, and others may receive dispute mediation training so they can help to resolve problems that are inherent in their work.

The ultimate goal of gang awareness and prevention activities is to provide safe and secure school campuses where students can learn and teachers can teach effectively. If successful prevention of gang involvement is the goal, students must be involved in school-based programs from an early age (Landre et al., 1997). One definitive way to accomplish this is to invest as much money in hiring elementary school counselors as school systems do in hiring high school counselors (Peep, 1996). School counselors are trained to work with schools, parents, and communities to address the social, emotional, and academic needs of all children while reducing risk factors for gang and criminal involvement.

Children who are economically deprived need to be provided with choices at school that will make dropping out less likely. Teaching methods and materials need to be evaluated for appropriateness to real-life situations. Instructional methods such as cooperative learning, cross-age tutoring, and team building can all help increase students' involvement and interaction with teachers. Changes in the power structure in school also help drive children away. Schools must provide a caring and nurturing environment that encourages students to be involved and connected with their peers and teachers.

School programs with the best chance for preventing gang involvement offer gang prevention topics, such as (a) consequences of gang membership, (b) gang resistance skills and assertiveness training skills, (c) coping and stress management skills, (d) decision-making skills, (e) conflict prevention and peer mediation, (f) character development and responsibility, and (g) drug and substance abuse prevention (Meeks et al., 1995; Miars, 1996). One program that presents a number of these gang prevention skills is Gang Resistance Education and Training (GREAT), initially introduced in the early 1990s as an 8-week lecture-based curriculum that was typically delivered by law enforcement officers (Esbensen, Peterson, Taylor, & Osgood, 2012). Studies of the initial program indicated few immediate benefits from the program in terms of reducing gang or delinquent activities. However, some effects were seen 3 to 4 years after the intervention was delivered. Because of the apparent lack of significant effectiveness, the program underwent a major transformation and now focuses on reducing gang and delinquent activity and developing a positive relationship with law enforcement. Components of the program are delivered in schools, community centers, and after-school care organizations, and the revised program yields significant results in several key areas, including lower rates of gang affiliation (Esbensen et al., 2012).

Return once again to the case of Christopher, our case study wannabe. A school counselor or teacher who had been able to identify the risk factors present in Christopher's home environment, coupled with his need for protection (by carrying a .25 pistol) as well as his feelings of being misplaced in school, may have been able to bring in additional resources to help Christopher get his needs met in other ways. A school counselor or social worker could work with Christopher around his home and family situation and resulting feelings, and a mentor could help Christopher create more safety in his surroundings. A tutor could have helped Christopher in his academic life early on so that he did not feel so inept at classroom activities. An athletic mentor or coach could help Christopher find a recreational activity or sport that allows him the same feelings of belonging, accomplishment, respect, and admiration that he longs for via gang activity. Christopher's strengths could have been capitalized on in a positive way, rather than being directed to his life of drugs, crime, and danger.

Community

Taylor (1990) suggested that available jobs and employment are necessary to reduce and control gang involvement. Gang members often get involved in gangs through drug trafficking or organized crime that yields a profit. Because most youth are attracted to material goods and the benefits that income brings, gang involvement is an attractive proposition to a child with little access to disposable income. If an individual has access to a reasonable income, he or she may be less likely to become gang involved or will have an easier time replacing some of the gang income if he or she chooses to escape from gang life.

Many communities have struggled with youth violence and gang development. A number of programs have been developed and implemented at local levels, and some have produced positive results. No one program, no set of strategies, can be considered the answer to the multifaceted and complex problem of gang involvement, however. As the 21st century unfolds, Americans need to be ready to take back the youth of our society from gangs. To do this, there must be dramatic changes in families, schools, communities, and this nation. No one group is able to do the work alone.

Intervention Strategies

Individual

Two strategies for dealing with individual gang members, especially those still on the fringes, are counseling and the use of psychodrama. Both of these intervention strategies have an effective therapeutic component and can be easily incorporated with other programs in schools, through community agencies, or in prisons. Counseling is most effective with marginal gang members or wannabes because it teaches new behavioral alternatives that allow these youth to become involved in constructive activities. Group counseling can provide opportunities for members to help each other gain insights and see their faulty thinking and behavior patterns. Group counseling can mimic the positive aspects of a gang interaction in that there is social norming, group cohesion, and group acceptance. Members are more comfortable and able to participate fully in the activity. Positive changes often occur through working in this type of group because all the members are working from a similar family and community background (Yablonsky, 2005).

Psychodrama differs from counseling because the primary activity is for the individual to work through his or her personal, home, and community problems by acting them out using an alter ego. The success of this intervention is rooted in the fact that if gang members are able to take a minute and work through some of their reactionary behavior in reality, chances are greater that the negative behavior can be thwarted. If, for example, a male gang member has reacted to a minor threat from one of his own gang by vowing to kill him, he can instead role-play through the drama in his head, work through some of the anger, and particularly work on what consequences await him if he goes through with this threat. Often, after psychodrama occurs, underlying causes may surface that have triggered an inappropriate reaction to a relatively minor problem. Counseling and psychodrama have great value when working with gangsters. They provide direct training to those involved, allow opportunities for individuals to vent their anger and rage in a controlled environment, and slow down events so that gangsters can take time to see and understand what is actually taking place.

Gangsters live in the moment and react to whatever stimuli are affecting them. They need a mechanism by which they are given a chance to think through their behavior or make changes in their initial behavioral reaction to the stimuli. Psychodrama and group counseling allow gangsters to learn from each other in an open environment that what causes their violent impulses is often based on the emotional, physical, or sexual abuse they may have received as young children in a dysfunctional family system (Yablonsky, 2005).

Family

Interventions addressing gang membership at a family level must take a multi-pronged approach. That is, interventions must address behaviors, attitudes, risk factors, and family stressors. First, many families whose children have gang involvement report that their children's schools do not provide adequate educational opportunities and a safe enough school climate for their children to learn and develop socially and emotionally (Horowitz, McKay, & Marshall, 2005). Parents have noted that when children feel unsafe at school, school is an undesirable place to be. Furthermore, many families are either single-parent families or families in which all adults work outside of the home. Therefore, children are often left unattended during after-school hours, especially in middle school, which is a primary risk point for gang recruitment. Furthermore, parents and guardians of gang-involved youth typically have experienced their own lifetime of risk factors and trauma. They may find themselves feeling untrusting of social service providers and law enforcement officials and may be hesitant to seek or accept assistance when needed. They may be hesitant to accept help with parenting for fear of losing custody of their child. In addition, many parents have limitations in their own education and employment pathways and may feel inept at being able to work with external systems to help their child gain access to assistance at school and with employment.

Outreach programs such as the Gang Comprehensive Model (Arciaga & Gonzalez, 2012) include elements of outreach wherein a social service worker can provide some service to the family at the family's home or within their neighborhood in a confidential and private manner. This privacy allows the family to be more open about their perceived needs so that the social service provider can then assist a treatment intervention team in providing appropriate referrals to service providers who may better be able to help the family with financial, psychological, and behavioral support. The Boys & Girls Clubs of America provides, among other services, a program called GITTO: Gang Intervention Through Targeted Outreach. This program is intended to address many needs that youth at risk have, including the need for more positive and productive parent–child communication and interaction. The program also seeks to provide parents with additional child care and after-school care plus parenting assistance and social support (Arbreton & McClanahan, 2002).

School

Schools are also beginning to be more of a clearinghouse for family resources by sending home information to parents via school newsletters and other community

---

Sidebar 12.6 ■ Case Study: Planning for Intervention

Consider the case of Christopher. What types of family interventions might you want to see used with Christopher and his family? What do you expect the outcome of these interventions to be? When determining treatment options, consider the entire system. That is, if Christopher's role as a gang member serves a purpose for the entire family or certain people in the family, the family may not share the common goal of getting Christopher out of the gang. Make a decision about your intervention entry point: Should you start with family interventions, individual interventions, or another route? Provide a therapeutic rationale for the decision, including a list of pros and cons for each decision.

■ ■ ■

publications. The intervention most needed in schools usually is during the hours of 3:00 p.m. until 7:00 p.m., which is often referred to by law enforcement as the prime time for crime. With good after-school programs, youth can be kept busy and will not have to spend time engaged in unproductive or unlawful activities (Moore, 1998). Many parent–teacher groups are beginning to see this need, and parent volunteers are investing their time with groups of youth after school by providing them with interesting and enjoyable activities.

Many schools are also used in the summer for remedial and recreational activities. Youth whose parents are unable to afford camps and sports activities need alternatives that provide safe and constructive programming for their children. School-based prevention and intervention programs may be integrated as part of a school safety project (Lassiter & Perry, 2009). In addition, school personnel and administrators need additional training and understanding about how to identify and contend with gang features as they emerge.

Community

One of the earliest interventions was begun by the New York City Youth Board in 1946. It was known as the detached worker project. This project had the following goals: (a) Reduce antisocial behavior, particularly street fighting; (b) increase friendly interactions with other street gangs; (c) increase democratic participation within the gangs; (d) broaden social horizons; (e) increase responsibility for self-direction; (f) improve the personal and social adjustment of the individual; and (g) improve community relations. In this model a professional, such as a social worker or police officer, works directly with a gang on its own turf. Each professional is assigned to a particular gang. Even though this approach had some success, the project worker often cannot provide the proper interventions commensurate with the level of gang involvement. Marginal gang members can often be helped by getting them to counseling groups, providing recreation to fill some of their time and connect them with more wholesome male role models, and providing job opportunities for them. Core gang members require a more intense level of intervention. Problems occur when project workers make incorrect diagnoses of gang structure and makeup. These programs also require that an effective police presence is available in the community (Yablonsky, 1997).

Another early program that emerged in cities like New York, Chicago, and Boston during the 1930s was known as the Adult Youth Association (AYA) approach. Settlement houses or community recreation centers were developed to deal with youth in these areas, where boredom, low economic status, and cultural differences were all contributing to the alienation of young men.

The AYA approach is primarily based on the premise that male youth, in particular, need good role models to learn basic acceptable socialization skills, and that the role models can be provided by community volunteers working with at-risk youth in recreational endeavors and other social activities. It is also based on the knowledge that even in ghetto areas it is not unusual to see known gang members involved in a pickup game of basketball. The success of this approach is based on the fact that community volunteers can better know and serve the needs of the community's youth because they are members of the same community (Yablonsky, 1997). This type of program often draws on its own success stories for future volunteers. Those at-risk individuals who were able to turn their lives around often return to their own neighborhoods to become the youth leaders and role models for the next generation.

Because the AYA is well integrated into each community, and the workers are members or returning members of that community, the chance of successful outcomes is raised. The fact that AYA uses recreation as a focus often leads to teams and leagues developing in one or more sports. Those at-risk youth who belong to these leagues often replace the idea of being in a gang with the idea of joining an athletic league and derive the positive aspects of this organization. Marginal gang members, who may disengage more easily because of their low level of gang involvement, may replace the benefits of gangs with those of a sports league. The most important aspect of any AYA is to allow the recreational and social activities to evolve naturally through the interaction of the local community volunteers and the youth. If communities bring already developed programs to neighborhoods without allowing for local youth to participate in the planning, the chance for success is diminished.

In recent years, gangs have continued to grow in numbers, strength, and violence. Many communities have attempted to fight back against gang proliferation and expansion by enacting more serious consequences to gang activity and involvement. On a federal level, HR 1279, known as the Gang Deterrence and Community Protection Act of 2005, was pushed through the House of Representatives as a measure that federalizes gang crimes and allows for 16- and 17-year-old gang members to be tried as adults (Bennefield, 2005). Furthermore, this measure states that the death sentence will be given to any person whose gang crime resulted in the death of another human. This act and its companion, S.2358, increased federal funding to $100 million over the span of 5 years to support antigang efforts and to share intelligence among law enforcement agencies so that joint prosecution of gang members can occur. A National Gang Intelligence Center would also be developed at the FBI, again to help create a network to more effectively fight gang activity (http://gangresearch.net).

The Office of Juvenile Justice and Delinquency Prevention, a division of the U.S. Department of Justice, presents a Comprehensive Gang Model that focuses on the work of "outreach workers" who work in targeted gang-laden neighborhoods. This model is currently being used in 20 communities across the United States, from rural to urban locations, with outreach workers leading the charge in each locale. The outreach workers build relationships with identified gang members to carry out the following goals: decrease the client's bond with the gang, decrease gang-related violence, support gang members and their families with accessing social and education services, and mentor gang members as positive adult role models (Arciaga & Gonzalez, 2012). Outreach workers work as part of an intervention team that oversees the project operations in any given location. The intervention team operates with the same goals as the outreach worker, but the outreach worker is not required to report all of the gang member's activities to the intervention team. Hence, the worker is kept free from concern of retaliation, loss of trust, or inability to effectively build rapport with the gang members. Instead, the outreach worker acts as a safe mentor and resource provider who can connect with the gang members in a meaningful, effective way. The outreach worker is required to report safety concerns and direct threats of harm; however, for the safety of the client and others, other manner of illegal activity is kept confidential (National Gang Center, 2010).

In addition to national efforts, several local governments have created programs to address the gang problems. Boston's Operation Ceasefire is a highly regarded and often replicated strategy of gang intervention that intends to reduce serious juvenile and gang violence in Boston (Braga, Kennedy, Waring, & Piehl, 2001; http://www.nationalgangcenter.gov/SPT/Programs/42). Many cities are replicating similar tactics, which include an emphasis on communicating to gang members that there will be swift, certain, and severe punishments for violent activities, coupled with a focus on catching and prosecuting offenders (Chermak & McGarrell, 2004; McGloin, 2005).

To be successful in preventing gang activity in communities, programs need a strong theoretical framework. However, this is an area that is extremely complex and not easily researched (Esbensen et al., 2012). The lack of systematic evaluation plans to determine the long-term effectiveness of prevention and intervention strategies is one major cause of promising programs being scrapped before they are fully implemented. Oftentimes the only data collected and used to judge success or failure are increases or decreases in crime statistics during new program implementation. Community programs also need a two-pronged program so as to include prevention as well as intervention and so the program is thorough enough to include all at-risk individuals who experience a wide range of risk features.

Adaptations for Diversity

Prevention and intervention strategies will be of little value to those who work to block gang involvement if there is not a basic understanding of the ethnic and cultural factors that influence individuals. People have always clustered together in groups for social interaction, protection, self-development, and simply because of their proximity to each other. Basic social expressions such as language, norms, sanctions, and values reveal valuable information. This information is critical when developing the best approaches to diverse gangs.

Because the United States is a pluralistic society in terms of culture, there are a variety of ethnic groups to address. There are also subcultures that are racial, ethnic, regional, economic, or social communities that are distinctly different from other dominant groups in society. Gangs can be considered a subculture unto their own.

Knowing that gangs represent diverse ethnic and cultural groups is of great importance when choosing approaches to block their influence and spread. In the case of Christopher, whose ethnic roots are African American, his cultural roots or learned experiences are steeped in the drug-infested and extreme poverty of his neighborhood home and place him at extremely high risk of joining a gang. It is easy to recognize that Christopher views the gang as a way of meeting his need to be part of a culture that offers him friends for social interaction, a unique language, a set of values, and codes to live and work by, even though the work is crime related.

For helping professionals who work with gangs, it is imperative that the ethnic and cultural backgrounds of specific gangs are reviewed as prevention programs are planned or interventions are undertaken. Uninformed assumptions about how gangs view the world or what norms or values they adhere to will not lead to successful outcomes. Providing opportunities that offer gang members a chance to reclaim ethnic pride or learn to function in an acceptable cultural milieu will enhance the likelihood of a successful outcome.

Summary

Gangs and gang members have had serious and tragic consequences on society as a whole for decades. The financial and individual losses to communities and families can be seen in towns large and small. Gang members are a diverse group, but they all seek to have their individual social and emotional needs met through gang involvement. Being part of a gang organization allows them to feel protected and affirmed by those who matter to them and to have a sense of belonging in an environment that alienates them from mainstream culture. Many factors in families, schools, and communities influence gang wannabes to become gang members. Thus it is important to intervene very early with potential gang members using interventions developed to combat the causes that are individual to each community while providing ongoing prevention activities. Effective laws and law enforcement are also needed. Diversity issues in gangs need to be addressed to find ways to solve the problems specific to a geographical region, large city, or small town in America. It is only when communities work collaboratively with all the resources they have toward strong prevention programs and effective intervention activities that progress will be achieved.

Useful Websites

CA.gov
   http://www.calema.ca.gov/PublicSafetyandVictimServices/Pages/Gang-Violence-Programs.aspx
Federal Bureau of Investigation
   http://www.fbi.gov/stats-services/publications/2011-national-gang-threat-assessment
Gang Resistance Education and Training
   http://www.great-online.org/
National Gang Center
   http://www.nationalgangcenter.gov/
Regional Information Sharing Systems
   http://www.riss.net/
Stance Cleveland
   http://www.clevelandstance.com/aboutgangs%20.asp
U.S. Department of Justice Archives
   http://www.justice.gov/archive/ndic/
U.S. Department of Justice, Bureau of Justice Assistance
   https://www.bja.gov/
U.S. Department of Justice, Office of Community Oriented Policing Services
   http://www.cops.usdoj.gov/
U.S. Department of Justice, Office of Justice Programs
   http://www.ojjdp.gov/

References

Allender, D. (2001, December). Gangs in middle America. *Law Enforcement Bulletin, 70*(12).
Alonso, A. A. (2004). Racialized identities and the formation of Black gangs in Los Angeles. *Urban Geography, 25,* 658–674.

Arbreton, A. J. A., & McClanahan, W. (2002). *Targeted outreach: Boys & Girls Clubs of America's approach to gang prevention and intervention.* Philadelphia, PA: Public/Private Ventures.

Arciaga, M., & Gonzalez, V. (2012, June). Street outreach and the OJJDP Comprehensive Gang Model. *National Gang Center Bulletin, 7.* Retrieved from http://www.nationalgangcenter. gov/Content/Documents/Street-Outreach-Comprehensive-Gang-Model.pdf

Bendixen, M., Endresen, I. M., & Olweus, D. (2006). Joining and leaving gangs: Selection and facilitation effects on self-reported antisocial behavior in early adolescence. *European Journal of Criminology, 3,* 85–114.

Bennefield, R. M. (2005, July/August). Experts fear new gang legislation will unfairly target minority youth. *The Crisis,* pp. 7–8.

Bernard, T. J. (1990). Angry aggression among the truly disadvantaged. *Criminology, 28,* 73–75.

Braga, A. A., Kennedy, D. M., Waring, E. J., & Piehl, A. M. (2001). Problem-oriented policing, deterrence, and youth violence: An evaluation of Boston's Operation Ceasefire. *Journal of Research in Crime and Delinquency, 38,* 195–225.

Campbell, A. (1987). Self-definition by rejection: The case of gang girls. *Social Problems, 34,* 451–456.

Campbell, A. (1992). *The girls in the gang.* Malden, MA: Blackwell.

Centers for Disease Control and Prevention. (2004). Youth Risk Behavior Surveillance Survey, 2003. *Morbidity and Mortality Weekly Report, 53*(SS02), 1–96.

Chermak, S., & McGarrell, E. (2004). Problem-solving approaches to homicide: An evaluation of the Indianapolis Violence Reduction Partnership. *Criminal Justice Policy Review, 15,* 161–192.

Covey, H. C., Menard, S., & Franzese, R. J. (1992). *Juvenile gangs* (Vol. 111). Springfield, IL: Charles C Thomas.

Densley, J. (2011). Ganging up on gangs: Why the gang intervention industry needs an intervention. *British Journal of Forensic Practice, 13,* 12–23.

Densley, J. A. (2012). Street gang recruitment: Signaling, screening, and selection. *Social Problems, 59,* 301–321.

Dukes, R. I., & Martinez, R. (1994). The impact of ethgender on self-esteem among adolescents. *Adolescence, 29,* 105–115.

Eitle, D., Gunkel, S., & Van Gundy, K. (2004). Cumulative exposure to stressful life events and male gang membership. *Journal of Criminal Justice, 32,* 95–111.

Esbensen, F. A., & Carson, D. C. (2012). Who are the gangsters? An examination of the age, race/ethnicity, sex, and immigration status of self-reported gang members in a seven-city study of American youth. *Journal of Contemporary Criminal Justice, 28,* 465–481.

Esbensen, F. A., Peterson, D., Taylor, T. J., & Osgood, D. W. (2012). Results from a multi-site evaluation of the GREAT program. *Justice Quarterly, 29,* 125–151.

Ezarik, M. (2002). How to avoid gangs: Money, power . . . gang life may have its perks, but its price tag is high. Here's what you can do to keep your life on track. *Current Health, 28,* 20–22.

Fagan, J. A. (1990). Social processes of delinquency and drug use among urban gangs. In C. R. Huff (Ed.), *Gangs and America* (pp. 183–219). Newbury Park, CA: Sage.

Federal Bureau of Investigation. (2012). *2011 national gang threat assessment: Emerging trends.* New York, NY: Morgan James.

Fishman, L. T. (1992, March). *The vice queens: An ethnographic study of Black female gang behavior.* Paper presented at the annual meeting of the American Society of Criminology, Chicago, IL.

Fitzpatrick, K. M. (1997). Fighting among America's youth: A risk and protective factors approach. *Journal of Health and Social Behavior, 38,* 131–148.

Gottfredson, M., & Hirschi, T. (1990). *A general theory of crime.* Stanford, CA: Stanford University Press.

Gray-Ray, P., & Ray, M. C. (1990). Juvenile delinquency in the Black community. *Youth and Society, 22,* 67–84.

Hagadorn, J. M. (1991). Gangs, neighborhoods, and public policy. *Social Problems, 38,* 529–541.

Hill, K. G., Lui, C., & Hawkins, J. (2001). *Early precursors of gang membership: A study of Seattle youth* (Juvenile Justice Bulletin). Washington, DC: Office of Juvenile Justice and Delinquency Prevention.

Hirschi, T. (1969). *Causes of delinquency*. Berkeley: University of California Press.

Horowitz, K., McKay, M., & Marshall, R. (2005). Community violence and urban families: Experiences, effects, and directions for intervention. *American Journal of Orthopsychiatry, 75*, 356–368.

Howell, J. C., & Lynch, J. P. (2000). *Youth gangs in schools*. Washington, DC: U.S. Department of Justice, Office of Justice Programs, Office of Juvenile Justice and Delinquency Prevention.

Hunt, G., Joe-Laidler, K., & MacKenzie, K. (2005). Moving into motherhood: Gang girls and controlled risk. *Youth and Society, 36*, 333–373.

Joe, K. A., & Chesney-Lind, M. (1995). Just every mother's angel: An analysis of gender and ethnic variations in youth gang membership. *Gender and Society, 9*, 408–430.

Johnson, S., & Mulhausen, D. B. (2005). North American transnational youth gangs: Breaking the chain of violence. *Trends in Organized Crime, 9*, 38–54.

Kivisto, P. (2001). Teenagers, pregnancy and childbearing in a risk society. *Journal of Family Issues, 22*, 1044–1065.

Klein, M. W. (2011). Comprehensive gang and violence reduction programs. *Criminology & Public Policy, 10*, 1037–1044.

Klein, M., Maxon, C., & Miller, J. (Eds.). (1995). *The modern gang reader*. Los Angeles, CA: Roxbury.

Knox, G. (1998). What do we know about the gang problem in American today? *Official Proceedings of the 1998 Second International Gang Specialist Training Conference, 1*, 419.

Krohn, M. D., Ward, J. T., Thornberry, T. P., Lizotte, A. J., & Chu, R. (2011). The cascading effects of adolescent gang involvement across the life course. *Criminology, 49*, 991–1028.

Landre, R., Miller, M., & Porter, D. (1997). *Gangs: A handbook for community awareness*. New York, NY: Facts on File.

Lassiter, W. L., & Perry, D.C. (2009). *Preventing violence and crime in America's schools: From put-downs to lock-downs*. Santa Barbara, CA: Praeger.

LeBinh, P. (1997). *Girl-only gangs: A bibliography*. (ERIC Document Reproduction Service No. ED413275)

Matza, D. (1964). *Delinquency and drift*. New York, NY: Wiley.

McCarthy, C. (1998). What are gang characteristics? *Official Proceedings of the 1998 Second International Gang Specialist Training Conference, 1*, 443.

McGloin, J. M. (2005). Policy and intervention considerations of a network analysis of street gangs. *Criminology and Public Policy, 4*, 607–636.

Meeks, L., Heit, P., & Page, R. (1995). *Violence prevention: Totally awesome teaching strategies for safe and drug free schools*. Blacklick, OH: Meeks Heit.

Miars, R. D. (1996). Stress and coping in today's society. In D. Capuzzi & D. R. Gross (Eds.), *Youth at risk: A prevention for counselors, teachers, and parents* (2nd ed., pp. 129–147). Alexandria, VA: American Counseling Association.

Miller, W. (1998). Lower class culture as a generating milieu of gang delinquency. *Journal of Social Issues, 14*, 5–19.

Molidor, C. E. (1996). *Female gang members: A profile of aggression and victimization*. (ERIC Document Reproduction Service No. EJ530433)

Moore, M. (1998). Investing in our children: Report on youth violence and school safety. *Official Proceedings of the 1998 Second International Gang Specialist Training Conference, 1*.

Morales, A. (1992). A clinical model for the prevention of gang violence and homicide. In R. C. Cervantes (Ed.), *Substance abuse and gang violence* (pp. 105–120). Newbury Park, CA: Sage.

National Gang Center. (2010). *Best practices to address community gang problems: OJJDP's comprehensive gang model*. Tallahassee, FL: Author.

National Gang Intelligence Center. (2011). *National gang threat assessment*. Retrieved from http://www.fbi.gov/stats-services/publications/2011-national-gang-threat-assessment/2011%20National%20Gang%20Threat%20Assessment%20%20Emerging%20Trends.pdf

Office of Juvenile Justice and Delinquency Prevention. (2000). *Comprehensive responses to youth at risk: Interim findings from the Safe Futures Initiative*. Washington, DC: Author.

Ojeda, A. (2002). *Juvenile crime: Opposing viewpoints*. San Diego, CA: Greenhaven Press.

Palmer, M. (1992). *Gang profiles*. Portland, OR: Northeast Coalition of Neighborhoods.

Peep, B. B. (1996). Lessons from the gang: What gang members think about their schools suggests new direction for classroom reform. *Social Administrator, 53,* 26–31.

Prothrow-Smith, D. (1987). *Violence prevention curriculum for adolescents*. Newton, MA: Education Development Center.

Ruble, N. M., & Turner, W. L. (2000). A systemic analysis of the dynamics and organization of urban street gangs. *American Journal of Family Therapy, 28,* 117–132.

Sharkey, J. D., Shekhtmeyster, Z., Chavez-Lopez, L., Norris, E., & Sass, L. (2011). The protective influence of gangs: Can schools compensate? *Aggression and Violent Behavior, 16,* 45–54.

Shulmire, S. R. (1996). *A comparative study of gang-involved and other adolescent women*. (ERIC Document Reproduction Service No. ED412477)

Skolnick, J. (1995). Gangs and crime as old as time: But drugs change gang culture. In M. Klein, C. Maxon, & J. Miller (Eds.), *The modern gang reader* (pp. 222–227). Los Angeles, CA: Roxbury.

Spergel, I. A. (1992). Youth gangs: An essay review. *Social Service Review, 6,* 121–140.

Spergel, I. A. (1995). *The youth problem*. New York, NY: Oxford University Press.

Spindler, A., & Bouchard, M. (2011). Structure or behavior? Revisiting gang typologies. *International Criminal Justice Review, 21,* 263–282.

Taylor, C. S. (1990). *Dangerous society*. East Lansing: Michigan State University Press.

Taylor, C. S. (1993). Female gangs: A historical perspective. In C. S. Taylor (Ed.), *Girls, gangs, women, and drugs* (pp. 13–47). East Lansing: Michigan State University Press.

Thrasher, T. (1926). *The gang: Study of 1,313 gangs*. Chicago, IL: University of Chicago Press.

Tremblay, R. E., Masse, L., Pagani, L., & Vitaro, F. (1996). From childhood physical aggression to adolescent maladjustment: The Montreal Prevention Experiment. In R. D. Peters & R. J. McMahon (Eds.), *Preventing childhood disorders, substance abuse, and delinquency* (pp. 268–298). Thousand Oaks, CA: Sage.

Tsunokai, G. T. (2005). A descriptive portrait of Asian gang members. *Journal of Gang Research, 12,* 37–57.

Walker-Barnes, C. J., & Mason, C. A. (2004). Delinquency and substance use among gang-involved youth: The moderating role of parenting practices. *American Journal of Community Psychology, 34,* 235–250.

Wilson, J. M., & Chermak, S. (2011). Community-driven violence reduction programs: Examining Pittsburgh's One Vision One Life. *Criminology & Public Policy, 10,* 4.

Wilson-Brewer, R., & Jacklin, B. (1990, December). *Violence prevention strategies targeted at the general population of minority youth*. Paper presented at the Forum on Youth Violence in Minority Communities: Setting the Agenda for Prevention, Atlanta, GA.

Wright, D. R., & Fitzpatrick, K. M. (2006). Violence and minority youth: The effects of risk and asset factors on fighting among African American children and adolescents. *Adolescence, 41,* 251–262.

Wyrick, P., & Howell, J. C. (2004). Strategic risk-based response to youth gangs. *Juvenile Justice, 9,* 20–29.

Yablonsky, L. (1997). *Gangsters: Fifty years of madness, drugs, and death on the streets of America*. New York, NY: New York University Press.

Yablonsky, L. (2005). *Gangs in court*. Tuscon, AZ: Lawyers & Judges Publishing.

Chapter 13

"It Takes a Village": Advocating for Sexual Minority Youth

John F. Marszalek III and Colleen R. Logan

Sexual minority youth, who have a different sexual orientation or gender identity (e.g., gay, lesbian, bisexual, transgender, and questioning) from other youth, in many ways are no different from their heterosexual counterparts when it comes to the challenging navigation of the tangled web of adolescence. It is a critically important and complex developmental stage that, regardless of sexual orientation and/or gender identity, is characterized by seeking independence from parental figures, exploring roles and rules, and experiencing burgeoning sexuality and deeper—often romantic—relationships with peers. However, some key differences emerge during this period that are important to both understand and value in the helping relationship. To be specific, sexual minority youth must face these often daunting developmental tasks while also coping with internalized and externalized homoprejudice and culturally sanctioned oppression. The terms *homoprejudice, biprejudice,* and *transprejudice* refer to the discrimination, hatred, verbal and physical harassment, and acts of violence that are directed at sexual minorities (Logan, 1996).

Fortunately for today's sexual minority youth, society has begun to shift and become more accepting of sexual minorities in general. This acceptance was clearly evidenced by President Barack Obama's recent inaugural address (Obama, January 21, 2013), where he noted, "Our journey is not complete until our gay brothers and sisters are treated like anyone else under the law for if we are truly created equal, then surely the love we commit to one another must be equal as well." The social climate is clearly changing, as evidenced by President Obama's unprecedented support of gay and lesbian equal rights as well as other recent landmark events such as multiple state legalization of gay and lesbian marriage and the increased visibility of openly gay and lesbian public officials. For example, during the 2012 elections, Tammy Baldwin became the first openly gay U.S. senator, and residents of Maine, Maryland, and Washington voted in favor of legal same-sex marriage in their states. Whereas only 27% of Americans supported same-sex marriage in 1996, over 50% of Americans stated they supported it in 2012 (USA Today/Gallup Poll, 2012). In addition, the positive portrayal of gay and lesbian characters on television shows such as *Glee, Smash, The New Normal,* and *Modern Family* has markedly served to significantly change the cultural landscape. Concurrently, sexual minorities are more visible than ever before in society, with 75% of lesbians and gays reporting they are open about their identities and 90% reporting they feel more accepted in their communities than in the past (USA Today/Gallup Poll, 2012). For sexual minority youth, this increased acceptance and visibility demonstrate to them that they are not alone and allow them to compare their feelings with those sexual minorities in the public eye, whereas sexual minority youth even 20 years ago, especially those youth living in rural areas, might have felt that there was no one else who felt the way they did.

Causal Factors

Nevertheless, although views have changed, a significant segment of society continues to view sexual minorities with suspicion and even outright hostility. Almost 90% of lesbian and gays and 63% of all Americans described discrimination based on sexual orientation to be a "serious problem" in our country; about 40% of both sexual minorities and all Americans believe that it is "difficult" for someone to live in the community as an openly lesbian or gay person (USA Today/Gallup Poll, 2012). Although homosexuality is typically not viewed as a disorder to be changed, and efforts to change sexual orientation are viewed as unethical and not supported by legitimate empirical research by the major medical and mental health professional organizations (e.g., American Counseling Association, American Psychiatric Association, American Psychological Association), many conservative religious groups continue to promote the notion that sexual orientation is a choice and should be cured through prayer and/or "reparative therapy"; in addition, over half of states permit employment discrimination based on sexual orientation (National Gay and Lesbian Task Force, 2012). As of this writing, the American Psychiatric Association (2000) continues to view a transgender person as disordered (i.e., gender identity disorder).

Society's divergent views on sexual orientation and gender identity mean that sexual minority youth hear mixed messages on whether or not it is acceptable to be lesbian, gay, bisexual, transgender, or questioning (LGBTQ); thus, they hear mixed messages on whether or not it is acceptable to come out. *Coming out* refers to the process of becoming aware of one's own sexual orientation or gender identity and sharing this identity with others. Although, for example, sexual minority youth are coming out at earlier ages than ever before (Ryan, 2009), 85% of middle and high school students surveyed by the Gay, Lesbian, and Straight Education Network (GLSEN; 2010) reported facing verbal harassment because of their sexual orientation identities, 40% reported physical harassment, and 19% reported physical assault. Facing a world that may or may not be safe, sexual minority youth are at a higher risk compared with other youth for depression (Almeida, Johnson, Corliss, Molnar, & Azrael, 2009). In fact, because sexual minority youth are 4 times more likely to attempt suicide than youth who are not sexual minorities (Centers for Disease Control and Prevention, 2011), suicide prevention programs such as

The Trevor Project (Trevor Project, 2013) and the It Gets Better Project were specifically created to reach out to these youth. Many sexual minority youth are even at risk in their families. In a recent survey (Durso & Gates, 2012) of U.S. agencies serving homeless youth, 40% of homeless youth were sexual minorities: 30% were lesbian or gay youth, 9% were bisexual youth, and 1% were transgender youth. Almost 70% of these youth were homeless because they had been rejected by their families, and more than half had faced physical, emotional, or sexual abuse at home. It is not surprising that 65% of the youth struggled with mental health issues such as depression and anxiety, and 53% reported using alcohol and drugs.

Increased depression, suicide rates, substance abuse, and health problems among sexual minorities can be attributed to "minority stress" (Meyer, 2003). Meyer described minority stress as the "excess stress to which individuals from stigmatized social categories are exposed as a result of their social, often a minority position" (p. 676). Like other minority groups in society, sexual minority youth have stress reactions to the both subtle and overt discrimination they experience in society. Many youth who have not come out fear being the object of bullying, harassment, and discrimination if others find out that they are LGBTQ. They may internalize the negative messages from society and others around them, leading to self-hate and feelings of aloneness. Some youth seek to cope with the feelings through substance abuse or unsafe sexual behaviors; unfortunately, some cannot cope and attempt suicide.

In this chapter, we discuss efforts to protect sexual minority youth from the risks associated with minority stress, and we discuss intervention efforts to use when they have symptoms of this stress that range from depression to self-harm. Prevention begins before parents, school personnel, community members, and the child herself or himself even know if a youth is LGBTQ. Prevention includes letting all children know that they will be loved regardless of their sexual minority or non–sexual minority status. It includes keeping an open dialogue with children so that they will feel safe coming out to others if they realize that they are lesbian, gay, bisexual, or transgender. In addition, they must feel safe coming to someone they can trust if they are questioning their identities, if they are being bullied, if they feel depressed, if they have suicidal ideations, or for any other reason. Prevention includes parents, school personnel, and community members demonstrating to youth that they are accepting of people regardless of who they are; this acceptance can be demonstrated by their reactions to sexual minorities in the community. Hence, prevention begins before youth come out as sexual minorities, it occurs when they come out to others, and it continues into adulthood.

Sidebar 13.1 ■ Not Just a Joke

Children listen to the jokes you tell, the look on your face, and the way you respond to someone else. Imagine a child who has heard you make fun of a gay couple in your neighborhood, heard you say that that transgender person, Rupaul, on television, is a freak. Imagine this child saw you support other parents who approached the school board to insist that they fire a teacher because she is an open lesbian. Imagine this child heard you say that "queers" are going to hell. What will happen if this child realizes that she or he is a sexual minority? How will your actions have affected this child? To what extent will this child have internalized your actions and comments?

■ ■ ■

Intervention, on the other hand, occurs when youth are not able to cope with their reactions to minority stress, for example, when they become depressed, become anxious, seek escape through alcohol or drugs, engage in unsafe sex, or have suicidal ideations. This is the time that families, schools, and communities need to move beyond prevention to intervene on behalf of youth. Although we present prevention and intervention in separate sections, they are intertwined when working with sexual minority youth. Intervening with a sexual minority youth who is depressed is not only a means to lessen the depression but a means to prevent suicide. Intervening when a sexual minority youth is being bullied is not only working to stop the bullying but working to prevent the youth from developing a low self-esteem through internalization of the bullying. Consequently, the line between prevention and intervention can be blurry when working with sexual minority youth. Nevertheless, the goals of both are the same: to protect and look after sexual minority youth as they develop into sexual minority adults.

Case Study

Ms. Hatherford was a relatively new principal at Valley Elementary School. Prior to accepting the principal position at the school, she had served as the volleyball coach at a local middle school. She also taught ninth-grade math and enjoyed positive relationships with both her colleagues and the students. She was pleased with her promotion and looked forward to her continued success as an academic leader and respected member of the community. That was until this year. She was admittedly puzzled by one of the fifth-grade girls and, in fact, wondered if the situation could explode and threaten her burgeoning career.

Emma, a popular fifth grader, always did well in school and loved to play sports, any kind of sports. She also loved to dress in very masculine clothing. She loved to wear boys' button-down shirts, pants, and even suit jackets. There was nothing that made her happier than when the other boys at school would give her their second-hand clothes and sports equipment. Her well-educated parents were supportive of Emma and would laugh with the other parents about Emma being a perpetual tomboy, dismissing it as just a phase. The other girls didn't seem to mind that Emma dressed like a boy because she was a good friend and great athlete and it really wouldn't make sense for her to wear skirts and dresses. The boys just thought she was lots of fun and would argue over who would get to have her on their teams.

At the beginning of fifth grade, Emma started announcing to her friends, teachers, and the school counselor that she was, indeed, a lesbian. In fact, she was looking forward to the fall dance because she had a big crush on one of her friends and surely they could attend the dance together. She felt very confident about her decision, citing shows like *Modern Family* as an illustration of how "gay is okay." Much to her surprise, her friends, both male and female, began to shun her and make fun of her. They would call her names like "dyke" and "lezzie." They left notes in her locker saying that she was "sick in the head" and "going to hell." The boys wouldn't play with her anymore, and the girls simply stopped talking to her completely. Every time she would pass a group of girls, she could hear them laughing and call her names. The saying that hurt most was "What are you, a freak? Are you a girl or a boy?" Emma was very clear that she was a girl and she wanted to be with girls romantically. Period.

Word spread around school like wildfire. Emma went to the school counselor for support but was told she was too young to know what she was feeling and, really, she hadn't even kissed a boy yet so how could she know that she didn't like boys? Emma felt that even the teachers were talking and whispering behind her back. As the other parents became aware of the situation they started to voice great distress and concern to Emma's parents as well as school officials. Suddenly, Emma was no longer invited to slumber parties and other events for girls. Emma started feeling ashamed and really bad about herself. She started making up illnesses so she could stay home and avoid school. Secretly she even wished she were dead.

Ms. Hatherford became more and more alarmed at the developing situation and called a meeting with Emma's parents in order to try and address the issues. Sure, the school had a strict no-bullying policy, but, really, couldn't Emma just keep her feelings to herself? "It would be so much easier," said Ms. Haverford. Emma's parents were completely supportive of Emma and her process of coming out. In fact, they demanded that Ms. Haverford "get with the times" and assure them in no uncertain terms that Emma was able to go to school in a safe and non-hostile environment. At the same time, other parents were calling and sending e-mails demanding that Emma stop talking about this foolishness or find somewhere else to go to school, as she was introducing topics they were not ready to address with their own children. Ms. Haverford started to wonder about whether or not she was the right person for this school. What if they started to question her ability to do her job? Or worse, what if they started to question her sexual orientation? Ms. Haverford knew this was irrational, but she couldn't help worrying that the situation could turn into a complete nightmare.

Prevention

When she was the First Lady of the United States, Hillary Clinton (1996) wrote that it takes a village to care for a child, and this is certainly true for sexual minority youth. In order to protect them from the risks discussed in the beginning of this chapter, prevention must be something that is the concern not only of their parents but also their schools and entire communities.

Individual

Becoming accepting of a sexual minority identity is affected by and affects overall identity development for sexual minority youth. Chickering and Reisser (1993) outlined tasks to be resolved in forming an overall identity, of which gender and sexual orientation identity are one of many: (a) comfort with body and appearance; (b) comfort with gender and sexual orientation; (c) sense of self in a social, historical, and cultural context; (d) clarification of self-concept through roles and lifestyle; (e) sense of self in response to feedback from valued others; (f) self-acceptance and self-esteem; and (g) stability and integration (p. 49). In other words, sexual minority youth not only are learning what it means to be a sexual minority, but they are learning about their whole selves.

It is not uncommon for sexual minority youth or people around them to confuse sexual orientation identity and gender identity. Sexual orientation identity involves one's sexual and emotional attraction to members of the opposite or same sex (Coleman, 1990; Shively & DeCecco, 1993), whereas gender identity is the belief a person has about his or her gender (i.e., do they identify as a male or a female?) and not one's actual biological sex. Theorists have developed identity

Sidebar 13.2 ■ Understanding Terminology

Do you know the following terms? Which of these terms relate to sexual orientation, and which relate to gender identity?

- *Lesbian* refers to females who are romantically and sexually attracted to other females.
- *Gay* refers to a person who is romantically and sexually attracted to persons of the same sex.
- *Bisexual* is used to indicate that a person is attracted to both males and females.
- *Transgender* is an umbrella term used to describe persons who experience their gender in a way that varies along a continuum from masculine to feminine.
- *Transsexuals* are a subgroup within transgender. The term refers to persons whose anatomy does not match the way they feel and who desire sex reassignment surgery or hormones.
- *Cross-dressers/drag queens/drag kings* are persons who dress and perform in female or male clothing for an act or performance.
- *Queer* is another term used by some to describe LGBTQ persons. It previously had a negative connotation. Many still view it negatively, but some LGBTQ persons are reclaiming it as a way to empower themselves.
- *Questioning* is used to describe persons who are questioning or exploring their sexual identity.
- *Intersex* is used to describe persons who naturally develop primary or secondary sex characteristics that do not fit neatly into societal definitions of what is male or female.

■ ■ ■

development models to describe the process of people first becoming aware of their same-sex feelings or gender identity and integrating these into their overall identities (e.g., Cass, 1979; Coleman, 1981/1982; Marszalek & Pope, 2008; Troiden, 1984). Research has shown that sexual orientation identity development is directly related to psychological adjustment (Marszalek, Dunn, & Cashwell, 2002; Miranda & Storms, 1989). In other words, being *closeted*, or keeping one's sexual orientation and/or gender identity secret, can lead to psychological distress (e.g., depression and anxiety) and affect identity development.

In the case of Emma, she has the support of her parents, and they are working to advocate for her in her school. Although the school is not being supportive and community resources are not in place, Emma can trust her parents to talk about her feelings and to help her find role models and allies. An *ally* refers to a person who confronts heterosexism, sexism, homoprejudice, and heterosexual privilege in both himself or herself and others; in addition, the ally does so out of concern for the well-being of sexual minorities and as a matter of social justice. Unlike Emma, many sexual minority youth feel completely isolated, because they are not sure in whom they can confide; this is especially true for LGBTQ youth in rural areas. Consequently, prevention of the risks discussed above will likely occur at the family, school, and community levels.

Family

When parents learn that their child is LGBTQ, it is crucial that they react with acceptance, support, and empathy. Researchers have found that LGBTQ youth whose families had accepted them were more likely to have greater self-esteem, social support, and overall health; in addition, they were less likely to experience

Sidebar 13.3 ■ Prevention Begins at Home

A parent described how she approached her 5-year-old daughter, Crystal, when she asked why Uncle John and Uncle Larry lived together and did not have wives. "Well," the mother said, "sometimes a man and a woman fall in love and get married; sometimes a man and a man fall in love and get married; and sometimes a woman and woman fall in love and get married."

"Oh," said her daughter. "They sleep in the same bed like you and daddy?"
"Yes," said the mother.
"And they kiss like you?"
"Well, I imagine they do."
"Okay," said her daughter and ran outside to play.

Imagine if Crystal turns out to be gay, herself, when she gets older. She'll likely know from encounters like this with her parents that her parents will accept her. For too many LGBTQ youth, however, either they hear parents, teachers, clergy, and other people talk about the evils of homosexuality or, in more cases, they hear nothing at all. Consequently, prevention should begin in families before parents even know the sexual orientation identity of their children. Imagine if Crystal turns out to be heterosexual when she gets older. How might this encounter with her mother affect the way she reacts to LGBTQ people she meets?

■ ■ ■

depression, substance abuse, and suicidal ideation and attempts and were less likely to engage in risky sexual behaviors that could increase the risk for becoming infected with HIV and other sexually transmitted diseases (Bouris et al., 2010; Ryan, Huebner, Diaz, & Sanchez, 2009; Ryan, Russell, Huebner, Diaz, & Sanchez, 2010). On the other hand, LGBTQ youth whose parents rejected them were more likely to experience depression, attempt suicide, use illegal drugs, engage in risky sexual behaviors, and internalize homoprejudice (Ryan et al., 2009; Willoughby, Doty, & Malik, 2010). In the case of Emma, her parents have provided her with an important inoculation against these risks. She is no doubt facing verbal harassment and stigmatization at school; however, she does not have to face these difficulties alone. Their engagement with her will be crucial to preventing her from experiencing the risks discussed above; in addition, she will have their assistance in finding peers, role models, and allies she can trust so that she does not feel alone.

Unlike Emma's parents, some parents may be shocked and even have a hard time accepting that their children are not the same people they thought they were. Parents may have had an expectation that their child would be heterosexual and imagined that child growing up and marrying someone of the opposite sex. Accepting their child's sexual orientation identity means having to grieve the loss of their dreams for their child. It is important, however, that parents express any negative views with a counselor or in a support group rather than with their children. Parents who are having difficulty accepting their children's LGBTQ identity can join a support group such as Parents, Families, and Friends of Lesbians and Gays (PFLAG) and meet other parents of LGBTQ children. If parents live in a rural area with no support groups or other resources available, they can access resources such as PFLAG and GLSEN on the Internet.

Ryan (2009) suggested the following reactions by parents when they learn that their child is LGBTQ to decrease the child's risk for developing health and mental health problems as an adolescent and an adult: (a) Talk about the child's LGBTQ identity, (b) respond with support and affection, (c) advocate for them and insist that others treat them with respect, (d) help them become involved in LGBTQ organizations, (e) introduce them to sexual minority adult role models, (f) welcome their sexual minority friends to the home, (g) support their gender expression, and (h) be positive about their ability to be happy as a sexual minority adult.

It's also important for parents to educate themselves about sexual orientation and gender identity so that they can talk to their children intelligently about their experiences. For example, some parents may believe myths they have heard such as someone chooses to be LGBTQ or that gender identity is the same as sexual orientation identity. Understanding the process of identity development and recognizing that a child's sexual orientation and gender identities are components of an overall identity (i.e., they are still the same children that they were before they came out to their parents) is important for challenging these myths; it is also important for developing a trusting relationship with youth so that they will be more likely to come to parents if they are being bullied, being harassed, or experiencing any other difficulties. In addition, parents can educate themselves on the community and school's climate for sexual minorities. For example, does the school have an antibullying policy and a nondiscrimination policy based on sexual orientation and gender identities? How does the school react if a child is bullied?

School

Schools have an important role in preventing the risks discussed in this chapter and providing a safe and supportive school climate for LGBTQ youth. The GLSEN (2011) recommended that schools have a Gay–Straight Alliance (GSA) group to provide education, support, and positive experiences for students. GLSEN also recommends that schools have an inclusive curriculum, make students aware of LGBTQ-supportive teachers and other school personnel, and create antibullying policies with protections for LGBTQ students. Because students in rural areas are less likely to have access to LGBTQ resources and more likely to face a hostile school climate, it's crucial that advocates in rural areas work to provide support for LGBTQ students (GLSEN, 2012). According to the GLSEN's 2011 National School Climate Survey, LGBTQ students in schools that had implemented these recommendations were less likely to hear anti-gay comments, less likely to be mistreated or feel unsafe because of their sexual orientation or gender expression, more likely to feel a part of the school, less likely to miss school, and more likely to continue their education beyond high school. In Emma's case, because her school has not implemented these policies, she is not receiving the protections she needs to feel safe. Her parents will need to advocate for her or consider finding a school that works to protect and affirm sexual minority youth. They might also work to find allies in the community or a national organization such as GLSEN to help them advocate for their daughter.

The U.S. Department of Health and Human Services (HHS; 2013) recommends that schools address bullying before it becomes a problem. First, they suggest that schools assess the degree to which bullying occurs, the response by students and school personnel, and the extent to which current prevention efforts are effective. Second, they stress the importance of including the whole community as much as possible to speak out against bullying and to be involved in the school's antibullying program. Third, they recommend that schools develop policies to establish a climate in which bullying is not acceptable. Fourth, they suggest that the school create a culture of acceptance, tolerance, and respect. Finally, they stress the importance of educating students and school personnel on school antibullying policies and how to respond appropriately when bullying does occur.

Community

Communities can offer programs that focus on preventing risks faced by sexual minority youth. For example, U.S. HHS (2013) provides training on developing community bully prevention programs. Not unlike their recommendations for schools, they suggest that communities begin by assessing the community climate on bullying. For example, communities can determine the youth most at risk, how often bullying occurs, the most frequent locations (e.g., schools, bus stops, after-school programs), and what the community is currently doing to address bullying, if anything. They stress the importance of involving as many community stakeholders as possible.

Community leaders can make sure that programs that exist are inclusive of sexual minority youth. When there are not programs, they can provide training. For example, The Trevor Project, a national LGBTQ youth suicide prevention program, offers workshops for educators and youth service providers in many large cities to train them on recognizing the warning signs, responding to warning signs, and understanding reasons that many LGBTQ youth are at risk for depression and suicide. In the case of Emma, an outside organization could provide training to school personnel and parents. Her parents might contact an outside organization such as PFLAG for support and ideas on how to best advocate for their daughter at the school.

If Emma's school is in a rural area, her parents are going to have a more difficult time finding supportive organizations and allies in the community to help them advocate for their daughter. GLSEN (2012) reported that LGBTQ youth in rural areas are more likely to be verbally harassed, feel unsafe in school, report that school personnel rarely intervene when students make homonegative or gender-biased comments, be physically assaulted, and be cyberbullied. In addition, LGBTQ youth in rural areas are less likely to feel a part of the school community, feel comfortable talking about LGBTQ issues in class or with school personnel, and attend a school with antibullying or nondiscrimination policies. GLSEN explained that adults in rural areas are more likely to have "conservative social beliefs," especially on LGBTQ issues such as same-sex marriage and the importance of nondiscrimination policies; this is especially true for rural areas in the South and Midwest.

Intervention

Sexual minority youth can now, more than ever, feel hope grounded in evidence that they will be accepted as integral members of society and equal in rights to their heterosexual counterparts. Even the traditionally anti-gay Boy Scouts organization is, at this writing, opening a dialogue rethinking policies that discriminate against gay leadership. In addition, today's sexual minority youth have online and community resources that were simply unheard of and unavailable in the past, and, as a result, we are seeing a significantly higher number of sexual minority youth coming out and living out with pride, connected to a community—virtual and otherwise.

Sadly, even with these significant steps toward equal rights there is still much work to be done. Homoprejudice abounds in many areas of the country, families are still unprepared for children coming out at even earlier ages, and communities of faith, in particular, struggle with how to serve and affirm—or not—sexual minorities.

Individual

Fedewa and Ahn (2011) conducted a comprehensive meta-analysis of the literature in order to determine the effects of homoprejudice and homonegativity on both heterosexual and sexual minority youth and found that sexual minority youth are 124% more likely to experience bullying as a result of their real or perceived differences than their heterosexual peers. The risks for sexual minority youth discussed in this chapter are not caused by innate characteristics attributable to their sexual orientation or gender identity but, rather, result from a response to discrimination, oppression, homoprejudice, and victimization (Diamond et al., 2011). Feeling different and inferior is enormously stressful and can only hinder the completion of the formative tasks of adolescence; daunting as those tasks are for everyone, they are compounded for those who are different in ways that society still claims a right to oppress. As illustrated by the case of Emma, she had always felt very comfortable wearing gender-non-conforming clothes and engaging in sports and other activities with boys. She didn't question her gender identity, and, quite frankly, no one else did either—she was popular with boys and girls and not perceived as "different." It is interesting that she was accepted by others when she was challenging the breadth of gender and yet shunned when she publicly acknowledged her different sexual orientation. Without support for her process, Emma could be at risk for depression, anxiety, and low self-esteem.

An important issue for sexual minority youth is deciding whether or not to come out to families, friends, and other important people in their lives. Not coming out means hiding an important part of their identities behind a mask of conformity. Accepting and embracing an LGBTQ identity can be a difficult task when youth are uncertain of the response they will receive from others. As discussed above, some sexual minority youth have faced rejection—being kicked out of their homes and/or subjected to physical or verbal abuse—so it's understandable that youth may be uncertain whether it is okay to come out. Not coming out, however, means not being able to receive the support they need and can lead to depression and anxiety. Consequently, sexual minority youth have a difficult decision to make in deciding with whom to share their sexual orientation or gender identity. GLSEN (2003) offered the following tips for youth trying to decide whether or not they should come out:

1. Because youth are under 18 and financially dependent on their caretakers, they need to consider whether or not there is a possibility they could be rejected and kicked out of the house, left to support themselves. In addition, if they fear harassment and abuse, they could consider waiting to come out until they feel safe and/or financially secure.
2. Youth should avoid acting impulsively and should access resources for LGBTQ youth. In some areas this may be joining a youth group at an LGBTQ community center that offers confidentiality or talking to a teacher or counselor advisor for the GSA at school who can ensure confidentiality. For many youth, especially those in rural areas, these options are not available; however, they can call an LGBTQ hotline and search for resources designed for LGBTQ youth on the Internet.

3. Youth can practice coming out with people they trust or with other LGBTQ youth prior to coming out to their families. If LGBTQ role models are known to be at a school or community center, youth can discuss what their coming out experiences were like.
4. Youth should not come out because they feel pressured by someone to do so but only when they are ready.
5. Youth should expect that family members may react at first with shock or challenge them. Knowing what to expect is important, as is providing family members with resources to educate themselves (e.g., PFLAG brochures).

Family

Rejection by parents and other family members because of one's sexual orientation or gender identity is particularly challenging and has been linked to a higher incidence of suicide attempts in sexual minority youth (Haas et al., 2010). Homelessness is also significantly higher in sexual minority youth, as it is estimated that 20%–40% of homeless youth are sexual minorities (Ray, 2006). Anti-gay and highly conservative religious beliefs are also highly correlated with parental rejection. Accordingly, it is an enormous task to help parents, family members, and other adults reconcile religious beliefs and accept and love their child regardless of sexual orientation or gender identity (Diamond et al., 2011). In the case example, Emma's parents were very accepting of Emma, regardless of her sexual orientation. As such, her parents are poised to serve as her advocate in the school environment that has already proven to be less than optimal and potentially hostile.

Haas et al. (2010) recommended the following initiatives to help reduce suicide in sexual minority youth: Develop awareness campaigns and educational programs for the general public that portray positive images of sexual minority youth, specifically target primary care physicians and pediatricians, and interface actively with community and organizational gatekeepers so that they are prepared to be first responders when a parent seeks help or information; build screening programs, hotlines, and other activities that identify at-risk sexual minority youth and direct them to safe and affirmative treatment; and restrict lethal means used for suicide, including guns, and discourage media coverage that glamorizes or normalizes suicide as a solution for challenges in life, even those that seem or are severe (Haas et al., 2010).

In a statewide survey of sixth, ninth, and twelfth graders in Minnesota, Eisenberg and Resnick (2006) found that family connectedness and perceived caring by adults was a significant deterrent to suicidal ideation and attempts at suicide or self-harm. Familial support is crucial, but it certainly doesn't need to be all or nothing. In other words, even lower levels of support, including implicit "tolerance," are better than outright rejecting and ostracizing a child from his or her primary source of support. Adult and extrafamilial support can also be found through peers, school personnel, and other adults and is very powerful in ameliorating the negative effects of rejection should it occur in the family of origin.

Parents also should be aware of the risk factors for children who are bullied and should watch for signs of bullying. According to the U.S. HHS (2013), children who are bullied often have several risk factors:

1. Their peers view them as different in some way. For example, they may look different (e.g., weight, early or late puberty, clothes, accent, and so forth).
2. Their peers view them as being "weak or unable to defend themselves."

329

3. They "are depressed, anxious, or have a low self esteem."
4. They "are less popular than others and have few friends."
5. They "do not get along well with others, [are] seen as annoying or provoking, or antagonize others for attention." (http://www.stopbullying.gov/at-risk/factors/index.html#atrisk)

Obviously, LGBTQ youth are different from the majority of their peers. When families suspect bullying, they need to work with the school to intervene. By keeping an open dialogue and not judging, parents can encourage youth to talk to them if they are being bullied. Parents can begin this dialogue by discussing bullying with youth before they are at risk and by establishing a trusting, nonjudgmental relationship. U.S. HHS (2013) suggested that parents should encourage youth to speak to someone they trust if they are being bullied or know about someone else being bullied and should discuss with them strategies for responding to bullies and for protecting themselves. In addition, parents should watch for signs of depression or anxiety or substance abuse. LGBTQ youth are more likely to commit suicide and/or abuse alcohol or drugs. In addition, they suggested that parents "encourage kids to do what they love," which can increase self-esteem and provide them with an opportunity to make friends with similar interests. Forcing a boy to play football who wants to play a musical instrument or preventing a girl from joining a sports team sends a signal to youth that there is something wrong with them if they do not have the same interests as their parents, siblings, or other boys and girls.

School

According to the 2011 National School Climate Survey conducted by the GLSEN, 80% of sexual minority youth reported being verbally harassed or physically harassed at school in the past year because of their sexual orientation. Over 60% of sexual minority students reported being verbally or physically harassed because of their gender expression or same-sex attraction. Eighty-five percent of sexual minority students heard "gay" used in a negative way or experienced derogatory name calling, such as "dyke," "fag," or "sissy." Sixty percent of sexual minority students reported feeling unsafe at school because of their sexual orientation, and 40% felt unsafe because of their gender expression. Some research has indicated that school personnel are 3 times more likely to challenge comments by students that are racist compared with comments that are homoprejudiced (GLSEN, 2012). These are critical statistics to understand while interfacing with sexual minority

Sidebar 13.4 ■ What Measures Would You Take?

Clearly the principal at Emma's school was unprepared to deal with Emma's feelings about her sexual identity. This unpreparedness could be because she never received training, or perhaps she was unable to see beyond her own homoprejudice and stereotypes. Maybe she was afraid to address the issues more directly because of potential backlash from parents and administration. If you were the principal, school counselor, or teacher, how would you work more effectively with Emma? What measures would you take to address the bullying and harassment? How would you address it with parents? Teachers? Administrators?

■ ■ ■

youth. Counselors cannot be lulled into complacency regarding the real risks that these kids face even as society shifts and changes.

Although these numbers are still daunting, the survey found for the first time both decreased levels of biased language and victimization and increased levels of student access to LGBTQ-related school resources and support; important changes are being made. This positive impact on the school environment was attributed to schools that hosted GSA groups, that had curricula that were not only inclusive but also included positive representations of LGBTQ people and events, and, finally, that had faculty and administrators who were actively supportive of their sexual minority students. These initiatives and climate changes do make a difference and need to be supported and initiated by counseling professionals, who are uniquely positioned to influence social and contextual change.

Antibullying programs are as effective as any other programs designed to reduce harmful behavior as long as the programs are well thought out and articulated; are long term versus "one shot/knee jerk reactions"; are developmentally appropriate; are culturally sensitive; and are specifically designed to support at-risk students, including sexual minority youth. That said, the absolutely crucial key to any harm-reducing program—whether it's antibullying or anti-drugs—is adult and parental involvement. Adults need to understand and acknowledge their own behavior in terms of whether they are actually implicitly or even explicitly promoting the harmful behavior, be it bullying, drug use, or inappropriate sexual behavior. Parents, teachers, and other adults have to honestly answer the question, "How am I contributing to and/or endorsing this type of behavior?" and commit to being a part of the solution, not the problem. And, undeniably, anti-harm programs are more effective when parents are involved and working in collaboration with the school and the community; educators cannot do this on their own. Anti-harm programs are just not as effective without parental buy-in, so parents have to get involved and put aside their personal struggles where they exist in order to create a safe environment for all children.

Community

Communities must continue to develop and build organizations that are safe and affirming of sexual minority youth and their families, who are often struggling and

---

Sidebar 13.5 ■ How Would You Help?

Imagine you are working as a counselor in private practice. The father of a 14-year-old boy makes an appointment with you because he is absolutely distraught. He tells you that his son has shared that he is gay and he wants to take his boyfriend to the junior high prom. He also shares with you that he is very religious, and although he has somewhat come to terms with the idea that his son is gay because he loves him dearly—albeit he is going straight to hell for his perverse proclivities—it is one thing to be gay at home but quite another to be gay in public! The father is at once angry and deeply sad. He sobs, "No one else knows how I feel or what it's like to have a gay child. I feel so alone and punished by God. Why me?"

How would you help your client? How would you help him reconcile his religion with this love for his son? How would you help him access community resources so that he would not feel like he is the only one?

■ ■ ■

need a place to land that provides security and safety as they explore and struggle with what it means to the family when a child comes out as LGBTQ. Needless to say, these programs are more likely to succeed with parental and familial support and involvement; families who have successfully traversed this challenge have a particularly important place at the table to provide guidance and a roadmap to support, acceptance, and ultimately affirmation. But even without parental support, these programs, including mentors and others who can provide affirmative support, can have such a positive influence on the development of sexual minority youth in terms of supplying a place of connection and affirmation. Counselors have unique skills in community organization and promotion of positive social change—even outside the counseling office, in systems such as schools and community centers—and must get involved to lead these kinds of efforts where they do not exist. In the case of Emma, there is an opportunity for the school to play a significant role in the understanding and acceptance of LGBTQ youth. Ideally, the school counselor, staff, and administrators could work together to create educational programs about how important it is to understand and accept differences. At the very least, the focus of these workshops would be that every student gets to go to school in a non-hostile environment, and, at best, the focus would be on fostering an appreciation and acceptance for diversity.

Advocates for Youth (2013) suggested an overall youth development program to serve youth at risk, such as LGBTQ youth and other youth who have little support in their communities. They argued that programs that focus on overall development are needed in addition to those programs that are focused on a specific issue; focusing on overall development will increase youth's motivation to avoid risky behaviors. Although geared for HIV/STD and teen pregnancy prevention groups, the strategies they outlined can apply to other groups focused on specific issues such as substance abuse or suicide. They suggest developing programs that do the following:

1. Focus on the assets and strengths of youth and help youth develop competence in all areas of wellness.
2. "Focus on the needs that young people themselves identity, and consider the multiple factors of young people's lives in developing an intervention" (p. 2).
3. Include youth in designing and implementing the program.
4. Include adults who are committed and treat youth with respect, not judgment.
5. Encourage the involvement of the whole community, and tailor the programs to the youth's culture, race/ethnicity, and socioeconomic background.
6. Seek community partnerships with other groups.

Adaptations for Diversity

Earlier in this chapter, we discussed how the increased depression, suicide rates, substance abuse, and health problems among sexual minority youth can be attributed to minority stress (Meyer, 2003). Sexual minority youth who have other minority statuses (e.g., race, culture, gender, religion) are double or triple minorities (Gonsiorek & Weinrich, 1991). For these minorities, they may face stigmatization because of one of their identities or because of multiple identities. Morales (1989) stated that a major developmental task for ethnic minority sexual minorities is resolving the conflicts between allegiances to two communities and integrating the different identities. In a similar manner, Rosario, Schrimshaw, and Hunter (2004), in their study of the coming out process of sexual minority youth, found that Black and Hispanic youth may have delayed identity integration as compared with White youth. For example, a Hispanic gay youth might face discrimination based on his ethnicity, his sexual orientation, or both. He may face pressure within his community to be heterosexual and believe that he must choose between his Hispanic family and community and the gay community; he may also be unsure if he will be accepted in a gay community that is majority White.

For school personnel, counselors, and allies, it is important to understand how various minority groups view LGBTQ people. For example, Negy and Eisenman (2005) compared college students' attitudes toward sexual minorities and found that African American students had more negative views as compared with White students; however, much of this difference was attributed to the role that churches played for many of the African American students. In a study by Diaz, Ayala, Bein, Henne, and Marin (2001), a majority of Latinos felt that they had to hide their sexual orientation from their families. Many Latinos have traditionally had a strong connection to the Catholic Church, which views homosexuality as sinful. As a consequence, some Latino youth who are Catholic may fear coming out because of having to face a choice between their religious identity and their sexual orientation or gender identity. Religion is obviously a factor for many White sexual minority youth who attend conservative Christian churches and are forced to choose between their religious and sexual minority identities. However, ethnic minority youth may have also been stigmatized because of their race or ethnicity and religion.

Consequently, as parents, school personnel, and community allies develop prevention and intervention programs, it is important to consider the intersections of sexual orientation identity, gender identity, racial/ethnic identity, and religious identity. It is also important to remember that according to Chickering and Reisser (1993), an overall identity includes not only sexual orientation and gender identities, but also physical appearance, ethnicity, social roles, and self-esteem. A sexual minority youth is more than his or her sexual orientation or gender identity; the youth is also developing these other aspects of his or her overall identity.

Summary

Sexual minority youth of today come out in a world that is more accepting of sexual minorities than ever before. They have role models on television and the Internet to emulate and celebrities such as Lady Gaga advocating for them through music and char-

---

Sidebar 13.6 ■ What Should You Do?

Imagine that you are a school counselor and an African American eighth-grade boy asks to talk to you. He says that he heard from another eighth grader that it is safe to talk to you. He tells you that he wonders if he might be gay, and he's not sure what he should do. His parents and he attend a church where the minister has been telling the congregation that it is a sin to be gay. He heard his father tell his mother that if he found out one of his children were gay, he would throw them out of the house. As this boy tells you his story, he looks down at the floor and speaks in a low, shaky voice. You think that he is likely depressed. What should you do?

■ ■ ■

ity organizations. Nevertheless, sexual minority youth still come out in a society that is conflicted about sexual orientation and gender diversity. LGBTQ youth in rural areas are more likely to face prejudice and discrimination than their counterparts in urban areas. Thus, there is still work to do to provide a world for sexual minority youth that is accepting and nurturing. By promoting prevention and intervention at all levels, we can continue working toward a day when it is not risky to be a sexual minority youth.

Useful Websites

Association for Lesbian, Gay, Bisexual & Transgender Issues in Counseling
    http://www.algbtic.org/
Gay, Lesbian, and Straight Education Network
    http://www.glsen.org
Gay–Straight Alliance (GSA) Network
    http://www.gsanetwork.org
Gender Spectrum
    http://www.transyouth.com
Human Rights Campaign
    http://www.hrc.org/resources
It Gets Better Project
    http://www.itgetsbetter.org
National Gay and Lesbian Task Force
    http://www.ngltf.org
Parents, Families, and Friends of Lesbians and Gays
    http://www.pflag.org/
Teaching Tolerance
    http://www.tolerance.org
The Trevor Project
    http:// www.thetrevorproject.com
U.S. Department of Health & Human Services, Stopbullying.gov
    http://www.stopbullying.gov/

References

Advocates for Youth. (2013). *Youth development: Strengthening prevention strategies.* Retrieved from http://www.advocatesforyouth.org/storage/advfy/documents/ythdevelop.pdf

Almeida, J., Johnson, R. M., Corliss, H. L., Molnar, B. E., & Azrael, D. (2009). Emotional distress among LGBT youth: The influence of perceived discrimination based on sexual orientation. *Journal of Youth and Adolescence, 38,* 1001–1014.

American Psychiatric Association. (2000). *Diagnostic and statistical manual of mental disorders* (4th ed., text rev.). Washington, DC: Author.

Bouris, A., Guilamo-Ramos, P. A., Shiu, C., Loosier, P. S., Dittus, P., Gloppen, K., & Waldmiller, J. M. (2010). A systematic review of parental influences on the health and well-being of lesbian, gay, and bisexual youth: Time for a new public health research and practice agenda. *Journal of Primary Prevention, 31,* 273–309.

Cass, V. C. (1979). Homosexual identity formation. A theoretical model. *Journal of Homosexuality, 4,* 219–235.

Centers for Disease Control and Prevention. (2011). *Sexual identity, sex of sexual contacts, and health risk-behaviors among students in grades 9–12.* Retrieved from http://www.cdc.gov/mmwr/pdf/ss/ss60e0606.pdf

Chickering, A. W., & Reisser, L. (1993). *Education and identity.* San Francisco, CA: Jossey-Bass.

Clinton, H. (1996). *It takes a village: And other lessons children teach us.* New York, NY: Simon & Schuster.

Coleman, E. (1981/1982). Developmental stages of the coming out process. *Journal of Homosexuality, 7,* 31–43.

Coleman, E. (1990). Toward a synthetic understanding of sexual orientation. In D. P. McWhirter, S. A. Sanders, & J. M. Reinisch (Eds.), *Homosexuality/heterosexuality: Concepts of sexual orientation* (pp. 267–276). New York, NY: Oxford University.

Diamond, G. M., Shilo, G., Jurgenson, E., D'Augelli, A., Samarova, V., & White, K. (2011). How depressed and suicidal sexual minority adolescents understand the causes of their distress. *Journal of Gay and Lesbian Mental Health, 15,* 130–151.

Diaz, R. M., Ayala, G., Bein, E., Henne, J., & Marin, B. V. (2001). The impact of homophobia, poverty, and racism on the mental health of gay and bisexual Latino men: Findings from 3 U.S. cities. *American Journal of Public Health, 91,* 927–932.

Durso, L. E., & Gates, G. J. (2012). *Serving our youth: Findings from a national survey of service providers working with lesbian, gay, bisexual, and transgender youth who are homeless or at risk of becoming homeless.* Los Angeles, CA: The Williams Institute with True Colors Fund and The Palette Fund.

Eisenberg, M. E., & Resnick, M. D. (2006). Suicidality among gay, lesbian and bisexual youth: The role of protective factors. *Journal of Adolescent Health, 39,* 662–668.

Fedewa, A. L., & Ahn, S. (2011). The effects of bullying and peer victimization on sexual minority and heterosexual youth: A quantitative meta-analysis of the literature. *Journal of GLBT Family Studies, 7,* 398–418.

Gay, Lesbian, & Straight Education Network. (2003). *Coming out: A guide to youth and their allies.* Retrieved from http://www.glsen.org/cgi-bin/iowa/all/news/record/1290.html

Gay, Lesbian, & Straight Education Network. (2010). *2010 national school climate survey.* Retrieved from http://www.glsen.org/cgi-bin/iowa/all/news/record/2624.html

Gay, Lesbian, & Straight Education Network. (2011). *2011 national school climate survey: LGBT youth face pervasive, but decreasing levels of harassment.* Retrieved from http://www.glsen.org/cgi-bin/iowa/all/library/record/2897.html?state=research&type=research

Gay, Lesbian, & Straight Education Network. (2012). *Strengths & silences: The experiences of lesbian, gay, bisexual and transgender students in rural and small town schools.* Retrieved from http://www.glsen.org/cgi-bin/iowa/all/library/record/2916.html?state=research&type=research

Gonsiorek, J., & Weinrich, J. (1991). *Homosexuality: Research implications for public policy.* Newbury Park, CA: Sage.

Haas, A. P., Eliason, M., Mays, V. M., Mathy, R. M., Cochran, S. D., D'Augelli, A. R., . . . Clayton, P. J. (2010). Suicide and suicide risk in lesbian, gay, bisexual, and transgender populations: Review and recommendations. *Journal of Homosexuality, 58,* 10–51.

Logan, C. R. (1996). Homophobia? No, homoprejudice. *Journal of Homosexuality, 31,* 31–53.

Marszalek, J. F., Dunn, M. S., & Cashwell, C. S. (2002). The relationship between gay and lesbian identity development and psychological adjustment. *"Q": The Journal of the Association of Gay, Lesbian, and Bisexual Issues in Counseling, 2.* Retrieved from http://www.aglbic.org/Q/Vol2Num1/

Marszalek, J. F., & Pope, M. (2008). Gay male identity development. In K. L. Kraus (Ed.), *Lifespan development theories in action: A case study approach for counseling professions* (pp. 294–327). Boston, MA: Lahaska Press.

Meyer, I. (2003). Prejudice, social stress, and mental health in lesbian, gay, and bisexual populations: Conceptual issues and research evidence. *Psychological Bulletin, 129,* 674–697.

Miranda, H. L., & Storms, M. (1989). Psychological adjustment of lesbians and gay men. *Journal of Counseling & Development, 68,* 41–45.

Morales, E. S. (1989). Ethnic minority families and minority gays and lesbians. *Journal of Homosexuality, 17,* 217–239.

National Gay and Lesbian Task Force. (2012). *State nondiscrimination laws in the U.S.* Retrieved from http://www.ngltf.org/downloads/reports/issue_maps/non_discrimination_1_12_color.pdf

Negy, C., & Eisenman, R. (2005). A comparison of African-American and White college students' affective and attitudinal reactions to lesbian, gay, and bisexual individuals: An exploratory study. *Journal of Sex Research, 42,* 291–298. doi:10.1080/00224490509552284

Obama, B. H. (2013). *Inaugural address* [Video webcast]. Retrieved from http://www.whitehouse.gov/the-press-office/president-barack-obamas-inaugural-address

Ray, N. (2006). *Lesbian, gay, bisexual and transgender youth: An epidemic of homelessness.* New York, NY: National Gay and Lesbian Task Force Policy Institute and the National Coalition for the Homeless.

Rosario, M., Schrimshaw, E. W., & Hunter, J. (2004). Cultural diversity and ethnic minority *Psychology, 10,* 215–228. doi:10.1037/1099-9809.10.3.215

Ryan, C. (2009). *Supportive families, healthy children: Helping families with lesbian, gay, bisexual & transgender children.* Retrieved from http://familyproject.sfsu.edu/files/English_Final_Print_Version_Last.pdf

Ryan, C., Huebner, D., Diaz, R. M., & Sanchez, J. (2009). Family rejection as a predictor of negative health outcomes in White and Latino lesbian, gay and bisexual young adults. *Pediatrics, 123,* 346–352.

Ryan, C., Russell, S., Huebner, D., Diaz, R., & Sanchez, J. (2010). Family acceptance in adolescence and the health of LGBT young adults. *Journal of Child and Adolescent Psychiatric Nursing, 23,* 205–213.

Shively, M. G., & DeCecco, J. P. (1993). Components of sexual identity. In L. D. Garnets & D. C. Kimmel (Eds.). *Psychological perspectives on lesbian and gay male experiences* (pp. 80–88). New York, NY: Columbia.

Trevor Project. (2013). *The Trevor Project programs.* Retrieved from http://www.thetrevorproject.org/Programs

Troiden, R. R. (1984). Self, self-concept, identity, and homosexual identity: Constructs in need of definition and differentiation. *Journal of Homosexuality, 10,* 97–109.

USA Today/Gallup Poll. (2012). *USA's shifting attitudes toward gay men and lesbians.* Retrieved from http://www.usatoday.com/story/news/politics/2012/12/05/poll-from-gay-marriage-to-adoption-attitudes-changing-fast/1748873/

U.S. Department of Health and Human Services. (2013). *Prevention at school.* Retrieved from http://www.stopbullying.gov/prevention/at-school/index.html

Willoughby, B. L. B., Doty, N. D., & Malik, N. M. (2010). Victimization, family rejection, and outcomes of gay, lesbian, and bisexual young people: The role of negative GLB identity. *Journal of GLBT Family Studies, 6,* 403–424.

Chapter 14

Death in the Classroom: Violence in Schools

Abbé Finn

On the morning of December 12, 2012, 20 children kissed their parents good-bye and went off to Sandy Hook Elementary School. By 9:40 a.m., they were dead. Although school rampage killings like this are rare (Rocque, 2012), the consequences are so horrible that when they happen time seems to stand still and the nation mourns. Even the students and faculty who survive are affected, perhaps forever (Hammond, 2009; Hughes et al., 2011). For a certain amount of time, attention is focused on the killer, and the press looks for reasonable motives and asks how this could have been prevented (Moore, Petrie, Braga, McLaughlin, 2003).

This chapter focuses on research into school violence and rampage (mass) killings. Psychological, sociocultural, and behavioral characteristics of school shooters are examined. School violence prevention and interventions are explored. Finally, the framework and composition of threat assessment teams are introduced. This chapter was written with the goal of increasing awareness and training professionals to recognize warning signs, assess students for risk of harming others, and prevent school violence.

Before the school shootings in the last half of the 1990s, there was little research conducted on the issue of school rampage shootings and school violence prevention (Furlong, Morrison, Skiba, & Cornell, 2004; Rocque, 2012). After the Columbine massacre in 1999, school safety concerns were catapulted onto the front pages and into the minds of most Americans. For example, before 1992 there were only 21 references in PsycINFO under the search topic "school violence," compared with 513 from 1999 to 2006. The outbreak of school shootings shined the light on the problem of youth violence. In the 10 years from 1992 to 2002, 234 children were killed in and around American schools (Centers for Disease Control and Prevention [CDC], 2006). Since 1996, there have been 60 school shooting incidents resulting in hundreds of deaths (Rocque, 2012). Many intervention programs were rushed into place in an effort to "do something" about the problem (Borum, Cornell, Modzeleski, & Jimerson, 2010; Furlong, Morrison, et al., 2004). Years later, the evaluative process was instituted to measure which programs were most helpful and which were ineffective.

Violence is a complex pattern of behaviors that can be understood by breaking down the behavior by indicators. These indicators are assessed from many sources, including the Youth Risk Surveillance Survey (YRSS), which collects data from high school students in the United States. This survey is funded by the CDC (2012). One of the indicators for future violence is the admission of carrying weapons. The YRSS (CDC, 2012) showed that in the 30 days prior to the survey, 16.6% of students carried a weapon at least one day. The rate is not equally distributed among males and females. The rate for males was 25.9%, and it was 6.8% for females. The prevalence rate decreased from 1991 to 1999 from 26.15% to 17.3%, but it has remained virtually unchanged since then (Eaton et al., 2012). In addition, the death rate at schools has remained constant since 2003, and 7.3% of students reported that they had been threatened or injured by weapons at school (Eaton et al., 2012). During the academic years from 1992–1993 to 1998–1999, there were approximately 30 murders on campus each academic year. Many of these were gang related and crimes of opportunity because of access to the victim at school (Borum et al., 2010).

In the 2009–2010 academic year there were 17 homicides (CDC, 2012). However, because murders at schools occur rarely, a single event like the rampage killings at Sandy Hook Elementary School can greatly affect the statistic; thus, yearly averages are not meaningful indicators of school violence.

The trend toward a decrease in the murder rate may reflect the impact of national policies developed to address the causes of school violence (Hong, Cho, Allen-Meares, & Espelage, 2011). Many intervention programs have been implemented, and some have been shown to be effective whereas others have not (U.S. Department of Health and Human Services [USDHHS], 2001a). Many were implemented without scientific investigation or any demonstration of efficacy (Elliott, 1998; Skiba & Knesting, 2002), and, contrary to logic, some interventions have been shown to increase the rate of violence (Derzon, 2006; Mendel, 2000).

Issues contributing to the problem of youth violence are multidimensional and caused by many factors working together (Eaton et al., 2012; Herrenkohl et al., 2000; USDHHS, 2001a). Some of these factors are explored in this chapter. *Violence* is defined as any action or threat of action that would result in intimidation, coercion, physical harm, personal injury, or death. The topic is examined from the perspective of the various types of prevention and intervention programs, with special attention paid to describe programs that have been evaluated and that demonstrate effectiveness.

The alarming rate of violence and the terrible consequences have raised national awareness and concern, which has resulted in public demand for the development and implementation of prevention and intervention programs to reduce the bloodshed (Borum et al., 2010; Furlong, Sharkey, Bates, & Smith, 2004). Interventions include the following: increased school security, zero tolerance policies, psychosocial profiling, school climate reform, social skills training, peer mediation programs, parent training, and the creation of threat assessment teams. To be effective, the prevention and intervention programs need to be based on the theoretical causes of youth violent behavior and must be evidence based (Borum et al., 2010).

Problem Definition

The decade from 1983 to 1993 marked a period described as a "violence epidemic" (Cook & Laub, 1998). No social class, neighborhood, or community in the United States was immune to the widespread consequences. Lasting physical and emotional scars were left on individuals, families, schools, and communities. Many children were killed or maimed during this time period (USDHHS, 2001a). Twenty-five percent of inner-city youth have been victims of or witnesses to extreme forms of violence. Community hostilities and violence often bleed into the school environment (Mulvey & Cauffman, 2001). This fact explains why many prevention and intervention programs coordinate their efforts across the school and community domains.

During this same period, the rate of violent crime committed by children and adolescents age 18 and younger rose by 1,000%. It has been estimated that violence costs the United States $508 billion a year: $90 billion is spent on the criminal justice system, $65 billion on security, $5 billion on the treatment of victims, $170 billion on lost productivity, and $178 billion in expenses to the victims (Illinois Center for Violence Prevention, 1998). It is estimated that children under the age of 20 committed one third of the murders in the United States. Among African American adolescent males, murder was the second leading cause of death (Center to Prevent Handgun Violence, 1990; James & Gilliland, 2001). Between 1985 and 1994 the rate of incarceration and arrest increased by 67% for young males and by 125% for young females (Dahlberg, 1998). Suicide, another extreme form of violence, was the third leading cause of death (Flannery, Singer, & Wester, 2001). Adolescent suicide and murder are highly correlated. Vossekuil, Reddy, Fein, Borum, and Modzeleski (2000) studied the student assailants in 37 school shootings and found that approximately 75% of the perpetrators had threatened or attempted suicide prior to committing the school shootings. Most school shooters plan to die on a battlefield of their own creation. Some have begged others to shoot them.

Schools, usually perceived as safe havens from violence, became part of the battleground. From the 1991–1992 to the 2001–2002 academic year, 92% of high schools and 87% of middle schools reported at least one incidence of violence each year. The violent incidents were unequally distributed, with 16% of the schools reporting 75% of the crime. Twenty percent of schools reported at least one serious violent incident. These incidents included rape, sexual assault, physical attack with and without a weapon, murder, and suicide. There were 60,719 incidents reported in the 2000 School Survey on Crime and Safety (National Center for Education Statistics, 2003). During the 1986–1987 academic year, the school crime report from the School Safety Council (1989) indicated that 3 million faculty, staff, students, and visitors were victims of crime in U.S. schools. From 1986 to 1990, 71 people were killed at U.S. schools; of these, 65 were students and 6 were employees. An additional 242 were held hostage at gunpoint, and 201 were seriously wounded (Center to Prevent Handgun Violence, 1990). For every hour that school was in session in the United States, 900 teachers were threatened, and approximately 40 teachers and more than 2,000 students were physically assaulted (Futrell, 1996; Shafii & Shafii, 2001). In a 1996 survey, 47% of teens responded that they thought violence was increasing in schools, with 10% reporting that they feared a classmate would shoot them. From February 1997 to April 1999, there were eight incidents of mass school shootings with at least 32 deaths (Chandras, 1999; Gibbs & Roche, 1999; King & Murr, 1998). More recently, between July 1, 2008, and June 1, 2009, there were 15 homicides and 7 suicides. During this same period, 10% of teachers were threatened by students and 6% of elementary teachers were attacked by students (Simone, Zhang, Truman, & Snyder, 2010). In addition, 2.2% of educators in secondary schools and 0.9% of elementary school teachers were victims of theft or violent crime (DeVoe, Peter, Noonan, Snyder, & Baum, 2005). According to the U.S. Department of Justice, Bureau of Statistics (2010), during the 2007–2008 academic year, 85% of public schools reported crimes, equaling approximately 2.0 million crimes. During this same period, 75% of schools in the United States experienced some type of violent event. A smaller portion (17%) experienced severe violence, including murder, rape, or other forms of sexual assault (Simone et al., 2010). Twenty-five percent of these attacks went unreported to the authorities. Other crimes committed at schools included possession of alcohol or other illegal drugs (27%), sale and distribution of drugs (12%), possession of a knife (43%), and possession of a firearm or explosive device (6%; U.S. Department of Education, 2004).

Most of the violence occurring in schools was not as extreme as school rampage shootings, and the majority of school violence occurs in undersupervised areas (Astor, Mayer, & Behre, 1999). Fearing victimization, 5% of the surveyed students reported that they were too intimidated to use the school restrooms and avoided particular hallways, locker rooms, and stairwells as well as school activities (DeVoe et al., 2005). This percentage is a decrease from 9% in 1998 (Elliott, Hamburg, & Williams, 1998).

Fortunately, there has been a slight but steady decline in violent crime among adolescents since this violence epidemic. However, the Report of the Surgeon General (USDHHS, 2001b) cautioned against complaisance. Although the rate of arrests of youthful offenders has declined, confidential self-reports indicate that the rate of potentially lethal acts of violence has remained unchanged.

Despite the decline in violence, the rate of arrests is still 70% higher than it was before 1983 (USDHHS, 2001b), and the number of mass murders or suicide paired with homicide at schools has increased, averaging five per year from 1994 to 1999 (USDHHS, 2001a). According to the National Center for Education Statistics and the U.S. Department of Justice, Bureau of Justice Statistics (2010), 8% of students reported they were victims of crime at school, and 5.4% reported carrying weapons on school property within the previous 30 days one or more times. These statistics continue to be a concern for schools and communities because these statistics mean that in a school of 2,000 students, 108 students (on one or more occasions) carried weapons to school during each month (Eaton et al., 2012). Therefore, on any given day there could be several students at school carrying weapons (Hermann & Finn, 2002). There is an erroneous belief that rampage killings are a recent phenomenon. In truth, the deadliest killing occurred in 1927 when Andrew Kehoe detonated bombs at the Bath Consolidated School, killing 44 people, including 38 school children. What has changed is the increased frequency of the rampage events and the number of multiple deaths (see Table 14.1). The data in Table 14.1

Sidebar 14.1 ■ Violence in Your Lifetime

On the basis of the statistics presented in the preceding pages, it is easy to see that violence in schools is not a new phenomenon, nor is it decreasing. As you think back to your days as an elementary or secondary student, are you able to identify situations that fit the examples set forth in this chapter? What was your reaction? What was the school's response? What measures were taken to eliminate the violent behaviors, and what was the fallout within and outside the school environment?

■ ■ ■

TABLE 14.1

Frequency Table for Number of School/College Rampage Killings in the United States by Decade

Variable	1920s	1930s	1940s	1950s	1960s	1970s	1980s	1990s	2000s	2010–2013
Number of rampage killings	1	2	1	1	3	3	3	14	7	8
Number killed	44	5	5	3	22	12	6	52	56	51

were collected from incidents where two or more people were killed at a K–12 school or a college/university. The evidence indicates an increase in rampage killings in American schools and colleges in the decades of the 1990s and 2000s as well as from 2010 to 2012. In the first 2 years of the 2010s, there have already been eight mass killings with 51 deaths. According to *USA Today* (Hoyer & Heath, 2012), on average there is a mass killing somewhere in America once every 2 weeks.

Students, educational professionals, parents, and community leaders are very concerned with school safety and are greatly distressed with the outbreak of youth violence. These worries translate to a national average of approximately 6% of students refusing to attend school on at least 1 day during the previous 30 days because of feeling unsafe while going to or from school or while at school (CDC, 2012). Most prevention programs follow the public health prevention model of primary, secondary, or tertiary prevention. Primary prevention programs identify characteristics that increase the risk of the public health problem and intervene with large heterogeneous groups through education or behavioral change. For example, with underage alcohol abuse, teens are encouraged through public service announcements not to drink and drive. Secondary prevention programs identify individuals or groups of people at risk for the specific problem and target them for intervention. An example of secondary prevention would be targeting teens who use drugs to receive counseling. Tertiary prevention programs attempt to limit the reoccurrence of a problem or further deterioration of people exhibiting symptoms of a public health problem (Lawler, 2000). A methadone clinic is an example of a tertiary or harm reduction program.

Case Study[1]

The day began at Thurston High in a deceptively normal way. Some students were arriving in a rush fearing they would be late, others were early and eating their breakfast while finishing their homework. Only the shooter had a premonition of the disaster that was about to strike. At 7:50 a.m. on May 21, 1998, 15-year-old Kip Kinkle arrived at school armed with a .22-caliber semiautomatic rifle concealed in the folds of his trench coat, two pistols, and a hunting knife tucked into the waistband of his pants. On his way down the hall, he encountered a student who had teased him for public display of affection at school. Without breaking stride Kip shot him in the head. Seconds later Kip passed another student, one he didn't even know, and shot him in the face. Moments before the first period bell rang, Kip strode

---

[1]This case study is drawn from a true case story. All of the information was drawn from publicly available news stories and legal documents.

into the cafeteria filled with approximately 400 students. Striding from the doorway he opened fire, emptying the rifle's 50-round clip. He shot into the crowd but sometimes fired point blank at specific students. When the chamber was empty, four boys tackled Kip to the ground in an attempt to halt the carnage. Kip continued to struggle and was able to reach one of his concealed handguns and shot several of the children who were restraining him. One of the boys was shot in the chest and had a collapsed lung. While on the ground, Kip begged the other students to shoot him. Later, the students, who had moments before been his targeted victims, said that shooting Kip had never crossed their minds even though they were holding Kip's guns. By the end of the day, Kip had killed 4 people and injured 20.

After his arrest, Kip was handcuffed and placed in an interrogation room. While in the cell he wriggled out of the handcuffs, removed a knife he had taped to his leg, and attacked a police officer. The officer escaped injury by subduing Kip with pepper spray. During the attack, Kip begged the officer to shoot him.

The killing spree had actually begun the afternoon before when Kip killed his father and then waited to ambush and kill his mother. Earlier that day, Kip had been arrested for buying a stolen gun and suspended from school for storing it in his locker. He was detained by police and released to his father's custody.

In the aftermath of these horrible events, people wondered how this could happen in a sleepy, all-American small town like Springfield, Oregon. However, upon closer examination, Kip gave many signals that he was in serious trouble.

Physically, Kip was small, standing 5 feet 5 inches, weighing 125 pounds, with red hair and freckles. He was emotionally immature, socially isolated, targeted for teasing by the bigger boys, and scholastically challenged. Both of his parents were very respected educators, and his older sister was an excellent student. In contrast, Kip struggled in school. Even though his parents were loving and caring, there was not a good fit between Kip and his family. They were intellectual and athletic, whereas he was a poor student who was awkward and clumsy. Kip was diagnosed with learning disabilities and was also suffering from depression. For a short time, he was treated by a psychologist and had been prescribed antidepressants, which he stopped taking. Adding to his depression, Kip had recently endured the breakup of a romantic relationship. After the shootings, Kip disclosed that he was hearing voices. Unfortunately, he failed to report to his psychologist that he was having auditory hallucinations. He had developed a fascination with the suicide pact in *Romeo and Juliet*. When the police arrived at his home to investigate his confessed murder of his parents, the soundtrack was blasting from Kip's stereo.

After the fact, students came forward with other information foreshadowing Kip's future violence. For example, Kip had reportedly bragged about skinning a live cat and also about making bombs. He made bombs and exploded them in an abandoned stone quarry. After the killings, police discovered 20 live bombs set to go off in his home. Some were large enough to cause collateral damage to the neighborhood, and their discovery resulted in the evacuation of 15 nearby houses. Kip nurtured a deep fascination with weapons and explosives. He had persuaded his parents to buy him several guns. Over the years he acquired an arsenal, which he kept hidden in the attic over his bedroom. On May 20th, Kip's father had brought him home from jail and told him that he was confiscating all of his guns. Kip later reported to the police that he felt compelled to kill his parents to spare them the shame he brought to the family (Dowling & Johnson, 1998; Kesey, 1998; Sullivan, 1998).

Sidebar 14.2 ■ Checking for Common Denominators

Using the case of Kip as a starting point, do you see any similarity between Kip's behaviors in Springfield, Oregon, and other school rampage shootings in locations such as Littleton, Colorado; Moses Lake, Washington; or Newtown, Connecticut? What do you see as the common denominators in these and other examples of rampage shootings?

■ ■ ■

Approaches to Prevention

Effective violence prevention programs share several common characteristics. Nine elements have been identified as necessary for programs to work: (a) clear policies; (b) skills training; (c) comprehensive multimodal approaches; (d) coordination among programs within and outside of the school; (e) changes to the physical plant; (f) at least 10 to 20 sessions; (g) training for the entire school staff, parents, and community; (h) multiple teaching methods; and (i) a sensitivity to the school and community culture (Henry, Farrell, & the Multisite Violence Prevention Project, 2004; Lawler, 2000). These elements were endorsed by Nation et al. (2003), with the addition of theory-driven approaches and outcome evaluation.

The first necessary component of an effective prevention or intervention program is a clear and consistent school policy. Schools should promote peaceful resolution to problems and discourage violence. The teachers, coaches, administrators, parents, and community members should be in agreement on the value of peaceful resolutions to problems. The second necessary component for the program is skills training for students, faculty, and parents. The skills training curriculum should include anger management, conflict resolution, how to take the social perspective of others, problem solving, peer negotiations, and active listening skills. Part of the peer negotiations training includes ways to resist peer pressure and techniques for making new friends. The third characteristic of successful programs is that they are comprehensive, integrated, and multimodal. They involve the community leaders, law enforcement, school personnel, and members of the press. A consistent message of peaceful resolution and antiviolence is encouraged and is infused into all forms of communication.

The fourth element is the coordination of all of the prevention programs. For example, the drug abuse prevention program is coordinated with the violence prevention program that is in concordance with the suicide prevention program and the teen pregnancy program. All share common elements of decision-making skills, peer refusal skills, social competency, and self-esteem. These skills are infused into the curriculum for subjects such as social sciences, health, physical science, and English composition. When learning is reinforced across the curriculum, more of the information is retained, and it is more likely to become part of students' daily lives. The fifth element concerns the physical design and administrative policies of the school. In effect, an assessment is made regarding security risks that are present in the school and these are remedied. For example, fences might be built around the school to control the access to school grounds, and outdoor lighting might be installed to improve the security for people attending school functions after dark. Administrative policy decisions are made to reduce congestion and increase adult supervision. Another example of administrative policy is the decision to require school uniforms to reduce the showing of gang colors, thereby reducing the influence of gangs at school. The sixth characteristic of programs that work is the amount of exposure that students have to the training program. Students need to have between 10 and 20 sessions the first year followed by repeated exposures (5 to 10 sessions) in the following years (Lawler, 2000). The more severe the problems and the greater the students' deficits, the more exposure they will require (Nation et al., 2003). Schools that have a high rate of new admissions to the school should include all new students in the prevention program in their first year.

The seventh characteristic involves training for the teachers, students, parents, and community. The program should begin with teacher and administrative in-service training before school starts in the early fall to set the stage for the entire year. Key student leaders should be identified and trained in the summer, with the rest of the student population exposed to the program as soon as school begins. The program should be integrated into the curriculum across all grades. The normative education should begin in kindergarten and continue throughout the entire school career.

The eighth characteristic of an effective program concerns a multimodal approach to learning. The students are exposed to the curriculum through a variety of teaching approaches, including role-plays, literature, quizzes, discussions, group projects, and current events. The final element necessary for an effective program is having programs and intervention procedures that are culturally sensitive to the needs of the school and community. All methods and principles of the program must be consistent with the ethnic and cultural makeup of the school and community (Lawler, 2000). Including the input of community and school members during the design phase of the program can ensure cultural sensitivity.

Daniels et al. (2010) conducted a qualitative study investigating the most important factors when intervening in planned school rampage shootings. Their outcomes are consistent with the information given above. Specifically, they discovered the following common elements among schools that foiled school rampage plots: a collaborative climate; effective crisis planning preparedness; training among students, personnel, and community members; and prevention programs, such as bullying prevention programs and policies. A strong relationship and shared trust between students, staff, and community members increases the likelihood that plans for mayhem will be disclosed to authorities and the violence will be prevented. Breaking the code of silence has been an important factor in the intervention and prevention of school violence.

Many of the effective youth violence prevention programs are shown to be cost beneficial. They can save taxpayers from the expenses of the criminal justice system, medical care of crime victims, social service costs for children supported while the parents are incarcerated, and increased work productivity of people who would otherwise spend their lives in jail (USDHHS, 2001b). The youth violence prevention programs that targeted specific populations of youthful offenders were most cost effective. These are secondary prevention programs because they target the people who are most likely to offend again and who come under the supervision of the legal system (Washington State Institute for Public Policy, 1999). Some of the prevention programs reduce violence through indirect means by preventing some of the conditions such as child abuse known to give rise to violence later on. The discussion of prevention programs is organized by their emphasis: the individual, family, school, and community levels.

Sidebar 14.3 ■ Common Elements of Violence Prevention

Of the nine common elements of effective violence prevention programs mentioned previously, which do you feel will have the greatest impact in reducing violence in the schools? Which would have the least? Given limited budgetary resources, if you were in charge of a program, which of the nine elements would you emphasize and why?

■ ■ ■

Individual

Psychosocial profiling is the most controversial individual youth violence prevention strategy. The controversy arises because although most youthful violent perpetrators fit some of the profile, many more will fit the profile but never become violent (Furlong, Bates, & Smith, 2001; Furlong, Sharkey, et al., 2004; Mulvey & Cauffman, 2001). Relying on the psychosocial profiles alone would result in many young people being falsely labeled as violent who would never commit a violent act (Vossekuil, Reddy, & Fein, 2001). A report by the Federal Bureau of Investigation (FBI) cautioned against an overreliance on profiling because there are no dependable profiles or distinguishing characteristics that reliably discriminate between people who commit violence and those who do not (O'Toole & the Critical Incident Response Group, 2000; USDHHS, 2001a). Consequently, in the worst case scenario, overreliance on a checklist of characteristics can overlook some violent youth if the checklist is too accurate or falsely identify some youth as dangerous who are not if the checklist is too sensitive (Baily, 2001; Finn & Remley, 2002). Instead, they recommend using threat assessment teams. The construction and theory behind threat assessment teams are described later in this chapter.

On the side of the debate favoring profiling, violent youth and school rampage killers share some common characteristics. For example, they usually are White, male, and middle class (Kimmel, 2008; Kimmel & Mahler, 2003), and most attacks take place in suburban or rural settings (Dejong, Epstein, & Hart, 2003; Luke, 2008; Rocque, 2012). To overlook psychosocial profiling as one of many tools to prevent violence may increase the risk of harm by ignoring what is known about violent students. Many educators fear that ignoring warning signs outlined by the psychosocial profile increases the school's liability (Lumsden, 2000; Williams, 2011). Theoretically, the greater the number of severe characteristics the youth presents, the higher the likelihood for violence (Bernes & Bardick, 2007; Finn & Remley, 2002; USDHHS, 2001b). The best use of psychosocial profiling is in identifying students who need counseling or some other form of supportive intervention (Baily, 2001; Finn & Remley, 2002; Hermann & Finn, 2002). It is hoped that if students get the appropriate intervention in a timely fashion, violence can be averted. Dwyer, Osher, and Warger (1998) identified early warning signs.

The following characteristics describe the perpetrators of the rampage school shootings. Almost all of the shooters were Euro-American males. The students who perpetrated the most severe acts of violence at schools planned them at least 2 weeks in advance. They had multiple reasons for their attacks and believed that they were justified in their actions. Seventy-five percent of the attackers held grievances against students, teachers, or administrators. They could not keep their violent plans to themselves and told others. Among the school shooters, 75% told friends or classmates. One school shooting perpetrator told a total of 24 acquaintances (Vossekuil et al., 2001). Certainly, the majority of people making threats never carry them out; however, most people who harm others have made threatening remarks. Some make clearly threatening statements listing time, place, targeted victims, and choice of weapons. For example, the shooters at Columbine presented a video in their media arts class describing their plan of attack. They also threatened and indeed shot another student they had specifically named on their Internet website (Gibbs & Roche, 1999). One of the shooters also posted the following on his website: "God I can't wait till I kill you people, Ill [*sic*] just go to some downtown area in some big ass city and blow up and shoot everything I can" (Immelman, 1999). In other cases, the students make obscure statements and threats through poetry, artwork, or journal writing (Dwyer et al., 1998).

Students who commit the most violent crimes show a fascination with weapons and ultraviolent films, video games, and music (Dwyer et al., 1998). Sometimes they mimic the dress, posture, and behavior of main characters from the films. The school shooters at Moses Lake, Oregon, and Littleton, Colorado, wore trench coats, modeling their clothing after antagonists in their favorite movies.

Violent youth are socially withdrawn or belong to the socially rejected, anti-social group (Borduin & Schaeffer, 1998; Kashani, Jones, Bumby, & Thomas, 1999; USDHHS, 2001a). Many also show symptoms of severe psychiatric disorders (Dwyer et al., 1998), with some hearing voices commanding them to commit the violent crimes. For example, the school shooters from Pearl, Mississippi, and Springfield, Oregon, had hallucinations. Both began their killing spree by shooting their parent(s). Many violent young people did not receive the appropriate level of psychiatric treatment or stopped taking their medication on purpose to increase their level of violence (James & Gilliland, 2001). Many engaged in angry outbursts at school and other public places or assaulted others with little provocation (Vossekuil et al., 2001), with the level of violence escalating rapidly.

Revenge was a common motive for the school shootings (Vossekuil et al., 2001). The perpetrators expressed a belief that their actions were justified because of previous histories of having been bullied by other students (Ross, 1996) or having had a failed romance. The shooters in Jonesboro, Arkansas; Pearl, Mississippi; and Springfield, Oregon, specifically targeted the girls they believed had wronged them.

There are several ways to classify the factors associated with youth violence. The Surgeon General report categorized the youth violence risk factors according to the size of the effect on the statistical outcome (USDHHS, 2001a). This research showed that a history of criminal offenses, substance abuse, weak social connections, antisocial delinquent peers, and belonging to a gang had the largest statistical impact on the outcome (USDHHS, 2001a). The factors associated with youth violence were further subcategorized by domain. Late-onset individual characteristics include all of the above plus risk-taking behaviors, commission of crimes, and violent acts toward others. However, the report also identified protective factors. These protective factors include being tolerant toward social differences, having a high IQ, having prosocial values, and believing that there are negative consequences for antisocial actions (USDHHS, 2001a).

Early-onset violence risk factors in the family domain include living in poverty, having parents who demonstrate antisocial behaviors, having a poor parent–child relationship, receiving poor parental supervision and discipline, living in a single-parent home, and having abusive or neglectful parents. Late-onset factors include low parental involvement and family conflict. Protective factors in the family domain include having warm, supportive, and involved parents who like the child's friends (USDHHS, 2001a).

Early-onset factors in the school domain include having poor school performance and having a poor attitude toward school and learning. In addition to the previous factors, late-onset factors contributing to violence include grade failure and retention. Factors that protect children from violence in the school domain include being involved in school activities, having a commitment to school, and getting recognition at school for success.

Factors in the peer group domain correlated with an early onset of violence are having a weak connection with friends and having friends who behave in an antisocial manner. Late-onset factors also include gang membership. The mitigating factor in the peer group domain is having friends with conventional values. In the community domain, only late-onset factors were identified. These included living in drug-infested, high-crime neighborhoods that are poorly organized and fail to meet the needs of the community (USDHHS, 2001a). Characteristics in the individual domain with early onset that increase the likelihood of violence include the following: having committed legal offenses, using substances, being male, acting out aggressively, being hyperactive, having a psychological disorder, being exposed to violence in the media, expressing antisocial behavior (individual, family, school, peer group, or community), and being younger when symptoms first appear (USDHHS, 2001a).

School Rampage Shooter Typology

Langman (2009) analyzed the school rampage shooters and placed them into three categories: traumatized, psychotic, or psychopathic. Langman studied the cases of 10 rampage school shooters in depth and found that three were what he called traumatized, five fit in the category of psychotic, and two were described as psychopathic.

The histories of the traumatized rampage killers included the following: having a parent who had been incarcerated, demonstrating violent behavior using a gun, having discontinuous parenting because of placement in foster care, experiencing a history of childhood abuse, and having at least one parent who abused substances. The traumatized rampage killer was a follower rather than the creator of the plan. These shooters do not show signs of psychosis or lack of conscience.

Psychotic rampage killers share symptoms of auditory and visual hallucinations, delusions, and paranoia. Some show symptoms of early-onset schizophrenia, with anxiety and exaggerated unreasonable fears. They are described by teachers and classmates as socially awkward. There also may be a history of mental illness among extended family members. None of the shooters in this investigation

Sidebar 14.4 ■ The Significance of Onset Risk Factors and Their Domains

Identifying early-onset risk factors related to youth violence seems to receive a good deal of support in the research literature. As you think about the three domains discussed (family, school, and peer group), which do you feel is the most significant and why? If you were to design a program aimed at evaluating each of these domains, where would you begin?

■ ■ ■

were on anti-psychotic medications, although some had complained about hearing voices. These psychotic rampage killers had not received the appropriate level of care to treat the severity of their pathology. These psychotic rampage shooters came from intact families with well-adjusted siblings. Most of the psychotic rampage killers studied were younger siblings who felt inferior when compared with their successful older siblings.

The psychopathic rampage shooters have histories of cruelty to small animals and vulnerable people. They lack empathy and believe that they are entitled to respect. They are skillful at managing their behavior in front of people they want to impress. Under other circumstances they are cruel and sadistic. They are also scam artists who are disruptive and prone to criminal behavior.

This practice of categorizing rampage shooters as traumatized, psychotic, or psychopathic is a useful way to classify and increase understanding. However, because of the small sample size, generalization of this information should be done with caution. The study should be repeated with a greater number of cases to see if the usefulness holds.

Lankford and Hakim (2011) compared school rampage killers with Middle Eastern "volunteer" suicide killers. The primary difference they found was the assumed political motivation for the Middle Eastern bombers. The commonalities between these two populations included the goal of notoriety, a history of childhood deprivation, and revenge-seeking behavior. If Langman's typology model were applied to the Middle Eastern mass killers, they would fit most consistently in the psychopathic group.

Family

Lasting changes with children can be made only if changes are also made in the family system. The earlier interventions are made, the better the outcome is for the child. Early intervention can improve prenatal care, reduce maternal drug use, and protect the developing fetus from the many negative consequences of these behaviors. One of the programs demonstrated to be effective is the Home Visitation by Nurses Program. It begins before the child is born and continues through the child's second birthday. The purpose of this program is to improve health outcomes by supporting and guiding young, often single women through the prenatal and postnatal period to the toddler years. In this program, the same nurse visits the young woman and her family twice monthly during the pregnancy and weekly following childbirth. The nurse gets to know the family and is able to train the mother in parenting skills. By taking this program to the mother's home, the nurses circumvent the problems young mothers have with transportation and other difficulties keeping appointments. Depending on the needs of the family, the nurse may visit once monthly after the child is 6 weeks old. The nurse advises the mother, monitors her health during the pregnancy, and monitors the child's health and development following delivery. The visits usually last between 1 and 1.5 hours. With low-income women, the program has demonstrated effectiveness through a 15-year follow-up. The women's behavior was healthier during pregnancy because of the intervention. This finding was especially true for the cessation of smoking and drinking while pregnant. There were fewer complications such as hypertension and kidney infections. There were significantly fewer cases of child abuse, neglect, and injuries to the children. The female participants also took more responsibility for their lives, including future pregnancy planning, reduction in welfare dependence, and reduction in substance abuse and illegal behavior. In a 16-year follow-up, the children whose mothers participated in this program had significantly fewer arrests and convictions and also had lower alcohol consumption. This program has been shown to be cost beneficial at a rate of at least 4:1. The cost of the program is recovered by the time the child reaches age 4. The future benefits extend to other children born to these mothers in later years (Lawler, 2000; Olds, Hill, Mihalic, & O'Brien, 1998; USDHHS, 2001a).

School

Derzon (2006) conducted a meta-analysis of 74 different school-based prevention programs. He found that most of the programs were implemented in the classroom, with the teacher delivering the curriculum once or twice a week during the regular classroom period. The teachers underwent an extensive amount of training, and most included all of the students in the class. Derzon concluded that most of the reviewed prevention programs were effective in reducing violence and antisocial behavior by 5% (some with greater impact). However, a few programs were unsuccessful and actually increased violence, antisocial behavior, and problem behavior over the comparison groups.

The earliest attempts to prevent school violence focused on improving school security. These security precautions include the mandated use of school uniforms, controlled access to schools, increased presence of uniformed security guards or police, the removal of hall lockers, and the installation of metal detectors. Some students and parents have questioned the right of administrators to search students and their belongings, but courts have consistently found that schools have this right in order to keep schools safe. They are granted this prerogative through the concept that teachers and administrators act in the role of the students' parents (*in loco parentis*). School personnel have an obligation to protect the children from others and themselves. The duty to protect students takes precedence over the students' right to privacy (Yell & Rozalski, 2000).

Many school districts have spent a great deal of their resources on the installation of metal detectors to halt the influx of weapons onto school campuses. For example, in 1 year, New York City spent over $28 million for this purpose (Kemper, 1993). At least 25% of the largest urban school districts use metal detectors (National School Safety Center, 1990). The cost of security and detection devices goes way beyond the initial investment in equipment. There is a continuous need for training, manpower, and maintenance of the detection devices. Trump (1997) warned that the school must react at a level consistent with the security threat in the school and community. He also stated that the security force must be trained in how to work with adolescents, de-escalation, and conflict resolution. If not, a poorly trained security force can decrease rather than increase safety.

With so many resources devoted to security, it is important to ask whether these measures are effective in reducing violence at schools. The CDC (1991) found that these devices were effective in reducing the number of students carrying weapons at school but had no effect on the number of students carrying weapons outside of school. Because the majority of the most serious violence and injury occurs outside of school property, these measures do not have an appreciable impact on the overall safety of children. Mercy and Rosenberg (1998) concluded that they could not find any studies investigating whether these measures decrease the incidence of gun violence at schools. However, it is reasonable to conclude that having fewer weapons in schools equals safer schools. Some communities have adopted community-policing policies to increase the safety of students walking to school. "Safe School Routes" are designated and community volunteers are on duty to observe the children as they pass twice daily. This program has been shown to increase the children's perception of safety with a minimal cost to the community (Mercy & Rosenberg, 1998).

The Bullying Prevention Program specifically addresses the most common form of violence occurring in schools (Batsche & Knoff, 1994). Bullying behavior can include coercive verbal comments, physical intimidation, or a combination of the two. It is sometimes more similar to chronic, systematic terrorism carried out by one or more people targeting a specific person (Furlong, Sharma, & Rhee, 2000). As a result, the child becomes a social outcast with a drastic reduction in self-esteem.

Victims of bullying tend to share certain physical characteristics, such as being overweight or underweight, being small in stature, or projecting general weakness. They also share certain personality characteristics, such as shyness, passivity, or (for males) effeminacy (Furlong et al., 2000; Olweus, 1997; Olweus, Limber, & Mihalic, 1999). In general, the bully has much more power than the victim. Olweus (1997) described two types of victims: passive or provocative. The passive types of victims are more anxious, insecure, introverted, shy, and quiet; demonstrate low self-esteem; and feel lonely and abandoned at school. Provocative victims show many characteristics of attention-deficit/hyperactivity disorder. In contrast to the passive victims, the provocative victims aggravate and annoy their attackers, leading to the harassment. This provocation in no way justifies the bullying that later takes place.

There are gender differences between the ways boys and girls bully. When boys bully they tend to use physical intimidation, abuse, and humiliating pranks. The pattern of behavior for girls is not so obvious but is just as emotionally damaging. Girls tend to tease and exclude girls who are targeted for bullying. In the United States, 23% of middle school children reported that they had been the targets of bullies on several occasions in the past 3 months (Olweus et al., 1999). The negative consequences of bullying are not limited to childhood. Many adults report lasting effects from their childhood bullying (Olweus, 1994). The bully also suffers negative consequences. Bullies, especially males, are more likely to break rules, act in other antisocial ways, use and abuse drugs, and commit crimes. Permitting bullies to act out also has a negative impact on the general classroom and school climate. Tolerance of bullying behavior creates a more hostile atmosphere (Olweus et al., 1999). In order for bullies to operate, there must be support by other classmates with tacit approval by teachers and administrators.

The Bullying Prevention Program confronts these behaviors by addressing the issues at the school, classroom, and individual levels. Intervention at the school level begins with an anonymous survey of the students regarding the nature, severity, and prevalence of bullying at the school. The school then holds a daylong meeting to discuss the results and plan the schoolwide intervention. The schoolwide plan targets areas on the school grounds requiring higher supervision. At the classroom level, rules are established that discourage bullying and intimidation. Classroom meetings are held with open discussions defining bullying behavior and describing the negative outcomes from bullying. Students are given an opportunity to discuss alternatives to bullying behavior. At the individual intervention level, children identified as bullies are given individual and group counseling to learn other more appropriate behavior. Children identified as victims are also given an opportunity for counseling. All of the parents of children receiving counseling are invited to participate in family counseling at the school. The counselors also act as consultants to the teachers who have students identified as bullies or victims of the bullies. The outcomes of the program showed a large and statistically significant reduction in the number of students reporting victimization by bullies. Other antisocial behaviors such as vandalism, violence, theft, and truancy were also significantly reduced. Students and teachers reported a significant improvement in school climate. There were significantly fewer discipline problems, there was an improved attitude toward scholastic activities, and there was improvement in the social relationships among students (Lawler, 2000; Olweus et al., 1999; USDHHS, 2001a). Other violence prevention programs target the members of the community.

Community

The Midwestern Prevention Project (MPP) is a primary prevention program and is an example of a broad-based community intervention program. It incorporates the mass media, educational systems, families, community, health care providers, and peer groups. The goal is to interrupt the pattern of addiction starting with tobacco use and progressing to alcohol use and abuse of other illegal substances. This prevention approach is multimodal, targeting students, parents, and community leaders in various domains. The drug abuse prevention message is transmitted in print and electronic media at least 31 times per year. The mass media campaign ranges from 15-second public service announcements to hour-long talk shows and continues for 5 years. Educational programs are offered to parents throughout the life of the program.

The program relies on support from the community to maintain the goal of drug use abstinence by youth. Communities support the ideals by refusing to sell drugs and alcohol to minors and offering activities that compete with the drug culture. The community also takes a lead in supporting community mental health centers for the treatment of drug abuse to decrease the demand for drugs. Law enforcement contributes to the program by controlling the supply side of the problem, diligently prosecuting both merchants who sell alcohol to underage children and drug dealers. Judges can mandate offenders to diversionary programs where they get treatment, maintain abstinence, or go to jail.

When Willie Sutton was asked why he robbed banks, he answered, "Because that's where the money is." Schools are the appropriate location for drug prevention programs because that's where the children are. The school portion of the MPP begins in the sixth or seventh grade. Teachers, counselors, and peer mediators are trained and take leadership roles in the program. The students participate in 10 to 13 class sessions in the first year, with at least 5 booster sessions the following year. The sessions focus on peer pressure and drug refusal and decision-making skills. At school, the message is supported by taking every opportunity across the curriculum to educate students about the risks of drug abuse.

Families support the program by modeling responsible behavior and refusing to serve alcohol to minors on any occasion. Parents also learn to recognize the early warning signs of drug use among their children and ways to confront their children when they begin experimentation. The parents refuse to tolerate any substance use. They are encouraged to model responsible alcohol use. To learn these skills, parents participate in parenting classes twice a year focusing on discipline and communication skills.

The MPP was an effective prevention program for children and also had an impact on the behavior of the parents. It resulted in a 40% drop in daily cigarette smoking among the student participants and a similar reduction in parental drug use. This drop resulted in more positive parent–child communications and relations. The program also resulted in a reduction in the demand for drug treatment because fewer people in the community initiated drug use to begin with (Lawler, 2000; Pentz, Mihalic, & Grotpeter, 1998; USDHHS, 2001a). The MPP had an impact on individuals and the entire community.

Intervention Programs

Intervention programs are synonymous with secondary prevention programs from the public health model previously discussed in the chapter. They are intended to interrupt behaviors that have already begun. They usually target particular groups of people who are either exhibiting the behavior or are at risk for this dangerous behavior. There is a price paid by individuals participating in intervention rather than prevention programs because they are already in trouble. Some damage may already have been done. On the other hand, because intervention programs target specific individuals, families, students in school, and community members, they are more cost effective. Only the people in need of care participate in the program.

Individual

Some programs focus on the school environment, others on family functioning, others on internal and interpersonal processes. The Promoting Alternative Thinking Strategies (PATHS) program is an example of the last. This program is designed for implementation in schools for children in kindergarten to fifth grades. The goal of the PATHS program is to reduce violence and high-risk behaviors while increasing prosocial behaviors and improving peer relationships. The curriculum contains developmentally appropriate activities promoting emotional competency and increasing understanding of self and others.

The teacher gets support from the project staff and coordinator in teaching the PATHS curriculum in regular and special education classrooms. It is integrated into the daily assignments. The materials consist of an instructor's manual and six volumes of lessons in three major units that are shared with the parents in parent meetings. The first unit teaches self-control and is covered in 12 lessons. The second unit focuses on feelings and interpersonal relationships taught in 56 lessons. The

---

Sidebar 14.5 ■ Prevention From a Family, School, and Community Perspective

From a prevention standpoint, on which of the following entities (family, school, community) would you place the most emphasis and why? On the basis of the one selected, where would you go to get direction and guidance? How would go about evaluating the results?

■ ■ ■

third unit concentrates on teaching the 11 steps to problem solving in 33 lessons. A supplementary unit reviews the principles of the program in 30 additional lessons. There are five themes in the PATHS program: self-control, emotional understanding, positive self-esteem, interpersonal relationships, and problem-solving skills. A total of 131 lessons are introduced over 5 years. Each lesson can last for up to five class meetings. The curriculum is based on a multimodal approach using direct instruction, pictures, role-plays, supplemental reading, and classroom discussions. Parents are notified about their child's progress through the mail. Homework assignments are designed to keep the parents involved with the curriculum and program goals. As a result of the program, participants significantly increased their ability to recognize and understand emotions and were better able to solve social problems and develop solutions. They also decreased aggressive or violent behavior. Teachers reported increased frustration tolerance and successful conflict resolution. In a 1-year follow-up study, the teachers reported that participants showed decreased sadness, increased self-esteem, decreased angry outbursts, decreased violence, and fewer conduct problems. The average cost of implementing the program over a 3-year period was $15 to $45 per year per student (Greenberg, Kusché, & Mihalic, 1998; Lawler, 2000; USDHHS, 2001a).

Family

The Functional Family Therapy (FFT) program targets young people who have demonstrated delinquent, substance-abusing, or violent behavior. Other participants have been diagnosed with oppositional defiant disorder, conduct disorder, or other disruptive behaviors. The program aspires to change the participant's behavior by increasing protective factors and reducing risk factors. One or two therapists (counselors, nurses, social workers, or physicians) are assigned to the youth and their families. They deliver counseling and other services to the youth and their families in their homes, schools, and clinics. There are five phases to the FFT program: engagement, motivation, assessment, behavior change, and generalization. In the engagement phase, the therapists establish a relationship with the youth and their families and are on the lookout for signs of premature termination. During the motivation phase, the therapists design interventions targeting maladaptive behaviors, emotions, and beliefs. They work to build a strong therapeutic alliance, trust, hope, and the change agenda. In the assessment phase, the therapists observe family interactions and analyze the strengths and weaknesses in the family system. During the behavior change phase, the therapists focus on communication training, basic parenting skills, contracting for behavior change, and recognition of behavior costs and consequences. The final phase is the generalization phase, in which newly acquired skills are implemented into other domains of the participants' lives. The therapeutic team individualizes the program to meet the needs of each family and maintains the goal to make long-term positive gains.

The FFT program has been shown to make positive changes with children diagnosed with conduct, oppositional defiant, disruptive, and other behavior disorders. There was a significant reduction in substance abuse and violent delinquent behavior by the termination of the program. The participants were much less likely to commit crimes and to need further contact with social service organizations. Younger children in the family also benefited from the counseling services, with a significant reduction in delinquent and substance abuse behaviors. The program costs approximately $1,350 to $3,750 for an average of 12 home visits. The costs are quickly offset when compared with the expense once a person enters the criminal justice system, with the loss of future income. The FFT model has been used for over 28 years with thousands of families (Alexander et al., 1998; Lawler, 2000; USDHHS, 2001a).

School

The theoretical basis for school violence prevention programs assumes that violence occurs in a cultural context. Therefore, to decrease violence in schools, there must be changes in the school environment. It is presumed that there are characteristics of the culture that promote the use of violence to meet the wants and needs of students. These characteristics can include an attitude that is permissive and encouraging of the use of force to achieve goals. Just think for a moment of the cheers heard at football games. Words such as *fight, beat*, and *hit* predominate. This attitude does not exist only at schools. Many children are instructed by their parents to hit back if someone hits them first. Because of the rise in concern over school violence, schools have adopted zero tolerance for violence. The driving force of zero tolerance is the belief that school violence occurs because the schools and communities have ignored warning signs that violence is imminent. There is a great deal of evidence demonstrating this belief; for example, the student perpetrators gave many clues regarding their intention to cause grievous harm, but the signs were overlooked in Littleton, Colorado; Pearl, Mississippi; Paducah, Kentucky; and Springfield, Oregon.

Zero tolerance is a concept that became popular during the so-called war on drugs. This get-tough policy implies that strict rules will be applied without any excuses for major as well as minor infractions. Overapplication of the policy with resulting negative consequences to individuals is considered an acceptable price to pay for safety (Skiba & Knesting, 2002). Under this policy, students are suspended or expelled for any weapons violation, threat to others, or use or sale of drugs at school. The Gun-Free Schools Act of 1994 made zero tolerance a national policy. It has been applied in districts to include any object that may be used as a weapon. Students and their parents are informed of the consequences of violating school policy. Many parents believe that this policy is carried to an extreme. For example, as a result of this policy, a 5-year-old child was expelled for wearing a toy axe as part of a firefighter's costume at a school Halloween party (Skiba & Knesting, 2002).

States have also enacted laws making it a crime to bring weapons to school, resulting in the suspension, expulsion, and arrest of offending students. Following the carnage of the 1980s and 1990s, this policy makes sense. Schools are caught in the dilemma of preventing violence through hypervigilance or repeating mistakes of the past by ignoring student threats. The courts have consistently upheld administrators' decisions to expel and discipline students bringing weapons to school, dealing or using drugs, or threatening other people (Skiba & Knesting, 2002; Yell & Rozalski, 2000). The controversy arises when administrators expel and suspend students for trivial offenses. An important research question is, Does zero tolerance reduce the risk of violence? Skiba and Knesting (2002) concluded that it does not. They believe that it might exacerbate student misbehavior and reduce student morale. The American Psychological Association Zero Tolerance Task Force (2008) analyzed the data and concluded that evidence does not support these policies. The task force found that schools with higher rates of expulsion and suspensions also had lower evaluation scores, lower academic achievement scores, and poorer school climate, and they had a 56% higher dropout rate. These findings were consistent even when socioeconomic factors were controlled. The task force also concluded that zero tolerance did not lead to lower violence rates (Cornell, Gregory, & Fan, 2011). This finding is supported by evidence in the case of Kip Kinkle, the school shooter near Springfield, Oregon. The day before he killed his parents and shot 24 people at school, Kip Kinkle was suspended and arrested for bringing a gun to school.

In many schools, the administrators ignore a certain amount of bullying and teasing because they perceive it as normal and harmless. In reality, experiencing bullying can have lasting negative effects on children. The person who is bullied may in turn become a bully, or the bullying may have a lasting impact on his or her self-confidence and self-esteem (Ross, 1996). The Secret Service National Threat Assessment Center identified school shooting perpetrators as students who had a past history of having been the victim of bullying, persecution, threats, and injury from peers. They associated a past history of bullying with 66% of the school shooting incidents (O'Toole & the Critical Incident Response Group, 2000; Vossekuil et al., 2001; Vossekuil, Fein, Reddy, Borum, & Modzeleski, 2002). In addition, schools that promote antisocial behavior over prosocial behavior increase the risk of violence and other antisocial activities. In contrast, recognizing and rewarding prosocial actions increases the occurrence of this behavior and decreases antisocial activities (Mattaini & Lowery, 2000).

Behaviorists have long been encouraging parents and teachers to catch children in the act of doing something right. However, children are often admonished, corrected, and punished as the main means of behavior control. Consequently, children can recite a litany of things that they are not supposed to do but are challenged to come up with things that they are *encouraged* to do. By changing the focus from punishment to praise, the focus changes from the negative to the positive. Mayer, Butterworth, Nafpaktitis, and Sulzer-Azaroff (1983) recommended written praise over spoken praise. They suggested that written notes praising students and parents are far more effective than spoken recognition. They used praise boards to recognize students' accomplishments on a daily or weekly basis. They found that merchants were willing to contribute to the program by issuing gift certificates as rewards for the students' accomplishments, which further builds a bridge from the school to the community. Community involvement has consistently been associated with effective school violence prevention and intervention programs (Lawler, 2000).

The Quantum Opportunities Program (QOP) is another example of a school-based violence intervention program. The QOP addresses the problem of violence intervention by increasing economic and educational opportunities for participants. This program targets specific groups of students. The goal of the QOP is to provide educational, social, and vocational opportunities to disadvantaged youth from the 9th through the 12th grades. The QOP provides an opportunity for 750 hours of education (computer instruction, tutoring for basic academic skills), service (community service, volunteering with agencies), and personal development activities (exposure to cultural activities, training in life skills, college planning, job preparation, and assistance with applications for scholarships). Approximately 20 students meet in each group with one adult throughout the year; the adult functions as a mentor, teacher, counselor, disciplinarian, and problem solver. Financial incentives are offered to the children for participating in the program. Results showed that there were substantial benefits for QOP participants. For example, they were more likely than the control group to graduate from high school (63% vs. 42%), more likely to attend college (42% vs. 16%), less likely to have children while in their teens (24% vs. 38%), and somewhat less likely to have been arrested (19% vs. 23%). The program costs $10,600 per participant over the 4 years and is considered cost beneficial because of reduced expenses for the criminal justice system and increased lifetime earnings by the participants because of their increased rate of high school graduation and secondary education (Flannery et al., 2003; Lattimore, Mihalic, Grotpeter, & Taggart, 1998; Lawler, 2000; USDHHS, 2001a).

Threat Assessment Teams

After reviewing the Columbine and other school rampage shootings, the Secret Service and U.S. Department of Education (Vossekuil et al., 2001) as well as the FBI (O'Toole & the Critical Incident Response Group, 2000) recommended that threat assessment teams function on campuses and communities. They suggested that the teams should use the protocols followed by the FBI and the Central Intelligence Agency, who are experts in assessing threats against politicians and other public figures (Cornell & Sheras, 2006).

After studying school rampage shooters and other school violence, the FBI and Secret Service concluded that lethal campus violence is rare and there is a need to take steps to prevent it (O'Toole & the Critical Incident Response Group, 2000; Vossekuil et al., 2001). They concluded that profiling students resulted in too many false positives because many students who show the characteristics do not, in fact, become violent. Therefore, they recommended that teams of professionals evaluate the student on the basis of characteristics, behavior patterns, and situational characteristics. The FBI identified several school shootings that were averted because teams were alerted, threats were reported, and prevention actions were taken (Cornell & Sheras, 2006; Fein et al., 2002; O'Toole & the Critical Incident Response Group, 2000).

The Virginia protocol was developed by the University of Virginia (Cornell, 2003; Cornell & Sheras, 2006) and has been applied to the assessment of students in elementary, middle, and high schools as well as on college and university campuses. This practice and protocol became more widespread following the shooting rampage at Virginia Polytechnic Institute and University in April 2007. Until then, many colleges and universities lacked sufficient policies and procedures to assess and manage crisis situations.

Threat assessment is based on several principles identified by the FBI and Secret Service (Cornell, 2003; Fein et al., 2002). The first is the assumption that it is possible to predict and prevent targeted violence, and that the violence is planned and well thought out. The second principle is that threats and violence occur in contextual settings. Sometimes threats are made without any real intention of carrying them out. The third assumption is that the assessment team will keep an open mind and will investigate the possibilities of risk. The fourth supposition is that the team will evaluate the facts rather than profiles. The fifth principle is that the team will gather evidence from multiple resources. These resources may include interviews with the student making the threat, the student's parents, the person threatened, and witnesses. The investigation may also include searching the student, the student's home, computer, locker, and so forth. Finally, the team determines if the student poses a threat, how serious the threat is, and what intervention should be made (Cornell & Sheras, 2006).

Threat assessment teams include the following professionals: mental health specialists (counselors, psychologists, and social workers), administrators, and law enforcement officers. Each has a role to play as a member of the team. The mental health professionals interview and evaluate the student. They have skills in working with troubled students. The administrator has the authority to establish policies and make leadership and administrative decisions. It is suggested that the school disciplinarian (principal or assistant principal) participate in the team. There are several administrative steps to be taken when creating a threat assessment team, including creating policies that grant the team power to investigate possible threats. This power might include searching lockers, students' cars, and students' property as well as questioning teachers, students, and their acquaintances. The role of the law enforcement officer is to conduct investigations inside and outside of the school and to access legal records and take legal action when necessary. The teams gather information from students, faculty, staff, and parents and share it across their professional domains (Bernes & Bardick, 2007; Cornell & Sheras, 2006). This process became a priority after the shooting on the Virginia Tech campus because it turned out that many people had been concerned about the young man who was the shooter. The lessons learned from this event resulted in the opening of communication among members of the academic community (Sulkowski & Lazarus, 2011). Threat assessment teams have been used in the Memphis School District with positive results (Strong & Cornell, 2008).

Community

The Multisystemic Therapy (MST) program is a community intervention program that has demonstrated effectiveness. It focuses on families, schools, and the community and targets violent, substance-abusing juvenile offenders from the ages of 12 to 17 years. The causes of the problems are viewed as stemming from the individual, family, and school factors; therefore, the interventions encompass all of these domains. The strengths that naturally occur within these areas are assessed and supported to encourage positive change. The MST program addresses the issues faced by families raising adolescents and empowers the participating youth to deal with problems in the schools, families, and community. The purpose is to improve parental disciplinary practices, improve family communication and family relationships, and decrease the power of deviant peer relationships while improving the participants' social skills and social relationships. Another goal is to improve the participants' school and vocational performance. The program mobilizes the support networks within the extended family, neighbors, and friends to back up the goals of the family. The MST program is another home-based program. The therapists focus on skill building for parenting, family therapy, and cognitive–behavioral approaches. Special attention is paid to the social networks that contribute to delinquency and drug abuse. The therapists work to remove the barriers to support services each family receives every week. The program usually includes 60 hours of therapeutic contact over 4 months. The length of involvement is determined by the needs of the family and client.

The MST program has been shown to be effective with serious juvenile offenders and where many other interventions have failed. The program has shown long-term results, including a 25% to 70% reduction in rearrests, improvement in family functioning, and decreased problems associated with mental health disorders. The average cost of the intervention per participant was $4,500. This program was determined to be the most cost-effective intervention for juvenile offenders (Henggler, Mihalic, Rone, Thomas, & Timmons-Mitchell, 1998).

Adaptations for Diversity

Children living in large, inner-city, ethnically heterogeneous neighborhoods characterized by high-density, high-poverty homes that are dilapidated and generally run down are more likely to live surrounded by crime (Smith & Jarjoura, 1988). These conditions describe most children attending large, inner-city schools. Ethnic heterogeneity is believed to cause an increase in crime because residents of diverse backgrounds are less likely to get to know each other and, therefore, are less likely to watch out for each other and their property (Taylor & Gottfredson, 1986). Children living in high-crime neighborhoods are at increased risk for victimization and for observation of crimes. Over 60% of inner-city youth have directly witnessed a shooting, and 50% have observed stabbings, with 60% of these resulting in deaths (Jenkins & Bell, 1994). The violent criminal activity in childhood is increased when children grow up in communities where the gangsters are the only ones with money and crime seems to pay. Children attending schools where they represent the ethnic minority are at a greater risk for violent victimization (U.S. Department of Justice, 1991). Therefore, school leaders should be sensitive to the need to protect children from each other. Administrators and teachers should be knowledgeable about diverse cultures and be sensitive to the needs of these children and their families. Schools must represent a safe haven for children from violence. Teachers and administrators must welcome students representing diverse backgrounds into the schools.

Each of the prevention and intervention programs described in this chapter was developed with the diverse ethnic, socioeconomic, and cultural makeup of the participants in mind. They were designed to include input from the students, their families, faculty, administrators, and community members. Many began with a needs assessment. This assessment is an important element because school violence has occurred at schools representing every type of community. Contrary to public expectations, the worst mass shootings have occurred at schools where there seemed to be few individual, family, or community indications of violence. Littleton, Pearl, Jonesboro, and Springfield are suburban, middle-class communities. The perpetrators were apparently affluent, White, male students. Because

Sidebar 14.6 ■ Intervention From an Individual, Family, School, and Community Perspective

From an intervention perspective, what do you see as the most effective starting point? Would you begin by working with the individual, the family, the school, or the community? On the basis of your choice, provide a rationale and indicate how you would integrate the other three entities.

■ ■ ■

school violence perpetrators defy stereotypes, each violence prevention or intervention program must be designed with the diverse population of the school and community in mind.

Summary

From 1983 until 1993, the United States was rocked by youth violence. The murder and suicide rates increased dramatically. In the years that followed, the unthinkable happened: Young men terrorized and murdered their classmates and teachers at school. Some of them began their killing sprees by murdering their parents. This explosion of violence caused students to fear for their lives while at school. These concerns have brought about many changes in the ways that schools operate.

Several programs have been initiated to prevent violence in the communities, homes, and schools. Schools have taken new security measures in an effort to help students feel safe. Administrators have also initiated zero tolerance policies to discourage students from making threats in and outside of school and have a plan to intervene when they do.

Experts on violence prevention have studied young violent offenders and have compiled lists of characteristics shared by the most violent. However, overreliance on this profiling can result in false positives. Many prevention and intervention programs have been designed to address maladaptive behaviors. These programs address school climate, community environment, family issues, interpersonal relationships, and career and educational opportunities. All of the reviewed prevention and intervention programs demonstrated their effectiveness and were cost beneficial. In addition, threat assessment teams have been created to assess individual students and enact appropriate interventions.

Youth violence is a complicated problem. Although there are no easy solutions to youth violence, there are prevention and intervention programs that work. Effective programs are comprehensive, coordinating individual, family, school, and community services. The programs are designed to last for an extended period of time. The implementation of these programs requires commitment from youth, families, schools, and communities.

To help students with their myriad of problems, schools should have full-service counseling centers with threat assessment teams at the building or district level. Here, students in need of intervention can be assessed, treated, and, when necessary, referred to other mental health professionals for the appropriate level of care. Parents and teachers should see themselves as partners, with similar goals to help every child achieve his or her full potential. Americans should never again mourn the loss of children to school violence. The following websites provide additional information relating to the chapter topics.

Useful Websites

American School Counseling Association: Helping Kids During Crisis
    http://www.schoolcounselor.org/content.asp?contentid=672
Center for the Prevention of School Violence
    http://www.ncdjjdp.org/cpsv/
Centers for Disease Control and Prevention (CDC): Understanding School Violence
    http://www.cdc.gov/violenceprevention/pdf/schoolviolence_factsheet-a.pdf

Early Warning, Timely Response: A Guide to Safe Schools
  http://www.ed.gov/about/offices/list/osers/osep/gtss.html
Facing Fear: Helping Young People Deal With Terrorism and Tragic Events
  http://www.redcross.org/article/0,1072,0_332_1005,00.html
Knowledge Path: Adolescent Violence Prevention: Guide to Safe Schools
  http://www.ed.gov/about/offices/list/osers/osep/gtss.html
National Alliance for Safe Schools
  http://mentalhealth.samhsa.gov/_scripts/redirect.asp?ID=587
New York University (NYU): Talking to Kids About School Violence
  http://www.aboutourkids.org/articles/talking_kids_about_school_violence
Safe and Healthy Schools: Practical Prevention Strategies
  http://www.schoolcounselor.org/store_product.asp?prodid=177
Safe Schools Healthy Students
  http://www2.ed.gov/programs/dvpsafeschools/index.html
Substance Abuse and Mental Health Services Association (SAMHSA)
  http://store.samhsa.gov/product/Mental-Health-Response-to-Mass-Violence-and-Terrorism-A-Training-Manual/SMA04-3959

References

Alexander, J., Barton, C., Gordon, D., Grotpeter, J., Hansson, K., Harrison, R., . . . Elliott, D. S. (1998). *Blueprints for violence prevention: Book 3. Functional Family Therapy*. Boulder, CO: Center for the Study and Prevention of Violence.

American Psychological Association Zero Tolerance Task Force. (2008). Are zero tolerance policies effective in schools? An evidentiary review and recommendations. *American Psychologist, 63,* 852–862.

Astor, R., Mayer, H., & Behre, W. (1999). Unowned places and times: Maps and interviews about violence in high schools. *American Educational Research Journal, 36,* 3–42.

Baily, K. (2001). Legal implications of profiling students for violence. *Psychology in the Schools, 38,* 141–155.

Batsche, G. M., & Knoff, H. M. (1994). Bullies and their victims: Understanding a pervasive problem in the schools. *School Psychology Review, 23,* 165–174.

Bernes, K., & Bardick, A. (2007). Conducting adolescent violence risk assessment: A framework for the school counselor. *Professional School Counselor, 10,* 419–427.

Borduin, C. M., & Schaeffer, C. M. (1998). Violent offending in adolescence: Epidemiology, correlates, outcomes, and treatment. In T. P. Gillotta, G. R. Adams, & R. Montemayor (Eds.), *Delinquent violent youth: Theory and interventions* (pp. 144–174). Newbury Park, CA: Sage.

Borum, R., Cornell, D., Modzeleski, W., & Jimerson, S. (2010). What can be done about school shootings? A review of the evidence. *Educational Researcher, 39,* 27–37.

Center to Prevent Handgun Violence. (1990). *Caught in the crossfire: A report on gun violence in our nation's schools*. Washington, DC: Author.

Centers for Disease Control and Prevention. (1991). *Attempted suicide among high school students, United States 1990*. Atlanta, GA: U.S. Department of Health and Human Services.

Centers for Disease Control and Prevention. (2006, June 9). Surveillance summaries. *Morbidity and Mortality Weekly Report, 55*(No. SS-5).

Centers for Disease Control and Prevention. (2012). *Understanding school violence fact sheet*. Atlanta, GA: National Center for Injury Prevention and Control.

Chandras, K. (1999). Coping with adolescent school violence: Implications for counselors. *College Student Journal, 33,* 302–311.

Cook, P., & Laub, J. H. (1998). The unprecedented epidemic in youth violence. In M. Yonry & M. H. Moore (Eds.), *Youth violence, crime and justice: A review of research* (Vol. 24, pp. 27–64). Chicago, IL: University of Chicago Press.

Cornell, D. (2003). Guidelines for responding to student threats of violence. *Journal of Educational Administration, 41*, 705–719.

Cornell, D., Gregory, A., & Fan, X. (2011). Reductions in long-term suspensions following adoption of the Virginia student threat assessment guidelines. *The National Association of Secondary School Principals Bulletin, 95*, 175–194.

Cornell, D., & Sheras, P. (2006). *Guidelines for responding to student threats of violence*. Longmont, CO: Sopris West.

Dahlberg, L. L. (1998). Youth violence in the United States: Major trends, risk factors, and prevention approaches. *American Journal of Preventive Medicine, 14*, 259–272.

Daniels, J., Volungis, A., Pshenishny, E., Gandhi, P., Winkler, A., Cramer, D., & Bradley, M. (2010). A qualitative investigation of averted school shooting rampages. *The Counseling Psychologist, 38*, 69–95.

Dejong, W., Epstein, J. C., & Hart, T. E. (2003). Bad things happen in good communities: The rampage shooting in Edinboro, Pennsylvania, and its aftermath. In M. H. Moore, C. V. Petrie, A. A. Braga, & B. L. McLaughlin (Eds.), *Deadly lessons: Understanding lethal school violence* (pp. 70–100). Washington, DC: National Academic Press.

Derzon, J. (2006). How effective are school-based violence prevention programs in preventing and reducing violence and other antisocial behaviors? A meta-analysis. In S. Jimerson & M. Furlong (Eds.), *The handbook of school violence and school safety* (pp. 429–441). Mahwah, NJ: Erlbaum.

DeVoe, J. F., Peter, K., Noonan, M., Snyder, T. D., & Baum, K. (2005). *Indicators of school crime and safety, 2005* (NCES 2006-001/NCJ 210697). Washington, DC: U.S. Government Printing Office.

Dowling, C., & Johnson, L. (1998, July). High school heroes. *Life, 21*, 52–62.

Dwyer, K., Osher, D., & Warger, C. (1998). *Early warning, timely response: A guide to safe schools*. Washington, DC: U.S. Department of Education.

Eaton, D., Kann, L., Kinchen, S., Shanklin, S., Flint, K. H., Hawkins, J., . . . Wechsler, H. (2012, June 8). Youth risk behavior surveillance, 2011–2012. *Morbidity and Mortality Weekly Report, 61*(4).

Elliott, D. S. (1998). Editor's introduction. In D. S. Elliott (Ed.), *Blueprints for violence prevention: Book 8. Multisensorial treatment foster care*. Boulder, CO: Center for the Study and Prevention of Violence.

Elliott, D., Hamburg, B., & Williams, K. (1998). *Violence in American schools*. Cambridge, England: Cambridge University Press.

Fein, R., Vossekuil, B., Pollack, W., Borum, R., Modzeleski, W., & Reddy, M. (2002). *Threat assessment in schools: A guide to managing threatening situations and to creating safe school climates*. Washington, DC: U.S. Secret Service and Department of Education.

Finn, A., & Remley, T. P. (2002). Prevention of school violence: A school and community response. In D. Rea & J. Bergin (Eds.), *Safeguarding our youth: Successful school and community programs* (pp. 19–27). New York, NY: McGraw-Hill.

Flannery, D., Singer, M., & Wester, K. (2001). Violence exposure, psychological trauma, and suicide risk in a community sample of dangerously violent adolescents. *Journal of the American Academy of Child and Adolescent Psychiatry, 40*, 435–442.

Flannery, D., Vazsonyi, A., Liau, A., Guo, S., Powell, K., Atha, H., . . . Embry, D. (2003). Initial behavior outcomes for the PeaceBuilders Universal School-Based Violence Prevention Program. *Developmental Psychology, 39*, 292–308.

Furlong, M., Bates, M., & Smith, D. (2001). Predicting school weapon possession: A secondary analysis of the Youth Risk Behavior Surveillance Survey. *Psychology in the Schools, 38*, 127–140.

Furlong, M., Morrison, G., Skiba, R., & Cornell, D. (2004). Methodological and measurement issues in school violence research: Moving beyond the social problem era. In M. Furlong, G. Morrison, R. Skiba, & D. Cornell (Eds.), *Issues in school violence research* (pp. 5–12). Binghampton, NY: Haworth Press.

Furlong, M. J., Sharkey, J. D., Bates, M. P., & Smith, D. C. (2004). An examination of the reliability, data screening procedures, and extreme response patterns for the Youth Risk Behavior Surveillance Survey. In M. J. Furlong, G. M. Morrison, D. G. Cornell, & R. Skiba (Eds.), *Issues in school violence research* (pp. 109–130). New York, NY: Haworth. (Simultaneously published in *Journal of School Violence*)

Furlong, M., Sharma, B., & Rhee, S. (2000). Defining school violence victim subtypes: A step toward adapting prevention and intervention programs to match student needs. In D. Sandhu & C. Aspy (Eds.), *Violence in American schools: A practical guide for counselors* (pp. 67–87). Alexandria, VA: American Counseling Association.

Futrell, M. (1996). Violence in the classroom: A teacher's perspective. In A. Hoffman (Ed.), *Schools, violence, and society* (pp. 3–19). Westport, CT: Praeger.

Gibbs, N., & Roche, T. (1999, December 20). The Columbine tapes. *Time*, 40–60.

Greenberg, M. T., Kusché, C., & Mihalic, S. F. (1998). *Blueprints for violence prevention: Book 10. Promoting Alternative Thinking Strategies (PATHS)*. Boulder, CO: Center for the Study and Prevention of Violence.

Hammond, J. (2009). The Columbine tragedy ten years later. *School Administrator*, *66*, 10–16.

Henggler, S. W., Mihalic, S. F., Rone, L., Thomas, C., & Timmons-Mitchell, J. (1998). *Blueprints for violence prevention: Book 6. Multisystemic therapy*. Boulder, CO: Center for the Study and Prevention of Violence.

Henry, D., Farrell, A., & the Multisite Violence Prevention Project. (2004). Design of the Multisite Violence Prevention Project. *American Journal of Preventive Medicine*, *26*, 12–19.

Hermann, M., & Finn, A. (2002). An ethical and legal perspective on the role of school counselors in preventing violence in schools. *Professional School Counseling*, *6*, 46–54.

Herrenkohl, T., Maguin, E., Hill, K., Hawkins, D., Abbott, R., & Catalono, R. (2000). Developmental risk factors for youth violence. *Journal of Adolescent Health*, *26*, 176–186.

Hong, J., Cho, H., Allen-Meares, P., & Espelage, D. (2011). The social ecology of the Columbine school shootings. *Children and Youth Services Review, 33*, 861–868.

Hoyer, M., & Heath, B. (2012, December 19). Virginia Tech, Fort Hood, Aurora, Sandyhook. *USA Today*, p. A1.

Hughes, M., Brymer, M., Chiu, W. T., Fairbank, J. A., Jones, R. T., Pynoos, R. S., . . . Kessler, R. C. (2011). Posttraumatic stress among students after the shootings at Virginia Tech. *Psychological Trauma: Theory, Research, Practice, and Policy, 3*, 403–411.

Illinois Center for Violence Prevention. (1998). *Fact sheets: Cost of violence*. Chicago, IL: Author.

Immelman, A. (1999). Indirect evaluation of Eric Harris. *USPP: Unit for the study of personality in politics*. Retrieved from http://www1.csbsju.edu/uspp/research/harris.html

James, R., & Gilliland, B. (2001). *Crisis intervention strategies* (4th ed.). Belmont, CA: Brooks/Cole.

Jenkins, E. J., & Bell, C. C. (1994). Violence among inner city high school students and posttraumatic stress disorder. In S. Freidman (Ed.), *Anxiety disorders in African Americans* (pp. 76–78). New York, NY: Springer.

Kashani, J., Jones, M., Bumby, K., & Thomas, L. (1999). Youth violence: Psychosocial risk factors, treatment, prevention, and recommendations. *Journal of Emotional and Behavioral Disorders, 7*, 200–211.

Kemper, P. (1993, Fall). Disarming youth. *California School Boards Journal*, 25–33.

Kesey, K. (1998, July 9). Land of the free, home of the bullets. *Rolling Stone*, 51–55.

Kimmel, M. (2008). Profiling school shooters' schools: The cultural contexts of aggrieved entitlement masculinity. In B. Agger & D. Lukes (Eds.), *There is a gunman on campus: Tragedy and terror on Virginia Tech* (pp. 65–78). Lanham, MD: Rowan & Littlefield.

Kimmel, M. S., & Mahler, M. (2003). Adolescent masculinity, homophobia and violence: Random school shootings 1982–2001. *American Behavioral Scientist, 46,* 1442–1464.

King, P., & Murr, A. (1998, June 1). A son who spun out of control. *Newsweek,* 32–33.

Langman, P. (2009). Rampage school shooters: A typology. *Aggression and Violent Behavior, 14,* 79–86.

Lankford, A., & Hakim, N. (2011). From Columbine to Palestine: A comparative analysis of rampage shooters in the United States and volunteer suicide bombers in the Middle East. *Aggression and Violent Behavior, 16,* 98–107.

Lattimore, C. B., Mihalic, S. F., Grotpeter, J. K., & Taggart, R. (1998). *Blueprints for violence prevention: Book 4. The Quantum Opportunities Program.* Boulder, CO: Center for the Study and Prevention of Violence.

Lawler, M. (2000). School-based violence prevention programs: What works? In D. Sandhu & C. Aspy (Eds.), *Violence in American schools: A practical guide for counselors* (pp. 247–266). Alexandria, VA: American Counseling Association.

Luke, T. W. (2008). April 16, 2007, at Virginia Tech—to multiple recipients: "A gunman is loose on campus. . . ." In B. Agger & T. W. Luke (Eds.), *There is a gunman on campus: Tragedy and terror on Virginia Tech* (pp. 1–28). Lanham, MD: Rowan & Littlefield.

Lumsden, L. (2000). Profiling students for violence. *ERIC Digest, 139.* (ERIC Document Reproduction Service No. ED446344)

Mattaini, M., & Lowery, C. (2000). Constructing cultures of peace and nonviolence: The PEACE POWER! toolkit. In D. Sandhu & C. Aspy (Eds.), *Violence in American schools: A practical guide for counselors* (pp. 123–138). Alexandria, VA: American Counseling Association.

Mayer, G. R., Butterworth, T., Nafpaktitis, M., & Sulzer-Azaroff, B. (1983). Preventing school vandalism and improving school discipline: A three year study. *Journal of Applied Behavior Analysis, 16,* 135–146.

Mendel, R. A. (2000). *Less hype, more help: Reducing juvenile crime; what works—and what doesn't.* Washington, DC: American Youth Policy Forum.

Mercy, J., & Rosenberg, M. (1998). Preventing firearm violence in and around schools. In D. Elliott, B. Hamburg, & K. Williams (Eds.), *Violence in American schools* (pp. 159–187). Cambridge, England: Cambridge University Press.

Moore, M., Petrie, C., Braga, A., & McLaughlin, B. (Eds.). (2003). Literature review. In M. Moore, C. Petrie, A. Braga, & B. McLaughlin (Eds.), *Deadly lessons: Understanding lethal school violence* (pp. 302–328). Washington, DC: National Academies Press.

Mulvey, E., & Cauffman, E. (2001). The inherent limits of predicting school violence. *American Psychologist, 56,* 797–802.

Nation, M., Crusto, C., Wandersman, A., Kumpfer, K., Seybolt, D., Morrissey-Kane, E., & Davino, K. (2003). What works in prevention. *American Psychologist, 58,* 449–456.

National Center for Education Statistics. (2003). *Violence in US public schools: 2000 school survey on crime and safety* (Statistical analysis report, NCE-2004-314). Washington, DC: Author.

National School Safety Center. (1990). *Weapons in schools* (NSSC resource paper). Malibu, CA: Author.

Olds, D., Hill, P., Mihalic, S., & O'Brien, R. (1998). *Blueprints for violence prevention: Book 7. Prenatal and home visitation by nurses.* Boulder, CO: Center for Study and Prevention of Violence.

Olweus, D. (1994). Bullying at school: Long term outcomes for the victims and an effective school based intervention program. In H. Rowell (Ed.), *Aggressive behavior: Current behavior* (pp. 97–130). New York, NY: Plenum Press.

Olweus, D. (1997). Tackling peer victimization. In D. P. Fry & K. Bjoerkqvist (Eds.), *Cultural variation in conflict resolution: Alternatives to violence* (pp. 215–231). Mahwah, NJ: Erlbaum.

Olweus, D., Limber, S., & Mihalic, S. F. (1999). *Blueprints for violence prevention: Book 9. Bullying Prevention Program*. Boulder, CO: Center for the Study and Prevention of Violence.

O'Toole, M. E., & the Critical Incident Response Group. (2000). *The school shooter: A threat assessment prospective*. Quantico, VA: Federal Bureau of Investigation.

Pentz, M. A., Mihalic, S. F., & Grotpeter, J. K. (1998). *Blueprints for violence prevention: Book 1. The Midwestern Prevention Project*. Boulder, CO: Center for the Study and Prevention of Violence.

Rocque, M. (2012). Exploring school rampage shootings: Research, theory, and policy. *The Social Science Journal, 49,* 304–313.

Ross, D. (1996). *Childhood bullying and teasing: What school personnel, other professionals, and parents can do*. Alexandria, VA: American Counseling Association.

School Safety Council. (1989). *Weapons in schools*. Washington, DC: U.S. Department of Justice.

Shafii, M., & Shafii, S. L. (2001). *School violence: Assessment, management, and prevention*. Washington, DC: American Psychiatric Association.

Simone, R., Zhang, J., Truman, J., & Snyder, T. (2010). *Indicators of school crime and safety: 2010*. Washington, DC: U.S. Department of Education.

Skiba, R., & Knesting, K. (2002). Zero tolerance, zero evidence: An analysis of school disciplinary practice. In R. Skiba & G. Noam (Eds.), *Zero tolerance: Can suspension and expulsion keep schools safe?* (pp. 17–43). San Francisco, CA: Jossey-Bass.

Smith, D., & Jarjoura, G. R. (1988). Social structure and criminal victimization. *Journal of Research in Crime and Delinquency, 25,* 27–52.

Strong, K., & Cornell, D. (2008). Student threat assessment in Memphis City schools: A descriptive report. *Behavioral Disorders, 34,* 42–54.

Sulkowski, M., & Lazarus, J. (2011): Contemporary responses to violent attacks on college campuses. *Journal of School Violence, 10,* 338–354.

Sullivan, R. (1998, October 1). A boy's life. *Rolling Stone*, 46–54.

Taylor, R., & Gottfredson, J. (1986). Environmental design, crime, and prevention: An examination of community dynamics. In A. J. Reiss, Jr., & M. Tony (Eds.), *Communities and crime* (pp. 244–262). Chicago, IL: University of Chicago Press.

Trump, K. (1997). Security policy, personnel, and operations. In A. Goldstein & J. Close (Eds.), *School violence intervention: A practical handbook* (pp. 265–289). New York, NY: Guilford Press.

U.S. Department of Education. (2004). *Crime and safety in America's public schools: Selected findings from the School Survey on Crime and Safety*. Washington, DC: Author.

U.S. Department of Health and Human Services. (2001a). *Youth violence: A report of the Surgeon General*. Rockville, MD: U.S. Department of Health and Human Services, Centers for Disease Control and Prevention, National Center for Injury Prevention and Control; Substance Abuse and Mental Health Services Administration, Center for Mental Health Services; and National Institutes of Health, National Institute of Mental Health.

U.S. Department of Health and Human Services. (2001b). Youth violence: A report of the Surgeon General: Executive summary. *American Journal of Health Education, 32,* 169–174.

U.S. Department of Justice, Bureau of Justice Statistics. (1991). *School crime: A national victimization survey report*. Washington, DC: U.S. Government Printing Office.

U.S. Department of Justice, Bureau of Justice Statistics. (2010). *School crime: A national victimization survey report*. Washington, DC: U.S. Government Printing Office.

Vossekuil, B., Fein, R., Reddy, M., Borum, R., & Modzeleski, W. (2002). *The final report and findings of the Safe School Initiative: Implications for the prevention of school attacks in the United States*. Washington, DC: U.S. Secret Service and U.S. Department of Education.

Vossekuil, B., Reddy, M., & Fein, R. (2001). The Secret Service Safe School Initiative. *Education Digest, 66,* 4–11.

Vossekuil, B., Reddy, M., Fein, R., Borum, R., & Modzeleski, W. (2000). *U.S.S.S. Safe School Initiative: An interim report on the prevention of targeted violence in schools*. Washington, DC: U.S. Secret Service, National Threat Assessment Center.

Washington State Institute for Public Policy. (1999). *The comparative costs and benefits of programs to reduce crime*. Olympia, WA: Author.

Williams, R. (2011). Threat assessment: What to consider. *School Counselor, 49,* 187–197.

Yell, M., & Rozalski, M. (2000). Searching for safe schools: Legal issues in the prevention of school violence. *Journal of Emotional and Behavioral Disorders, 8,* 187–197.

Chapter 15

"Escaping Reality": Adolescent Substance Abuse

Matthew V. Glowiak

Childhood is unique in that it is marked by rapid physical and psychological changes. With these changes comes instability: instability in personality characteristics, instability with relationships, and instability of hormones. As adults we sometimes forget how stressful childhood really is. Although for some the biggest trauma was being dumped the evening of prom, for others it was staying up all night to care for a sick parent. Sometimes families move a lot. Many school systems like to switch up peer groups as students advance in grade. Then, after so many years we go from attending one school to another that is generally larger with its own new microcosm. Our bodies and appearances continue to change while pop culture continues to evolve our looks further. Strengths, skills, and talents differ from person to person—one may be glorified here but frowned upon there. Adjusting to fit in along each step of the way comes easily for some yet very poorly for others. In attempting to belong to one social group, another, or a combination of several, strategies to fit in may also differ significantly. Whereas some groups strive to succeed in productive activities, others find solace in lethargy or excitement in risk-taking behaviors. It is any one or a culmination of these factors that may lead toward and facilitate a problem with substance abuse or dependence.

In some cases drug dependence comes to those most unsuspecting. In an article written by Sari Harrar (2012), readers learn of the case of Tim Rader—an all-American kid who grew up in northeastern Pennsylvania and had it all going for him (high school quarterback and local hero) until tragically being diagnosed with cancer. What followed was an unfortunate bout with drugs that led to devastating consequences.

> The pain pills came into my life with cancer treatment . . . I was a strong 17-year-old and the doctors didn't hold back—I got codeine, morphine, whatever I needed. I was very young, very scared and kind of in denial about the whole experience. I still remember how it felt when I took a dose. For two brief minutes I didn't care that I was bald, I didn't care that I might die, I didn't care that I couldn't play football. The fear that had been so strong went away. I cherished that little escape and waited for the next one. It planted a dangerous seed. (Harrar, 2012)

The years to follow were marked by high and low periods. During college Tim began to get his life back on track and upon graduation had a high-paying job, fiancé, and upscale apartment. After not taking so much as a Tylenol for over a year, his world came crashing back down one day during a doctor's visit when he faced his old foe.

> I took one. The next day I took three. Then I took them all. I woke up the next morning still wearing my suit. I started stealing from doctors, forging prescriptions, moving on to other things like heroin. I was out of control. Ultimately, I ended up in a crack house in Philadelphia with a gun in my hand, ready to take my own life. (Harrar, 2012)

Tim's story is a sad one. Here we have a well-intentioned kid who suddenly fell victim to circumstance. Or did he? It is important to ask what makes Tim's fall to substances any different from any other child who might identify as plastic, jock, nerd, Goth, stoner, emo, or any other group to which today's youth identify. The reality is that drugs are generally bigger than an individual's willpower or physical ability to fend off. Although it is true that most adolescents who experiment with drugs appear to enter adulthood unscathed, the reality is that substances do pose harm to one's physical and psychosocial well-being. Considering that youth are at the peak of their most critical developmental stages as well, there are additional concerns with substance abuse that must be taken into consideration.

The aim of this chapter is to provide the reader with an overview of adolescent substance abuse. Given space constraints, this chapter is able to address only some of the more pressing concerns, commonly used substances, and most widely used approaches. To be more specific, in this chapter I define substance abuse and explain exactly how it affects the adolescent—mentally, physically, and socially. Substances discussed in this chapter include alcohol, marijuana, inhalants, ecstasy, methamphetamine, and prescription and over-the-counter (OTC) drugs. To address concerns in these areas, I discuss various means of prevention and intervention. Because there are numerous ways for counselors to address a substance

---

Sidebar 15.1 ■ Self-Perceptions of Substance Use and Abuse

Here is a good point to stop and take a moment to introspect. Think about your own level of substance use and how it affects your life. Think about the various reasons why and when you use. Has your level of use changed over the years? After a few minutes spend a few more thinking about your perceptions of others. Do you have any frustrations or biases? Digging deeper, think about your feelings concerning child and adolescent substance use. Have your feelings changed since growing from a child into adult? If so, in what ways?

■ ■ ■

abuse problem, depending on the specific individual and situation, some general suggestions are provided. For more information on adolescent substance abuse, please be sure to view the additional resources provided at the end of this chapter.

Problem Definition

The Centers for Disease Control and Prevention (CDC) is a government-run organization with a primary focus on the health of the nation. Its website (CDC.gov) is an extremely credible resource that provides various information on topics such as healthy living, environmental health, and diseases and conditions along with the latest national data and statistics to back it up. In terms of youth substance use and abuse, the most recent data and statistics reveal some serious concerns. The 2011 assessment of the nation was conducted using the Youth Risk Behavior Surveillance System (YRBSS), which "monitors six types of health-risk behaviors that contribute to the leading causes of death and disability among youth and adults" (CDC, 2012, "Abstract"). It is administered every 2 years to 9th- to 12th-grade adolescents in all public and private high schools throughout the country.

Whether one is surprised or not by any of these numbers given in Sidebar 15.2—in any direction, larger or smaller than anticipated—the fact remains that a significant number of youth living in the United States have experienced some type of mind-altering substance. Like any other assessment or study, there are some gaps that must be considered with the YRBSS. First, although it is administered to every school, it may be conducted with a minimum of one grade level per school. Second, the assessment had an 81% school response rate with 87% of students participating (totaling 71% overall). Thus, there was a sizeable amount of nonparticipation. Third, of the students who did participate there is always the likelihood that (despite measures to protect privacy) some provided false responses in an attempt to protect themselves; therefore, there is the possibility of these numbers being slightly to significantly higher in some areas. So for those who thought some numbers were lower than expected, there is still the chance that they are actually higher; and for those who thought these numbers were already high, it should be apparent that professional counselors have some work to do.

One difficulty in working with substance abuse and dependence is that there is a large gray area. In other words, there is no clear-cut definition as to what is acceptable at what age by each person in every circumstance. For instance, one individual might say all drugs and alcohol are bad, whereas another might say

---

Sidebar 15.2 ■ Latest Youth Drug and Alcohol Statistics as Provided by the Centers for Disease Control and Prevention (2012)

- 10.3% of youth smoked a whole cigarette for the first time prior to 13 years old.
- 20.5% of youth drank alcohol for the first time prior to 13 years old.
- 8.1% of youth tried marijuana for the first time prior to 13 years old.
- 23.1% of youth have used marijuana at least once.
- 11.4% of youth have at least once either sniffed glue, breathed the contents of aerosol spray cans, or inhaled any paints or sprays to get high.
- 8.2% of youth have used ecstasy at least once.
- 20.7% of youth have taken prescription drugs without a doctor's prescription at least once. (CDC, 2012)

■ ■ ■

it's okay if the user is of age and obeys the law. Then there are those who feel as though some drugs should be legal, with only the "most dangerous" of drugs being banned. In addition there are those who think everyone should be free to do whatever they want as long as the individual using does not present any clear or imminent harm to self or others. Take the legalization of marijuana for instance. Since it became illegal in the 1930s, millions of people have continued to push for its legalization. What started with the legalization of medical marijuana in the early 2000s has now led toward its recreational use in controlled situations within states that allow it. Another differentiation regarding alcohol and other substance use lies with the reason that people use these substances. For example, some people use to relax, whereas others use to celebrate; some use to escape reality, and others use to mask some type of emotional distress. Once again, individuals may point fingers at which reason to use is better or worse than another, but the reality is that any amount of use of any substance does have at least some minimal effect on one's mental and physical well-being. Fortunately, most individuals who do use alcohol and other substances are able to do so in moderation without having any severe consequences. Unfortunately, there are those who begin to allow substances to take over each and every facet of their lives.

Pharmacokinetics of Drugs

Despite the type of drug used, method of ingestion, and individual using it, there is a very specific process that each drug goes through in the human body:

1. The medication is absorbed into the systemic circulation (i.e., oral, rectal, IV [intravenous], transdermal, inhalation).
2. The drug and metabolites are distributed in tissues.
3. The drug is metabolized.
4. The drug and metabolites are eliminated from the body. (Perazella & Parikh, 2005, p. 1130)

It is during the metabolism of the drug that the user feels its effects. Depending on the drug, its potency, and the method of intake, the effects may take place more or less quickly for a longer or shorter duration of time.

The Nervous System

The nervous system is the processing center by which everything else functions. It is a very complex system that is composed of all the body's nerve tissues (Ophardt, 2003). Nerves are like messengers that transmit, receive, and initiate responses to various stimuli. With the help of neurotransmitters, these messages travel from one neuron to the next through synapses—the small gaps between cells (Christopher & Dana Reeve Foundation, 2013). These synapses take on a domino-like effect whereby one signal triggers another, and another, and so on. Subsystems of the nervous system include the central nervous system (CNS), the peripheral nervous system (PNS), the somatic nervous system, and the autonomic nervous system (sympathetic and parasympathetic).

The CNS is composed of the brain and spinal cord. As a collection point for nerve impulses, it controls most functions of the body and mind. "Like a central computer, it interprets information from our eyes (sight), ears (sound), nose (smell), tongue (taste) and skin (touch), as well as from internal organs such as the stomach" (Christopher & Dana Reeve Foundation, 2013, para. 1). In addition, it is the center of emotion, thought, and memory (University of Pittsburgh, 2013). The spinal cord, then, is made up of bundles of nerve fibers. Bones protecting the spinal cord form a canal that runs all the all down from the brain to the center of the spine. The spinal cord and brain are connected by the brain stem—a region that controls involuntary functioning, such as hunger, thirst, body temperature, blood pressure, and breathing.

The PNS is made up of all nerves outside of the brain or spinal cord. It interacts with the CNS by connecting all the rest of the body's parts to it. "The peripheral (sensory) nervous system receives stimuli, the central nervous system interprets them, and then the peripheral (motor) nervous system initiates responses" (Ophardt, 2003, "Introduction," para. 1). Functions of the somatic nervous system are voluntary and conscious, whereas those of the autonomic nervous system are involuntary. The sympathetic system, then, stimulates activity in the body and the parasympathetic system calms it down. When the entirety of the nervous system works in harmony, messages are relayed from one point to another like a well-oiled machine. When drugs or alcohol become involved, however, these messages become irregular in accordance with the type of substance consumed.

Synapses and Neurotransmission

Neurotransmitters are the chemicals that help messages pass through each synapse. "To transmit an action potential message across a synapse, neurotransmitter molecules are released from one neuron (the 'pre-synaptic' neuron) across the gap to the next neuron (the 'post-synaptic' neuron). This process continues until the message reaches its destination" (Christopher & Dana Reeve Foundation, 2013, para. 1). Major neurotransmitters include the following: acetylcholine, dopamine, serotonin, endorphins, norepinephrine, and gamma aminobutyric acid (GABA). Each of these neurotransmitters and their corresponding receptors has different functions that contribute toward the overall functioning of the body. Table 15.1 provides a list of major neurotransmitters, their function in the nervous system, and the way in which various drugs act upon them.

Drugs and Their Affects on Neurotransmission

Neurotransmission in the synapse occurs through a series of five stages: (a) release of the neurotransmitter, (b) interaction with the receptor, (c) degradation of the neurotransmitter, (d) diffusion from the receptor, and (e) resynthesization or restoration of the neurotransmitter (Ophardt, 2003). When drugs enter the system they act on and modify processes in these different stages. There are four ways in which they may do this:

1. Drugs can mimic certain neurotransmitters.
2. Drugs may also block the effects of neurotransmitters by fitting into receptor sites and preventing neurotransmitters from acting.
3. Drugs may affect the length of time a neurotransmitter remains in the synaptic gap.
4. Drugs may increase or decrease the amount of neurotransmitter released (Lane Community College, 2008).

TABLE 15.1

Major Neurotransmitters

Neurotransmitter	Function	Drug and Its Effects
Acetylcholine	Excitatory 1. Muscle contractions in motor neurons 2. Memory formation, learning, and intellectual function (in the hippocampus)	Nicotine: increases the release of acetylcholine
Dopamine	Excitatory 1. Voluntary muscle control 2. Attention, learning, and memory 3. Emotional arousal	Amphetamines: primarily increase dopamine and norepinephrine levels (to some extent serotonin) and activate the sympathetic nervous system
Endorphins	Inhibitory 1. Pain perception 2. Sexuality, pregnancy, and labor 3. Positive emotions (associated with aerobic exercise)	Opiates: increase the production of endorphins
Gamma Aminobutyric Acid (GABA)	Inhibitory 1. Relay messages to other neurons 2. Balance and offset excitatory messages	Alcohol, Valium, and Xanax: increase GABA activity to slow brain activity and inhibit action potential
Norepinephrine	Excitatory and inhibitory 1. Heartbeat and arousal 2. Learning and memory 3. Eating	Amphetamines: primarily increase dopamine and norepinephrine levels (to some extent serotonin) and activate the sympathetic nervous system
Serotonin	Excitatory or inhibitory 1. Mood 2. Sexual behavior 3. Pain perception 4. Sleep 5. Eating behavior 6. Maintaining a balanced body temperature and hormonal state	Ecstasy (MDMA): may destroy serotonin nerve cells in moderate or high doses Prozac: prevents the reuptake of serotonin so that more is available

Note. Information is from Lane Community College (2008).

Drug Availability and Variation

Despite all the laws that have been placed against drugs, people continually find a way to manufacture, distribute, and consume them. Should a drug become illegal, distributors will find a way to sell it in the black market, create a substitute, or begin production of something entirely new. In fact, some 25.6% of youth have offered, sold, or given an illegal drug to someone on school property (CDC, 2012). Today some of the more commonly used illegal drugs by adolescents include the following: amphetamines (i.e., black beauties, white bennies), methamphetamines (i.e., meth, speed, crank, crystal, ice, fire, glass), cocaine (i.e., coke, snow, nose candy, blow), heroin (i.e., smack, horse, brown sugar, junk, dope), phencyclidine (i.e., PCP, ozone, rocket fuel, angel dust), lysergic acid diethylamide (i.e., LSD, dots), and ecstasy (i.e., X, E, XTC, eccy, love drug). For those not interested in illegal drugs, there are other options. Adolescents may easily access OTC drugs that are not illegal, including cough suppressants (e.g., Robitussin, Coricidin Cold & Cough, Nyquil), stimulants (e.g., NoDoz, Vivarin), or painkillers with sleep aids (e.g., Tylenol PM, Advil PM). Prescription pills have also become a major concern. These drugs may be easily snuck out of the house and distributed to others. Furthermore, adolescents may fake symptoms to the family doctor in an attempt to acquire these drugs. From that point they might distribute as well. The most commonly abused prescription drugs include the following: opioids (e.g., OxyContin, Vicodin), CNS depressants (e.g., Xanax, Valium), and stimulants (e.g., Concerta, Adderall; NIDA for Teens, 2013). Another concern involves random household items being used as inhalants (e.g., air freshener, correctional fluid, canned whipped cream, and permanent markers). These seemingly not-so-dangerous chemicals (to misinformed youth) have been proven to cause Sudden Sniffing Death Syndrome in 22% of first-time users (Foundation for a Drug-Free World, 2012). To a great extent, then, it is some of the more easily acquired drugs (or chemicals) that adolescents abuse that lead toward the most significant problems. There are numerous drugs available, and this chapter examines more closely the following: nicotine, alcohol, marijuana, inhalants, ecstasy, methamphetamine, and prescription and OTC drugs.

Nicotine

Nicotine comes in many forms: cigars, cigarettes, e-cigarettes, transdermal patches, pills, gum, chewing tobacco, smokeless tobacco, snuff, and snus. With each of these the milligrams of nicotine differs, as does the method of ingestion. Smoking has been heralded as the "single most preventable cause of death in our society" (Oral Cancer Foundation, 2010, "Cigarettes"). According to the Oral Cancer Foundation (2010), cigarette smoking accounts for

- a 10- to 12-year decrease in life expectancy;
- a 90% addiction rate;
- more than 430,000 (or one in every five) deaths in the United States per year; and
- more deaths "than AIDS, alcohol, drug abuse, car crashes, murders, suicides, and fires—combined!" (Oral Cancer Foundation, 2010)

Aside from deaths by smoking, other forms of smokeless tobacco may prove just as dangerous. For instance, in India and Sri Lanka chewing tobacco has led to an alarming incidence of oral cancer that accounts for about 50% of all cancers combined (Oral Cancer Foundation, 2010). Although tobacco use is legal at age 18, evidence continues to prove that it is dangerous at any age and at any time. To discourage smokers from smoking and improve the health of nonsmokers, various states have already begun imposing tax hikes on tobacco purchases along with restricted smoking areas (e.g., no public smoking in restaurants or bars).

Alcohol

Although legal for adults 21 and over in the United States, alcohol presents a myriad of concerns for individuals of all ages. With about 70.8% of youth having had at least one alcoholic beverage at least once (CDC, 2012), alcohol is the most commonly tried substance. In terms of youth, there are a variety of risk factors that lead toward use, abuse, and dependence. According to the National Institute on Alcohol Abuse and Alcoholism (NIAAA; 2000), these factors include the following: genetic risk factors, biological markers, childhood behavior, psychiatric disorders, suicidal behaviors, parenting, family environment, peers, expectancies, trauma, and advertising. Alcohol, or ethanol, comes in many varieties that suit one's taste (e.g., beer, wine, champagne, spirits, liqueurs) and desired level of intoxication (i.e., alcohol percentage, number of shots per drink). Although drinks vary, the defined standard for a drink is 12 grams of pure alcohol (i.e., 12-ounce bottle of beer or wine cooler, 5-ounce glass of wine, 1.5 ounces of 80-proof distilled spirits). Therefore, when clients say they've had a drink, it is important to note whether it is a bottle of beer or a three-shot mixed drink because one will intoxicate the youth much faster and to a greater intensity than the other.

Statistics from the American Medical Association (2013) have revealed that half of the 11 million or so underage American youth who consume alcohol drink to excess (with excess being defined in terms of five or more drinks in a row, once or more within a 2-week period). A common activity practiced by youth is that of drinking games, whereby participants take a drink in accordance with whatever the rules prescribe. Some games include beer pong, taps (flip-cup), card games, darts, word associations, or any other agreed upon activity. Depending on the type of drink consumed as well as personal factors (e.g., weight, gender, amount of food consumed prior), one's blood alcohol level may fluctuate significantly. According to NIAAA (2000), however, only a minority of these youth meet criteria for alcohol dependence as established by the *Diagnostic and Statistical Manual of Mental Disorders* (4th ed., text rev.; *DSM-IV-TR*; American Psychiatric Association, 2000). Beyond physical health risks (i.e., liver damage, kidney failure, brain damage), excessive drinking by youth has also contributed toward the following:

- approximately half of all teen vehicular accidents (the leading cause of death among teens);
- suicides, homicides, and fatal injuries (the second leading cause of death among teens);
- approximately two thirds of the sexual assaults and date rapes experienced by teens and college students; and
- an increase in HIV and other sexually transmitted diseases (STDs) attributable to failure to practice safe sex (American Medical Association, 2013).

To a degree, alcohol may be considered a gateway drug in that its use by especially young children oftentimes correlates with later use of other substances. The mentality at this young age is that "if I am breaking the law already, what's the harm in trying something else?" Crossing boundaries becomes easier and easier as more boundaries are crossed. Even if the youth's use of alcohol does not develop into another substance abuse problem, the level of severity may lead toward even more devastating consequences than anything else.

It is important that youth have someone to monitor, positively influence, and in some cases discipline them when they begin participating in this type of risk-taking behavior. Although it may not always be apparent whether or not a child has a problem with alcohol, there are some signs to watch for. Such signs may include the following:

- unkempt appearance;
- red, flushed cheeks;
- attempts to cover breath (e.g., with gum or mints);
- failure to meet curfew;
- eye contact avoidance;
- locked doors as well as being silent and uncommunicative;
- secretive phone calls;
- reckless driving;
- change of friends;
- continued use of excuses for misbehavior (most nonsensical);
- truancy, loss of interest, or grade decline at school;
- depression; and
- failure to fulfill responsibilities or priorities (Alcoholism Guide, 2012).

Lowered inhibitions are a major concern with alcohol use. Aside from an increased risk of reckless driving and misbehavior, using alcohol also increases the probability youth will engage in unsafe sex, will demonstrate risk-taking behaviors, will make more poor judgment calls, and will have suicidal ideation or attempts. Many of these signs may also be applied toward all of the other drugs in the sections to follow. As a rule of thumb, a sudden and intense change in behavior for the negative might prove indicative of a substance disorder.

Marijuana

Perhaps no other drug is referred to more often as a gateway drug than marijuana. For years this drug has gotten the bad rap of being responsible for people's interest and participation in other, "harder" drugs. Unlike alcohol, which has been socially acceptable again in the United States since the end of Prohibition in 1933, marijua-

---

Sidebar 15.3 ■ Case Study: Daniel

Daniel is a 16-year-old high school student who has had his fair share of life experience. Although he is a high school weightlifting champion, is a black belt in karate, is an honor roll student, and holds a job, he has lived a difficult life. At age 2 he was placed in foster care when his mom was killed in a drunk driving accident and his father was not able to care for him. Though he was adopted by a loving, supportive family at age 5, his foster parents continually faced financial hardship. Daniel lived in a small apartment (where he shared a bedroom with two other brothers), walked to school, wore tattered clothing, and never had any of the latest technology. As a result, he was picked on and did most everything on his own. His interest in weightlifting and karate began as a plight to defend himself. Although his success in both activities greatly enhanced his self-esteem, he has been suspended on multiple occasions for getting into fistfights with classmates. During the middle of sophomore year Daniel met Silver, a new transfer. The two began hanging out. Their favorite activities were working out, practice fighting, and driving around in Silver's car. Silver had a secret, though. After being friends for 2 months, he revealed that he likes to dabble in drugs and alcohol. Reluctant at first, Daniel decided to take his first shot.

Think: Though Daniel has only taken a single shot, are there any warning signs for a potential problem in the future? If so, what are the warning signs? Why are they warning signs? Do you feel as though there is any need for prevention measures in this situation? If so, why and which ones?

■ ■ ■

na has not gained more significant social support until recently. Thus, its status as a drug makes it closer to other drugs than, say, alcohol. As with alcohol use, many similar warning signs are present with marijuana use. Rather than strong-smelling breath and slurred speech, however, the child may come home with red eyes and stink of an unusual odor. Marijuana (also known as pot, grass, herb, weed, Mary Jane, ganja, reefer) contains some 400 chemicals, including delta-9-tetrahydrocannabinol (THC), the main psychoactive ingredient (NIDA for Teens, 2013). Thus, the strength or potency of the marijuana is directly correlated to its THC level. It triggers the release of dopamine, which makes users feel euphoric or high. This is why THC content has continued to increase in potency since modified growing techniques arose in the 1970s. Marijuana may be smoked, brewed, or cooked. If smoking is the preferred method, inhalation may take place through a joint (cigarette), blunt (cigar), bong (large water pipe), bowl (pipe), hitter (small pipe), tin can, gas mask, or vaporizer. Because drug paraphernalia is illegal to possess, youth may purchase various means of disguising it. These products may include but are not limited to the following: cigarette look-alike hitters, hitter boxes, beverage containers (i.e., cans, bottles), markers/highlighters, lipstick, or even manmade rocks. In terms of brewing, marijuana is generally made in tea. Those who opt to cook marijuana generally eat it in brownies, cookies, cakes, or other baked goods.

Marijuana use by adolescents has revealed a correlation that directly relates to adult social acceptance. The NIDA for Teens (2013) revealed a decline in use from the late 1990s until the mid-to-late 2000s, with an increase ever since—an increase to the extent that more teens now smoke marijuana than cigarettes.

> In 2012, 6.5 percent of 8th graders, 17.0 percent of 10th graders, and 22.9 percent of 12th graders used marijuana in the past month—an increase among 10th and 12th graders from 14.2 percent, and 18.8 percent in 2007. Daily use has also increased; 6.5 percent of 12th graders now use marijuana every day, compared to 5.1 percent in the 2007. (NIDA, 2012a, "Illicit Drug Use," para. 1)

Other recent trends of concern involve the creation of synthetic marijuana (e.g., spice, K2), which contains herbal mixtures laced with synthetic cannabinoids. Although this type of marijuana may not appear on certain drug tests, it is not a safe alternative to the real deal.

Because smoking marijuana is partaking in the activity of smoking, the same risk factors involved in cigarette smoking are of concern for marijuana smokers. The reality is that marijuana smoke contains similar levels of tar and up to 50% more carcinogens then cigarettes (Moore, Augustson, Moser, & Budney, 2005). Thus, there are similar rates of various forms of cancer and other respiratory problems associated with its use. THC affects brain functioning by binding to cannabinoid receptors in brain cells (NIDA for Teens, 2013). This process interferes with learning and memory, which accounts for the stereotypical jokes that make fun of users' impaired short-term memory. Next, THC interferes with balance and coordination. The subsequent slower reaction times generally impair physical activity or driving. Because this combination makes many activities more difficult to do, users develop a perceived lack of motivation. In addition, it may increase heart rate by 20 to 50 beats per minute, which may be especially problematic for those with heart problems. Continued marijuana use may lead to addiction. Research assessed by the NIDA (2012a) reported that approximately 9% of users become addicted—a number that increases among those who start young (about 17%) and daily users (to 25%–50%). Those reporting long-term use do tend to experience some withdrawal symptoms (e.g., irritability, sleeplessness, decreased appetite, anxiety, craving) when they attempt to abstain or quit the drug altogether.

Inhalants

The U.S. Consumer Product Safety Commission (CPSC; 2013) estimates that over 1,000 different products are commonly abused. Many of these are common household or classroom items, including air fresheners, correctional fluid, permanent markers, highlighters, bleach, gasoline, paint, compressed air for computers, and so forth. To a great extent, these products are even more dangerous than any other drug as indicated by the extremely high percentage (23%) of deaths by first-time users (Foundation for a Drug-Free World, 2012). Because of their practical use, these products are extremely difficult to monitor or control. For instance, a 14-year-old could easy walk into an office supply store and purchase compressed air, markers, highlighters, and correctional fluid. A teen thinking he is being extra cautious might even throw in some notebooks, pencils, and folders for good measure.

Current studies have not revealed any particular type of individual who might be more likely to use or abuse inhalants (U.S. CPSC, 2013). There are, however, some common signs to tell if a child is abusing inhalants:

- unusual breath or clothing odor;
- slurred or disoriented speech;
- drunken-like appearance;
- signs of the chemical on the child (e.g., Wite Out on fingernails);
- red eyes and/or runny nose;
- mouth sores and/or spots;
- nausea and/or appetite loss; and
- mood swings consistent with anxiety, excitability, irritability, or restlessness (U.S. CPSC, 2013).

Should the child be approached while under the influence of inhalants, there may be the need to immediately contact the nearest poison control center or 911.

Because of the toxicity of the chemicals contained in these inhalants, physical damage to the body is a likely result. Just as inhalants may kill an individual on the first attempt, they may also cause permanent damage from just a single use. Such damage may be extensive and affect multiple systems within the body. In terms of the CNS, inhalants may directly affect the brain, cerebral cortex, cerebellum, ophthalmic nerve, PNS, and acoustic nerve (National Inhalants Prevention Coalition, 2013). Cellular death in these regions may lead to sensory disorders, psychological disorders, sight disorders, personality change, memory impairment, hallucinations, learning disabilities, trembling, loss of coordination, slurred speech, tingling, numbness, paralysis, or deafness, just to name a few! Because inhalants cause oxygen blockage or chemical poisoning in the blood stream, the heart, lungs, liver, and kidneys may become damaged or cease functioning. In addition, there is the subsequent deterioration of muscle and bone marrow that results from chronic and continued use. Clearly the consequences of inhalant use are severe enough to warrant professional counseling services.

Sidebar 15.4 ■ Counseling Approaches for Daniel

Since having his first shot with Silver, Daniel continued drinking over the following weeks. After throwing up after the first time he drank, he found that he enjoyed beer. Over the next month he would spend one weekend night out with Silver, and they would drink beer. Though five beers did the trick the first time, the following weeks it took seven, eight, and eventually twelve beers to do the job. Concerned that drinking so much beer would make him gain weight and become sluggish, he became curious to try something legal that would still give him a euphoric sensation. Silver knew just the trick! After a solid month of drinking, the two teens went to the grocery store and picked up some canned whipped cream, correctional fluid, and air freshener. Knowing how dangerous inhalants can be, Daniel opted out of the air freshener but tried the canned whipped cream and correctional fluid. The feeling he got in return was better and faster acting than alcohol. In addition, he did not feel any apparent effects upon returning to school on Monday.

Think: Though Daniel opted out of the air freshener, what was the harm in him trying the canned whipped cream and correctional fluid? Is Daniel fooling himself by thinking that these inhalants are a better alternative than alcohol? On the basis of his current progression, how might a counselor best approach Daniel?

■ ■ ■

Ecstasy

In the 1970s MDMA (3,4-methylenedioxy-methamphetamine) was developed to assist in psychotherapy. It was in 1985 that the Drug Enforcement Agency (DEA) classified it as a Schedule I substance, claiming it had no recognized medicinal purpose and a high abuse potential. Although the drug might not have served a medical purpose, the general public quickly found a way to put it to use. Once popular at dance clubs or raves, MDMA has steadily become popular among other demographics. MDMA works by increasing the activity of serotonin, dopamine, and norepinephrine. "The body normally releases serotonin a little at a time, but Ecstasy dumps it all" (Street Drugs, 2012, "Ecstasy," para. 4). It has psychoactive properties similar to those of the stimulant amphetamine, and the hallucinogen mescaline leaves users with "feelings of increased energy, euphoria, emotional warmth and empathy toward others, and distortions in sensory and time perception" (NIDA, 2012b, "DrugFacts: MDMA (Ecstasy)," para. 1). Users may refer to this experience as "rolling." Unlike with other drugs, many users claim that the effects are subtle yet intense in that they are personal in nature. As explained by Dr. Shulgin of *A Chemical Love Story*, "(With 100 mg) MDMA intrigued me because everyone I asked who had used it answered the question, 'What's it like?' in the same way: 'I don't know.' 'What happened?' 'Nothing.' And now I understand those answers. I too think nothing happened. But something seemed changed" (Shulgin & Shulgin, 2009, "Qualitative Comments," para. 1). In other words, the drug experience becomes something that leaves an impact on the mindset of the user; the experience is more than the drug.

Although most users swallow ecstasy in its pill form, some users crush and snort it, take it rectally as a suppository, inject it in its liquid form, or smoke it. These differences alter the metabolism of the drug, which alters the onset, duration, and intensity of the experience. On average, users begin to feel warm, tingly, and a bit lightheaded as it kicks in, and the effects last about 3 to 6 hours (TheDEA.org, 2013). Side effects of use vary depending on the amount taken, frequency of use, and length of time it is used. Although rare-to-moderate users may have minimal permanent effects, chronic users may suffer from severe and pervasive side effects to the extent of being potentially life threatening. While intoxicated (or shortly thereafter), users might experience the following: pupil dilation, dry mouth, minor visual effects, nystagmus (involuntary eye movements), diminished attention span, bruxism (teeth clenching/grinding), digestive upset/loss of appetite, difficulty urinating, and difficulties regulating body temperature. Body temperature regulation is especially frightening as there may be occasions where users experience hyperthermia (drastic increase in body temperature) that may reach as high as 108°F (Street Drugs, 2012). This is an area of concern, because such an occurrence "can result in liver, kidney, or cardiovascular system failure or even death" (NIDA, 2012b, "What Are Other Health Effects of MDMA?" para. 2). To combat some of these side effects, users will drink excessive amounts of water and consume 5-HTP, Vitamin C, or other antioxidants. Longer lasting effects outside of the period of intoxication include confusion, drug cravings, impotence, problems with attention and memory, sleeping problems, psychological disturbances (e.g., depression, anxiety), cardiovascular damage, and brain damage.

Because MDMA is a synthetic drug, users must watch that their pills are actually pure MDMA and not some fake pill that may include one or a combination of multiple more dangerous chemicals. Common fakes include amphetamine, caffeine, codeine, DXM, ephedra, ketamine, MDA, methamphetamine, and PCP (Street Drugs, 2012). In other instances, users like to mix the effects of MDMA with other drugs—an act known as "candy-flipping." These drugs might include alcohol, cocaine, GHB, LSD, methamphetamine, mushrooms (psilocybin), ketamine, and Viagra. Such interactions might significantly increase the chances of any one or a combination of side effects occurring. Because the drug increases people's desire to touch one another, unsafe sexual practices are also of concern (NIDA, 2012b). In some cases, once individuals experience sex under the drug, sex without it is never the same. Hence a desire to continue using the drug ensues or dissatisfaction with succeeding sexual experiences becomes the norm. This is yet another means by which psychological disorders are exacerbated.

Methamphetamine

Methamphetamine (meth) is an extremely addictive synthetic CNS stimulant. Although it was also created (and is in some rare cases still used) for medical purposes, its highly addictive property has it listed as a Schedule II drug (NIDA, 2012c). The drug in its various forms may be smoked, injected, inhaled, or even swallowed. It is most common for people to smoke it in its crystalline form. Because it is synthetic and may be made using store-bought goods, anyone with the knowledge of how to create meth may do so. The most important ingredient is pseudoephedrine, an item that may be picked up at any drug store. Knowing this, some stores prohibit cold medication sales to minors or place a limit on the number that may be purchased. The remaining ingredients are toxic in nature and actually resemble the chemistry of some types of bombs—a reason why meth labs have a high likelihood of exploding if the chemist is not careful (MethProject.org, 2012).

According to the NIDA (2011), some 13 million people age 12 and over have abused meth at some point in their lifetime, and about 353,000 are current users. The good news, if there is any good news when it comes to meth, is that use rates among youth have been on the decline. The NIDA's 2010 Monitoring the Future Survey revealed that the rate of use among 8th to 12th graders significantly declined between 1999 and 2007 and has leveled off from that point onward. Perhaps this decline is attributable to drug education that has stressed how dangerous this drug actually is. Or perhaps it is because other drugs (e.g., marijuana, MDMA) are more popular among today's youth. In all likelihood it is a combination of factors. For users, this manmade drug is significantly less expensive than its counterpart (cocaine). Given the low cost, then, it is something that may be affordable to those of lower socioeconomic status. Although anybody living anywhere may become addicted to meth, cost is a major contributor to the meth epidemic occurring in impoverished communities, rural regions, and minority populations. More specifically, particular problems have been reported in the Midwest, Hawaii, and the West Coast (NIDA, 2011). Thus, various anti-meth organizations have been established throughout the country.

The effects of meth on one's physical and mental state cannot be overstated. When meth enters the brain it forces the release of dopamine while also blocking transporters to cause the dopamine to get trapped within the synapse (MethProject.org, 2012). This overstimulation is experienced as a feeling of intense euphoria to the user. Because the dopamine transporters are blocked, brain cells cannot recycle dopamine. Thus, there is literally less and less dopamine available after each subsequent high. Consequently, users feel compelled to abuse larger quantities of the drug in attempt to relive that first, most immaculate high—hence the phrase "chasing the dragon." In due time the brain chemistry changes to the extent that so little dopamine is released that the user no longer experiences feelings of pleasure. This loss of dopamine may also cause cognitive impairment, poor memory retention, and motor dysfunction (MedlinePlus, 2013). Other adverse health effects may entail irregular heartbeat, increased blood pressure, violent mood changes, severe mental disorders, open sores, severe dental problems (meth mouth), muscle degradation, appetite loss, poor hygiene, and a host of severe mental disorders (e.g., meth-induced psychosis, anxiety, depression, confusion, insomnia). Because of its tendency to sometimes cause paranoia, panic, and other aversive effects, meth has been directly linked to violent episodes, murders, and other criminal activities (Stevens & Smith, 2009). All in all, this drug is extremely dangerous.

Prescription and OTC Drugs

Equally frightening as, if not even more so than, all of the other drugs previously mentioned is the misuse and abuse of prescription and OTC drugs. In a survey conducted to reveal how many Americans had abused a prescribed drug within the past 30 days, over 6 million people aged 12 or older had used such drugs for nonmedical use at least once—a number that came out higher than the number of cocaine, heroin, hallucinogen, MDMA, and inhalant use combined (DuPont, 2010). In addition, "In 2008, 4.7% of high school seniors used OxyContin nonmedicinally, 9.7% used Vicodin, 5.8% used sedatives, 6.2% used tranquilizers, and 2.4% used Ritalin" (DuPont, 2010, p. 128). Should this trend continue, the future drug epidemic will shift from meth to prescription and OTC drugs. According to Maxwell (2011), "The epidemic is characterized by a number of different factors which contributed to the problem, including inappropriate or incorrect prescribing; a variety of drug sources (both legal and illegal); belated governmental response;

and aggressive marketing for off-label use by pharmaceutical companies" (p. 264). Because these drugs are legal and may prove easier to acquire than some illegal drugs, they are an attractive option for youth. In terms of getting in trouble with the law, they also pose less of a threat. Why risk arrest with heroin when carrying a couple OxyContin carries with it much less severe legal consequences? In addition, there are some people who become addicted to prescription and OTC drugs out of ignorance: They assume that because a drug was prescribed or is sold over the counter it must not have any deleterious effects. If one were to pay attention to the fine print and fast talk of those drug advertisements on TV, the Internet, and other media, though, it would be apparent that this is not the case. Symptoms for some of the most seemingly harmless drugs may include anything from skin sores to liver damage to heart failure. Individuals who are ill or require particular medical assistance may also be at risk. The story of Tim Rader at the beginning of this chapter is an excellent example.

When abusing prescription and other OTC drugs, most people do not pay attention to the extremely important factors that are generally considered by medical professionals. These factors include one's weight, susceptibility to dangerous side effects, age, gender, and past and current medical conditions in addition to possible reactions caused when the medication is used in combination with other drugs. Failure to pay attention to any one or a combination of these factors may result in consequences as severe as death. Although prescription drugs are generally more powerful than OTC drugs, OTC drugs are not any less dangerous (NIDA for Teens, 2013). High dosages of these medications, especially in conjunction with alcohol use, may produce catastrophic effects—a reason why some OTC medications hold restrictions for minors. In 2006, there were over 38,000 drug-induced overdose deaths in the United States, a record high that surpassed any other year prior (DuPont, 2010).

Prevention and Intervention

Counselor Considerations and Characteristics

In order to best serve any client in any capacity, professional counselors are required by the American Counseling Association's (ACA's) *Code of Ethics* (ACA, 2005) to jointly work with their clients to create a unique treatment plan that

---

Sidebar 15.5 ■ Daniel's Diagnosis and Treatment

Because purchasing inhalants was getting somewhat expensive, Daniel started to think of yet another replacement that would help them still have a good time but not cost them any more money. Then he had a thought! About 2 years ago his foster father had a bad accident at work and was prescribed Vicodin and Ambien to take at night. Since the accident his foster father has taken the medication regularly, and his doctor refills his prescriptions without question. With a seemingly endless supply of Vicodin and Ambien in sight, the boys ditched inhalants for prescription pills.

Think: At this point do you think that Daniel might have a diagnosable substance disorder? If so, what? How would you treat it? Have any additional critical factors been layered into this case study?

■ ■ ■

most appropriately addresses their needs (A.1.c). With that there are some questions to consider:

1. Is the client substance abusive or dependent? How severe?
2. What are the environmental factors weighing on the client (e.g., social life, school, parents, relationships, and so forth)?
3. How is the client responding on an emotional level?
4. Is the client motivated to change?
5. Are there any other diagnosable disorders present?
6. What is the best course of intervention and maintenance?

Although there are plenty of other questions to consider as well, these really help paint a comprehensive picture as to what lies ahead.

The most effective youth substance abuse counselors generally hold personal characteristics or skills that are compatible for this type of counseling. Dealing with substance disorders requires a lot of persistence, energy, and even hope. For some children, issues more urgent than the substance abuse are present. This may realistically be the case for the following: children of parents who have substance disorders; adolescents who are victims of physical, sexual, or psychological abuse; adolescents with mental health problems (e.g., depression and suicidal ideation); gay, lesbian, bisexual, or transgender youth; bullying victims; children in poverty; minorities; and physically disabled adolescents. Even as a counselor of another discipline it is important to consider such disorders, as they may prove comorbid within another primary diagnosis. Thus, "it is essential that all mental health professionals understand the process of abuse and addiction, the etiology of addiction, the individual, family, societal costs; and available treatment modalities" (Stevens & Smith, 2009, p. 19).

Diagnosing Substance/Medication-Induced Disorders

Because all theories, approaches, treatment plans, and so on are all predicated upon evidence-based research, it is vital that this information is as up to date as possible. Thus, the *Diagnostic and Statistical Manual of Mental Disorders* (*DSM*) has undergone a number of revisions (in 1968, 1980, 1987, 1994, and 2000) since its original publication in 1952. The *DSM-5* (American Psychiatric Association, 2013) has recently been released and seeks to strengthen the diagnosis criteria for substance use disorders while using less stigmatizing language. Unlike the *DSM-IV-TR*, this newer edition does not separate the diagnoses of substance abuse and dependence. Rather, it diagnoses substance use along a spectrum of mild to moderate to severe.

Criteria for substance/medication-induced mental disorders as diagnosed by the *DSM-5* (2013) include:

A. The disorder represents a clinically significant symptomatic presentation of a relevant mental disorder.
B. There is evidence from the history, physical examination, or laboratory findings of both of the following:
    1. The disorder developed during or within 1 month of a substance intoxication or withdrawal or taking a medication; and

    2. The involved substance/medication is capable of producing the mental disorder.

C. The disorder is not better explained by an independent mental disorder (i.e., one that is not substance- or medication-induced). Such evidence of an independent mental disorder could include the following:

    1. The disorder preceded the onset of severe intoxication or withdrawal or exposure to the medication; or

    2. The full mental disorder persisted for a substantial period of time (e.g., at least 1 month) after the cessation of acute withdrawal or severe intoxication or taking the medication. This criterion does not apply to substance-induced neurocognitive disorders or hallucinogen persisting perception disorder, which persist beyond the cessation of acute intoxication or withdrawal.

D. The disorder does not occur exclusively during the course of a delirium.

E. The disorder causes clinically significant distress or impairment in social, occupational, or other important areas of functioning.

    (American Psychiatric Association, 2013, p. 488)

Substance-related disorders include: alcohol-related disorders; caffeine-related disorders; cannabis-related disorders; hallucinogen-related disorders; inhalant-related disorders; opioid-related disorders; sedative-, hypnotic-, or anxiolytic-related disorders; stimulant-related disorders; tobacco-related disorders; and other (or unknown) substance-related disorders. Severity of the *DSM-5* (2013) substance use disorders is contingent upon the specific characteristics of a particular substance and are based upon the number of criteria met: a) mild disorders meet 2–3 criteria, b) moderate disorders meet 4–5 criteria, and c) severe disorders meet 6 or more. Additionally, the *DSM-5* (2013) added the new criterion of craving or urge to use a substance while recurrent legal problems has been eliminated.

Factors Contributing to Substance Abuse in Youth

Sobeck, Abbey, Agius, Clinton, and Harrison (2000) found that early-age onset of experimental substance use was the best predictor of later substance abuse. Those who experimented before sixth grade were found to have poorer decision-making skills, more susceptibility to peer pressure, more negative perceptions of school, and less confidence in their skills than those who did not. Even for those youth who do not experiment with substances, adolescence itself presents the opportunity for emotional and behavioral concerns. According to Fontaine, Archer, Elkins, and Johansen (2001), "Adolescents tend to report more unusual symptoms suggestive of serious psychopathology and deviant social views, greater impulsivity and rebelliousness, and more isolation and alienation from their social environment, in a manner that is consistent with traditional views of adolescence as a turbulent stage of development" (pp. 265–266). Because childhood and adolescence are marked by a rate of growth and development exceeding that reached at any other point in life, experiences occurring during these years may have an impact lasting the rest of the youth's life (Santrock, 2007). The sections to follow explain how evidence-based therapy may be applied toward each critical area.

Evidence-Based Therapy

The most successful therapy models are those that are multidimensional and work across the critical areas of the individual, family, school, and community

(Guo, Hawkins, Hill, & Abbott, 2007). Within these critical areas are numerous factors that may perpetuate use, abuse, and addiction. Such factors may entail extreme poverty, easy availability of substances, parental alcoholism, high levels of family conflict, lenient school policies, association with peers who use, a sensation-seeking disposition, academic failure, and psychopathology. Two evidence-based approaches that successfully work at the individual, family, school, and community level are behavioral management (e.g., contingency management) and cognitive behavior therapy (CBT; Dennis, Dawud-Noursi, Muck, & McDermeit, 2003). Behavioral management approaches aim to replace maladaptive substance use behaviors with healthier, more functional ones. Here the clinician will find it advantageous to determine the adolescent's positive reinforcements. The question to ask is, "What else could the child be doing to break this cycle of abuse?" Rather than skip seventh period to hang out with delinquent friends, a better approach might entail attending class and joining an extracurricular activity. CBT approaches, however, incorporate one's cognitions (e.g., thoughts, knowledge, experiences, emotions) and implement multiple components derived from classical conditioning, operant conditioning, and social learning perspectives (e.g., self-monitoring, avoidance of stimulus cues, modeling, coping-skills training, assertiveness training, communication skills, anger management, relapse prevention).

Because changing one's behavior is not an easy feat, clinicians must generally follow a process that not only encourages behavioral change but also terminates the original maladaptive behavior. Prochaska and DiClemente's (1982) transtheoretical model using the motivational interviewing (MI) approach has revealed six notable stages of change: (a) pre-contemplation, (b) contemplation, (c) preparation, (d) action, (e) maintenance, and (f) termination (Wood, 2006). Each stage is unique and holds a specific goal that must be completed in order to proceed to the following stage. By processing change one step at a time, the opportunity for effective behavioral change is significantly increased; however, not meeting the youth where he or she is at might break trust in the relationship and impede progress.

Individual

On an individual level, there are a variety of options to meet the child's or adolescent's needs (e.g., psychosocial, socioeconomic, physical) and fit with his or her current available resources (e.g., money, transportation). For instance, any number of community mental health agencies, hospitals, crisis hotlines, various shelters, and private practice therapists may appropriately provide some type of basic-to-advanced counseling services. During therapy, the clinician should explore the child's or adolescent's lived experience at home, at school, and with peers (Stevens & Smith, 2009). In addition, the clinician should explore levels of anger and feelings of belonging, hopelessness, self-efficacy, and self-esteem. Another important individual component resides in motivation to change. The fact is that one can wish a substance disorder away or see the best clinician in the country, but if that client is not willing to put forth the effort needed to change, nothing will happen. Strategies involving MI use Rogerian principles to prepare and subsequently engage clients in treatment. To do this effectively, counselors are strongly encouraged to (a) express empathy, (b) develop discrepancy, (c) roll with resistance, and

(d) support self-efficacy (Capuzzi & Stauffer, 2011). Once the client acknowledges the reality and severity of the substance disorder and wants to do something about it, the process of change may begin. Therefore, MI is particularly useful during the pre-contemplation and contemplation stages as "an empathic, gentle, and skillful type of counseling that helps practitioners have productive conversations" (Substance Abuse and Mental Health Services Administration, 2011).

Family

Evidence indicates that biological predispositions may be passed from one generation to the next, therefore increasing the likelihood that succeeding generations will also suffer from substance-related disorders (Stevens & Smith, 2009).

> Genetically influenced factors may be important in how the effects are experienced. For instance, the individual's personality, level of anxiety, rate of metabolism, and the nervous system's sensitivity to the drug may all contribute to the final balance between a positive and negative experience of the first ingestion of a drug that will influence the individual's decision to try again. (Stevens & Smith, 2009, pp. 94–95)

Combining this disposition with the wrong environmental factors may lead toward the youth's propensity to use.

One would be remiss not to consider the child's home environment as one of, if not the, most important environmental considerations. Aside from passing on their genes, parents have a significant impact on the child's environment. If caregivers (e.g., relative, foster home, foster parent) are raising the child, these individuals will also have a significant impact on the child. Home is where a child learns, experiences, and receives or is denied love, nourishment, shelter, protection, hygiene, support, knowledge, recreation, and so on. Social cognitive theory "posits that response patterns to particular stimuli are learned through either experience or observation" (Fireman & Kose, 2002). Thus, one's self-system in learning results from a combination of experiences that facilitate (a) vicarious reinforcement, (b) symbolic activities, (c) forethought activity, (d) self-regulatory capabilities, (e) self-reflecting capability, (f) self-efficacy, and (g) self-reinforcement (Malone, 2002). In other words, children tend to mimic the behaviors of their parents or caregivers (Santrock, 2007). To this extent, pervasive familial discord or substance abuse increases the likelihood of negative consequences.

> This makes the children in these families at high risk for the development of a variety of stress-related disorders, including conduct disorders, poor academic performance and inattentiveness. Children in substance-abusing families are socially immature, lack self-esteem and self efficacy, and have deficits in social skills. (Stevens & Smith, 2009, p. 257)

Should the metaphorical apple not fall far from the tree, the child may fall prey to the same traps the parent or caregiver had. Survey results from a quantitative study by Guo et al. (2007) revealed that "strong bonding to school, close parental monitoring of children and clearly defined family rules for behavior, appropriate parental rewards for good behaviors, high level of refusal skills and strong belief in the moral order predicted a lower risk for alcohol abuse and dependence at age 21" (p. 754). Unfortunately, this type of environment is not always available or provided; and even in cases where it is, there are always exceptions. Take for instance the adolescent who just went through her first breakup. Upset to the point she thinks her world might end, she begins using drugs to make the pain go away. The examples are many, but the point is that any little environmental factor might prove powerful enough to trigger the onset of drug-related behavior. Regardless, a healthy familial relationship serves as a buffer between the child and all other aspects of the environment that might prove harmful (Carr, Moore, & Robinson-Kurpius, 2005; Hart & Robinson-Kurpius, 2005).

Approaches intentionally designed to work with youth within the familial context, such as multidimensional family therapy and others, seek both to understand how familial influences impact the substance use and to create treatment plans that help the home achieve a healthy dynamic (NIDA, 2009). Communication dynamics between the parents (or caregivers) and the child are significant. Although content is important, parents and clinicians must also pay attention to associated feelings and nonverbal cues. Does what the youth says make sense? Is there another explanation for deviant behavior, or do the patterns fall in line with those symptomatic of a particular substance disorder? Any inconsistencies warrant further exploration (Stevens & Smith, 2009). An additional behavioral intervention involves applying logical consequences for deviant behaviors. This approach challenges youth to assume responsibility for their behaviors. Logical consequences, by this token, may be applied both firmly and consistently, and positive reinforcements can be applied for desired behaviors. This type of behavioral contracting requires that deviant and desired behaviors be clearly defined and agreed upon. For instance, coming home 15 minutes late without calling might be reason for one night's grounding, whereas being dropped off by a police officer because of public intoxication might be reason for an entire month's grounding without driving privileges. Terms of the contract may be renegotiated as necessary.

School

The school setting is an excellent place for alcohol and drug education, prevention, and intervention strategies. These strategies may be either formal or informal but must address those factors involved in the etiology of substance abuse and involve some behavioral, cognitive, and affective strategies components (Hart & Robinson-Kurpius, 2005). In addition, multicomponent approaches are better than one-dimensional ones. That is, the more in depth the approach gets over a broader spectrum of related topics, the more equipped the youth becomes to approach a similar situation in the future.

If done well, something as simple as hosting an inspirational speaker during an assembly may go a long way. Hanging posters with drugs facts and statistics throughout the school may make certain students think twice before using substances or at the very least make better, safer decisions when they do. Short workshops that focus on information and skill-based training (e.g., assertiveness, decision-making skills) may help students make informed decisions about substance use (McWhirter, McWhirter, McWhirter, & McWhirter, 2007). These workshops can help students identify critical situations and circumstances where they might need to use some of these skills. Then, a more creative strategy may involve having students pledge sobriety for a semester or school year. Perhaps an incentive for such a program is a school-sponsored event or small scholarship toward college. The important thing is that the delivery of the message is one that works for that specific audience.

Formal, ongoing educational programs are another approach toward alcohol and drug education, prevention, and intervention. One such example that has been met with proven success in numerous studies is the D.A.R.E. (Drug Abuse Resistance Education) America program (D.A.R.E. America, 2012). D.A.R.E. uses police officers to provide educational information and share stories that scare kids straight. Here children are issued the "dare," or challenge, to "Just say no!" when approached with alcohol and drugs. Organizations like Operation Snowball actually band together abstinent students and educate them to impart safer practices to their friends. Furthermore, they offer training sessions (to groups of students and parents) that cover a broad variety of topics dealing with substance use issues (Operation Snowball, 2012). Whether hosting groups, seeing students individually, or providing psychoeducational information to entire classrooms, school counselors may also make an impact. By working with a third party, the child may divulge the critical information underlying the substance issue. Working through that issue (or issues), the child may begin to focus on the substance issue. For real changes to occur, however, students must believe in the counselor as an advocate, not someone who is there simply to scold or punish. Unfortunately, today's economy makes it difficult for many schools to afford a school counselor.

One must never discount the influence one's cohort has over beliefs, experiences, behaviors, and so on. If birds of a feather truly do flock together, it is important that they flock toward the right direction. Thus, naturally occurring peer groups are effective ways of relaying information to youth (Robinson-Kurpius, 2000). Groups along these lines that help may also be formal or informal. For instance, a member of the football team who has daily practice and games on the weekend might not have time to partake in substance abuse; or if that individual does find the time to develop a problem, the team may band together to help the teammate out. In organizations like Operation Snowball, peers educated on the topic may facilitate these groups. Those who take the peer group seriously may share and learn from peer experiences and difficulties. There is also comfort simply in knowing that one is not alone. For example, attendees who have never used may appreciate having the support of other abstinent students. Peer pressure does affect these students too!

Community

The community itself may also prove to be a valuable asset in combating youth alcohol and drug abuse. As identified by McWhirter et al. (2007), there are five types of community-based programs that address youth substance abuse: (a) drug-free programs, (b) residential treatment facilities, (c) day-care programs, (d) aftercare programs, and (e) therapeutic communities (TCs). Drug-free programs are generally offered as an outpatient service for children who use, and they also help keep children from using drugs in the first place. A child may attend a program like this both after school and on weekends, depending on the severity of use. These programs might facilitate open discussions, educational activities, or counseling services. For more serious issues that require inpatient services, residential treatment facilities focus on long-term recovery. By immersing youth who use in a program day in and day out (under constant supervision), residential treatment programs help adjust maladaptive thoughts and behaviors into healthier, more appropriate ones. Day-care programs are a bit less structured and focus more on academic learning and counseling as well as supervised social activities. Aftercare programs, then, target those who have been discharged from previous treatments (i.e., residential treatment). Similar to the process in residential treatment programs, the process in aftercare programs may be ongoing and focus on lifelong change. Finally, TCs are live-in communities that treat substance abuse as a disorder of the whole person; the focus is on mutual help as the primary agent of change. TCs are built on the principles of (a) community separateness; (b) a focus on the community, rather than personal, use of space; (c) community activities; (d) the view that community members are peers and role models; (e) work with staff who are rational authorities, role models, facilitators, and guides; (f) a structured day; (g) a phased therapeutic process; (h) job functions; and (i) peer groups (Jainchill, 2006). In summary, the TC essentially combines the efforts of all of the other groups into one so that the youth has the absolute best chance at maintenance and recovery.

Additional community-based efforts oftentimes involve the collaboration of groups (e.g., parents and teachers, teachers and city officials, city officials and the police department). Although D.A.R.E. primarily focuses its efforts on educating youth, it is not uncommon for police to offer resources to parents of such youth or align with others as a community task force to design community-wide prevention and intervention programs. Outside of school-sponsored after-school activities, Boys and Girl Scouts of America, Boys and Girls Clubs, and community YMCAs and YWCAs all provide enriching activities for youth. Though these programs do not specifically offer assistance in the area of substance abuse or counseling, they do foster productive behavior and meaningful relationships.

The Disease Model

Perhaps one of the most publically known treatments for alcoholism is the 12-step program facilitated through Alcoholics Anonymous. Beginning with admitting powerlessness to alcohol and culminating with the achievement of a spiritual awakening, alcoholics go through a series of 12 steps that each gradually removes them further and further from the substance until they finally regain control. The foundation of this program is built on the first step: acknowledging alcoholism as a disease to which the alcoholic is powerless (Kurtz, n.d.). Rather than view a substance disorder as something behavioral (i.e., deviant) or environmentally induced (i.e., substance-abusing peers, broken home), it is viewed in terms of a disease. "The disease model pervades addictions research and practice, despite evidence that addictive behaviour is not inevitably progressive, degenerative, or incurable; not unrelated to complex sociocultural and psychological factors; and that addictive behaviours are often similar to other behaviours which do not carry the same 'diagnosis'" (Larkin, Wood, & Griffiths, 2006, p. 208). Under the disease model clients may come to terms with their addiction, believing that it is something bigger than themselves—they have no control without help. "While the path to drug addiction begins with the voluntary act of taking drugs, over time a person's ability to choose not to do so becomes compromised, and seeking and consuming the drug becomes compulsive" (NIDA, 2009, "Drug Addiction Is a Complex Illness," para. 1).

Thus, "slips" or "lapses" constitute a return to the disease and negate all progress that the person has made in recovery before the relapse (Stevens & Smith, 2009). Whether the alcoholic gives himself or herself to God or another higher power, the point is submission to the drug. The individual is never fully cured but may eventually possess the power to control the alcoholism. Programs of this type may also be adjusted to work with those addicted to other drugs or with family members of those who are controlled by addiction.

Medication

Though professional counselors currently do not possess the licensure required to prescribe medication, it is important to consider and be familiar with the various benefits that current medications offer within different aspects of the treatment process. For instance, medications offer help in suppressing withdrawal symptoms during the detoxification process (NIDA, 2009). Medications may also be used to help repair brain functioning, prevent relapse, and diminish cravings, which is how medications such as methadone help curb the use of severely addictive drugs like heroin. Other drugs like disulfiram, or anabuse, discourage use by interfering with the degradation of the drug (in this case alcohol) so that those who use it are overcome with an ill feeling. Though these medications have proven useful in clinical trials, they are more often than not a supplement to a full-blown treatment plan that also includes some type of behavioral and/or cognitive modification. Simply replacing one drug with another is not how substance disorders are resolved.

Multicultural Considerations

Given that an individual's thoughts and actions are influenced by culture (Sue & Sue, 2008), it is appropriate to consider culture when working with substance use disorders. Diversity goes well beyond skin color. It includes everything within Hays's (2008) ADDRESSING format: Age and generational influences, Developmental disability, Disability acquired later in life, Religion and spiritual orientation, Ethnic and racial identity, Socioeconomic status, Sexual orientation, Indigenous heritage, National origin, and Gender. Thus, counselors must carefully attend to each of these factors. The *ACA Code of Ethics* (ACA, 2005) deems it unethical for any counseling professional to act in a manner that strays from that of clear, understandable, collaborative, and culturally appropriate practice (A.2.c). After all, "the primary responsibility of counselors is to respect the dignity and to promote the welfare of clients" (A.1.a.).

Unfortunately, there are many cases where minorities face oppression and discrimination, even when in "professional" situations. For instance, minorities are continuously subject to stereotypes, harassment, unequal opportunities, less pay, and so on (Coogan & Chen, 2007). Because many traditional psychological theories are rooted in Eurocentric male data, current beliefs and interventions must be modified to the unique client. This is perhaps the counselor's most significant challenge: to respectfully and effectively meet the needs of diverse persons. Therefore, minority-friendly treatments like multicultural therapy and feminist therapy may be used alone or in conjunction with one another as appropriate and may always be incorporated into a comprehensive substance treatment plan (Sharf, 2008). By understanding the client's culture in the context of the environment, the counselor may more easily understand the substance use disorder. Even with

> ### Sidebar 15.6 ■ Advance Your Clinical Opinion
>
> After reading this chapter and becoming familiar with the case of Daniel and Silver, what is your overall clinical opinion? As Daniel's counselor, what type of treatment approach would you take? Why? Defend your stance using evidence-based information.
>
> ■ ■ ■

clients of dominant demographics, it is always important to consider the cultural factors that shape the entirety of the individual.

Summary

1. Despite all the laws that have been enacted against drugs, people continually find a way to manufacture, distribute, and consume them. For those who for whatever reason do not have access to or choose not to use illegal drugs, there are still other options for abuse, including using prescription and OTC drugs and inhalants.

2. One difficulty in working with substance issues is society's varied opinion. Whereas one individual might believe all drugs (including alcohol) are bad, another might believe it's okay if the user meets legal restrictions. Then there are those who feel as though some drugs should be legalized while others remain banned.

3. Major neurotransmitters include the following: acetylcholine, dopamine, serotonin, endorphins, norepinephrine, and GABA. Neurotransmission in the synapse occurs through a series of five stages: (a) release of the neurotransmitter, (b) interaction with the receptor, (c) degradation of the neurotransmitter, (d) diffusion from the receptor, and (e) resynthesization or restoration of the neurotransmitter. The user experiences euphoria when drugs enter the system and modify these stages.

4. Substance use appears to follow societal and legal trends. Alcohol, which is legal at age 21, has been used by 70.8% of youth—a number higher than any other substance. Marijuana, a controversial drug that has recently gone through various stages of legalization, has been used by 23.1% of youth.

5. Behavioral change takes course over six notable stages: (a) pre-contemplation, (b) contemplation, (c) preparation, (d) action, (e) maintenance, and (f) termination.

6. The most successful therapy models are those that are multidimensional across individual, family, school, and community modalities. Specific treatments include but are not limited to the following: individual counseling, group counseling, family counseling, parental education, psychoeducational presentations/workshops, drug-free programs, residential treatment facilities, day-care programs, aftercare programs, TCs, ongoing educational programs, and community collaboration.

7. Regardless of the client, counselors should always incorporate demographic factors across Hays's (2008) ADDRESSING format: Age and generational influences, Developmental disability, Disability acquired later in life, Religion and spiritual orientation, Ethnic and racial identity, Socioeconomic status, Sexual orientation, Indigenous heritage, National origin, and Gender.

Useful Websites

Centers for Disease Control and Prevention
  http://www.cdc.gov
Foundation for a Drug-Free World
  http://www.drugfreeworld.org
National Inhalants Prevention Coalition
  http://www.inhalants.org
National Institute on Alcohol Abuse and Alcoholism
  http://www.niaaa.nih.gov
National Institute on Drug Abuse
  http://www.drugabuse.gov
National Institute on Drug Abuse for Teens
  http://teens.drugabuse.gov

References

Alcoholism Guide. (2012). *Adolescent alcoholism: Adolescent alcohol abuse*. Retrieved from http://www.the-alcoholism-guide.org/adolescent-alcoholism.html

American Counseling Association. (2005). *ACA code of ethics*. Alexandria, VA: Author.

American Medical Association. (2013). *Facts about youth and alcohol*. Retrieved from http://www.ama-assn.org/ama/pub/physician-resources/public-health/promoting-healthy-lifestyles/alcohol-other-drug-abuse/facts-about-youth-alcohol.page

American Psychiatric Association. (2000). *Diagnostic and statistical manual of mental disorders* (4th ed., text rev.). Washington, DC: Author.

American Psychiatric Association. (2012). *APA corrects* New York Times *article on changes to DSM-5's substance use disorders*. Retrieved from http://dsmfacts.org/issue-accuracy/apa-corrects-new-york-times-article-on-changes-to-dsm-5s-substance-use-disorders/

American Psychiatric Association (2013). *Diagnostic and statistical manual of mental disorders* (5th ed.). Washington, DC: Author.

Capuzzi, D., & Stauffer, M. (2011). *Career counseling: Foundations, perspectives, and applications* (2nd ed.). New York, NY: Routledge.

Carr, E. M., Moore, E. G. J., & Robinson-Kurpius, S. E. (2005). *The role of fathers in adolescent girls' at-risk behaviors*. Paper presented at the American Educational Research Association annual meeting, San Francisco, CA.

Centers for Disease Control and Prevention. (2012). *Youth online: High school Youth Risk Behavior Surveillance System (alcohol and other drug use)*. Retrieved from http://apps.nccd.cdc.gov/youthonline/App/QuestionsOrLocations.aspx?CategoryID=3

Christopher & Dana Reeve Foundation. (2013). *What is the central nervous system?* Retrieved from http://www.christopherreeve.org/site/c.ddJFKRNoFiG/b.4452157/k.3E9D/What_is_the_Central_Nervous_System.htm

Coogan, P. A., & Chen, C. P. (2007). Career development and counselling for women: Connecting theories to practice. *Counselling Psychology Quarterly, 20*, 191–204.

D.A.R.E. America. (2012). *Research/resources/evaluations*. Retrieved from http://www.dare.com/home/Resources/Default5647.asp?N=Resources&M=16&S=0

Dennis, M. L., Dawud-Noursi, S., Muck, R. D., & McDermeit, M. (2003). The need for developing and evaluating adolescent treatment models. In S. J. Stevens & A. R. Morral (Eds.), *Adolescent substance abuse treatment in the United States: Exemplary models from a national evaluation study* (pp. 3–34). New York, NY: Haworth Press.

DuPont, R. L. (2010). Prescription drug abuse: An epidemic dilemma. *Journal of Psychoactive Drugs, 42*, 127–132.

Fireman, G., & Kose, G. (2002). The effect of self-observation on children's problem solving. *Journal of Genetic Psychology, 163,* 410–423.

Fontaine, J. L., Archer, R. P., Elkins, D. E., & Johansen, J. (2001). The effects of MMPI-A *t*-score elevation on classification accuracy for normal and clinical samples. *Journal of Personality Assessment, 76,* 267–281.

Foundation for a Drug-Free World. (2012). *The truth about inhalants: International statistics.* Retrieved from http://www.drugfreeworld.org/drugfacts/inhalants/international-statistics.html

Guo, J., Hawkins, J. D., Hill, K. G., & Abbott, R. D. (2007). Childhood and adolescent predictors of alcohol abuse and dependence. *Journal of Studies on Alcohol and Drugs, 62,* 754–762.

Harrar, S. (2012). *Teen prescription drug abuse: How it begins.* Retrieved from http://www.philly.com/philly/blogs/healthy_kids/Teen-prescription-drug-abuse-how-it-begins.html

Hart, S., & Robinson-Kurpius, S. E. (2005). Relationship of personality, parent and peer attachment to adolescent girls' sexual behavior. In S. Kurpius, B. Kerr, & A. Harkins (Eds.), *Handbook for counseling girls and women* (pp. 257–273). Mesa, AZ: Nueva Science.

Hays, P. A. (2008). *Addressing cultural complexities in practice* (2nd ed.). Washington, DC: American Psychological Association.

Jainchill, N. (2006). Adolescent therapeutic communities: Future directions for practice and research. In H. A. Liddle & C. L. Rowe (Eds.), *Adolescent substance abuse: Research and clinical advances* (pp. 313–332). Cambridge, England: Cambridge University Press.

Kurtz, E. (n.d.). Alcoholics Anonymous and the disease concept of alcoholism. *Alcoholism Treatment Quarterly.* Retrieved from http://www.bhrm.org/papers/AAand%20DiseaseConcept.pdf

Lane Community College. (2008). *Summary of the known major neurotransmitters.* Retrieved from http://media.lanecc.edu/users/kime/ch2neurotrans.pdf

Larkin, M., Wood, R. T. A., & Griffiths, M. D. (2006). Towards addiction as relationship. *Addiction Research & Theory, 14,* 207–215.

Malone, Y. (2002). Social cognitive theory and choice theory: A compatibility analysis. *International Journal of Reality Therapy, 22,* 10–13.

Maxwell, J. C. (2011). The prescription drug epidemic in the United States: A perfect storm. *Drug and Alcohol Review, 30,* 264–270. doi:10.1111/j.14653362.2011.00291.x

McWhirter, J. J., McWhirter, B. T., McWhirter, E. H., & McWhirter, R. J. (2007). *At risk youth: A comprehensive response* (4th ed.). Pacific Grove, CA: Brooks/Cole.

MedlinePlus. (2013). *Methamphetamine.* Retrieved from http://www.nlm.nih.gov/medlineplus/methamphetamine.html

MethProject.org. (2012). *Meth: Not even once.* Retrieved from http://www.methproject.org

Moore, B. A., Augustson, E. M., Moser, R. P., & Budney, A. J. (2005). Respiratory effects of marijuana and tobacco use in a U.S. sample. *Journal of General Internal Medicine, 20,* 33–37.

National Inhalants Prevention Coalition. (2013). *Damage inhalants can do to the body & brain.* Retrieved from http://www.inhalants.org/damage.htm

National Institute on Alcohol Abuse and Alcoholism. (2000). *Alcohol alert.* Retrieved from http://pubs.niaaa.nih.gov/publications/aa37.htm

National Institute on Drug Abuse. (2009). *DrugFacts: Treatment approaches for drug addiction.* Retrieved from http://www.drugabuse.gov/publications/drugfacts/treatment-approaches-drug-addiction

National Institute on Drug Abuse. (2011). *Declines in methamphetamine abuse by youth.* Retrieved from http://www.drugabuse.gov/publications/topics-in-brief/methamphetamine-addiction-progress-need-to-remain-vigilant

National Institute on Drug Abuse. (2012a). *DrugFacts: High school and youth trends.* Retrieved from http://www.drugabuse.gov/publications/drugfacts/high-school-youth-trends?

National Institute on Drug Abuse. (2012b). *DrugFacts: MDMA (ecstasy)*. Retrieved from http://www.drugabuse.gov/publications/drugfacts/mdma-ecstasy

National Institute on Drug Abuse. (2012c). *DrugFacts: Methamphetamine*. Retrieved from http://www.drugabuse.gov/publications/drugfacts/methamphetamine

National Institute on Drug Abuse for Teens. (2013). *Prescription drug abuse*. Retrieved from http://teens.drugabuse.gov/facts/facts_rx1.php

Operation Snowball. (2012). *Trainings*. Retrieved from http://www.os-iti.org/code/os-conf.html

Ophardt, C. E. (2003). *Nervous system—overview*. Retrieved from http://www.elmhurst.edu/~chm/vchembook/661nervoussys.html

Oral Cancer Foundation. (2010). *Types of tobacco*. Retrieved from http://oralcancerfoundation.org/tobacco/types_of_tobacco.htm

Perazella, M. A., & Parikh, C. (2005). Pharmacology. *American Journal of Kidney Diseases, 46,* 1129–1139.

Prochaska, J. O., & DiClemente, C. C. (1982). Transtheoretical therapy: Toward a more integrative model of change. *Psychotherapy: Theory, Research and Practice, 19,* 276–288.

Robinson-Kurpius, S. E. (2000). Peer counseling. In A. E. Kazdin (Ed.), *Encyclopedia of psychology*. Washington, DC: American Psychological Association and Oxford University Press.

Santrock, J. W. (2007). *A topical approach to life-span development* (3rd ed.). New York, NY: McGraw-Hill.

Sharf, R. S. (2008). *Theories of psychotherapy and counseling: Concepts and cases* (4th ed.). Belmont, CA: Brooks/Cole, Cengage Learning.

Shulgin, A., & Shulgin, A. (2009). *Pihkal: A chemical love story* (#109 MDMA). Retrieved from http://www.erowid.org/library/books_online/pihkal/pihkal109.shtml

Sobeck, J., Abbey, A., Agius, E., Clinton, M., & Harrison, K. (2000). Predicting early adolescent substance use: Do risk factors differ depending on age of onset? *Journal of Substance Abuse, 11,* 89–102.

Stevens, P., & Smith, R. L. (2009). *Substance abuse counseling: Theory and practice* (4th ed.). Upper Saddle River, NJ: Pearson Education.

Street Drugs. (2012). *Ecstasy*. Retrieved from http://www.streetdrugs.org/html%20files/ecstasy.html

Substance Abuse and Mental Health Services Administration. (2011). *Training*. Retrieved from http://www.samhsa.gov/co-occurring/topics/training/skills.aspx

Sue, D. W., & Sue, D. (2008). *Counseling the culturally diverse: Theory and practice* (5th ed.). New York, NY: Wiley.

TheDEA.org. (2013). *The art of rolling*. Retrieved from http://thedea.org/letsroll.html

University of Pittsburgh. (2013). *About the brain and spinal cord*. Retrieved from http://www.neurosurgery.pitt.edu/neuro_oncology/brain/about.html

U.S. Consumer Product Safety Commission. (2013). *A parent's guide to preventing inhalant abuse*. Retrieved from http://www.cpsc.gov/cpscpub/pubs/389.html

Wood, C. (2006). Career counseling for clients with addictive behaviors. In D. Capuzzi & M. Stauffer (Eds.), *Career counseling: Foundations, perspectives, and applications* (pp. 445–472). Boston, MA: Pearson Education.

Chapter 16

Nowhere to Turn: The Young Face of Homelessness

Melissa A. Stormont and Rebecca B. McCathren

The face of a homeless person is often the face of a child or teenager, on the streets with no place to call home (Corliss, Goodenow, & Austin, 2012; Swick, 2010). Families with small children now represent approximately 37%, or more than one third, of the homeless population in the United States (National Center on Family Homelessness, 2011). The National Center on Family Homelessness (2011) has reported that up to 1.6 million children are homeless in the United States each year. This translates to 1 in 45 children.

Given these prevalence estimates, every educational professional needs to be aware of the characteristics of children and youth who are homeless and the resources available to address their needs (National Center on Family Homelessness, 2011). Children who are homeless are at great risk for academic, social, emotional, and behavioral problems in school (Children's Defense Fund, 2005; Davey, 2004; National Center on Family Homelessness, 2011). Many homeless youth do not attend school at all and are very likely to be the victims of abuse and to engage in destructive behaviors (Corliss et al., 2012; Haber & Toro, 2004; National Center on Family Homelessness, 2011). For young people who are homeless, it is evident that their educational needs will be met only through collaborative outreach efforts and interventions from teachers, counselors, administrators, and communities.

Accordingly, this chapter first describes the problem of homelessness for two specific groups: children living with their families and youth living alone. To define the problem of homelessness, the characteristics of both groups are presented first, followed by specific contributing factors for homelessness for each group. Next, the chapter describes the strategies for prevention and intervention with young people who are homeless from individual, family, school, and community perspectives. Adaptations for diversity are addressed in the final section and include additional considerations for working with single mothers and increasing knowledge of different cultures to enhance cultural sensitivity.

Problem Definition

Homelessness means having a primary residence that is a public or private shelter, emergency housing, hotel or motel, or any other public space, including public parks, cars, abandoned buildings, or aqueducts (National Coalition for the Homeless, 2009). Other definitions of homelessness also include those individuals who have to double up in housing with friends and family members or live in overcrowded housing conditions because of the loss of their housing (National Coalition for the Homeless, 2009). The latter definition includes those individuals who are homeless and living in rural areas where there are more limited shelter facilities (National Coalition for the Homeless, 2009). Regardless of how homelessness is defined, being homeless means more than not having a fixed place to sleep. People who are homeless have nowhere to put the things they cherish, things that connect them to their past. Youth who are homeless have often lost contact with their family and friends, and families who are homeless may have to uproot their children from school. More specific characteristics and contributing factors to homelessness for children and youth are presented next.

Children and Families Who Are Homeless

Characteristics

From the most recent statistics available, it is clear that families are the fastest growing group of homeless and now account for approximately 37% of the homeless population (Paquette, 2011). The majority of homeless families include a single mother and two young children (Paquette, 2011). The average age of the children is 6 years old, and 42% of children who are homeless are under the age of 6 (Paquette, 2011).

Demographically, children who are homeless are from all geographical areas and ethnic backgrounds. Although many assume that homelessness is an urban problem, the rate of homelessness may be more than twice as high in small towns or rural areas (Fisher, 2005). In rural areas, people who are homeless are more apt to be female, married, and working (Fisher, 2005). In addition, the population is less intractable, with a higher percentage being homeless for the first time and homeless for a shorter length of time than for those in urban areas (Fisher, 2005). Children who are homeless also represent different ethnicities. However, a disproportionate number of minorities, especially African Americans and Latinos, are represented in the homeless population (Haber & Toro, 2004; Paquette, 2011). Approximately 42% of homeless families are from African American backgrounds, and an additional 20% of families are from diverse cultural backgrounds (Paquette, 2011). Children's needs may vary according to their different cultural backgrounds, which will need to be addressed in a culturally sensitive way. These adaptations for diversity are presented later in the chapter.

Children who are homeless are at risk for moving, some many times. Some statistics report that as many as 97% of children who are homeless move each year (Paquette, 2011). Each time children move, instructional time is lost and children fall further behind their same-age peers. Every year, 40% of children who are homeless change schools once, and 28% change schools twice. Sadly, as many as one third of children who are homeless are retained once (Institute for Children and Poverty & Homes for the Homeless, 2005; National Center on Family Homelessness, 2011), and 20% of children who are homeless do not attend school at all (National Coalition for the Homeless, 2006). Multiple barriers are present that discourage homeless children from attending school. For example, they may not have school records, immunization records, a permanent address, transportation, school supplies, gym shoes, or appropriate clothing (National Center on Family Homelessness, 2004). Removing barriers and increasing school attendance are critical parts of prevention and intervention efforts and are addressed later in this chapter.

The lack of appropriate health care is another serious concern for children living in conditions that will increase their vulnerability for getting sick (National Center on Family Homelessness, 2011; Swick, 2010). According to the National Center on Family Homelessness (2011), homeless children are in poor health 4 times as often as children from middle-class families. They also have much higher rates of illness and experience stomach ailments 5 times as often, ear infections twice as often, and asthma more often than other children. Approximately 11% of children experiencing homelessness have asthma. Children who are homeless are also at high risk for social, emotional, and behavioral problems, with over two thirds having significant or clinical problems in these areas (Davey, 2004). The emotional problems faced by children who are homeless begin as early as preschool (National Center on Family Homelessness, 2004). Unfortunately, mental health treatment services are also lacking for this population (National Center on Family Homelessness, 2004).

Children living in homeless conditions are also at risk for experiencing stressors that further contribute to risk for serious emotional and behavioral problems. Children are at risk for having been exposed to domestic violence (Anooshian, 2005; Swick, 2010). They are 3 times more likely than children who are not homeless to have been the victim of sexual abuse and twice as likely to have been the victim of physical abuse (National Center on Family Homelessness, 2004). They are also at risk for being placed in foster care. Each year, more than one in five homeless children experience being separated from their families (Paquette, 2011). Overall, to place children's lives in context, consider Maslow's (1968) hierarchy of needs, whereby shelter, security, and food must be obtained before one reaches higher order needs such as psychological and self-actualization needs. While homeless children are not getting their most basic needs fulfilled, their psychological health is also at stake. Children who are homeless have very adult worries. To be specific, 74% worry about their housing situation, 58% report concerns that they will have no place to sleep at night, and almost all worry about their families and are concerned something bad will happen to them (National Center on Family Homelessness, 2011). Children who are homeless also report missing their friends, which further contributes to their risk for social–emotional problems (Anooshian, 2005). The case study presented below illustrates the potential impact of homelessness on young children.

Case Study

It was 3:00 a.m. At a local gas station, a man was trying to bum $5 worth of gas off the attendant as his family waited, shivering, in their junky car. The attendant obliged the family and called a local homeless shelter asking if they would let the family stay even though their doors were closed for the night. The children arrived at the shelter hungry and cold. Their parents tucked them in and stayed up for a while chatting with the volunteers. They were homeless because their father lost his job as a result of an illness, and they couldn't pay their bills or rent. He tried to find another full-time job, but there weren't any available. He had a series of part-time jobs, but they just didn't pay enough to cover rent, electricity, and their other expenses. They tried to survive in their trailer without heat, lights, or hot water, but they all just kept getting sick and that cost even more money. For the children, seeing how sad their dad was and how scared their mom was made everything even worse. They tried to be good, but it was hard when all they wanted to do was go home.

The children woke up and ate breakfast. Their clothes were wrinkled. They were dirty and extremely tired. They went to school after less than 3 hours of sleep with a lot more on their minds than reading and math. What will their teachers think when they fall asleep in class? How will they get food for lunch? What will their peers think? Will the other kids notice they didn't change clothes? Will someone say something mean about needing a bath? In addition to worrying about how they look, they are also concerned about how to make friends and talk with others in their class. They have had to grow up too fast. Their worries are not the same as those of other children. They are worried about their next meal and where they will seek shelter. They are worried about their parents and if they'll be okay. They are worried about what else might happen. Even though they have adult worries, their needs are the same as other children. They need a home and all of the securities that come with it. They also need an education.

Factors That Contribute to Family Homelessness

How do families become homeless? The overarching cause of homelessness is poverty. As illustrated in the case study above, many families teeter on the brink of homelessness by living paycheck to paycheck, and when one bill cannot be paid they may become homeless. Approximately 15% of people living in the United States meet the criteria for poverty (U.S. Census Bureau, 2012). Recently family incomes have declined, leaving more families at risk for poverty (U.S. Census Bureau, 2012). The factors related to poverty that contribute to and perpetuate homelessness include low wages, a decline in public assistance, lack of affordable housing, and inadequate physical and mental health care (National Coalition for the Homeless, 2009). These factors are briefly described.

Low wages and lack of well-paying jobs contribute to both poverty and homelessness (National Coalition for the Homeless, 2009). As the gap between rich and

---

Sidebar 16.1 ■ Self-Awareness: Who Is Vulnerable?

Think about the many things the children will be taking to school with them each day they are living in such stressful conditions. Do you think most professionals in schools know when children are vulnerable for homelessness? How could you increase awareness among teachers about homelessness and children's characteristics when they are experiencing homelessness? Consider the factors, discussed in this section, that contribute to homelessness and think about how we can raise public awareness of these issues.

■ ■ ■

poor has grown, those making minimum wage have been disproportionately affected (National Coalition for the Homeless, 2009). The purchasing power of the minimum wage in 2004 was 26% less than in 1979 (Economic Policy Institute, 2005). Although a Congressional plan was supposed to be enacted to increase the federal minimum wage to $9.50 by 2011 (National Coalition for the Homeless, 2009), currently in 2013 the federal minimum wage is $7.25 (U.S. Department of Labor, 2012). Therefore, homeless shelters house many full-time workers, and in at least 11 out of 19 cities those numbers are increasing (U.S. Conference of Mayors, 2008). Although lack of jobs and associated income can cause homelessness, having a job does not necessarily ensure housing.

Reductions in public assistance have also contributed to rates of poverty and homelessness. Welfare reform repealed the largest cash assistance program, Aid to Families With Dependent Children (AFDC), and replaced it with Temporary Assistance for Needy Families (TANF). However, TANF has not been able to provide support at the same levels that AFDC did, and that support has lessened over time. For example, TANF provided cash support to 68 out of every 100 families living in poverty in 1996, but by 2010, TANF provided cash supports to only 27 out of every 100 families living in poverty (Trisi & Pavetti, 2012). During this same period of time, the number of families with children living in poverty increased by 17% and the number of children living in poverty increased by 12% (Trisi & Pavetti, 2012). In addition, in 1995 AFDC was responsible for lifting more than 60% of children out of deep poverty. By 2005, TANF's results were just 21%. This cutback has left holes in the safety net. Without these benefits to fall back on, many families with children were and are destined for economic hardship and homelessness (Institute for Children and Poverty, 2001).

Lack of affordable housing contributes to poverty and homelessness. When the task of trying to obtain affordable housing interacts with the low wages that people who are impoverished receive, finding housing becomes almost impossible (National Center on Family Homelessness, 2004; National Coalition for the Homeless, 2006). The National Coalition for the Homeless (2009) reported that currently a worker would need to earn $14.97 per hour to afford a one-bedroom apartment and $17.84 to afford a two-bedroom apartment. (Remember that the federal minimum wage is $7.25, and the minimum wage for states ranges from $5.15 an hour up to a high of $9.04 per hour, substantially below what is needed for housing; U.S. Department of Labor, 2012.)There has been a 41% increase in fair market rent from 2000 to 2009 (National Low Income Housing Coalition, 2009), with the minimum wage clearly not keeping pace. The increase in the costs of housing has contributed to overcrowding, families paying large portions of their income for housing, homelessness, and the risk of homelessness (National Coalition for the Homeless, 2009).

Housing assistance could help families access stable housing and prevent homelessness. However, the demand for housing assistance far exceeds the resources, and in 2004 families spent an average of 35 months on wait lists (National Coalition for the Homeless, 2009). The prospects of additional low-income housing in the future are dubious. In fact, about 200,000 rental units are destroyed every year, leaving fewer available for low-income renters (National Coalition for the Homeless, 2009). The U.S. Conference of Mayors (2008) cited the lack of affordable housing as the number one cause of homelessness. The recent increase in foreclosures has also affected low-income renters. About 40% of the homes foreclosed on were rental units, requiring the renters to move. But frequently there are not comparable homes available. With more than 12 million homeowner households spending more than 50% of their income on housing, there is not money left to provide health care or adequate nutrition or to build a safety net to prevent them from becoming homeless. According to the U.S. Census Bureau (2012), the median household income declined significantly from 2007 to 2011.

The health care system in the United States is also severely lacking. Poor physical health is often cited as a contributing factor to becoming homeless. According to the U.S. Census Bureau (2012), approximately 13.8% of children living in poverty have no health care and 25.4% of people living in households with less than $25,000 have absolutely no health insurance. It is important to note that the census bureau refers to "households"; thus, the currently homeless population is most likely not counted in these numbers. Individuals who are homeless experience high rates of chronic and acute health problems, so their lack of health insurance is especially problematic. They are also more likely to have hypertension, physical problems such as skin diseases, respiratory infections, drug or alcohol abuse or addiction, and mental health disorders (National Coalition for the Homeless, 2009). However, for homeless people or those at risk for homelessness, there are not adequate resources to effectively help those with mental illness (National Coalition for the Homeless, 2009). Issues of poverty, physical and mental illness, and remediating skill deficits are rarely included as a part of treatment but are blatant barriers to a potential life of stability and self-sufficiency. The programs that do exist are often unable to meet the service demands.

Another important contributing factor for homelessness is being raised in homeless conditions. That is, many youth who are homeless and living in shelters or on the street were raised in families who experienced homelessness (Haber & Toro, 2004). Many of these youth then have children and recreate the cycle of homelessness for another generation. In a study of homeless adolescent females from New York City and Denver, Colorado, researchers found that almost 50% either were pregnant or had been pregnant (Kral, Molnar, Booth, & Watters, 1997). Research has not documented what happens to young homeless youth who become pregnant. However, because the majority of homeless mothers are in their 20s (Burt, Aron, Lee, & Valente, 2001), it is likely that there is considerable overlap between homeless youth and homeless families (Haber & Toro, 2004). Most research on homeless families has excluded families headed by teen mothers, and most studies of homeless youth have not specifically looked at those who are mothers (Haber & Toro, 2004). Thus, the characteristics and contributing factors for these groups (children, families, and youth) need to be understood for prevention purposes. Characteristics and additional contributing factors for youth who are homeless are presented next.

Sidebar 16.2 ■ Self-Awareness: The Causes of and Biases Related to Homelessness

Consider the many causes of homelessness. Do you have any biases related to causes of homelessness that should be addressed? Do you feel the general public blames people who are homeless, or are they informed of the many potential contributing factors? The recent recession and increase in foreclosures may have supported increased empathy toward people who work but can't maintain housing—what are your thoughts?

■ ■ ■

Youth Who Are Homeless

Characteristics

The Center for Law and Social Policy (2003) estimated that the number of homeless youth is between 500,000 and 1.3 million. The range is quite large because the number of adolescents who are homeless is difficult to calculate (Harber & Toro, 2004; National Alliance to End Homelessness, 2013). Some adolescents may run away from home and stay with friends for a few nights before returning to their families (National Alliance to End Homelessness, 2013). Others may leave for the night after a fight with their parents but go home the next morning. Should they be included in the count? Youth who are homeless also tend to move around quite frequently and may stay in different shelters or different places. Overall, youth who are homeless fit into two broad categories: those who live in shelters or other makeshift arrangements and those who have spent time on the streets (Haber & Toro, 2004). However, living arrangements for homeless youth are fluid, and most youth who have lived on the street have also had other living arrangements in shelters, with other relatives, or with friends (Haber & Toro, 2004; National Alliance to End Homelessness, 2013). Therefore, time spent on the street could be considered an indication of the severity of homelessness.

Homeless youth in shelters are often experiencing homelessness for the first time and usually have not been homeless for long (Haber & Toro, 2003). When researchers specifically studied demographic characteristics of youth living in shelters, either the numbers of males or females were the same or more were female (Heinze, Toro, & Urberg, 2004). In contrast, adolescents who were living on the street were more likely to be male (Cauce et al., 2000). Unlike the demographic characteristics of homeless families, 57% of homeless youth are Caucasian, 17% are African American, 15% are Hispanic, and 11% are from other ethnic groups (Hammer, Finkelhor, & Sedlak, 2002).

In terms of more specific behavioral characteristics, youth who are homeless have been found to have extremely high rates of oppositional defiant disorder (40% to 51%; Cauce et al., 2000; McCaskill, Toro, & Wolfe, 1998; Toro & Goldstein, 2000). Although researchers removed "running away from home" as one of the criteria for the diagnosis, many homeless youth engage in other behaviors associated with the diagnosis. For example, in one study 23% of the homeless youth reported stealing, 14% reported breaking into homes, 20% sold drugs, and 2% reported selling sex for money (Whitbeck, Hoyt, & Ackley, 1997). It is sad to note that many of the youth stated that they engaged in these behaviors to pay for housing or food (Haber & Toro, 2004).

Drug and alcohol use and abuse are also more common in homeless youth and may appear at younger ages than for housed youth (Boesky, Toro, & Bukowski, 1997). Greenblatt and Robertson (1993) found that rates of drug and alcohol abuse were 5 to 8 times higher in adolescents who were homeless. Toro and Goldstein (2000) found that homeless youth had significantly higher rates of both alcohol and drug use. According to recent research, when youth who are homeless do abuse substances they are more likely to be experiencing multiple stressors and more likely to report that they contemplate suicide (Bannon et al., 2012). In addition to drug and alcohol use, homeless youth engage in high-risk sexual behavior, including unprotected sex (Lombardo & Toro, 2004; Whitbeck & Hoyt, 1999) and unprotected sex with intravenous drug users (Rotheram-Borus, Parra, Cantwell,

Gwadz, & Murphy, 1996). The repercussions of such high-risk behaviors include contracting sexually transmitted diseases such as AIDS (Lombardo & Toro, 2004; National Coalition for the Homeless, 2006; Sweeney, Lindegren, Buehler, Onorato, & Janssen, 1995). Rates of HIV and AIDS are between 2 and 10 times higher for youth who are homeless as compared with housed youth (National Coalition for the Homeless, 2006). Youth who are homeless may be engaging in so-called survival sex whereby partners provide drugs, shelter, or money in exchange for sex (Anderson et al., 1996; National Coalition for the Homeless, 1999). In a multisite study, Anderson and colleagues (1996) found that up to 41% of the homeless youth interviewed had participated in this type of sexual activity.

The National Alliance to End Homelessness (2013) provided suggestions for matching interventions to different types of homeless youth. The suggested framework matches a tiered approach to prevention by understanding the different levels of need for support. They categorize youth as low risk, transient, and high risk. The levels of risk are conceptualized based on characteristics of youth (age, mental health needs, substance use) and their connectedness to protective factors (e.g., families, schools).

Factors That Contribute to Homelessness in Youth

In an effort to prevent homelessness in youth, it is important to understand life conditions that are also associated with the onset and sustainment of homelessness. As illustrated in the case of Latisha in Sidebar 16.4, many homeless youth become homeless because of chronic negative experiences at home, including physical or sexual abuse, neglect, or parental drug addiction (National Alliance to End Homelessness, 2013; National Coalition for the Homeless, 2009). Maltreatment and neglect are substantially higher in youth who become homeless than in the broader group of adolescents (Haber & Toro, 2004; National Coalition for the Homeless, 2009). One study found that half of homeless youth reported being asked to leave their homes by their parents, and almost half (47%; National Coalition for the Homeless, 2009) reported being sexually abused (Rew, Taylor-Seehafer, Thomas, & Yockey, 2001). Other research with a large sample of homeless youth found that 50% of youth reported being sexually abused at some point in their life (Rew, Fouladi, & Yockey, 2002). In addition to being the victims of maltreatment, youth who became homeless also reported higher rates of being verbally or physically abusive toward their parents (Haber & Toro, 2003).

Other research has investigated more specific family factors that may contribute to alcohol abuse and homelessness in teenage youth (McMorris, Tyler, Whitbeck, & Hoyt, 2002). The approach used to frame the relationships among family and youth characteristics was a risk amplification model (McMorris et al., 2002). Youth who were homeless and abused alcohol had a history of parental alcohol abuse, parental rejection, and physical and sexual abuse. The youth who reported higher rates of alcohol use had spent more time on the streets, had spent more time with deviant peers, and had engaged in antisocial or self-deprecating acts to survive on the street. Research has also investigated characteristics that were associated with resilience in youth (Rew et al., 2001). Youth who were more likely to believe in their own competence and were more accepting of themselves (i.e., high ratings of resilience) were less likely to report feeling lonely and hopeless and engaging in risky behaviors.

Another subgroup of adolescents who are at increased risk for becoming homeless is those who are in foster care (National Coalition for the Homeless, 2009). In fact, the National Center on Family Homelessness (2004) identified being in foster care as one of only two risk factors in childhood to predict homelessness in adulthood. According to their estimates, 20% of all homeless mothers had been in foster care during their childhoods. In another study, 29% of youth who were homeless had a history of foster care (Nyamathi et al., 2012). Another group of youth who are at risk for becoming homeless is those who have serious psychiatric problems (National Coalition for the Homeless, 2009). Researchers followed adolescents who had been treated in a residential program for 5 years postdischarge; a large percentage (33%) had experienced homelessness at least once after being discharged, with half of these youth having this experience within a year after being discharged (Embry, Stoep, Evens, Ryan, & Pollock, 2000). In addition to early psychiatric disorders, youth who were more likely to experience homelessness had a history of physical abuse and drug or alcohol abuse (National Coalition for the Homeless, 2009). A final group with rates of homelessness at 6 times more than their peers is those who are gay, lesbian, bisexual, or transgender (National Coalition for the Homeless, 2006), and prevention and intervention efforts need to be sensitive and responsive to this subgroup of individuals (National Alliance to End Homelessness, 2013).

Approaches to Prevention

Because of the negative effects of homelessness described in the previous sections, it is crucial to focus efforts on prevention for young children and their families and youth who are homeless. It is clear that homelessness is a complicated social issue that will require a multilevel and multisystem approach. Providing permanent affordable housing is only part of the solution. Ending homelessness is a matter of providing people with opportunities for housing, decent wages, health insurance, treatment for health problems, and an education. Strategies for ending homelessness include prevention and intervention, which are closely related. Many strategies can be deemed prevention when they target people who are currently housed but at risk for becoming homeless and can be deemed intervention when they target the homeless (Haber & Toro, 2004). Using a prevention science model, research can help inform mediators and moderators of homelessness, which can then be used to target interventions for vulnerable populations (Stormont, Reinke, & Herman, 2010). The following sections address specific preventive strategies that can be used for individuals (youth), families, schools, and community agencies.

Individual

It is critical to support follow-up outreach and intervention efforts for youth who are included in treatment programs. If youth are in treatment programs and have a history of family maltreatment, then it is even more critical to provide outreach and support for these individuals. If youth have a history of physical abuse in their families, they may be less likely to seek or to receive support from their families upon release and may continue a destructive pattern of substance abuse.

Another group of youth to target for prevention is those in foster care (Nyamathi et al., 2012). Research has found that a substantial number of youth and adults who are homeless lived in foster care when they were children

(Nyamathi et al., 2012). Given the lack of strong family connections for many in foster care, it appears that when youth age out of the system they have no place to go (Haber & Toro, 2004; National Center on Family Homelessness, 2004; National Coalition for the Homeless, 2006). Prevention strategies for these youth could include connecting them with resources in the community to support their transition to adult life. The resources that are critical for youth who are at risk for sudden displacement include those that help them establish housing and employment and those that teach life skills (Ferguson, 2012).

After youth become homeless, it appears that younger adolescents may be in a better position for professionals to assist them and help get them off the streets (Milburn et al., 2005). They rely more on other people and are more at risk for gang affiliations, possibly because they have difficulty making it alone on the streets (Unger et al., 1998). Early intervention is very important with adolescents who are living on the streets because the health risks are substantially higher for adolescents who have been on the street for more than 1 year (Unger, Kipke, Simon, Montgomery, & Johnson, 1997).

Overall, as illuminated in the case study given in Sidebar 16.4, youth who are homeless are typically in situations in which they feel that they have nowhere to turn. Prevention efforts need to target these youth to assist them in reestablishing or creating supportive relationships.

Family

Although it seems obvious, the best way to prevent homelessness for families is to identify families at risk for homelessness and provide support services. It is more cost effective to spend money preventing homelessness by preventing evictions (e.g., providing vouchers to landlords for past payments, legal assistance, cash assistance programs), keeping families in shared housing situations, strengthening family connections, and assisting families who are living in condemned buildings by providing them with transition help than it is to support families in shelters once they become homeless (Lindholm, 1996; Mayock, Corr, & O'Sullivan, 2011).

Another prevention strategy is to create "alternative families" to prevent homelessness (Haber & Toro, 2004). For example, a family might live with an elderly woman, who is less apt to be homeless than younger women with children, and provide caretaking tasks in exchange for rent. Such arrangements may be feasible as an alternative to becoming homeless or may be an intervention for a family who is homeless. More important than cost-effectiveness is the fact that once families are homeless, the road to reestablishing self-sufficiency is much more difficult, and the effects of homelessness on children may be traumatizing not solely because of the lack of permanent housing but also because of the other risks that may accompany homelessness.

Sidebar 16.3 ■ Self-Awareness: The Need for More Support for Family Stability

Did you know how extensive the risk is for homelessness if youth are in foster care? What can you do in your professional role to reduce the risk for this population? How can you help support increased family stability (foster or biological) with this group and increased efforts for youth to be successful when they are emancipated? Consider Latisha in the following case study and the factors that are contributing to her risk and needs for prevention efforts.

■ ■ ■

Sidebar 16.4 ■ Case Study: Latisha

Latisha entered the shelter that her high school counselor had told her about. She was tired, scared, confused, and a little dizzy. How did she get here? Although she knew the answer to the question, it still felt so desperate not to have anyone to turn to and nowhere to go besides a homeless shelter. She is 15, and she is pregnant. She left home because she couldn't handle the physical abuse of her stepfather anymore, especially after she found out she was pregnant. She also figured she would get quite the beating when her parents found out about her pregnancy. Latisha is still going to school, and she confides in her counselor.

The days living in the shelter become weeks. Latisha can stay at the shelter for 1 month, and then she hopes she will have a placement in a house for pregnant teens. Her counselor is working with community agencies to help Latisha and meets with her daily to see how she is doing. One of her counselor's major concerns is that Latisha has allowed the father of her child, a much older and married man, to reestablish communications with her. He is a known drug dealer, and, although Latisha denies it, her counselor believes that he is abusive.

■ ■ ■

School

Youth who are homeless are often hard to reach if they are not currently in school. However, when youth are in school, community and school efforts can be focused on targeting youth who are having problems in school or problems with their families and providing appropriate services (Mayock et al., 2011). In fact, many adolescents who run away report they had recent school stresses, including failing a grade, being expelled, or having particular problems with teachers (Rotheram-Borus et al., 1996).

Another strategy for preventing homelessness for families includes providing comprehensive prevention services to low-income families and their children, particularly those who have additional risk factors. Many early childhood programs that target children living in poverty function as prevention programs for many later risks, including homelessness (Haber & Toro, 2004). These programs support children when they provide high-quality child care that prepares young children to succeed in school. These programs also make it more likely that parents will be able to work because child care is affordable (Haber & Toro, 2004). When programs focus directly on parents, they may also help prevent homelessness. Finally, when schools participate fully in the broader community and provide education and supports to families, it is more likely that families will be able to avoid homelessness and that children and youth will remain housed. Schools can also prevent homelessness by providing a wide variety of supervised after-school programs for children and adolescents so that parents can work and not worry about their children's supervision (Chen et al., 2004).

Sidebar 16.5 ■ Case Study: Understanding Latisha's Needs

What are Latisha's strengths and needs that should be considered when working with her? If she does not continue to go to school, what increased risk factors will be present? How could systems work together to make sure she, and her baby, don't fall through the cracks? Why might Latisha be interested in connecting with the father of her child?

■ ■ ■

Community

Some recent community efforts have addressed preventing homelessness for both families and individuals. Although more needs to be done, the Department of Housing and Urban Development reported that the Homelessness Prevention and Rapid Re-Housing Program (HPRP), created by the Recovery Act, has prevented at least a million people from becoming homeless. The program provided $1.5 billion to support efforts preventing homelessness during the recent economic downturn (Recovery.gov, 2012).

Effective community-based prevention strategies have included rental insurance, credit counseling, utility payments, and funds to pay for relocation and new housing. Many communities have successfully decreased their homeless populations through these efforts, including Chicago, Denver, New York, and Portland, among others (National Alliance to End Homelessness, 2013). Unfortunately, these funds were time limited and the money had to be spent by September 2012. It is hoped that communities that experienced success will be able to access other funding sources to continue prevention efforts.

Intervention Strategies

Given a problem of this magnitude, prevention efforts currently are not affecting a large percentage of the homeless population. Accordingly, it is critical that professionals also understand interventions that can be applied to families and individual youth who are homeless. Specific interventions that can be applied in school settings for children and youth are also discussed, followed by efforts to intervene at the community level. As you read through the following intervention strategies, consider the two case examples presented in this chapter and reflect on the strategies that may be appropriate.

Individual

To work effectively with homeless adolescents, it is important to understand the barriers to providing services to this population and the needs of this population. The immediate needs of adolescents include their physical needs for shelter, clothing, and food and their medical needs, including education on behaviors that will place them at risk for HIV infection and other sexually transmitted diseases (Nyamathi et al., 2012). When educators and service providers attempt to reach out to street youth, it is important to understand the day-to-day lifestyle of adolescents who are living on the streets (Altena, Brilleslijper-Kater, & Wolf, 2010). In addition, many adolescents may distrust adults and, therefore, will not access services. So the question is, How can professionals work with this population of homeless youth?

The first goal of intervention, whenever possible, is to involve both the adolescent and his or her parents or a significant family member in setting goals and developing interventions (Haber & Toro, 2004). This strategy may be particularly effective for youth who are newly homeless (Milburn et al., 2005). Auerswald and Eyre (2002) found that homeless youth are most receptive to intervention when they are newly homeless or when they are in crisis. Other research has also underscored the need to support family bonds and relationships and to attempt to reestablish family connections quickly after youth become homeless (Mayock et al., 2011; Milburn et al., 2005). A program in Australia, called Reconnect, has provided family intervention to 23,000 youth and their families, and 70% of the participants had a positive change as a result of the intervention (Regan, 2003).

Because of the high rates of HIV, pregnancy, and sexually transmitted diseases in homeless youth, a number of intervention programs have focused on health care (Altena et al., 2010). One recommendation is to have programs that are specifically designed for youth (e.g., substance abuse, counseling, medical care) streamlined and accessible in one place (Nyamathi et al., 2005). There have been successful programs documented in the literature, including storefront services for youth to drop in and pick up information about AIDS (Lloyd & Kuszelewicz, 1995). Focus groups that are led by adults who have similar demographic characteristics, and who have possibly been homeless themselves, is another intervention option. One study (Rotheram-Borus, Koopman, Haignere, & Davies, 1991) used a comprehensive intervention program that included small-group sessions facilitated by a trained leader with a similar demographic background and included individual counseling when needed. The intervention included information on (a) general knowledge of HIV and AIDS, (b) the importance of using coping skills effectively, and (c) resources available to adolescents (Rotheram-Borus et al., 1991). Findings from this study were that the number of sessions that adolescents participated in was associated with a reduction in high-risk behavior and an increase in consistent condom use.

Another suggested model for working with youth who are homeless includes strengths-based case management (Nyamathi et al., 2005). This model includes frequent interactions between youth who are homeless and a designated case manager who provides intensive support. This type of case management may result in more appropriate, individualized services for youth, and the formation of a positive relationship may also function as an additional intervention (Haber & Toro, 2004). It is clear that limited outreach efforts may serve only as a bandage and not provide the level of support that youth who are homeless need. Gleghorn, Marx, Vittinghoff, and Katz (1998) found that higher levels of contact between case workers and clients resulted in higher rates of follow-through on the part of the client and lower rates of risky behavior. Thus, a consistent and sensitive outreach approach that provides ongoing information in many different formats on the risks of certain behaviors appears to be the best intervention option. There is much more research needed in this area, as a recent systematic review of the literature found only 11 studies on interventions and outcomes for homeless youth (Altena et al., 2010). The most promising intervention was using cognitive behavior approaches. It is also important to note that some interventions had negative effects on targeted outcomes. Additional school-based interventions are presented later.

Family

Interventions for families who are homeless are provided both at a systems level, whereby the focus is on the family as a whole, and at an individual level, whereby the focus is on the individual family members. The first type of intervention is to provide housing and to help parents connect with the supports and services that are available in their communities. The second is to provide intervention designed to lessen the negative impact on the children who are homeless. These include interventions designed to positively affect the parent–child relationship as well as interventions targeting children's long-term positive outcomes. Specific studies are discussed below.

According to the National Alliance to End Homelessness (2013), the most effective intervention for family homelessness is to provide permanent housing quickly. Most families who lose their housing do so because of an unexpected event. If housing is provided quickly, the majority of families spend a very brief time in shelters and are able to continue on with their lives. For families with caregivers who have mental health or substance abuse issues, or who have a history of homelessness, supportive housing may be the intervention of choice. Two studies (Gerwitz, 2007; Hong & Piescher, 2012) have examined supportive housing as a way to support the mental health of the children. Gerwitz (2007) described a collaboration between the community agencies involved with supportive housing and a university. They found that many children living in supportive housing had emotional and behavioral problems and that the service providers did not have the skills or knowledge to work effectively with the children. The goal of the project was to increase staff expertise to help them support caregivers and their children in order to increase the mental health of the children. The model includes providing professional development for the service providers in the supported housing facilities related to mental health and child development as well as providing intervention to the children who are demonstrating either internalizing or externalizing behaviors. Unfortunately, no outcome studies have been published to document the results of the interventions.

A second study (Hong & Piescher, 2012) compared children in supportive housing and children who were homeless and found that the children in supportive housing had better school attendance, changed schools less often, and had higher math skills. They also were less likely to have protective services involved in their families than children who were homeless. Thus, for families who have ongoing risks, supportive housing may be an effective way to support both the caregivers and the children.

Additional interventions have been used to promote positive parent–child relationships and to increase parenting skills. These interventions are important because parenting quality for families who are homeless is associated with academic performance and has a protective effect on young children (Herbers et al., 2011). Although most of the intervention studies targeted small numbers of children or parents, they have shown positive results. One intervention, the multiple family group model, has been implemented using weekly meetings and, more recently, has been executed within a weekend retreat (Davey, 2004). The content of the intervention is the same, regardless of the format. In this model, four to five families meet regularly with counselors to learn positive coping skills that focus on parenting, communication strategies, and how to deal with stress. Although some of the time is spent with the children in one group and parents in another, most of the time is spent with all of the children and parents together. Families are supported in recognizing their strengths, positively communicating with each other, and clarifying the roles that each member in a family serves. In general, parents found their experience to be beneficial for the entire family.

Intervention has also targeted parents and their infants and toddlers who are homeless. Parent–child advocates were taught how to coach mothers to improve the quality of their interactions with their young children (Kelly, Buehlman, & Caldwell, 2000). The results showed that mothers increased their contingent responsivity as well as their ability to stimulate and respond in ways that support positive social–emotional development. A similar intervention conducted with homeless families was used to teach parents how to support the language development of their preschool-age children (O'Neil-Pirozzi, 2009). The results showed that parents were able to learn and use language support strategies. Neither of these studies looked at the effect of the interventions on the children's development. However, it is encouraging that while experiencing the stress of homelessness, these mothers wanted to learn new ways of interacting with their children and were able to learn new skills.

A case study using filial therapy with a mother who was homeless because of domestic violence and her young son shows promise (Kolos, Green, & Crenshaw, 2009). Filial therapy is a type of play therapy where the parent takes the role of the therapist. In this study, the 5-year-old son was experiencing behavior problems, including aggression toward peers, tantrums, and defiance with adults. The mother was taught a set of strategies for engaging her son in play in a way that followed his lead and acknowledged his feelings. Both the mother and son benefitted from the intervention. The mother felt more confident in her ability to interact with her son and felt increased competence in her parenting skills. Her son's aggressive behavior, tantrums, and defiance all decreased, and he was able to develop friendships with peers.

Finally, play therapy was done with children who were homeless (Baggerly, 2004). A therapist provided play therapy to one or two children at a time. Each child got one to two sessions each week. As a result of the play therapy, children's self-perceptions of their competence increased, their self-esteem increased, and they had lower levels of anxiety and also lower levels of some aspects of depression. The results of the studies discussed all showed positive results for interventions targeting the entire family (e.g., supportive housing) and interventions that target individuals in the family.

School

School counselors' knowledge and sensitivity to serving homeless children in the schools make them the best coordinator of resources for these individuals. School counselors could coordinate efforts to educate teachers and administrators on the characteristics and educational needs of children who are homeless. According to a 2002 reauthorization of the McKinney-Vento Act, school districts need to have a person in charge of educating professionals and communities about homelessness (National Coalition for the Homeless, 2006). That person should ensure that homeless children are receiving an appropriate education and that parents know their children's rights within the educational system (National Coalition for the Homeless, 2006). The McKinney-Vento Homeless Assistance Act was enacted to attempt to alleviate barriers for school attendance for children who are homeless (Institute for Children and Poverty, 2003; National Coalition for the Homeless, 2006). According to this act, families of children who are homeless have the right to choose which school their children will attend, including the school their child attended before the family became homeless or the school closest to their temporary living conditions. Families also have the right to enroll their children in school even if they do not have current immunizations, proof of residency, or any school records (Institute for Children and Poverty, 2003; National Coalition for the Homeless, 2006). Although clear gains have been made since the 1980s when an earlier act was established, children who are homeless still encounter barriers. To obtain more specifics regarding their rights, the district liaison needs to work closely with parents who are experiencing homelessness or who are at risk for homelessness.

School counselors and this liaison could work together to provide in-service training for teachers on general information related to homelessness, children's characteristics, suggested classroom modifications, and ways to facilitate positive self-esteem and success in school. In addition, school counselors need to work with teachers to ensure that teachers are providing a supportive, nurturing classroom environment. Ensuring teachers provide a compassionate classroom is extremely important because many teachers have negative views of homeless children and their families, and these views affect the children and families and prevent teachers from providing the best possible instruction and supports (B. Powers-Costello & Swick, 2011; E. Powers-Costello & Swick, 2008). If we consider the children and youth from the case examples described earlier, it is easy to discern that they will have potential needs for support. Counselors should help teachers determine supports that are feasible for them to use, and then both counselors and teachers could provide the needed support.

Because children and youth who are homeless, particularly those with a history of homelessness, usually struggle academically, teachers, counselors, or school psychologists should administer quick, informal assessments to students who are homeless, and teachers should begin instruction in content areas at a place where the students can succeed (Bos & Vaughn, 2006; Stormont, 2007). Teachers should also be very systematic and not assume that students have gone through the curriculum with the same consistency as their peers. Instruction may need to be modified, and assignments may need to be adapted. Instruction modifications could include allowing completion of in-class assignments in groups and tailoring independent work according to students' interest areas. Teachers can also use technology, cooperative learning, and peer tutoring. The number of accommodations and modifications that could be used is beyond the scope of this chapter to describe. The critical academic supports that both children and youth need include individualized instruction and homework assignments that fit their achievement levels, their after-school environments, and their personal learning styles and interests; such tailored instruction and assignments will help support the students' motivation to stay in school.

There are many small changes a teacher can make in terms of homework assignments. If students have difficulty completing written work, a teacher can adjust the amount of work required by students or change the output requirements (e.g., recite a story into a tape recorder instead of writing it out). Teachers should modify homework assignments for students who have no place to study after school (Stormont, 2007). Modifications could include allowing early access to the library or classroom, work with peers, and after-school and weekend homework support at school or at a library. Teachers need to access family members, shelter professionals, and professionals in school who would be willing to assist with homework completion or other academic enrichment activities (Nabors et al., 2004).

In addition to academic needs, children and youth who are homeless have social, emotional, and behavioral needs. Counselors should take the lead to make sure that teachers are sensitive to students' well-being at all times. Research has documented that teachers have reported negative perceptions of the manageability of homeless children (B. Powers-Costello & Swick, 2011). Teachers should be aware of the physical as well as emotional risk factors associated with homelessness. For younger children, teachers should use strategies that can promote social and emotional well-being. Teachers can make other arrangements if children celebrate their birthdays by bringing treats. They could enlist the support of the Parent-Teacher Association or another parent to bring treats for children who are homeless if that would be a burden for their families. Or teachers could work with counselors and lunch staff to use kitchen space to make treats for the class. It may also mean a lot to students if they have a consistent place in the classroom to work and to post their work.

Another strategy for supporting children who are homeless would be to develop a circle of friends for children to seek out if they need assistance and individuals who have specific responsibilities for supporting children in different settings (Turnbull, Turnbull, Erwin, & Soodak, 2006). For example, an assistant principal (or another person) could be in charge of making sure a child arrives at school and could contact families when children are absent. This person could then determine barriers to school attendance, and professionals could try to problem solve how to overcome barriers. Overcoming barriers to attending events at school is also important to increase children's connectedness to school (B. Powers-Costello & Swick, 2011).

Another way to support both academic and social–emotional needs is for school professionals to help children transition more smoothly from one school to another. Teachers could keep a work and assessment folder for children who are at risk for moving to save instructional time at their next school (Stormont, 2007). Making the transition to a new school smooth for children also helps to ensure that they feel welcome. This folder could have an introduction to the child written by his or her current classmates (e.g., including likes, dislikes, strengths) that the teacher at the new school could use to introduce the child to his or her classmates (Stormont, 2007). This folder should also include recent assessment data, work samples, and the sending teacher's phone number for consultation. This folder could be sent with the child's family and presented upon arrival at the new school.

For youth who are homeless, teachers and counselors should develop transition support plans to help students connect the content they are learning in school to work and life after school. Special education teachers and school psychologists could be accessed to help in this process. Transition plans are especially important for youth who are living in foster care. Programs that include vocational training, academic enrichment, and individual counseling are appropriate for older youth who are homeless given the complexities of their lives (Ferguson, 2012; Nabors et al., 2004). For youth who have mental health issues as well as limited education, job skills, and life skills, the probability that they will be able to break the cycle of homelessness without extensive support is dubious (Ferguson, Xie, & Glynn, 2012). Thus, a wraparound approach in which schools streamline the mental health services that students need while providing an appropriate education is critical for youth who are homeless (Nabors et al., 2004).

Community

Many of the strategies presented in this intervention section include community support. From a community perspective, resources in some areas may be rich, and partnerships among schools, businesses, and shelters could be quickly established and sustained to support children and youth who are homeless. Communities could then drive the establishment of after-school programs, day camps in the summer or on the weekends, and comprehensive and accessible mental and physical health services. In other communities, the school system is the most plentiful resource, and prevention and intervention efforts would need to come from the schools.

Most communities can and should support efforts to keep children and youth who are homeless in school. Community advocates could help identify those students who are not currently receiving an education. Community outreach representatives could begin by setting up networks with local shelters and emergency housing facilities. It is also important to have continuous lines of communication open with local shelters and churches that house students currently in school. Volunteers could be recruited to get parents and youth who are homeless involved and interested in education. Community volunteers could also be recruited to be mentors for children and youth who are homeless. Mentors could be responsible for meeting with young students at least once a week and could be a source of support and advocacy. Parent sponsors could also be solicited to provide resources for a particular child or youth who is homeless. These sponsors could provide, for example, birthday treats, school supplies, or clothing.

Another important goal for school and community professionals working with families is to remove barriers to receiving adequate health care. Community and school programs need to link families with the information they need regarding services they can access. For example, outreach programs such as Healthcare for the Homeless are available to provide health care for the uninsured (National Coalition for the Homeless, 1999). Information on community resources for free immunizations can also be provided to families through outreach efforts.

There are resources for schools and communities to access through local and state improvement grants (National Coalition for the Homeless, 2006). Local grant funds could help support outreach efforts for identification purposes, school attendance and transportation, local resource coordination, the establishment of after-school and summer programs, and the distribution of school supplies. State grants could help with professional development, technical assistance, and the development of educational materials for dissemination (National Coalition for the Homeless, 2006).

Adaptations for Diversity

The primary focus of this chapter has been on children, families, and youth who are homeless. There are other groups of people who experience homelessness who have characteristics that need to be considered when designing appropriate supports, including single mothers and people from culturally diverse backgrounds.

Single Mothers

Research has shown that about 85% of homeless families are headed by a single female (National Center on Family Homelessness, 2004). It is clear that single mothers with children are a distinct subgroup within the population of the homeless, and they have different psychological and demographic characteristics (Anooshian, 2005). The needs of mothers with small children are also important to consider. Homeless mothers are also more likely to report greater degrees of psychological distress than homeless single women without children.

The psychological distress for homeless mothers appears to be much greater than the distress of poverty alone. Thus, even though mothers caring for children appear to have less major substance abuse and mental health problems than other homeless people, research has found that mothers living in shelters have substance abuse problems at high rates. In fact, 40% of homeless women report having experienced drug or alcohol dependence during their lives (National Center on Family Homelessness, 2004). The psychological distress related to being a homeless mother may be attributable to the precipitating events to homelessness and/or the lack of outside support available once homeless (Anooshian, 2005).

One of the precipitating events to homelessness for mothers is domestic abuse (Anooshian, 2005; National Coalition for the Homeless, 2009). Research has found that up to 50% of women are homeless because they are fleeing domestic abuse (National Coalition for the Homeless, 2009). Unfortunately, if violence occurs in a specific residence, landlords can evict the residents, even women who have been abused (National Coalition for the Homeless, 2009). Women who are homeless have also experienced more violence overall than other women. According to the National Center on Family Homelessness (2004, p. 3), "The frequency of violence in the lives of homeless mothers is staggering." For example,

- 63% have been violently abused by an intimate male partner.
- 27% have required medical treatment because of violence by an intimate male partner.
- 25% have been physically or sexually assaulted by someone other than an intimate partner.
- 66% were violently abused by a childhood caretaker or other adult in the household before reaching the age of 18.
- 43% were sexually molested as children.

The lack of support that homeless mothers report is another major consideration for working with this diverse population (Anooshian, 2005). Mothers living in homeless conditions may not trust other adults, which will likely impact the supports their children can access (Anooshian, 2005). Mothers who are homeless appear to receive less emotional support from friends and family. In one study that included predominantly African American mothers, researchers documented that mothers in low-income housing saw and/or talked to more friends and relatives on a weekly basis than mothers who were homeless (Letiecq, Anderson, & Koblinsky, 1998). Furthermore, mothers who were homeless reported there were fewer people that they could count on in times of need and less family support in the last 6 months than mothers in low-income housing. Thus, another factor to consider for mothers who are not receiving much support from relatives and friends is that they may face a major child care dilemma. The following quote eloquently describes the plight of single mothers with children:

> It is obvious that these mothers are extraordinarily stressed and are facing almost insurmountable problems of single parenting under the difficult circumstances of poverty, lack of extended family support, lack of affordable child care available to them if they could work, and are without a home. In reality, any smaller combination of these circumstances could render almost anyone immobilized, and it is highly unlikely that any improvement can occur without ongoing social assistance and interpersonal support. (Dail, 1993, p. 59)

Cultural Diversity

In addition to cultural differences related to marital status and gender, ethnicity and geographical location need to be considered when working with homeless

Sidebar 16.6 ■ Case Study: Supporting Latisha

Consider Latisha from the case example. Is she at risk for becoming a single homeless mother with her new baby? Why? What prevention and intervention efforts discussed in this chapter could be used to help improve her situation and minimize risks for negative outcomes for herself and her baby?

■ ■ ■

children. There is extreme disparity between the percentage of cultural diversity in the general population and the percentage of people from culturally diverse backgrounds who are homeless. In fact, researchers have documented the percentage of homeless persons from culturally diverse backgrounds to be as high as 85% in certain areas (Danseco & Holden, 1998). Research on people who were homeless across the United States found that 42%–61% were from African American backgrounds (Institute for Children and Poverty & Homes for the Homeless, 2005; National Coalition for the Homeless, 2009).

With this knowledge, preventive outreach approaches should target community and state-run services that serve minority groups, particularly African Americans, and support families who are teetering on the brink of homelessness. Once African American mothers become homeless, it is very important to provide linkages with social service organizations and other sources of support. Research has shown that this group may be particularly subject to alienation or a lack of support from family and friends (Letiecq et al., 1998). It is important to note that the triggers to homelessness also appear to be somewhat culturally related. Caucasians are more likely to have become homeless because of domestic abuse, and people from Hispanic backgrounds may be more likely to become homeless because of language barriers that cause difficulty accessing social services (Institute for Children and Poverty & Homes for the Homeless, 2005).

There is also a misconception in the general public that homelessness is an urban problem. Rural homelessness may be increasing at a faster rate than urban homelessness, and the demographic characteristics of the rural homeless are different from those of the urban homeless. Specifically, rural people who are homeless are more likely to be Caucasian than their urban counterparts (Herron & Zabel, 1995; National Coalition for the Homeless, 2006). Native Americans and migrant workers who are homeless are also predominantly in rural areas (National Coalition for the Homeless, 2006). Another important consideration for working with homeless populations in rural areas is that it may be more difficult to identify rural families who are homeless because they may have a stronger support network and may be living in temporary residences with family and friends or because they may be living in wooded camp areas or other remote areas (Aron & Fitchen, 1996).

Overall, it is important to remember to honor cultural diversity when working with all families. It is important always to be culturally sensitive without being stereotypic (Turnbull et al., 2006). Some examples of arrangements that professionals providing services to families who are homeless could make to be culturally sensitive include ensuring that the provider and the family have a language and cultural match, having flexible hours and accepting walk-ins, and using clergy or respected members of cultures in interventions (Turnbull et al., 2006; Watson, 1996).

Summary

It is clear that children and youth who are homeless suffer physically, psychologically, socially, and academically. It is unconscionable that many of these children and youth are not being served when a portion of this population could be readily identified through homeless shelters, foster care, and other social agencies. Research on homeless children and youth is growing but still scarce despite the large numbers of homeless youth in the United States. More information regarding children and youth who are homeless and the barriers they face within and outside of the school system is needed. In addition, state departments of education must recognize the prevalence of homelessness and fund programs designed to support coordinated outreach, prevention, and intervention efforts. Without more concentrated efforts for prevention and intervention, youth who are homeless will continue to be at risk for growing up uneducated, in poor health, and at risk for recreating the cycle of homelessness with their children.

Useful Websites

Horizons for Homeless Children
  http://www.horizonsforhomelesschildren.org
Institute for Children, Poverty and Homelessness
  http://www.icphusa.org/Publications/Reports/
National Alliance to End Homelessness
  http://www.endhomelessness.org
National Center for Homeless Education
  http://www.naehcy.org
The National Center on Family Homelessness
  http://www.familyhomelessness.org
National Coalition for the Homeless
  http://www.nationalhomeless.org

References

Altena, A. M., Brilleslijper-Kater, S. N., & Wolf, J. R. L. M. (2010). Effective interventions for homeless youth: A systematic review. *American Journal of Preventive Medicine, 38*, 637–645.

Anderson, J. E., Cheney, R., Clatts, M., Faruique, S., Kipke, M., Long, A., . . . Wiebel, W. (1996). HIV risk behavior, street outreach and condom use in eight high-risk populations. *AIDS Education and Prevention, 8*, 191–204.

Anooshian, L. J. (2005). Violence and aggression in the lives of homeless children: A review. *Aggression and Violent Behavior, 10*, 129–152.

Aron, L. Y., & Fitchen, J. M. (1996). Rural homelessness: A synopsis. In J. Baumchi (Ed.), *Homelessness in America* (pp. 81–85). Phoenix, AZ: Oryx Press.

Auerswald, C., & Eyre, S. L. (2002). Youth homelessness in San Francisco: A life cycle approach. *Social Science and Medicine, 54*, 1497–1512.

Baggerly, J. (2004). The effects of child-centered group play therapy on self-concept, depression, and anxiety of children who are homeless. *International Journal of Play Therapy, 13*, 31–51.

Bannon, W. M., Jr., Beharie, N., Olshtain-Mann, O., McKay, M. M., Goldstein, L., Cavaleri, M. A., . . . Lawrence, R. (2012). Youth substance use in a context of family homelessness. *Children and Youth Services Review, 34*, 1–7.

Boesky, L. M., Toro, P. A., & Bukowski, P. A. (1997). Differences in psychosocial factors among older and younger homeless adolescents found in youth shelters. *Journal of Prevention and Intervention in the Community, 15,* 19–36.

Bos, C. S., & Vaughn, S. (2006). *Strategies for teaching students with learning and behavior problems* (6th ed.). Boston, MA: Pearson/Allyn & Bacon.

Burt, M., Aron, L. Y., Lee, E., & Valente, J. (2001). *Helping America's homeless: Emergency shelter or affordable housing?* Washington, DC: Urban Institute Press.

Cauce, A. M., Paradise, M., Ginzler, J. A., Embry, L., Morgan, C. J., Lohr, Y., & Theofelis, J. (2000). The characteristics and mental health of homeless adolescents: Age and gender differences. *Journal of Emotional and Behavioral Disorders, 8,* 230–239.

Center for Law and Social Policy. (2003). *Leave no youth behind: Opportunities for Congress to reach disconnected youth.* Washington, DC: Author.

Chen, C., Dormitzer, C. M., Gutieerrez, U., Vittetoe, K., Gonzales, G. B., & Anthony, F. C. (2004). The adolescent behavioral repertoire as a context for drug exposure: Behavioral autarcesis at play. *Addiction, 99,* 897–906.

Children's Defense Fund. (2005). *The state of America's children.* Washington, DC: Author.

Corliss, H. L., Goodenow, C. S., & Austin, S. B. (2012). "Sexuality and homelessness in Los Angeles public schools"; Corliss et al. respond. *American Journal of Public Health, 102,* 202.

Dail, P. W. (1993). Homelessness in America: Involuntary family migration. *Marriage and Family Review, 19,* 55–75.

Danseco, E. R., & Holden, E. W. (1998). Are there different types of homeless families? A typology of homeless families based on cluster analysis. *Family Relations, 47,* 159–165.

Davey, T. L. (2004). A multiple-family group intervention for homeless families: The weekend retreat. *Health and Social Work, 29,* 326–329.

Economic Policy Institute. (2005). *Minimum wage: Frequently asked questions.* Available from http://www.epinet.org

Embry, L. E., Stoep, A. V., Evens, C., Ryan, K., & Pollock, A. (2000). Risk factors for homelessness in adolescents released from psychiatric residential treatment. *Journal of the American Academy of Child and Adolescent Psychiatry, 39,* 1293–1299.

Ferguson, K. M. (2012). Merging the fields of mental health and social enterprise: Lessons from abroad and cumulative findings from research with homeless youths. *Community Mental Health Journal, 48,* 490–502.

Ferguson, K. M., Xie, B., & Glynn, S. (2012). Adapting the individual placement and support model with homeless young adults. *Child & Youth Care Forum, 41,* 277–294.

Fisher, M. (2005). *Why is U.S. poverty higher in nonmetropolitan than metropolitan areas?* Corvallis, OR: Rural Poverty Research Center. Retrieved from http://www.rprconline.org/WorkingPapers/WP0504.pdf

Gerwitz, A. H. (2007). Promoting children's mental health in family supportive housing: A community–university partnership for formerly homeless children and families. *Journal of Primary Prevention, 28,* 359–374.

Gleghorn, A. A., Marx, R., Vittinghoff, R., & Katz, M. H. (1998). Association between drug use patterns and HIV risks among homeless, runaway and street youth in Northern California. *Drug and Alcohol Dependence, 51,* 219–227.

Greenblatt, M., & Robertson, M. J. (1993). Lifestyles, adaptive strategies, and sexual behaviors of homeless adolescents. *Hospital and Community Psychiatry, 44,* 1177–1183.

Haber, M., & Toro, P. A. (2003, June). *Parent–adolescent violence as a predictor of adolescent outcomes.* Poster session presented at the biennial conference on Community Research and Action, Las Vegas, NM.

Haber, M. G., & Toro, P. A. (2004). Homelessness among families, children, and adolescents: An ecological–developmental perspective. *Clinical Child and Family Psychology Review, 7,* 123–164.

Hammer, H., Finkelhor, D., & Sedlak, A. J. (2002). *Runaway/thrown away children: National estimates and characteristics*. Washington, DC: U.S. Department of Justice, Office of Juvenile Justice and Delinquency Prevention.

Heinze, H., Toro, P. A., & Urberg, K. A. (2004). Delinquent behaviors and affiliation with male and female peers. *Journal of Clinical Child and Adolescent Psychology, 33*, 336–346.

Herbers, J. E., Cutuli, J. J., Lafavor, T. L., Vrieze, D., Leibel, C., Obradovi, J., & Masten, A. S. (2011). Direct and indirect effects of parenting on the academic functioning of young homeless children. *Early Education and Development, 22*, 77–104.

Herron, N. L., & Zabel, D. (1995). *Bridging the gap: Examining polarity in America*. Englewood, CO: Libraries Unlimited.

Hong, S., & Piescher, K. (2012). The role of supportive housing in homeless children's well-being: An investigation of child welfare an educational outcomes. *Children and Youth Services Review, 34*, 1440–1447.

Institute for Children and Poverty. (2001). *A shelter is not a home: Or is it?* Retrieved from http://www.homesforthehomeless.com/PDF/reports/Shelter.pdf?Submit1=Free+Download

Institute for Children and Poverty. (2003). *Miles to go: The flip side of the McKinney–Vento Homeless Assistance Act*. Retrieved from http://www.homesforthehomeless.com/PDF/merchandise/MilestoGo.pdf?Submit1=Free+Download

Institute for Children and Poverty & Homes for the Homeless. (2005). *Homelessness in America: Part 2. A statistical reader*. Retrieved from http://www.icpny.org/PDF/merchandise/HIA2%20final.pdf?Submit1=Free+Download

Kelly, J. F., Buehlman, K., & Caldwell, K. (2000). Training personnel to promote quality parent–child interaction in families who are homeless. *Topics in Early Childhood Special Education, 20*, 174–185.

Kolos, A. C., Green, E. J., & Crenshaw, D. A. (2009). Conducting filial therapy with homeless parents. *American Journal of Orthopsychiatry, 79*, 366–374.

Kral, A. H., Molnar, B. E., Booth, R. E., & Watters, J. K (1997). Prevalence of sexual risk behavior and substance use among runaway and homeless adolescents in San Francisco, Denver, and New York City. *International Journal of STD and AIDS, 8*, 109–117.

Letiecq, B. L., Anderson, E. A., & Koblinsky, S. A. (1998). Social support of homeless and housed mothers: A comparison of temporary and permanent housing arrangements. *Family Relations, 47*, 415–421.

Lindholm, E. N. (1996). Preventing homelessness. In J. Baumohl (Ed.), *Homelessness in America* (pp. 187–200). Phoenix, AZ: Oryx Press.

Lloyd, G. A., & Kuszelewicz, M. A. (Eds.). (1995). *HIV disease: Lesbians, gays, and the social services*. New York, NY: Haworth Press.

Lombardo, S., & Toro, P. A. (2004). *Risky sexual behaviors and substance abuse among homeless and other at-risk adolescents*. Unpublished manuscript, Department of Psychology, Wayne State University.

Maslow, A. H. (1968). *Toward a psychology of being* (2nd ed.). New York, NY: Van Nostrand.

Mayock, P., Corr, M. L., & O'Sullivan, E. (2011). Homeless young people, families and change: Family support as a facilitator to exiting homelessness. *Child and Family Social Work, 16*, 391–401.

McCaskill, P. A., Toro, P. A., & Wolfe, S. M. (1998). Homeless and matched housed adolescents: A comparative study of psychopathology. *Journal of Clinical Child Psychology, 27*, 306–319.

McMorris, B. J., Tyler, K. A., Whitbeck, L. B., & Hoyt, D. R. (2002). Familial and "on-the-street" risk factors associated with alcohol use among homeless and runaway adolescents. *Journal of Studies on Alcohol, 63*, 34–44.

Milburn, N. G., Rotheram-Borus, M. J., Batterham, P., Brumback, B., Rosenthal, D., & Mallett, S. (2005). Predictors of close family relationships over one year among homeless young people. *Journal of Adolescence, 28,* 263–275.

Nabors, L. A., Weist, M. D., Shugarman, R., Woeste, M. J., Mullet, E., & Rosner, L. (2004). Assessment, prevention, and intervention activities in a school-based program for children experiencing homelessness. *Behavior Modification, 28,* 565–578.

National Alliance to End Homelessness. (2013). *Rapid re-housing and prevention: Local progress.* Retrieved from http://www.endhomelessness.org/pages/local_progress

National Center on Family Homelessness. (2004). *Homeless children: America's new outcasts.* Newton, MA: Author. Retrieved from http://www. familyhomelessness.org

National Center on Family Homelessness. (2011). *The characteristics and needs of families experiencing homelessness.* Retrieved from http://www.familyhomelessness.org/media/306.pdf

National Coalition for the Homeless. (1999). *Health care and homelessness* (NCH Fact Sheet No. 8). Retrieved from http://nch.ari.net/health.html

National Coalition for the Homeless. (2006). *Homeless youth* (NCH Fact Sheet No. 13). Retrieved from http://www.nationalhomeless.org

National Coalition for the Homeless. (2009). *Why are people homeless?* Retrieved from http://www.nationalhomeless.org/factsheets/why.html

National Low Income Housing Coalition. (2009). *Out of reach 2009.* (Available from the National Low Income Housing Coalition, 1012 14th Street, Suite 610, Washington, DC 20005).

Nyamathi, A., Branson, C., Kennedy, B., Salem, B., Khalilifard, F., Marfisee, M., . . . & Leake, B. (2012). Impact of nursing intervention on decreasing substances among homeless youth. *The American Journal on Addictions, 21,* 558–565.

Nyamathi, A. M., Christiani, A., Windokun, F., Jones, T., Strehlow, A., & Shoptaw, S. (2005). Hepatitis C virus infection, substance use and mental illness among homeless youth: A review. *AIDS, 19,* 34–40.

O'Neil-Pirozzi, T. M. (2009). Feasibility and benefit of parent participation in a program emphasizing preschool child language development while homeless. *American Journal of Speech-Language Pathology, 18,* 252–263.

Paquette, K. (2011). *Families experiencing homelessness.* Retrieved from Homelessness Resource Center website: http://homeless.samhsa.gov/Resource/View.aspx?id=48807

Powers-Costello, B., & Swick, K. J. (2011). Transforming teacher constructs of children and families who are homeless. *Early Childhood Education Journal, 39,* 207–212.

Powers-Costello, E., & Swick, K. J. (2008). Exploring the dynamics of teacher perceptions of homeless children and families during the elderly years. *Early Childhood Education Journal, 36,* 241–245.

Recovery.gov. (2012). *Preventing homelessness.* Retrieved from http://www.recovery.gov/News/featured/Pages/Preventing-Homelessness.aspx

Regan, P. (2003, April). *Youth homelessness and early intervention: The Reconnect experience.* Paper presented at the Third National Homelessness Conference, Beyond and Divide, Brisbane, Queensland, Australia.

Rew, L., Fouladi, R. T., & Yockey, R. D. (2002). Sexual health practices of homeless youth. *Journal of Nursing Scholarship, 34,* 139–145.

Rew, L., Taylor-Seehafer, M., Thomas, N. Y., & Yockey, R. D. (2001). Correlates of resilience in homeless adolescents. *Journal of Nursing Scholarship, 33,* 33–40.

Rotheram-Borus, M. J., Koopman, C., Haignere, C., & Davies, M. (1991). Reducing HIV sexual risk behaviors among runaway adolescents. *Journal of the American Medical Association, 266,* 1237–1241.

Rotheram-Borus, M. J., Parra, M., Cantwell, C., Gwadz, M., & Murphy, D. A. (1996). Runaway and homeless youths. In R. J. DiClemente, W. B. Hansen, & L. E. Ponton (Eds.), *Handbook of adolescent health risk behavior* (pp. 369–391). New York, NY: Plenum Press.

Stormont, M. (2007). *Fostering resilience in young children vulnerable for failure: Strategies for K–3.* Columbus, OH: Pearson/Merrill/Prentice Hall.

Stormont, M., Reinke, W. M., & Herman, K. C. (2010). Using prevention science to address mental health issues in schools. *Psychology in the Schools, 47,* 1–3.

Sweeney, P., Lindegren, M. L., Buehler, J. W., Onorato, I. M., & Janssen, R. S. (1995). Teenagers at risk of human immunodeficiency virus Type 1 infection. *Archives in Pediatric Adolescent Medicine, 149,* 521–528.

Swick, K. J. (2010). Responding to the voices of homeless preschool children and their families. *Early Childhood Education Journal, 38,* 299–304.

Toro, P. A., & Goldstein, M. S. (2000, August). *Outcomes among homeless and matched housed adolescents: A longitudinal comparison.* Poster presented at the annual convention of the American Psychological Association, Washington, DC.

Trisi, D., & Pavetti, L. (2012). *TANF weakening as a safety net for poor families.* Retrieved from Center on Budget and Policy Priorities website: http://www.cbpp.org/cms/index.cfm?fa=view&id=3700

Turnbull, A., Turnbull, R., Erwin, E., & Soodak, L. (2006). *Families, professionals, and exceptionality: Positive outcomes through partnerships and trust* (5th ed.). Upper Saddle River, NJ: Pearson/Merrill/Prentice Hall.

Unger, J. B., Kipke, M. D., Simon, T. R., Montgomery, S. B., & Johnson, C. J. (1997). Homeless youths and young adults in Los Angeles: Prevalence of mental health problems and the relationship between mental health problems and substance abuse disorders. *American Journal of Community Psychology, 25,* 371–394.

Unger, J. B., Simon, T. R., Newman, T. L., Montgomery, S. B., Kipke, M. D., & Albornoz, M. (1998). Early adolescent street youth: An overlooked population with unique problems and service needs. *Journal of Early Adolescence, 18,* 325–348.

U.S. Census Bureau. (2012). *Income, poverty and health insurance coverage in the United States: 2011.* Retrieved from http://www.census.gov/prod/2012pubs/p60-243.pdf

U.S. Conference of Mayors. (2008). *2008 status report on hunger & homelessness.* Available from http://usmayors.org/uscm/home.asp

U.S. Department of Labor. (2012). *Wages.* Retrieved from http://www.dol.gov/dol/topic/wages/minimumwage.htm

Watson, V. (1996). Responses by the states to homelessness. In J. Baumohl (Ed.), *Homelessness in America* (pp. 172–178). Phoenix, AZ: Oryx Press.

Whitbeck, L. B., & Hoyt, D. R. (1999). *Nowhere to grow: Homeless and runaway adolescents and their families.* New York, NY: Aldine de Gruyter.

Whitbeck, L. B., Hoyt, D. R., & Ackley, K. A. (1997). Abusive family backgrounds and victimization among runaway and homeless adolescents. *Journal of Research on Adolescence, 7,* 375–392.

Chapter 17

"This Isn't the Place for Me": School Dropout

Lea R. Flowers and Dawn M. Robinson-McDonald

Concerns about at-risk youth and the national dropout rate have existed for decades. Dropping out of school presents a serious national, state, and local problem. Researchers, administrators, and educators have sought to gain a greater understanding of the causes of academic underachievement in hopes of identifying an effective course of prevention for youth at risk (Lynch, Hurford, & Cole, 2002). In the National Center for Education Statistics (NCES; 2012) Longitudinal Study, researchers examined dropout statistics on the basis of grade level, gender, race, and ethnicity among a nationwide school-age sample. Results revealed that U.S. dropout rates increased as grade level increased: The lowest dropout rate was 2.6%, for the ninth grade, whereas the highest dropout rate was 5.1% for 12th grade. Racial and ethnicity data revealed the lowest dropout rate was among the Asian/Pacific Islander students, at 1.9%. Dropout rates were higher among American Indian/Alaska Native, Black, and Hispanic students at 6.7%, 5.5%, and 5.0%, respectively. Results of nationwide analysis of dropout rates associated with gender revealed males in every state had a higher dropout rate than females. This study also looked at a comparison between high school dropout rates in the 2008–09 and 2009–10 school years. The results were mixed; there was an increase of at least 1% in Delaware, Illinois, and Louisiana. However, in states such as Mississippi, New Mexico, and Wyoming there was a decrease of 1% or more.

The current labor force is vastly different from those of past agrarian and industrial economies; the demands and complexities require an increased skill set and expertise (Harvey, 2001). Currently, we live in a growing global and technology-based economy; thus, medium-income jobs for poorly educated workers have become more and more scarce. School dropouts will likely face significant challenges as they are not adequately prepared to compete in the modern competitive work force, which naturally results in a cycle of poverty and unemployment (Mayer, 2002, as cited in Campbell, 2003). On average, the median annual income for adults without a high school diploma in 2010 was $21,000 versus $29,900 for those with a high school diploma or its equivalent (NCES, 2012). High school dropout comes at a significant cost, and society suffers when students do not complete their education. The nation's economy expends approximately $240 million per year in costs associated with dropping out in terms of tax contributions, Medicaid/Medicare, welfare dependence, and jail/prison systems (Belfield & Levin, 2007). As of October 2009, 3.0 million young people between the ages of 16 and 35 had dropped out of school (NCES, 2012).

The negative effects that result from dropping out do not end with monetary and career limitations: Dropouts 25 years and older typically have a poorer quality of health than non-dropouts, regardless of income (Pleis, Ward, & Lucas, 2010). Dropping out of school tends to create a mindset and environmental norms that are often associated with substance abuse, crime, and other delinquent high-risk behaviors. There are disproportionately high percentages of minorities in prison and on death row who dropped out of school.

Historically, educational policy or issues relating to dropout were not addressed by the federal government. Each state developed and implemented its own policies and programs and designed distinct ways to measure their schools' effectiveness. However, that way of doing things changed when the No Child Left Behind Act of 2001 (Pub. L. No. 107-110) became a federal law. This law has broadened the role of the federal government into educational policy in a more direct way than it ever has been in the history of the United States. The No Child Left Behind Act created measures that hold schools directly accountable for dropout rates, providing additional funding for effective schools and steep penalties for schools that are not effective. Federal law requires that all students in K–12 be assessed each year in order to reflect adequate yearly progress. The primary tool used to measure effectiveness is high-stakes testing as well as school completion (Sunderland, Kim, & Orfield 2005).

Another federal effort designed to increase high school completion was a push to create a nationwide norm for the compulsory attendance age. The compulsory attendance age is the minimum age students must reach before they can withdraw completely from school as an independent. The compulsory attendance age for most states is 16 or 10th-grade completion. There was a push federally to increase the compulsory attendance age to 18 years old. Supporters of this idea believed creating a nationwide age limit would create consistency and accountability throughout the country for at-risk students, who are often transient. Proponents also believed that because almost a third of high school students are dropping out of school nationwide, resulting in a weaker work force and economic strain, the age increase would send a strong message to youth and their families about the importance of education. Supporters also thought that increasing the age to 18 could be more effective if the federal government incentivized it by attaching potential for schools to obtain prime federal education grant funding to support programs for at-risk students. Some advocates for the age increase also believed that as a result there would be an increase in postsecondary, higher education and career aspirations.

Increasing the compulsory attendance age was not well received by many states. The idea of the federal government being involved in any type of mandates regarding their educational policies, particularly the age limit, posed a significant hurdle for some legislators to win acceptance from their constituency. Critics of this change spoke out because they felt increasing the compulsory attendance age to 18 would increase school overcrowding and school violence because the schools would be filled with students who were no longer academically engaged and would likely saddle the school administrators with disciplinary problems.

Homeschool advocacy groups, such as the Home School Legal Defense Association (HSLDA; 2007), have been adamantly against raising the compulsory attendance age to 18 years old. For instance, the Senate File 96 legislation in Wyoming included the increase from 16 to 18 compulsory attendance clauses with an additional section that required parents to meet with school officials in order for students to be exempt from this ruling. Homeschool advocacy groups felt this legislation was excessive in that it violated their families' freedoms and imposed additional burdens with reporting requirements.

Other researchers found legislation or mandates to increase the compulsory attendance age from 16 to 18 had no correlation with high school completion rates. However, programs specifically designed to meet the needs of at-risk students did improve completion rates.

The school dropout rate continues to be a national, state, and local concern. Researchers, administrators, and educators must continue to search for both intervention and prevention programs to stem this growing problem. This chapter provides a definition of the problem as well as approaches to prevention and intervention from an individual, family, school, and community perspective. Case studies are used not only to demonstrate these approaches but also to clarify many of the issues involved in this increasing problem. Attention is also directed to issues of diversity and the part it continues to play in assessing and addressing the school dropout rate. Given that school dropout rates have continued to rise, all entities involved with youth need to direct their attention to finding solutions to this growing problem.

Problem Definition

Schools determine effectiveness by the dropout rate. The schools or districts with low dropout rates are thought to have higher effectiveness, whereas schools with high dropout rates are deemed as having a lower effectiveness (Chapman, Laird, Ifill, & Kewal Ramani, 2011). The cause of student dropout cannot be measured in isolation of impeding factors. Numerous individual, family, and structural factors contribute

---

Sidebar 17.1 ■ Case Study: Designing Effective Prevention and Intervention Services That Would Meet Stephanie's Needs

Stephanie is a 15-year-old Latina female in the 10th grade. Stephanie lives with her mother, twin brother, and her older sister. Stephanie was in the gifted/high achiever program in elementary and middle school. Since fifth grade, Stephanie's grades have been declining, and Stephanie has begun hanging out with a group of students who teachers frequently report are skipping school. Stephanie does not get along with her mother. Stephanie has missed more than 20 days of school from August through December; she says she doesn't see the purpose of going to school.

What are some programs and services that may be effective in decreasing the likelihood that Stephanie will drop out of school?

■ ■ ■

Sidebar 17.2 ■ **Case Study: Evaluating School Policies and Practices to Meet Paul's Needs**

Paul is a 14-year-old African American male. He was in the gifted/high achiever program in elementary school and made all As and Bs in middle school. Paul lives with his mother in a single-parent household. His mother works two jobs to support the family. His mother referred him to the school counselor because his grades have dropped since he began at his new high school, which is a predominantly White high school. His teachers report that he is frequently sleeping in class and is not completing assignments. He stated that he doesn't feel as if he belongs in his school and that he isn't interested in school anymore.

What are some school policies and practices that may impact Paul's experiences? What are some ways that school staff can determine the impact that school practices and policies have on students? How can school staff work to create systemic change in addressing policies and practices that may affect Paul and other students?

■ ■ ■

to students' decisions to leave school (Newcomb et al., 2002; Velez & Saenz, 2001; Wayman, 2002b). The most common reasons students do not complete high school derive from "life interruptions," such as having increased responsibilities at home, becoming pregnant, or working. Other reasons stem from decreased motivation and lack of desire to remain in the school setting, recurrent poor academic performance, truancy, expulsion, and grade retention (Southwest Educational Development Laboratory, 2002) as well as lack of engagement in extracurricular activities and environmental factors, such as having a sibling or parent who dropped out of school or living in a single-parent family with minimal postsecondary education. Historically, students of families with low socioeconomic status and African American and Latino students have had lower rates of high school completion than their peers.

Causal Factors

The underlying causes of school dropout are complex and multidimensional (Christenson, Sinclair, Lehr, & Godber, 2001). Although the label *dropout* has been applied to large numbers of students who do not finish school, such a label fails to adequately represent the fact that youth who drop out of school are a diverse group who leave school for many different reasons. Bickel, Bond, and LeMahieu (1986) noted that the term *dropout* is potentially misleading because it implies that school dropout is an event instead of a process and that the student is the sole decision maker in the process. These researchers suggested that in actuality, some students do not really drop out but merely "fade out" after a period of feeling alienated from school, whereas other students may be subtly or not so subtly "pushed out" of school by school administrators who do not want to deal with the struggling student any longer. Still other students are "pulled out" by more important life demands on their time, such as parenting or having to work. Regardless of the reasons for school dropout, school personnel and counselors who work with these youth cannot afford to passively watch the levels of school attrition increase.

Case Study

Charles is a 14-year-old African American male in the sixth grade. He reports that he does not like going to school and has struggled academically since around the second or third grade. Charles was retained in the first grade and the third grade.

Charles is currently reading at a third-grade level, and his math skills are also at the third-grade level. He was tested but did not qualify for special education services in both the third grade and again in the fifth grade. His teachers report he typically does not complete homework or class assignments and is frequently written up for behavior concerns. School faculty and staff describe him as an unmotivated student. His mother is overwhelmed. She thinks he would be better off taking his General Education Development certificate and getting a job because he is "flunking out" of all of his classes. When Charles was asked what he plans to do once he graduates from high school, he stated he did not plan to graduate and expected he would likely drop out at the end of the school year.

Charles's mother and father divorced when he was in the second grade. His mother remarried when he was in the fourth grade but separated within a year. Since the separation, Charles has not seen his stepfather, and he and his mother have moved several times in between periods of homelessness. They have stayed in shelters, with family and friends, or in hotels.

Charles's mother has a high school education. His biological father dropped out of school in tenth grade. Charles's mother has been unemployed for more than a year and is no longer eligible for unemployment benefits.

Approaches to Prevention

Individual

School counselors work as leaders, advocates, and systemic change agents to assist all students in developing their academic, personal/social, and career potential (American School Counselor Association [ASCA], 2012). It is essential that school counselors consult and work collaboratively with stakeholders within the school community. Their role is to design culturally and developmentally appropriate comprehensive school counseling programs. These services should effectively address the needs of all students, particularly those within diverse populations.

By addressing systemic factors that may impact individual students at risk, the school counselor endeavors to prevent or at least reduce school dropout. Likewise, mental health counselors who work within the community can work collaboratively with the school counselor with counseling approaches that focus on personal/social issues that are connected to academic success.

There are several risk factors that put Charles at an increased risk for dropping out of high school: (a) living in a single-parent household, (b) experiencing frequent moves and homelessness, (c) having a parent who dropped out, and (d) being an African American male (Jozefowicz-Simbeni, 2008). Effective counseling prevention programs must be tailored to meet the individual needs of each student at risk of dropping out.

Sidebar 17.3 ■ Self-Awareness: Becoming an Agent of Systemic Change

Dropout prevention and intervention often requires that we work collaboratively as systemic change agents. What are some ways that you can work in school communities as a systemic change agent to reduce student dropout? What do you believe are some possible barriers to working toward systemic change? What are some ways that you can overcome some of these barriers to success when working toward systemic change?

■ ■ ■

Students at risk benefit from interventions that integrate ecological counseling approaches (Abrams, Theberge, & Karan, 2005; Bronfenbrenner, 1979; Conyne & Cook, 2004). School and community counselors use ecological approaches that enable them to address the systemic issues that are involved when a student is at risk of dropping out of school. During the initial school counseling session(s), the counselor may determine Charles's needs, identify his worldview, identify his sources of support, evaluate any risk factors that may contribute to his being at risk, identify potential barriers to success, and set goals for sessions.

There is evidence to support the fact that solution-focused brief counseling can be effective in school settings (Franklin, Moore, & Hopson, 2008). A solution-focused approach would enable a counselor to work with Charles from a strengths approach and identify times that he has experienced success. Counseling techniques that use play can increase Charles's self-confidence (Bagger & Parker, 2005) and assist him in working through issues of grief and loss (Fiorini & Mullen, 2006). Play techniques such as sand trays and drawings can assist counselors in examining Charles's worldview. During the initial session, the counselor may ask Charles to depict or show his world by using a sand tray or by drawing. While Charles is completing his sand tray or drawing, the counselor can observe and track the themes and placements of how Charles uses the manipulatives within the sand tray. This process of observation helps the counselor discover how he views his world without seeming intrusive with probing questions. Using play helps the counselor and student build trust and rapport. The play becomes the student's mode of expression. Students are often receptive to nondirective sand tray approaches because they do not have to use verbal language to express themselves on topics that may be difficult to discuss.

By analyzing the completed sand tray, the counselor may discover themes of how Charles conceptualizes his personal world. The themes that were illuminated from Charles's sand tray suggested that he may view his world as a place where he often feels lonely and unloved as well as a place in which "people always leave." The counselor can label this as a theme of grief and loss. Children and adolescents experiencing grief and loss often show a decrease in academic performance, particularly in the absence of adequate social support.

At this point the central theme of the counselor's work with Charles could revolve around the theme of grief and loss. Charles has experienced layers of loss, beginning with his mother and biological father divorcing when he was in the second grade. Then he developed a new bond with his mother's second husband, which resulted in another layer of loss when his mom and stepfather separated. Counselors could focus intervention strategies on teaching Charles coping strategies to deal with his unresolved grief and loss of these relationships. Students who are in families of divorce typically benefit from group counseling that includes goals that are specifically tailored for the issues that derive from having fractured family systems. Such small groups and classroom guidance lessons within the school setting can focus on teaching students coping strategies. Once Charles develops trust and rapport with others by interacting within the small group of students who have had similar experiences, he may feel many of his thoughts and fears regarding his family situation will be normalized and validated throughout the group process.

Self-esteem is another area for the counselor to work on with Charles. His lack of motivation and the fact that he frequently gives up on things he doesn't feel he can do right are clear indications that Charles experiences feelings of inadequacy. Therefore, it is important for the counselor to set Charles up for success by creating opportunities where he can experience a sense of mastery through activities within the counseling sessions. Study skills and interventions that focus on self-esteem can be designed by the school counselor, then implemented in classroom guidance and/or small groups. To address other counseling needs that may affect Charles's academic success, the school counselor may collaborate and refer him to a counseling agency within the community that can continue working on his goals and offer support to decrease his risk of dropping out.

Family

School counselors, community counselors, teachers, administrators, and others within the school community can provide families with support. They can assist Charles's family by providing strategies that the family can use to help him experience academic success in school. Some strategies that may be helpful for families who have students at risk of dropping out are to provide consistency and encouragement, keep the lines of communication open with the school, seek support, provide real-world experiences of concepts at home, stress the importance of obtaining a high school education, and know your rights.

Provide Consistency and Encouragement

Charles's family system is strained by a multitude of stressors, which could inevitably have a long-term impact on his health and well-being. When faced with difficult family and financial situations, it is important that parents provide as much consistency as possible. By continuing with daily routines such as having a consistent time for homework, bedtime, and other routines, children and adolescents can experience a sense of normalcy. Charles's parents can encourage him by recognizing the amount of effort that he puts into tasks. This acknowledgment is important because Charles has very little confidence in his abilities. Through encouragement, Charles can learn to become self-motivated to complete tasks.

Keep the Lines of Communication Open With the School

Parental involvement is one of the key factors in determining student success in schools. Thus, it is essential that Charles's parents communicate regularly with his teachers and school counselor. Through regular communication, Charles's parents can be aware of missed homework and assignments as well as behavior concerns, and they can work with teachers to develop a plan to help Charles experience academic success in school.

Seek Support

Communities and schools have services available to students that are not always advertised. Families may be unaware of these resources if they do not advocate for themselves. For instance, Charles and his family could benefit from family counseling. Many families in similar financial situations as this family may think the cost of family counseling is unaffordable. However, there are agencies that can provide family and individual counseling with fees based on a sliding scale ranging from minimal cost to free of charge, depending on the family's economic situation. The family needs to advocate for itself by contacting the child's school to find out about the resources that are available in the school and community. Likewise, many schools provide free tutorial service before and/or after school. Charles could benefit from daily tutoring that focuses on teaching basic skills and concepts. By knowing what services are available, Charles's parents can determine what programs and services would be beneficial for him. In addition, the school counselor and/or school social worker can help the family identify other community resources, such as food, shelter, and basic daily living needs to help address the family's limited economic and housing situation.

Provide Real-World Experiences With Concepts at Home

The family can participate in daily games and activities to help increase Charles's proficiency in basic math and reading skills. Also, by incorporating real-life situations as examples of how information he learns in school transfers within real-life situations—for example, as the family shops for groceries, pays bills, and does other daily tasks—Charles can apply both math and reading concepts.

Stress the Importance of a High School Education

Parents can stress the importance of a high school education. By seeing differences in the income levels between students who drop out of school and high school graduates, Charles may gain an understanding of the long-term consequences of not completing high school. Although it may be financially beneficial to the family at the current time for him to get a job, the long-term benefits of getting a high school diploma can be far more beneficial financially. It is important that Charles's family encourage him to stay in school and emphasize the long-term benefits of Charles completing high school.

Know Your Rights and Advocate for Your Child

It is important that parents are aware of their rights regarding their children's education. The well-informed and active parent of the at-risk student is one of the most powerful tools against school dropout. It is imperative that parents, in this case Charles's mother, be aware that they do have rights and have at least a basic understanding of those rights. Parents have a right to request a meeting to discuss their child's education. In some cases, the student may not qualify for special education services or have an individualized education plan (IEP); however, there are other programs that provide assistance and accommodations for students within the classroom setting, such as the 504 plan.

School retention is often an ineffective strategy in meeting the needs of students (Poland, 2009). Charles was retained in both first grade and third grade. However, it appears that retention was not an effective strategy. In situations like this, parents must use their rights and understand they have a voice in the decision-making process of their child's academic journey. Decisions for students should never be made unilaterally by a particular teacher, counselor, or administrator. Decisions are made by a team in an open and transparent way. Parents are an integral part of that team approach. The most effective plans are person-centered, where the student is present at the meetings and also has a voice in the decisions that are being made on his or her behalf. In Charles's situation, it is clear that retaining him twice was not effective. Retaining him again would increase his likelihood of dropping out; therefore, retention should not be considered an effective option for Charles.

School

Bridge Gaps Within the School Community

Schools must work to meet the needs of all students by identifying and providing ways to bridge the gaps within the school community. To address the needs of students who are struggling, schools need regular communication between and among school counselors, teachers, school social workers, school administrators, parents, students, and other stakeholders. School staff in elementary, middle, and high school must work together as they design programs and services to meet the diverse needs of students.

Often there are programs in elementary schools that may have been effective but are not linked to what is done in the middle or high school. If Charles began a mentoring and tutorial program in fifth grade and was showing success through these services, but he began sixth grade and no one was aware of this successful program, then the school staff would not know that it could be replicated to assist Charles. To be most effective there should be a transition of services from Charles's elementary school to middle school and then to high school; that is, there should be a continuity of services as he matriculates throughout his school experience. This type of cohesion among the professionals who serve at-risk students would strengthen the development and implementation of programs such as tutoring and mentoring. In addition, school staff who work directly with the students could communicate regularly so that they know what programs or strategies have been effective or ineffective in working with the at-risk students. If students move outside of the school community, which they often do, the school counselor and other school staff could share information with the student's new school. School staff could perhaps consider attaching a brief summary to go along with his records that provides a condensed overview of Charles's social, emotional, and academic context. This type of overview would be helpful for the professionals at the receiving school to have a snapshot of the student before reviewing his entire record.

Schools can provide ongoing opportunities for Charles's parents to meet with school staff to discuss his progress. Semi-monthly parent conferences could provide Charles's parents with an opportunity to meet regularly with his teachers and other educators within the school setting. Schools can also hold parent conferences and meetings in apartment complexes, agencies, and organizations within the community so that school staff are easily accessible to parents. In addition, schools can work with the local community to prevent students from dropping out of school. Area businesses could work with Charles's school to encourage students to stay in school. The school could work with area businesses that might provide incentives for attending school, possible employment opportunities, and opportunities for students to connect what they are learning in school to daily life.

Build Relationships With Students and Families

Charles's school must work to maintain a positive relationship with Charles and his family. Faculty and staff can examine current practices and policies that could be perceived as being unwelcoming to Charles and his family. Anonymous parent surveys, needs assessments, and focus groups could assist Charles's school in gathering information from parents and students about their perceptions of interactions within the school as well as the overall culture and climate of the school. Charles's school would want to ensure that all interactions, practices, and procedures communicate both respect and an appreciation of diversity and that everyone feels welcome.

Sidebar 17.4 ■ Self-Awareness: Evaluating Beliefs, Practices, and Policies

Often we have beliefs that affect our practices in working with students. What we think and believe shapes our daily interactions with students and parents. Many students who drop out of school report that school practices and policies reflected a lack of care and concern about them.

What do you believe about all students? When you reflect on the following groups, what are your beliefs?

- students with disabilities
- English language learners
- males
- females
- White students
- African American students
- Latino students
- Asian students
- students who are undocumented
- lesbian, gay, bisexual, transgender, and questioning students
- gifted/high achiever students

How may your beliefs affect your daily interactions with students? What are some common school practices and policies that may communicate (a) that a student or parent is not welcome or (b) that there is a lack of concern for certain groups?

■ ■ ■

School and community counselors can provide trainings for school faculty and staff on ways to build positive relationships with students and parents. Trainings could focus on developing verbal and nonverbal communication skills, dealing with conflicts, and understanding the worldview of parents and students. Faculty and staff can build relationships with Charles and his parents by being visible, being easily accessible, and showing interest in their concerns. Charles's teachers must also keep the lines of communication open with his parents. Charles's teachers can communicate with his parents through phone, e-mail, and face-to-face interactions. They can make the parents aware when Charles has missed class, when he is having behavior concerns, and if he does not complete class assignments. It is also equally important for Charles's teachers to inform his parents when he has done well in school and what worked for him on those days.

Charles's teachers can build a relationship with him by learning about his interests, finding out what is most important to him, and taking time to meet with him individually. Charles's teachers can use the information about his interests in designing lessons that engage him. Charles's teachers, school counselors, and other educators working with Charles can also take the time to visit his community. Often school faculty and staff come to work but have not become familiar with apartment complexes and other communities that students live in. Faculty and staff could hold parent nights at local apartment complexes or churches and could go visit the communities so that they have a better understanding of their students; such visits would also help to build relationships with students and families in their school communities.

Track Attendance

Schools can regularly track the attendance of students and meet with students who have attendance concerns. For students like Charles, tracking attendance can serve as a means of school dropout prevention, as he expects he will drop out of school at the end of this year. Tracking attendance holds the student accountable and may give students a sense that someone cares about their whereabouts. It is sometimes the role of the school counselor to meet with students who have had a significant number of absences or are frequently late to identify issues that cause them to miss school, then work with students and their families to address potential obstacles.

Provide Opportunities for Parental Involvement

Parental involvement is one of the primary predictors of students dropping out of school (Jozefowicz-Simbeni, 2008; White & Kelly, 2010). The school can provide opportunities for parents to be involved in their child's education. The school can also provide parental workshops on topics that address the specific needs of the parents within the school. For instance, a parental workshop on the parent and child relationship during the time when the student is transitioning from elementary to middle school would help parents understand what to expect during that transitional period. Encouraging parents to volunteer in the school setting is important. Often parents do not feel welcome in the school environment. In Charles's case, if he and his mother both felt connected to the school as a vital source of support and involvement within their community, they might not feel as discouraged and his mother might not have such low expectations for him. There are many ways parents can volunteer in the schools: Often they can help in the parent resource center, assist the classroom teacher, and/or assist the support staff.

A parent resource center should be developed in the school to help foster a bridge to work collaboratively with community agencies with joint sponsored programs and services that address the needs of the students and increase parental involvement. The school can be a place where a sense of community is fostered for the students and their families; for instance, literacy classes or ESL (English as a second language) classes could be held at the school to strengthen the parents' skills. In Charles's case his mother could benefit from programs and services that help her to find resources for housing and employment and that provide her with education on how to work with Charles on basic math and reading skills at home. In the age of accountability, it is essential that the programs and services have data to evaluate effectiveness and determine program modifications that may be necessary.

Provide Programs and Services That Meet the Needs of the School Community

School administrators, school counselors, teachers, school social workers, school psychologists, and other school staff must work together to identify and meet the needs of their community. Formal and informal needs assessments can be used to determine the needs of a school community. In school communities in which parents may have difficulties with obtaining employment and/or need educational or career training, schools can serve as a resource for families.

School and Class Size

Fostering the development of a sense of community at school includes advocating for smaller schools and structuring school activities to include ample opportunity for students to bond with adults and peers at school (Marcus & Sanders-Reio, 2001). Schools with low teacher/student ratios retain students until graduation more than schools with higher ratios (Baker et al., 2001). Large teacher/student ratios limit the ability of teachers to monitor students' outcomes carefully and minimize the opportunity for the development of supportive teacher–student relationships.

Counselors need to remain cognizant of the benefits of low teacher/student ratios and promote small class sizes when possible.

Provide Additional Academic Support

Many students at risk of dropping out of school need additional academic support (White & Kelly, 2010). There is a need for programs and services for students who are struggling academically but do not qualify for special education services. School tutorial and supplemental enrichment programs can be effective in decreasing the rate of students at risk of dropping out of school (Somers & Piliawsky, 2004). School tutorial programs can assist students so that they are able to complete class assignments and homework; in addition, they can teach students basic skills in reading and math and can help students learn and reinforce concepts that have been taught in the classroom setting. Many schools provide tutorial services before and after school. Charles could attend tutorial programs so that he does not fall further behind in school; however, if Charles's school provides tutorial programs but the teachers do not have the training to teach basic math and reading skills to a middle school student, these services may not be effective. Middle and high school teachers who provide tutorial services must be trained to teach basic skills to older students, as many students who are at risk of dropping out of school often may not have grasped the basic skills in reading and/or math and may need additional support. Charles could also benefit by being in an inclusive environment in which he has a teacher who is trained to meet his needs. Peer tutoring programs can also be effective in working with students academically.

Mentoring Programs

Mentoring programs within the school can serve as a means of connecting students with positive role models in the community. Schools can work collaboratively with agencies that have reputable mentoring programs, such as Big Brothers/Big Sisters, to match students with mentors or can design their own mentoring programs.

Provide an Opportunity for a Sense of Belonging and Connectedness

Students who are at risk of dropping out of school are often no longer interested in being engaged within the school setting. The process of disengaging from school is sometimes subtle and occurs over time with a series of academic failures and unfulfilling, meaningless academic experiences. Students often communicate experiences of not having a sense of belonging and not feeling connected to their schools (Bost & Riccomini, 2006). School extracurricular activities and clubs can serve as a means of helping students to have a sense of belonging in their school environment. Charles lost interest in school because he did not feel connected and did not feel as if he was able to be successful at anything. Charles loves art, and because his local school has a variety of activities for Charles to become involved in, he may be able to find something that he enjoys and that would enable him to have a sense of mastery.

Community

Collaboration Between School and Community Counselors

School and community counselors must work together to meet the needs of students who are at risk of dropping out of school. School counselors can refer Charles and his family for individual and family counseling services. School counselors

Sidebar 17.5 ■ Self-Awareness: School and Community Counselors Working Together

It is essential for school and community counselors working with students who are at risk of dropping out of school to work together in meeting students' needs. What are some ways that school and community counselors can work together to address the needs of students who are at risk of dropping out of school? What are some barriers that school and community counselors may face in keeping the lines of communication open? What are some ways that school and community counselors can ensure that they are able to work to overcome some potential barriers to communication?

■ ■ ■

must first get a release of information so that they are able to share information such as grades, behavior reports, and any other information that may be pertinent to Charles's success with the community counselor. It is essential that school and community counselors network and develop rapport and relationships among themselves so that they can have a positive alliance to work effectively to meet the academic, personal/social, and career needs of students like Charles.

Work With Community Businesses

School counselors and educators in the school community can work with area businesses in the community to promote student success. They can work with apartment complexes and churches to hold events for families, can encourage employees at area businesses to volunteer at their school, and can work with the community to assist in showing how concepts that they teach in their classes can be used in the real world.

Teaming/Collaborating as Systemic Change Agents

School counselors, community counselors, educators, and parents can work as leaders and advocates in their communities to effect systemic change. They can work collaboratively to influence policies and procedures at the local, state, and national levels that focus on meeting the needs of all students. When stakeholders team up and collaborate together, they can have a great effect on prompting systemic changes that need to be addressed to meet the needs of all students.

Sidebar 17.6 ■ Case Study: Teaming/Collaborating to Meet Junior's Needs

Junior is a 12-year-old Latino male in the seventh grade. Junior lives with his mother and three siblings. He was born in the United States, but his parents and one of his older siblings were born in Mexico. Junior reports that he was doing well in school until around the fourth grade, when his father moved to Florida to support his family financially. Junior reports that he and his father are close, and he talks with his father over the phone on Sunday evenings.

Junior's teacher referred him because he appears to be unmotivated in his classes and frequently does not complete assignments. He also told one of his teachers that he plans to drop out of school. Junior made all As prior to the fourth grade. He wants to do well in school, but he is not sure how.

How can the school community work collaboratively to address Junior's needs? What are some specific strategies and interventions that can help Junior to be successful? How can you use an ecological perspective in working with Junior?

■ ■ ■

Case Study

Michelle is a 16-year-old Hispanic female who is an eighth-grade student at a local middle school. Her parents are involved in her education and want her to excel in school. Michelle and her family are undocumented; she and her family moved to the United States from Mexico when Michelle was in the fourth grade. Michelle and her family live in the South, and Michelle frequently talks about experiences with being mistreated because she is undocumented. She reports feelings of hopelessness as a result of her experiences. Michelle's parents do not speak English, but Michelle and her two younger siblings speak English fluently. Michelle has been receiving ELL (English language learner) services in her subject area courses. In sixth grade, Michelle was frequently suspended from school for fighting with peers, and it was reported that Michelle was hanging out with local gang members. Michelle was retained in sixth grade because she had more than 20 unexcused absences, was not passing the majority of her classes, and did not pass the state achievement test at the end of the school year.

Michelle dropped out of school last year and returned to school at the beginning of this school year. Michelle stated that she previously dropped out of school because she felt that school was too hard and reported that she is considering dropping out of school again for the same reason. She stated that she has the most difficulty in math, but she enjoys other subject areas in school because she likes the teachers. She reported that no matter how hard she tries, she has not been able to pass her math class. Although Michelle has had difficulties in school in the past, she reports that she would like to graduate from high school and has been coming to school more frequently in the past couple of weeks.

Michelle has an extensive trauma history and has reported that she was sexually abused when she was in fifth grade. It is important to Michelle to help her family, and she has been working two jobs so that she can assist the family financially. Her jobs require her to work late; thus, she is often sleepy in class.

Although there are various approaches that can be effective in working with Michelle, an ecological counseling approach would address the systemic factors that Michelle is dealing with that contribute to her being at risk of dropping out of school. Ecological counseling examines microsystem, mesosystem, exosystem, and macrosystem influences in a client's day-to-day life.

Intervention Strategies

Individual

At the individual level, counselors using an ecological approach as an intervention strategy would focus on exploring Michelle's perception of her environment and the meanings that she makes from the interactions in her environment. During the initial meeting with Michelle, it is essential that the counselor work to build a positive relationship with her. Rapport is important: Michelle needs to trust her counselor and perceive him or her as a genuine and authentic person who is reliable. Play techniques such as sand trays, drawings, and/or genograms may be used in the initial sessions to assist in building rapport and highlighting Michelle's day-to-day experiences by prompting Michelle to make something in the sand tray or in a drawing that shows her world. Through the initial assessment, the counselor could determine Michelle's strengths, motivation for change, and sources of support and could work to identify Michelle's academic, personal/social, and career goals. In this case, Michelle's strengths include parental support, her relationships with her teachers, and the fact that she is willing to work hard when there is something of interest to her (e.g., supporting her family).

The next level is the microsystem level. At this level, the counselor needs to work with Michelle to identify choices that she makes that at times impede her ability to excel in school. It is important that students have an awareness of the barriers that impede their academic success. In addition, a counselor can work with Michelle to identify different systems that are involved in her day-to-day life and the way that these systems impact her thoughts, feelings, and behaviors as well as the role these systems have played on her academic, personal/social, and career development. For instance, Michelle's school and/or community counselor can work with Michelle to identify macrosystems, such as cultural barriers to success like ethnicity and gender. In addition, at the macrosystem level, schools and communities can work with Michelle to explore her experiences of being undocumented and the ways that her culture affects her experiences.

A counselor can help Michelle to identify her career goals. Michelle is often hard on herself when she does not achieve her goals. The counselor can then work with her with a focus on how her negative self-talk neither adds to her image of self nor helps her to refocus and achieve her goals. The counselor can assist Michelle and her family in identifying strengths and sources of support. Michelle's supportive family is a strength, and Michelle's desire to be able to support her family can be a motivating factor in Michelle excelling academically, particularly when she is able to see the connection that a solid education has on her ability to assist her family in the future.

When students have experiences of past sexual abuse and/or trauma, it is often necessary for the school counselor to provide a counseling referral to a mental health professional within a community agency. It is essential for the school counselor to thoroughly review his or her referral sources that are appropriate and can meet the specific needs of the student and the student's family. In this case, it is important that the agency can provide services for Spanish-speaking individuals.

The ecological approach works very well with other theoretical interventions. It lends itself to the ideal framework for an integrative approach. Theoretical interventions from cognitive-behavioral, Adlerian, and solution-focused counseling perspectives are some of the interventions most commonly integrated with the ecological approach. Cognitive-behavioral counseling could assist Michelle in exploring irrational beliefs and negative self-talk. Adlerian counseling techniques could be used to help Michelle identify her early recollection of experiences as well as to create a sense of belonging and feelings of connectedness. Solution-focused counseling could also be used to identify her ideal world or how she would like for things to be in her environment and focus on her strengths, resources, and times that she has been successful in order to determine what may work best in addressing her needs.

Family

Mesosystems include the interaction between microsystems in a client's environment. The interaction between the school and community would be considered as part of Michelle's mesosystem. Counselors can support families of at-risk students by including families in designing and implementing services to meet the needs of students. By involving parents in the planning process, schools and communities are able to increase the effectiveness of interventions. Parents can provide valuable input on ways to assist their children because they have expertise in knowing their children and an awareness of strategies that can assist them. Michelle's parents can help to determine resources that are needed to assist her. Family counseling and child–parent relationship training can also be beneficial to improve the relationship between Michelle and her parents and to draw on her strengths (Michelle's support from her parents).

School

School counselors can work with school administrators to evaluate current school policies and practices and determine whether changes need to be made to meet the needs of students. For instance, school counselors and administrators may determine that the ratio of students to teachers is significantly high and thus students are not able to get the support that they need. They may determine that a school-within-schools approach or other approaches that have evidence to support their effectiveness may be more beneficial in their school environment. Wraparound services that take into account diversity can also be helpful in meeting Michelle's needs and the needs of other students who have dropped out of school (Fries, Carney, Blackman-Urteaga, & Savas, 2012).

Community

In the community, counselors can be advocates for schools and students. Counselors can promote the value of providing all students with a quality education. Counselors can also assist schools in obtaining human and financial resources from the community. For example, counselors can engage in collaborative relationships with community social service agencies so that appropriate referrals can be provided to students.

At the exosystem level, there are policies at the local, state, and national level that impact Michelle's daily experiences. Michelle's counselors can advocate for policies at the local, state, and national level that address the needs of undocumented students. Many students who are undocumented lose hope because, given current legislation, they cannot see the benefit of obtaining a high school diploma. Often their parents are first-generation immigrants who may have fears and lack of trust for individuals within the broader exosystem level. They may not feel they have a voice in what happens or how their day-to-day experiences are shaped. There is often an external locus of control, where the belief is that forces outside of the self have the greatest impact on the individual's ability to succeed.

Because Michelle is working in the community, the school counselor and other school staff can work with Michelle, her parents, and her employers to develop a work schedule that is more conducive to her educational success. If Michelle continues to work late hours, the likelihood of her struggling academically and not being successful academically increases.

Counselors can encourage school–community collaboration by providing students with direct access to community and business leaders. This task can be accomplished through activities such as inviting professionals from the community to the school to talk to students about political issues or career opportunities in the community. Activities involving community members can help students see the value of staying in school. One activity that can be helpful for all students is having a nontraditional career day that incorporates members of the community to discuss job opportunities relating to a skill or trade job (e.g., construction workers; beauticians; barbers; plumbers; heating, ventilation, and air conditioning technicians; artisans; mechanics; and bakers) and their personal experiences with school. These guest speakers could offer advice on the importance of staying in school. The career day could extend into job shadowing or mentorship opportunities. These types of activities give students relevant real-life experience of the tangible possibilities for completing school.

Adaptations for Diversity

Our society is becoming increasingly diverse culturally. The statistics on minority students' high dropout rates are indicative of a school system that has been slow to respond to this cultural diversity. The failure of schools to respond to cultural diversity can also be viewed as a failure of schools to capitalize on the dynamic resources and opportunities for learning created by cultural pluralism. Wayman (2002a) explained that schools can respond to the reality of a pluralistic society by developing curricula that are more inclusive of minorities and promote cultural sensitivity within the school climate. These types of interventions not only would help minority students but also could benefit all students by promoting tolerance for differences.

Culture, ethnicity, students' learning differences, and family socioeconomic status can be considered risk factors for student dropout. However, these factors can also be viewed as positive attributes of the learning community. For example, fostering pride in students' cultural heritage can lead to increased self-esteem and tolerance for differences. Furthermore, using the resources and social support inherent in many communities can benefit all students.

Counselors can help make school a comfortable place for every student. Workshops for school personnel on multicultural issues seem to be indicated. Counselors can also sponsor activities and clubs related to pride in diversity. Counselors can help make sure that students who need ESL classes or other academic support receive the services they need. Finally, counselors can take an active role in promoting home–school communication and increasing parents' involvement in school.

Summary

School dropout is a serious social problem. Large numbers of dropouts place a burden on unemployment and welfare services as well as the criminal justice system. The correlation between ethnicity and student dropout is particularly disturbing considering that the Hispanic population is the largest minority population in the United States and remains one of the fastest growing U.S. populations (Velez & Saenz, 2001). Because the trend of increased school dropout is likely to continue, school systems need to work harder to address the needs of all students.

Counselors can be instrumental in providing successful prevention and intervention efforts for students at risk for school dropout. Best practices for professional school counselors are to advocate for all students. Counselors can facilitate the development of self-esteem in students, and they can help school personnel, students, and their parents become aware of the negative implications of current school policies such as retention. Counselors should work collaboratively to encourage positive teacher–student interactions, foster family support and healthy peer relationships, and engage members of the community in school activities. Counselors can also help schools create environments that promote inclusion for all ethnic groups and academic success for all students. Furthermore, counselors can help students become more educationally resilient by providing interventions, such as promoting optimism, teaching students how to effectively manage stress, and helping students learn from the challenges they encounter. Professional school counselors make a significant contribution toward the academic, career, and personal/social success of all students. Professional school counselors work in a leadership role (ASCA, 2001) with all entities relating to the betterment and well-being of the students.

Useful Websites

Ad Council
http://www.adcouncil.org/Our-Work/Current-Work/Education/High-School-Dropout-Prevention
National Dropout Prevention Center/Network
http://www.dropoutprevention.org/
National Education Association
http://www.nea.org/home/DropoutPrevention.html
SolutionsforAmerica.org
http://www.solutionsforamerica.org/healthyfam/dropout_prevention.html
U.S. Department of Education Digest of Education Statistics
http://nces.ed.gov/programs/digest/d11/tables/dt11_114.asp
U.S. Department of Education Fast Facts
http://nces.ed.gov/fastfacts/display.asp?id=16
U.S. Department of Education What Works Clearinghouse
http://ies.ed.gov/ncee/wwc/PracticeGuide.aspx?sid=9

References

Abrams, K., Theberge, S. K., & Karan, O. C. (2005). Children and adolescents who are depressed: An ecological approach. *Professional School Counseling, 8,* 284–292.

American School Counselor Association. (2001). *Position statement: The professional school counselor and dropout prevention/students-at-risk.* Retrieved from http://www.school-counselor.org/files/positions.pdf

American School Counselor Association. (2012). *ASCA national model: A framework for school counseling programs* (3rd ed.). Alexandria, VA: Author.

Bagger, J., & Parker, M. (2005). Child-centered group play therapy with African American boys at the elementary school level. *Journal of Counseling & Development, 83,* 387–396.

Baker, J. A., Derrer, R. D., Davis, S. M., Dinklage-Travis, H. E., Linder, D. S., & Nicholson, M. D. (2001). The flip side of the coin: Understanding the school's contribution to dropout and completion. *School Psychology Quarterly, 16,* 406–426.

Belfield, C. R., & Levin, H. M. (2007). *The price we pay: Economic and social consequences of inadequate education.* Washington, DC: Brookings Institution Press.

Bickel, W. E., Bond, L., & LeMahieu, P. (1986). *Students at risk of not completing high school. A background report to the Pittsburgh Foundation.* Pittsburgh, PA: Pittsburgh Foundation.

Bost, L. W., & Riccomini, P. J. (2006). Effective instruction: An inconspicuous strategy for dropout prevention. *Remedial and Special Education, 27,* 301–311.

Bronfenbrenner, U. (1979). *The ecology of human development: Experiments by nature and design.* Cambridge, MA: Harvard University Press.

Campbell, L. (2003). As strong as the weakest link: Urban high school dropout. *High School Journal, 87,* 16–28.

Chapman, C., Laird, J., Ifill, N., & Kewal Ramani, A. (2011). *Trends in high school dropout and completion rates in the United States: 1972–2009* (Publication No. NCES 2012006). Retrieved from National Center for Education Statistics website: http://nces.ed.gov/pubsearch

Christenson, S. L., Sinclair, M. F., Lehr, C. A., & Godber, Y. (2001). Promoting successful school completion: Critical conceptual and methodological guidelines. *School Psychology Quarterly, 16,* 468–484.

Conyne, R. K., & Cook, E. P. (2004). *Ecological counseling: An innovative approach to conceptualizing person–environment interaction.* Alexandria, VA: American Counseling Association.

Fiorini, J., & Mullen, J. (2006). *Counseling children and adolescents through grief and loss.* Champaign, IL: Research Press.

Franklin, C., Moore, K., & Hopson, L. (2008). Effectiveness of solution-focused brief therapy in a school setting. *Children & Schools, 30,* 15–26.

Fries, D., Carney, K. L., Blackman-Urteaga, L., & Savas, S. A. (2012). Wraparound services: Infusion into secondary schools as a dropout prevention strategy. *NASSP Bulletin, 96,* 119–136.

Harvey, M. W. (2001). Vocational–technical education: A logical approach to dropout prevention for secondary special education. Preventing school failure. *Alternative Education for Children and Youth, 45,* 108–113.

Home School Legal Defense Association. (2007, November 7). *Raising the compulsory attendance age fails to achieve significant results.* Retrieved from http://www.hslda.org/

Jozefowicz-Simbeni, D. M. H. (2008). An ecological and developmental perspective on dropout risk factors in early adolescence: Role of school social workers in dropout prevention efforts. *Children & Schools, 30,* 49–62.

Lynch, S., Hurford, D. P., & Cole, A. (2002). Parental enabling attitudes and locus of control of at-risk and honors students. *Adolescence, 37,* 527–550.

Marcus, R. F., & Sanders-Reio, J. (2001). The influence of attachment on school completion. *School Psychology Quarterly, 16,* 427–444.

National Center for Education Statistics. (2012). *Annual earnings of young adults 2012.* Retrieved from http://nces.ed.gov/programs/coe/indicator_er2.asp

Newcomb, M. D., Abbott, R. D., Catalano, R. F., Hawkins, J. D., Battin-Pearson, S., & Hill, K. (2002). Mediational and deviance theories of late high school failure: Process roles of structural strains, academic competence, and general versus specific problem behaviors. *Journal of Counseling Psychology, 49,* 172–186.

No Child Left Behind Act of 2001, Pub. L. No. 107–110, § 1425 (2002).

Pleis, J. R., Ward, B. W., & Lucas, J. W. (2010). *Summary health statistics for U.S. adults: National Health Interview Survey 2009* (Publication No. NCHS 249:2010). Retrieved from Centers for Disease Control and Prevention website: http://www.cdc.gov/nchs/data/series/sr_10/sr10_249.pdf

Poland, S. (2009, November). Grade retention: School districts are leaving too many children behind. *District Administration,* 209.

Somers, C. L., & Piliawsky, M. (2004). Drop-out prevention among urban, African American adolescents: Program evaluation and practicum implications. *Preventing School Failure, 48,* 17–22.

Southwest Educational Development Laboratory. (2002, November). *Why students drop out: Perceptions of educators, parents, and students.* Retrieved from http://www.sedl.org/rural/atrisk/why.html

Sunderland, G. L., Kim, J. S., & Orfield, G. (2005). Introduction. In G. L. Sunderland, J. S. Kim, & G. Orfield (Eds.), *NCLB meets school realities: Lessons from the field* (pp. xxv–xxxvi). Thousand Oaks, CA: Corwin Press.

Velez, W., & Saenz, R. (2001). Toward a comprehensive model of the school leaving process among Latinos. *School Psychology Quarterly, 16,* 445–467.

Wayman, J. C. (2002a, February/March). Student perceptions of teacher ethnic bias: A comparison of Mexican American and non-Latino White dropouts and students. *High School Journal,* 27–37.

Wayman, J. C. (2002b). The utility of educational resilience for studying degree attainment in school dropouts. *Journal of Educational Research, 95,* 167–178.

White, S. W., & Kelly, F. D. (2010). The school counselor's role in school dropout prevention. *Journal of Counseling & Development, 88,* 227–235.

Chapter 18

A Nation at Risk: Bullying Among Children and Adolescents

Jennifer E. Beebe

Bullying has recently gained significant attention from professionals in academia, education, and the community at large because of the widespread prevalence of bullying behaviors among school-aged children (Cole, Cornell, & Sheras, 2006). This attention has been further heightened by the alarming increase in school shootings over the past decade (Fein et al., 2002; Harlow & Roberts, 2010; Limber, 2006). The media has been, and continues to be, at the forefront of reporting incidents of bullying and is a leading contributor to the heightened awareness surrounding this issue. Counselors have responded to this heightened awareness by examining the complexities of bullying and developing prevention efforts, education, and intervention efforts—such as presentations, courses, websites, and legislation—to address this ongoing concern.

Although bullying has generated increased attention recently, the topic of bullying has been a concern for decades, with several reviews of literature dedicated to the topic of bullying (see Espelage, Bosworth, & Simon, 2000; Hoover, Oliver, & Hazler, 1992; Smith & Brain, 2000). Historically bullying was not always viewed as a concern that warranted attention, as it was once accepted as a normal part of childhood (Campbell, 2005; Limber & Small, 2003). However, in the last two decades, attitudes have changed and bullying is being viewed as a serious concern that warrants attention (Shariff, 2008). Bullying continues to be the most prominent form of aggression and victimization experienced by children (Nansel, Overpeck, Haynie, Ruan, & Scheidt, 2003) and continues to remain a pervasive problem in the United States and internationally (Olweus, 1997).

This chapter examines bullying and highlights the definition, prevalence, and impact of this behavior among children and adolescents. In addition, it provides information on several approaches to prevention and intervention strategies, with an emphasis on individuals, families, schools, and communities. This chapter is guided by key research, issues of diversity, and effective practices.

Problem Definition

Bullying definitions can vary; however, for the purpose of this chapter, bullying behavior is defined as an aggressive behavior (Nansel et al., 2001; Olweus, 1993) with the presence of the following characteristics: (a) There is an intent to cause another harm, (b) the behavior is repeated over time, and (c) there is an imbalance of power (e.g., the student is physically bigger or more popular; Olweus, Limber, & Mihalic, 1999). Bullying can include physical aggression (e.g., hitting and kicking), verbal aggression (e.g., name calling and threats), and relational aggression (e.g., gossiping and rumor spreading; Crick & Grotpeter, 1995; Scaglione & Scaglione, 2006).

Recently, another form of bullying has arisen as a result of technology. Cyberbullying is when an individual or group uses information and electronic mediums to perpetrate deliberate, repeated, and hostile behavior that is intended to harm others (Belsey, 2006). Cyberbullying can take place in several venues and occur through different electronic mediums, such as e-mail, instant messaging, chat rooms, social networking sites, and blogs.

In this chapter, the terms *bully*, *victim*, and *bully–victim* are used to discuss bullying behaviors. In earlier research it was common practice to divide individuals into one of two mutually exclusive groups, the bully and the victim. Recently, there is a third group that has emerged, which is referred to as the bully–victim. The bully–victim is someone who may engage in bullying behaviors one day and experience bullying victimization the next. It is important to remember that bullying is a behavior that is not static but dynamic, which means that the bullying relationship is unique and is ever-changing (Espelage & Swearer, 2003). Children assume different roles at different times. Therefore, the terms *bully*, *victim*, and *bully–victim* are used in this chapter. The term *bully* is used to describe the child who perpetrates bullying behaviors. The term *victim* refers to the individual who is the target of the bullying behavior, and the term *bully–victim* refers to the child who both engages in bullying behavior and is also victimized by others.

Prevalence of Bullying

Bullying has generated interest internationally as well as in the United States. The first large systematic research study on bullying was conducted by Olweus, a Norwegian researcher, in 1983. This study was conducted with 130,000 students, with the participants ranging from the second to the ninth grade. Findings indicated that 9% of the students reported victimization, 7% indicated that they engaged in perpetrating bullying behaviors, and 2% reported both engaging in perpetrating and experiencing victimization (Olweus, 1983).

Since this study, there have been several examinations that further highlight the prevalence of bullying. For instance, Nansel and colleagues (2001) conducted the first study in the United States that used a nationally representative sample. They distributed a self-report questionnaire to over 15,686 sixth- to tenth-grade students. The findings revealed that 17% of the participants had been bullied, 19% of the participants had bullied others, and 6% of the participants had both been bullied and bullied another. Overall, as a result of their findings, Nansel et al. (2001) estimated that one in three children and adolescents in the United States are involved in bullying, as either a bully, victim, or bully–victim. In a more recent study (Finkelhor, Ormond, Turner, & Hamby, 2005), several researchers conducted telephone interviews with youth and their parents. Findings revealed that an estimated 22% had been physically bullied, and 25% had been teased or emotionally bullied.

Impact of Bullying

Mental Health–Related Outcomes

As a result of bullying behaviors, children and adolescents may experience physical and psychological consequences that include anxiety, depression, low self-esteem, loneliness, increased at-risk behaviors, psychological distress, poor social adjustment, isolation, attention-deficit disorder, conduct disorder, and suicidal ideation (Kowalski, Limber, & Agatston, 2008; Kumpulainen, Rasanen, & Puura, 2001; Olweus, 1993; Young et al., 2009). As the frequency of bullying victimization increases, there is a greater likelihood for the prevalence of suicidal ideation, depression, and loneliness (Rigby, 1996; Van der Wal, de Wit, & Hirasing, 2003). Research findings (Van der Wal et al., 2003) suggest that depression and suicidal ideation are more common among children who report being victims of relational aggression (e.g., rumor spreading and social isolation).

School-Related Outcomes

Bullying behaviors result not only in some serious psychological problems but also in several negative consequences related to academic development and success in school. Children and adolescents involved in bullying are more likely to have lower school satisfaction and receive lower grades (Eisenberg, Neumark-Sztainer, & Perry, 2003). These concerns are likely to result in increased absences from school and truancy problems. Consequently, students may miss out on opportunities to develop a connection to their peers and the school environment. Research findings (Bonny, Britto, Klostermann, Hornung, & Slap, 2000; Johnston, O'Malley, Bachman, & Schulenberg, 2006) have demonstrated a positive association between academic achievement, healthy behavior, and attachment or connection to school. Thus, students who feel more connected to school are more likely to earn higher grades and to engage in healthy behavior. Children and adolescents who are repeatedly bullied are at risk for missing out on important opportunities afforded by education.

Consequences for the Bully

In addition to examining the impact of bullying behavior on the victim, it is important to consider the consequences that the bully may experience as well. Research that has focused on the bully suggests the presence of multiple mental health problems, such as alcohol and substance abuse, depression, aggressive behavior, and weak caregiver–child relationships (Ybarra & Mitchell, 2007). An earlier study (Ybarra & Mitchell, 2004) found that young perpetrators of bullying behavior were more likely to experience psychosocial challenges, including problem behavior, substance use, depressive symptomatology, and a low school commitment. These participants also reported previous bullying victimization, social rejection, violence, low emotional warmth at home, and low socioeconomic status (SES). Although the impact of bullying behaviors is well researched and documented from the victim's perspective, research that examines the bully's perspective is lacking. However, research does indicate that bullies are at risk for increased academic, social, emotional, and behavioral problems (Glew, Fan, Katon, Rivara, & Kernic, 2005; Seals & Young, 2003). For instance, bullies are at risk for peer rejection, delinquency, criminality, violence, and suicidal ideation (Marsh, Parada, Craven, & Finger, 2004). More recent research (Ma, Phelps, Lerner, & Lerner, 2009) contends that perpetrators of bullying behavior experience academic problems and have school attendance problems.

Overall, because of the impact and consequences of bullying victimization, bullying is considered to be a serious form of violence and should not be taken lightly (Batsche & Knoff, 1994). It is essential to develop effective prevention and education efforts beginning in elementary school.

Case Study: Conner

Conner is a 13-year-old African American boy who is in seventh grade. He attends a middle school that is located in an urban setting and comes from a low to middle socioeconomic background. Beginning in third grade, Conner was picked on in school. The bullying behaviors included name calling, isolation, and physical aggression such as pushing, hitting, and kicking. During fifth grade Conner began to bully others. He began to name call, push, and shove. By the end of sixth grade, Conner had very few friends and was not doing well in school. His grades dropped from a B average in all subjects to a low C in sixth grade.

Now in seventh grade, Conner is struggling academically and missed 15 days of school before the first report period in November. In addition to having an increase in absences, Conner is tardy to first period three out of the five days of the week. Conner hates going to school and is often depressed and anxious, has suicidal thoughts, and feels terrible about who he is. His parents are very worried about Conner. They feel hopeless, powerless, and deeply saddened that their child is having such a negative school experience.

Conner and his parents were hopeful that the transition to middle school would eliminate the bullying; however, this was not the case. The school counselor is meeting with Conner's mom and dad this week to inform them of the current situation and to develop a support plan for Conner.

Approaches to Prevention

Implementing prevention efforts to eliminate or at least decrease the incidence of bullying has generated a copious amount of research over the years (Espelage

Sidebar 18.1 ■ Self-Awareness: The Consequences of Bullying Victimization and Perpetration

There are several consequences of bullying for the bully, victim, and bully–victim. What are some of the consequences that both victims and perpetrators may experience? Review the section titled "Impact of Bullying" to become familiar with the specific outcomes that may occur among children. As counselors, why do you think it is important to be aware of and knowledgeable about the effects of bullying? How can this information facilitate your prevention and intervention efforts?

■ ■ ■

& Swearer, 2003, 2008; Olweus, 2005; Ttofi & Farrington, 2011). Some of this attention has been given to individual characteristics and special populations that have been identified as at risk for becoming bullies, victims, and bully–victims (Cook, Williams, Guerra, Kim, & Sadek, 2010; Espelage & Swearer, 2003; Finkelhor et al., 2005; Nansel et al., 2001; Rose & Espelage, 2012; Shetgiri, Lin, Avila, & Flores, 2012). Identification of predictors for bullying-related behavior can provide a foundation for prevention efforts to decrease bullying among children (Tolan, Guerra, & Kendall, 1995). This chapter highlights several prevention approaches from the perspective of the individual, family, school, and community.

Individual

Individual counseling with Conner could have helped him in several ways. If counseling had been initiated in third grade, Conner may not have suffered from depression, social isolation, withdrawal, and academic difficulties. He also may not have engaged in bullying others. During the counseling session, Conner would have learned how to identify, express, and cope with his feelings and emotions related to the bullying. Also, the counselor may have encouraged Conner to join a group that focused on assertiveness skills, friendship skills, and self-esteem. Furthermore, Conner and the counselor could have met with his parents to discuss what was happening at school and develop a support plan earlier. Both individual and group counseling would have had multiple benefits for Conner. In third grade Conner was the victim of bullying, and by fifth grade Conner began to demonstrate perpetration behaviors. As a result, Conner transitioned into the role of bully–victim, which represents the most at-risk group of youth (Swearer, Espelage, & Napolitano, 2009). Perhaps the combination of counseling, support from his parents, and resources at school would have contributed to a different outcome for Conner. Prevention is key to eliminating the short-term and long-term psychological and academic consequences of bullying.

Individual Factors and Bullying

This section briefly examines a few selected individual factors that are related to bullying behaviors. Prevention efforts aimed at high-risk individuals may help reduce the prevalence of new bullying cases among a specific population. If counselors understand the antecedents of bullying, their prevention measures may be effective in interrupting any maladaptive behaviors (Tolan et al., 1995).

Gender. Previous studies on bullying contend that males are victims of bullying more frequently than their female counterparts (Finkelhor et al., 2005; Olweus, 2005). Males also perpetrate bullying behaviors more and engage in physical aggression (e.g., hitting, punching, and kicking behaviors) more frequently (Olweus, 2005). Conversely, females are more likely to engage in indirect bullying, including gossiping, social isolation, and rumor spreading, more frequently than their male counterparts (Crick & Grotpeter, 1995). A recent meta-analysis examining bullying and victimization among children and adolescence over the past 30 years found that males participated in bullying as the bully, victim, and bully–victim more frequently than the females in the samples (Cook et al., 2010).

Race/ethnicity. There are limited studies—particularly recent ones—that examine race/ethnicity and bullying. However, an earlier study revealed that African American students in the United States indicated less bullying victimization compared with White or Hispanic youth (Nansel et al., 2001). In a subsequent study, African American males were more likely to be categorized as a bully or a bully–victim compared with their White peers (Juvonen, Graham, & Schuster, 2003). It is interesting that in a recent study examining parental characteristics associated with bullies, the researchers found that both Latino and African American children were more likely to be bullies than their White or Asian/Pacific Islander peers (Shetgiri et al., 2012).

Age and transitions. Additional predictors that increase children's likelihood that they may experience bullying victimization include age and transitions. According to research (Nansel et al., 2001; Seals & Young, 2003), there is an increase in bullying behaviors among early adolescence (i.e., 11–13 years old) and a decrease in bullying among high school–aged students (i.e., 14–18). These studies highlight the need for prevention efforts to be implemented during transition periods (i.e., elementary to middle school). Transitions increase the likelihood that bullying perpetration will occur (Hazler, 1996; Pellegrini & Bartini, 2001). During these periods, children are more at risk for maladaptive behaviors such as bullying. The transition from elementary to middle school is an important developmental milestone as children begin to focus on peer and social relationships. These relationships can serve as either supports or barriers in their adjustment in a new school setting (Birch & Ladd, 1996).

Children with disabilities. Children with disabilities have been overrepresented as both bullies and victims (Rose & Espelage, 2012). Victimization rates of bullying among students with disabilities have been reported to be as high as 50% (Dawkins, 1996). Reasons for this overrepresentation may be linked to a lack of social skills among students with disabilities. For instance, students may have difficulty with social cues and social processing, which may contribute to this particular group of students being at risk for bullying victimization (Crick & Dodge, 1996). Although there is some debate in the literature about the victimization rates among students with disabilities, researchers suggest that culture, social contextual factors, and differences that exist among subgroups of students with disabilities may account for some of these discrepancies (Cornell, Sheras, & Cole, 2006; Rose & Espelage, 2012).

Lesbian, gay, bisexual, and transgender (LGBT) students. The LGBT student population is at risk for both bullying behavior and victimization. A recent study by Kosciw, Greytak, Diaz, and Bartkiewicz (2010) found that out of 7,261 LGBT student participants, 85% between the ages of 13 and 21 were verbally harassed (called names or threatened) at school because of their sexual orientation and 63.7% were harassed because of their gender expression. An alarming finding was that 40% of the sample indicated they were physically harassed (e.g., pushed or shoved) at school in the past year because of their sexual orientation and 27.2% because of their gender expression.

A step toward decreasing the prevalence of bullying behaviors is to increase understanding of the bully dynamic. Bullying does not happen in isolation but is the result of many factors. It is important to examine the bullying relationship from a social ecological perspective, which suggests that interactions between individuals, families, peer groups, school, community, and societal norms may be related to roles (i.e., bully, victim, or bully–victim) that children and adolescents adopt in the bully dynamic (Rose & Espelage, 2012). Developing a more comprehensive

> ## Sidebar 18.2 ■ Self-Awareness: The Therapeutic Relationship and Counselor Self-Awareness
>
> An important element in counseling is the therapeutic relationship. This relationship provides the foundation for effectiveness and success. To build the relationship, the counselor must be aware of the client's developmental stage, SES, culture, and other environmental factors that may influence the client's choices. At the same time, the counselor should be aware of how his or her own cultural background and experiences have influenced attitudes, values, and biases about psychological processes.
>
> What are some your own personal experiences, emotional triggers, individual differences—such as race, ethnicity, SES, culture, or environmental factors—that you would have to consider when counseling a bully, victim, and bully–victim? How do you think your own background and cultural experiences may affect the therapeutic relationship?
>
> ■ ■ ■

understanding of the individual characteristics associated with bullying provides counselors with the necessary information to develop effective prevention and intervention strategies. In addition to individual factors, there are also contextual factors that relate to bullying and victimization. Contextual factors are composed of family/home environment, school climate, community factors, peer status, and peer influence (Cook et al., 2010). These factors are addressed the next section of this chapter.

Family

Family plays an integral role in helping to prevent bullying among children and adolescents. In a recent meta-analysis (Ttofi & Farrington, 2011), researchers concluded that parent training and education are important components to curbing bullying. Further research has suggested that high parental involvement and increased maternal warmth are related to a decrease in bullying (Bowes et al., 2009). It is not surprising that bullying has been associated with low parental monitoring and high family conflict (Espelage et al., 2000). Additional protective factors include high parental involvement and communication with children and adolescents. Families who are more involved and help their children with homework, meet their children's friends, and have consistent and ongoing communication are less likely to have children associated with bullying behaviors (Shetgiri et al., 2012).

Involving families in antibullying efforts is essential to decreasing victimization and bullying behaviors. In a recent meta-analysis that examined individual and contextual predictors of bullying, researchers found that family and home environment are significantly related to bullying victimization and perpetration (Cook et al., 2010). Family antibullying efforts could include involving parents or guardians in antibullying conferences or trainings (Olweus et al., 1999). In addition, parents or guardians should be invited to participate in developing antibullying policies at school (Sharp & Thompson, 1994).

A multilayered approach to prevention should be considered. A three-pronged prevention approach is recommended that includes reaching out to the families in the community, providing behavioral parent training, and establishing a system at school that allows students to report bullying behaviors and is not punitive (Sherer & Nickerson, 2010). It is important to take into consideration individual and contextual characteristics to prevent the onset of bullying behaviors.

School

Incidents of bullying behavior in schools have increased significantly and are of special concern because of the school shootings that have occurred in the past decade. Accordingly, there has been increased attention to prevention efforts and the reduction of bullying victimization in schools (Berger, 2007). In response to this growing concern, prevention programs have been implemented across the nation. Prevention programs have been developed to address empathy, social skills, and problem-solving skills (Frey, Nolan, Van Schoiack Edstrom, & Hirschstein, 2005). These programs have had some success at contributing to positive changes and have been associated with decreasing bullying victimization (Ttofi & Farrington, 2011).

The most successful prevention programs aim to change the broader school environment rather than just the individual (Atlas & Pepler, 1998; Sherer & Nickerson, 2010). According to several researchers (Atlas & Pepler, 1998; Garrity, Jens, Porter, Sager, & Short-Camilli, 1997; Larson, Smith, & Furlong, 2002), the most effective strategy for preventing and minimizing bullying at schools is a systematic, multilayered approach that focuses on bullies, victims, bystanders, families, and communities. An additional recommendation for effective prevention programming is to coordinate efforts between primary, secondary, and tertiary strategies. An example of this model is Positive Behavior Support (PBS; Sprague & Golly, 2004). PBS is a comprehensive, multilevel approach that aims to improve educational outcomes and addresses social development for all students. Assumptions of PBS purport that approximately 80% of students will require primary prevention strategies, 15% of students will require secondary prevention strategies, and 5% will require tertiary strategies (Espelage & Swearer, 2008).

Examples of primary prevention strategies include schoolwide efforts such as adopting school rules and consequences for bullying behavior, implementing classroomwide strategies in which teachers and students discuss bullying and related issues, developing antibullying committees (teachers, administrators, counselors, parents, bus drivers, and any other relevant school personnel), and increasing overall school awareness related to bullying (Espelage & Swearer, 2008). Secondary prevention strategies consist of implementing specific classroom curricula that address bullying, bystander intervention, friendship-making skills, and how to report bullying incidents (Brown, Low, Smith, & Haggerty, 2011). Finally, examples of tertiary strategies include providing individual counseling or developing a functional behavioral assessment for the bully. This assessment will allow the counselor to understand the antecedents that may be related to the problematic behavior (Ross & Horner, 2009).

The Development of Antibullying Policies

A positive outcome of the increased attention to bullying is the development of legislation and policies to combat bullying in schools. Out of the 50 states, 49 have adopted antibullying laws. Currently, Montana is the only state that has not adopted an antibullying law (American Foundation for Suicide Prevention, 2012). Antibullying policies in schools provide a framework that will help the school community to prevent, educate, identify, and intervene in a systematic manner. Policies should implement a task force that is composed of teachers, parents, counselors, administrators, community members, and any other relevant school personnel. It is vital that the school community assist in the policy development in order for the program to be successful.

Antibullying policies should define bullying behaviors, outline how incidents will be reported, identify investigation and disciplinary actions, provide training for school staff and faculty, and address how the policy will be evaluated (see Swearer et al., 2009, for more specific policy practices). In addition to outlining specifics about bullying, the policy should address comprehensive harassment/assault policies that specifically highlight race, religion, disabilities, sexual orientation, gender identity, and gender expression. It is important that antibullying policies have a well-defined and effective system in place for reporting and addressing situations (Kosciw et al., 2010).

School Climate

Another factor to consider when examining preventive interventions, bullying behaviors, and victimization is school climate. *School climate* refers to the rules, values, structure, and norms that are unique to each school in which the quality and character of social interactions are affected (Cohen, McCabe, Michelli, & Pickeral, 2009). Research specific to school climate has revealed that students attending schools high in conflict are more likely to experience an increase in verbal and physical aggression (Kasen, Berenson, Cohen, & Johnson, 2004). Additional factors related to school climate include students' level of safety, belonging, and connectedness at school. For example, findings from a study revealed that students who were victims of bullying were less likely to report a sense of safety and belonging at school (Waasdorp, Pas, O'Brennan, & Bradshaw, 2011). A sense of belonging, connection, and safety are all important factors that are related to school adjustment (Glew et al., 2005).

The school climate can affect many variables and several different populations in the school setting. For instance, in a recent report (Kosciw, Greytak, Diaz, & Bartkiewicz, 2010) of LGBT youth, 61% of participants indicated that they felt unsafe at school because of their sexual orientation and 40% of the sample reported that they did not feel safe at school because of how they expressed their gender. An unsafe climate was related to absenteeism, low educational aspirations, low academic achievement, and poor psychological well-being. A positive school climate is an important protective factor in preventing at-risk behaviors such as bullying, harassment, and aggressive attitudes (Klein, Cornell, & Konold, 2012).

In order to foster a positive school climate, schools should increase opportunities for social skills training and organize schoolwide assemblies that address bullying, race, sexual orientation, and disabilities. Education efforts should aim to increase awareness of, knowledge about, and ability to identify resources or supports for students. Teachers should establish classroom rules against bullying, harassment, and discrimination. They should identify consequences and conduct regular class discussions related to bullying (Olweus, 1993). Classroom discussions should address discrimination, stereotypes, and differences in order to combat oppression in our schools. Implementation of educational information into the curriculum and use of cooperative group work are additional prevention strategies. It is vital to address problem-solving skills, conflict resolution, and information on social–emotional learning in the classroom (Frey, Hirschstein, et al., 2005). Cultivating a safe, positive school climate for our children is essential for their academic, personal, and social development.

Staff Education and Training

It is important to have ongoing education for counselors, teachers, administrators, and other relevant school personnel. Education related to bullying should be focused on the following: identifying at-risk populations (e.g., LGBT students and students with disabilities), increasing awareness and knowledge of bullying behaviors, identifying predictors and protective factors, and providing opportunities for discussion of attitudes and perceptions of bullying. In addition, it is integral to understand teachers' attitudes and perceptions of bullying and at-risk populations in order to cultivate a safe school environment. Some research has suggested that teachers do not feel confident in their ability to address bullying, intervene when biased or derogatory language is being used, or do anything when a student reports an incident of bullying (Boulton, 1997; Kosciw et al., 2010). As a result, it is imperative that educational opportunities are provided to address staff and faculty attitudes and perceptions, identify interventions, and highlight protocols that address how to report incidents in the school.

Outlining specific interventions and ways that the faculty and staff can advocate for a safe school climate for all students is essential. Training staff and faculty affords ongoing support and has resulted in teachers' abilities to handle bullying incidents (Newman-Carlson & Horne, 2004). A consistent recommendation noted in the literature highlights the importance of adopting a comprehensive schoolwide prevention strategy that aims to increase positive interactions between students and teachers (Barrett, Bradshaw, & Lewis-Palmer, 2008). This recommendation suggests the importance of educating and training our school personnel in order to help cultivate positive experiences for children and adolescents in our schools.

Implications

There have been several seminal meta-analytic reviews (Merrell, Gueldner, Ross, & Isava, 2008; Polanin, Espelage, & Pigott, 2012; Ttofi & Farrington, 2011) of bullying prevention programs in the past 10 years. For instance, Merrell and colleagues (2008) examined preventive interventions and discovered positive effects for only one third of the outcomes evaluated in the 16 studies. In a later meta-analysis by Ttofi and Farrington (2011), results revealed that bullying decreased on average by 20% to 30% and victimization decreased by 17% to 20%. Overall, findings are somewhat mixed regarding the effectiveness of bullying prevention programs

Sidebar 18.3 ■ Case Study: The Need for Antibullying Policies in Schools

Ava is a very shy 13-year-old Latina girl. Mom brought Ava to counseling because she had difficult making friends, became anxious in social situations, and had become increasingly withdrawn in the past several months. As the counselor began to work with Ava it became clear that she was having problems with bullying at school.

Ava shared with the counselor several experiences where she had been subject of gossip, rumors, aggression, social isolation, and teasing by four girls in her class. In the most recent incident, this group of girls sent her hurtful messages via instant messaging. The messages stated "You are so ugly," "Learn how to speak English," and "Go back to where you come from." School personnel have an obligation to create a safe environment for all students. How could an antibullying policy help to create a safe climate for Ava? Does your local school have an antibullying policy?

■ ■ ■

(Swearer, Espelage, Vaillancourt, & Hymel, 2010). Disagreement in the literature highlights the importance of considering the unique characteristics of the school and the community in which the prevention program will be implemented. The importance of addressing individual factors (e.g., race, disability, and sexual orientation) and contextual factors (i.e., family, school, peer relationships, community) needs to be taken into consideration. Results from prevention efforts vary because of the wide use of self-report measures, lack of a strong theoretical base in preventive intervention programs, and the dearth of empirically based efforts that guide work with perpetrators of bullying behaviors. Overall, results of programs may be more effective if there were more attention focused on the small percentage of the school population that engaged in bullying behaviors (Swearer et al., 2010).

Community

Planning and implementing prevention efforts should include collaboration with multiple partners, including those from the community. Increasing community partnerships by working in collaboration with families, schools, and community agencies to promote a positive climate is integral to prevention (Swearer et al., 2009). Shetgiri and colleagues (2012) conducted a study examining how community characteristics impact bullying behaviors. Their findings revealed the children in the sample who lived in neighborhoods where people were helpful and watched out for each other's children were less likely to engage in bullying behaviors. Conversely, children living in communities labeled as unsafe were more likely to engage in bullying behaviors. This information highlights the importance of developing relationships with neighbors, local churches, and community organizations. In addition, this information suggests how the reduction of bullying in our communities is related to a positive community climate.

Partnering with local community members and organizations to establish a vision and agenda related to bullying is the first step in prevention. Increasing awareness in the community through posters, plays, forums, town-hall meetings, advertisements, and radio commercials are examples of ways to collaborate. There are several websites that provide information and resources for how to partner with community members. For example, the Department of Health and Human Services provides resources for community members specific to the prevention of bullying. See the section titled "Useful Websites" at the end of the chapter for specific details.

As previously discussed, there are multiple risk factors associated with bullying behaviors. Therefore, it is important to highlight efforts that serve as protective factors, helping to prevent bullying behaviors, such as increased social support, supportive friends, a positive school climate and community, and a supportive family (Swearer et al., 2009). Counselors can work individually with students like Conner, but they should also be aware of and be proactive in addressing the systemic influences that support bullying behavior. It is imperative to approach this pervasive problem from a multilayered, systemic, and collaborative approach.

Intervention Strategies

Interventions to address bullying can take place on a variety of levels. Once it has been assessed that the child or adolescent is a bully, victim, or bully–victim, it is essential

Sidebar 18.4 ■ Self-Awareness: The Importance of Protective Factors and Prevention

Both families and school personnel can do a tremendous amount to prevent bullying in schools. It is evident from the research that there are several protective factors for children and adolescents that may contribute to limiting their involvement with bullying. For instance, a positive school climate, supportive family and peers, and positive community climate can serve as barriers to reduce involvement and minimize the impact of bullying behaviors. What are some prevention measures that you can implement to facilitate an antibullying environment in your home, school, or community?

■ ■ ■

to determine what appropriate intervention strategy to use. This section explores possible interventions strategies for individuals, families, schools, and communities.

Individual

An effective intervention at the individual level is individual counseling. Individual counseling serves as an appropriate intervention for several reasons. First, the child or adolescent may have been a victim of bullying behaviors for many years and as a result have experienced some psychological repercussions, such as anxiety, depression, social isolation, and suicidal ideation. Second, individual counseling may better meet the multiple needs of the child than a schoolwide bully-intervention model. Individualized attention will allow the counselor to develop specific goals and identify additional resources that the child may require. It is critical to intervene in this matter because children who experience chronic victimization are at risk for developing serious psychosocial concerns such as anger, depression, and anxiety. Furthermore, children who are chronically victimized may be at risk for engaging in bullying behavior later in life. Interventions should be developed for the specific child and adolescent and include assessments (Swearer et al., 2009).

Individual counseling sessions with victims should focus on identifying, expressing, and learning healthy ways to cope with their feelings and emotions. Other areas of attention could include teaching interpersonal, friendship-making, and assertiveness skills (Smith, Shu, & Madsen, 2001). The focus of the individual counseling sessions with bullies should be on anger management, conflict resolution, and social skills (DeRosier, 2004; Swearer et al., 2009). School staff should meet individually with bullies and victims immediately after an incident has occurred to communicate expectations and provide support and resources (Olweus, 1993).

Additional interventions at the individual level include programs such as the Bullying Intervention Program (BIP; Swearer & Givens, 2006). This program involves a counselor working one-on-one with the individuals who bully. The theoretical underpinnings of the BIP purport that the social and cognitive perceptions of students involved in bullying are equally as important as aggressive attitudes and behaviors (Swearer et al., 2009). This intervention was developed as an alternative response to school suspensions and expulsions. The BIP is a 3-hour intervention that is one-on-one. Students who have participated in this program have endorsed behavioral and psychosocial concerns that would best be addressed in a more individually focused setting (Espelage & Swearer, 2008).

Group Counseling

In the case study of Conner, group counseling could have served as an appropriate intervention in third grade. Conner would have benefited from participating in a group at school that included training in assertiveness and in friendship-building skills and that addressed emotions such as anxiety, depression, and aggression. The group would have served as a place of safety and a resource for Conner. In addition, he would have had the opportunity to develop friendships with his peers and a relationship with the school counselor. As a result, Conner may have communicated what was happening and been able to explore his feelings and emotions. Also, the school counselor could have collaborated with the teacher and his parents to ensure that the bullying stopped. Perhaps the combination of group counseling and the collaboration among school personnel would have resulted in a different outcome for Conner. Consequently, Conner would have been able to focus on his academic and personal social development in third grade and the years to follow.

Research suggests that intervention efforts should incorporate psychoeducational groups (Swearer et al., 2009). These groups can focus on skill building with victims that include social skills, self-esteem, interpersonal problem solving, and friendship skills (Sharp & Cowie, 1994; Smith et al., 2001). Groups for bullies should address anger management strategies, conflict resolution, cognitive retraining, social skills, and empathy training (DeRosier, 2004; Espelage et al., 2000). The group will serve as a safe place for the child and may facilitate the development of friendships among members.

Essential elements to be mindful of for both individual and group counseling are the therapeutic relationship, developmentally appropriate interventions, and the identification of goals. Establishing a trusting relationship with the child or adolescent is always an important factor to consider. The development of a genuine, open relationship that provides a safe place for the child is essential for a successful therapeutic outcome. In addition, this relationship may teach the child how to trust individuals and may help the child learn to identify characteristics that are essential for a healthy relationship. Developmentally appropriate interventions and expectations are important factors to consider when working with children or adolescents. Often children do not have the language ability, cognitive development, emotional maturation, or social maturation to address their feelings and emotions. Therefore, counselors should be aware of different ways to work specifically with children that allow them to explore their feelings and emotions. Implementing bibliotherapy, scrapbooking, journaling, the use of puppets, and art are just a few useful tools for working with children and adolescents.

Family

The importance of open communication between children and adolescents and their families cannot be stressed enough. Families can serve as a protective factor for victimized children by offering support and decreasing stress. Most important, family support can contribute to eliminating further victimization (Hunter & Borg, 2006). Unfortunately, prior research findings reveal that children may not disclose to their parents that they are experiencing bullying victimization (Fekkes, Pijpers, & Verloove-Vanhorick, 2005). Establishing a positive relationship that is characterized by open communication will increase the likelihood that children and adolescents will disclose this information to their family.

Children and adolescents are products of their environments and their family systems. Parents or guardians, siblings, and grandparents teach us communication, social, relationship, and social emotional skills, both positive and negative. Consequently, parents or guardians should consider what messages and skills they are teaching their children and adolescents at home. It is also important to consider what children and adolescents are being exposed to at home. Television, video games, exposure to aggression, and exposure to graphic material should be limited in the home. Research suggests that exposure to violence in media increases the likelihood of aggression and violent behavior among children and adolescents (Anderson et al., 2003). Therefore a home environment that consists of positive role models, open communication, and developmentally appropriate media are important factors to consider. Counselors and other personnel who work closely with bullies and victims should partner together with families to develop a system of support for children and adolescents.

Partnering with families is critical to intervening in bullying and to decreasing the future incidence of it; thus, communication between schools and families is an important aspect to addressing bullying. Parents are often unsure about how to respond to their child's complaints about being bullied. Some parents want to contact the aggressor's parents. However, this situation creates a risk for interfamily conflict and deprives the children of the opportunity to engage in conflict resolution. Parents can help their children by teaching children how to manage themselves when confronted by a bully or exploring why their child may be engaging in bullying behavior. Parents should encourage children to ask for help when needed. The use of role-plays can be a useful strategy in teaching children how to handle situations (Roth & Van Der Kar-Levinson, 2002).

School

As mentioned earlier, primary, secondary, and tertiary are three categories that are used to classify prevention efforts. These same categories can be used to categorize intervention efforts in schools. Primary (Tier 1), secondary (Tier 2), and tertiary (Tier 3) efforts are discussed in this section. Characteristics of Tier 1 programs include increasing faculty and staff awareness of bullying, cultivating a positive school climate and respectful environment, and teaching faculty and staff how to report bullying behaviors (Lund, Blake, Ewing, & Banks, 2012). Many programs have had success with decreasing bullying victimization and with promoting social and behavioral changes (Merrell et al., 2008). The most widely known

---

Sidebar 18.5 ■ Case Study: What Are Some Steps Maria's Parents Can Take to Help Her?

Maria is a bilingual, Hispanic 12-year-old girl in a predominantly upper middle-class White suburb. She struggles with obesity and is very shy. Maria loves to read and learn! She has always done well in school; however, since she has started middle school she has been suffering from stomachaches and headaches. Her parents are very concerned and have taken her to the doctor several times this year. The physician indicated that there was nothing wrong with Maria. How can you help parents respond to this type of situation? What systems are in place in your home and school that encourage sharing of feelings and emotions?

■ ■ ■

evidence-based program is the Olweus Bullying Prevention Program (OBPP; Lund et al., 2012; Merrell et al., 2008; Schroeder et al., 2012). This program is guided by four important guidelines. Adults at school should (a) demonstrate warmth, express positive interest, and get involved in students' lives; (b) identify consequences for intolerable behavior; (c) implement non-hostile and peaceful consequences when the rules are not followed; and (d) act as authoritarian and positive role models (Olweus, 1993, 2001; Olweus et al., 2007).

Other evidence-based intervention programs are Steps to Respect/Second Step (Frey, Hirschstein, & Guzzo, 2000; Frey, Hirschstein, et al., 2005) and Bully Busters (Newman, Horne, & Bartolomucci, 2000). Both of these programs have some evidence of decreasing aggression and bullying behaviors. Specifically, the Steps to Respect program has demonstrated a decrease in victimization among participants (Frey et al., 2000). This program was developed specifically for elementary students and focuses on increasing prosocial behavior and decreasing aggression. This information is promising and should be considered integral given that bullying is considered to be an aggressive behavior (Olweus et al., 1999). Therefore, if aggressive behaviors at the elementary level are decreased among children, the likelihood that they will engage in bullying behaviors may not be as probable. This outcome is also consistent with findings from a recent meta-analysis that suggested that bullying interventions should focus on aggression and how it affects bullying (Merrell et al., 2008).

Tier 2 interventions (classroom-level and small-group interventions) focus on social skills development, small groups, individual counseling, or peer mentoring (Whitted & Dupper, 2005). Benefits of Tier 2 interventions include curtailing the goals of the groups on the basis of the unique and individualized needs of the students. For example, a small group can be conducted for LGBT youth who have experienced verbal harassment and don't feel safe at school. Classroom-level interventions should establish rules specific to bullying, encourage class discussions that address what bullying is and how to intervene if students observe it happening in the classroom, and integrate bullying prevention material in the class curriculum (Whitted & Dupper, 2005). Important information to integrate into the curriculum should include accurate education on race, sexual orientation, and disabilities. It is also important that the teacher be consistent with implementing consequences when bullying behaviors occur.

Classroom guidance lessons are additional appropriate Tier 2 interventions (Young et al., 2009). Collaboration among professionals in the school system is also encouraged. School counselors can partner with school psychologists or social workers to deliver classroom lessons. It is important that the guidance lesson address a need that was revealed by the needs assessment. For example, if the needs assessment indicates that bullying is prevalent among fifth-grade students, the guidance lesson (intervention) should address what specific type of bullying is occurring. Next, the counselor can implement developmentally appropriate strategies for working with fifth graders. Benefits of conducting classroom guidance lessons with all of the fifth-grade classes include a chance to educate the whole class on bullying, increase opportunities to develop empathy, and educate students on bystander intervention. Therefore, in this scenario implementing a guidance lesson would serve multiple purposes.

Tier 3 is composed of individual or targeted interventions for bullies and victims. Examples of Tier 3 intervention programs include individual counseling for the bully, victim, or bully–victim. There is little research that demonstrates the effectiveness of Tier 3 interventions among bullies and victims. In a recent review (Merrell et al., 2008) that evaluated bullying interventions over a 30-year span, findings indicated scarce empirical support for the effectiveness of Tier 3 bullying interventions.

Data-Driven Interventions

The first step that should be taken when implementing interventions in the school is to conduct a needs assessment. Assessing the problem, determining the prevalence and incidence of bullying, as well as understanding what types of bullying (i.e., verbal, physical, or relational aggression) are occurring in the school is essential to guide the intervention(s) that will be used.

Interventions that are implemented need to be purposeful and goal oriented. It is essential to also consider how you will measure change. How will you know if the interventions that you use are creating a positive difference? As a result, it is important not to be reactive; rather, be proactive and mindful of how services are implemented and assessed. Keep in mind a couple of tips when implementing interventions. First, data should always guide the interventions that you will implement. Second, use valid and reliable surveys or instruments to collect the information that will you will use to analyze your results. Third, consider the demographics and unique characteristics of your school. Fourth, use evidence-based interventions that have undergone rigorous empirical evaluation. In order for an intervention to be considered evidence-based, the intervention must demonstrate strong, consistent, and replicable results in experimental or quasi-experimental studies (American Psychological Association, 2003). Time is limited in the school setting; however, it benefits all involved to take the time to ensure that the interventions that will be used are appropriate for the school setting and are evidence-based. Again, the most beneficial programs are multilayered and implement interventions at the individual, peer, family, schools and community levels (Cook et al., 2010).

Community

Establishing school-to-community relationships is vital to eliminating bullying from our schools and communities. Partnering with local organizations such as the Boys and Girls Club, community libraries, churches, neighborhood watch groups, and local parent groups are some ways to extend your efforts into the community. According to Dappen and Isernhagen (2006), schools are an ideal setting for partnerships with businesses, schools and colleges, and community organizations. Community partnerships are vital for several reasons. First, community organizations can help to further spread similar messages that are being taught in the school setting, such as tolerance, prosocial behaviors, and education on bystander intervention. Second, mentorship relationships can be cultivated with the diverse organizations in your community. School-based mentoring programs have been found to contribute to academic success and prosocial behaviors, specifically for at-risk students (Randolph & Johnson, 2008). The reduction of alcohol and drug use, teen parenting, gang membership, and peer violence are other reasons to establish mentor relationships with community organizations. Specific prosocial behaviors that are influenced by these partnerships are increased self-confidence, better interpersonal skills, and improved relationships (Dappen & Isernhagen,

Sidebar 18.6 ■ Case Study: Would Trey Benefit From a Mentor?

Trey is a 17-year-old African American male. He attends an urban high school and is from a low socioeconomic neighborhood. He is in his junior year and is struggling academically. Trey has missed 12 days of school, and it's only October. He lives alone with his mom and younger sister. He hates going to school and would prefer to just get a job and drop out of high school. He is not connected to anything or anyone at his school. Overall, he does not feel that he belongs at his school and can't wait for high school to be over. Trey is at risk for becoming a bully, a victim, or a bully–victim. What are some ways that a community-based mentor could help Trey? How could this relationship help to increase his academic, personal/social, or career development?

■ ■ ■

2006). Establishing and sustaining relationships with your local community organizations has many benefits for curbing bullying in your community and schools.

Adaptations for Diversity

There are many individual and contextual dynamics related to bullying, given that bullying is a behavior that occurs when there is a power imbalance (Olweus et al., 1999) and is also the result of many contextual factors, such as school, peer groups, societal norms, and the individual (Swearer et al., 2009). It is important to consider how race/ethnicity, culture, gender, SES, disabilities, and sexual orientation contribute to the bullying relationship. For instance, Graham and Juvonen (2001) noted that the least predominant racial/ethnic group at a school is most likely to be bullied. At the same time, students from the most predominant racial/ethnic group at a school are more likely to be bullies.

In a seminal research study conducted by Nansel and colleagues (2001), it was found that Hispanic students reported both bullying victimization and perpetration at an increased frequency compared with their African American peers. In a more recent study, low-SES African American students from an urban community were more likely to be classified as a bully compared with their Hispanic peers (Peskin, Tortolero, & Markham, 2006). This finding is consistent with other research that supports that African American students are more likely to be identified or perceived to be a bully (Juvonen et al., 2003). These findings suggest the importance of attending to the racial and cultural dynamics that occur in schools and communities.

In addition to race and ethnicity, it is important to attend to other contextual variables, such as poverty. According to Shetgiri et al. (2012), findings revealed that children living in poverty were twice as likely to be bullies as children who did not live in poverty. This finding highlights the importance that contextual variables (e.g., SES) have on the context of bullying. In order to combat historical and institutional oppression, it is essential that counselors examine the cultural and systematic implications that lead to poverty and decreased access to resources. These findings suggest that preventive bullying efforts should be more focused on helping poor youth instead of exploring the prevalence of bullying behaviors across race and ethnicity. Counselors should advocate for children and adolescents who come from marginalized and disenfranchised backgrounds in order to ensure equity, access, and resources to combat the increased risk for engaging in bullying behaviors. A study (Kosciw et al., 2010) that examined LGBT youth in the United States discovered that 62% of students did not even report incidents of harassment or assault at school because of a perception that no action would be taken by school personnel in advocating for this population. This finding highlights the continued effort that is needed in order to ensure that children and adolescents feel safe and supported in order to succeed academically, personally, and emotionally.

Counselors can play a pivotal role in combating oppression and identifying gaps and needs in their schools and community. To successfully help students who come from historically oppressed backgrounds, counselors must promote environments that facilitate social justice (Holcomb-McCoy & Chen-Hayes, 2011). According to Flynn (1995), social justice includes equity, equality, and fairness in the distribution of resources. Therefore, it is critical to first determine if this is a gap that is occurring in your system, that is, your school or community. As a result of your findings, prevention and intervention efforts should be taken in order to bridge the gap. Also, it is important to increase your own multicultural competence as a counselor. Be mindful to examine your own cultural or ethnic heritage. This exploration will increase your self-awareness, which is critical to becoming a multiculturally competent counselor (Corey, Corey, & Callanan, 2006).

Summary

This chapter has addressed how approaches to prevention and intervention strategies can benefit individuals, families, schools, and communities. It is integral that prevention and intervention efforts address the specific needs of clients, families, schools, and communities. Using needs assessments, evaluation components, and evidence-based prevention and interventions strategies can help contribute to the reduction and elimination of bullying. Finally, counselors must be aware of the influence of families, communities, and social contexts when working with bullies, victims, and bully–victims. The importance of approaching this epidemic from a collaborative effort among professionals is essential for successful outcomes.

Useful Websites

Bully Police USA
   http://bullypolice.org
Bullying.org
   http://www.bullying.org/
Cyberbully411
   http://www.cyberbully411.com/
Cyberbullying Research Center
   http://www.cyberbullying.us/
Gay, Lesbian and Straight Education Network (GLSEN)
   http://www.glsen.org/cgi-bin/iowa/all/home/index.html
Hazelden Foundation
   http://www.violencepreventionworks.org/public/bullying.page
MedlinePlus
   http://www.nlm.nih.gov/medlineplus/bullying.html
Safe Schools Coalition
   http://www.safeschoolscoalition.org/index.html

Stopbullying.gov
  http://www.StopBullyingNow.hrsa.gov
Talk, Trust and Feel Therapeutics
  http://www.angriesout.com/bullylessons.htm
ThinkBe4YouSpeak.com
  http://www.thinkb4youspeak.com/TheCampaign/

References

American Foundation for Suicide Prevention. (2012). *AFSP state anti-bullying laws overview.* Retrieved from http://www.afsp.org/files/Misc_/Public_Policy/State_Research/State_Anti_Bullying_Memo_Updated_10_5_2012.pdf

American Psychological Association. (2003). *Task force on evidence-based interventions in school psychology.* Washington, DC: Author.

Anderson, C. A., Berkowitz, L., Donnerstein, E., Huesmann, L. R., Johnson, J. D., Linz, D., . . . Wartella, E. (2003). The influence of media violence on youth. *Psychological Science in the Public Interest, 4,* 81–110. doi:10.1111/j.1529-1006.2003.pspi_1433.x

Atlas, R. S., & Pepler, D. J. (1998). Observations of bullying in the classroom. *The Journal of Educational Research, 92,* 86–97.

Barrett, S., Bradshaw, C., & Lewis-Palmer, T. (2008). Maryland state-wide PBIS initiative. *Journal of Positive Behavior Interventions, 10,* 105–114. doi:10.1177/1098300707312541

Batsche, G. M., & Knoff, H. M. (1994). Bullies and their victims: Understanding a pervasive problem in the schools. *School Psychology Review, 23,* 165–174.

Belsey, B. (2006). *Cyber bullying: An emerging threat to "always on" generation.* Retrieved from http://www.cyberbullying.ca

Berger, K. (2007). Update on school bullying at school: Science forgotten? *Development Review, 27,* 90–126. doi:10.1016/j.dr.2006.08.002

Birch, S. H., & Ladd, G. W. (1996). Interpersonal relationships in the school environment and children's early school adjustment: The role of teachers and peers. In J. Jaana & K. R. Wentzel (Eds.), *Social motivation: Understanding children's school adjustment* (pp. 199–225). New York, NY: Cambridge University Press. doi:10.1017/CBO9780511571190.011

Bonny, A., Britto, M., Klostermann, B., Hornung, R., & Slap, G. (2000). School disconnectedness: Identifying adolescents at risk. *Pediatrics, 106,* 1017–1021. doi:10.1542/peds.106.5.1017

Boulton, M. (1997). Teachers' views on bullying: Definitions, attitudes and ability to cope. *British Journal of Educational Psychology, 67,* 223–233. doi:10.1111/j.2044-8279.1997.tb01239.x

Bowes, L., Arseneault, L., Maughan, B., Taylor, A., Caspi, A., & Moffitt, T. E. (2009). School, neighborhood, and family factors are associated with children's bullying involvement: A nationally representative longitudinal study. *Journal of the American Academy of Child & Adolescent Psychiatry, 48,* 545–553. doi:10.1097/CHI.0b013e31819cb017

Brown, E. C., Low, S., Smith, B. H., & Haggerty, K. P. (2011). Outcomes from a school-randomized control trial of Steps to Respect. *School Psychology Review, 40,* 423–443.

Campbell, M. (2005). Cyber bullying: An old problem in a new guise? *Australian Journal of Guidance & Counseling, 15,* 68–76. doi:10.1375/ajgc.15.1.68

Cohen, J., McCabe, E. M., Michelli, N. M., & Pickeral, T. (2009). School climate: Research policy, practice, and teacher education. *Teachers College Record, 111,* 180–213.

Cole, J. C. M., Cornell, D. G., & Sheras, P. (2006). Identification of school bullies by survey methods. *Professional School Counseling, 9,* 305–313.

Cook, C. R., Williams, K. R., Guerra, N. G., Kim, T. E., & Sadek, S. (2010). Predictors of bullying and victimization in childhood and adolescence. *School Psychology Quarterly, 80,* 65–83. doi:10.1037/a0020149

Corey, G., Corey, M. S., & Callanan, P. (2006). *Issues and ethics in the helping professions* (7th ed.). Pacific Grove, CA: Brooks/Cole.

Cornell, D., Sheras, P. L., & Cole, J. C. M. (2006). Assessment of bullying. In S. R. Jimerson & M. J. Furlong (Eds.), *Handbook of school violence and school safety: From research to practice* (pp. 191–209). Mahwah, NJ: Erlbaum.

Crick, N. R., & Dodge, K. A. (1996). Social information-processing mechanisms in reactive and proactive aggression. *Child Development, 67,* 993–1002. doi:10.1111/1467-8624.ep9704150179

Crick, N. R., & Grotpeter, J. K. (1995). Relational aggression, gender, and social–psychological adjustment. *Child Development, 66,* 710–722. doi:10.1017/S0954579400007148

Dappen, L., & Isernhagen, J. C. (2006). Urban and nonurban schools: Examination of a statewide student mentoring program. *Urban Education, 41,* 151–168.

Dawkins, J. L. (1996). Bullying, physical disability and the pediatric patient. *Developmental Medicine & Child Neurology, 38,* 603–612.

DeRosier, M. E. (2004). Building relationships and combating bullying: Effectiveness of a school-based social skills group intervention. *Journal of Clinical Child and Adolescent Psychology, 33,* 196–201.

Eisenberg, M. E., Neumark-Sztainer, D., & Perry, C. L. (2003). Peer harassment, school connectedness, and academic achievement. *Journal of School Health, 73,* 311–316.

Espelage, D. L., Bosworth, K., & Simon, T. R. (2000). Examining the social context of bullying behaviors in early adolescence. *Journal of Counseling & Development, 78,* 326–333.

Espelage, D. L., & Swearer, S. M. (2003). Research on school bullying and victimization: What have we learned and where do we go from here? *School Psychology Review, 32,* 365–383.

Espelage, D. L., & Swearer, S. M. (2008). Current perspectives on linking school bullying research to effective prevention strategies. In T. W. Miller (Ed.), *School violence and primary prevention* (pp. 335–353). New York, NY: Springer.

Fein, R., Vossekuil, B., Pollack, W., Borum, R., Modzeleski, W., & Reddy, M. (2002). *Threat assessment in schools: A guide to managing threatening situations and to creating safe school climates.* Washington, DC: U.S. Department of Education.

Fekkes, M., Pijpers, F. M. I., & Verloove-Vanhorick, S. P. (2005). Bullying: Who does what, when and where? Involvement of children, teachers and parents in bullying behavior. *Health Education Research, 20,* 81–91.

Finkelhor, D., Ormond, R., Turner, H., & Hamby, S. L. (2005). The victimization of children and youth: A comprehensive, national survey. *Child Maltreatment, 10,* 5–25. doi:10.1177/1077559504271287

Flynn, J. P. (1995). Social justice in social agencies. In National Association of Social Workers (Ed.), *Encyclopedia of social work* (19th ed., pp. 2174–2179). Washington, DC: NASW Press.

Frey, K. S., Hirschstein, M. K., & Guzzo, B. A. (2000). Second Step: Preventing aggression by promoting social competence. *Journal of Emotional and Behavioral Disorders, 8,* 102–112.

Frey, K. S., Hirschstein, M. K., Snell, J. L., Van Schoiack Edstrom, L., MacKenzie, E. P., & Broderick, C. J. (2005). Reducing playground bullying and supporting beliefs: An experimental trial of the Steps to Respect program. *Developmental Psychology, 41,* 479–491.

Frey, K. S., Nolan, S. B., Van Schoiack Edstrom, L., & Hirschstein, M. K. (2005). Effects of a school-based emotional competence program: Linking children's goals, attributions, and behavior. *Journal of Applied Developmental Psychology, 26,* 171–200.

Garrity, C., Jens, K., Porter, W., Sager, N., & Short-Camilli, C. (1997). *Bully proofing your school.* Longmont, CO: Sopris West.

Glew, G. M., Fan, M. Y., Katon, W., Rivara, F. P., & Kernic, M. A. (2005). Bullying, psychosocial adjustment, and academic performance in elementary school. *Archives of Pediatric and Adolescent Medicine, 159,* 1026–1031.

Graham, S., & Juvonen, J. (2001). An attributional approach to peer victimization. In J. Juvonen & S. Graham (Eds.), *Peer harassment in school: The plight of the vulnerable and victimized* (pp. 44–72). New York, NY: Guilford Press.

Harlow, K. C., & Roberts, R. (2010). An exploration of the relationship between social and psychological factors and being bullied. *Children and Schools, 32,* 15–26.

Hazler, R. J. (1996). *Breaking the cycle of violence: Interventions for bullying and victimization.* Washington, DC: Taylor & Francis.

Holcomb-McCoy, C., & Chen-Hayes, S. F. (2011). Culturally competent school counselors: Affirming diversity by challenging oppression. In B. T. Erford (Ed.), *Transforming the school counseling profession* (3rd ed., pp. 90–109). Boston, MA: Pearson.

Hoover, J. H., Oliver, R., & Hazler, R. J. (1992). Bullying: Perceptions of adolescent victims in the midwestern USA. *School Psychology International, 13,* 5–16. doi:10.1177/0143034392131001

Hunter, S. C., & Borg, M. G. (2006). The influence of emotional reaction on help seeking by victims of school bullying. *Educational Psychology, 26,* 813–826.

Johnston, L. D., O'Malley, P. M., Bachman, J. G., & Schulenberg, J. E. (2006). *Monitoring the future national results on adolescent drug use: Overview of key findings.* Rockville, MD: National Institute on Drug Abuse.

Juvonen, J., Graham, S., & Schuster, M. (2003). Bullying among young adolescents: The strong, weak, and troubled. *Pediatrics, 112,* 1231–1237.

Kasen, S., Berenson, K., Cohen, P., & Johnson, J. G. (2004). The effects of school climate on changes in aggressive and other behaviors related to bullying. In D. L. Espelage & S. M. Swearer (Eds.), *Bullying in American schools: A social–ecological perspective on prevention and intervention* (pp. 187–210). Mahwah, NJ: Erlbaum.

Klein, J., Cornell, D., & Konold, T. (2012). Relationships between bullying, school climate, student behaviors. *School Psychology Quarterly, 27,* 154–169. doi:10.1037/a0029350

Kosciw, J. G., Greytak, E. A., Diaz, E. M., & Bartkiewicz, M. J. (2010). *The 2009 National School Climate Survey: The experiences of lesbian, gay, bisexual and transgender youth in our nation's schools.* New York, NY: GLSEN.

Kowalski, R. M., Limber, S. P., & Agatston, P. W. (2008). *Cyber bullying: Bullying in the digital age.* Malden, MA: Blackwell.

Kumpulainen, K., Rasanen, E., & Puura, K. (2001). Psychiatric disorders and the use of mental health services among children involved in bullying. *Aggressive Behavior, 27,* 102–110.

Larson, J., Smith, D. C., & Furlong, M. J. (2002). Best practices in school violence prevention. In A. Thomas & J. Grimes (Eds.), *Best practices in school psychology* (4th ed., Vol. 2, pp. 1081–1097). Bethesda, MD: National Association of School Psychologists.

Limber, S. P. (2006). The Olweus Bullying Prevention Program: An overview of its implementation and research basis. In S. Jimerson & M. Furlong (Eds.), *Handbook of school violence and school safety: From research to practice* (pp. 293–307). Mahwah, NJ: Erlbaum.

Limber, S. P., & Small, M. A. (2003). State laws and policies to address bullying in schools. *School Psychology Review, 32,* 445–455. doi:10.1080/15388220.2010.519375

Lund, E. M., Blake, J. J., Ewing, H. K., & Banks, C. S. (2012). School counselors' and school psychologists' bullying prevention and intervention strategies: A look into real-world practices. *Journal of School Violence, 11,* 246–265. doi:10.1080/15388220.2012.682005

Ma, L., Phelps, E., Lerner, J. V., & Lerner, R. M. (2009). The development of academic competence among adolescents who bully and who are bullied. *Journal of Applied Developmental Psychology, 30,* 628–644.

Marsh, H. W., Parada, R. H., Craven, G. R., & Finger, L. (2004). In the looking glass: A reciprocal effects model elucidating the complex nature of bullying, psychological determinants and the central role of self-concept. In C. S. Sanders & G. D. Phye (Eds.), *Bullying implications for the classrooms* (pp. 63–110). Orlando, FL: Academic Press.

Merrell, K. W., Gueldner, B. A., Ross, S. W., & Isava, D. M. (2008). How effective are school bullying intervention programs? A meta-analysis of intervention research. *School Psychology Quarterly, 23,* 26–42. doi:10.1037/1045-3830.23.1.26

Nansel, T. R., Overpeck, M. D., Haynie, D. L., Ruan, W. J., & Scheidt, P. C. (2003). Relationships between bullying and violence among U.S. youth. *Archives of Pediatric Adolescent Medicine, 157,* 348–353. doi:10.1001/archpedi.157.4.348

Nansel, T. R., Overpeck, M. D., Pilla, R. S., Ruan, W. J., Simons-Morton, B., & Scheidt, P. (2001). Bullying behaviors among U.S. youth: Prevalence and association with psychosocial adjustment. *Journal of the American Medical Association, 285,* 2094–2100. doi:10.1001/jama.285.16.2094

Newman, D. A., Horne, A. M., & Bartolomucci, C. L. (2000). *Bully Busters: A teacher's manual for helping bullies, victims, and bystanders, grades 6–8.* Champaign, IL: Research Press.

Newman-Carlson, D., & Horne, A. M. (2004). Bully Busters: A psychoeducational intervention for reducing bullying behavior in middle school students. *Journal of Counseling & Development, 82,* 259–267.

Olweus, D. (1983). Low school achievement and aggressive behavior in adolescent boys. In D. Magnusson & V. Allen (Eds.), *Human development: An interactional development and treatment of childhood aggression* (pp. 411–448). Hillsdale, NJ: Erlbaum.

Olweus, D. (1993) *Bullying at school.* Oxford, England: Blackwell.

Olweus, D. (1997). Bully/victim problems in school: Facts and intervention. *European Journal of Psychology of Education, 12,* 495–510. doi:10.1007/BF03172807

Olweus, D. (2001). Peer harassment: A critical analysis and some important issues. In J. Juvonen & S. Graham (Eds.), *Peer harassment in school* (pp. 3–20). New York, NY: Guilford Press.

Olweus, D. (2005). A useful evaluation design, and effects of the Olweus Bullying Prevention Program. *Psychology, Crime, & Law, 11,* 389–402. doi:10.1080/10683160500255471

Olweus, D., Limber, S. P., Flerx, V., Mullin, N., Riese, J., & Snyder, M. (2007). *Olweus Bullying Prevention Program: Schoolwide guide.* Center City, MN: Hazelden.

Olweus, D., Limber, S., & Mihalic, S. (1999). *The bullying prevention program: Blueprints for violence prevention.* Boulder, CO: Center for the Study and Prevention of Violence.

Pellegrini, A. D., & Bartini, M. (2001). Dominance in early adolescent boys: Affiliative and aggressive dimensions and possible functions. *Merrill-Palmer Quarterly, 47*(1).

Peskin, M., Tortolero, S., & Markham, C. (2006). Bullying and victimization among Black and Hispanic adolescents. *Adolescence, 41,* 467–484.

Polanin, J. R., Espelage, D. L., & Pigott, T. D. (2012). A meta-analysis of school-based bullying prevention programs' effects on bystander intervention behavior. *School Psychology Review, 41,* 47–65.

Randolph, K. A., & Johnson, J. L. (2008). School-based mentoring programs: A review of the research. *Children & Schools, 10,* 177–185.

Rigby, K. (1996). Peer victimization and the structure of primary and secondary schooling. *Primary Focus, 10,* 4–5.

Rose, C. A., & Espelage, D. L. (2012). Risk and protective factors associated with the bullying involvement of students with emotional behavior disorders. *Behavioral Disorders, 37,* 133–148.

Ross, S. W., & Horner, R. H. (2009). Bully prevention in positive behavior support. *Journal of Applied Behavior Analysis, 42,* 747–759. doi:10.1901/jaba.2009.42-747

Roth, B., & Van Der Kar-Levinson, F. (2002). *Secrets to school success: Guiding your child through a joyous learning experience.* Beverly Hills, CA: Association of Ideas Publishing.

Scaglione, J., & Scaglione, A. R. (2006). *Bully-proofing children: A practical, hands on guide to stop bullying.* Lanham, MD: Rowman & Littlefield Education.

Schroeder, B. A., Messina, A., Schroeder, D., Good, K., Barto, S., Saylor, J., & Masiello, M. (2012). The implementation of a statewide bullying prevention program: Preliminary findings from the field. *Health Promotion Practice, 13,* 489–495. doi:10.1177/1524838810386887

Seals, D., & Young, J. (2003). Bullying and victimization: Prevalence and relationship to gender, grade level, ethnicity, self-esteem, and depression. *Adolescence, 152,* 735–748.

Shariff, S. (2008). *Cyber-bullying: Issues and solutions for the school, the classroom and the home.* New York, NY: Routledge Taylor & Francis Group.

Sharp, S., & Cowie, H. (1994). Empowering students to take positive action against bully-ing. In P. K. Smith & S. Sharp (Eds.), *School bullying: Insights and perspectives* (pp. 108–131). London, England: Routledge.

Sharp, S., & Thompson, D. (1994). How to establish a whole-school anti-bullying policy. In S. Sharp & P. K. Smith (Eds.), *Tackling bullying in your schools: A practical handbook for teachers* (pp. 193–212). London, England: Routledge.

Sherer, Y. C., & Nickerson, A. B. (2010). Anti-bullying practices in American schools: Perspec-tives of school psychologists. *Psychology in the Schools, 47*, 217–229. doi:10.1002/pits.20466

Shetgiri, R., Lin, H., Avila, R. M., & Flores, G. (2012). Parental characteristics associated with bullying perpetration in U.S. children aged 10 to 17 years. *American Journal of Pub-lic Health, 102*, 2280–2286. doi:10.2105/AJPH.2012.300725

Smith, P. K., & Brain, P. (2000). Bullying in schools: Lessons from two decades of research. *Aggressive Behavior, 26*, 1–9.

Smith, P. K., Shu, S., & Madsen, K. (2001). Characteristics of victims of school bullying: De-velopmental changes in coping strategies and skills. In J. Juvonen & S. Graham (Eds.), *Peer-harassment in school: The plight of the vulnerable and victimized* (pp. 332–351). London, England: Guilford Press.

Sprague, J. R., & Golly, A. (2004). *Best behavior: Building positive behavior support in schools.* Longmont, CO: Sopris West Educational Services.

Swearer, S. M., Espelage, D. L., & Napolitano, S. A. (2009). *Bullying prevention & interven-tion: Realistic strategies for schools.* New York, NY: Guilford Press.

Swearer, S. M., Espelage, D. L., Vaillancourt, T., & Hymel, S. (2010). What can be done about school bullying? Linking research to educational practice. *Educational Researcher, 39*, 185–200. doi:10.3102/0013189X09357622

Swearer, S. M., & Givens, J. E. (2006, March). *Designing an alternative to suspension for middle school bullies.* Paper presented at the annual convention of the National Association of School Psychologists, Anaheim, CA.

Tolan, P. H., Guerra, N. G., & Kendall, P. C. (1995). A developmental–ecological perspec-tive on antisocial behavior in children and adolescents: Toward a unified risk and intervention framework. *Journal of Consulting and Clinical Psychology, 63*, 579–584. doi:10.1037/0022-006X.63.4.579

Ttofi, M. M., & Farrington, D. P. (2011). Effectiveness of school-based programs to reduce bullying: A systematic and meta-analytic review. *Journal of Experimental Criminology, 7*, 27–56. doi:10.1007/s11292-010-9109-1

Van der Wal, M. F., de Wit, C. A. M., & Hirasing, R. A. (2003). Psychosocial health among young victims and offenders of direct and indirect bullying. *Pediatrics, 111*, 1312–1317. doi:10.1542/peds.111.6.1312

Waasdorp, T. E., Pas, E. T., O'Brennan, L. M., & Bradshaw, C. P. (2011). A multilevel per-spective on the climate of bullying: Discrepancies among students, school staff, and parents. *Journal of School Violence, 10*, 115–132. doi:10.1080/15388220.2010.539164

Whitted, K. S., & Dupper, D. R. (2005). Best practices for preventing or reducing bullying in schools. *Children & Schools, 27*, 167–175.

Ybarra, M. L., & Mitchell, K. J. (2004). Online aggressor/targets, aggressors, and targets: A comparison of associated youth characteristics. *Journal of Child Psychology and Psychia-try, 45*, 1308–1316. doi:10.1111/j.1469-7610.2004.00328.x

Ybarra, M., & Mitchell, K. (2007). Prevalence and frequency of Internet harassment in-stigation: Implications for adolescent health. *Journal of Adolescent Health, 41*, 189–195. doi:10.1016/j.jadohealth.2007.03.005

Young, A., Hardy, V., Hamilton, C., Biernesser, K., Sun, L.-L., & Niebergall, S. (2009). Empowering students: Using data to transform a bullying prevention and intervention program. *Professional School Counseling, 12*, 413–420.

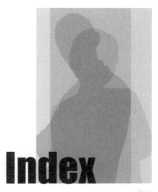

Index

Figures and tables are indicated by f and t following the page number.

A

Aasheim, L. L., 291
Abaied, J. L., 140–141, 142
Abbey, A., 383
Ablon, S. L., 95, 102
Abramson, L. Y., 97
Abstinence-only programs, 268–269
Abuse and neglect
    child abuse, 75, 147–148
    development period and, 10
    in dysfunctional families, 74–82
        impact of, 76–79
        incidence of, 75–76
        prevention of, 81–82
    neglect effects, 78
    race and ethnicity, incidence of, 75
    trauma effects, 76
ACA (American Counseling Association), 381, 389
Acculturation, 175, 183
Acetylcholine, 371, 372t
Achievement expectations, 241
Acquaintance rape, 279
Acting out, 241
Action research, 59
Adams, P., 79
ADHD (attention-deficit hyperactivity disorder), 59,
   113, 127
Adjunct services, 38
Adler, N. E., 267–268
Adlerian counseling techniques, 435
Adolescence, use of term, 9
Adult role models, 30
Adult Youth Association (AYA), 311–312
Advocates for Youth, 332

AFDC (Aid to Families with Dependent Children), 399
Affective disorders, 10
African Americans
    binge eating and, 200
    brief structural family therapy and, 88
    bullying and, 445–446, 457
    as counselors, 54
    dropout problem and, 421
    gangs and, 293, 301
    HAWK Federation, for black males, 113
    homelessness and, 396, 401, 414
    incidence of abuse among, 75
    multiracial families, 173–174
    murder, as leading cause of death, 339
    nonresident fathers, 174
    PTSD and, 157
    racial identity model for, 179–180
    STARS programs, 113
    suicide rates of, 230
Africentric Youth and Family Rites of Passage Program,
   116–117
Age
    bullying and, 446
    compulsory school attendance and, 422–423
    eating disorders and, 200
    impact of risk and protective factors, 27
    incidence of abuse and, 75
Agius, E., 383
Ahn, S., 328
AIDS, 272–278. *See also* Sexually transmitted diseases
   (STDs)
    HIV/AIDS Education Law, 80
    intervention strategies, 276–278
    prevention approaches, 273–276
    risk factors, 273

Aid to Families with Dependent Children (AFDC), 399

Alarm phase of stress, 141

Alcohol. *See also* Substance use and abuse
 fetal alcohol syndrome and fetal alcohol effects, 24
 homelessness and, 402
 underage drinkers, 24
 use and abuse of, 369, 373–375

Alderfer, M., 73

Allostatic load, 142

Alvarado, G. F., 129

Amato, P. R., 72

AMCD (Association for Multicultural Counseling and Development), 182

American Bar Association, 281

American Counseling Association (ACA) *Code of Ethics,* 381, 389

American Medical Association, 374

American Psychiatric Association, 144, 320

American Psychological Association, 354

American School Counselor Association (ASCA), 85

Amphetamines, 372, 372*t*

Anderson, G. E., 10

Anderson, J. E., 402

Anderson, W. P., 101

Angelou, Maya, 191

Anorexia nervosa (AN)
 atypical, 208
 binge eating/purging type, 202
 defined, 202–203
 etiology of, 203–204
 media and, 197
 mortality rate and, 198
 nutritional restabilization, 213
 pharmacological treatment for, 214
 restrictive type, 202
 socioeconomic status level and, 200–201

Antibullying policies, 448–449

Anticipatory guidance in schools, 155

Appalachia Educational Laboratory, 108, 110

Approach–avoidance coping model, 153–154

Archer, R. P., 383

Aronson, M., 93

Aryan Nation, 302

ASCA (American School Counselor Association), 85

Asian gangs, 300–301

Assertiveness training, 34

Assimilation, 175

Association for Multicultural Counseling and Development (AMCD), 182

Athletes and eating disorders, 220–221

At-risk adults parenting, 70

At-risk behaviors
 dysfunctional families, 82–83
 prevalence of, 23–24
 risk factors, 26

At-risk youth
 behaviors and causal factors, 9–13
 defined, 6–8
 foundational perspective, 5–15
 origins of causal factors, 13–14
 overview, 3–5
 population of, 8–9
 prevention and crisis management paradigm, 15–18

Attendance tracking, 430–431

Attention-deficit hyperactivity disorder (ADHD), 59, 113, 127

Auerswald, C., 406

Austin, S. B., 199

Australia
 child and family abuse, 147
 eating disorders study, 200–201
 Reconnect (homeless program), 406–407

Autonomic nervous system, 370, 371

Autonomy, 51

AYA (Adult Youth Association), 311–312

Ayala, G., 333

B

Baird, A., 199

Baldwin, Tammy, 320

Balis, T., 232

Barber, L. W., 11

Bartkiewicz, M. J., 446

Basch, C. E., 266, 269

Bath Consolidated School (1927 mass killing), 340

Battle, J., 94

Beane, J. A., 96

Becker, B., 46

Beckett, R., 79

BED. *See* Binge eating disorder

Beebe, J. E., 441

Behavioral management approaches, adolescent substance abuse, 384

Behaviors. *See* Causal factors

Bein, E., 333

Beintner, I., 213

Belief systems, 49

Benard, B., 47, 50–51, 53

Bender, K., 150

Bendixen, M., 295

Benoit, R. B., 97

Be proud! Be responsible! program, 277–278

Berger, R., 155

Berkowitz, S. J., 156

Bernay, T., 95

Bickel, W. E., 424

Big Brother/Big Sister, 305

Binge eating disorder (BED)
 diagnosis of, 206–207
 etiology of, 207–208
 gender and, 200
 in male population, 198
 nutritional restabilization, 213
 race and ethnicity factors for, 200

Biological changes, stress of, 141

Biological models for mood disorders, 131

BIP (Bullying Intervention Program), 452

Bipolar disorders, 126–127, 131

Biprejudice, 319

Biracial youth. *See also* Multiracial youth
 defined, 179
  identity models, 179–180
  sociocultural context, 170–171

Bisaga, K., 218

Bisexual, defined, 324

Bjorck, J. P., 94
Bloods, 301
Blyth, D. A., 94
Body Project, 211–212
Bond, L., 424
Bonding, family, 30
Borum, R., 339
Bower, B., 101
Boy Scouts, 327, 388
Boys & Girls Clubs of America, 113, 191, 310, 388
BPP (Bullying Prevention Program), 350–351
Braeges, J. L., 152
Brain and central nervous system. *See* Central nervous system (CNS)
Brentro, L. K., 116
Breslau, N., 129
Brewer, M. M., 80
Brief structural family therapy (BSFT), 88
Brokenleg, M., 116
Brooks, K., 10
Brooks, R. B., 60
Brown, J., 79
Bulimia nervosa
    diagnosis of, 204–206
    etiology of, 206
    gender and, 199–200
    multiple psychiatric disorders and, 198
    nutritional restabilization and, 213
    pharmacological treatment for, 214
    socioeconomic status level and, 200–201
Bullies, consequences for, 443–444
Bully Busters, 455
Bullying, 441–463
    antibullying policies, 448–449
    case study, 444
    children with disabilities and, 446
    data-driven interventions, 456
    definition, 442–444
    diversity
        adaptions for, 457–458
        incidence of, 445–446
    gender and, 350, 445
    HHS recommendations, 326–327
    impact of, 443–444
    intervention strategies, 451–457
        community, 456–457
        family, 453–456
        individual, 452–453
        school, 454–456
    prevalence of, 442–443
    prevention, approaches to, 444–451
        community, 451
        family, 447
        individual, 445–447
        school, 448–451
    race and ethnicity, 445–446
    risk factors, 329–330
Bullying Intervention Program (BIP), 452
Bullying Prevention Program (BPP), 350–351
Burch, B., 146
Burchell, J. L., 151
Bureau of Justice Statistics, on violence in schools, 340
Burgeson, R., 94

Buri, J. R., 99
Burnett, J. W., 101
Burnout, 141
Burrow-Sanchez, J. J., 107
Burt, C. E., 94
Butterworth, T., 355
Byrne, D. G., 151

C

Camp Elsewhere, 113
Canada
    child and family abuse in, 147
    Montreal Preventive Treatment Program, 304
    teen pregnancy rates, 266
Cantor, D., 95
Capra, Fritof, 56
Capuzzi, D., 3, 23, 229, 237
Careers discourse for resilience, 56–57
Caring relationships, 51
Carlock, C. J., 95, 98–99, 100
Carlton-Ford, S., 94
Carter, P., 146
Cashwell, C. S., 113
Casual gang membership, 300
Casual-register discourse patterns, 52, 55–56
Causal factors
    behaviors and, 7, 9–13
    for dropout problem, 424
    for dysfunctional families, 12–13, 70–80
    family perspective on, 12–13
    home perspective on, 12–13
    for low self-esteem, 98–104
        environmental influences on, 103–104
        individual influences on, 100
        parental influences on, 98–100
        physical influences on, 103
        psychological influences on, 102–103
        social influences on, 101–102
    mental health perspective on, 12
    for mood disorders, 126–131
    for multiracial youth, 171–179
        academic and behavioral problems of, 175–176
        community acceptance of, 172
        education and career goals, 177–178
        ethnic identity and self-esteem, 176–177
        families of, 172–174
        immigrant youth and families, 175
        language and communication, 178
        parentification and, 179
    origins of, 13–14
    school perspective on, 10–11
    for stress and trauma, 143–153
        child and family abuse, 75, 147–148
        chronic illness, 147
        divorce and marital dissolution, 24, 148–149
        economic stress, 149
        gender differences, 152
        home and family stress, 147
        homelessness, 150
        interpersonal stress, 152–153

(Continued)

Causal factors *(Continued)*
    for stress and trauma *(continued)*
        life event stressors, 143
        military families, 150
        mood disorders and, 129–131
        natural disasters, 145–146
        occupational stress, 150
        school stress, 151
        sexual identity/gender expression, 151–152
        traumatic stress, 129–130, 143–145
CD (conduct disorder), 127
Census Bureau, 24, 170, 400
Center for Ecoliteracy, 56
Center for Law and Social Policy, 401
Centers for Disease Control and Prevention (CDC)
    Be proud! Be responsible! program, 277–278
    community prevention programs for youth, 275
    HIV rate among youth, 273
    mental health problems after Hurricane Katrina, 145
    metal detectors in schools, 349
    prevalence of at-risk behaviors, 24
    suicide statistics, 229
    Youth Risk Behavior Surveillance Survey, 200, 338, 369
Central Area Youth Association, 112–113
Central Intelligence Agency (CIA), 356
Central nervous system (CNS)
    alcohol and, 373–375
    inhalants and, 377
    methamphetamines and, 379–380
    nicotine and, 373
    substance use and, 370–371, 372*t*
CFTSI (Child and Family Traumatic Stress Intervention), 156
Chapman, P. L., 97
Cheadle, J., 72
A Chemical Love Story (Shulgin), 378
Chen C. P., 107
Chermak, S., 292
Chickering, A. W., 323, 333
Child abuse, 75, 147–148
Child Abuse Prevention and Treatment Act (1973), 74
Child and Family Traumatic Stress Intervention (CFTSI), 156
Childhood obesity, 207
Children's Defense Fund, 6
Chlamydia, 272, 273, 277
Christakis, D., 73
Christenson, S. L., 10
Chronic illnesses, 73, 147
CIA (Central Intelligence Agency), 356
Cicchetti, D., 46
Cigarette smoking. *See* Tobacco smoking
Circle conversations, 52
Clark, D. B., 95
Class distancing, 55
Class size, 431–432
Clinton, Hillary, 323
Clinton, M., 383
CNS. *See* Central nervous system
Cocaine, 301, 372
Code of Ethics (ACA), 381, 389
Cognitive-behavioral therapy (CBT), 384

Cognitive change strategies, 34–35
Cohen, D. A., 276
Cohen, K., 143
Cohen, L. H., 94
Coiro, M. J., 73
Coley, R. L., 174
Collens, P., 143
Columbine High School shootings (1999), 337, 346
Combs, J. L., 207
Committee for Children, 280
Commonwealth Fund Survey, 200
Communication skills
    circle conversations, 52
    interpersonal, 33–34
    multiracial youth's language, 178
    of suicidal youth, 241
    technology and, 179
Community
    bullying problem and
        intervention strategies for, 456–457
        prevention approaches for, 451
    diverse youth and
        intervention strategies for, 190–191
        prevention approaches to, 186
    dropout problem and
        intervention strategies for, 436–437
        prevention approaches to, 432–433
        situations putting youth at risk, 27
    dysfunctional families and, 86–87
        capacity building and, 87
        parent education and, 86–87
    eating disorders and
        intervention strategies for, 216
        prevention approaches to, 212–213
    gang membership and
        intervention strategies for, 311–313
        prevention approaches to, 308–309
    homelessness and
        intervention strategies, 411–412
        prevention approaches to, 406
    mood disorders and, 134–135
    racial and ethnic minorities, acceptance of, 172
    rape and date rape
        intervention strategies for, 283–284
        prevention approaches to, 281
    school violence and
        intervention programs, 357–358
        prevention approaches to, 351–352
    self-esteem and, 111–113
    sexually transmitted diseases and
        intervention strategies for, 277–278
        prevention approaches to, 275–276
    sexual minority youth and
        intervention, approaches to, 331–332
        prevention, approaches to, 327
    stress and trauma prevention, 156–157
    substance abuse and, 387–388
    suicidal behavior and
        intervention strategies for, 256–257
        prevention approaches to, 244–248
    teen pregnancy and
        intervention strategies for, 272
        prevention approaches to, 270

Community Promise program, 277

Community resources and prevention programming, 37

Compas, B. E., 152, 153

Competencies, programs to develop, 157, 188

Competitive Abstinence Education Grant Program, 272

Comprehensive Gang Model, 312

Concepcion, J. I., 79

Condom use, 278

Conduct disorder (CD), 26, 127

Conflict resolution education, 307

Conger, R. D., 149

Conrath, J., 5

Consistency, 427

Consumer Product Safety Commission (CPSC), 377

Continuing effects/youth sex offenders and abuse, 79–80

Contract writing, 255

Conyne, R. K., 17, 28, 29, 232

Cooke, C., 142

Copenhagen, L., 52

Coping skills, 36, 153–154, 188

Cordero, E. D., 199

Counselors
    diverse youth and, 189–190
    dropout problem and, 425, 427, 432–433
    substance abuse and, 381–382

Cox, N., 151

CPSC (Consumer Product Safety Commission), 377

Craft, L., 231

Crips, 301

Crisis management, 17–18, 249–256

Crisis response plans, 31–32

Crisp, A., 219

Croll, J. K., 210

Cross, W. E., 179–180

Cross-dressers, defined, 324

Cultural approaches. *See also* Multicultural Counseling Competencies; Multiracial youth
    to diverse youth, 182–184
    in STD counseling, 274
    in substance abuse counseling, 389–390

Cultural dislocation, 116

Cultural diversity. *See* Diversity; Multiracial youth

Curriculum-based interventions, and dysfunctional families, 85

Cyberbullying, 327, 442

D

Daniels, J., 344

D.A.R.E. (Drug Abuse Resistance Education), 387, 388

Data-driven interventions for bullying, 456

Date rape. *See* Rape and date rape

Davidson, K, 109

Davis, T., 10

Day-care programs, 388

Debriefing, stress and trauma events, 146, 155

DECIDE model, 35

DeLeel, M. L., 200

Delgado, M., 113

Delta-9-tetrahydrocannabinol (THC), 376

Dependable Strengths Articulation Process (military program), 109

Dependable Strengths Assessment Training (DSAT, Washington State), 109

Depression, 26, 131–132, 231, 236, 241–242, 443

Derzon, J., 349

Detached worker project, 311

DeVries, M. W., 157

Diagnostic and Statistical Manual of Mental Disorders
    Fourth Edition (DSM-IV-TR), 126, 150, 201–202, 204, 242, 374, 382
    Fifth Edition (DSM-5), 126, 128–129, 201–202, 204, 382–383

Diagnostic issues and mood disorders, 126–131

Diaz, E. M., 446

Diaz, R. M., 333

Dickinson, K. A., 99

DiClemente, C. C., 384

Disabilities
    bullying and, 446
    multicultural considerations, 389
    resilience of youth with disabilities, 59–60
    within the family, 73

Disasters, 145–146

Discourse patterns for resilience, 52–57
    careers, 56–57
    poverty, 55–56
    racism, 54–55
    risk, 53–54

Dishion, T. J., 105

Disidentification, 177

Diversity
    acculturation, 175, 183
    adaptations for
        athletes, 220–221
        bullying, 457–458
        dropout problem, 437
        dysfunctional families, 87–88
        eating disorders, 216–221
        gang membership, 313
        mood disorders, 135–136
        multiracial youth, 191–192
        resilience and, 60–61
        school violence, 358
        self-esteem, 115–118
        sexual minority, counseling of, 332–333
        stress and trauma, 157
        substance abuse, 389–390
        suicidal behavior, 257–258
        youth, 191–192
    contextual and historical considerations, 183–184
    cultural considerations, 182–184
    eating disorders and, 216–221
    in gang membership, 300–303
    homelessness and, 412–414
    incidence of abuse and, 75
    intervention strategies for, 186–191
        community, 190–191
        family, 188–189
        FRIENDS program, 188
        individual, 186–188
        multiracial youth, 186–191
        school, 189–190

(Continued)

Diversity *(Continued)*
    multiracial, 169–196
        academic and behavioral problems of,
            175–176
        biracial and multiracial in context,
            170–171
        case study, 180–181
        community acceptance of, 172
        culturally appropriate approach, 181–184
        education and career goals, 177–178
        ethnic identity and self-esteem, 176–177
        families of, 172–174
        identity models, 179–180
        immigrant youth and families, 175
        language and communication, 178
        parentification and, 179
        prevention approaches to, 185–186
        racially and ethnically diverse families,
            172–174
    poverty and, 189–190
    rape and date rape, 284
    school counselors and, 189–190
    suicide and, 230–231, 233
Divorce and marital dissolution, 24, 72, 148–149, 426
Dixon-Saxon, S. V., 139
Dodder, L., 93
Domestic violence, 24, 413
Donovan, J. E., 95
Dopamine, 371, 372*t*, 378, 380
Drag queens and drag kings, defined, 324
Drew, J. J., 197
Dropout problem, 421–440
    African American youth, 421
    attendance tracking, 430–431
    case study, 424–425, 434
    causal factors, 424
    counselors and, 425, 427, 432–433
    defined, 423–424
    diversity, adaptations for, 437
    Hispanic youth, 421
    impact on income and future employment, 25,
      422
    intervention strategies for, 434–437
        community, 436–437
        family, 435–436
        individual, 434–435
        school, 436
    mentoring programs, 432
    prevention approaches to, 425–433
        community, 432–433
        family, 427–428
        individual, 425–427
        school, 429–432
    rate of, 23
    retention, 428
    school and class size, 431–432
    sense of belonging and connectedness, 432
    situations putting youth at risk, 26–27
    structural characteristics leading to, 11
    teacher/student ratios and, 431–432
Drug abuse. *See* Substance use and abuse
Drug Abuse Resistance Education (D.A.R.E.), 387, 388
Drug-free programs, 387

Dryfoos, J. D., 24
DSAT (Dependable Strengths Assessment Training),
  109
*DSM-IV-TR. See Diagnostic and Statistical Manual of
  Mental Disorders, Fourth Edition*
*DSM-5. See Diagnostic and Statistical Manual of Mental
  Disorders, Fifth Edition*
Dukes, R. I., 295
Dupper, D. R., 189
Dwyer, K., 345
Dykeman, C., 69
Dysfunctional families, 71–95
    abuse and neglect, 74–80
        family structure and, 76, 77*f*
        impact of, 76–79
        incidence of, 75–76
        prevention, 81–82
    at-risk adults parenting, 70
    at-risk behaviors of, 82–83
    at-risk youth, family role of, 82–83
    causal factors, 12–13, 70–80
    community and, 86–87
        capacity building and, 87
        parent education and, 86–87
    definitions of, 69–70
    denial, 72
    diversity, adaptations for, 87–88
    family intervention, postabuse, 83
    individual and
        abuse prevention, 81–82
        counseling, 80–81
    malevolent dynamics, impact of, 82
    moderate dysfunction, 69–70
    parental conflict, 70–72
    parentification of children, 72–73, 179
    prevention approaches to, 80–87
        abuse prevention, 81–82
        community approach, 86–87
        family approach, 82–83
        individual counseling, 80–81
        postabuse family intervention, 83
        school approach, 84–86
    school and, 84–86
        curriculum-based interventions, 85
        mentoring programs, 85
        physical and sexual abuse education for
          children, 85–86
        preservice and in-service needs, 84–86
    serious illness and disability within the family,
      73, 147
    severe dysfunction, 70

E

Early indicated preventive interventions in schools,
  155
Eating disorder not otherwise specified (EDNOS),
  201–202
Eating disorders, 197–227
    anorexia nervosa
        atypical, 208
        binge eating/purging type, 202
        defined, 202–203

etiology of, 203–204
　　media and, 197
　　mortality rate and, 198
　　nutritional restabilization, 213
　　restrictive type, 202
　　socioeconomic status level and, 200–201
　binge eating disorder
　　diagnosis of, 206–207
　　etiology of, 207–208
　　gender and, 200
　　in male population, 198
　　nutritional restabilization, 213
　　race and ethnicity factors for, 200
　bulimia nervosa
　　diagnosis of, 204–206
　　etiology of, 206
　　gender and, 199–200
　　multiple psychiatric disorders and, 198
　　nutritional restabilization, 213
　　pharmacological treatment for, 214
　　socioeconomic status level and, 200–201
　consequences of, 198
　defined, 201–202
　developmental period and, 10
　diversity, adaptations for, 216–221
　　athletes, 220–221
　　ethnicity, 216–218
　　gay, lesbian, bisexual, transgender,
　　　219–220
　　males, 199–200, 218–219
　　women, 199–200, 216–218, 220–221
　intervention strategies for, 213–216
　　community, 216
　　family, 215–216
　　individual, 213–215
　　school, 216
　media and, 197
　night eating syndrome, 208
　prevention approaches to, 209–213
　　community, 212–213
　　family, 210–211
　　individual, 210
　　school, 211–212
　purging disorder, 202, 208
　risk factors, 198–201
　　age, 200
　　family characteristics, 201
　　gender, 198–199
　　race and ethnicity, 200
　　socioeconomic status level, 200–201
　unspecified feeding or eating disorder, 208
Ebata, A. T., 154
Economic impact of school dropouts, 25
Economic stress, 149
Ecstasy, 369, 372*t*, 373, 378–379
Edible Schoolyard, 56–57
Edmondson, J. H., 108
Education, importance of, 428
Educational perspective, 10–11
Education Department, 11, 356
Eisenberg, M. E., 329
Eisenman, R., 333
Eitle, D., 294

Ekstron, R. R., 11
Elaboration likelihood model, 280
Elective mutism, 178
Elias, M. J. K., 107
Elkins, D. E., 383
Ellen, J. M., 267–268
Elliott, G. C., 96
Emotional well-being, 233
Emotion-focused coping, 154
Employment potential and school dropouts, 25
Empowerment and prevention efforts, 29
Encouragement, 427
Endorphins, 371, 372*t*
Enns, C., 101
Environmental influences
　mood disorders and, 131
　on low self-esteem, 103–104
　resilience and, 51
ERASE-Stress program, 155
Erikson, E. H., 176, 265
Eron, L. D., 107
Eskilson, A., 93
Ethnic groups. *See* Diversity; *specific ethnicity*
Evaluation procedures, 38
Evidence-based interventions
　bullying, 455, 456
　eating disorders, 198
　family-based treatment, 88
　substance use and abuse, 382, 383–384
Exhaustion phase of stress, 141
External support, 232–233
Eyre, S. L., 406

F

Falk, G., 270
Falkner, J., 169
Family, 385–386. *See also* Dysfunctional families
　bullying problem and
　　intervention strategies for, 453–456
　　prevention approaches to, 447
　diverse youth and
　　intervention strategies for, 188–189
　　prevention approaches to, 185
　dropout problem and
　　intervention strategies for, 435–436
　　prevention approaches to, 427–428
　　situations putting youth at risk, 27
　eating disorders and
　　intervention strategies for, 215–216
　　prevention approaches to, 210–211
　　as risk factor, 201
　gang membership and
　　intervention strategies for, 310
　　prevention approaches to, 305–306
　homelessness and
　　intervention strategies for, 407–409
　　prevention approaches to, 404
　home perspective and, 12–13
　incidence of abuse, 75–76
　low-self-esteem prevention, 105–107
　mood disorders prevention, 132–133

(Continued)

Family *(Continued)*
    multiracial youth
        intervention strategies for, 188–189
        prevention approaches to, 185
    perspective on at-risk youth, 12–13
    rape and date rape
        intervention strategies, 283
        prevention strategies, 280
    residence status, urban vs. rural, 76
    school violence and
        intervention programs for, 353–354
        prevention approaches to, 348–349
    sexually transmitted diseases and
        intervention strategies for, 276–277
        prevention approaches to, 274
    sexual minority and
        diversity, adaptations for, 332–333
        intervention, approaches to, 329–330
        prevention strategies, 324–326
    stress and trauma prevention, 154
    stress from, 147
    substance abuse and, 385–386
    suicidal behavior and
        intervention strategies for, 249–256
        prevention approaches to, 243–244
    teen pregnancy and
        intervention strategies for, 271
        prevention approaches to, 269
Family bonding, 30
Family values, 171, 179
Farbverow, N., 238
Farr, C., 79
Farrington, D. P., 450
Federal Bureau of Investigation (FBI), 293, 312, 356
Fedewa, A. L., 328
Feeding and Eating Disorders Not Elsewhere Classified (FED-NEC), 202
Fein, R., 339
Felbeck, K., 170
Felix, E. D., 117
Females. *See* Women
Fetal alcohol syndrome and fetal alcohol effects, 24
FFT (Functional Family Therapy), 353–354
Filial therapy, 409
Fine, M., 11, 53
Finn, A., 337
Fishman, L. T., 299
Five Cs of competency, 157
Flowers, L. R., 10, 11, 421
Flunitrazepam (Rohypnol), 283
Folkman, S., 142
Fontaine, J. L., 383
Forbes, N., 146
Formal-register discourse patterns, 52, 55–56
Foster care and homelessness, 403, 404, 411
Foundational perspective, 5–15
Frandsen, K. J., 241
Frey, D., 98–99
FRIENDS program, 188
Functional Family Therapy (FFT), 353–354

G

Gamma-aminobutryic acid (GABA), 371, 372*f*
Gamma hydroxy butyrate (GHB), 283
Gangbangers, 297
Gang Comprehensive Model, 310
Gang Deterrence and Community Protection Act (2005), 312
Gang Intervention Through Targeted Outreach (GITTO), 310
Gang membership, 291–317. *See also* Violence
    active gang roles, 297
    alphabets, codes, and symbols used by, 307
    case study, 303
    causal factors, 293–303
    defined, 291, 292–293
    diversity, adaptations for, 313
    ethnic gangs, 300–303
        African American, 301
        Asian, 300–301
        Hispanic, 301–302
        white supremacist groups, 302–303
    graffiti, 298
    history of, 292–293
    Internet and, 293
    intervention strategies for, 309–313
        community, 311–313
        family, 310
        individual, 309
        school, 310–311
    involvement factors, 293–300
        females in gangs, 298–300
        gang characteristics, 295–296
        gang member characteristics, 296–298
        recruitment, 295
    Mafia, 292
    non-active gang roles, 297
    police perception of, 297
    prevention approaches to, 303–309
        community, 308–309
        family, 305–306
        individual, 304–305
        school, 306–308
Gang Resistance Education and Training (GREAT), 308
Garbarino, J., 78
Garfinkel, A., 146
Garfinkel, B. D., 234
Garland, A. F., 231
Garnier, H. E., 11
Gay, defined, 324. *See also* Sexual minority youth
Gay, Lesbian, and Straight Education Network (GLSEN), 320, 326, 327, 328–329
Gelgand, J. C., 265
Gelkopf, M., 155
Gender differences
    bullying, 350, 445
    coping with stress, 152
    depression, 135
    incidence of abuse, 75
    suicide, 233
Gender expression, 151–152

Gender identity, 177, 323–324
Gender socialization, 152
General adaptation syndrome (GAS), 141
Genetically influenced factors
    alcohol abuse, 374
        depression and suicide, 231, 236
        eating disorders, 204, 206
        mood disorders, 129, 131–132, 133
        posttraumatic stress, 144
        substance-related disorders, 385
Gentry, J. H., 107
Gerwitz, A. H., 408
GHB (gamma hydroxy butyrate), 283
GITTO (Gang Intervention Through Targeted Outreach), 310
Gleghorn, A. A., 407
Glenn, H. S., 100, 102, 114–115
Global self-esteem, 96
Glowiak, M. V., 367
GLSEN (Gay, Lesbian, and Straight Education Network), 320, 326, 327, 328–329
Glue sniffing, 369
Goertz, M. E., 11
Goldstein, M. S., 401
Gonorrhea, 272, 273
Gonzales, N. A., 157
Gottlieb, B. H., 155
Graber, J. A., 152
Graf, R. C., 93
Graham, S., 457
GREAT Program (Gang Resistance Education and Training), 308
Greenblatt, M., 401
Gregg, S., 59
Greytak, E. A., 446
Grief and loss, 426
Grieve, F., 199
Griffin, J., 8
Grilo, C. M., 217
Gross, D., 3, 23, 44, 229
Group counseling, 214, 453
Guilt, 241
Guindon, M. H., 95–96, 107
Gun-Free Schools Act (1994), 354
Gunkel, S., 294
Guo, J., 385
Guttman, E., 78
Gysbers, N. C., 85

H

Haas, A. P., 329
Haddock, L. R., 169
Hafen, B. Q., 241
Hagino, O., 127
Hains, A. A., 108
Hakim, N., 348
Haldane, B., 109
Haley, M., 265
Hall, D. W., 269
Hall, G. S., 10, 265
Hamachek, D., 107

Harpine, E. C., 232
Harrar, Sari, 367
Harrington, R., 116
Harrison, K., 383
Hauora (health and well-being philosophy), 61
Hawaii State Department of Health, Maternal and Child Health Branch, 94
HAWK Federation, 113
Hays, P. A., 389
Hazler, R. J., 94
Health and Human Services (HHS), 326, 327, 329–330, 451
Healthcare for the Homeless program, 412
Heariold-Kinney, P., 11
Henne, J., 333
Henry, A. F., 230
Heppner, P. P., 101
Hermann, M., 10, 11
Heroin, 301, 368, 373
HHS (Health and Human Services), 326, 327, 329–330
High expectations, 51
High School and Beyond (Department of Education), 11
Hipwell, A., 200
Hirschi, T., 294
Hispanic youth
    brief structural family therapy and, 88
    bullying and, 446, 457
    dropout problem and, 421
    gangs and, 301–302
    homelessness and, 396, 401, 414
    incidence of abuse among, 75
    multigenerational home sharing, 176
    PTSD and, 157
    suicide and, 231
    teen pregnancy and, 266–267
HIV. *See* AIDS; Sexually transmitted diseases (STDs)
Hoberman, H. M., 234
Home. *See* Family
Homeless Assistance Act (2002 reauthorization), 409
Homelessness, 395–419
    alternative families and, 404
    case study, 397–403
    children and families
        characteristics of, 396–397
        contributing factors, 398–400
    defined, 396
    demographic characteristics of, 396
    developmental period and, 10
    diversity, adaptations for, 412–414
        cultural diversity, 413–414
        single mothers, 412–413
    drug and alcohol use and, 401–402
    healthcare, lack of, 397, 400
    intervention strategies for, 406–412
        community, 411–412
        family, 407–409
        individual, 406–407
        school, 409–411
    maltreatment and neglect, 402
    mothers and violence, 413

(Continued)

Homelessness *(Continued)*
    pregnancy and, 407
    prevention approaches to, 403–406
        community, 406
        family, 404
        individual, 403–404
        school, 405
    sexually transmitted diseases and, 402, 407
    stress and trauma of, 150
    students and mentors, 412
    youth, 401–402
        characteristics of, 401–402
        contributing factors, 398–400
Homelessness Prevention and Rapid Re-Housing
    Program (HPRP), 406
Home School Legal Defense Association, 423
Home Visitation by Nurses Program, 348
Homoprejudice, 319
Homosexuals. *See* Sexual minority youth
Hopelessness/helplessness, 240
Housing, cost and availability of, 399
Housing and Urban Development (HUD), 406
Houston, K. B., 142
HPRP (Homelessness Prevention and Rapid Re-Hous-
    ing Program), 406
Hsu, L.K.G., 217
Huberty, T. J., 239
Hughes, T. L., 200
Humphrey, J. H., 155
Hunt, G., 299
Hunter, J., 333
Hurricane Gustav, 146
Hurricane Katrina, 145–146

I

Immigrant youth, multiracial families, 175
Incarceration, rate of, 339
Income potential and school dropouts, 25
Indicated prevention programming in schools, 155
Individualized educational programs (IEPs), 59
Individual level
    bullying problem
        intervention strategies for, 452–453
        prevention approaches to, 445–447
    dropout problem
        intervention strategies for, 434–435
        prevention approaches to, 425–427
    dysfunctional families, 80–82
    eating disorders
        intervention strategies for, 213–215
        prevention approaches to, 210
    gang membership
        intervention strategies for, 309
        prevention approaches to, 304–305
    homelessness
        intervention strategies for, 406–407
        prevention approaches to, 403–406
    low self-esteem, 100
    mood disorders, 131–132
    multiracial youth
        intervention strategies for, 186–188
        prevention approaches to, 185

rape and date rape
    intervention programs, 282
    prevention strategies, 280
school violence
    intervention programs, 352–353
    prevention approaches to, 345–348
sexually transmitted diseases (STDs)
    intervention strategies for, 276
    prevention approaches to, 274
sexual minority
    intervention, approaches to, 328–329
    prevention strategies, 323–327
stress and trauma prevention, 153–154
substance abuse, 384–385
suicidal behavior
    intervention strategies for, 249–256
    prevention approaches to, 243
teen pregnancy
    intervention strategies for, 270–271
    prevention approaches to, 268–269
Informal gang membership, 300
Ingersoll, G., 10
Inhalants, use of, 369, 373, 377
Inpatient treatment, 214–215
Internal control theory, 294–295
Internet
    eating disorders and, 213, 215
    gang membership and, 293
Interpersonal communication for prevention, 33–34
Interpersonal stress, 152–153
Interracial marriages, 170–171, 173
Intersex, defined, 324
Intervention strategies
    in community context. *See* Community
    for diversity, 186–191
    for dropout problem, 434–437
    for eating disorders, 213–216
    in family context. *See* Family
    for gang membership, 309–313
    for homelessness, 406–412
    in individual context. *See* Individual
    for rape and date rape, 281–284
    in school context. *See* Schools
    for school violence, 352–358
    for sexually transmitted diseases, 276–278
    for sexual minority youth, 327–332
    for substance use and abuse, 381–388
    for suicidal behavior, 249–257
    for teen pregnancy, 270–272
Isaacs, J. B., 150
Ishiyama, F. I., 116
Isolation, 240
It Gets Better Project, 321

J

Jacobi, C., 213
Jacobs, J. K., 11
Janosik, E. H., 32
Jason, L. A., 104
Jimerson, S. R., 10
Joe-Laidler, K., 299
Johansen, J., 383

Johnson, D. S., 97
Johnson, D. W., 107
Johnson, R. T., 107
Jones, D. J., 110
Justice Department, 24, 312
Juvonen, J., 457

K

Kaplan, H. B., 93, 95, 101
Katz, D. A, 142
Katz, M. H., 407
Kauai study, 48–49
Kazak, A. E., 73
Keel, P. K., 217
Kehoe, Andrew, 340
Kelder, S., 86
Kelly, F. D., 10
Kelly, T. M., 95
Kennison, J. A., 113
Kerwin, C., 179–180
Kessler, R., 145
Ketamine, 283
Kigin, T. J., 241
Kim, L. S., 157
Kimchi, K. J., 154
Kinkle, Kip, 341–342, 355
Kitashima, M., 49–50, 54
Klein, M., 296
Klindera, K., 104
Klingman, A., 155
Knesting, K., 354
Kosciw, J. G., 446
Kraizer, S., 108
Kruczek, T., 140, 146
Kryah, R., 232
Kumamoto, C. C., 117
Kushman, J. W., 11

L

Lachance, C. R., 268
Lambie, I., 79
Langman, P., 347
Lankford, A., 348
Lapan, R., 85
Latinos. *See* Hispanic youth
Lazarus, R. S., 142
Lee, A., 79
LeMahieu, P., 424
Lemoire, S. J., 107
Leone, J. E., 221
Lepkowski, W., 109
Lesbian, 163, 219, 324. *See also* Sexual minority youth
Lesbian, gay, bisexual, transgender, or questioning (LGBTQ) youth, 320. *See also* Sexual minority youth
Levine, M. P., 210
Lewis, R. E., 43, 54
LGBTQ youth, 320. *See also* Sexual minority youth
Life event stressors, 143
Life skills for prevention, 30, 33, 428
Lipka, R. P., 96

Litman, R., 238
Living, reasons for, 233
Locus of control and low self-esteem, 97
Logan C. R., 125, 319
Lord, S., 99
Loth, K. A., 210
Lott, B., 55
Lovell, P., 150
Low-income, as risk factor, 26. *See also* Poverty
Low self-esteem. *See* Self-esteem
LSD (Lysergic acid diethylamide), 373
Lubeck, S., 53
Lucia, V. C., 129
Luthar, S. S., 46
Lynch, K. G., 95

M

MAAT Center for Human and Organizational Enhancement Inc., 113, 116
Macfarlane, A. H., 60
Machismo, 274
Mack, J. E., 95, 102
MacKenzie, K., 299
Madison-Colmore, O., 116
Mafia gangs, 292
Males
    eating disorders among, 199–200, 218–219
    rate of incarceration among, 339
Maltreatment, defined, 75, 147
Maori special education, 60–61
Maples, M. F., 109
Marianismo, 274
Marijuana use, 369, 370, 375–377
Marin, B. V., 333
Marital dissolution, 148–149
Marsella, A. S., 157
Marszalek, J. F., III, 319
Martin, M. D., 171
Martin, W., 182
Martinez R., 295
Martin Luther King Jr. Middle School (Berkeley, California), 56
Marx, R., 407
Masche, J. G., 94
Masculinity, 101
Maslow, A. H., 397
Masten, A. S., 45, 46
Maton, K. L., 111
Matza, D., 293
Maxon, C., 296
Maxwell, J. C., 380
Mayer, G. R., 355
McCarthy, C., 306
McCathren, R. B., 395
McClellan, M. C., 11
McDowell, J., 95
McGee, R., 98
McKinney-Vento Homeless Assistance Act (2002 reauthorization), 409
McMahon, S. D., 117
McWhirter, A. M., 35, 46, 157
McWhirter, B. T., 46, 126–127, 157

McWhirter, E. H., 46, 157

McWhirter, J. J., 33, 35, 46, 157, 188, 241, 387

MDMA (Ecstasy), 372*t*, 378–379

Meadus, R. J., 133

Medeiros, B. L., 174

Media. *See also* Social media
    anorexia nervosa and, 197
    bullying awareness and, 441
    eating disorders and, 197, 199
    societal standards for youth and, 14
    television and self-esteem, 102, 171–172
    violence in, 454

Meggert, S. S., 93

Mellin, E. A., 94

Menderwald, J., 104

Mental health perspective, 12

Mental illness
    homelessness and, 400, 403
    statistics of in U.S., 25

Mentoring programs
    anti-bullying and, 456
    dysfunctional families and, 85
    gang member involvement and, 305
    homeless students and, 412
    school dropout problem and, 432

Mercy, J., 349

Merrell, K. W., 450

Metal detectors in schools, 349

Methadone, 389

Methamphetamines, 372, 379–380

Mettee, S., 93

Meuhlbauer, G., 93

Meyer, I., 321

Midwestern Prevention Project (MPP), 351–352

Milburn, J., 151

Military service, 109, 150

Miller, J., 296

Miller, J. A., 200

Mindfulness training groups, 214

Mirabito, N. S., 151

Mitchell, L. K., 97

Modzeleski, W., 339

Mohay, H., 146

Molidor, C. E., 299

Monitoring the Future (MTF) Survey, 380

Montana State Board of Education, 6

Montreal Preventive Treatment Program, 304

Mood disorders, 125–138
    causal factors, 126–131
    depression. *See* Depression
    diagnostic issues, 126–131
    diversity, adaptations for, 135–136
    individual and, 131–132
    prevention, 131–135
        community, 134–135
        family, 132–133
        individual, 131–132
        school, 133–134

Moore, J. L., 116

Moore, S. E., 116

Moos, R. H., 154

Morales, A., 294

Morales, E. S., 332

Morbidity and mortality, causes of among youth, 24

Moreau, D., 94

Motivational interviewing, 271, 384–385

MPP (Midwestern Prevention Project), 351–352

MST (Multisystemic Therapy), 357–358

MTF (Monitoring the Future) Survey, 380

Mufson, L., 94

Mullany, B., 268

Mullis, R. L., 97

Multicultural Counseling Competencies, 188

Multidisciplinary approach to prevention, 16–17

Multiple family group model, 408

Multiple marginality, 294, 300

Multiracial youth, 169–196. *See also* Diversity
    adaptations for diversity, 191–192
    case study, 180–181
    causal factors, 171–179
        academic and behavioral problems of, 175–176
        community acceptance of, 172
        education and career goals, 177–178
        ethnic identity and self-esteem, 176–177
        families of, 172–174
        immigrant youth and families, 175
        language and communication, 178
        parentification and, 179
        technology and, 179
    culturally appropriate approach, 181–184
    defined, 170–171
    identity models, 179–180
    intervention strategies, 186–191
        community, 190–191
        family, 188–189
        individual, 186–188
        school, 189–190
    prevention approaches to, 185–186
        community, 186
        family, 185
        individual, 185
        school, 186
    sociocultural context, 170–171

Multisystemic Therapy (MST), 357–358

Murray, N., 86

Myers, J. E., 108

N

Nafpaktitis, M., 355

Nagarajan, T., 117

Nahum, D., 80

Name calling, 187, 209

Nansel, T. R., 442–443, 457

Nassar-McMillan, S. C., 113

Nation, M., 343

National Alliance to End Homelessness, 402, 408

National Campaign to Prevent Teen Pregnancy (NCP-TUP), 267

National Center for Children in Poverty, 149

National Center for Education Statistics (NCES), 24, 340, 421–422

National Center on Family Homelessness, 395, 397, 403, 413

National Commission on Excellence in Education, 6
National Dropout Prevention Center, 26
National Eating Disorder Screening Program (NEDSP), 200
National Gang Intelligence Center, 293, 312
National Gang Threat Assessment, 300
National Incidence Study of Child Abuse and Neglect (NIS), 75–76, 85
National Institute on Alcohol Abuse and Alcoholism (NIAAA), 374
National Institute on Drug Abuse for Teens (NIDA), 167, 376
National Institutes of Health (NIH), 198, 275
Nationalist Socialist Vanguard, 303
National School Climate Survey, 330
National Teen Dating Violence Prevention Initiative, 281
"A Nation at Risk" (National Commission on Excellence in Education), 6
Native Americans
    binge eating and, 200
    homelessness and, 414
    sexually risky behaviors, 268
    suicide rates for, 231, 257
    youth theater program, 118
Natural disasters, 145–146
NCES (National Center for Education Statistics), 340
NCPTUP (National Campaign to Prevent Teen Pregnancy), 267
NEDSP (National Eating Disorder Screening Program), 200
Needs assessments, 37
Neglect. *See* Abuse and neglect
Negy, C., 333
Nelson, J., 100, 102, 114–115
Nervous system. *See* Central nervous system
Networking
    community-wide, 87
    school counselors and teachers, 84
    social support, 232–233
Neumark-Sztainer, D., 210
Neurotransmitters, 371, 372*t*
New York City Youth Board, 311
New Zealand, 60–61
NIAAA (National Institute on Alcohol Abuse and Alcoholism), 374
Nicotine use, 372*t*, 373
NIDA (National Institute on Drug Abuse for Teens), 167, 376
Night eating syndrome, 208
NIH (National Institutes of Health), 198
Nitza, A., 232
No Child Left Behind Act (2001), 422
Nonverbal communication, 34
Norepinephrine, 371, 372*f*

O

Obama, Barack, on gay equality, 319
OBPP (Olweus Bullying Prevention Program), 455
Occupational stress, 150
ODD (oppositional defiant disorder), 127, 401

Office of Juvenile Justice and Delinquency Prevention, 312
Okech, A. P., 116
Older gangsters (OGs), 297
Olive, L. S., 151
Olweus, D., 350, 442
Olweus Bullying Prevention Program (OBPP), 455
O'Neill, S. K., 218
Operation Ceasefire, 313
Operation Snowball, 387
Opiates, 372*t*
Opportunities to participate and contribute, 51
Oppositional defiant disorder (ODD), 127, 401
Oral Cancer Foundation, 373
Ordway, A. M., 197
Orpinas, P., 86
Orr, D., 10
Osher, D., 345
Other-directedness, 241
Ott, M. A., 270
Ousley, L., 199
Outdoor Adventure Group, 111–112
Overstreet, S., 146
Over-the-counter (OTC) drugs, 373, 380–381
Oxnam, P., 79
OxyContin, 373, 381

P

Palmer, M., 300
Parasympathetic nervous system, 371
Parcel, G., 86
Parental ability to nurture and support, 26
Parental conflict, 70–72
Parental influences on low self-esteem, 98–100
Parental involvement, 29, 427, 431. *See also* Family
Parental rights, 428
Parent-child advocates, 408
Parent consultation, 84
Parent education, 86–87
Parentification of children, 72–73, 179
Parent monitoring, 86–87
Parent resource centers, 431
Parents, Families, and Friends of Lesbians and Gays (PFLAG), 325, 372
Parent sponsors, for homeless children, 412
PATHS (Promoting Alternative Thinking Strategies), 352–353
Patterson, G. R., 105
Paulu, N., 11
PBS (Positive Behavior Support), 448
PD (purging disorder), 202, 208
Pearson, C. M., 207
Peer drug use, 387
Peer facilitation (peer helping), 28, 33, 34
Peer groups, 13, 26, 176
Peer mediation, 33
Peer tutors, 33
Peripheral nervous system (PNS), 371
Perren-Klinger, G., 157
Peterson, A. C., 152

PFLAG (Parents, Families, and Friends of Lesbians and Gays), 325, 372
Pharmacokinetics of drugs, 370–372
Pharmacological treatment
for bulimia, 214
for depression, related to suicidal ideation, 242
Phencyclidine, 373
Phillips, M. G., 267–268
Philosophical meaning and resilience, 50
Phinney, J. S., 116, 176
Physical abuse effects, 77
Physical and sexual abuse education for children, 85–86
Physical influences on low self-esteem, 103
Pianta, R. C., 69, 80
Planned Parenthood, 274
Planning programs for prevention, 36–38
Play therapy, 409, 426
Poertner, J., 189
Policies and procedures, for prevention programs, 38
Pollack, J. M., 11
Ponterotto, J. G., 180
Portes, P. R., 94
Positive Behavior Support (PBS), 448
Postolache, T. T., 232
Poston, W. S. C., 180
Posttraumatic stress disorder (PTSD), 127, 144, 146, 154, 156, 157
Poverty
bullying and, 457
diverse youth and, 189–190
gangs and, 294
homelessness and, 398
PTSD and, 157
resilience and, 55–56
stress from, 149
Powell, M. J., 125
Pregnancy. *See* Teen pregnancy
Prescription drug use, 369, 373, 380–381. *See also* Substance use and abuse
Prevention, approaches to
adult role models, 30
applicable in more than one context, 29
bullying, 444–451
community, 451
family, 447
individual, 445–447
school, 448–451
cognitive change strategies, 34–35
collaborative, 29
in community context. *See* Community
coping with stress, 36
crisis-management paradigm and, 15–18
cumulative and transferable efforts, 28
defining qualities of, 27–30
diverse youth, 29
dysfunctional families, 80–87
abuse prevention, 81–82
community approach, 86–87
family approach, 82–83
individual counseling, 80–81
postabuse family intervention, 83
school approach, 84–86
early in life span, 28–29

eating disorders, 209–213
community, 212–213
family, 210–211
individual, 210
school, 211–212
empowerment and, 29
in family context. *See* Family
focus of efforts on identifiable groups, 28
gang membership, 303–309
community, 308–309
family, 305–306
individual, 304–305
school, 306–308
group based, 28
individual based, 28
in individual context. *See* Individual
in-service training, 30
interpersonal communication, 33–34
life skills for, 30, 33, 428
mood disorders, 131–135
community and, 134–135
family and, 132–133
individual and, 131–132
school and, 133–134
multidisciplinary approach, 16–17
multiracial youth, 185–186
community, 186
family, 185
individual, 185
school, 186
new dysfunction, reducing incidence of, 28
overview, 23–27
parental involvement, 29
planning programs, 36–38
population based, 28
primary prevention, 17, 30–31, 32–36
proactive, 28
in school context. *See* Schools
school dropout problem, 425–433
school violence, 343–352
secondary prevention, 17–18, 31–32
self-esteem, 104–113
self-management and self-control, 35–36
sexual minority youth, 323–327
community, 327
family, 324–326
individual, 323–324
school, 326–327
significance and importance of, 23–24
social skills training, 30
stress and trauma, 153–157
community, 156–157
family, 154
individual, 153–154
school, 155–156
substance use and abuse, 16–17, 381–388
suicide, 243–248
targeting more than a single system, 29
teen pregnancy, 268–270
tertiary prevention, 17–18, 32
work world connections, 30
Prevention programming and community resources, 37

Prevention science model, 403
Prison population and school dropouts, 25
Problem-focused coping, 154
Problem-solving skills, 51, 233, 242
Prochaska, J. O., 384
Profiling, 345, 356
Promoting Alternative Thinking Strategies (PATHS), 352–353
Prospective design, 48
Prothrow-Smith, D., 307
Provocative victims, 350
Prozac, 372*t*
Pshyhotic rampage killers, 347–348
Psychodrama, 309
Psychoeducational groups, 214
Psychological debriefing, 146, 155
Psychopathic rampage killers, 347–348
Psychosocial control theory, 294
Psychosocial profiling, 345
PsycINFO, 337
PTSD. *See* Posttraumatic stress disorder
Public assistance, 399
Purging disorder (PD), 202, 208

Q

Quantum Opportunities Program (QOP), 355–356
Queer, defined, 324
Questioning (sexual identity), 320, 324

R

Race. *See* Diversity; Multiracial youth
Racial identity models, 179–180
Racism discourse for resilience, 54–55
Rader, Tim, 367–368
Ramirez, S., 217
Ramirez-Valles, J., 111
Rampage shooting incidences in schools, 14, 337, 340–342, 341*t*, 347–348
Randall, P., 217
Rape and date rape, 278–284
    date rape drugs, 283
    definition of, 279
    intervention strategies for, 281–284
        community, 283–284
        family, 283
        individual, 282
        school, 283
    prevention approaches to, 279–281
        community, 281
        family, 280
        individual, 280
        school, 280–281
    risk factors for women, 279
Rap music, 298
Reading level of adult population, 23
Reality therapy, 277
Reasoner, R. W., 108
Reconnect (Australian homelessness program), 406–407
Recovery Act (2009), 406

Reddy, M., 339
Red Eagle Soaring (RES), 118
Referral options, 38, 84
Reid, J. B., 105
Reisser, L., 323, 333
Relationships, students and families, 429–430
Relaxation, 108
Religion
    resilience and, 50
    suicide and, 233–234
Renken, R. H., 85
Replicating Effective Programs Plus (REP+), 277
Report of the Surgeon General
    on suicide, 229
    on violence in schools, 340, 346
RES (Red Eagle Soaring), 118
Reschly, A. L., 10
Research on prevention programs, 36–37
Residence status, urban vs. rural, 76
Residential treatment facilities, 387–388
Resilience, 43–65
    changing perspectives and practices, 50–52
    coping and adjustment characteristics, 15
    defined, 46–47
    development of concept of, 48–50
    discourse patterns for, 52–57
        careers discourse, 56–57
        poverty discourse, 55–56
        racism discourse, 54–55
        risk discourse, 53–54
    diversity, adaptations for, 60–61
    effective practices, 44–45
    factors, perspectives, and practices, 47–52
    fostering approaches, 57–59
    key research, 44
    professional possibilities, 45
    protective factors, 49
    spirituality, religion and philosophical meaning, 50
    within community, 49
    within family, 49
    within individual, 50–51
    youth with disabilities and, 59–60
Resistance and refusal training, 34
Resistance phase of stress, 141
Resnick, M. D., 329
Response-oriented views on stress and trauma, 141–142
Restorative justice, 52
Restrepo, A., 152
Retrospective design, 48
Richardson, G., 79
Risk amplification model, 402
Risk discourse, for resilience, 53–54
Risk factors
    for AIDS, 273
    for bullying, 329–330
    for eating disorders, 199–201
    ethnicity as, 200
    gender as, 135, 198–199
    race as, 200
    for rape and date rape, 267–268

(Continued)

Risk factors (*Continued*)
　　for sexually transmitted diseases, 273
　　socioeconomic status level as, 200–201
　　for suicide, 231–232
　　for teen pregnancy, 267–268
Roberson, G., 59
Roberts, R., 109
Robertson, M. J., 401
Robinson-McDonald, D. M., 421
Rock, D. A., 11
Rogerian principles, 384–385
Rohypnol, 283
Rosario, M., 333
Rosenberg, M, 349
Rosengard, C., 267–268
Rudolph, K. D., 140–141, 142
Rumberger, R. W., 11
Rural homelessness, 414
Rural vs. urban residence status, 76
Ryan, C., 325

S

Safe School Routes, 350
Sale, E., 232
Salloum, A., 146
Salsman J., 140, 146
Saltzman, A., 101
Sanchez, L., 127
Sandhu, D. S., 104, 105, 107
Sandy Hook Elementary School shootings (2012), 337
Satcher, D, 229
Satir, V., 95
Schaffner, B., 154
Schiraldi, V., 10
Schlegel, P., 107
Schneidman, E., 238
Schoen, A., 183
School counselors and diverse youth, 189–190
Schooler, D., 216
Schools
　　bullying problem and
　　　　intervention strategies for, 454–456
　　　　prevention approaches to, 448–451
　　class size, 431–432
　　climate or culture, 449
　　dropout problem. *See* Dropout problem
　　dysfunctional families and
　　　　curriculum-based interventions, 85
　　　　mentoring programs, 85
　　　　physical and sexual abuse education for
children, 85–86
　　　　preservice and in-service needs, 84–86
　　eating disorders and
　　　　intervention strategies for, 216
　　　　prevention approaches to, 211–212
　　gang membership and
　　　　intervention strategies for, 310–311
　　　　prevention approaches to, 306–308
　　homelessness and
　　　　intervention strategies for, 405
　　　　prevention approaches to, 405
　　mood disorders and, 133–134

multiracial youth and
　　intervention strategies for, 189–190
　　prevention approaches to, 186
peer support groups, 33
perspective on at-risk youth, 10–11, 26
rape and date rape and
　　intervention programs for, 283
　　prevention approaches to, 280–281
restorative justice in, 52
retention by, 428
school violence and
　　intervention programs for, 354–357
　　prevention approaches to, 343–352
security systems in, 349
self-esteem and, 107–111
　　district-level recommendations, 110
　　policy recommendations, 110
sexually transmitted diseases and
　　intervention strategies for, 277
　　prevention approaches to, 274–275
stress and trauma prevention, 155–156
stress from, 151
substance abuse and, 386–387
suicidal behavior and
　　intervention strategies for, 256–257
　　prevention approaches to, 244–248
teen pregnancy and
　　intervention strategies for, 271–272
　　prevention approaches to, 269–270
violence in. *See* Violence
School Safety Council, 339
School stress, 151
School Survey on Crime and Safety, 339
School violence, 337–365
　　case study, 341–342
　　community prevention efforts, 156
　　defined, 339–341
　　diversity, adaptations for, 358
　　intervention programs, 352–358
　　　　community, 357–358
　　　　family, 353–354
　　　　individual, 352–353
　　　　school, 354–357
　　prevention approaches to, 343–352
　　　　community, 351–352
　　　　family, 348–349
　　　　individual, 345–348
　　　　school, 349–351
　　rampage shooting incidences, 14, 337, 340–342,
　　　　341*t*, 347–348
　　threat assessment, 345, 356–357
Schrimshaw, E. W., 333
Scribner, R., 276
Search Institute, 151
Sears, S. J., 151
Seasonal affective disorder, 126
"Second chance" opportunities, 49
Secret Service National Threat Assessment Center,
　　355, 356
Seeley, J. W., 78
Selective self-esteem, 96
Selective serotonin reuptake inhibitors (SSRIs), 242
Self-acceptance, 96

Self-concept, 96
Self-efficacy, 97, 233
Self-esteem, 93–124
    adaptations for diversity, 115–118
    causal factors, 98–104
        environmental influences on, 103–104
        individual influences on, 100
        parental influences on, 98–100
        physical influences on, 103
        psychological influences on, 102–103
        social influences on, 101–102
    community and, 111–113
        Central Area Youth Association, 112–113
        other programs, 113
        STAR I and II, 113
        YMCA teen services, 112
    cultural dislocation and, 116
    definitions of, 95–96
    Dependable Strengths Articulation Process, 109
    Dependable Strengths Assessment Training, 109
    dropout problem and, 426–427
    ethnic identity and, 176–177
    gang membership and, 307
    indicators of, 96–98
    prevention approaches to low self-esteem, 104–113
        community, 111–113
        family, 105–107
        global, 114–115
        individual, 104–105
        school, 107–111
    school and, 107–111
        district-level recommendations, 110
        policy recommendations, 110
    suicide and, 240
Self-management and self-control for prevention, 35–36
Self-monitoring, 35–36
Self-reinforcement, 36
Seligman, M.E.P., 97
Selye, Hans, 141
Sense of purpose and future, 51
September 11, 2001, terrorist attack, 14
Serious illnesses, 73, 147
Serotonin, 371, 372*f*
Sexual abuse effects, 78
Sexual assault, 279
Sexual behaviors, developmental period of youth
    and, 10
Sexuality, 265–290
    AIDS and other STDs, 272–278
        intervention strategies, 276–278
        prevention approaches, 273–276
        risk factors, 273
    case study, 266
    diversity, adaptations for, 284
    gender identity and, 177
    rape and date rape, 278–284. *See also* Rape and
        date rape
        intervention strategies, 281–284
        prevention approaches, 279–281
        risk factors for women, 279
    sexually transmitted diseases. *See* AIDS; Sexually
        transmitted diseases (STDs)
    sexual predators, 166, 282

teen pregnancy
    intervention strategies for, 270–272
    prevention approaches to, 268–270
    risk factors, 267–268
Sexually transmitted diseases (STDs), 272–278. *See also*
    AIDS
    homelessness and, 402, 407
    intervention strategies for, 276–278
        community, 277–278
        family, 276–277
        individual, 276
        school, 277
    prevention approaches to, 273–276
        community, 275–276
        family, 274
        individual, 274
        school, 274–275
    risk factors, 273
Sexual minority youth, 319–336
    bullying among, 446–447
    case study, 322–323
    causal factors, 320–322
    coming-out process, 151–152, 320
    diversity, adaptations for, 332–333
    eating disorders and, 199, 219–220
    homelessness and, 403
    identity and, 135, 151–152, 323–324
    intervention, 327–332
        community, 331–332
        family, 329–330
        individual, 328–329
        school, 330–331
    mood disorders and, 135
    prevention strategies, 323–327
        community, 327
        family, 324–326
        individual, 323–324
        school, 326–327
    safety at school, 449
    stress and, 151–152
    suicidal behaviors and, 234
    terminology and, 324
Sexual trauma, 282
Seymour, F., 79
Shaffer, D., 231
Sharaf, A. Y., 105
Shaw, H., 217
Shectman, Z., 108
Sheets, R. H., 117
Shetgiri, R., 451, 457
Short, J. F., 230
Shulgin, A., 378
Shulmire, S. R., 299
Sieber, C., 11
Sim, T. N., 100
Simmons, R. C., 94
Simpson, M., 109
Single mothers and homelessness, 412–413
Skiba, R., 354
Skinheads of America, 303
Skolnick, J., 296
Smetana, J. G., 152
Smith, D. C., 104, 105, 107

Smith, G. T., 207
Smith, R. S., 45, 48–49
Smoking. *See* Marijuana use; Tobacco smoking
Smolak, L., 210
Snyder, J., 105
Sobeck, J., 383
Social and life-skills training, 30
Social competence, 51
Social influences on low self-esteem, 101–102
Social media, 179, 239, 293, 295
Social network, 232–233
Societal standards for youth, 14
Socioeconomic status
 child abuse and neglect, 75–76
 eating disorders, 200–201
Solution-focused approach, 426, 435
Somatic nervous system, 371
Sontag, L. M., 152
Spergel, I. A., 295
Spirituality and resilience, 50
Sprang, G., 142
SSRIs (selective serotonin reuptake inhibitors),
 242
Staff development, 38, 450
Stanard, R. P., 94
Stanger-Hall, K. F., 269
STARS I and II, 113
Stauffer, M. D., 197
STDs. *See* Sexually transmitted diseases
Stein, J. A., 11
STEP (Systematic training for effective parenting),
 86
Steps to Respect/Second Step program, 455
Stevens, P., 8
Stice, E., 217
Stimulus-oriented views on stress and trauma,
 140–141
Stormont, M. A., 395
Storytelling, 57–59
Strain theory, 294
Strengths-based case management, 407
Stress and trauma, 139–164
 adolescence and, 10
 causal factors, 143–153
  child and family abuse, 147–148
  chronic illness, 147
  divorce and marital dissolution, 24,
   148–149
  economic stress, 149
  gender differences, 152
  home and family stress, 147
  homelessness, 150
  interpersonal stress, 152–153
  life event stressors, 143
  military families, 150
  natural disasters, 145–146
  occupational stress, 150
  school stress, 151
  sexual identity/gender expression, 135,
   151–152
  traumatic stress, 143–145
 defined, 140
 diversity, adaptations for, 157

 perspectives on, 140–143
  response-oriented views, 141–142
  stimulus-oriented views, 140–141
  as transaction between person and
   environment, 142–143
  trauma and posttraumatic stress, 143–145
 posttraumatic stress. *See* Posttraumatic stress
  disorder (PTSD)
 prevention approaches to, 153–157
  community, 156–157
  family, 154
  individual, 153–154
  school, 155–156
 suicide and, 131, 240–241
Stress resistance, 78–79
Structured narratives, 57–59
StudentBodies (Internet-based program), 213
Substance use and abuse, 367–393
 age of beginning experimentation, 8–9
 counselor considerations and characteristics,
  381–382
 defined, 369–370
 diagnosing, 382–383
 disease model, 388–389
 diversity, adaptations for, 389–390
 drug availability and variation, 372–381
  alcohol, 373–375
  ecstasy, 373, 378–379
  inhalants, 373, 377
  marijuana, 370, 375–377
  methamphetamines, 372, 379–380
  nicotine, 373
  over-the-counter, 380–381
  prescription, 373, 380–381
 evidence-based therapy, 383–384
 factors contributing to, 383
 intervention strategies for, 381–388
  community, 387–388
  family, 385–386
  individual, 384–385
  school, 386–387
 medication for, 389
 multicultural considerations, 389–390
 pharmacokinetics of drugs, 370–372, 372*t*
 prevention approaches to, 16–17, 381–388
  community, 387–388
  family, 385–386
  individual, 384–385
  school, 386–387
Sudden Sniffing Death Syndrome, 373
Sue, D., 182
Sue, D. W., 182
Suicide, 229–263
 adolescent prevalence of, 24
 adolescent stress and, 10
 behavioral cues, 236–238
 bullying and, 443
 case study, 242–243
 defined, 230–242
 diversity, adaptations for, 257–258
 ethnic and gender differences, 230–231
 intervention strategies for, 249–257
  community, 256–257

family, 249–256
    individual, 249–256
    school, 256–257
methods, 231
myths and misconceptions about, 234–236
personality traits and, 240–242
precipitants, 234
prevention approaches to, 243–248
    community, 244–248
    family, 243–244
    individual, 243
    school, 244–248
profile of, 236
protective factors, 232–234
risk factors, 131, 231–232
school and community preventions
    administrators, 244–245
    classroom presentations, 247–248
    collaboration with administrators, 244–248
    counseling options, 246–247
    faculty and staff in-service, 245–246
    legal considerations, 248
    parent education, 247
    preparation of crisis teams, 246
sexual minority youth and, 327
thinking patterns and motivations, 239–240
verbal cues, 238–239
Sulzer-Azaroff, B., 355
Sun, Y., 85
Supportive housing, 408
Support services, 427–428
Surgeon General. *See* Report of the Surgeon General
Survival sex, 402
Sutton, Willie, 351
Swadener, B. B., 53
Swartz-Kulstad, J., 182
Sweeney, T. J., 108
Sympathetic (somatic) system, 371
Synapses, 371
Systematic training for effective parenting (STEP), 86
Szapocznik, J., 88

T

TANF (Temporary Assistance for Needy Families), 399
Targeted population, 29, 37
Taylor, B., 107
Taylor, C. B., 213
Taylor, C. S., 299, 308
Teacher/student ratios, 431–432
TEAM program, 109
Teasdale, J. D., 97
Technology. *See also* Social media
    intrapersonal relationships and, 179
    used in gang membership, 293
Teen pregnancy, 266–272
    adolescent stress and, 10
    intervention strategies for, 270–272
        community, 272
        family, 271
        individual, 270–271
        school, 271–272

    prevention approaches to, 268–270
        community, 270
        family, 269
        individual, 268–269
        school, 269–270
    risk factors, 267–268
Teen Pregnancy Prevention Initiative, 272
Teen Pregnancy Prevention Program, 272
Television. *See* Media
Temporary Assistance for Needy Families (TANF), 399
Terr, L., 76
Terrorist attacks of September 11, 2001, 14
Tertiary prevention, 17–18, 32, 155
Text messaging, 215
THC (Delta-9-tetrahydrocannabinol), 376
Theodore, L. A., 200
Therapeutic communities (TCs), 387
Thomas, K. A., 151
Thompson, E. A., 105
Thrasher, T., 292
Threat assessment teams, 345, 356–357
Tobacco smoking, 279, 352, 369, 373, 376
Toro, P. A., 401
Tragedy response plans, 31–32
Transactional-ecological model of human
    development, 48, 50
Transgender, defined, 324. *See also* Sexual minority
    youth
Transitioning
    bullying during periods of, 446
    from elementary to middle school to high school,
        429
    to new school, 411, 429
Transprejudice, 319
Transsexuals, defined, 324
Transtheoretical model, 384
Trauma. *See* Stress and trauma
Traumatized rampage killers, 347
Trenholm, C., 269
Trevor Project, 321, 327
Trost, A., 217
Trump, K., 349
Tsunokai, G. T., 294, 301
Ttofi, M. M., 450
Tutorial services, 432
Type II trauma and abuse, 76
Type I trauma and abuse, 76

U

Unemployment and school dropouts, 25
Unger, M., 47
United Kingdom
    child and family abuse, 147
    teen pregnancy rates, 266
    white supremacist groups, 302
United Nations, 275
University of Montreal (depression research), 132
University of Virginia (threat assessment), 356
Unspecified feeding or eating disorder, 208
Urban vs. rural residence status, 76
U.S. Conference of Mayors, 399
U.S. News & World Report on girls' self-esteem, 101

V

Valium, 372*t*, 373
Van Bockern, S., 116
Van Gundy, K., 294
Velkoff, P., 239
Vernon, A., 187
Vess, J., 79
Victims of bullying, 350, 355, 442
Violence. *See also* Gang membership
domestic, 24
early-onset risk factors, 346–347
homeless mothers and, 413
late-onset risk factors, 346–347
in media sources, 454
prevention programs, characteristics of, 343–352
research dealing with developmental periods
and, 10
in schools, 337–365
bullying, 326–327, 329–330, 350–351, 355
Bureau of Justice Statistics, 340
community and, 156, 351–352, 357–358
defined, 339–341
diversity, adaptations for, 358
family and, 348–349, 353–354
incidences of, 14, 337
individual and, 345–348, 352–353
intervention programs, 352–358
metal detectors and, 349
National Center for Educational Statistics,
340
prevention approaches to, 343–352
Report of the Surgeon General, 340, 346
School Survey on Crime and Safety, 339
threat assessment teams, 345, 356–357
Violence Against Women Act (amended 2005), 281
Virginia Polytechnic Institute and University shootings (2007), 356
Virginia protocol (threat assessment), 356
Vittinghoff, R., 407
Vossekuil, B., 339

W

Wages, statistics on, 398–399
Wagner, B. M., 152, 153
Walsh, D. J, 69, 80
Walsh, E., 105
Walters, K. P., 126–127
Wannabes, 297
Warger C., 345
Washington, E. D., 117
Waters, Alice, 56
Watson, B. C., 110
Wayman, J. C., 437
Webb, N. B., 76

Weil, V., 232
Weller, E., 127
Weller, R., 127
Wellness, resilience and, 45
Werner, E. E., 45, 46, 47, 48–49
Weston, M., 59
West Virginia Education Association, 108, 110
Whaley, A. L., 116
Wheel of Wellness, 108
Whipple, A. D., 10
White, J., 108
White, M. A., 217
White, S., 199
White, S. W., 10
White Aryan Resistance, 303
White supremacist groups, 302–303
Wiley, G., 93
Williams, T., 98
Wilson, J. M., 292
Witmer, J. M., 108
Women
domestic violence and, 24, 413
eating disorders, 199–200, 216–218, 220–221
in gangs, 298–300
rape and date rape. *See* Rape and date rape
rate of incarceration among, 339
single mothers and homelessness, 412–413
Work world connections as prevention approach, 30
"A Write Way," 58
Writing interventions, 57–59

X

Xanax, 372*t*, 373

Y

Yablonsky, L., 296, 297
Yanish, D. L., 94
Yau, J., 152
YMCA teen services, 112, 388
Young Parenthood Program, 272
Youth Risk Behavior Surveillance Survey (YRBSS),
200, 338, 369
Youth with disabilities. *See* Disabilities

Z

Zady, M. F., 94
Zapolski, T.C.B., 207
Zero tolerance, 354–355
Ziedenberg, J., 10
Zigler, E., 231
Zimmerman, M. A., 111
Zoot Suit Riots (1943), 301